# THE ESSENTIAL HISTORY OF MANCHESTER UNITED

FOREWORD BY NORMAN WHITESIDE

IVAN PONTING AND CLIFF BUTLER

WH S

First published in 2003
by Headline Book Publishing
for WHSmith, Greenbridge Road, Swindon SN3 3LD

10 9 8 7 6 5 4 3 2 1



ISBN 0 7553 1269 4

Design by designsection, Frome, Somerset

All photos by Colorsport except Manchester Evening News pages 9, 13, 19, 42, 49, 80, 96, 104, 105, 108 and Popperfoto pages 14, 15, 22, 72, 74 (bottom 2)

The authors would like to acknowledge the admirable work of various historians and statisticians who have been down this road before. Useful sources of information included the following: *Manchester United: The Complete Record* by Ian Morrison and Alan Shury, Breedon Books; *Manchester United* by Percy M. Young, William Heinemann; *There's Only One United* by Geoffrey Green, Hodder and Stoughton; *Winners and Champions* by Alec Shorrocks, Arthur Barker; *The Manchester United Football Books* by David Meek, Stanley Paul; *Matt, United and Me* by Jimmy Murphy, Souvenir Press; *Soccer at the Top* by Matt Busby, Weidenfeld & Nicolson; *Manchester United and Beyond* by Bill Foulkes, Bluecoat Press; *Manchester United: The Official History* by David Meek and Tom Tyrrell, Hamlyn; *The Official Manchester United Illustrated History*, Carlton Books; *Managing My Life* by Alex Ferguson, Hodder and Stoughton; *Manchester United Player by Player* by Ivan Ponting, Polar Publishing; *Manchester United Yearbooks*, edited by Cliff Butler; *Rothmans Football Yearbooks*, Headline; *Manchester United Pictorial Record & Club Record*, various authors, Temple Nostalgia; *The United Alphabet* by Garth Dykes, ACL & Polar; *The Complete Encyclopaedia of Manchester United* by Tony Matthews & John Russell, Britespot; *The PFA Premier & Football League Players' Records 1946-1998* by Barry Hugman, Lennard Queen Anne Press; *Football League Players' Records 1888-1939* by Michael Joyce, SoccerData

Printed and bound in Great Britain by Clays Ltd, St Ives PLC, Bungay, Suffolk

HEADLINE BOOK PUBLISHING
A division of Hodder Headline
338 Euston Road
London NW1 3BH

www.headline.co.uk
www.hodderheadline.com

# Contents

# Foreword
# By Norman Whiteside

I have an admission to make, one that makes me feel a bit sheepish, as I sit down to write a few words about the club which means so much to me and to millions of people all over the world. When I was growing up in Belfast, my entire family were mad-keen supporters of Manchester United, but I wasn't. Not that my allegiance resided anywhere else, it was just that I was barmy about the game without following any specific team. My tunnel-vision for playing left me with no time for watching. But then something happened to change my outlook. I was discovered by Bob Bishop, the famous scout who had unearthed such gems as George Best, Sammy McIlroy, David McCreery and Jimmy Nicholl, and I crossed to Manchester at the age of 12. When I saw the great players at close quarters and experienced the atmosphere of Old Trafford, I was smitten, and will remain so for as long as I live. Memories of my early years as a Red Devil are still vivid in my mind, particularly of my weekend jaunts from Ireland to play for United's junior teams. Every Friday the club would fly me over in time for a match on the Saturday morning, and I can still visualize the puzzled expressions of my fellow passengers, mostly businessmen in smart suits, as they gazed at this big skinhead in Doc Marten boots and duffle coat.

Things went pretty well for me in Manchester and I made my first-team entrance as a 16-year-old substitute for Mick Duxbury at Brighton in April 1982. Ray Wilkins scored the only goal of the game, a rare one for him, and my £16 weekly wage was boosted by a win-bonus of £800, even though I was on the field for only 12 minutes. I thought: 'This will do for me!' A few weeks later I managed to score on my full debut, when we beat Stoke, and what has been described as a footballing fairytale continued as, that summer, I became the youngest player ever to appear in the World Cup finals, a record previously held by Pele.

The pace didn't exactly slow down in my first full season in the United team, as I contributed goals in the semi-finals and finals of both domestic cup competitions, chalking up a few more firsts in the process, and coming to terms with my new existence. Over the next few campaigns I was privileged to play alongside some magnificent footballers – I'd say Bryan Robson was the greatest of them all – in a team which served up sensational entertainment under an enlightened manager who didn't bother what you did off the field as long as you produced the goods on it. It was Big Ron Atkinson who converted me from striker to midfielder, recognizing that I didn't have the pace for a frontman at the top level but that I had a decent footballing brain, and who in 1985 led us to our second FA Cup final victory in the space of three years. That Wembley meeting with Everton was one of the most dramatic games of my career, and I was fortunate enough to play a key role.

A season later that team threatened to scale even grander peaks and during our opening sequence of ten straight wins there was a genuine belief that nothing was beyond us. We felt unbeatable and it was a shame that we didn't go on to claim the title, but that's life. A little later Alex Ferguson arrived and, contrary to what you might have read in the newspapers, he and I had an excellent professional relationship, and a friendship which lasts to this day. Some of the lads liked to let their hair down when they were off duty, and I was one of them, but we did it at the right time, like any group of young fellows at the end of their working week.

Down the years I had my share of injuries and operations and I was forced to retire with knee problems at 26, but I'm not complaining. I count myself lucky to have enjoyed ten years in the big time and those endless sessions in medical rooms aroused an interest which ultimately led me into my second career as a podiatrist, looking after footballers' feet. Meanwhile, I still maintain close links with Manchester United, who will always be my club. Even in my last two years as a player, which I spent with Everton, I always made sure there was an apprentice on standby to keep me up to date with the United score. These days I continue to play a small part in the Old Trafford set-up by working in corporate hospitality on match days, and I love the ongoing sense of belonging.

As you will read between these covers, United can look back on a history of unrivalled richness and drama, and I am delighted that Sir Alex is maintaining that tradition with a vengeance. Over the past dozen or so years his teams have accumulated an unprecedented haul of silverware and everyone fortunate enough to pull on the famous red jersey continues to strive alongside manager and board to achieve even more glory. I'm happy to say that I can't see them failing.

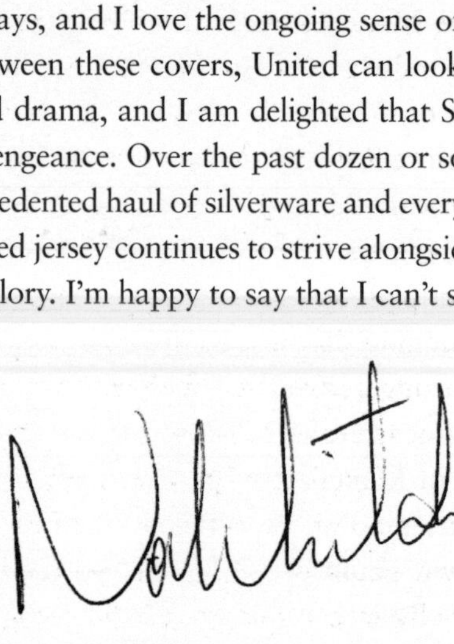

Norman Whiteside

# Chapter One: 1878-1906
# Enter the Heathens

A tantalizing whiff of mystery lurks at the very source of the Manchester United legend. Astonishingly enough, nobody can say exactly when that mightiest, starriest and most romantic of footballing institutions first drew breath. It is accepted that United's predecessor club was formed by and for railway workers in 1878, but no definitive records exist. Real Madrid, Arsenal, Liverpool – they can all pinpoint the month, the day, practically the minute of their birth. The Red Devils? Throughout their epic history, little has ever been that simple.

What is certain is that modern football is the product of the social reform which swept through mid-Victorian England. All too belatedly, the toiling masses in factories, mills and every manner of sweatshop across the land were granted their liberty on Saturday afternoons. It was a sweet and welcome release, but it created a vacuum of free time and organized sport became a prime means of filling it. Thus the rough-and-tumble game which had existed for centuries in different versions assumed new seriousness, uniformity of rules was attained with the formation of the Football Association in 1863 and the first national competition, the FA Cup, was launched nine years later.

In Cottonopolis, the Manchester area, enthusiasm for football burgeoned exuberantly, nowhere more so than in the railway shunting yards at Newton Heath, just northeast of the city centre. Duly, as the passion took hold, the Lancashire and Yorkshire Railway Company's Dining Room Committee was asked by men of their carriage and wagon works division for permission to start their own team, together with enough money to get it off the ground. By then the LYR, perhaps fearful of the effects of mushrooming alcohol abuse, was already running 'improvement' classes for its employees. Now it was decided that sporting activity fell within this remit and thus was born the Newton Heath Lancashire and Yorkshire Railway Cricket and Football Club, the forerunner of Manchester United.

The beginnings were modest, reflected by the first pitch at North Road, Monsall, a flint-strewn patch of land near the railway depot, which rain would transform rapidly into a quagmire. Changing rooms? Initially, they were a good half a mile away at the Three Crowns, a pub on the Oldham Road, then at the Shears Hotel, situated at a similar distance. In bad weather the trek to and from the venue must have been intimidating, but we're not talking here of pampered millionaires, rather of hardy souls who played football purely for the love of it.

There is no verification of specific opponents faced in the late 1870s, though matches must have been played against rival LYR departments, such as the engine drivers and maintenance men, and teams formed by workers from neighbouring parts. Such encounters were not reported by newspapers so details are scant and the first even vaguely reliable mention of a contest involving the green-and-gold-shirted Heathens – they adopted the colours of the LYR – is of an away meeting with Bolton Wanderers reserves on 20 November 1880, which resulted in a 6-0 defeat. However, their standard improved quickly, prompting a first entry in the Lancashire Cup in 1883-84, and although they were drubbed 7-2 by Blackburn Olympic, significant progress was being made. This was confirmed by reaching the final of the inaugural Manchester Cup in 1884-85, where they were beaten by Hurst, from Ashton-under-Lyne.

A year later Newton lifted the trophy in front of 8,000 supporters at Whalley Range, upsetting Manchester FC 2-1 through a disputed winning goal which might have been ruled out for both handball and offside. Whatever, that breakthrough victory ushered in an era of dominance in the competition, encompassing further triumphs in 1888, 1889, 1890 and 1893, and also signalled their first entry in the FA Cup, which ended in bizarre elimination at the first hurdle. Facing Fleetwood Rangers (away) in October 1886, they fought out a creditable 2-2 draw, but when asked to play extra-time they refused and the referee awarded the tie to Fleetwood.

Despite such turbulence, the side's exploits were bringing such prestige to LYR that the players were given time off work to train. From such a position it was but a short step to professionalism, which was becoming ever-more prevalent at many clubs even before it was legalized in 1885. Top players were attracted by the offer of outside jobs, a form of 'shamateurism' which now became unnecessary. Around this time there was an influx of Welsh internationals at North Bank, including marksman Jack Doughty, his brother Roger, a half back, and full back Jack Powell, recruited from Bolton and made skipper. Scot Pat McDonnell made a more remarkable entrance, walking from Glasgow to Manchester in search of a job on the railways and a berth in the side, both of which he achieved.

Against the background of an explosion of public interest, the Football League was formed in 1888, comprising a dozen clubs from the industrial North and Midlands. Though they were getting better, perhaps Newton Heath did not feel quite strong enough to apply for first-time membership, and after their bid to enlist a year later attracted only one vote, they banded together with a group of other clubs of similar stature to form the Football Alliance. In 1891 they made a renewed bid for a place among the elite, this time receiving not a single vote, but their time was at hand. Come 1892 the League opted to expand into two divisions and Newton Heath, having finished as runners-up to Nottingham Forest in the Alliance, were admitted to the top flight, while Ardwick – later to become Manchester City – joined the new Second Division.

## Newton Heath Join the Football League

This momentous milestone for the Heathens was marked by independence from the railway company – henceforth, LYR was dropped from the club's title – and the appointment of Alf Albut, formerly of Aston Villa, as the club's first paid secretary. Unfortunately, any thought that Newton's struggles were behind them proved misguided. The financial commitments of league football were intimidating, a share flotation flopped and concessionary travel to away games was no longer available following the severance of links with LYR, who added further pressure by hiking up the North Road rent. Years of horrendous, backs-to-the-wall cash problems were to follow, periodically threatening the club's existence, and life proved tough on the field, too.

*A Newton Heath team from 1892. Robert Donaldson, third from the left in the front row, scored their first league goal in their first league match, against Blackburn Rovers.*

The first season of league competition kicked off against Blackburn Rovers, one of the most powerful sides of the age, having won the FA Cup five times in eight seasons. In the circumstances, the new boys performed nobly, being edged out only by the odd goal in seven at Ewood Park, where ex-Rover Bob Donaldson opened Newton Heath's scoring account against his former colleagues. The combative Scottish spearhead netted again a week later in Manchester's first taste of First Division football, a 1-1 draw with Burnley, but although he continued to register regularly, the Heathens garnered only two points from their first six games.

Against all rational expectation, a first victory arrived sensationally in mid October when Wolverhampton Wanderers, who would lift the FA Cup in the spring, were annihilated 10-1 at North Road, with the trusty Donaldson contributing the club's first league hat-trick and Willie Stewart adding another three. At the time of writing, that stands as the record league win by either the Heathens or the Red Devils. However, this proved to be one of only six league victories during a discouraging campaign which ended with Newton Heath five points adrift at the bottom. Temporary salvation was at hand, though, thanks to the system of 'Test Matches' which involved the top three teams in the Second Division meeting the bottom three in the First for the right to play at the higher level. Newton were pitted against Small Heath, eventually to become Birmingham City, who were champions of the second flight, and the Manchester side managed a 1-1 draw at Stoke. Hero of the hour was right winger Alf Farman who scored the goal, and he became more of a celebrity after his hat-trick in the Bramall Lane replay was the centrepiece of a rousing 5-2 triumph.

Off the pitch, matters were less satisfactory. Nobody loved the cloying claypit that was North Road, but at least it was home, and that summer Newton Heath faced eviction by LYR, who believed the field should be used by all its employees, not just footballers. Even then, land was not easy to come by in a sprawling city, but an exhaustive quest produced dividends in the shape of Bank Street, Clayton, three miles from Newton Heath. Here the playing surface, while still tending towards marshiness, was an immeasurable improvement on its predecessor, but the move threw up new difficulties for the cash-strapped Heathens. They were unable to retain the stands recently and expensively erected at North Street, which they sold cheaply to the LYR. Then, although new landlords the Bradford and Clayton Athletic Company helped to make necessary improvements at Bank Street, the club was involved in extra expenditure it could ill afford.

A decent playing season would have helped. Alas, it wasn't to be, despite a thrilling fightback to defeat Burnley on the opening day. That first Bank

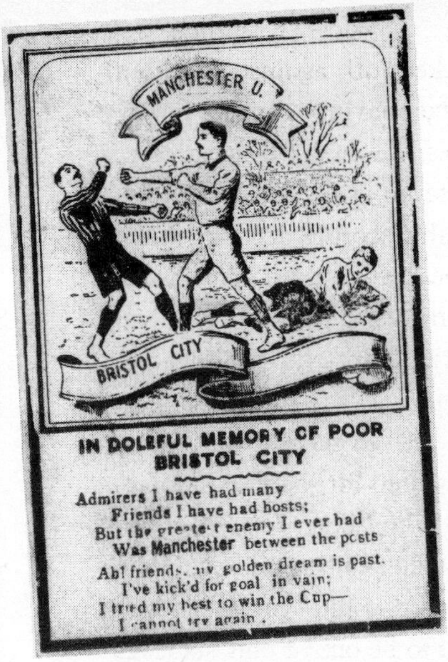


*A humorous card, with illustration and rhyme, commemorating Manchester United's victory over Bristol City in the 1909 FA Cup final.*

Street fixture attracted 10,000, but it would be misleading to imply the supporters were any more affectionate towards the new headquarters than the old.

True, no longer did they have to trudge through ankle-deep slime, but Bank Street was situated windward of a chemical works and now the crowd was assailed by the foul stench which spewed forth from a forest of tall chimneys. Opponents were none too impressed, either, and some maintained, perhaps not wholly seriously, that Newton Heath had an arrangement with the chemical company to step up production when the home team was losing, thus creating extra fumes to undermine the visitors.

After the beating of Burnley, the Heathens' fortunes dipped disastrously, with only five more league wins leaving them propping up the First Division table for the second successive season. Once again they met the Second Division table-toppers in a 'Test Match' but this time they lost, to Liverpool, and became the first Football League club ever to suffer relegation.

## Relegation Gloom

Now began a truly parlous period in the club's history, though playing-wise Newton had found their true competitive level in the lower echelon. In 1894-95 they remained unbeaten at home, thus finishing third and qualifying for another 'test', which was lost to Stoke City. The highlight was putting 23 goals past Walsall Town Swifts at Bank Street, although only nine of those strikes are to be found in the record books. The anomaly occurred because the Heathens hammered the Swifts 14-0, only for the Midlanders to complain to the League about the bog-like state of the pitch; the protest was upheld, a rematch ordered – and this time the hosts were restricted to a mere nine-goal margin.

Promotion was coveted, for both sporting and financial reasons, and Newton went close again in 1896-97. Resplendent in new colours of white shirts and blue shorts, they were runners-up to Notts County, but then failed to progress through a new mini-league play-off system.

As the 20th century dawned they could point to a succession of further near misses, including three fourth places, and an ecstatically greeted first success in the locally prestigious Lancashire Cup, overcoming Blackburn in the 1898 final. In addition, the fans had some fine players to cheer, the likes of prolific marksman Joe Cassidy, the redoubtable full back pairing of Harry Stafford and Fred Erentz and the versatile Walter Cartwright, of whom it was once written that 'a team of Cartwrights would lick creation!' But all that did little to alleviate a cash crisis which was in danger of spiralling out of control, despite the tireless efforts of new secretary James West and the loyal skipper Stafford. Results had taken a downturn, too, and after a disappointing tenth-place finish in 1900-01, extinction was beckoning.

Nothing short of a miracle, it seemed, could save Newton Heath. Then, right on cue, one materialized in the shape of a St. Bernard's dog named Major. At least, so legend has it, and it should be stressed that numerous versions of the story have been told, each with subtle variations. Who is to say, at the distance of more than 100 years, which details are fact and which are colourful embellishment? Whatever, here are the bones of it.

In spring 1901, the club staged a four-day grand bazaar in St. James's Hall, Oxford Street, Manchester, to raise the money needed to stave off bankruptcy. Huge effort had gone into organizing the event, generous patrons of which included Manchester City FC, but by the end of the third day it seemed likely that profits would fall short of the minimum £1,000 needed urgently. Now it was that Major, Harry Stafford's animal, entered the picture. That day he had been wandering amiably between the stalls with a barrel around his neck, his owner hoping that he would attract donations. Around closing time Major dodged out of a side entrance and an exhaustive search failed to locate him. Eventually, he turned up at the home of a rich businessman, brewer John Henry Davies, who took a shine to the stray, believing he would make a desirable pet for his young daughter. Duly the man of means tracked down the Heathens' skipper, who regaled him with details of Newton's pressing need, evidently firing his imagination in the process. The upshot was that lucky Miss Davies was presented with a new pet and the club had made first contact with the man destined to save it.

## The Heathans Find a Saviour

The fruits of that fateful encounter became evident a year later when, with Newton Heath some £2,670 in debt and facing a winding-up order, the inspirational Stafford dropped a welcome bombshell at a shareholders' meeting in the New Islington Hall. He announced that he and four local

*John Henry Davies, the wealthy benefactor who rescued Newton Heath in 1902 with his money and forward-thinking business acumen.*

businessmen, including John Henry Davies, were each willing to invest £500, thus restoring Newton to an even financial keel. In the circumstances, the Football Association agreed to the re-forming of the club, the heaven-sent band of benefactors replaced the existing directors and it was decided that a change of name was needed. With Manchester City spoken for already, what would it be? Manchester Central was put forward, but then knocked back because it sounded like a train station. Its proponents pointed out that given the club's railway origins it was eminently suitable, but the fact that Manchester actually boasted a Central Station, on land now occupied by the G-MEX Exhibition Centre, proved decisive.

## Manchester United are Born

Another much-favoured suggestion was Manchester Celtic, presumably in reference to the plentiful Scots and Welshmen who had served Newton Heath, but that was rejected as too narrow, and it was left to Louis Rocca, destined to become a talent-spotting legend over half a century, to come up with... Manchester United. The new title, announced on 28 April 1902, was accompanied by another change of colours. Soon enough those red shirts and white shorts would burn themselves vividly into the public consciousness. Now John Henry Davies revealed himself as a true enterprising visionary. Though not a football man previously, he recognized the vast potential of a successful club in Manchester and brought his business acumen to bear. Administration became more efficient, cash was made available for new players and soon both results and attendances were improving.

Certainly United's first campaign offered a considerable step forward from Newton Heath's last. The opening game produced a 1-0 victory at Gainsborough Trinity, with the honour of scoring the reconstituted club's first goal going to Charlie Richards. This was followed by success in United's inaugural Clayton fixture, another single-goal triumph, this time courtesy of

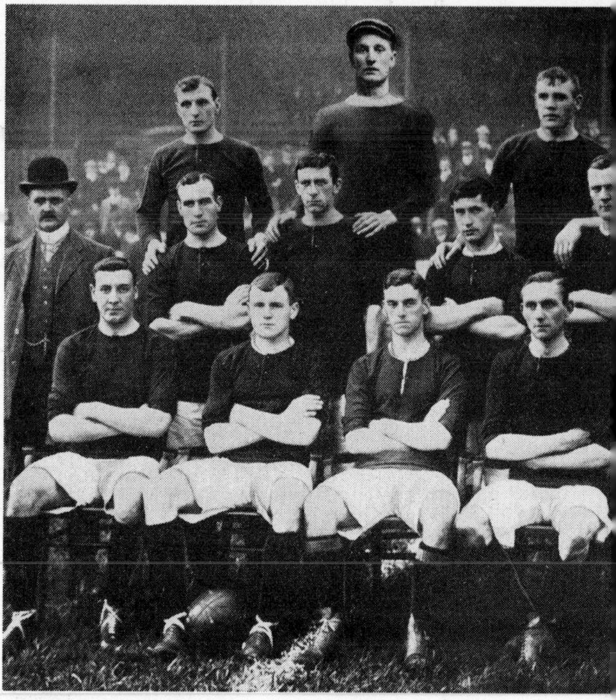

*A team from 1905, l-r: back row – Downie, Moger, Bonthron; middle – Mangnall (sec), Picken, Sagar, Blackstock, Peddie; front – Beddow, Roberts, Bell, Arkesden.*

a strike by winger Daniel Hurst in front of 15,000 fans.

That level of momentum was not maintained, but local enthusiasm was racheting ever higher, as demonstrated by the 40,000 crowd which crammed Bank Street for the 1-1 draw in the Manchester derby on Christmas Day. Meanwhile, supporters were demanding promotion with increasing impatience and even a fifth-place finish, ten slots higher than in the previous term, was not enough to quell vehement criticism. As a result, possibly, West felt under such pressure that he resigned.

The full circumstances of his unexpected exit remained cloudy, even more so a year later when both he and Stafford were suspended by the FA for making illegal payments to players, a practice which was widespread and carried less of a stigma in those days when footballers' pay packets were less bloated than they were to become. For Stafford, so instrumental in keeping Newton Heath from going under, it was a cruel blow and he declared, with a ring of truth: 'Everything I have done has been in the best interests of the club.' Happily in later years he emerged from the shadows with his honour intact and when he moved overseas for health reasons, he was helped on his way by a £50 gift from United's directors.

## The First Manager

No matter what the moral injustice or otherwise of the pair's original sentence, United were the beneficiaries by the appointment in September 1903 of Ernest Mangnall as West's successor. Nominally he was the secretary, but in reality he was the club's first manager, certainly as that job description is understood in modern times. A shrewd Lancastrian, recruited from Burnley, he preached a gospel of physical fitness and team spirit while maintaining that players should be given a ball only once a week, and although that latter part of the Mangnall doctrine seems monstrous today, his results brooked no argument.

In his first season United rose to third place in the Second Division, finishing a point behind promoted Woolwich Arsenal, but more significant were the massive strides towards constructing an outstanding team with Davies's cash. The most notable arrival was centre half Charlie Roberts, a magnificent all-rounder destined to become one of the most influential of all United leaders, who was enlisted for £400 from Grimsby Town. Before long he would join local product Dick Duckworth and South African-born Scot Alex Bell in a flinty but stylish half back line admired far and wide.

Expectations rose in autumn 1904, and with the rearguard increasingly tight and the attack ever more bountiful, the Reds embarked on an 18-match unbeaten run which included 14 straight wins. However, Easter defeats by Chesterfield and champions-elect Liverpool cost them dearly and Bolton pipped them by three points for the vital runners-up position. Despite the setback, any sane evaluation of Mangnall's progress would have been overwhelmingly positive but with restive supporters in no mood to listen to reason, he understood that promotion was imperative in 1905-06.

With the inspirational Roberts elevated to the captaincy, and with Jack Picken, Jack Peddie and Charlie Sagar supplying goals aplenty, the team rose to the challenge. They clinched their place in the upper echelon by holding third-place Chelsea to a draw at Stamford Bridge, watched by 60,000 people on Good Friday, 13 April.

*Sixteen goals from Charlie Sagar helped Manchester United finally gain promotion to Division One in 1906.*

The prize was made mathematically safe by beating Leeds City at Elland Road and as there were still two games to spare, Manchester United's celebration party was delayed until the season's final day. By then Bristol City had secured the title but that

*Billy Meredith had been suspended by rivals Manchester City but Ernest Mangnall saw his potential and snapped him up. The 'Welsh wizard' became the star of the first great United side.*

hardly mattered as the Reds crushed Burton United 6-0 at Bank Street.

On that joyous afternoon even a sudden snowstorm and the obnoxious odours from the chemical works could not sour the exultant mood. Clayton echoed to the crackling of fireworks and a crowd of 16,000 rejoiced with such wild abandon that there was even a flower fight, the fans pelting each other with buttonholes. If ever there was an occasion when missiles hurled by spectators were acceptable, this was it. But as the mayhem died down, thoughts turned to the future, begging the question: would United be good enough for the top flight? There were always prophets of doom, but genuine optimism had been engendered by the 5-1 trouncing of FA Cup holders Aston Villa in that term's competition, a stirring achievement not devalued even by capitulation to Woolwich Arsenal in the quarter-final.

So Manchester United's prospects were realistically bright and, as it turned out, the ever-canny Ernest Mangnall had a few aces up his sleeve as he knew where he could find a posse of high-quality footballers who would transform his club into England's finest. He turned his gaze just a few miles away to Hyde Road, where Manchester City were being ripped apart by a scandal over financial irregularities. Mangnall's attention was focused most acutely on a bandy-legged fellow with gaunt cheekbones and a heavy moustache, whose trademark was a toothpick which he rolled from one corner of his mouth to the other as he ran down the wing.

# Chapter Two: 1906-19
## Edwardian Aces

When Manchester City were all but disembowelled by the Football Association for making illegal payments to players, Manchester United profited overwhelmingly from their neighbour's turmoil. After winning the FA Cup and finishing as championship runners-up in 1904, City were one of the leading powers in the land, but the following year their world began to disintegrate when their best player, the brilliant Welsh international winger Billy Meredith, was suspended for three years. It was alleged that he had attempted to bribe Alec Leake of Aston Villa to fix the outcome of a match, and then compounded his problems by trying to obtain payment from his employers during the course of his ban.

It seemed that his outlook could hardly have been bleaker, but Ernest Mangnall sensed an opportunity and in May 1906, clearly believing that the draconian sentence would never be served in its entirety, the canny United boss pounced to sign the star for £500. There was a shaft of light on the Meredith horizon, but for City the worst was yet to come when an FA investigation revealed that they had made over-the-odds payments to their footballers. Five directors resigned, 17 players past and present were banned for life from representing the club and suspended from all football until January 1907. Poor City, who were plainly guilty but no more so than most of their leading contemporary rivals, had no alternative but to sell their players or leave the League. In the early winter of 1906, they staged an auction at the Queen's Hotel in Manchester's Piccadilly and an expectant posse of top managers and chairmen assembled in anticipation of picking up some bargains.

However, they had reckoned without the shrewdness of Ernest Mangnall, who scooped the lot of them by approaching his transfer targets before the sale. He acquired the signatures of Herbert Burgess, the most coveted full back in the English game; the free-scoring Sandy Turnbull and Jimmy Bannister, another fine marksman. Not surprisingly, many of his fellow bosses were practically apoplectic with rage, but it was to no avail. He had broken no rules and now he had the basis of Manchester United's first great team.

Already the Reds had made a solid if unspectacular start to First Division life, but the arrival of the high-quality quartet from Hyde Road – Meredith's suspension had been commuted to end at the same time as those of the other ex-City men, a case of natural justice being done – brought about a further marked improvement.

The debut of Mangnall's new combination attracted a crowd of 40,000 to Bank Street for the visit of Aston Villa on New Year's Day 1907 and the classy recent acquisitions did not disappoint. Indeed, they offered a beguiling taste of delights in store by a spirited victory and it was distinctly symbolic that the only goal of the game was scored by Turnbull from a Meredith cross.

Gradually they attained admirable consistency, losing only four games during the remainder of that term and climbing to an eighth-place finish, thus building a firm platform for a genuine title challenge in 1907-08. That bid got off to an auspicious start with three straight wins, including a 4-0 home thumping of Liverpool to which Turnbull contributed a hat-trick, and such was the side's growing confidence that they shrugged off a defeat by Middlesbrough to embark on a sequence of ten successive triumphs which sent them well clear at the top of the table by late autumn.

## The First Championship

Clearly they were the outstanding team in the League and, just six years after Newton Heath had perished in penury, Manchester United claimed the club's first title. The final margin over runners-up Aston Villa was a crushing nine points, and it could have been even more emphatic but for a bout of chronic complacency in the weeks after the prize had been secured.

Mangnall's line-up was exhilarating yet solid. Clearly Meredith, eventually to be hailed as football's first superstar, was the most eye-catching component, both making and taking goals from the right flank, but this was no one-man effort. Unarguably the heartbeat of the team was the mighty half back trio of Duckworth, Roberts and Bell, while rearguard operations were in the safe hands of former Southampton goalkeeper Harry Moger, either Dick Holden or George Stacey at right back, with the diminutive but dynamic Burgess on the left flank of defence. Up front Sandy Turnbull, whose power was matched by his subtlety and stealth, proved the principal threat with 25 league goals from a mere 30 outings, a club record until it was beaten by Jack Rowley in 1946-47. England international left winger George Wall offered magnificent support with 19 strikes and the other regular forwards were the clever inside right Jimmy Bannister and energetic spearhead Jimmy 'Trunky' Turnbull, acquired from Southern League Leyton at the end of the previous campaign.

Immediately after being crowned as English Champions, United set off on a brief tour of three European capitals – Prague, Vienna and Budapest –

*The 1908 championship-winning side, l-r: back – Downie, Burgess; third row – Taylor (director), Nuttall (assistant director), Stafford (director), Broomfield, Stacey, Duckworth, Holden, Bell, Moger, Bacon (trainer), Mangnall (secretary); second row – Picken, Bannister, Jimmy Turnbull, Roberts (captain), Halse, Sandy Turnbull; front – Meredith, Wall. Trophies: FA Charity Shield, League Championship Cup, Manchester Cup.*

apparently seeing themselves as football missionaries. Evidently supporters in Czechoslovakia and Austria were duly impressed but not so the fans of the Hungarian side, Ferencvaros, who rioted after watching the visitors annihilate their favourites 7-0. In truth it had been an utter mismatch, with Moger the custodian striding forward to net from the penalty spot, an act which underlined United's superiority but maybe not their diplomacy. As they left the pitch, the players were set upon by a screaming mob, some of whom were brandishing pistols and daggers, and police on horseback drew their swords to see the Reds to safety.

In the circumstances, perhaps, the team was lucky to arrive home in one piece, ready to kick off the new term with a replay of the first-ever Charity Shield encounter, which had resulted in a 1-1 draw with Southern League champions Queens Park Rangers back in April at Stamford Bridge. At the second time of asking, United coasted to a 4-0 triumph, thanks largely to three goals from Sandy Turnbull.

*Charlie Roberts captained United to their FA Cup win in 1909 and made over 300 appearances as one of the finest centre halves of his generation.*

That impressive form was carried into the new league season, which began with a seven-game unbeaten run. 'Trunky' was in particularly compelling early form, netting in each of the opening five games, and he was ably abetted by little Harold Halse, a prolific recent acquisition from Southend.

The cry went up from the Bank Street terraces that retaining the title would be a formality but an erratic interlude was followed by a post-Christmas free-fall from grace so demoralizingly complete that only one win was garnered from the last 15 matches. But for that buoyant start, United would have been facing the ignominy of relegation and as it was they could finish no higher than 13th.

There was no satisfactory reason for such a dismal transformation, though the players' oft-stated discontent with the gruesomely tacky Clayton pitch would not have helped and neither did their simmering resentment over what they saw as pathetically poor wages.

Such theories, however, hardly square with the Reds' stirring FA Cup exploits during that same term. After squeaking single-goal wins over non-league Brighton and high-riding Everton, they humbled Blackburn Rovers 6-1 at Bank Street, with each of the Turnbulls – the two Scottish sharpshooters were not related – contributing hat-tricks. That set up another all-Lancashire confrontation, against Burnley at Turf Moor, where United experienced a gargantuan slice of quarter-final good fortune. With the playing surface part sheet-ice and part slushy gluepot, the hosts took a deserved one-goal lead, which they held until midway through the second half, when a sudden blizzard swept down from the Pennines.

The markings were obliterated and, with the increasingly atrocious conditions making a mockery of football, referee Herbert Bamlett – who will crop up again in this story, but in a markedly different role – put an end to proceedings some 20 minutes from time. At least, he tried to, but he was too numbed and exhausted to signal the end, eventually fumbling the whistle into the custody of Charlie Roberts, who was only too happy to oblige with a prolonged blast.

Having thawed out, the sides met again for a rematch four days later, and this time United, evidently anxious to capitalize on their reprieve, performed far more convincingly and won 3-2 to reach the last four. Now, though, the knockout progress of Mangnall's men, still unremittingly poor in their bread-and-butter fixtures, appeared likely to come to an unceremonious halt. Their semi-final opponents were Newcastle United, who were on their way to their third First Division crown in five seasons and seemed a fair bet to become the first club since Aston Villa, a dozen years earlier, to complete the League and FA Cup 'Double'.

## FA Cup Success

But with the Reds' first final beckoning, what remained an essentially high-quality side rose to the occasion and overcame the Magpies, Halse grabbing the only goal of a tight encounter at Bramall Lane. Though the game was fiercely contested, the spirit between the two camps was upliftingly sporting, as exemplified by the Geordies' memorable gesture in waiting for 15 minutes, in torrential rain aboard an open coach, so they could applaud their conquerors. When they realized what had happened, Charlie Roberts and company, who had been celebrating in their dressing room oblivious of their soaking opponents, were acutely embarrassed. The fans, of course, were consumed by other emotions. At that point in football's development, the FA Cup, with all its attendant glamour and the drama of sudden death, exceeded even the League Championship in terms of prestige, and the red half of Manchester was awash with tension and anticipation as the day of the final approached.

The opponents were Bristol City, who were second favourites despite finishing five places above United in the First Division table and the clash was given added spice because the West Countrymen's leading light was Billy Wedlock, the relatively tiny but extremely skilful centre half who denied Charlie Roberts a regular England berth. Here, it seemed, was the ideal opportunity to compare the merits of the two rivals, thrown into direct opposition on the national game's gala day. In the event, though Wedlock did well, it was United's captain who prevailed, dominating the middle of the field while 34-year-old Meredith sparkled on the wing, although the overall standard of play never came remotely close to reflecting the importance of the occasion. Sadly, as so often occurs in a final, the two teams cancelled each other out and a flintily dour contest was settled by a single first-half strike from the reliable Sandy Turnbull. Ironically, the Reds marksman was not really fit enough to play and only shortly before kickoff had contemplated withdrawing because of a knee injury, but his skipper, seeing him correctly as the potential key ingredient, insisted on risking him.

Clad imposingly in a white shirt with a deep red 'V' – both clubs usually wore red so they changed for the final, the Robins settling on blue – Roberts accepted the trophy from Lord Charles Beresford, commander-in-chief of the Channel Fleet. The massive Manchester contingent at the Crystal Palace stadium erupted with glee. If anything, the scenes of celebration were even more tumultuous when United took the FA Cup home three days later, with massive crowds gathering outside Manchester Central station and lining the streets as the party passed triumphantly in carriages, to the strains of 'Hail the Conquering Hero Comes', to a reception at the Town Hall.

That day in Albert Square, all appeared to be sweetness and light in the world of Manchester United, but bitter disharmony lay in wait. Within a few weeks, the players were locked out of Bank Street and threatening a strike that would have paralysed English football. Essentially the problem was over

*The 1909 FA Cup final at Crystal Palace, v Bristol City. Sandy Turnbull (out of shot) scores the 22nd-minute winning goal as Bristol City goalkeeper Clay is beaten. Watching are United players, (in white) Billy Meredith (left) and Harold Halse.*

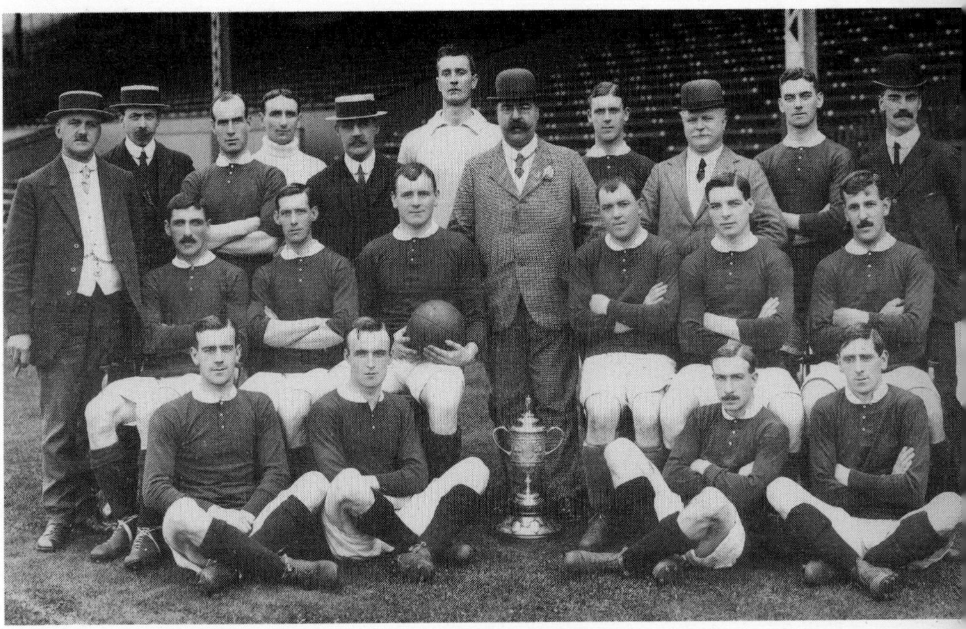

*A team from 1911, with a replica of the FA Cup, assembled to commemorate the 1909 FA Cup win, l-r: back row – Mangnall (sec/man), Bacon (trainer), Picken, Edmonds, Mr Murray (dir), Moger, John Henry Davies, Homer, Mr Lawton (dir), Alex Bell, Mr Deakin (dir); middle row – Meredith, Duckworth, Roberts, Sandy Turbnbull, West, Stacey; front row – Whalley, Hofton, Halse, Wall.*

the players' union, which had been formed in 1898 but then practically died on its feet until independent spirits such as Roberts and Meredith gave it new impetus a decade later. The principle under debate was whether the Union of Professional Footballers should be allowed to join the Federation of Trades Union, the League and FA taking the view that if it did then players might become involved in wider disputes in support of, say, miners, engineers or railway workers.

The argument concerned the whole English game, but the chief crusaders were the United contingent and it was at Bank Street where the issue came to a head. Suspended without pay and banned from entering their own headquarters, the players trained instead at the Manchester Athletic Ground in Fallowfield, where they posed for a famous team photograph in which Roberts is holding a placard bearing the defiant legend 'The Outcasts FC'.

With the 1909-10 season only five days away, the deadlock remained, with the authorities still attempting to enforce their edict against union membership and Roberts leading his men with the same inspiration that he

**50 Greatest Players**

**CHARLIE ROBERTS Defender**

**Born:** Darlington, 6 April 1883

**Joined Manchester United:** 1904 **From:** Grimsby Town

**Debut:** 23 April 1904 v Burton United, League

**Appearances:** 302 **Goals:** 23

**Left Manchester United:** 1913 **For:** Oldham Athletic

**Honours won with United:** Division One championship 1908, 1911; FA Cup winner 1909

Charlie Roberts was one of the great centre halves of his generation and also the first United skipper to get his hands on the league championship trophy and the FA Cup. The tough, no-nonsense defender joined United from Grimsby in 1904 and fast became a pivotal figure in secretary Ernest Mangnall's plans to build a side to compete against the best. The masterplan reached fruition in 1908 when Roberts led United to their initial league title and 12 months later when the club lifted the FA Cup for the first time. He was also captain in 1911 when the championship trophy found a home at Old Trafford for the first time. Roberts, a founding member of the Players' Union (later the Professional Footballers' Association), was capped three times for England, a figure that would have been increased but for his outspoken views and loyalty to the players' cause.

brought to his on-field captaincy. With 'the Thin Red Line' refusing to budge, a strike seemed inevitable and Bradford City, due to be United's first opponents of the new season, were warned that the game was in jeopardy.

But on the eve of that Bank Street clash, the employers changed their tune. In what some observers perceived as a backdown, others a truce, but which was most likely a fudge, the union was recognized, bans were lifted and arrears of pay were handed over. It seemed that the players had won a priceless victory by their courageous stand and certainly Roberts and company were to be congratulated, but still the clubs enjoyed iniquitous power over their employees, a situation which would not be righted for another half a century. Still, it was a major relief to football-hungry fans when the new term got under way with a home victory over the Yorkshiremen, though the main focus of that campaign was to be less on the team, which proved rather unpredictable and finished fifth in the First Division, and more on the club's headquarters.

## Welcome to Old Trafford

For a long time it had been increasingly obvious that Bank Street, with its vile smell and inhospitable surface, was wholly unsuitable for the ambitious club. Meanwhile, John Henry Davies had acted with imagination and generosity, loaning £60,000 of his personal fortune towards the establishment of a state-of-the-art stadium with an 80,000 capacity in the southwest of the city. Thus Manchester United bade farewell to Clayton on 22 January 1910 with a 5-0 win over Spurs, and welcomed Liverpool to kick off the Old Trafford era four weeks later on 19 February. With a characteristic disregard for Mancunian sensibilities, the Anfielders ruined the Reds' housewarming, recovering from a deficit of 3-1 to win 4-3, but at least there was no doubting the magnificence of the new ground. Complete with the biggest grandstand in the League, it boasted fabulous facilities far removed from the game's Victorian norm. A gymnasium, massage room, plunge baths, bars, lifts, tearooms... it must have seemed like a pleasure dome in comparison to the spartan facilities of earlier days and it might have been on a different planet to the Three Crowns. Certainly the move had proved timely, not only because of the much-needed modernity, but also because United's old home had become unsafe. Shortly after their departure, gales wrecked a wooden stand, carrying the debris across the road and damaging several houses. Luckily no one was hurt, but had it happened when a crowd was present the consequences would have been catastrophic.

Though that landmark season had finished anti-climactically football-wise, the Reds made up for it in their first full campaign at Old Trafford, when the league crown was lifted for the second time in four years. Buoyed by the signing of Nottingham Forest centre forward Enoch 'Knocker' West, Mangnall's team got off to a flying start with a 2-1 win at Woolwich Arsenal's Manor Ground and went on to entertain royally, the forward line of Meredith, Halse, West, Sandy Turnbull and Wall earning frequently rapturous acclaim. For all that, though, the side lacked consistency, and when the climax of the season approached the initiative in the title race had passed to Aston Villa.

### A Second Title

Certainly when the Midlanders beat United in the Reds' penultimate game it looked as though they would prevail, as the pair were level on points and Villa had a match in hand. But then the favourites could only draw with Blackburn, giving them a one-point advantage to take into the final day. United could only win and hope for the best and even after thumping third-placed Sunderland 5-1 in their last game, there was still agonizing uncertainty for footballers and fans alike as they sweated on the result from Anfield, where a Villa victory would have secured the prize.

The tremulous scene was captured by Charlie Roberts in an interview with the old *Saturday Post*: 'At the end of the game our supporters rushed across the ground in front of the stand to wait for the final news from Liverpool. Suddenly a tremendous cheer rent the air and was renewed again and again and we then knew we were the champions once again.' Villa had been beaten 3-1 and United had triumphed by a single point.

It was a marvellous achievement, underlining the stature of Mangnall's creation as arguably the finest team of the Edwardian age – only Newcastle could reasonably take issue with that verdict – but also it signalled the end of an era, the final flourish of Manchester United's first great team. Thereafter, it would be no fewer than 41 years before the Reds could claim the mantle of English champions once again and untold travail would be suffered in the meantime.

There were hints of the difficulties to come during the early months of 1911-12 when the team blew hot and cold, with their Charity Shield meeting with Southern League champions Swindon Town at Stamford Bridge in September being one of the warmer occasions. United won a staggeringly open contest 8-4, with Harold Halse netting six times in succession, a once-in-a-lifetime display which was later recalled with wonder by Billy Meredith, when he told the *Manchester Football Chronicle*: 'Nobody else could get a kick of the ball but Halse and every time he scored he said to the Swindon goalkeeper "I'll be back in a minute!"'

For most of a lacklustre campaign, however, there was precious little to enthuse over, certainly in comparison to the rousing deeds of recent seasons. Frequent absences of key players through injury and illness were partly to blame for the disappointment of finishing 13th in the First Division pecking order and it might have been worse. There were only four victories after the turn of the year and but for a late surge, which included five points in the last three games and an unlikely triumph over newly-crowned champions Blackburn Rovers, the Reds might have faced demotion.

Overall, there was an inescapable impression that the team was passing its peak. That said, only Meredith among the key players had reached the veteran stage and, like Stanley Matthews later in the century, he was a rare exception, a seemingly indestructible individual whose effectiveness was not withered by age. Whatever the reason for the rapid decline, it would appear that wise fellow Ernest Mangnall might have sensed storm clouds on the Old Trafford horizon and supporters were stunned in August 1912 by his sudden departure to take over the reins of Manchester City. Undoubtedly United were the poorer for the departure of the man who had transformed their

*Enoch 'Knocker' West was bought to bolster the strikeforce for the 1910-11 season and his 19 goals helped United win their second championship.*

footballing fortunes since his arrival nine years earlier. Not only was he one of the best judges of a player in the land and a charismatic fellow adept at communicating with his charges, but also he was an expert publicist and an able administrator with plenty of working capacity left in him. Duly he spent a dozen productive years at Hyde Road, guiding City through testing times of their own.

Mangnall's successor as secretary-manager was J.J. Bentley, an older man who was vastly experienced in administration, and who deserved considerable credit for guiding United to fourth place in 1912-13, as well as winning the Lancashire Cup for the second time in their history, which was welcomed as an important success. However, the fans' mood was soured by the summer shock of losing Charlie Roberts to neighbouring Oldham Athletic, who paid a club record £1,750 to sign the man who had been United's first Captain Marvel, the cornerstone of all their major triumphs.

Unexpectedly Bentley's side, which retained Stacey, Duckworth, Meredith, West and Wall from the 1910-11 title-winning team, began 1913-14 in splendid fettle. They dropped only two points in their opening ten games, only to crumble distressingly to 14th place by season's end, by which time the retention of the Lancashire Cup offered scant consolation.

Now United's problems intensified. Attendances plummeted as a result of of falling standards on the pitch and restrictions on public movement dictated by the outbreak of World War I. The recruitment of John Robson from

## Great Managers – 1903-12

### ERNEST MANGNALL

United's first purple patch coincided with Ernest Mangnall being appointed club secretary in 1903. He had previously held a similar post with Burnley. Mangnall was to develop into one of the foremost football administrators of the early 20th century. He inherited a struggling club, which had been relegated to Division Two at the end of season 1893-94 and in the intervening years had threatened, on several occasions, to make the return to the top grade without being successful. Mangnall, in collaboration with chairman and club benefactor John Henry Davies, set about transforming the team into one capable of mixing it with the best. His first two seasons saw United finish third in the table and then in 1905-06 they were promoted as runners-up. United's first really great side, which included Harry Moger, Charlie Roberts, Billy Meredith and George Wall, gradually changed their fortunes and in 1908 the league championship arrived at Bank Street. The FA Cup followed a year later and in 1911 another title was added to the honours' list. Mangnall also oversaw the club's move from its less than ideal Bank Street ground in Clayton to the then 80,000 capacity Old Trafford. He moved across town to join neighbours Manchester City in 1912.

Brighton as manager brought no improvement and in 1914-15 the Reds finished a mere point above relegated Chelsea, their plight emphasized by erstwhile stalwart Charlie Roberts leading Oldham to the runners-up spot.

Thereafter the League and FA Cup were abandoned for the duration of the conflict, being replaced by regional emergency competitions, and the Reds' downward spiral gathered pace. With steadily decreasing income through the turnstiles and with the expensive upkeep of Old Trafford to fund, there was a return to dire financial straits. In 1915 the gloom deepened when three United players – Sandy Turnbull, 'Knocker' West and Arthur Whalley – were suspended for life over a betting scandal, along with four from Liverpool and one from Chester. Then came the sickening news that the popular Turnbull had been killed in action while fighting for the Footballers Battalion in Arras, France.

Manchester United had reached a traumatic watershed and for now, it seemed, the only way was down.

# Chapter Three: 1919-39
# When the Cupboard was Bare

After World War I, Manchester United embarked on two rollercoaster decades in which the club's fortunes on and off the pitch veered between numbing mediocrity and outright awfulness. That's not to say there were no new heroes for the fans to cheer – well, there was Joe Spence, at least – but the fellow who made the most dramatic and meaningful contribution to the Old Trafford cause during these wilderness years was not a footballer, but a visionary local businessman. James Gibson was the saviour of the club when it faced bankruptcy in the early 1930s and he remained its benignly shrewd patriarch until his death in 1951. But before examining in detail the timely intervention of the Manchester-born clothing magnate, a look at the seasons preceding United's financial crisis is in order.

When peacetime competition resumed in 1919-20, the Reds were much reduced from their Edwardian pomp. John Robson was still the manager, but few players remained from before the conflict although, amazingly, one of the handful who did was Billy Meredith. Only just, though. During the war the great man had guested for Manchester City and now he wanted to stay with them. However, he became involved in a complicated dispute with United over the projected move and the upshot was that he was still a Red, and still a considerable asset, despite having recently entered his 46th year as the new campaign commenced.

Because of the disagreement, Meredith was not part of the United team which faced Derby County at the Baseball Ground in the first official league game for more than four years. The line-up read: goalkeeper John Mew, full backs Charlie Moore and John Silcock, a half back trio of James Montgomery, Clarrie Hilditch and Arthur Whalley (reprieved from his earlier ban), and a forward line comprising James Hodge, Wilf Woodcock, Joe Spence, Arthur Potts and Fred Hopkin.

Woodcock scored the goal which secured a creditable point against the Second Division champions of 1914-15 and when the Reds lost only one of their first dozen matches, there was widespread optimism that the success of the Mangnall era might be replicated. The populace was eager for entertainment after the privations of war so attendances were healthy, echoing the positive message emanating from Robson's side. But sad, rapid and comprehensive disillusionment was in store. The New Year brought a chronic dip in performance and even the return to the team of the dissatisfied Meredith, whose railing against the exploitation of players by clubs in general was wholly understandable, could not prevent a dismal slump into 12th place at season's end.

## A Period of Decline

Further drab fare followed in 1920-21, when United finished 13th in the First Division, and springtime brought further dismay to the supporters when it was announced that Billy Meredith was to rejoin Ernest Mangnall at City. It was a shame that this great footballer's final days at Old Trafford should have been marred by financial fall-outs but while he made only 14 appearances and scored one goal in his farewell term, he remained enormously popular to the last. Back with City, he made a nonsense of the evidence on his birth certificate by playing on at the top level, cutting a dash in a 1924 FA Cup semi-final when only months short of his 50th birthday.

Meanwhile, the mere mortals he had left behind him at Old Trafford were labouring ever more drearily, despite the heroic efforts of centre forward Joe Spence. The sparky northeasterner scored in six successive autumn outings, including an exhilarating hat-trick in the 3-1 home triumph over Mangnall's and Meredith's Manchester City, but that was a rare high point.

The atmosphere was not lifted by the affable Robson stepping down through ill health in October. At first he served as assistant to his replacement, former Airdrieonians boss John Chapman, but his illness worsened and within three months he was dead. Confronted with a gargantuan task and saddled with a team in which only Spence, Hilditch and Silcock could be described as top-drawer performers, the new manager struggled from the outset. Not unexpectedly he beefed up his squad with two Scottish signings – centre half Neil McBain from Ayr United who acquitted himself well, and marksman William Henderson from Airdrie, who did not. There followed a disastrous sequence of results and a nosedive to the foot of the table which led to a first demotion since Newton Heath days.

Chapman's men made a sprightly beginning to life in the Second Division, and were given an early boost by the signing of attacking centre half Frank Barson, a former blacksmith and celebrated hard man, from Aston Villa for £5,000. A rumbustious Yorkshireman with a reputation for confrontations with authority, Barson was said to have pulled a pistol on one occasion when the Villa boss had annoyed him, and there were countless tales of his physical strength, including an account of a seven-mile trek through heavy snow

*Hard man Frank Barson was brought in to add backbone to the fading team of the 1920s.*

immediately before turning out for Villa against United at Old Trafford.

Unperturbed by the maverick aspect of the Barson character, the Reds saw the England international as the inspiration they needed to lead them back to the top flight, and so keen were they to sign him that club president John Henry Davies, still powerful in the brewery trade, offered him the licence of a pub as an inducement. He accepted and his presence in the team proved uplifting as the Reds completed a reasonably buoyant campaign, finishing in fourth place, three points adrift of promoted West Ham. But if that had seemed like a dawn, it was a false one, as Barson and company dragged their feet to 14th place in 1923-24. It was a horribly anti-climactic season in which the most notable achievement involving United belonged to Oldham's Sam Wynne in the Latics' 3-2 victory at Boundary Park, when the largely unsung full back nudged his way into the headlines by netting twice for each side.

The 1924-25 term began on a light-hearted note when a combined United and City team met a Liverpool and Everton hybrid at City's new headquarters, Maine Road, in a testimonial match for Ernest Mangnall, who was leaving the Blues to become a director of Bolton Wanderers. The more serious business over the subsequent nine months produced the Reds' most memorable postwar season to date as, with Barson massively influential at the core of a niggardly rearguard, they earned promotion as runners-up to Leicester, clinching the position with a goalless draw at Barnsley on the last day.

The immediate aim in 1925-26 was consolidation, and ninth place in the top flight achieved that, while the admirable Spence, by now employed on the right wing, underlined his quality with a succession of effective displays which earned him an England call-up in May. At Old Trafford, now, the most familiar cry from the supporters was: 'Give it to Joe!'

The season was not without its pain, however. In January a stirring sequence of victories was rudely interrupted by a 6-1 home thrashing at the hands of City, and the humiliation of United supporters appeared to be

**50 Greatest Players**

**BILLY MEREDITH Forward**

**Born:** Chirk, 30 July 1874

**Joined Manchester United:** 1906 **From:** Manchester City

**Debut:** 1 January 1907 v Aston Villa, League

**Appearances:** 335 **Goals:** 36

**Left Manchester United:** 1921 **For:** Manchester City

**Honours won with United:** Division One championship 1908, 1911; FA Cup winner 1909

Billy Meredith was a mega-star in the days when media-hyped titles hadn't even been invented. A lavishly talented winger, he could be best described as the Ryan Giggs of the pre-World War I era. He came from the land of the Red Dragon, was a crowd-pleaser and was dubbed the 'Welsh wizard' by his admirers. He was arguably *the* star of United's first great side that captured the league championship in 1908 and 1911 and the FA Cup in 1909. And he was also one of the rare individuals to be acclaimed by both United and City supporters in Manchester. Meredith collected 48 caps for Wales winning the final one, against Northern Ireland, when he was just four months short of his 46th birthday.

complete when the Blues cuffed their team aside 3-0 in an FA Cup semi-final at Bramall Lane, a particularly demoralizing result in view of recent failures in the knockout competition. Soon, though, it was the Red contingent who were laughing as their rivals lost the final to Bolton Wanderers, then were relegated a week later.

## Managers Come and Go

Now United, who had played host to their first full international when Scotland beat England 1-0 in April 1926, appeared to have a platform from which to push on towards the summit of the English game but, beneath the surface, all was not well at Old Trafford. An indifferent start to 1926-27 was followed by a bombshell from the Football Association, who dispatched a telegram to the Reds' board which read as follows: 'For improper conduct in his position as secretary-manager of your club, Mr J.A. Chapman is suspended from taking any part in football or football management during the present season.'

The nature of Chapman's alleged misdemeanour has never been revealed, but it was sufficiently serious for the directors to sack him on the spot, handing responsibility for team affairs to skipper Clarrie Hilditch. The new player-boss presided over an up-and-down winter which declined into a doleful spring and in April he was replaced by Herbert Bamlett, who had formerly held the managerial reins at Oldham, Wigan Borough and Middlesbrough. Bamlett was also an ex-referee, who at 32 had been the youngest to take charge of an FA Cup final in 1914, but was best remembered in the United camp as the man who was too cold to blow his whistle when their tie with Burnley had been abandoned in a blizzard back in 1909, when the trophy had finished up at Old Trafford.

If that was seen as a favourable omen for the Bamlett reign, then it turned out to be sadly misleading. Season 1927-28 brought toil and disappointment on the pitch, where the continued excellence of 22-goal Spence was the only significant beacon of light, and grief off it with the death in October of John Henry Davies. Personal considerations apart, the loss of such a generous benefactor was ominous at a time when the club's financial situation was mirroring the worsening economic depression in the world at large. The fact that Bamlett's team came 18th in the First Division, a mere point above doomed Tottenham Hotspur, was hardly mitigated by appearance in the FA Cup quarter-finals or even a last-day 6-1 annihilation of Liverpool, to which Spence contributed a hat-trick.

The 1928-29 campaign offered marginally more hope, a late sequence of victories lifting the Reds to midway in the table. But form was unremittingly poor in 1929-30 when only two points separated the Reds from the drop, and FA Cup defeat by Third Division Swindon Town at Old Trafford emphasized their sorry plight.

As if that was not humbling enough, the standard of play reached a new low at the outset of 1930-31, when Manchester United lost their first dozen games, scoring 14 goals while conceding a barely credible 49. A victory in the 13th match, at home to Birmingham on the opening day of November, produced rapturous applause but it was tinged with irony. There was no fooling the paying customers, who were dwindling alarmingly but understandably in number, and they knew that the Reds had declined into a desperately poor side by First Division standards.

By then the fans were already holding public meetings to debate the crisis, culminating in a five-point plan of action which was presented to the club in the form of an ultimatum. The revolutionaries wanted a change in management, new players, a revamped scouting system, the raising of money through a share issue and the election of five shareholders to the board. If all of this was not forthcoming, then they threatened a boycott of the imminent home meeting with Arsenal. The response from Old Trafford was a deafening silence, but at that point the majority of fans were not ready to vote with their feet and 23,406 turned up to witness the Gunners' 2-1 win. By then the players were the subject of scathing public criticism, but they found a champion in former skipper Charlie Roberts, long since retired, who blamed rotten management for the mess.

For their part, the board sounded a distinctly pathetic note, pointing to bad luck and injuries, but they did not make a decisive move until April when, with relegation inevitable, they dismissed Bamlett and asked Walter Crickmer to combine his duties as club secretary with those of team manager. Ironically the season ended on an untypically entertaining note when the Reds and Middlesbrough shared eight goals at Old Trafford, but only 3,969 people were there to watch and the result could not disguise the poverty of United's position, nine points adrift at the bottom of the table.

## United are Relegated

As 1931-32 began, the future could not have looked much blacker. Debts continued to mount, the football was dreadful and even the traditionally eternal August optimism of fans everywhere had evaporated, as demonstrated by the attendance of 3,507 for the opening home game, a 3-2 defeat by Southampton. In Crickmer, nevertheless, United were blessed with a magnificent servant who, assisted by faithful chief scout and general factotum Louis Rocca, strove tirelessly to improve a side which continued to rely heavily on the indefatigably brilliant Joe Spence.

To the workaholic Walter, who had enlisted as an office boy shortly after the Great War and would continue to be an Old Trafford bulwark until he lost his life in the Munich disaster some 40 years later, would fall the trauma of discovering the full seriousness of the club's situation. Shortly before Christmas 1931, he wrote a cheque to cover the players' wages and called at the bank to collect the cash, an apparently routine task. But this time was different; this time he was turned away; the cupboard was bare. Now, surely, Manchester United were doomed, first to bankruptcy and then, with a grisly inevitability, to extinction. Others had perished in the same manner and the Reds were not exempt from the financial slump which was gripping the whole of the capitalist world.

But then one man, appalled by the prospect, had a bright idea. Sports writer Stacey Lintott, who had been following the story in his professional capacity, now took a crucial hand in shaping its outcome by appealing for help to the wealthy head of a hugely successful local clothing company. James Gibson had made a fortune producing military uniforms during the war, then expanded his operation by selling to railways, local authorities and other civilian outlets when hostilities ceased. Like John Henry Davies, the rescuer of United some three decades earlier, he was not a football fan at the time his attention was drawn to the club, but he believed in the benefits of sport, he loved the city passionately and he did not want it to be deprived of one of its most cherished institutions. Accordingly, he announced that he would pay the players' wages, bought a turkey for every member of staff (a club tradition that had looked like going by the board that year) and made £2,000 available to cover pressing expenses.

## A New Benefactor is Found

Gibson made his longer-term intentions clear to the *Manchester Guardian* on 22 December: 'Though I have decided to see United through the coming month, I am not prepared to be a milch cow... unaccountable inertia is responsible for United's downfall. I do not blame the public for staying away. The board of management has never taken the public into their confidence and they could not expect them to keep rolling up while a hush-hush policy has been adhered to. I am at the head of United now and if the public will back me and give any justification for carrying on, I will assure them that the United will not fail. Manchester is surrounded with large towns to support two first-class teams. It will be some time before anyone can establish a winning team and I do not intend to try immediately.'

The effect on the beleaguered club was electric. In the match which preceded his declaration, against Bristol City on 19 December, the crowd had numbered 4,697; the attendance for the first game afterwards, when Wolves visited on Christmas Day, was 33,123.

The fans had spoken every bit as eloquently as he had hoped and he was particularly moved by the receipt of a one shilling postal order from a working man whom the pressures of everyday life would not allow to attend games, but who was keen to contribute his mite to the Reds' salvation. Duly the new chairman appointed his own set of directors – the former board had taken the only conceivable course by resigning –

*New chairman James Gibson provided welcome financial support for a United in serious trouble.*

*Scott Duncan was taken on by James Gibson as team boss when United were in the doldrums of Division Two. He lead them to championship glory in 1935-36.*

and soon he confirmed plans to sign a new manager and players.

The renaissance began euphorically with a 3-2 victory over Wolves in that fateful yuletide confrontation and although the effect was rather spoiled by a 7-0 Boxing Day defeat at Molineux, Crickmer's side rallied in the spring to secure 12th place in the Second Division. No great shakes for a club of United's stature, but considering the tumultuous background against which it was achieved, it was eminently acceptable.

That summer, true to his word, James Gibson began to invest heavily in the Reds' future, modernizing the ground and recruiting Scott Duncan from Cowdenbeath as team boss, thus allowing Crickmer to concentrate exclusively on his administrative duties once more. However, as Gibson had warned, there would be no magical transformation to the team. Duncan spent lavishly on new players, most of them fellow Scots including Neil Dewar from Third Lanark and Willie Stewart from Cowdenbeath, but United were a dozen points short of promotion in 1932-33, then slumped in a potentially calamitous way in 1933-34.

Inevitably by then, several erstwhile bastions were departing. Joe Spence, who scored 168 goals in 510 games for a side which often was not worthy of him, joined Bradford City; there was the retirement of loyal, gentlemanly wing half and stand-in manager, Clarrie Hilditch, and the stalwart full back Jack Silcock would leave to wind down his career in a distinctly anti-climactic way with an unsuccessful trial at Oldham come season's end. In their prime, they were all men who could lift an ailing team and their replacements, to be blunt, were not quite up to scratch.

Not surprisingly, then, the closing weeks of 1933-34 were distressingly fraught, with the hitherto unthinkable prospect of Third Division football looming large despite the springtime recruitment of four new faces: goalkeeper Jack Hacking from Oldham, right back Jack Griffiths from Bolton and wing halves Willie Robertson and Bill McKay from Stoke and Bolton respectively. When the Reds lost at West Ham in early April, they appeared to be doomed, but then a win and three draws set up a stomach-churning last-day encounter with fellow strugglers Millwall.

### The Only Way is Up

As they ran out at the Den, United had plumbed the lowest depth in their history to date, standing in 21st place in the Second Division. The situation was clear-cut: a defeat or a draw would condemn Scott Duncan's men to relegation; a victory would send the Lions down in their place. More hung on this desperate encounter than on any cup final... and this time the Manchester Reds did not disappoint. Against the expectations of all but the most optimistic of their followers, and despite being reduced to ten fit men through an injury to Ernie Hine, United prevailed 2-0 thanks to goals from Tom Manley and Jack Cape. The names of the team Duncan picked that day deserved to be enshrined forever on the club's roll of honour: between the posts stood Hacking; Griffiths and Tom Jones were the full backs; Robertson, ball-playing stopper Bill Vose and McKay made up the half back line; and the front five were Cape, Hugh McLenahan, Jack Ball, Hine and Manley.

Back home the fans whooped as if a championship had been lifted, but a sense of perspective was necessary. Using no fewer than 38 players, United had just completed a sorry Second Division campaign in which they had

**50 Greatest Players**

**JOE SPENCE Forward**

**Born:** Throckley, 13 December 1898

**Joined Manchester United:** 1919 **From:** Scotswood

**Debut:** 30 August 1919 v Derby County, League

**Appearances:** 510 **Goals:** 168

**Left Manchester United:** 1933 **For:** Bradford City

Joe Spence, like Billy Meredith, was a crowd-pleaser but unlike the Welsh star he was to negotiate his lengthy stint at United without collecting any silverware. But Spence was always a great favourite among United followers and for much of the time almost single-handedly carried their hopes and dreams that something better may be around the corner. An exciting and gifted forward, such was his popularity that supporters were heard to shout: 'Give it to Joe!' when events weren't going in the right direction. Spence was capped twice by England and won the Third Division (North) title with Chesterfield in 1936 – scant reward for a player who'd given so much to the game.

*United's Second Division championship-winning side, 1935-36, l-r: back row – Gibson (chairman), Ferrier, Griffiths, Breedon, Curry (trainer), Hall, Porter, Manley, Duncan (manager); middle – Cape, Mutch, Bamford, Brown (captain), Rowley, McKay, Vose; front – Bryant, Robertson, Owen, Redwood.*

been trounced by the likes of Grimsby Town, Bradford Park Avenue and even bottom-placed Lincoln City. Meanwhile, Manchester City, riding high in the top flight and being inspired by a cultured Scottish wing half who went by the name of Matt Busby, had won the FA Cup. The fact that the Reds' leading scorer during that harrowing season had been Neil Dewar with eight league goals emphasized the need for more firepower and it arrived in the form of George Mutch from Arbroath in May, Wrexham's Tommy Bamford in October and Harry Rowley of Oldham in December. That had the desired effect, with Mutch a particular success, contributing 18 strikes towards a fifth-place finish which resulted in a marked improvement in attendances.

## Fortunes are Up and Down

That upward trend was confirmed joyously in 1935-36 when Duncan shuffled his team as little as possible and United carried off the Second Division title, finishing a point ahead of runners-up Charlton Athletic. This first major honour for a quarter of a century was based on a doughty defence, in which Vose was outstanding, and the goals of the ever-present Mutch, who netted 21 times and was ably supported by Rowley (19), Bamford (16) and Manley (14). Now United fans believed a glorious new era was beckoning, and so there was, but not yet. In 1936-37 they failed to come to terms with life among the elite and crashed back to earth with a thud, finishing 21st and making an instant return to the lower grade. For the Reds' long-suffering followers, it hardly helped that Manchester City were the new champions.

Gradually, as the clamour for better players rose to a crescendo, the realization was dawning at Old Trafford that the future should be based on youth, but United were unlucky that one promising youngster who made his debut that term saw his career curtailed cruelly by a potentially crippling disease of the spine. Rookie centre half Walter Winterbottom was being touted as an England possible after excelling with a compelling blend of strength and intelligence in United's hard-pressed rearguard. That dream died, but the articulate Lancastrian turned instead to coaching and ended up as his country's first and longest-serving manager, between 1946 and 1962.

For Scott Duncan, though, time was running out at Old Trafford. After registering only five wins in the first 14 matches of the new Second Division season, and disagreeing with chairman Gibson over the need for more spending on the team, the Scot resigned in November. Back into temporary harness climbed the dependable Walter Crickmer who, abetted once more by Louis Rocca and aided nobly by trainer Tom Curry, oversaw a dramatic turnaround in fortune. Crickmer's first match in his second stint at the helm was at Chesterfield, where Bamford struck four times in a 7-1 victory and a Salford-born 18-year-old inside forward called Stan Pearson made an encouraging debut. That was the start of a storming sequence which saw United beaten only once in 13 matches as other young men, such as the stylish, softly-spoken Irishman Johnny Carey and abrasive, goal-hungry Black Countryman Jack Rowley, made their presence felt.

As impetus built towards a hitherto unexpected promotion bid, February brought two fascinating developments. The first was a reported offer of £6,000 plus a part-exchange player to sign the incomparable Stanley Matthews from Stoke City, where he had become unsettled. In the event, the English game's brightest star would continue to shine for the Potters, with whom he patched up his differences, until his move to Blackpool in 1947.

Of more far-reaching significance to the Old Trafford cause was a proposal to launch the Manchester United Junior Athletic Club (MUJAC), which was to form the basis of the most productive youth policy in the land. James Gibson's statement of club policy could hardly have been firmer when he said: 'We have no intention of buying any more mediocrities. Our aim is a United composed of Manchester players.'

## 50 Greatest Players

**JOHN SILCOCK Defender**

**Born:** Wigan, 15 January 1898

**Joined Manchester United:** 1916 **From:** Atherton

**Debut:** 30 August 1919 v Derby County, League

**Appearances:** 449 **Goals:** 2

**Left Manchester United:** 1934 **For:** Oldham Athletic

Jack Silcock was the archetypal loyal servant that provides continuity and stability at any football club. The Lancastrian patrolled United's defence with distinction throughout his lengthy career at the club, linking up with keeper Jack Mew and fellow rearguard specialist Charlie Moore on numerous occasions. The trio amassed close on 1,000 appearances between them for the club, but none collected any senior honours while at United. Silcock and Mew were capped by England. Silcock played for his country on three occasions, but on the club front his 18 years were rewarded with little more than the pride of knowing that he'd given loyal and unstinting service through some of the most unsuccessful years in United's history. He later continued his career in the Manchester area with Oldham Athletic and Droylsden.

### A Return to the Top Flight

Meanwhile, though, the focus was firmly on bouncing back to the top division, which was achieved with a 2-0 home triumph over Bury in front of 53,604 spectators on the season's final day, when the unfortunate Sheffield United were pipped for the runners-up spot by the merest fraction of a goal. The glee of Reds fans, already unconfined, was heightened still further by the supreme irony of Manchester City being relegated only 12 months on from their title triumph, a stunning reversal of fortunes for the two passionate rivals.

The 1938-39 campaign produced rather uneasy consolidation and a mid-table finish, which was something of a relief in the light of recent ups and downs. In March Old Trafford registered its record attendance, when 76,952 squeezed in to watch Wolves beat Grimsby Town in an FA Cup semi-final, but by then football was operating in the shadow of impending war. The following season was only three games old when it was abandoned after German tanks had trundled into Poland. Come the outbreak of peace six years later, Manchester United had acquired a new manager, a certain Matt Busby.

# Chapter Four: 1939-52
# The Miner's Son with a Vision

The smart young man in the trilby hat puffed thoughtfully on his pipe as he surveyed the scene of ruin spread out before him. It was the autumn of 1945 and Matt Busby was about to start work as manager of Manchester United, a football club on its knees. The devastation which met the eyes of the unassuming yet compellingly ambitious Scot was comprehensive. Though Old Trafford had never been a specific target for Hitler's bombs, the close proximity of the Trafford Park industrial estate, the Manchester Ship Canal and the docks made the Reds' headquarters vulnerable should the marksmanship of the Luftwaffe drift only slightly awry, and that was exactly what had happened twice during the fear-ridden winter and spring of 1940-41.

United had been comparatively lucky on 22 December, when the ground had suffered enough damage for the Christmas Day meeting with Stockport County in the North Regional League to be reversed. However, it was a different story when the German raiders returned on the night of 11 March. This time most of the main stand was destroyed, the dressing rooms and offices were wrecked, the playing surface was hideously scorched and pock-marked. Club secretary Walter Crickmer, a member of the Police Volunteer Reserve, was called out as Old Trafford continued to burn and he recalled later: 'It was a heartbreaking sight. I tried to reach the dressing rooms to save the kit, but I couldn't get near.'

It was the most extensive devastation suffered by any league club during the war and the four years since the bombs had fallen had done nothing to heal the scars. As Busby reflected on his decision to throw in his lot with United, the stand remained a contorted shell, a large bush sprouted on the pitch, weeds were creeping over the terracing and the only training area for the players was the cindered car park. To make matters worse, his new employers were some £15,000 in debt, an intimidating sum at a time of severe austerity in postwar Britain. How much wiser it might have seemed to accept an offer from his current club, Liverpool, to become player-coach and assistant boss at Anfield, or to work his way up the managerial ladder through the likes of either Reading or Ayr United, both keen to enlist him.

But Busby was beguiled by the vast potential of Manchester United and, given the club's lack of recent success, Old Trafford offered a relatively clean slate on which he could inscribe his signature. A strong character and a natural leader who had captained Scotland in wartime internationals, he was mature beyond his years after losing his father at the age of six and enduring a tough upbringing as the family's eldest son in the Lanarkshire mining village of Orbiston. He was a visionary, too, and brought with him a fundamentally fresh approach to the job. For instance, he was a passionate believer in team spirit, having seen other clubs founder for the lack of it, and he reckoned he could foster it best by donning a tracksuit to spend time with his players, a near-revolutionary touch which caused some of his pin-striped fellow bosses to scoff, although before too long, they were changing their tune.

## Busby Takes Charge

After making up his mind, Busby acted with typical decisiveness. First he insisted on a five-year contract instead of the proffered three-year agreement because it was clear to him that a lasting transformation involved long-term commitment; and then he made the most important signing of his life by recruiting Jimmy Murphy as his assistant. The pair had been friendly since their playing days – Matt had been a wing half with Manchester City and Liverpool, Jimmy filling the same role for West Bromwich Albion – but it was during their Army service that the shrewd Scot had identified the fiery, loquacious Welshman as his ideal right-hand man. A few minutes listening

*Old Trafford suffered the most serious bomb damage of any of the league clubs during the war. Undaunted, Matt Busby rebuilt the team and stadium and propelled United into a period of unparalleled success on the field.*

to Murphy's passionate fervour as he talked football to a group of players at a sports centre in Bari, Italy, prompted Busby to declare: 'If you fancy a job when you are demobbed, Jimmy, come and look me up at Old Trafford.' Thus one of the game's most inspirational and perfectly balanced partnerships came into being. They were destined to remain in productive harness together for more than a quarter of a century, experiencing highs and lows the like of which would have been impossible to imagine back in 1945, and producing three supremely entertaining sides in the process.

In view of the parlous state of the club, most observers expected a lengthy period of team-building before the Reds re-emerged as a major power, but their record in the first six years of the Busby-Murphy reign makes nonsense of that notion. In the League they finished second, second, second, fourth, second and first in 1951-52, and picked up the FA Cup in 1948. The team pioneered the modern tradition of Manchester United, always daring to flow forward so that it might entertain and emerge victorious, but never afraid to risk gallant defeat. In terms of soul, if not of accumulated silverware, it was a combination which nudged genuine greatness.

Crucially, although cash was in short supply, when Matt and Jimmy surveyed the footballing assets at their disposal they were rich men. Four players who would form the basis of the side had already made their entrances before the war. There was the personable Dubliner Johnny Carey, who developed into one of the most accomplished of all British full backs; Stan Pearson, the subtly intelligent, supremely incisive schemer-cum-scorer who hailed from Salford; dynamic centre forward Jack Rowley, who somehow escaped the scouting net of his local club, Wolverhampton Wanderers; and that granite bulwark of a centre half Allenby Chilton. Also at Old Trafford already were the versatile, eager and deceptively skilful John Aston, who would form such a magnificent full back partnership with Carey; Henry Cockburn, an endlessly combative, superbly constructive wing half; the dashing Charlie Mitten, an uncannily adept manipulator of a football who was destined to become an all-time Old Trafford favourite on the left wing; feisty little inside right Johnny Morris, an irrepressible Lancastrian whose boundless ability was matched by his raw bravery; and goalkeeper Jack Crompton, the very antithesis of flamboyance but reassuringly consistent and a top-rate athlete.

What they did not constitute, however, was a ready-made team: that was where Busby and Murphy came in. For instance, before excelling so influentially as a right back, and later at right half, Carey had been a stylish but ultimately unremarkable inside forward; Aston, too, majored as an attacker in his youth and occasionally he would return to the front as United's need dictated, but it was with a No. 3 on his back that he reached his zenith; Chilton was a grindingly industrious wing half, but it wasn't until he became a stopper that he revealed his full potential. All these important switches came about – and briskly, too – through the insight and imagination of Matt Busby and Jimmy Murphy.

Still, though, it was evident to the manager that the picture was not quite complete. He needed a right winger and to find him his eyes turned to his homeland, where they lighted upon a balding thirty-something dismissed by the majority of pundits as being past his pomp. In addition, Jimmy Delaney of Celtic and Scotland was written off widely as an unacceptably high fitness risk, being dubbed 'Old Brittlebones' in reference to previous career-threatening arm and shoulder injuries. But Busby was confident about the pedigree of his former international team-mate and duly in February 1946 he paid £4,000 to secure the veteran's services. In truth, even the United boss saw it as a short-term acquisition, yet Delaney was to vindicate Matt's judgment handsomely.

As well as being a penetrative flank runner and a tellingly accurate crosser, Jimmy scored vital goals, too, relishing the perceptive service of inside forwards Morris and Pearson. Then, when his Old Trafford day was done and he left to join Aberdeen as a 36-year-old, Delaney attracted a fee of £3,500. Thus, if his wages are discounted – and for a club watched by massive crowds, as United were during the late-1940s boom, they amounted to peanuts – the Reds had incurred a net expenditure of £500 in exchange for nearly half a decade of sensationally effective service. Certainly his team-mates were in no doubt as to his value. The effervescent Mitten gave him the nickname of '100mph Jim' and Morris, with whom he formed a dazzling right wing partnership, said: 'He was the biggest bargain Matt Busby ever struck. I always knew exactly where he was and I could send him the ball without looking up. He was a great fellow, too.'

That sort of warmth and loyalty was typical of the team ethos engendered by the rookie boss and described in revealing detail by Crompton: 'We were such a close-knit bunch that any one of us could have spoken for the other ten, and that despite the usual mix of personalities you would find anywhere. We had our extroverts like Johnny Morris and jokers like Charlie Mitten, who was always quick-witted and light-hearted, while a lot of us were quieter. John Carey, the skipper, was a diplomat with a touch of the blarney, while Allenby Chilton was our leader on the field, a screamer and a shouter but always one of the lads. There were no prima donnas. We were all broke together, all on the bus together, all on a level.'

The arrival of Delaney had been too late to take part in the first official competition of the postwar era, the 1945-46 FA Cup. For that season only it had been decided that the ties should be two-legged affairs and peacetime operations were resumed against Accrington at Peel Park, where United earned a 2-2 draw. Stanley were disposed of comfortably in the second leg, which was played at Maine Road, the headquarters of Manchester City, who would rent their home to their neighbours until the blitzed Old Trafford was restored to use in 1949. That victory attracted a modest attendance of 15,339, but it had the salutary effect of stirring up cup fever which had lain dormant throughout the war. Unfortunately, Reds fans suffered an instant cure as their heroes fell to Preston North End in the next round.

## Building a Team for the Future

However, they made a more positive start to the first league campaign of the brave new era in 1946-47, winning their first five games while racking up a total of 14 goals and conceding two. The fourth of those games, a 5-0 annihilation of Liverpool to which Pearson contributed a hat-trick, summed up the exhilarating appeal of Busby's lovely side. They flowed forward like molasses over glass, utterly outclassing the Merseysiders who, as events would prove by season's end, were no mean performers themselves. At that stage United were being described, ludicrously prematurely, as champions elect, but the early momentum was not maintained. Suddenly, the bewildering interchanges of position which had been central to their success appeared to be confusing the Reds as much as their opponents, then injuries to Carey and Mitten further disrupted the rhythm.

Now the manager showed his mettle, tinkering successfully with his combination by the addition of inside right Morris, freshly returned from army service in the autumn, and introducing Aston, until then a rather

*Henry Cockburn, a battling wing half in Matt Busby's first great team, and a medal winner in the 1952 title-winning side.*

moderate performer as a forward or wing half for the reserves, at left back. The new pair slotted in smoothly and the Reds achieved a new consistency which saw them finish creditably as runners-up to Liverpool in the title race, a mere one point adrift and rueing a 1-0 defeat at Anfield.

Though disappointed to be pipped, Matt Busby professed himself satisfied by his first season at the helm at Old Trafford, one in which he had moulded a collection of contrasting talents into an exciting unit. Perhaps even more importantly, he had established himself at the vanguard of a new breed of manager, one who would brook no interference from the board over matters of selection, one who identified his own transfer targets and decided who he wanted to sell. In short, after a brief battle of wills with the autocratic James Gibson, he had established complete sovereignty over football matters, which amounted to a revolution from the pre-war days when directors took advice from their managers before following their own wishes. Busby deserves massive credit for this shift, but so does Gibson, who demonstrated the decisiveness and wisdom which had fashioned his own business empire in recognizing that the club would benefit from having a professional in a position of genuine power.

Thus season 1947-48 began on a note of sky-high optimism, which seemed justified as three points were garnered from two early meetings with the reigning champions. There was no doubt that the Manchester Reds were the most entertaining team in England but once again, infuriatingly, United's consistency unravelled, with only one victory being claimed during September and October, virtually stifling their latest championship bid.

However, a marked midwinter upsurge during which the 'Famous Five' forward line of Delaney, Morris, Rowley, Pearson and Mitten meshed to sublime effect, inspiring a 14-game unbeaten run, moved Busby to predict in January: 'I think we can win the FA Cup.' These were no hollow words. Genuinely he believed his side was on the brink of achieving something special, though always he was seeking to fine-tune it, as he did by promoting wing half John Anderson from reserve to first-team regular following a marvellous display against Middlesbrough's brilliant Wilf Mannion.

## Success in the FA Cup

The season took on renewed impetus from the day the Reds travelled to Villa Park for the third round of the FA Cup. In sheeting rain and cloying mud, two fine sides fought out a titanic contest which ended 6-4 in United's favour, setting them up for a Wembley charge. What was to follow in the remainder of the cup campaign was to define that memorable team's niche in the club's

## Great Matches

**FA CUP THIRD ROUND** — **Villa Park, 19 January 1948**

| Aston Villa 4 | Manchester United 6 | Attendance: 71,401 |
|---|---|---|
| Edwards 2 | Rowley | |
| Smith | Morris 2 | |
| Dorsett (pen) | Pearson 2 | |
| | Delaney | |

Here was the cup tie with everything – ten goals, two storming comebacks, lengthy passages of exquisite football and a nerve-shredding finale, all played out in an ocean of mud in front of a roaring multitude. Villa aimed for a fast start and they stuck to their plan, seizing the lead after some 14 seconds through Edwards without a United man touching the ball. The problem for the Midlanders was that the Reds had plenty of time in which to retaliate, which they did to spectacular effect. Within seven minutes Rowley headed an equalizer from a Mitten cross, which signalled a relentless bombardment of the Villa goal by the visitors, whose dazzling display of passing and movement was all the more remarkable for being performed in a quagmire.

Man-of-the-match Morris put them ahead, then Pearson, Morris again and Delaney added further strikes to stretch the interval lead to a daunting and surely decisive 5-1. Game over? Not a bit of it. Villa came out spitting fire and within a minute Edwards had scored direct from a corner. As rain sheeted down, Smith popped home a rebound from Dorsett's free kick to make it 5-3. Soon Chilton downed the combative Ford and Dorsett thundered home from the spot, then the crowd went berserk as Villa were denied a sensational equalizer when a Ford strike was ruled out for handball. The final word, though, was left to United's Pearson, who netted calmly from a Mitten corner only two minutes from the end of a truly classic encounter.

**Aston Villa:** Jones, Potts, Parkes, Dorsett, Moss, Lowe, Edwards, Martin, Ford, Brown, Smith
**Manchester United:** Crompton, Carey, Aston, Anderson, Chilton, Cockburn, Delaney, Morris, Rowley, Pearson, Mitten
**Referee:** H. Bent

folklore. Facing First Division opposition at every hurdle, and still unable to play at Old Trafford, they demoralized Liverpool 3-0 at Goodison Park, eased to a comfortable 2-0 triumph over Charlton Athletic at Huddersfield, then crushed Preston North End – Tom Finney, Bill Shankly et al – at Maine Road. In the semi-final they encountered Derby County at Hillsborough, where a Stan Pearson hat-trick secured a 3-1 victory and the first visit to Wembley in United's history. There they would meet a Blackpool side featuring the biggest star in the game, Stanley Matthews, as well as England marksman Stan

Mortensen, in what was to be described at the time as the most breathtaking exhibition of club football the famous stadium had ever hosted.

Though the force appeared to be with the Reds – they were on course to finish as runners-up to Arsenal in the League, while the Seasiders were ensconced in mid-table – their preparation for the game was disrupted by two disputes, one between the players and the club over bonuses, and another between the players and the press over payments for interviews. In addition, Jack Crompton was enduring a traumatic time, being distraught at the recent death of his sister and suffering from an excruciatingly painful abscess in his back, which seemed certain to keep him out of the final. The medics declared that he had no chance of regaining fitness, but a last, desperate visit to a surgeon at Ancoats hospital while the rest of the United party headed south worked a minor miracle. Thus, thanks in no small measure to his phenomenal fitness – he would train all day, given the opportunity – Jack walked out at Wembley after all, bandaged so thoroughly that he didn't need his jockstrap.

As well as Blackpool, United were facing the Matthews factor. The Reds were immensely popular with neutral fans – what a contrast with today! – but the Seasiders carried majority public backing through a sentimental desire to see Stan realize his lifetime's ambition of claiming an FA Cup winner's medal. The theory was that, at 33, the newly-crowned inaugural Footballer of the Year would never get a better chance. In the event he would play in another two finals before gaining the coveted gong as a 38-year-old in 1953. However, back in 1948, at 12 minutes past three on 24 April, it seemed as though the Matthews dream would come true by teatime, Blackpool having taken the lead through Eddie Shimwell's penalty after Chilton had felled the charging Mortensen. Soon, Rowley levelled, but Mortensen restored the Seasiders' lead two minutes before the interval, during which there were words of quiet inspiration from Busby and Carey backed up by a few choice imprecations from the abrasive Chilton.

For all that, Blackpool continued to hold sway until 21 minutes from the end when the wily workaholic Morris, distinctly sore from an ankle injury which he had concealed from his boss, planted a quickly-taken free kick on to the head of Rowley, and United were back on terms. Now the Reds attacked compellingly, but the 'Pool were not done and looked set to regain the ascendancy when Mortensen bore down on Crompton, only for the doubtlessly uncomfortable keeper to save at full stretch. Then, conscious of the need for urgency, he hurled the ball instantly to Anderson, who set up Pearson for a majestic goal to make it 3-2 after 80 minutes.

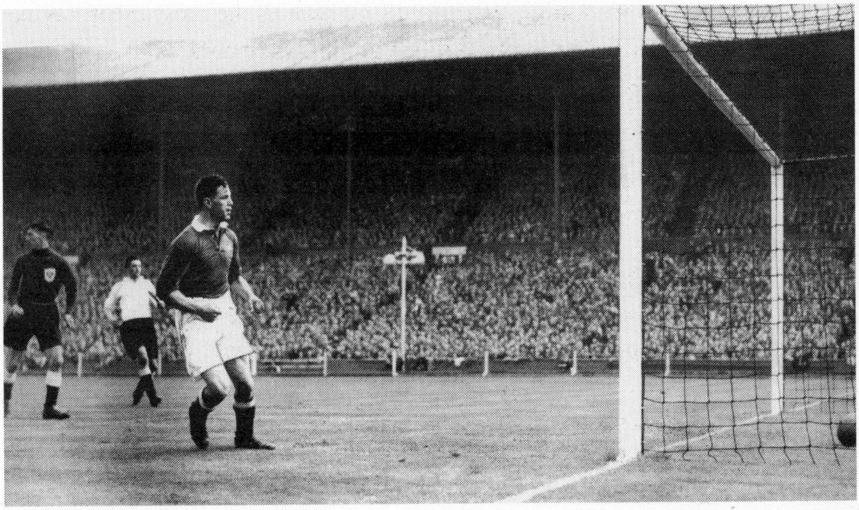

*Rowley scores United's first equalizer in the 1948 FA Cup final against Stanley Matthews' Blackpool. He scored again in a 4-2 win that brought the cup back to Manchester. Below, the programme of the final where United denied Matthews the cherished trophy.*

All that remained was for Anderson, the least-trumpeted member of the side, to fashion his own moment of personal glory with a sudden, dipping 40-yarder. A few minutes later Carey was leading his blue-shirted Reds – both they and the Tangerines had changed colours to avoid a clash – in joyous procession to receive the trophy from King George VI, while the bitterly disappointed but admirably gracious Matthews declared: 'We were beaten by a great team and I offer them my heartiest congratulations.'

Stan's own day of days was still five years down the line; meanwhile, it seemed likely that Matt Busby's glorious creation would have plenty to celebrate in the near future. Having suffered only a handful of defeats since the autumn of 1947, they were favourites for the 1948-49 league crown but another near miss was in store. This time the majority of pundits were surprised by the emergence of Portsmouth, a beautifully co-ordinated side which was damned all too frequently by faint praise but which romped away with the title by five clear points, leaving the Reds to contemplate their third successive second-place finish. At one point, after they had put a total of 22 goals past

Bournemouth, Bradford (who took Busby's men to a second replay), Yeovil Town and Hull City, it seemed that United might retain the FA Cup, but they fell to Wolves in a semi-final replay and finished trophyless.

In March, too, they had suffered what was arguably an even more grievous loss with the shock transfer of 25-year-old Morris to Derby County for what was then a British record fee of £24,500. Johnny was a key member of the team and didn't want to leave, but he disagreed with the club over the thorny matter of a testimonial and he asked for a transfer. Anderson, too, was allowed to leave and, sadly, it would not be long before the exit of another top performer, left winger Charlie Mitten. His departure, at the end of the 1949-50 campaign in which the Reds had bade farewell to Maine Road and returned to a refurbished Old Trafford but had slipped to finish fourth in the table, was understandable.

Even though leading English clubs were making colossal profits during the postwar football boom, a top player picked up a mere £8-per-week during the season, falling to £6 in the summer. No wonder they were disgruntled and no wonder Mitten accepted a £10,000 signing-on fee to join the Colombian club, Santa Fe of Bogota. As he put it succinctly: 'If I'd stayed at United for 25 years I wouldn't have made anything like that. I could have bought a row of houses with what the Colombians gave me and there was a wonderful weekly wage on top. I had to go.' But he was horribly unfortunate. When he left Manchester, Colombia was outside FIFA so he became an outlaw and when the South Americans were readmitted he was suspended, fined, then eventually packed off to Fulham.

Busby's team fragmented further in 1950-51, with the veteran Delaney joining Aberdeen and injured goalkeeper Crompton being replaced by Reg Allen. But with the infusion of a few youngsters, United made progress by regaining the First Division runners-up slot, which they occupied for the fourth time in five seasons. That said, it must have been a mighty relief when United finally finished on top of the pile in 1951-52, especially for the six FA Cup winners still playing regularly for the first team. For Carey, Aston, Chilton, Cockburn, Rowley and Pearson, all in their thirties, it must have felt like time was running out in their quest for title glory, but they made it in the end.

Reinforced by the £25,000 summer arrival from Birmingham City of tenacious little right winger Johnny Berry, who had tormented the Reds repeatedly in recent years and who had been the subject of several previous bids by Busby, United got off to a decent start. Boosted by three Rowley hat-tricks inside three weeks, they won five of their first seven games, but then ran into indifferent form and, having lost six times by mid-November, the

## 50 Greatest Players

**CHARLIE MITTEN Forward**

**Born:** Rangoon, 17 January 1921

**Joined Manchester United:** 1936 **From:** Juniors

**Debut:** 3 August 1946 v Grimsby Town, League

**Appearances:** 162 **Goals:** 61

**Left Manchester United:** 1950 **For:** Santa Fe (Colombia)

**Honours won with United:** FA Cup winner 1948

Although he signed on the dotted line to become a professional early in 1938, Charlie Mitten had to wait until August 1946 to make his league debut for the club as World War II intervened. He was 25 years of age by the time the 1946-47 season opened, but he wasted no time in establishing his place in Matt Busby's first great side. A talented winger with an eye for goal, Mitten was an important member of the United team which lifted the FA Cup in 1948. His future looked assured at Old Trafford, but in 1950 he was tempted to try his luck in Colombia where the financial rewards way outstripped those available in Britain. He returned after a year playing for Santa Fe in Bogota only to face a six-month ban and fine by the FA. He later signed for Fulham and played for Mansfield.

championship prognosis looked gloomy once again. The rollercoaster progress continued with a run of 16 matches without defeat to take them to the top in March, then a mini-slump in the spring which left them neck-and-neck with Arsenal and Portsmouth with six games to play. Cue a piece of inspired management by Busby, switching speedy young full back Roger Byrne to the left wing, and he responded with seven goals which were crucial to a successful run-in comprising four victories and two draws.

### United Grab the Title at Last

The prize was all but secured in the penultimate game, a 3-0 home win over Chelsea, after which the Gunners could only pip United if they won 7-0 at Old Trafford on the final Saturday. In the event the Reds thrashed their rivals 6-1 and finished four points clear, Rowley notching yet another hat-trick which took his league tally for the season to 30, a new club record. Versatility had been a major theme of the triumph. Apart from redeploying Byrne, Matt had used Carey at right back and right half, Aston at centre forward and left back, Rowley at centre forward and on the left flank, and Pearson in both inside forward roles.

*The championship-winning side of 1952, l-r: back row – Curry (trainer), Crickmer (sec); Gibson, MacLean, Whittaker, Petherbridge (directors); Matt Busby (manager); middle row – Downie, Rowley, Aston, Allen, Chilton, Byrne, Pearson; front row – Berry, Carey, Cockburn, McNulty.*

Medals went to Carey, Aston, Cockburn, Chilton (the only ever-present), Allen, Pearson (22 goals), Rowley, Berry, Johnny Downie (Morris' replacement, who chipped in with 11 strikes), Byrne, full backs Tom McNulty and Billy Redman, wing half Don Gibson and winger Ernie Bond. Two men unlucky to miss out were winger Harry McShane, who played 12 times when the gong qualification was 14, and the faithful Crompton, who made nine appearances.

Poignantly, Manchester United's first championship for 41 years, and their third ever, was not witnessed by the man who had ensured the club's survival some two decades earlier, James Gibson having died in September 1951. How he would have relished this new eminence, which none could deny was a just reward for phenomenal consistency in the six seasons immediately following World War II. As Matt Busby put it, perhaps a tad idealistically: 'I don't believe there's another club or set of supporters in the land who would begrudge us this success.' For the endlessly ambitious Scot, though, this was merely the end of the beginning.

# Chapter Five: 1952-58
# The Incomparable Babes

A revolution was fomenting in Manchester, one which would sweep all before it on the football fields of England, then go on to resonate exuberantly across Europe. It stemmed from the vision of Matt Busby who, while taking his first steps in management back in the 1940s, espoused the notion that the only way to lay solid foundations for lasting success was through youth. Accordingly, every appointment to his backroom staff was tailored to that ultimate requirement. Naturally, he needed men capable of embellishing the performance of his then-current first team, which consisted mainly of experienced individuals in their mid-twenties, but the ability to work imaginatively with youngsters was regarded as compulsory.

Thus Busby surrounded himself with the likes of his inspirational assistant, the cheerily demanding Jimmy Murphy; avuncular but firm senior coach Bert Whalley, a former United player; trainers Tom Curry and Bill Inglis; physiotherapist Ted Dalton; and chief scout Joe Armstrong, who unearthed countless gems during his long service at Old Trafford, not least because of his gift for charming the parents of future stars. Under the benevolent aegis of this hand-picked backroom brigade evolved the Busby Babes – a tag which, incidentally, was loathed by the United boss – and not a moment too soon. At an early stage in 1952-53 it became distressingly obvious to Matt that his title winners of the previous

*Johnny Carey was a versatile player and one of Busby's early stalwarts who, as captain, saw United win the FA Cup in 1948 and the championship in 1952.*

campaign were past their best and that the painful business of breaking up the edifice which he had so lovingly constructed could not be postponed if the club was going to avoid a slide towards mediocrity.

He outlined his intentions, boldly and decisively, declaring that he would not need to make repeated forays into the transfer market because there was plenty of young talent worth hundreds of thousands of pounds on the books already. There were those who scoffed, believing that here was just another bluffer promising 'jam tomorrow', but Busby knew he was sitting on a goldmine. Of the reigning champions, Byrne and Berry were not yet in their prime and others of the new wave had been blooded, such as goalkeeper Ray Wood, centre half Mark Jones, wing half Jeff Whitefoot and utility man Jackie Blanchflower. Beyond that his newly-launched youth team – United would lift the inaugural FA Youth Cup in the 1952-53 season and hold it for the first five years of its existence – contained an array of immensely gifted boys, many of whom were destined to become household names. That same term United slipped to eighth place in the table, but a new raft of rookie debutants included intelligent and skilful inside forward John Doherty, graceful winger David Pegg, uncompromising defender Bill Foulkes, incisive

**50 Greatest Players**

**JOHNNY CAREY Defender**

**Born:** Dublin, 23 February 1919

**Joined Manchester United:** 1936 **From:** St James's Gate

**Debut:** 25 September 1937 v Southampton, League

**Appearances:** 346 **Goals:** 18

**Left Manchester United:** 1953 (retired)

**Honours won with United:** Division One championship 1952; FA Cup winner 1948

Manchester United have been served by several great captains and John Carey is up there with the best of them. Matt Busby and Jimmy Murphy could have scarcely wished for a better lieutenant to interpret their plans on the field as they assembled the first great United side of the post World War II era. Carey led by example and there was nothing he wouldn't do for the good of the club – a point highlighted by the fact that he played in every outfield position except outside left and even turned out as goalkeeper in an emergency against Sunderland in February 1953. Despite his versatility it was as an accomplished full back for United and Ireland that he gained his fame. And it was from a place in United's defence that he led them to the FA Cup in 1948 and the championship in 1952. A gently-spoken and well-liked man, he captained the Rest of Europe against Great Britain in 1947 and was named Footballer of the Year in 1949.

marksman Dennis Viollet and an awesome all-rounder by the name of Duncan Edwards.

In addition, the manager made what proved to be his last major purchase for nearly half a decade, beating off competition from nearly 20 rivals to sign the rumbustious centre forward Tommy Taylor from his hometown club, Barnsley, in the March of 1953. For many months Matt had been hunting a long-term successor to the still-vigorous but ageing Jack Rowley and now he broke the Reds' transfer record by paying the Tykes £29,999, the odd pound going to an Oakwell tea lady so as not to saddle his new recruit with the burden of becoming a £30,000 footballer. Not that Taylor appeared prone to that type of pressure, his character an attractive fusion of irrepressible ebullience and feet-on-the-ground good sense, and he made an explosive early impact by netting twice on his debut in a 5-2 home victory over Preston North End, then adding five more goals before the summer recess.

Such is the nature of football, however, that as one new star makes his scintillating entrance to the footballing firmament, so an old one sinks below the horizon's rim, and this time it was the evergreen Carey's turn to depart, having made a mammoth contribution to the United cause. 'Gentleman John' accepted a coaching job with the Reds but did not linger long with the club he had served so majestically since crossing the Irish Sea some 17 years previously, becoming manager of Blackburn Rovers a few months later. While Carey was assessing the possibilities at Ewood Park, his former comrades at Old Trafford were making such a disappointing start to 1953-54 that by late October Busby opted for a dramatic acceleration of his changing of the guard. After experimenting successfully in a convenient friendly at Kilmarnock, he made up his mind to press Edwards, Blanchflower and Viollet into regular first-team duty.

## Busby's Babes Revitalize United

The effect was electric as the hitherto hiccuping Reds achieved creditable draws against Huddersfield Town and Arsenal, then hammered a total of ten goals past Cardiff City and Blackpool in the next two fixtures. Now the point of no return in the youth-inspired transformation had been reached and the Babes' fearless attacking approach brought only three defeats between mid-October and mid-March. They finished fourth in Division One, nine points adrift of champions Wolves, but now Busby had produced firm evidence that he was on the right track.

Suddenly, erstwhile critics were changing their tune, predicting that the new United would carry all before them in 1954-55, but the new campaign turned out to be one of essential consolidation. Yet more tyros were given

*Known as the 'Gunner' for his explosive shot, Jack Rowley was prolific postwar goalscorer. He finally made way for Busby's Babes in the mid 1950s.*

their chance – notably the jaunty Salford-born wing half Eddie Colman, the dashing Mancunian winger Albert Scanlon and Billy Whelan, a quiet, courteous Dubliner who was soon to emerge as one of the most exciting inside forwards of his generation. Meanwhile, the last of the postwar greats, Chilton and Rowley, followed Pearson and Cockburn to the exit door, having demonstrated their stature as men as well as footballers by selflessly assisting with the development of the boys who were about to take their jobs.

The season produced plenty of exhilarating, swashbuckling football – a 6-5 victory at Stamford Bridge will live forever in the memories of all those lucky enough to be present – but inconsistency was rife, as exemplified by 15 league defeats including a 5-0 Old Trafford humbling by Manchester City and an unceremonious FA Cup ejection at Maine Road.

Still, fifth place in the First Division was no mean feat for such a green combination, the lads gained priceless experience – for example, Taylor and Viollet knocked in 20 league goals apiece – and also there was an unusual story to savour, concerning one of the side's less vaunted members. When Bill Foulkes had signed for United, he had been reluctant to give up his job in a Lancashire coalmine because it had seemed far more secure than professional football. Though Matt Busby was uneasy about employing part-timers at senior level, so keen was he to retain the services of the redoubtable and ruthless full back that he agreed to Foulkes continuing with his shifts at Lea Green colliery, near St Helens, and training on two evenings a week.

Incredibly enough by modern standards, Bill retained that status when he won a regular first-team berth in 1953, and was still completing an honest week's toil underground when he was picked for England to face Northern

Ireland in Belfast in October 1954. Duly, on the Tuesday before the midweek game he completed a morning shift at Lea Green before linking up with his international colleagues to cross the Irish Sea, then he performed impressively alongside clubmates Wood and Byrne in a 2-0 victory, before heading back to the mine for his Thursday shift. Unfortunately for the 22-year-old, who had played only 20 or so senior games at that time, there was to be no happy sequel in the form of further caps. Ludicrously he was discarded after that one sound display in the No. 2 shirt and later, when he had switched to his preferred position of centre half, he was never offered a chance. It was an episode which reflected appallingly on the England selection committee which held sway at that time and Bill Foulkes was by no means the only victim of their perversity.

Happily, however, he continued to thrive at club level, eventually forsaking King Coal in favour of full-time employment at Old Trafford, and he played a key role in subsequent successes despite being pressed into National Service. In another scenario which appears outlandish in the 21st century, in 1955-56 Foulkes struck an agreement with Busby that he would play in any match for which he turned up. The problem was that he was stationed at

## 50 Greatest Players

**STAN PEARSON Inside forward**

**Born:** Salford, 11 January 1919

**Joined Manchester United:** 1935 **From:** Juniors

**Debut:** 13 November 1937 v Chesterfield, League

**Appearances:** 346 **Goals:** 149

**Left Manchester United:** 1954 **For:** Bury

**Honours won with United:** Division One championship 1952; FA Cup winner 1948

Stanley Pearson's playing career was interrupted by World War II, but the Salford-born inside forward learnt his early football at the famed Adelphi Lads' Club before joining United as an amateur in 1935. It was the first steps of a glorious career that was to see him play a vital part in the re-emergence of United as one of the game's top clubs during the years immediately after the close of the War in 1945. Pearson was a member of the all-star forward line that enjoyed FA Cup glory against Blackpool in 1948 and he was still playing when the club claimed their first league title since before World War I in 1952. A terrific footballer and prolific scorer Pearson was also a full England international with eight caps to his name.

Aldershot and could not guarantee that he would be granted leave of absence from his duties as a driver with the Royal Army Service Corps.

So keen was Bill to maintain the impetus of his United career that frequently he went AWOL from his barracks, foxing the military police who haunted the railway stations in their ceaseless quest for errant soldiers, by disguising himself as a businessman, complete with attache case and trilby, with his coat collar turned up. He recalled: 'Luckily I was never rumbled, but it was pretty stressful at times and I was glad when the club eventually agreed to fly me to matches.'

Astonishingly, all that cloak-and-dagger activity had no immediate effect on Foulkes' performances for a side which swept all before it as the Babes began to blossom luxuriantly in the autumn of 1955. They started solidly, then faltered with a trio of perplexing September defeats before embarking on a triumphant midwinter and topping it all off with a 14-match unbeaten sequence to take the title by 11 points, a truly swingeing margin in those far-off, two-for-a-win days. It was an exuberant, precocious, omni-talented team, average age a mere 22, and unquestionably it takes its place among the finest ever assembled in this country or abroad.

Missing only one match between the posts was the quick-footed Ray Wood, who as a teenager had sprinted for money in the pit villages of his native Northeast. He had begun his football career with Newcastle United, then progressed at Darlington before being recruited by Matt Busby for £5,000 in December 1949. A sudden injury crisis led to an emergency debut a few days later, ironically against former employers, the Magpies, and he made light of a torrential downpour to shine in a 1-1 draw at Old Trafford. Thereafter, the 18-year-old worked diligently at honing his craft, biding his time to supplant Jack Crompton, and later Reg Allen, while demonstrating his athleticism by scoring six goals in three outings at centre forward for the Reds' A-team. Wood re-emerged in his specialist position to claim a regular club spot in 1953-54 and went on to garner three England caps during his mid-1950s prime.

Foulkes and Byrne, the captain, formed the customary full back pairing, though Bill, perhaps eventually worn down a tad by those aforementioned army commitments, slipped out of the side in the spring and the ungainly but effective Ian Greaves stepped in to earn a medal on merit. The half back line was anchored by ever-present stopper Mark Jones, a homely Yorkshireman whose engagingly gentle off-the-field persona was in vivid contrast to his fearsomely rugged mode of play. Particularly commanding in the air, Jones might have been quarried from the same vein of northern rock as his predecessor Allenby Chilton, and there seemed every prospect that he might graduate to international stature as a certain initial crudeness gradually receded from his game.

The quality of the wing halves verged on the sublime. As the campaign began the right-sided slot was occupied by Jeff Whitefoot, whose perceptive distribution, intelligent positional sense and spirited tackling would have marked him out for longevity at virtually any other First Division club. Unfortunately for him, he was being pursued by the younger Eddie Colman, a diminutive, endlessly energetic ball of creativity and a master of the mazy dribble, who usurped the more stately Whitefoot's berth in November and never showed the slightest sign of relinquishing it. At left half was the incomparable Duncan Edwards, a man-mountain and an England regular, though still in his teens, and the possessor of pretty well every attribute any footballer could need.

As for the forwards, collectively and individually, they simply dazzled. The wingers, Johnny Berry on the right and left-sided David Pegg, offered a striking contrast in styles. Berry was a spiky little fighting cock, years ahead of his time in that he was ever eager to scrap back and harass opponents in the manner of a modern midfielder, and he was skilful and penetrative, too.

## 50 Greatest Players

**ALLENBY CHILTON Defender**

**Born:** South Hylton, 16 September 1918

**Joined Manchester United:** 1938 **From:** Seaham Colliery

**Debut:** 2 September 1939 v Charlton Athletic, League

**Appearances:** 392 **Goals:** 3

**Left Manchester United:** 1955 **For:** Grimsby Town

**Honours won with United:** Division One championship 1952; FA Cup winner 1948

Allenby Chilton was a hard-as-nails centre half who provided the rock on which Matt Busby's first great side was built. Reliable and loyal, Chilton appeared in his last league game for United in February 1955 having played in every one of the previous 165 Division One fixtures, 16 years after he had made his league debut on 2 September 1939. War was declared the following day and Chilton's professional football career was put on hold. The resumption of organized football in 1946 saw Chilton immediately installed as the team's defensive pivot. He went on to be a member of the sides that won the FA Cup in 1948 and championship in 1952. He later moved into management at Grimsby Town, Wigan Athletic and Hartlepools United.

Pegg was a smoother operator, seeming almost to float over the surface as he left opponents in his wake on a typically elegant dribble. In harness they were as devastating a pair as Delaney and Mitten had been before them, and praise does not come higher than that.

## Busby's Youngsters Come of Age

The two principal marksmen were leader of the line Tommy Taylor and the deeper-lying Dennis Viollet, a prolific duo who complemented each other perfectly. The effervescent Taylor was peerless in the air, possessed boundless stamina and strength, and far more all-round ability than he was credited with; Viollet was a more subtle operator, full of flair and creative ideas, a finely-honed rapier of a footballer. Both were quick and resilient, and both scored goals freely, Taylor's 1955-56 tally being 25 and Viollet's 20.

That left the other inside forward slot, the only position on which it appeared Matt Busby could not make up his mind during the Babes' first trophy-winning campaign. He started with the cultured Irishman, Jackie Blanchflower, in the No. 8 shirt, then switched to John Doherty. However, the sharp-witted Mancunian was hampered by the knee injury which was destined to bring his career to a premature end before the decade was out, and he was replaced by Billy Whelan, a majestic performer who lacked nothing but outright pace. Doherty returned in the spring and it is anyone's guess who would have seized the long-term initiative if bad luck and then stark tragedy had not intruded. The only other man to qualify for a medal was Welsh international utility forward Colin Webster, a robust, industrious dasher not sprinkled with stardust in the manner of his team-mates but an extremely valuable member of the squad.

Yet for all the fabulous ability at Manchester United's disposal, they suffered one crushing lowlight during the Babes' first title campaign, a 4-0 FA Cup hammering by Second Division Bristol Rovers. Lacking only the injured Edwards from their first-choice line-up, Matt Busby's men were given a comprehensive runaround in the Eastville mud by the Pirates' classy front duo Geoff Bradford and Alfie Biggs, both marvellous players who, with all due respect to Rovers, were worthy of a more exalted stage.

Bill Foulkes recalled the day: 'We just disintegrated and got exactly what we deserved. Probably we had been too confident and Matt was not happy. I don't know if it was a coincidence, but on the train journey back to Manchester he became so upset about our card school that he grabbed everything on the tables, the cards and even the money, and threw it out of the window. On the way down a few of the lads, myself included, had lost

*The championship-winning team of 1955-56, l-r: back row – Taylor, Jones, Wood, Foulkes, Edwards; front – Whelan, Colman, Berry, Viollet, Pegg, Bent; Skipper Byrne was absent through injury.*

some wages, which he thought was bad for team spirit and he might have linked that to our unexpected defeat. It's a tribute to the respect in which he was held that nobody so much as murmured when he ended our game so abruptly. We knew we had let ourselves and the club down and felt he was entitled to be angry.'

In fact, the Babes were fiercely proud of their universally revered father figure and never more so than in the summer of 1956 when he stood tall to champion the cause of European football in the face of narrow-minded opposition from the domestic game's hidebound authorities. When the European Cup had been launched a year earlier, Chelsea, as the holders of the First Division title, were invited to take part, but turned down that golden chance at the behest of the Football League, who believed that involvement in continental competition would be harmful to English interests, that the League and FA Cup would suffer as a result of the necessary extra commitment of overseas travel. No matter that, only a

## 50 Greatest Players

**JACK ROWLEY Forward**

**Born:** Wolverhampton, 7 October 1920

**Joined Manchester United:** 1937 **From:** Bournemouth & Boscombe Athletic

**Debut:** 23 October 1937 v Sheffield Wednesday, League

**Appearances:** 424 **Goals:** 211

**Left Manchester United:** 1955 **For:** Plymouth Argyle

**Honours won with United:** Division One championship 1952; FA Cup winner 1948

Jack Rowley's career was interrupted by World War II, but he became one of the greatest goalscorers ever to pull on the famous red shirt. He had football in his blood – his father played the game while brother Arthur was, like Jack, a prolific goalscorer. He claimed four goals in only his second outing for the first team – an early explosive goal-scoring blast from the player who would go on to become known as 'The Gunner' to United supporters. His proficiency in front of goal was a vital element in the club's successes of the late 1940s and early 50s. He netted twice in United's 1948 FA Cup final win over Blackpool and claimed 30 goals as the club won the league title in 1952. An England international, he later enjoyed several seasons in football management.

couple of years earlier, the Hungarians had twice demolished the England team with ravishingly destructive displays, highlighting the existence of a vibrant football world beyond these shores, one from which it was imperative to learn if creeping stagnation was to be avoided.

Happily, Busby was made of sterner and more imaginative stuff than the woefully weak-kneed Stamford Bridge regime. He declared, and his plucky chairman Harold Hardman backed him wholeheartedly, that Manchester United must blaze a trail into Europe. He spoke, with vision, passion and utter conviction, of fresh horizons, new standards against which to measure the best our own clubs had to offer and, crucially, the enlightened Stanley Rous, then secretary of the FA secretary, agreed to sanction the great adventure. If Matt Busby had seen the future and was desperate to embrace it, then his team was no less keen. Wincing at the poignancy of his words in the light of the tragedy which was to overtake the club at Munich in 1958, Bill Foulkes declared: 'We were thrilled at the prospect, desperate to face different opponents in foreign lands and to experience air travel...'

Not that United neglected domestic concerns in 1956-57, making an imperious start to the successful defence of their First Division crown with ten victories and two draws in their opening dozen games. The penultimate match of that blistering sequence, against Charlton Athletic at Old Trafford, carried extra significance in that it marked the senior debut of a shy young fellow from the Northumberland mining village of Ashington. With Tommy Taylor absent on international duty, the No. 9 shirt was handed to Bobby Charlton, who was five days short of his 19th birthday but recognized already as a special talent. What the manager didn't know, however, was that his blond bombshell was carrying an injury to his favoured right foot, but was disguising it so as not to forfeit his first senior opportunity. In the event it hardly mattered as Charlton contributed two goals with his left to United's 4-2 triumph, and thereafter he was content to shoot with either foot, as keepers all over the globe were to discover to their cost over the next 18 years.

Though Taylor reclaimed his place for the next match, as the season wore on Bobby returned for two productive spells as a deputy for the injured Dennis Viollet, netting ten times in 14 outings, enough to earn his first championship medal. This time the winning margin was eight points, three fewer than in the previous term, yet that could not conceal the giant strides being made by an increasingly confident and mature side. In 1956-57 they totalled 64 points compared to 60 a year earlier, and rattled in 103 goals, 20 more than in 1955-56. Taylor was nudged off the pinnacle of the scoring chart by the unassuming Dubliner Billy Whelan, who registered 26 hits in 39 appearances despite spending much of his time in withdrawn positions.

The Red Devils, to quote their latest nickname, dominated the League from start to finish, hitting an irresistible peak in the first three weeks of February, when they won 4-2 at Maine Road, thrashed Arsenal 6-2 at Old Trafford and eclipsed Charlton 5-1 at the Valley, finding time in between to record one of their most stupendous European triumphs against Bilbao and to knock Everton out of the FA Cup.

## Another Title Secured

With the title race being sealed by Easter and the temperature mounting in the other competitions, Matt Busby opted to field eight reserves at home to a strong Burnley side yet still won 2-0. On the same afternoon, that awesome demonstration of all-round strength was compounded by a 3-1 Central League triumph at Turf Moor by a reserve side which contained nine members of the all-conquering youth team. At that point United boasted the most formidable squad ever assembled in the history of English football, with high-quality cover in every position, and it was no exaggeration to contend that they could have fielded two teams capable of finishing simultaneously in the First Division's top six.

They were backed heavily to become the first club in the 20th century to achieve the League and FA Cup 'Double', and they came within an ace of doing so, only to fall victim to a malign twist of fate. Their path to Wembley had been punctuated by rude shocks from unfancied opposition which revived bad memories of their humbling by Bristol Rovers a year earlier. First Hartlepools United fought back to level terms from a three-goal deficit at Victoria Park only for Whelan to scupper their celebrations with a late winner; then Bournemouth, who had knocked out Wolves and Spurs on their way to the quarter-finals, led at the interval only to lose by the odd goal in three.

The Red Devils' opponents beneath the twin towers were Aston Villa, a tidy enough mid-table First Division side, but not considered a realistic threat to the champions' 'Double' dream. That all changed in the sixth minute when a header from Villa's onrushing Peter McParland was caught safely by United goalkeeper Ray Wood, only for the Irish international winger to continue his charge. Wood remembered vividly what happened next: 'I held the ball to my chest and swayed, thinking McParland would pass by me harmlessly. But he must have lost his cool and lunged forward, banging into me with his head, knocking me unconscious and fracturing my cheekbone.'

Unquestionably it was a reckless challenge at best, and it would have warranted instant dismissal in modern times, but referee Frank Coultas saw nothing wrong. Thus, in those days before the use of substitutes, United were

*Ray Wood seen in the 1957 FA Cup final a split second before the infamous shoulder charge by Peter McParland of Aston Villa which resulted in Wood being stretchered off. He returned to the match later but United lost the final and with it a chance of the 'Double'.*

## Great Matches

**EUROPEAN CUP, QUARTER-FINAL, 2ND LEG** **Maine Road, 6 February 1957**

**Manchester United 3** **Athletic Bilbao 0** **Attendance: 70,000**
**Viollet**
**Taylor**
**Berry**

On a night of tumultuous drama at the home of Manchester City, where the Red Devils were entertaining Bilbao because their own floodlights were not ready to use, Matt Busby's team pulled off one of the most stirring of all comebacks by a British team in European competition. Trailing 5-3 from the first leg, United battered away relentlessly at the Spaniards' defence, but the visitors held firm until the 42nd minute, when a stinging drive from Edwards was cleared off the line and Viollet pounced to reduce the deficit. The second period followed a similar pattern and twice United thought they had broken through, only for efforts from Viollet and Whelan to be disallowed for offside. Then Pegg fired wide from six yards and the massive crowd bayed with frustration after 70 minutes when Taylor finally slipped his marker but shot against an upright. An instant later, though, Taylor latched on to Colman's swiftly-taken free kick and cracked the ball into the roof of Carmelo's net to make it 5-5 on aggregate.

Now United went for the kill while the Basques resisted courageously, but Spanish hopes of a replay were confounded by a dazzling interchange of positions by Taylor and right winger Berry. The Reds' spearhead surged down the touchline and swept past Garay, before shaping to shoot from a narrow angle; instead he rolled a perfect pass inside to Berry, who netted gleefully to complete what the *Daily Express* recorded breathlessly as 'the greatest victory in soccer history.'

**Manchester United:** Wood, Foulkes, Byrne, Colman, Jones, Edwards, Berry, Whelan, Taylor, Viollet, Pegg

**Athletic Bilbao:** Carmelo, Orue, Canito, Mauri, Garay, Maguregui, Arteche, Marcaido, Etura, Merodio, Gainza

**Referee:** A. Dusch

condemned to struggle on with ten men, with Jackie Blanchflower taking over in goal and the tottering custodian returning as a groggy passenger on the wing shortly before the interval.

Ironically it was McParland who fired Villa into a two-goal lead midway through the second period and when Taylor reduced the arrears with seven minutes remaining, the courageous Wood went back between the posts as the Red Devils mounted an unavailing late assault. Blanchflower, who had been converted to centre half with such success that he had unseated no less a rival than the colossus Jones, deserved immense praise for his competent display, but the team had been critically unbalanced by the reshuffle and the outcome was hardly surprising.

The third strand of a momentous season was an heroic first European Cup campaign which began with a 2-0 victory in Brussels against Anderlecht, who were annihilated 10-0 in the second leg at Maine Road, used because Old Trafford's floodlights were not ready. It wasn't that the Belgian champions were a poor side, far from it, but they were unprepared for United's enchantingly fluid movement and some ruthless finishing, especially from Viollet, who netted four times. Every forward scored except Pegg, ironically the outstanding performer and the creator of four goals for his colleagues, who made unavailing attempts to get him on the scoresheet late in the game.

## United Shine in Europe

In the next round a 3-0 home advantage over Borussia Dortmund was almost frittered away as the Germans snatched two late goals, but then the Reds were indebted to Wood for his superb display in a goalless draw on a bleak Ruhr evening to ensure their progress to the quarter-finals. The European Cup's reputation for enthralling drama and football of the highest quality was enhanced still further by the two last-eight encounters with Athletic Bilbao. Despite excelling in Spain on a swamp-like pitch which appeared to consist of equal amounts of snow and mud, United had fallen victim to a succession of brilliant counter-attacks and were 5-2 down with the final whistle looming. Cue Whelan with the goal of a lifetime, jinking past three defenders in the oozing morass and firing home from 25 yards. Still the Reds needed something akin to a second-leg miracle, and they achieved it with an unforgettable 3-0 triumph on the most emotion-charged night of their Maine Road tenure.

The semi-final brought an even more daunting test when United were paired with the holders, Real Madrid, who were replete with footballing artists such as the lordly Argentinian centre forward cum play-maker Alfredo di Stefano; Hungary's 'Galloping Major', the phenomenally prolific Ferenc Puskas; and Spaniard Francisco Gento, probably the world's paciest and most powerful winger. Though they resisted nobly and were never outclassed in front of 135,000 supporters at the cavernous Bernabeu stadium, they succumbed 3-1 to their brilliant hosts, all the goals arriving in the second half. For once there was little doubt that the Busby Babes had been beaten by a superior team and in the return leg the Spaniards provided suitably eminent opposition for Old Trafford's first European match under lights.

## Great Matches

**FOOTBALL LEAGUE DIVISION ONE** **Highbury, 1 February 1958**

| Arsenal 4 | Manchester United 5 | Attendance: 63,578 |
|---|---|---|
| Herd | Edwards | |
| Bloomfield 2 | Charlton | |
| Tapscott | Taylor 2 | |
| | Viollet | |

As an epitaph for the pre-Munich Babes, no game could have been more memorable. United surged forward irresistibly from the first whistle and broke through after ten minutes when Viollet set up Edwards to beat Kelsey with a skimming 20-yard scorcher. The Reds extended their advantage when man-of-the-match Scanlon dashed some 70 yards down the left flank before squaring for Bobby Charlton to double the lead, and the outcome appeared to be inevitable when Scanlon and Morgans sent in Taylor for the third goal shortly before the break. Perhaps United fell prey to complacency, and they were punished ruthlessly as the Gunners hit back with three goals in four minutes around the hour mark. First Herd, later to become a Red Devil himself, volleyed in a Bowen lob, then Bloomfield contributed a quickfire brace, converting a Groves knockdown and equalizing with a diving header from Nutt's low cross.

Suddenly, all the impetus was with Arsenal, but United were not champions for nothing. Charlton and Scanlon combined to create an adroitly headed goal by Viollet, and Taylor netted from a narrow angle to make it 5-3 after slick work by Colman and Morgans. Even then, the Gunners refused to lie down. Tapscott scampered through to reduce the arrears again after 77 minutes, the prelude to a late siege on the visitors' goal, but to no avail. Both sides had contributed colossally to a feast of football. How appalling to reflect that five days later, one team would be decimated by tragedy.

**Arsenal:** Kelsey, Stan Charlton, Evans, Ward, Fotheringham, Bowen, Groves, Tapscott, Herd, Bloomfield, Nutt

**Manchester United:** Gregg, Foulkes, Byrne, Colman, Jones, Edwards, Morgans, Charlton, Taylor, Viollet, Scanlon

**Referee:** G.W. Pullin

A comeback of Bilbao proportions was needed if the Red Devils were going to reach the final at the first attempt, but that never looked likely as the visitors soaked up early pressure, then stretched their aggregate lead to 5-1 in a ferocious contest. Second-half goals from Taylor and Charlton salvaged a draw on the night and a measure of pride, but United's first foray into Europe had ended, albeit with their honour enhanced by a rousing campaign.

*Albert Scanlon was in scintillating form in the encounter with Arsenal in February 1958 that showed the Busby Babes in all their glory before the Munich disaster.*

Back on the home front in 1957-58, Busby's team started at such a gallop, scoring 22 times in their first six games and taking 11 points out of a possible 12, that a third successive title seemed likely. But then an outbreak of inconsistency saw them toppled from pole position by Stan Cullis' hard-running Wolves and the United boss dipped into his resources to reshape his side. Out went Blanchflower and back came Jones, Berry was replaced by teenage Welsh flankman Kenny Morgans, Charlton stepped in for Whelan and Albert Scanlon, a locally-born, breathtakingly bold wing flier, took over from Pegg.

In addition, in December Matt Busby paid Doncaster Rovers £23,500 to make Northern Ireland international Harry Gregg the world's most expensive goalkeeper, thus sidelining Ray Wood, who had recovered fitness but never seemed quite the same player after his Wembley trauma. The sweeping changes offered yet further proof, as if any were needed, of Busby's acute managerial acumen. Immediately the revamped side starting winning, and they would not lose again until the calamity of Munich reshaped their future in the grisliest manner imaginable.

For now they advanced on all fronts, renewing their interest in the championship, breezing through two rounds of the FA Cup and seizing a 2-1 advantage over Red Star Belgrade in the quarter-finals of the European Cup, thanks to a rare goal from Eddie Colman and another from Bobby Charlton, who was becoming a gratifyingly frequent scorer.

And so, on the first day of February 1958, a revitalized Manchester United rolled up at Highbury where, together with Arsenal, they captivated the sporting world by shading a spellbinding nine-goal classic. As they prepared to fly out to Yugoslavia for the return contest with Red Star, there seemed to be nothing beyond the compass of Matt Busby's Babes.

# Chapter Six: 1958
# Utter Desolation

Not even the bank of swirling fog which shrouded Manchester's Ringway airport in the early morning of 3 February 1958 could douse the spirits of the United party as they boarded an airliner for Belgrade, where they would meet Red Star in the second leg of a European Cup quarter-final. The Red Devils were still bubbling in the aftermath of the Highbury cliffhanger and, while not underestimating the task awaiting them in Yugoslavia, given the slender lead they had chiselled out at Old Trafford three weeks earlier, they were confident that they would progress to a second successive semi-final.

It was a tribute to what they had achieved already in their short careers that most of their fans, and the wider footballing community, shared the players' faith. It also said plenty about the unique position United occupied in the national psyche in the middle to late 1950s.

While a gigantic gulf separated Busby himself from the rock'n'roll culture that was burgeoning at that time, his new team of young players was the sporting embodiment of it. They weren't rebels as such, but they were young, fresh and exhilaratingly precocious, and as they destroyed opponent after opponent with flowing, upliftingly entertaining football, they seemed set to sweep all before them for the foreseeable future.

*Duncan Edwards, the multi-talented star of Busby's team of untouchables, whose life was brutally curtailed by the Munich crash at the age of 21, having earned a first England cap at just 19.*

**50 Greatest Players**

**JOHNNY BERRY Forward**

**Born:** Aldershot, 1 June 1926

**Joined Manchester United:** 1951 **From:** Birmingham City

**Debut:** 1 September 1951 v Bolton Wanderers, League

**Appearances:** 276 **Goals:** 45

**Left Manchester United:** 1958 (enforced retirement after Munich)

**Honours won with United:** Division One championship 1952, 1956, 1957

There are few more exciting sights in football than an orthodox winger going about his business and there have been few better exponents than Johnny Berry in Manchester United's history. Matt Busby signed the diminutive wide-man from Birmingham City to fill the void left by the departure of Jimmy Delaney to Aberdeen and the United manager wasn't disappointed. Berry, with his neat, clever wing play, became a firm favourite of the Old Trafford crowd as United's second great side of the post World War II era took shape. He won three league championship medals and was in the FA Cup final side which lost 2-1 against Aston Villa in 1957. Capped four times by England, his career was brought to a premature close due to the injuries sustained in the Munich air disaster.

To add an extra dimension to the impression that these new Red Devils were a breed apart, a thoroughly modern phenomenon divorced from postwar stuffiness and austerity, came the club's defiance of the league's anti-European edict. Where Chelsea had tugged their collective forelock and shuffled into line, the pioneering Busby would have no truck with such insularity and United's mould-breaking image continued to mushroom accordingly.

Thus when they touched down in bleak, Communist-controlled Belgrade, they were greeted with feverish excitement from the Yugoslavian fans, who must have viewed them as the epitome of western sporting glamour. However, any hero-worship was quick to dissipate when the game began in bright sunshine on a pitch on which 'the last remnants of melting snow produced the effect of an English lawn flecked with daisies' as the *Guardian*'s Don Davies, so soon to lose his life, put it so lyrically.

United tore straight into the attack and within 90 seconds they were in front, Taylor having raced clear of his markers to free Viollet, who shot coolly past Red Star's famous keeper, Beara. With Colman and Edwards controlling the midfield, the visitors hit a vein of irresistible form and Charlton struck two wonderful goals to establish a 5-1 aggregate advantage at the interval. But just as Arsenal had fought back four days earlier, so Red Star revived sensationally. With the crowd roaring in fury at what it saw as the English champions' excessively physical approach – their star Dragoslav Sekularac had been spreadeagled spectacularly by Edwards, but only after the Belgrade playmaker had ripped open Morgans' knee with his studs – the hosts fought back to make it 3-3 (5-4 overall) with three minutes remaining. Thereafter, United's heroic rearguard held firm and a semi-final berth was secured.

The men who rose to the occasion so magnificently in what proved to be the valedictory performance of the original Busby Babes were Gregg in goal, full backs Foulkes and Byrne, a half back line of Colman, Jones and Edwards, and an attack comprising Morgans, Charlton, Taylor, Viollet and Scanlon. How macabre it is to reflect that within 24 hours, four of those boys would be dead and another, the seemingly indestructible young leviathan Duncan Edwards, would be dying. For the moment, though, joy was unconfined in the United party, particularly as for the remainder of their Belgrade sojourn all hint of local animosity evaporated and they were feted royally at a lavish banquet. After that, and it was not early by then, a few of the players headed for the city's bright lights while the rest retired to their hotel for a game of cards, which went on into the small hours.

## 50 Greatest Players

**ROGER BYRNE Defender**

**Born:** Gorton, Manchester, 8 February 1929

**Joined Manchester United:** 1949 **From:** Juniors

**Debut:** 24 November 1951 v Liverpool, League

**Appearances:** 280 **Goals:** 20

Lost his life in the Munich air disaster, February 1958

**Honours won with United:** Division One championship 1952, 1956, 1957

Manchester lad Roger Byrne was one of the finest full backs ever to grace a football field, but he could quite easily have made his name as a wing forward. His league debut against Liverpool at Anfield in November 1951 was at left back, a slot he retained for four months. He was then moved forward to play the final six games of the campaign on the left wing, scoring seven goals as United swept to the title. Byrne registered his displeasure when opening the following season on the wing and he was soon restored to his preferred defensive role. It was the start of a brilliant career that was so grievously cut short by the Munich air disaster. As club skipper he led United to the league title in 1956 and 1957 as well as skippering them in the 1957 FA Cup final against Aston Villa. Byrne was also an established England star with 33 caps to his credit.

*The Manchester United team prepare to board their aeroplane at Ringway airport for the journey to Belgrade prior to their European Cup tie against Red Star.*

So it was a bleary-eyed group which assembled, after a brief rest, for the flight home to Manchester via a refuelling stop in Munich. Before take-off there was delay caused by the temporary loss of Johnny Berry's passport but soon the chartered twin-engined Elizabethan was flying through a blizzard, then dropping down smoothly to land safely in the snowy Bavarian capital.

## Flight to Disaster

At this point most of the players were still in high spirits, with only habitually poor flyers – such as Mark Jones and Roger Byrne – showing even the slightest hint of apprehension. There was some larking about with snowballs as they trooped from the plane for coffee at the terminal while the fuel was being taken on, then footballers, officials, pressmen and the handful of other passengers returned to their seats. Card schools prepared to resume while a few people settled back in their seats for a much-needed nap as the plane, with pilots James Thain and Kenneth Rayment in the cockpit, accelerated smoothly down the runway. Then came the first hint of trouble, as Bill Foulkes recalled: 'Just as we were anticipating the sensation of lift-off there was a frantic screeching of brakes and we slithered to an unexpected halt.'

No explanations were offered as Lord Burleigh (the Elizabethan's name) was turned around, but a second run was similarly aborted. Suddenly Foulkes felt uneasy: 'It flashed across my mind that there might be something wrong with the aircraft, though still I had total confidence in the pilots, their procedure and the plane itself. After all, they were the professionals.'

Understandably, however, some of the passengers were seriously perturbed, including Frank Swift, the former Manchester City and England goalkeeper, now travelling in his capacity as a writer with the *News of the World*. 'What the hell's going on here?' he wanted to know, and it was announced that there had been a mechanical fault, though nothing serious. Everybody disembarked once more and at this point Duncan Edwards, apparently believing that all flights for the day had been cancelled, sent a telegram to his landlady in Manchester, advising that he would not be home until the following day. But almost immediately they were called back to the plane and this time, although there was no sign of panic, the atmosphere was tense with anxiety. On the flight deck Captain Thain, who was in overall charge, and Captain Rayment were sharing the controls. The Elizabethan reached 117 knots, the point after which it was unsafe to abandon take-off. Suddenly the speed dropped and Rayment shouted 'Christ! We can't make it.'

## 50 Greatest Players

**EDDIE COLMAN Half back**

**Born:** Salford, 1 November 1936

**Joined Manchester United:** 1952 **From:** Juniors

**Debut:** 12 November 1955 v Bolton Wanderers, League

**Appearances:** 108 **Goals:** 2

Lost his life in the Munich air disaster, February 1958

**Honours won with United:** Division One championship 1956, 1957

Pint-sized Eddie Colman was raised in the terrace streets of Salford that were later to be immortalized in *Coronation Street*, the world's longest running television soap. In fact, from the area of his childhood, he could most likely have seen Old Trafford had it not been for the forest of cranes that dominated the skyline on Manchester Docks. Accordingly, it was a short journey down Trafford Road to the world famous football ground he would grace until his life was tragically cut short in the Munich air disaster. Colman, one of the stars of United's all-conquering FA Youth Cup sides of the mid-1950s, was a fans' favourite who collected a league championship medal at the end of his first season as a first-teamer. He added a second 12 months later and was in the 1957 FA Cup final team that went down 2-1 to Aston Villa.

## The Munich Air Crash

Thain recalled later: 'I looked up and could see a lot of snow, a house and a tree in the path of the aircraft... I was convinced we could not get between the house and the tree... I put my head down and waited for the impact of the crash. The aircraft went through a fence, crossed a road and the port wing hit the house. The wing and part of the tail were torn off and the house caught fire. Luckily the people in the house were unscathed.' The cockpit smashed into a tree and part of the fuselage hit a fuel hut, which exploded.

Bill Foulkes recounted his version of what happened on that third take-off attempt in his autobiography, *Manchester United and Beyond*: 'Roger Byrne joked that it was all or nothing this time. Billy Whelan, a devout Roman Catholic who might have made an excellent priest, murmured that whatever was coming, he was ready. Then we started to taxi forward again, and I was hit by the strongest possible feeling of foreboding. Something told me that we were not going to make it. It came to me that we should not be attempting to take off this third time in such terrible weather. By this time all the cards had stopped. I crouched right down, jamming my head into my chest, well below the level of the top of the seat, and strapping myself in so tightly that I could hardly breathe. I have little doubt that these precautions saved my life.

'As we accelerated down the runway I peered out of the window at the snow racing past. My last memory is of pushing a pack of cards hurriedly into my side pocket. The engines were surging but there was a peculiar note, as though they could not really get going, and the movement of the aircraft seemed decidedly sluggish. Then, just at the moment when we should have been getting off the ground, there was the first of a series of three sickening bumps. The first must have been the aircraft hitting a perimeter fence, the second when the pilot pulled up his wheels and the third, and loudest, when we hit a house. I just had time to think to myself "This is it" before I had the sensation of being thrown all over the place. Then there was darkness.'

Foulkes was one of the lucky ones, but when he regained his bearings a little while after scrambling out through a jagged hole in Lord Burleigh's fuselage, his numbed senses took in a scene of heart-rending devastation.

*The Munich air crash, left, clockwise from the top: the Munich air crash clock outside Old Trafford; a memorial window in honour of Duncan Edwards, Busby Babe and England footballer who lost his life – the St. Francis Church, Dudley; Matt Busby unveils a memorial plaque at Old Trafford to the victims of the crash ; survivor Dennis Viollet with his wife Barbara and children Stephanie (6) and Roger (1) after he arrived back home at Davyhulme following the crash; a newspaper with the details of the horrific news.*

**50 Greatest Players**

**DUNCAN EDWARDS Wing half**

**Born:** Dudley, 1 October 1936

**Joined Manchester United:** 1953 **From:** Juniors

**Debut:** 4 April 1953 v Cardiff City, League

**Appearances:** 177 **Goals:** 21

Lost his life in the Munich air disaster, February 1958

**Honours won with United:** Division One championship: 1956, 1957

Duncan Edwards lost his life at the tragically tender age of 21 in the Munich air disaster, but the young colossus had already made an indelible impression on the football world. His name, his reputation and his contribution to United's success during mid-1950s meant that more than 45 years later he would still be regarded by many as the greatest Manchester United star of them all. There is little need to itemize Edwards' attributes for he possessed all the elements that a top player requires, and he utilized them to stunning effect. He was the star in United's all-conquering FA Youth Cup winning sides, the proud owner of two league championship medals and appeared in the 1957 FA Cup final. He gained his first full England cap midway through his 19th year and looked set for a footballing career to compare with the very best.

The plane was sliced in half, parts of the wreckage were blazing fiercely and, worst of all, the snowy ground was littered with bodies. After taking stock of the carnage he joined Harry Gregg, who had already climbed back into the twisted metal to rescue a baby and a woman, in attempting to help survivors. The Irishman, later embarrassed to be hailed as a hero but that's what he was by any reckoning, felt convinced that Ray Wood, Albert Scanlon, Dennis Viollet and Bobby Charlton were dead. Mercifully he was wrong on each count although some of his comrades, such as Roger Byrne, were clearly beyond assistance; others, including Matt Busby and Jackie Blanchflower, lay groaning in the slush and mud.

### Tragic Loss

The final toll was horrendous. The dead players were Roger Byrne, Tommy Taylor, Eddie Colman, Billy Whelan, Mark Jones, David Pegg, Geoff Bent, and Duncan Edwards was soon to join their number. Other fatalities were secretary Walter Crickmer, trainer Tom Curry, coach Bert Whalley; journalists Alf Clarke, Don Davies, George Follows, Tom Jackson, Archie Ledbrooke, Henry Rose, Eric Thompson and Frank Swift; crew members Kenneth Rayment and Tom Cable; courier BP Miklos and passenger Willie Satinoff.

Jackie Blanchflower and Johnny Berry were maimed beyond the possibility of future sporting endeavour, while Charlton, Viollet, Scanlon, Wood and Morgans were injured but, like Gregg and Foulkes, would all play again. In the long term, however, Morgans, and to some extent Scanlon, would never be the same exciting performers that they had been pre-Munich.

Nearly half a century on from the first horror, there remains a catalogue of harrowing images and impressions from the aftermath of the crash. There was the fearfully hurt Matt Busby, fighting for his life in an oxygen tent and whispering to Jimmy Murphy, whose duties as Wales' manager had prevented him from travelling to Belgrade: 'Keep the flag flying, Jimmy. Keep things going till I get back.' There was Duncan Edwards, who had been given a 50-50 chance of survival, joking indomitably with the assistant boss about the kickoff time for the next match. There was the distraught Murphy slumped weeping and alone after hearing that Duncan's great fighting heart had stopped beating. There were survivors, missing their chums but not knowing the full extent of the tragedy, asking nurses where the 'other' hospital was. For Foulkes and Gregg the trauma was heightened by a return to the wreckage, where they came across the belongings of the friends they had lost.

## 50 Greatest Players

**TOMMY TAYLOR Forward**

**Born:** Barnsley, 29 January 1932

**Joined Manchester United:** 1953 **From:** Barnsley

**Debut:** 7 March 1953 v Preston North End, League

**Appearances:** 191 **Goals:** 131

Lost his life in the Munich air disaster, February 1958

**Honours won with United:** Division One championship 1956, 1957

In the opinion of many United supporters, who had the privilege of watching Tommy Taylor during his goal-plundering pomp of the mid-1950s, there will never be a more complete United centre forward. Taylor combined all of the elements required to survive in the ultra-demanding role of leading the attack to awesome effect. He was the perfect spearhead to the Matt Busby team that looked destined to dominate football at home and in Europe until fate stepped in. His fabulous scoring record was rewarded with two league championship medals and 19 England caps. He also scored in the 1957 FA Cup final against Aston Villa at Wembley when United lost 2-1. Manchester United and England were robbed when he lost his life aged 26.

## 50 Greatest Players

**LIAM WHELAN Forward**

**Born:** Dublin, 1 April 1935

**Joined Manchester United:** 1953 **From:** Home Farm

**Debut:** 26 March 1955 v Preston North End, League

**Appearances:** 98 **Goals:** 52

Lost his life in the Munich air disaster, February 1958

**Honours won with United:** Division One championship 1956-57

Liam 'Billy' Whelan was another of the clinical finishers that Matt Busby had at his disposal during the glory days of the mid-1950s. Tommy Taylor, Dennis Viollet and Whelan terrorized defences as United claimed two league titles and embarked on a couple of fabulous European Cup campaigns. His calm, assured manner belied his ruthlessness when chances presented themselves in front of goal. His goals-per-game ratio ranks among the best in United history. Like so many of his contemporaries he was destined for a glittering career until fate intervened. He didn't play in the European Cup quarter-final, second leg against Red Star in Belgrade, but travelled as a member of the squad on the doomed flight.

The families of each victim suffered their own pain, but for the relatives of Geoff Bent there was the excruciating irony that the reserve full back was added to the party only at the last moment as a possible deputy for Roger Byrne, who had picked up a thigh injury against Arsenal. The skipper passed a late fitness test and Bent was not required to face Red Star, but he perished with the rest. At the other end of the emotional spectrum there was Ronnie Cope, a promising young centre half who had expected to travel and was so disappointed to be left out to make way for Bent at the last moment that, before the news came through, he had considered a transfer request.

The cause of the accident took a long time to determine. At first accusing fingers were pointed at James Thain, whom it was alleged did not ensure the wings were free from ice. But the pilot, who has since died, battled with dignity for 11 years through four enquiries, and eventually cleared his name when the official cause was recorded as a build-up of melting snow on the runway which prevented the plane from reaching take-off speed.

Back in early February 1958, it was difficult to envisage how Manchester United could go on. But, nobly heeding the unbearably poignant plea from his stricken manager, Jimmy Murphy ensured that they did.

# Chapter Seven: 1958-63
# Back from the Brink

The task facing Jimmy Murphy was Herculean. As well as coming to terms with his own grief – and he was a friend of every Manchester United player and official who had perished at Munich – it was his responsibility to ensure that the club did not sink into oblivion in the months after the tragedy. While Matt Busby was beginning the long struggle to recover from his horrific injuries, Murphy headed for home with Harry Gregg and Bill Foulkes, the only two able-bodied crash survivors among his playing staff. The overland journey proved hellish for the pair, who suffered mental torture every time there was a squeal of train brakes, but Murphy nursed them through.

Manchester was a city in mourning and nothing symbolized that grief more harrowingly than the row of bodies in the Old Trafford gymnasium, where they lay before being consigned to the individual families ahead of the funerals. In the midst of this nightmare, Murphy contemplated the footballing future – and it appeared unremittingly bleak. Not only was he shorn of so many Busby Babes, but he had also lost coach Bert Whalley and trainer Tom Curry, a double void he moved rapidly to fill by re-enlisting former Old Trafford hero Jack Crompton, who had been working for Luton Town.

Though United's next two league fixtures were postponed, Jimmy had less than two weeks to assemble a team to meet Sheffield Wednesday in the fifth round of the FA Cup. There was plenty of talent in the Red Devils' junior sides but the pressing need was for experience. The authorities waived the rule preventing individuals from playing for more than one club per season in the FA Cup and United signed Stan Crowther, the abrasive young Aston Villa wing half who had faced them at Wembley nine months earlier. In addition they recruited the veteran Blackpool midfield general Ernie Taylor, who had recently lost his son in an accident and was eager for a

*Jimmy Murphy, Matt Busby's right-hand man for so many years, on whom the grievous burden fell of marshalling the shattered United after the crash.*

change of scene. Beyond that, although there was no shortage of sympathetic pronouncements from other clubs, none of them was willing to release key players, so it was very much a patchwork combination which ran out to meet Wednesday on a night of near-hysterical emotion at Old Trafford.

*Bill Foulkes leads the makeshift team out as captain for the first game after the Munich disaster. The Reds won 3-0 against a subdued Sheffield Wednesday.*

Because of the uncertainty, the teamsheet in the programme was left blank and these are the names which were announced shortly before kickoff for the supporters to ink in. Harry Gregg, Bill Foulkes (captain), Ian Greaves, Freddie Goodwin, Ronnie Cope, Stan Crowther, Colin Webster, Ernie Taylor, Alex Dawson, Mark Pearson and Shay Brennan. The front page of that programme carried a moving message from chairman Harold Hardman, which included this uplifting declaration of intent: 'Although we mourn for our dead and grieve for our wounded, we believe that great days are not done for us... the road back may be long and hard, but with the memory of those who died at Munich, of their stirring achievements and wonderful sportsmanship ever with us, Manchester United will rise again.'

For Sheffield Wednesday it was an impossible situation. Their skipper, Albert Quixall, destined soon to play his own crucial part in the Red Devils' renaissance, reflected later that he and his team-mates simply did not want to be there. It was as though they were intruders at a private wake and, understandably, they were nowhere near their considerable best as they were swept aside by United's unlikely amalgam of rookies, reserves, new recruits and two men, Gregg and Foulkes, who were still reeling from the aftershock of Munich.

### A Shattered United Rebuild Under Murphy

Murphy's marvels triumphed 3-0, thanks largely to two goals from 20-year-old debutant Shay Brennan, an inside forward cum wing half who would develop eventually into a high-quality right back, but who was filling the outside left slot for the first time in his professional life. As he put it many years later: 'I had as little idea about playing on the wing as the man in the moon.' The third goal came from Dawson, a dauntingly muscular centre forward who was two days short of his 18th birthday, and it was fashioned by the rugged but skilful inside forward Pearson, himself only 18 and another making his senior entrance. Both boys would go on to serve United well, particularly the prolific Dawson, but neither forged a long-term career at Old Trafford, their subsequent development being hindered, perhaps, by being pitched unavoidably into the limelight before they were ready.

For now, though, the Reds could not worry too deeply about the future, instead throwing themselves into their fixture backlog and pursuing their FA Cup campaign amid constant transfer speculation. But although the rumour machine suggested the return of former Babe Jeff Whitefoot from Grimsby Town, the acquisition of legendarily gritty Bolton full back Tommy Banks and even the arrival of Hungary's 'Galloping Major', the fabulous Ferenc Puskas, no more deals were completed.

Happily, Murphy's resources were bolstered immeasurably by the comeback in early March of Munich survivor Bobby Charlton for the FA Cup quarter-final clash with West Bromwich Albion. The Reds' achievement in drawing 2-2 at the Hawthorns was considerable, and their subsequent victory at Old Trafford, secured by a late Webster winner after surviving frenetic Albion pressure, was utterly glorious. Not surprisingly, league results fell away – after Munich there was only one win in the 14 games that remained – but when the cup semi-final draw paired United with Second Division Fulham, the belief began to grow that Murphy's team could pull off a sporting miracle at Wembley.

The Cottagers, inspired by England schemer Johnny Haynes, offered stern resistance, however, and would have prevailed at Villa Park but for a thunderously struck late equalizer from Charlton. Thus reprieved, United triumphed 5-3 in the replay at Highbury with Dawson contributing a hat-trick. Astoundingly, they had booked their place in the final only seven weeks on from the calamity in Bavaria. During that surreal period of fiercely conflicting emotions, Murphy's brave band had negotiated a fantastic journey, but now the debilitating strain of increasingly unrealistic expectations began to tell. Though their fervour remained irrepressible, their form was poor as they completed a draining spell of 11 league games in 29 days leading up to their Wembley assignation with Bolton Wanderers.

The Trotters were doughty adversaries, a physically rigorous, no-frills First Division outfit quite properly unswayed by the sentimental groundswell of

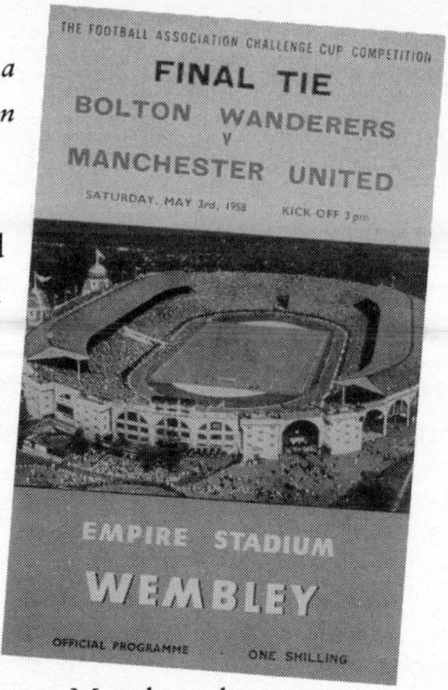


*Winning the FA Cup in May 1958 would have been a wonderful tonic for United, but it wasn't to be and Bolton came away 2-0 victors on the day.*

goodwill which the Red Devils had generated nationwide. Managed by former United player Bill Ridding, they were desperate to make up for their own FA Cup final disappointment of five years earlier, when a Stanley Matthews-inspired Blackpool had recovered from a 3-1 deficit to claim the trophy. Though he looked heart-rendingly fragile as he hobbled along with a walking stick, the Wembley presence of Matt Busby lifted the Manchester fans, but it was fitting that the honour of leading out the team fell to Jimmy Murphy, who had been the club's inspiration through that tumultuous spring. The stand-in boss named this line-up: Gregg, Foulkes, Greaves, Goodwin, Cope, Crowther, Dawson, Taylor, Charlton, Viollet, Webster. The inclusion of Viollet was a gamble, given that he had only recently returned to action following his Munich injuries, while Pearson could count himself unlucky to be omitted and there were no places either for Brennan or the fit-again Morgans.

In the quarter and semi-finals, Dame Fortune had smiled on United at crucial moments, but on the big day she deserted them with a vengeance. They fell behind after only three minutes when a deflection fell to Nat Lofthouse and England's dreadnought of a centre forward netted with alacrity. There were no more first-half goals, the outcome being effectively decided by a dramatic sequence of action ten minutes after the interval when two major breaks went the Wanderers' way. First Charlton beat goalkeeper Eddie Hopkinson with a pulverizing drive which crashed off the inside of an upright before rebounding into the custodian's arms. Almost immediately the focus shifted to the opposite end where Dennis Stevens – a cousin of United's Duncan Edwards, incidentally – let fly with a powerful drive which Harry Gregg palmed into the air. As the Ulsterman completed his catch, the combative Lofthouse barged into him at full bore, depositing goalkeeper and ball into the net – and the referee signalled a goal. Even in 1958, when keepers were not the protected species they have since become, it looked the most blatant of fouls, but the decision stood and, with the largely inexperienced Reds looking increasingly forlorn, Bolton went on to complete a comfortable 2-0 victory.

*A young Bobby Charlton survived the Munich air crash and went on to win all the major honours the game had to offer, including a World Cup medal in 1966.*

In truth, on the balance of play they deserved it, having been the more powerful and controlled unit during the game, but it was a bitter pill for the United camp to swallow after enduring such a grievous season. Typically the ailing but proud Busby took the defeat with ineffable grace, limping into the Bolton dressing room and congratulating every opponent in turn.

Back in Manchester the next day, the Red Devils were greeted by countless thousands of supporters, many of them with tears streaming down their faces, yet still that seemingly endless term was not at an end. In all the furore which had surrounded the fairytale progress to Wembley, it had been easy to forget that, way back in February in Belgrade, they had qualified for the semi-finals of the European Cup. Now, only five days after falling to Bolton, they took on mighty AC Milan at Old Trafford, and staggered the sporting world by beating them 2-1. The Red Devils fought like furies in that unforgettable first leg, coming back from a goal behind to carry the day with a late penalty, dispatched with icy aplomb by Ernie Taylor after Dennis Viollet had been baulked by Cesare Maldini. Suddenly another impossible dream hove tantalizingly into view, only to be shattered brutally in the second leg at the San Siro, where the Italians overwhelmed their gallant and overstretched opponents 4-0.

## Problems in Europe

The most astonishing aspect of the tie was the absence from both games of Bobby Charlton, who was constrained to remain with the England party during their series of World Cup warm-up games while his club was contesting one of the most momentous ties in their history. The FA's draconian decision, rendered all the more heartless in the light of the recent tragedy which had devastated the club's resources, would simply not be countenanced today, and was received with understandable gall at the time. Incredibly, soon United were to be the victims of yet another outrage by callous authority when the Football League, in an act of stupendous small-mindedness, refused to allow them to accept an invitation to enter the 1958-59 European Cup alongside their successors as First Division champions, Wolves.

The League ruled that the offer, extended in sympathy over Munich and in recognition of their recent sterling contribution to the continental scene, must be spurned because the Reds had not qualified in the accepted manner, as champions. At this distance it is impossible to discern whether there was an element of vengeance for what the League saw as United's cavalier attitude to that body's opposition to European Cup entry in 1956, but the impression of seriously sour grapes was inescapable.

Busby wasted no time on futile recriminations, however, instead looking boldly towards the future. Months earlier, wracked with pain and grief as he lay in a hospital bed, he had entertained genuine doubts about continuing as a football manager, being assailed by feelings of guilt about leading so many of his Babes to their deaths. But having cast such thoughts aside, he set to work on the reconstruction of Manchester United, a task he reckoned would take at least five years. Having resumed the Old Trafford reins in the summer of 1958, he determined that a creative inside forward was his top priority, and that September he smashed the European transfer record by paying Sheffield Wednesday £45,000 for Albert Quixall.

## Busby Returns

At that time the blond Yorkshireman, with his mesmeric ball skills, baby-faced looks and preference for very short shorts, was dubbed 'the golden boy of English football'. But although his signing was seen as a massive coup for Busby, at first he struggled to settle and United went seven games without a win following his arrival. Quixall became increasingly embarrassed, and later reflected: 'The manager was very patient, telling me to

*Albert Quixall, the 'golden boy', was Matt Busby's first big signing for United on returning to management after the Munich disaster.*

relax and play my normal game, but I didn't find that easy. It sounds daft but I think I was trying too hard, what with having that big fee on my napper, and it was only when I started doing what came naturally that matters improved.'

Another factor, perhaps, was the arrival in November of Warren Bradley, a diminutive but fiercely combative England amateur international right winger. The notion was that he and two colleagues from top amateur club Bishop Auckland, Bob Hardisty and Derek Lewin, would strengthen the Reds' reserves, thus freeing some of the promising youngsters for senior action. However, Bradley did so well that he earned a regular first-team slot with his new club and within six months had ascended to the full international stage.

For United he melded effectively with Quixall and by early winter the Red Devils were the most attractive side in the country once again, albeit temporarily. Amazingly, in view of the depredations of Munich, they lost only three First Division games between mid-November and season's end, finishing as runners-up to Stan Cullis' Wolves and firing a century of goals. It is an achievement which remains arguably the most underrated in the club's history, though there are still those who pay generous homage, particularly to that free-scoring forward line. One of them is Bill Foulkes: 'They played some of the most dazzling football I've ever seen, and it's a shame that it has always tended to be overshadowed by both the pre-Munich side and the wonderful team of the 1960s. The interplay between the inside trio of Quixall, Viollet and Charlton was exceptional, and the wingers, Bradley and Scanlon, were magnificent too.'

Charlton struck 29 times to record the most prolific season of his career, while Viollet scored 21 and Scanlon 16, a total of 66 goals from three men who had recently survived an air crash. Thus Charlton and Viollet had confirmed their pre-Munich excellence, but the case of Scanlon remains distinctly perplexing. Before the accident he had just claimed a regular place in the side, but a combination of physical injuries and psychological scars meant that he did not play again until August 1958. Immediately he struck such compelling form that he won England under-23 and Football League recognition, and didn't miss a league match all season. But thereafter his standard tailed off and he was sold to Newcastle, where he never settled and slipped away to complete his playing days in the lower divisions. Charlton's subsequent temporary switch to the left flank, a succession of niggling injuries and possible delayed trauma from the disaster have been advanced as theories to explain the premature burn-out of one of the most exciting performers in the top flight. Whatever the truth, it amounted to a crying shame.

Foulkes was another who suffered from debilitating after-effects of Munich. Though blessed with an iron constitution, he lost weight rapidly and did not relish the responsibility of the captaincy. In due course he relinquished it and rebuilt his career by switching from right back to centre half, but not before enduring a period of excruciating anguish. It seems clear in retrospect that after the crash he needed rest and counselling, neither of which were forthcoming in an era when people were expected to grit their teeth and get on with life, no matter what the circumstances. Still, despite his distress, the doughty Lancastrian remained a bulwark of Busby's team for another ten years. He was the team's sole ever-present in 1959-60 when United racked up more than 100 goals for the second successive term – including 32 from Dennis Viollet, a new club record in league outings which remained unbroken in 2003 – but slipped to seventh place in the table as they conceded 80.

By the midway point of that campaign it was clear that, having given his second wave of youngsters plenty of chances, the manager needed reinforcements if he was to rebuild United to anything like their former level, and duly he paid West Bromwich Albion £30,000 for the signature of wing half Maurice Setters. The arrival of the crunchingly hard West Countryman was particularly timely as another ball-winner, Wilf McGuinness, had recently sustained a serious leg injury. At first there were hopes of a recovery, and the effervescent Mancunian battled manfully for two years to save his career before admitting defeat and joining the coaching staff. It was a savage blow to a promising young fellow whose natural gifts were limited, but whose phenomenal dedication and work-rate had already earned him two full England caps. He was destined, however, to surface again, a decade down the line in the Manchester United story.

One of the more heartening aspects of 1959-60 was the splendid generosity of Real Madrid in meeting the Red Devils for two friendlies, home and away, to keep them in touch with the European scene. The Spaniards won 6-1 at Old Trafford and 6-5 at the Bernabeu, but the results mattered less than the fact that, despite their temporarily reduced circumstances, United were still competing with the best.

## Young Talent Boosts the Team

A demoralizingly disappointing start to 1960-61 brought further investment that November in the shape of left back Noel Cantwell, whose £29,500 arrival from West Ham signalled the end for his fellow Irishman Joe Carolan. Genial Joe was capable enough, but maybe lacked the class and ruthlessness to thrive in the top flight, a shortfall which also accounted for the exits of

## 50 Greatest Players

**DENNIS VIOLLET Forward**

**Born:** Manchester, 20 September 1933

**Joined Manchester United:** 1950 **From:** Juniors

**Debut:** 11 April 1953 v Newcastle United, League

**Appearances:** 293 **Goals:** 179

**Left Manchester United:** 1962 **For:** Stoke City

**Honours won with United:** Division One championship 1956, 1957

Dennis Viollet was probably one of the most under-rated of the galaxy of stars Matt Busby assembled into the Busby Babes during the mid-1950s. He rarely commanded the headlines in the way many of his team-mates could, but he was undoubtedly a hugely talented footballer and well at home in the teams of the day that seemed to have no obvious deficiencies. A consummately stylish forward and instinctive goalscorer, Viollet's striking record stands comparison with many great players. A survivor of the Munich air disaster, his Old Trafford days saw him win two league championship medals and participate in the 1958 FA Cup final after having recovered from injuries sustained in the crash. He later played for several other clubs including Stoke City, whom he helped to claim the Second Division title in 1963. Viollet eventually settled in the USA when his playing days came to a close.

full back Ian Greaves, centre half Ronnie Cope and wing half Freddie Goodwin around the turn of the decade. Cantwell brought poise, stability and leadership to the team, which profited also from Foulkes and Brennan settling at centre half and full back respectively. There was encouraging input, too, from a buoyant wave of rookie talent which included wing half cum inside forward Nobby Stiles, inside forward or winger Johnny Giles, wing half Jimmy Nicholson and the maturing spearhead Alex Dawson, who celebrated New Year's Eve with a hat-trick in the 5-1 humbling of Manchester City at Old Trafford.

That term Dawson netted 16 times in 28 outings, helping United revive to finish seventh for the second successive year, but Busby did not believe that the 20-year-old Aberdonian's all-round game was equal to the task of leading the line in the long term, and in the summer of 1961 he was replaced by Arsenal's Scottish international David Herd. That autumn Dawson departed to newly-relegated Preston North End, where he performed admirably, scoring freely and winning renown as 'The Black Prince of Deepdale', though without quite managing to suggest that Busby had made the wrong decision.

*Johnny Giles was one of the group of rookies brought on by Busby in the early 60s to help revitalize United.*

At Old Trafford, meanwhile, all was not well in 1961-62, either on the field or off it. Recent defensive frailties were heightened by number-one goalkeeper Harry Gregg's ongoing injury problems, while his daredevil deputy, David Gaskell, suffered fitness problems, too. Though the rearguard had been bolstered by the introduction of Tony Dunne, a quick and clever Irish full back signed for next-to-nothing from Shelbourne, the midfield lacked cohesion and Herd took time to settle up front, top-scoring with a mere 14 goals.

Considering the lack of firepower, it came as a shock to most observers when Busby elected to sell the proven marksman Dennis Viollet to Stoke City in January. Still not past his pomp at 28, and recently elevated to full England status, he appeared to be exactly the type of experienced goal-getter needed by a team in the process of regeneration. Though he never bore a grudge, and demonstrated his timeless class by going on to help the Potters lift the Second Division title in his first season at the Victoria Ground, Viollet was hurt by that unexpected exit, never fully explained. Rumours abounded about behind-the-scenes disagreements with the club, but they were never confirmed and the transfer remains shrouded in mystery to this day.

Certainly if there was strife between Busby and Viollet, it was not the only discord rippling the surface of the Old Trafford pond in the early 1960s. There was a group of players, among whom the articulate, fair-minded Cantwell was prominent, who believed passionately that more structured coaching was needed urgently at the club, while others were content with the status quo as represented by the manager's preference for allowing his footballers to express themselves untrammelled by modern theory. Cliques developed and team spirit suffered at times, a situation reflected by United's plunge to 15th place at the end of 1961-62, their lowest ebb since Munich. The supporters, not mollified by a run to the semi-finals of the FA Cup, began to stay away, and with Matt Busby looking increasingly careworn, the future began to take on a forbidding aspect. But just when a fresh spark was desperately needed, duly it arrived in the irrepressible form of Denis Law.

## The Brilliant Scot

United shattered the British transfer record by paying Italian club Torino £115,000 for the brilliant Scot in August 1962. Like the contrastingly placid Bobby Charlton, Law was a world-class performer, an inside forward whose skill, opportunism, bravery and sheer puckish presence was central to the uplifting transformation that followed. Not that the Reds suddenly became a team of world-beaters. An interlude of painful transition was in store, commencing with the woeful autumn of 1962 which yielded only three victories with a third of the season gone. Charlton had been missing because of a hernia, but even when he returned in October the team lacked the creativity which would bring the best out of the potent pairing of Law and Herd.

So, as the seemingly interminable winter of the Big Freeze ground towards a belated spring, the manager made another inspired dip into the transfer market, shelling out £53,000 to Celtic for the penetrative if occasionally tempestuous play-maker Paddy Crerand. The newcomer took time to become accustomed to English football, however, and as he picked up a win-bonus only once in his first 11 league outings, the spectre of relegation loomed unthinkably large. Indeed, but for a distinctly fortunate draw at Maine Road three matches from the end, secured by a late Quixall strike, United might have taken the plunge. As it was City went down instead and

*The FA Cup final of 1963 brought hard-earned glory back to the rebuilt Reds. Here, David Herd scores goal number two after Leicester City's Gordon Banks failed to hold a Bobby Charlton shot. United went on to win 3-1.*

the Red Devils could turn their attention to the saving grace of an otherwise abysmal term, the FA Cup. They had reached the final thanks to victories over Huddersfield, Aston Villa, Chelsea, Coventry and Southampton, who proved taxing opponents in a scrappy, unbearably tense semi-final at Villa Park, where Law had scrambled an untidy winner. Now they faced Matt Gillies' high-riding Leicester City, a side short on flair but long on organization and spirit, and which richly merited their status as favourites.

On a picture book Wembley afternoon in late May, the anxieties of that chronic winter melted away as Manchester United awoke belatedly from hibernation. After surviving a predictably shaky opening, Busby's stellar collection of outstanding individuals gelled exquisitely, their sumptuous moves flitting like sunshine across Wembley's lush, green carpet.

At the heart of it all was Crerand, passing like a god and controlling the rhythm of the contest, while Charlton offered touches of genius, Giles and Quixall probed intelligently and Herd contributed two goals. But the crowning glory was Denis Law. He was everywhere, his incandescent quality flashing across the afternoon like a bolt of summer lightning, and he gave United the lead with a goal to treasure in the memory.

Crerand pounced on a loose throw-out by newly-capped England keeper Gordon Banks, then speared a defence-splitting pass to Law, who swivelled sweetly to net with a crisp, low drive into the corner of the net. Thereafter Law was uncontrollable, tormenting the Foxes' rearguard relentlessly and it was surprising that he didn't add to his personal tally. However, Herd dispatched a rebound from a trademark Charlton thunderbolt and then, after Ken Keyworth had reduced the arrears, the ex-Gunner completed the 3-1 scoreline by shooting home after Banks had spilled a Giles cross.

Though the Reds' defence had not been sorely pressed, contrary to most pre-match predictions, Gaskell had performed efficiently after a fitful beginning, Dunne and skipper Cantwell had been a complementary full back pairing – Tony waspishly quick, Noel a stately anticipator of events – while Foulkes and Setters had been their usual formidable selves. Of those who didn't make the line-up Gregg, who was fit again after injury, was unfortunate, especially as his noble Old Trafford career would never be crowned by a major medal. Stiles and Brennan, too, had strong cases for inclusion, but their day would come.

For the team as a whole, it was a comprehensive triumph and a handsome vindication of Busby's rebuilding efforts over half a decade. Now the players, the supporters, the entire football world could see that the Manchester United bandwagon was rolling again.

# Chapter Eight: 1963-68
# Glory Unconfined

A rude awakening was awaiting all who believed that FA Cup glory heralded an instant return to the promised land of serial silverware. It was delivered by Everton, the champions, in a merciless Charity Shield drubbing at Goodison Park in August 1963. United lost 4-0 but, far worse, they were practically humiliated and Matt Busby reacted decisively for the league opener against Sheffield Wednesday. Out went the right wing pairing of Giles and Quixall, centre forward Herd and goalkeeper Gaskell, who was carrying an injury as usual. In came three young forwards, Ian Moir, Phil Chisnall and David Sadler, and Harry Gregg, still an able custodian but plagued by fitness doubts. It was a typically bold move and it carried far-reaching consequences for Quixall and Giles. The 30-year-old one-time captain of Sheffield Wednesday appeared to have suffered premature burn-out and while it was poignant to see such an extravagant talent shuffle off to Oldham Athletic for a nominal fee a year later, at least it was clear that his best days were behind him.

Not so those of Giles, who was 22 and bounteously equipped for a long-term future at the top. However, he was a fiercely independent individual not averse to arguing with his eminent manager, and in August 1963 he was sold to Leeds for £37,500. It turned out to be a shrewd piece of business for the Yorkshiremen as the Dubliner matured into one of the cleverest (and hardest) midfield generals the British game has known.

Conversely, Giles missed out on a key role in Busby's third great team, which began to take engaging shape in 1963-64, though not before further radical shuffling of the pack. Each of the three rookies was given an extended senior run, and each did well, but not well enough for their demanding boss. Accordingly Moir, an entertaining but mercurial winger, and Chisnall, a sweet-passing inside forward with an eye for goal, were soon

*Keeper Harry Gregg, a survivor of the Munich disaster, never won any honours at United but his bravery won him an army of fans.*

dispatched to Blackpool and Liverpool respectively, while Sadler receded temporarily to the periphery, resurfacing later in midfield and winning England caps as a central defender. Herd was restored to lead the attack, netting 27 times in all competitions, an admirable return which nevertheless was dwarfed by Law's astonishing tally of 46 goals in 41 outings. No wonder he was crowned European Footballer of the Year for 1964. Other changes included the purchase, trial and swift rejection of Chelsea's skilful but ponderous Graham Moore at inside right, the springtime replacement of Maurice Setters by Nobby Stiles as Bill Foulkes' partner at the heart of the rearguard, and the reintroduction of Shay Brennan at the expense of Noel Cantwell, with Tony Dunne switching from right back to left.

## George Best Joins the Team

But it was two further adjustments which most enchanted the Old Trafford faithful as the Red Devils leapt from 19th in 1962-63 to the runners-up spot, four points adrift of Liverpool. Bobby Charlton was granted his heart's desire of moving from the left wing to a deep-lying central role, where he meshed sublimely with Paddy Crerand and, at home to West Bromwich Albion on 14 September, Busby introduced a pale, skinny 17-year-old from Belfast, name of George Best. His public profile was non-existent, but within the club excitement was already running high about the boy's stunning potential. Harry Gregg, for one, had been given the runaround by his callow countryman in a training session and knew that he had encountered something special. After contributing to a 1-0 win on his debut, Best returned to the youth team – which that term he would help to secure the FA Youth Cup – before resuming senior duty at home to Burnley in late December, two days after United had been humbled 6-1 at Turf Moor. Operating nominally on the left wing, George roamed at will, tantalizing the Burnley defence with his untrackable runs and ceaseless invention, scoring once as the Reds claimed a 5-1 revenge win. Thereafter he was in the side for keeps, sharing in the progress to an FA Cup semi-final, which was lost to West Ham on a Hillsborough mudheap, and in a European Cup-Winners' Cup campaign which culminated in the most inept display United have ever given against continental competition.

Having recovered from a 2-0 first-leg deficit to knock out holders Spurs in the previous round, then tanned Sporting Lisbon 4-1 at Old Trafford in the quarter-final opening leg, the trip to Portugal was seen as a virtual formality. But, conceivably distracted by a dispute over bonuses, the players under-performed chronically, plunging to a 5-0 defeat. Busby was livid, and pledged privately that no team of his would ever suffer such humiliation again. Thus the defence was tightened by the regular selection of Stiles, and at season's end England winger John Connelly arrived from Burnley at a cost of £56,000, while a hitherto obscure goalkeeper, Dubliner Pat Dunne, was recruited for £10,500 from Shamrock Rovers. The fees were not exorbitant, although they represented significant outlay at a time when the club was spending heavily on ground improvements ahead of the 1966 World Cup finals, but both men were to prove worth every penny in 1964-65 as the Red Devils became champions for the first time since Munich.

### The Title Regained at Last

After a couple of early stumbles, Dunne – no relation to full back Tony – replaced Gaskell between the posts and it was 16 games before he finished on the losing side. There followed a worrying midwinter hiatus, but crucial springtime victories over their principal title rivals – an exhilarating 4-0 crushing of Tommy Docherty's pert young Chelsea at Old Trafford and an edgily attritional triumph over Leeds at Elland Road – cleared the way for a smooth run-in. The crown was effectively claimed when Arsenal were beaten 3-1 on the same night as Don Revie's men were held by Birmingham, and only a 17-0 last-day reverse at Aston Villa could have deprived the Red Devils of the prize. In the event they lost 2-1 and were declared champions on goal average, pipping Leeds by approximately 0.6 of a goal.

**50 Greatest Players**

**HARRY GREGG Goalkeeper**

**Born:** Magherafelt, 25 October 1932

**Joined Manchester United:** 1957 **From:** Doncaster Rovers

**Debut:** 21 December 1957 v Leicester City, League

**Appearances:** 247

**Left Manchester United:** 1966 **For:** Stoke City

Harry Gregg was acclaimed as the 'Goalkeeper of the Tournament' after appearing for Northern Ireland in the 1958 World Cup in Sweden – a terrific accolade that was even more meritorious considering that four months earlier he had survived the Munich air disaster. Gregg had only been a United player for two months at the time of the crash after being transferred from Doncaster Rovers for £23,500, then a record for a keeper. Tough and brave, sometimes to the point of being foolhardy, he won a special place in United hearts with his unique brand of goalkeeping. He won no major honours with United although he was in the 1958 FA Cup final side that lost 2-0 to Bolton Wanderers after having been barged over the line by Nat Lofthouse while still in possession of the ball.

Quite properly, praise was rained on the incomparable trinity of Charlton, Law and Best. Never before had a British team boasted three such exceptionally gifted individuals, and there has been no such celestial collaboration since. The beauty of it all was that they complemented each other ideally, rarely getting in each other's way. Charlton's primary beat was the midfield, where he sprayed long-distance passes, wrong-footed opponents with his gazelle-like runs, worked himself to a standstill and carried a howitzer shot in either foot. Law was at the sharp end, a fizzing firecracker of a predator blessed with blinding reflexes, a comprehensive range of skills, courage that could be terrifying and an unsurpassable rage to win. As for Best, he was everywhere and he had everything. If ever these islands produced the perfect footballer, then he was it.

Yet this was no three-man extravaganza. The other two attackers, winger Connelly and centre forward Herd, were fine footballers in their own right. Lancastrian Connelly, who had picked up his first title medal with Burnley in 1959-60, was an admirably direct foil to fellow flanker Best and his 15 goals were integral to the success. John was a tough customer, too, ever-ready to chase back and tackle like a ball-winning wing half, offering splendid cover for Crerand's creative meanderings. Herd was an ultra-reliable, 20-goals-a-season man, making nonsense of the vilification visited on his head by mindless barrackers, who had treated him as a scapegoat for disappointing team displays during the early part of his Old Trafford tenure.

The attack was completed by yet another thoroughbred, Paddy Crerand, the quick-tempered, slow-moving wing half whose imaginative distribution provided ideal service to the pacy flair merchants, but attention should also be lavished on a hugely underrated defence. When the championship chips were down in the spring, the combination of Pat Dunne, Brennan, Tony Dunne, Bill Foulkes and Nobby Stiles conceded just six goals in a dozen games, their contribution a monument to concentration and simplicity. True, Pat Dunne was far more impressive as a shot-stopper than as a claimer of crosses, but such was the aerial dominance of the granite-hard Foulkes, the pace and cuteness of the full backs and the abrasive Stiles' immaculate reading of the game that the custodian was rarely exposed.

Overall it was a wonderful team, well worthy of the treble to which it aspired. However, it pulled up fractionally short in both knockout competitions, falling to Leeds after a replay in a bitterly fought FA Cup semi-final, and bowing out of the Inter-Cities Fairs Cup at the same stage. Once again it was the European exit which irked Busby the most, especially as the tie with Ferencvaros went to a third match following a draw on aggregate,

## 50 Greatest Players

**NOEL CANTWELL Defender**

**Born:** Cork, 28 February 1932

**Joined Manchester United:** 1960 **From:** West Ham United

**Debut:** 26 November 1960 v Cardiff City, League

**Appearances:** 146 **Goals:** 8

**Left Manchester United:** 1967 (retired)

**Honours won with United:** FA Cup winner 1963

Cantwell had been well established in West Ham United's defence when Matt Busby paid £29,500 for him in 1960. The United boss was still rebuilding his side following the Munich air disaster and in Cantwell saw many of the attributes that Johnny Carey had brought to his first great side after the War. The Republic of Ireland international proved to be a valuable addition to United's gradually strengthening squad and he made an important contribution as the Reds returned to the status of a trophy-winning side, collecting the FA Cup as captain in 1963. He didn't appear in sufficient games to win a medal in the 1965 and 1967 title-winning sides, but his experience provided a major factor behind the scenes. Tipped as a likely successor to Matt Busby he moved on in 1967 to cut his managerial teeth at Coventry. Many expected him to return to Old Trafford, but he went to several clubs before changing tack to work in the licensed trade.

but the setback merely sharpened his desire for the ultimate prize, which his side had qualified to contest yet again in 1965-66.

For Manchester United, though not for their England men, that turned out to be a season of mammoth frustration. The team had not changed drastically although, with Pat Dunne deemed of insufficient quality for the long term, Gregg and occasionally Gaskell minded the net, while skipper Cantwell and young winger John Aston – son of the identically named United stalwart of the 1940s and early 1950s, by now an Old Trafford coach – enjoyed lengthy runs. They were never remotely consistent enough to challenge Liverpool for the league title, finishing ten points adrift in fourth place, and once again they were beaten in two semi-finals, which was becoming a distressing habit.

### A Classic Performance in Europe

The European Cup had topped the club's agenda and it had seemed tantalizingly within reach after they had dispatched HJK Helsinki, ASK Vorwarts and mighty Benfica, racking up 22 goals against six conceded over

## Great Matches

**EUROPEAN CUP, QUARTER-FINAL, 2ND LEG Stadium of Light, 9 March 1966**

**Benfica 1**
Brennan o.g.

**Manchester United 5**
Best 2
Connelly
Crerand
Charlton

**Attendance: 75,000**

With the Red Devils taking a meagre one-goal advantage from the first leg, Benfica might have expected Matt Busby's men to take no risks during the opening phase, but after less than a quarter of an hour, a Best-inspired United had surged into a 3-0 lead and the Eagles were doomed to their first European reverse in front of their own fans. The rout began on six minutes when Dunne flighted a free kick and Best lost his marker to nod the first. Some five minutes later a raking Gregg clearance was glanced by Herd to Best, and the untameable Irishman darted beyond two defenders before lashing a low cross-shot home.

United drove forward relentlessly and, a further two minutes in, Law duped two Portuguese before slipping a pass to Best. This time the inspired 19-year-old switched the ball to Connelly, who sidefooted the third with alacrity. Benfica were utterly demoralized and might have been humiliated before the interval, but for fabulous Pereira saves from Herd and Charlton. Brennan presented Benfica with an own goal after 52 minutes, and Gregg made several characteristically courageous interventions to deny Torres and Eusebio, but it was the Reds who finished in total control, with Crerand firing in a fourth goal and Charlton dummying several opponents to stroke home a fifth. Even by the standards of Busby's scintillating team, this was a display to enshrine in the memory.

**Benfica:** Costa Pereira, Cavem, Germano, Cruz, Pinto, Coluna, Augusto Silva, Jose Augusto, Eusebio, Torres, Simoes
**Manchester United:** Gregg, Brennan, Dunne, Crerand, Foulkes, Stiles, Best, Law, Charlton, Herd, Connelly
**Referee:** C. Lo Bello

*When George Best returned from the Benfica match wearing a sombrero he was dubbed 'El Beatle'. Here seen with John Fitzpatrick (left) and David Herd.*

the six matches. The 5-1 quarter-final trouncing of Eusebio and company in Lisbon's Stadium of Light stands to this day as United's most spectacular display on foreign soil. Against a Benfica side not far descended from their opulent peak, the Red Devils were unstoppable, particularly Best, whose life was changed forever when he arrived back in England wearing a sombrero and was dubbed 'El Beatle' by the newspapers. Thereafter, a combination of his pop idol looks and racy lifestyle, together with his continuing emergence as a footballing genius, ensconced him permanently in the media spotlight. Eventually, both he and United would suffer grievously for it, but for the moment the personable Irishman could revel in his new-found fame, though his progress was jolted by a knee injury. George needed a cartilage operation, and though he was patched for the first leg of the European semi against Partizan in Belgrade, he was not at his most effective. United lost 2-0 and then, with Best sidelined, could manage only a 1-0 victory at Old Trafford. Three days later, with several others suffering from knocks and strains, they were beaten by a single Everton goal in an FA Cup semi-final at Burnden Park.

It was a dismal climax to a term which had promised so much but which had foundered on lack of squad depth when injuries and fatigue bit deep in the spring. It did have its magical moments, though, quite apart from the Lisbon goal-fest. Notably there were two unforgettable league clashes with Tottenham Hotspur, both of which ended in 5-1 wins for the home side, each game garnished with a goal of unperishable quality. At White Hart Lane in October, Spurs' Jimmy Greaves seized possession inside the centre circle, then waltzed past five challenges before planting the ball deftly into the United net. Two months later, with players ankle-deep in a muddy Old Trafford morass, Bobby Charlton met a headed clearance on the half-volley some 30 yards from goal and the rising ball appeared to gather jet-propelled pace as it rocketed into the roof of Jennings' net. Here was proof, twice over, that football can produce sequences of deathless beauty which shimmer in the memory even though their relevance in any other context has long since withered.

For both of those scorers, and for Stiles and Connelly, there was to be a tumultuous addendum to the domestic season as they took part in England's victorious World Cup campaign. Charlton, shortly to be voted European Footballer of the Year for 1966, and Stiles went all the way to the final, while Connelly and Greaves were discarded after appearing earlier in the tournament. That summer, which brought such ecstasy to English fans, was not without its turbulence for Matt Busby. Denis Law, no less, doubtlessly having noted the massive crowds which paid to watch the Red Devils, and perhaps distracted by tales of footballers lining their pockets when they switched clubs, declared

*John Connelly scored a goal in United's infamous 5-1 thrashing of Benfica in 1966 and went on to appear for England in that year's World Cup campaign.*

that he would leave unless he received a substantial bonus to re-sign. Some managers might have panicked and caved in, but not Busby. Instead he placed Law on the transfer list, a decision he announced publicly before telling his fellow Scot. Duly Matt and Denis sorted out a new financial package, but every other United player got the message about who was the boss.

In addition, Busby was panned by critics for not plunging into the transfer market. He was urged to buy two of England's World Cup winners, Blackpool's Alan Ball and Geoff Hurst of West Ham, but Ball went to Everton, Hurst remained at Upton Park and United's money remained in the bank until September. At that point, perplexed by a switchback start to the term, the United boss broke the world transfer record for a goalkeeper for the second time in less than a decade. The new man was England under-23 international Alex Stepney, a £50,000 acquisition from Chelsea who had only recently arrived at Stamford Bridge from Millwall, believing that he was earmarked to replace the Blues' Peter Bonetti. However, Stepney joined the Red Devils after making only one league appearance for Chelsea.

With the injury-plagued Gregg, the previous most expensive custodian, past his best, and neither Gaskell nor Pat Dunne fitting Busby's bill, the confident Londoner was a much-needed addition to a still-impressive side for which Tony Dunne, Crerand, Stiles, Best, Law, Charlton and Herd remained automatic selections. The veteran Foulkes, too, would demonstrate his indestructibility yet again, despite constant newspaper talk about replacing him with Mike England of Blackburn Rovers, but autumn brought further changes.

The consummately professional John Connelly, still only 28 with his powers undiminished, experienced a difference of opinion with the manager and was sold to newly-demoted Blackburn for £40,000. At first he was replaced by pushing Herd wide and re-introducing David Sadler at centre forward, but by mid season Aston, a specialist winger, had claimed a regular berth.

At the back Brennan was dropped, with the increasingly splendid Dunne switching to the right defensive flank and local youngster Bobby Noble taking the No. 3 shirt. Sadler, meanwhile, was demonstrating priceless versatility, contributing stints as a replacement stopper for Foulkes in midwinter, returning to the front line when Herd suffered a broken leg in the spring, and even doing competent duty in midfield. The upshot was that United settled to title-winning form; after losing to Sheffield United on Boxing Day, they embraced the classic championship formula of winning at home and drawing away, shaking off a pack of pursuers of which John Carey's Nottingham Forest were the most persistent. The prize was lifted on the penultimate Saturday with a 6-1 annihilation of West Ham at Upton Park, a fittingly majestic display to crown the Reds' seventh title triumph.

### A Seventh Title

Significantly, this time there had been no European or protracted FA Cup distractions. Another key difference was the presence of the reliable Stepney, of whom Busby declared: 'Without him I don't think we would have won the championship.' But there was a tragic side to 1966-67, too. At 21, Bobby Noble had emerged as a full back of staggering potential, exceedingly quick, relentlessly abrasive and an astoundingly mature reader of the game for one so young. After ousting Brennan in the autumn he was an ever-present until April, when he suffered grievous injuries to head, chest and leg in a car accident following the goalless draw at Roker Park. For a time Bobby's very survival was in doubt, but although his life was spared, he never played again despite valiant, heart-rending attempts at a comeback. It was a crushing blow to the multi-talented youngster who had skippered the likes of Best, Sadler and Aston to FA Youth Cup glory in 1964, and for whom a golden future had appeared to beckon at both club and international level.

How Noble would have adorned Manchester United's next great challenge, a renewed assault on the European Cup in 1967-68. As it was his absence offered fresh opportunity to Brennan and an opening for young Francis Burns, a classy Scottish left back who held his place for most of an eventful season, only to lose it at the unforgettable climax. Back in the summer, though, Matt Busby was contemplating another vacancy, that of a marksman to operate alongside Law following the serious injury to Herd. Transfer speculation was rife, with Hurst being mentioned again along with Welsh stars Ron and Wyn Davies, but the manager decided that a quiet local lad from the same Collyhurst school as Nobby Stiles was the man to fill the void. Duly 18-year-old Brian Kidd shone on the summer tour of Australia and impressed in the 3-3 Charity Shield draw with Spurs, a ravishingly entertaining game which featured two incandescent passages of play.

One was a freak, when Spurs keeper Pat Jennings lofted a towering clearance which caught on the Old Trafford breeze and bounced over the head of the stranded Stepney for the strangest goal of the season. The other was down to pure genius, as Law danced round several tackles in a shoulder-dropping left wing dash before rolling the ball inside for the charging Charlton to unloose a first-time 25-yard piledriver which poor Jennings can barely have glimpsed. It was an extravagant flourish which summed up the swashbuckling appeal of Busby's lovely team which, after losing their First Division opener at Goodison Park, were beaten only twice more in a blistering 25-match sequence. Now another championship appeared theirs for the taking as they cantered into a five-point lead.

But, weakened by injuries to Foulkes and Law, and concentrating on Europe come the spring, they fell prey to chronic inconsistency. A 3-1 defeat by Joe Mercer's Manchester City at Old Trafford in March proved particularly damaging and the local rivals were locked together on 56 points at the top of the table with one match to play. The Reds looked to have the easier task at home to lowly Sunderland, but they lost 2-1 while the Blues triumphed 4-3 at Newcastle to earn the Blues' first title since 1937.

Under normal circumstances, the United faithful would have despaired, but this time there was the little matter of Europe's premier club prize to console them. The continental campaign had kicked off in a comparatively low key with a simple 4-0 home victory over Hibernians of Malta, a team of part-timers coached by a priest, and continued with a goalless draw in the Gzira Stadium. The first leg of the second round brought another stalemate, against PK Sarajevo in Yugoslavia. On the run of play United were a trifle lucky, but Busby's men endured extreme provocation from over-physical opponents and deserved their draw. Back at Old Trafford, goals from Aston and Best secured a 2-1 win to set up a tough quarter-final against Gornik Zabrze.

The first game in Manchester was a top-quality affair, with United attacking relentlessly and the Poles defending skilfully but without the violent excesses of the Yugoslavians. An own-goal by Florenski and a late flick by Kidd furnished a decent advantage to take to Katowice but it was only just enough. On a surface of packed snow and ice, the Reds fought a match-long rearguard action in which rookie man-marker John Fitzpatrick was outstanding, losing 1-0 but going through to their fourth European Cup semi-final on a 2-1 aggregate.

**50 Greatest Players**

**DAVID HERD Forward**

**Born:** Hamilton, Lanarkshire, 15 April 1934

**Joined Manchester United:** 1961 **From:** Arsenal

**Debut:** 19 August 1961 v West Ham United, League

**Appearances:** 264 (1) **Goals:** 145

**Left Manchester United:** 1968 **For:** Stoke City

**Honours won with United:** Division One championship 1965, 1967; FA Cup winner 1963

Herd was a master striker in his own right but playing in a side that contained three of the greatest players of their, or any other, age meant that he was he always going to struggle in the media's acknowledgement stakes. That wasn't, however, the case with United's supporters who were never slow to show their appreciation of Herd's brilliant goal-scoring qualities. Herd's father, Alec, was a team-mate of Matt Busby during the 1930s at Manchester City and the family links were further strengthened when the Reds' boss paid Arsenal £35,000 for the Scottish international in the close season of 1961. Herd became a vital part of the set-up that was to bring success to the club over the next few years.

In the last four, United were paired with Real Madrid, still the most illustrious name in world football, if hardly the incomparable force they had been in the 1950s. For the Old Trafford instalment, Matt Busby recalled Denis Law, who had been struggling with a knee injury, a telling factor in the club's deteriorating First Division fortunes. Though 'The King' was unable to perform at his imperious best, he contributed gamely as the Red Devils stormed forward in wave after wave of attacks. But the Spaniards defended resolutely and intelligently and the hosts were restricted to a solitary goal, plundered by Best with a venomous drive from an Aston dispatch.

Conventional wisdom made Real warm favourites for the second leg, especially with Law now removed from the firing line for the remainder of the season. With an onslaught inevitable, Busby opted for additional experience in defence, drafting in Foulkes even though the faithful 36-year-old stopper was nursing knee trouble, and Brennan, whose canny positional sense might counter the pace of Gento. Despite the careful planning, United opened calamitously at the Bernabeu, conceding first-half goals to Pirri, Gento and Amancio, with only a flukily sliced own goal by Zoco to show in reply. Worse still, they had been given a thorough runaround by Real, and there seemed little hope as they trooped disconsolately to the dressing room at half-time.

Privately, perhaps, Busby was plumbing his own depths of despair as the vision of European glory appeared to be receding for yet another year. But he found within him a grain of hope, pointing out to his players that they were only one behind on aggregate, that there was still time to recover. It was then that Real Madrid made a fatal mistake. Believing that they had won, they began the second half in showboating mode, playing keep-ball and strolling long before it was safe to do so. United fought on and when Sadler tucked away a scrappy goal to level the tie some 20 minutes from time, the Spanish champions reacted with consternation, thus encouraging the Reds to go for the kill.

Foulkes recalled what happened next: 'We won a throw-in on halfway and, although I did not usually pile forward, something told me this was the time to get moving. I snapped to Nobby "Stay here, I'm going up" and he asked me what the hell I was doing. I showed for the ball but Paddy Crerand threw it to George Best. George hared down the wing past several tackles, and I kept going, too. As he looked up I was the only United player in the box. I thought he would never pass to me and that he would attempt to score at the near post. But as he feinted one way, wrong-footing the defenders, I knew what was in his mind. I had seen him do it so often before. So I took three steps back and, sure enough, he rolled it into my path. All I had to do was sidefoot it into the net. It all seemed unreal, like I was frozen in time. When everyone came to congratulate me, the first thing I did was to tell Nobby to stay back because there were still 15 minutes to go. He said "You miserable bugger", and George wondered why I wasn't showing any emotion, but I saved all that for later.'

It was a remarkable, but utterly characteristic reaction from the level-headed Foulkes, who had just scored the most important goal in United's history. With Madrid now shocked and stumbling, the Reds had completed a stunning comeback and they cruised into their first European Cup final, winning 4-3 on aggregate. And so to the biggest night of all, when Wembley provided the venue, old foes Benfica the opposition. For both club and player, it was a shame that United were deprived of Law, forced to watch the game on television from a hospital bed after undergoing a knee operation, but he was with them in spirit on that tumultuous occasion. There was heartache, too, for young Francis Burns, omitted in favour of Shay Brennan after playing in the first seven matches of the European campaign, but for the rest there was only joy and fulfilment as the Eagles of Lisbon were grounded comprehensively.

The normal 90 minutes was unbearably tense, with United appearing to have triumphed through a rare Charlton header, only to concede a late equalizer and, so nearly, an even later winner. But then came the most expansive, exhilarating first period of extra-time conceivable, with goals from Best, Kidd and Charlton ensuring that Matt Busby's 12-year quest should reach a successful conclusion.

## A European Dream Comes True

Every man on the Red Devils' teamsheet contributed titanically to that ultimate glory. Goalkeeper Stepney will live forever in United folklore for preventing Eusebio, 'The Black Panther', from hammering the goal which would have scuppered Busby's dream; full backs Brennan and Dunne covered like men possessed; Foulkes snuffed out the giant Torres, while Stiles largely shackled his world-class partner, Eusebio; the creativity of Crerand and two-goal Charlton in midfield was matched only by their prodigious workrate, which left them so dehydrated on a searingly humid evening that

### 50 Greatest Players

**BILL FOULKES Defender**

**Born:** St Helens, 5 January 1932

**Joined Manchester United:** 1951 **From:** Juniors

**Debut:** 13 December 1952 v Liverpool, League

**Appearances:** 688 **Goals:** 9

**Left Manchester United:** 1970 (retired)

**Honours won with United:** European Cup winner 1968; Division One championship 1956, 1957, 1965, 1967; FA Cup winner 1963

Bill Foulkes will be always regarded as one of the great names in the annals of Manchester United. His record of 688 appearances in all competitions remains second only to Bobby Charlton's. Foulkes burst into the United side as a full back in 1952 but it was as a rock solid, totally dependable centre half that he will be best remembered. He was an established star before the Munich air disaster and having survived the tragedy he went on to remain a club stalwart for another 12 years. He collected four league championship medals, played in three FA Cup finals – picking up a winners' medal in 1963 – and in 1968, at the grand age of 36, he was in the side that defeated Benfica to win the European Cup. Capped once by England, he went into management following his playing days and was employed by clubs as diverse as Witney Town in Oxfordshire and Mazda Hiroshima in Japan.

## Great Matches

**EUROPEAN CUP FINAL** — **Wembley, 29 May 1968**

**Manchester United 4** — **Benfica 1** — **Attendance: 100,000**

Charlton 2 — Graca
Best
Kidd

**After extra-time**

On a stiflingly hot Wembley evening, Matt Busby's blue-shirted Red Devils never scaled the heights of dazzling virtuosity which saw them destroy Benfica in Lisbon two years earlier, but they did what was necessary – they won the European Cup. United made a fast start and although Eusebio administered a fright when he shivered Stepney's bar with a sudden screamer from 25 yards, they shaded the first half, regretting only that Sadler had spurned their two most inviting openings. He made amends, though, after 53 minutes when his cross from the left reached Bobby Charlton, who rose at the near post to dispatch a copybook glancing header just inside the far upright. Now United threatened to take control and an equalizer seemed beyond Benfica until the 79th minute when Torres

*United's and Bobby Charlton's first goal, a header into the corner. Charlton's second was United's fourth, in extra-time, to seal a famous victory.*

finally managed to win an aerial battle with the mighty Foulkes, the ball running free for Graca to net emphatically from a narrow angle. Soon Eusebio might have carried the day but, through on Stepney, he elected for power rather than precision and the keeper saved heroically to take the contest into extra-time. Now, when it mattered most, the Red Devils hit their stride with a vengeance. Three minutes in, Stepney launched a massive clearance, Kidd nodded on and Best nipped past Jacinto, rounded keeper Henrique and rolled the ball home. A minute later man-of-the-match Aston won a corner which was taken by Charlton and, though Kidd's first header was saved, he celebrated his 19th birthday by scoring from the rebound. Finally, Charlton accepted a return pass from Kidd on the right and scored United's fourth with a first-time looping shot. The second half of extra-time passed on a wave of euphoria as Matt Busby's version of the holy grail was secured.

**Manchester United:** Stepney, Brennan, Dunne, Crerand, Foulkes, Stiles, Best, Kidd, Charlton, Sadler, Aston
**Benfica:** Henrique, Adolfo, Humberto, Jacinto, Cruz, Graca, Coluna, Augusto, Eusebio, Torres, Simoes
**Referee:** C. Lo Bello

*George Best's extra-time goal in that saw United triumph for the first time in Europe, beating Benfica 4-1 on a steamy night at Wembley.*

**50 Greatest Players**

**PAT CRERAND Half back**

**Born:** Glasgow, 19 February 1939

**Joined Manchester United:** 1963 **From:** Celtic

**Debut:** 23 February 1963 v Blackpool, League

**Appearances:** 397 **Goals:** 15

**Left Manchester United:** 1971 (retired)

**Honours won with United:** European Cup winner 1968; Division One championship 1965, 1967; FA Cup winner 1963

'When Crerand plays well, United play well' was an oft-used phrase in the 1960s that perfectly illustrated the considerable part the former Celtic half back played in the re-emergence of United as one of the game's top clubs. He arrived at Old Trafford from Celtic early in 1963 and was looked on as the final piece of the post-Munich jigsaw, becoming a major influential figure over the next few years. The gritty, highly-skilled Glaswegian supplied another dimension to the team that was to destined to become the Busby/Murphy collaboration's third great side. Crerand, a pass-master who could drop the ball at a team-mate's feet from 40 yards and more, won an abundance of silverware in his time at United.

they were unable to attend the post-match banquet; Sadler, too, laboured nobly, passed sensibly and put the trauma of several missed opportunities behind him to set up Charlton's ice-breaker; Kidd led the line with verve and maturity on his 19th birthday and chipped in with the third goal; Best terrified and tormented the Benfica rearguard into resorting to violence, but even that could not prevent his sensational strike to restore the Reds' lead with his 32nd goal of the season; and the hitherto untrumpeted Aston, who shredded the Portuguese rearguard with sheer pace, seizing the supreme moment to give the performance of a lifetime and emerge as man of the match.

For everybody connected with the club, but especially for Munich survivors Busby, Charlton and Foulkes, winning the European Cup represented the culmination of a uniquely emotional sporting journey. It had encompassed a confrontation with blind authority, the death of dear comrades and a tortuous but ultimately uplifting climb to the very pinnacle of achievement. Now the question was: could United stay there?

# Chapter Nine: 1968-77
## A Time of Turbulence

Though Old Trafford was still bathed in the luxuriant glow of European Cup glory, Manchester United stood at one of the key crossroads in the club's history at the outset of 1968-69. In retrospect, it is easy to see that they took one wrong turning after another, but nothing seemed clear cut at the time. The brutal truth was that the Red Devils had lifted the continental crown with a brilliant but ageing team of whom, arguably, only Stepney, Dunne, Sadler, Kidd, Aston and European Footballer of the Year-elect Best were not beyond their peak. They also had a veteran manager who, though he would always remain an inspirational leader, would hardly have been human had he not been ready for a rest after all he had endured.

Certainly, as Bobby Charlton brandished aloft that yearned-for trophy at Wembley in May 1968, any suggestion that Old Trafford would be playing host to Second Division opponents within six years would have been greeted with incredulous contempt. But from this distance it is possible to contemplate an agonizing catalogue of might-have-beens. If only early steps had been taken to bring about an appropriate managerial succession; if only it had been recognized that a club of such imperious stature required an experienced and proven operator at its helm; if only the need for root-and-branch rebuilding had been addressed before it became urgent; if only George Best, appalled by what he perceived as lack of ambition all around him, had been arrested in his lurch towards self-destruction (not that he was blameless himself), then the subsequent grisly decline might have been avoided.

That said, there remained plenty of challenges to entice the newly-knighted Sir Matt as he commenced his 23rd campaign at the club in August 1968: the defence of the hard-won European pot, a renewed assault on the league title and a first tilt at the World Club Championship, a two-legged encounter with Estudiantes de la Plata of Argentina. United were reinforced for this triple crusade by the £117,000 acquisition of Burnley winger, Willie Morgan. Like Best, he was part of the modern pop culture, being the first footballer in the world with his own fan club, and he had bags of talent, too, the type of player who would excite the demanding Old Trafford faithful.

Though he took time to settle, the newcomer was in the line-up for the late-September clash with Estudiantes in Buenos Aires. Clash? It was more like a war.

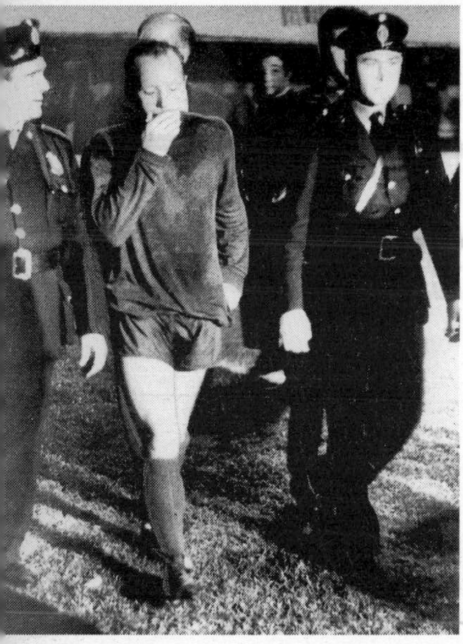

*Nobby Stiles is sent off and escorted from the pitch after having been dubbed 'El Bandito' by the Argentinians in a nasty clash with Estudiantes in the World Club Championships.*

Sporting relations with the Argentines having been fouled by Alf Ramsey's reference to their team as 'animals' during the 1966 World Cup, the locals seized on England's Nobby Stiles as a target for revenge. Accordingly he was vilified in the official programme as 'brutal' and introduced to fans as 'El Bandito'. During the game he was kicked, punched and head-butted. Finally, after merely waving an arm at a linesman in protest at an offside call, he was dismissed and banned from the second leg.

The match itself was a travesty, with the Reds subjected to outrageous violence and they were content to escape with a 1-0 defeat and all their limbs intact. Afterwards, Matt Busby, never a whinger in normal circumstances, declared angrily: 'Holding the ball out there put you in danger of your life.' There was slightly more order in the Old Trafford return, but still it was an unattractively attritional contest in which the visitors scored an early goal – through Juan Ramon Veron, whose son became a Red Devil in 2001 – and the hosts a late one courtesy of Morgan, so the world title, irreparably tarnished, went to Estudiantes.

United's domestic form was fitful and their eventual league position of 11th reflected their mediocrity. They were never far from the headlines, though, partly because of steady progress in the European Cup to set up a plum semi-final with AC Milan, but more specifically due to Busby's January announcement that he would relinquish control of team affairs at season's end. He was not departing, however, but moving 'upstairs' as general manager.

## Matt Busby Takes a Back Seat

Naturally there was intense speculation about the succession, with such names as Don Revie and Jock Stein being advanced, but the rumour mill was laid to rest in April with the revelation that 31-year-old Wilf McGuinness would step up from looking after the reserves to become chief coach. He would be in charge of first-team selection, coaching, training and tactics, while Sir Matt would remain responsible for all other matters affecting the club and players. The effervescent Mancunian was no greenhorn, having helped Alf Ramsey prepare his victorious World Cup side and guided England youth, but he was a contemporary of many of his top players, which posed questions of authority. In the short term he took a back seat as Busby led United on one last European assault, which was to end in controversy. A 2-0 defeat in the San Siro was fair enough, but after Charlton had dispatched a narrow-angled scorcher in the 70th minute of the second leg, Law touched a Crerand chip over the Milan line, but the ball was hacked away and no goal was given. Busby was gracious in defeat, though some Stretford Enders were not, showering Italian keeper Cudicini with missiles.

That summer the spotlight shifted inexorably to McGuinness, who was handed vast responsibility but without a fraction of the control upon which Busby himself had insisted when he had been appointed. Despite his confident

## Great Managers – 1945-69, 1970-71

### SIR MATT BUSBY

Matt Busby took charge of United early in 1945 and was immediately faced with similar problems to those that Ernest Mangnall had encountered almost 40 years before. The club, potentially one of the biggest in the country, had grossly underachieved since before World War I, the Luftwaffe had massively damaged Old Trafford, and finance was in short supply. Undeterred, he and his newly-recruited assistant, Jimmy Murphy, set to transforming the club into one of the most successful in English football and a sporting institution known around the globe. Busby's first great side claimed the FA Cup in 1948 and the league title four years later. Then, it was the turn of the legendary 'Busby Babes' to add two league championships in the mid-1950s and go within an ace of becoming the first team in the 20th century to win the 'Double'. It was also around this time that United, on Busby's insistence, became the first English club to enter the European Cup. The tragic Munich air disaster in 1958 robbed United of their young, and potentially, great side and almost their inspirational manager. Mercifully, Busby recovered from his serious injuries and proceeded to rebuild yet again. It took a little time but United were eventually returned to the summit with two league titles, the FA Cup and, to universal acclaim, the European Cup in 1968. Knighted for his services to the game he later joined United's board of directors and was also club president until the time of his death in 1994.

air, Wilf gave the unavoidable impression of a rookie on probation, especially with Sir Matt lurking in the background, and the initial report was not encouraging. After taking only one point from the first three games, he dropped Charlton and Law for the visit to Everton, a bold move and a risky one. United lost 3-0 and the illustrious duo were restored, but there was an ominously unstable look to the team which was addressed by the £80,000 purchase of Scottish centre half Ian Ure from Arsenal.

Certainly a new stopper was a priority, with the redoubtable Foulkes – who had thought he had retired to concentrate on coaching duties only to be recalled with a gammy knee at the age of 37 when youthful successor Steve James had experienced a crisis of confidence – clearly unable to continue. Now United embarked on a spell of eight league games unbeaten, but behind the scenes the atmosphere was far from tranquil, with not all the players fully supportive of the new regime. Later McGuinness would assert that he had not wanted Ure, who was not a long-term success, but had been overruled by Busby, and that he had been denied his own transfer preferences.

The chief coach was hampered, too, by injuries which sidelined Stiles and Law for most of the season, so in the circumstances he did well to steer United to an eighth-place league finish and to the semi-finals of both domestic cups. However, defeats in those games against high-profile rivals, Manchester City in the League Cup over two legs and Leeds after three meetings in the FA Cup, dealt telling blows to club morale, which tumbled further through the deteriorating behaviour of Best. The Irishman was suspended for knocking the ball out of a referee's hands, then bounced back to underline his overriding value to the team by notching a double hat-trick in that term's 8-2 FA Cup drubbing of Northampton Town. Best's off-the-field irresponsibility was highlighted by continued media coverage of his sexual exploits and McGuinness himself located his errant star in a girl's bedroom on the afternoon of the first Leeds replay. In addition, George was becoming increasingly dependent on alcohol as his life spiralled out of control, so it is remarkable that he played so brilliantly, so often.

In June 1970 McGuinness was upgraded to team manager, but his problems multiplied. There were no major signings, most of his youngsters were below-par, and the stalwarts were getting long in the tooth. League form was dreadful but progress to the League Cup semi-finals in December might have offered a temporary lifeline had United not bowed out to Third Division Aston Villa. All that remained was a 4-4 Boxing Day draw with Derby County before the axe fell on poor Wilf. Initially he accepted his old job back but soon pride dictated that he left the club to which he had devoted his working life and which he loved to the point of distraction. At first his health suffered, but happily he made a full recovery to manage elsewhere before becoming a physiotherapist, then tasting success as an after-dinner speaker.

Meanwhile, Sir Matt, whose recommendation of McGuinness as his successor had been based partly on belief in Wilf's abilities and partly on a desire for a member of the club 'family' to take over, reluctantly became caretaker boss. He was accorded the whole-hearted backing from his entire staff which McGuinness had been denied and results improved so radically that the Reds climbed to eighth place by season's end. Even Busby, though, could not induce the rehabilitation of Best, whose own mounting frustration with the United scene was reflected by more wild living, silly tantrums, missed training sessions and even being hours late for a disciplinary hearing in London. Incredibly, such was his natural physical resilience, that he scored twice on Sir Matt's farewell game as manager, a 4-3 victory over Manchester City at Maine Road.

### Difficult Times Ahead for O'Farrell

Now, sooner than expected, United needed another new boss. This time they looked as far as Leicester and Filbert Street where Frank O'Farrell had built a reputation for sound judgement and integrity, and had just led Leicester

**50 Greatest Players**

**NOBBY STILES Half back**

**Born:** Manchester, 18 May 1942

**Joined Manchester United:** 1957 **From:** Juniors

**Debut:** 1 October 1960 v Bolton Wanderers, League

**Appearances:** 395 **Goals:** 19

**Left Manchester United:** 1971 **For:** Middlesbrough

**Honours won with United:** European Cup winner 1968; Division One championship 1965, 1967

If fame hadn't embraced Nobby Stiles before the 1966 World Cup final, it certainly had after England had beaten West Germany 4-2 after extra-time to claim the Jules Rimet trophy. Anyone who watched English football's finest triumph, and the celebrations which followed, will never forget the heart-warming sight as Nobby cavorted around Wembley Stadium displaying the famous trophy and a huge toothless grin. The image is one of the most enduring of the entire tournament. Stiles, who hailed from Collyhurst, north Manchester, remained a firm favourite with the Old Trafford crowd throughout his time at the club. They appreciated his fierce determination, tireless effort and dedication to the Red cause. He was one-third of the brilliant half back line, along with Bill Foulkes and Pat Crerand, that served United so well during the mid- to late-1960s.

*Frank O'Farrell reigned over a brief resurgence in United's form but, plagued by Best's out-of-control lifestyle, he finally made way for Tommy Docherty.*

City to the Second Division title. Once a polished wing half with West Ham and Preston, and a graduate of the famous Upton Park academy of soccer thinkers, the quiet Irishman was promised a free hand. Busby relinquished the position of general manager and joined the board.

United started the season under a cloud, being ordered to play their first two home games at least 25 miles from Old Trafford as punishment for a knife-throwing incident during the previous term. It did not affect the team, though, as Arsenal were beaten at Anfield and West Brom at Stoke. Indeed, after emphasizing the need to tighten the defence, which he addressed by giving extended opportunities to full back Tommy O'Neil and centre half Steve James, O'Farrell presided over a spectacular surge to the summit of the First Division based on sparkling attack. Successfully deploying erstwhile striker Alan Gowling and winger Willie Morgan in midfield, he played to the renowned strengths of Law, Charlton and particularly Best as United entertained royally throughout the autumn and moved five points clear in the championship race.

Though Best was drinking ever more heavily, it was impossible to tell from his performances and some of his goals, notably an enchanting sprint through the massed rearguard of Sheffield United which he capped by a pinpoint cross-shot at full stretch, were unperishable gems. There was delight, too, from another son of Belfast, 17-year-old Sammy McIlroy, who scored on his debut in a 3-3 draw with Manchester City. All the while, though, there were critics who maintained that O'Farrell's bubble would burst, and so it proved. On New Year's Day United suffered the first of seven successive defeats, Best's personal predicament intensifying so that he could no longer compensate for overall deficiencies and eventually the Reds managed only a comparatively abject eighth-place league finish.

As matters worsened O'Farrell had conducted two significant transfers, acquiring the polished Scottish international defender Martin Buchan from Aberdeen for £125,000 and recruiting goal-scoring winger Ian Storey-Moore for a further £200,000 from Nottingham Forest. Both made an instant impact, but experienced contrasting fortunes at Old Trafford. Buchan went on to become skipper and exert massive influence for over a decade, poor Storey-Moore was to be forced by injury into premature retirement.

That May the Best crisis deepened when he went missing instead of reporting for duty with Northern Ireland and he fetched up in Marbella, Spain, where he announced his retirement on the eve of his 26th birthday. Clearly George was in a state of pitiable confusion and soon he changed his mind, but 1972-73 would bring only further grief.

The Reds got off to an abysmal start and the purchase of two strikers – £200,000 Ted MacDougall from Bournemouth and Manchester City's Welsh international warhorse Wyn Davies, who cost £25,000 – made scant difference. With the Best scenario plaguing O'Farrell, and with Charlton and others outraged at the latitude extended to their temperamental team-mate, there was little hope of recovery and in December, following a 5-0 humbling at Crystal Palace which left United one place off the bottom, the boss was sacked. With Busby and chairman Louis Edwards said to have dealt with Best behind their manager's back, it was easy to feel sympathy for O'Farrell, but he was always

## 50 Greatest Players

**TONY DUNNE Defender**

**Born:** Dublin, 24 July 1941

**Joined Manchester United:** 1960 **From:** Shelbourne

**Debut:** 15 October 1960 v Burnley, League

**Appearances:** 534 (1) **Goals:** 2

**Left Manchester United:** 1973 **For:** Bolton Wanderers

**Honours won with United:** European Cup winner 1968; Division One championship 1965, 1967; FA Cup winner 1963

The words 'unsung hero' could have been coined for Tony Dunne, a virtual fixture in United's defence during the trophy-winning years of the 1960s. Compact, efficient and hugely reliable, he rarely got the plaudits that were lavished on his better-known team-mates, but that wouldn't have worried the quietly-spoken Dubliner. He joined United from League of Ireland club Shelbourne and it proved to be one of Matt Busby's shrewdest moves, for Dunne went on to become one of the greatest full backs to serve the club. Noel Cantwell and Shay Brennan were in possession of the full back berths when he arrived at the club, so it took him a while to become established. Once ensconced in the side he was all but immovable and collected a pocketful of medals, while at the same time serving his country in wonderful style.

*Denis Law, known as 'the King' by the United fans, was the most renowned striker of his generation and won honours galore at Old Trafford.*

a remote figure whose reign was summed up by Law, who declared that he had arrived a stranger and left a stranger.

That criticism could never be levelled at his successor, Tommy Docherty, who walked out of the Scotland job to realize his lifetime's ambition of taking United's reins. The controversial, wise-cracking Doc was faced with an uphill fight if demotion was to be avoided and he addressed the task in whirlwind style.

Within days of arrival be began signing players, most of them fellow Scots. Full back Alex Forsyth cost £100,000 from Partick Thistle; elegant play-maker George Graham was priced at £120,000 from Arsenal; mammoth stopper Jim Holton, a virtual unknown, swelled the coffers of Shrewsbury Town by £80,000; tiny Celtic striker Lou Macari spurned Bill Shankly's Liverpool to join Old Trafford in a £200,000 deal; Dubliner Mick Martin, a midfielder from Bohemians, made a further £25,000 dent in the bank balance.

## The Flamboyant Doc Takes Charge

The blast of bracing Caledonian air signalled new hope for the gloomy legions who continued to pour through the turnstiles. It was exemplified in the home clash with West Ham, in which Holton's rugged commitment earned instant folk-hero status and Macari salvaged a late point with a thrillingly opportunistic finish. Over the next three months as the Red Devils scrapped for their lives, the football was never pretty but gradually confidence bloomed where there had been only despair and safety was procured by the ultimately comfortable margin of seven points.

Come the end of the campaign, however, there was more than a little blood on the Old Trafford carpet, which had been stained already by the £170,000 departure of MacDougall to West Ham in March. None of it belonged to Bobby Charlton, who announced his retirement at 35, having rounded off his majestic United career by playing a sterling role in avoiding relegation. George Best was temporarily out of the equation, his future on hold while he strove to sort out his turbulent life. However, there were unlooked-for exits for Denis Law, Tony Dunne and David Sadler, European Cup winners all.

The departure of Law, revered by the fans like few other Red Devils before or since, was handled with a particular lack of sensitivity, as he learned of his free transfer from the TV in an Aberdeen bar. As for Dunne and Sadler, both still had plenty to offer – which they demonstrated amply at Bolton and Preston respectively – but the new boss wanted his own men around him as he pressed on with his Old Trafford revolution.

Distressingly, though, the longed-for renaissance was not yet imminent. A grim first-day display at Highbury in August 1973 proved the harbinger of a doleful autumn and winter in which the football was awful and the results even worse. With the side deep in travail, George Best was welcomed back for his last chance in October, and a few vintage touches from the now-portly Irishman lit up a rare win, against Birmingham City. It spoke volumes,

### 50 Greatest Players

**DENIS LAW Forward**

**Born:** Aberdeen, 24 February 1940

**Joined Manchester United:** 1962 **From:** Torino

**Debut:** 18 August 1962 v West Bromwich Albion, League

**Appearances:** 398 (6) **Goals:** 237

**Left Manchester United:** 1973 **For:** Manchester City

**Honours won with United:** Division One championship 1965, 1967; FA Cup winner 1963; European Footballer of the Year 1964

There have been several pretenders to his throne in the years since his reign came to an end but he was the original and arguably the only true 'King' of the Stretford End. Law was an instant hit with the Old Trafford faithful following his record-breaking £115,000 transfer from Torino in the summer of 1962 where he had endured a traumatic 12 months having joined the Piedmont club from Manchester City. He scored on his debut against West Bromwich Albion at Old Trafford and never looked back as he embarked on a new phase of his career that was to see him become one of the finest strikers ever to pull on the famous red of United and Scotland's dark blue. He helped United to win the FA Cup in his first season, played a major role in capturing two league titles, but sadly was injured and unavailable for selection when United won the European Cup in 1968. Law would be many fans' choice in a poll to find the most popular United star of all-time and would certainly figure in the top five of any list of the club's greatest players.

though, that when Alex Stepney netted from the penalty spot he became the club's joint leading scorer. Best, by now a grotesque parody of his former self, departed the team forever at the turn of the year and soon the hitherto unthinkable prospect of relegation took on a terrible reality. In the spring, with the situation virtually hopeless, Docherty decided that if he was taking United down then he would do so in style, and swapped his negative tactics for an adventurous approach which offered the fleeting possibility of escape.

Boosted by the £60,000 arrival of striker cum midfielder Jim McCalliog from Wolves, United took ten points from a possible 12, but when they played host to Manchester City in their penultimate fixture, a miracle was needed: the Reds had to win, but Norwich had to beat Birmingham, too, and neither happened. Though they would have been doomed anyway, it was poignantly symbolic that the goal which highlighted their fate was backheeled by the recently-ousted Denis Law, whose marked glumness after ball hit net underlined his own sadness at United's plight. As if the day was not dismal enough already, a pitch invasion by Stretford Enders caused abandonment with a

## 50 Greatest Players

**BOBBY CHARLTON Forward/Midfielder**

**Born:** Ashington, 11 October 1937

**Joined Manchester United:** 1953 **From:** Juniors

**Debut:** 6 October 1956 v Charlton Athletic, League

**Appearances:** 759 **Goals:** 249

**Left Manchester United:** 1973 **For:** Preston North End

**Honours won with United:** European Cup winner 1968; Division One championship 1957, 1965, 1967; FA Cup winner 1963; European Footballer of the Year 1966; Footballer of the Year 1966

Having survived the horror of the Munich air disaster Bobby Charlton proceeded to become one of football's greatest exponents. As one of the famed 'Busby Babes' he was tipped for a place at the top of the tree, but few could have envisaged just how big a star the Ashington-born player would become. Charlton possessed most of the vital assets needed in the make-up of a top player and they were blended into one of the finest attacking midfielders the British Isles has ever produced. Respected around the globe for his gentlemanly approach to the game, he collected virtually every major honour available. He joined the board of directors at Old Trafford when his playing days were over, but he will probably be best remembered for the thunderous long-range shooting that had goalkeepers quaking in their boots the world over.

few minutes remaining, and subsequent erection of spiked steel barriers around the ground. It seems they had been attempting, in their wanton idiocy, to secure a replay; all they achieved was to heap shame on their club.

## That Sinking Feeling

At that point it was difficult to draw many positives. For instance, Brian Kidd, having lost impetus when he should have been approaching his prime, would soon leave for Arsenal; Macari had made little impact in his front-running role, and several youngsters were not making expected progress. Against that, Stepney, Buchan, Holton and Morgan had performed nobly and a few rookies had done well, notably McIlroy and midfielders Brian Greenhoff and Gerry Daly. With prophets of calamity predicting that Docherty's team would struggle to cope with the raw realities of Second Division life, a ray of hope appeared in the May procurement of marksman Stuart Pearson from Hull City in exchange for £170,000 plus fellow striker Peter Fletcher.

That optimism mushroomed on a sunny afternoon at Brisbane Road when United opened their 1974-75 account with a brisk 2-0 victory over Leyton Orient. Three more straight wins lifted them to the top of the table and they stayed there for the remainder of a barnstorming campaign which is remembered fondly by the generation of fans who roared Docherty's swashbuckling young team to promotion at their first attempt. True, meeting unfamiliar opponents such as York City and Bristol Rovers on equal terms took a bit of getting used to, but so exciting was the fare served up by the new United that no one could legitimately complain. Glittering high spots included home victories over fellow high-riders Aston Villa and Sunderland, while moronic vandalism by travelling Reds supporters at Norwich, when the team tasted defeat for the first time in September, was the gruesome lowlight.

One other miserable aspect was the broken leg suffered by Holton in the 4-4 draw at Sheffield Wednesday in December, the first of a cruel succession of mishaps which prevented Big Jim from playing another senior game for the club. Happily he qualified for a medal, as did goalkeeper Stepney, full backs Forsyth and Stewart Houston, captain and central defender Buchan, midfielders Morgan, Greenhoff, Daly, McCalliog and Macari (converted from a striker to splendid effect), and front-runners Pearson and McIlroy. Also there were notable contributions from stand-in stoppers Steve James and Arnold Sidebottom, and winger Steve Coppell, a callow Merseysider who excelled when introduced in place of Morgan during the run-in.

The presentation of the Second Division championship trophy, which coincided with the 4-0 beating of Blackpool on the last day, provoked mass

## 50 Greatest Players

**GEORGE BEST Forward**

**Born:** Belfast, 22 May 1946

**Joined Manchester United:** 1961 **From:** Juniors

**Debut:** 14 September 1963 v West Bromwich Albion, League

**Appearances:** 470 **Goals:** 179

**Left Manchester United:** 1974 **For:** Dunstable Town

**Honours won with United:** European Cup winner 1968; Division One championship 1965, 1967; European Footballer of the Year 1968; Footballer of the Year 1968

Few would argue that the brilliant Ulsterman was the greatest player the British Isles has ever produced, and quite possibly the most complete footballer of all time. Sumptuously gifted in every facet of the game, he could single-handedly turn a match in his team's favour, and did so on numerous occasions during a ten-year career that had the Old Trafford crowd mesmerized. He was worth the entrance fee on his own and it was no surprise that the dark-haired, handsome lad from Belfast quickly became a favourite with female supporters and football's first 'pop-star' personality. Sadly, it was his media-hyped celebrity status and excesses away from the game that contributed to his premature departure from Old Trafford. He later appeared for several other clubs, but George Best will always be remembered with glowing affection by those lucky enough to have witnessed his pomp as one of United's magnificent 'Charlton-Best-Law' triumvirate.

ecstasy spiced with an invigorating sense of resurrection at nightmare's end. Now there was unbridled optimism about the future, and it was justified gloriously by Docherty's fearless young blades.

### Back in the Top Flight

Strengthened only by the addition of the experienced Tommy Jackson, a fetch-and-carry midfielder freed by Nottingham Forest, and with the versatile Greenhoff now partnering Buchan in central defence, United exploded on to the First Division scene with six wins in their opening eight games, their dynamic verve and buccaneering spirit threatening to carry all before them. Reinforced in November by the £80,000 purchase of gifted left winger Gordon Hill from Millwall, and with youngsters such as full back Jimmy Nicholl and perennial substitute and utility man David McCreery stepping in at need, United topped the table in January. Come April they were still in the hunt for the League and FA Cup 'Double' but inexperience told as they slipped behind Liverpool and Queens Park Rangers to finish third.

Rather less expected was their Wembley FA Cup defeat by Second Division Southampton. After scoring twice to overcome a top-notch Derby County in the semi-final, the irrepressible 'Merlin' Hill cracked good-naturedly: 'Who are Southampton?' He soon found out as the Saints brought off a stupendous upset, the recently transferred McCalliog adding irony to injury by setting up the only goal of the contest for Bobby Stokes. Never mind that McIlroy hit the bar for United, the Reds never got going and the triumph of Lawrie McMenemy's zestful combination was thoroughly merited. Docherty declared: 'We'll be back to win next year!'

He was right, although not before a rather anti-climactic league season in which United dazzled periodically, only to let themselves down with unexpected lapses. A perfect example was the home encounter with Tottenham in September when they raced into a two-goal lead through Coppell and Pearson, captivating Old Trafford's biggest crowd of the season with the sweetest football imaginable, only to fall away and lose 3-2.

Perhaps feeling that guile and nous was needed to temper a surfeit of dashing impetuosity, Docherty enticed Stoke to sell Jimmy Greenhoff, Brian's older brother, for £120,000 in November. One of the most accomplished Englishmen never to win a full cap, he slotted in alongside Pearson, with McIlroy moving into midfield and Daly forfeiting his place. The quicksilver 'Pancho' and the deliciously subtle newcomer gelled immediately, both majoring on deft control and first-touch lay-offs. They interchanged positions to mesmerizing effect, confronting opponents with an ever-changing set of problems.

Though the title was already out of reach when Greenhoff arrived, he was a key factor in the FA Cup run, his contributions including a brace in the 'revenge' victory over Southampton in a fifth-round replay and a volleyed opener in the 2-1 semi-final triumph over Leeds, his first club. Still to come was the even more devastating, albeit involuntary, strike which was to decide the destination of the trophy.

Liverpool provided daunting Wembley opponents, having already won the championship and booked their place in the European Cup final, in which they would overcome Borussia Möenchengladbach. Kopites were confident that the Anfield Reds were on the verge of a then-unique treble, and their faith was not shaken by a goalless first half which their side had shaded. But with Buchan dominating Kevin Keegan, United began the second period at a gallop and soon Pearson fired them in front. When Jimmy Case equalized within two minutes, it seemed likely that the favourites would prevail but, another

*Stuart Pearson scores United's first goal in the 1977 FA Cup final against Liverpool. They went on to win 2-1 and blow the Anfield team's chance of winning a record-breaking treble.*

180 seconds into the action, fate took a hand. Greenhoff battled for possession with Tommy Smith and the ball ricocheted to the onrushing Macari, whose wild shot was flashing hopelessly wide. But then the ball cannoned off the chest of Greenhoff, looping unstoppably over Ray Clemence and beyond defender Phil Neal into the net. Whether it was a product of dedicated practice on the training ground or not, it was enough to win the cup!

The treble-busting line-up was Stepney in goal, Nicholl and Albiston at full back, Buchan and Brian Greenhoff in central defence, a midfield quartet of Coppell, Macari, McIlroy and Hill, with Pearson and Jimmy Greenhoff up front and McCreery arriving as a substitute for Hill. Every Red Devil played his heart out, but none more so than 19-year-old Albiston who, called in to replace injured Stewart Houston, quelled the threat of Liverpool flyer Steve Heighway. Albiston's generosity in offering his medal to Houston was hugely appreciated by his fellow Scot, though it was declined with thanks.

Afterwards United fans speculated joyously about what their team could go on to achieve under Docherty, but a few weeks later he was sacked following the revelations of his romance with Mary Brown, the wife of club physiotherapist Laurie. Quite what bearing such personal business had on his professional life in the 'enlightened' late 1970s was never satisfactorily explained, but Manchester United were looking for a new manager.

# Chapter Ten: 1977-86
# Chalk and Cheese

In the summer of 1977, Manchester United were about to undergo a drastic transformation. The reason? Tommy Docherty had just been ejected from the management seat and Dave Sexton was about to move in. The brands of football espoused by the two men contrasted as vividly as their personalities. The Doc's preferred game was heart-on-sleeve, helter-skelter, adventurous, while the newcomer favoured a far more cautious, measured and methodical approach. Ironically, the career paths of the two men had much in common, both having guided the fortunes of Chelsea and Queens Park Rangers before responding to the summons from Old Trafford. When Sexton's call came, just over a week after the dismissal of Docherty, he was looking back on a successful three-year stint at Loftus Road, the high-spot of which was finishing as runners-up to Liverpool in 1975-76. Now he passed up a chance to coach Arsenal to take up the United challenge.

Dave's new team began their league campaign with a flourish, a Macari hat-trick providing the centrepiece of a 4-1 victory at Birmingham. However, a miserable seven-day spell in September turned the season prematurely sour. Defeats at Maine Road and at home to Chelsea sandwiched a 1-1 draw in St Étienne in the European Cup-Winners' Cup, not a bad result on the face of it, but the night was scarred by serious crowd disturbances. In consequence United were banned summarily from the competition, a decision promptly commuted to a £7,500 fine and the order to play the home leg at least 200 kilometres away from Manchester.

Reds chairman Louis Edwards, who had not shrunk from condemning violence by United fans in the past, now stood up for the travelling supporters, declaring that a combination of

*Alex Stepney was first-choice keeper at Old Trafford for 12 years during a period that saw United win the European Cup and be relegated to Division Two.*

*Battling forward Joe Jordan was brought in from rivals Leeds by Dave Sexton to beef up the attack.*

over-enthusiastic policing and lack of segregation were to blame for the incident. Happily the players were unfazed, overcoming the Frenchmen 2-0 in the return at Home Park, Plymouth, but their resilience did not extend to league form, which nosedived as autumn wore on. The mood was not lightened by a 4-0 away hammering by FC Porto, and although a Steve Coppell-inspired fightback produced an enthralling second leg – United won 5-2 at Old Trafford, bowing out 6-5 on aggregate – criticism of the new regime began to mount as the team became ensconced in the wrong half of the First Division table.

Sexton's first radical step was to axe veteran goalkeeper Alex Stepney in favour of Irishman Paddy Roche, who had demonstrated immense natural talent but an apparent lack of self-belief when given earlier opportunities by Docherty. This time Roche was granted a lengthy settled sequence, from November to March, but never emerged as a dominant figure.

## Sexton Makes Changes

As pressure increased, the manager launched an ambitious New Year excursion into the transfer market, enraging Leeds fans by signing warrior centre forward Joe Jordan for £350,000 and his pal Gordon McQueen, a towering centre half, for £500,000, then a staggering fee for a defender. Most Old Trafford regulars welcomed McQueen, believing that the rearguard needed beefing up, but there were reservations about Jordan. Connoisseurs of the slick-passing style espoused by Pearson and Greenhoff could scarcely credit that the partnership was being broken up to accommodate what they saw as a mere battering ram and a player much vilified west of the Pennines during his Elland Road days. Jordan, admittedly a fearsomely physical operator, was far more subtle and intelligent than his detractors allowed, and he worked hard to mature into an outstanding all-round performer.

In the short term, though, the Red Devils were an inconsistent side relying ever-more on organization rather than flair, as reflected by the deep role handed to one winger, Steve Coppell and the unpopular sale of another, Gordon Hill,

*Gordon McQueen followed Joe Jordan from Leeds. His towering presence was felt in defence for seven years.*

to Derby for £250,000 in April. The policy shift was emphasized by the identity of the buying manager, one Tommy Docherty. Hill had been a lavish entertainer with an impressive strike-rate for a flankman – 51 goals in 134 appearances – though sometimes he infuriated team-mates by his relaxed approach to defensive duties; enough, in fact, to induce exasperated skipper Martin Buchan to clip his ear during one game!

A mid-table finish left fans disenchanted, feeling that more should have been achieved with the exciting resources assembled by Docherty, but they faced a second season of league mediocrity in 1978-79 and attendances began to fall. Hampered by long-term injury to Pearson but boosted by the emergence of teenage marksman Andy Ritchie, who contributed ten goals in 16 starts, Dave Sexton made two significant changes. After giving Roche another extended opportunity in goal, he reacted to a 5-1 humbling by Birmingham by agreeing a £440,000 fee for Coventry's Jim Blyth, only for the Scot to fail his medical. The upshot was an opening for Gary Bailey, a tall, blond, confident youngster, who impressed on his debut, keeping a clean sheet in a win over Ipswich Town, and he made the position his own.

The other newcomer was little Mickey Thomas, a selflessly industrious left-sided midfielder, signed from Wrexham for £300,000 to fill the slot vacated by the more flamboyant but less methodical Hill. For all his apparent ordinariness, the Welshman played an integral part in the high-spot of United's season. After featuring solidly throughout an FA Cup run which offered a welcome distraction from league toil, Thomas put in the most influential display of his United career, slaving tirelessly through a dramatic semi-final with Liverpool which ended 2-2 at Maine Road. The Anfielders, who were on their way to another title, had gone ahead through Kenny Dalglish, then strikes from Jordan and Brian Greenhoff had given the Red Devils the initiative, only for a rare Alan Hansen goal to secure a replay at Goodison Park.

Now it seemed likely that Sexton's underdogs had blown their chance, a theory propounded relentlessly, if not altogether wisely, by the Liverpool

**50 Greatest Players**

**ALEX STEPNEY Goalkeeper**

**Born:** Mitcham, 18 September 1942

**Joined Manchester United:** 1966 **From:** Chelsea

**Debut:** 17 September 1966 v Manchester City, League

**Appearances:** 539 **Goals:** 2

**Left Manchester United:** 1978 **For:** Dallas Tornado

**Honours won with United:** European Cup winner 1968; Division One championship 1967; FA Cup winner 1977

Matt Busby persuaded Alex Stepney to move north from Stamford Bridge barely four months after he'd made the somewhat shorter northerly journey from Millwall to Chelsea. A fee of £50,000, then a world record for a goalkeeper, changed hands on both occasions. Stepney was pitched in to make his debut in the Old Trafford Derby against Manchester City. It was the start of a long and distinguished career that was to see him encounter the highs and lows of life at one of the world's great clubs. He was a member of United sides that won the league title, FA Cup and European Cup and was also an ever present in season 1973-74 when United were relegated to Division Two. Remarkably, he was also the team's leading goalscorer for several months during that campaign after finding the net twice from the penalty spot.

play-maker Graeme Souness prior to the re-match. Thus, with their motivation level massaged beyond even the fever pitch which is normal for any meeting with their northwest rivals, United battled like men possessed and from a cunning Thomas cross Jimmy Greenhoff headed a late winner. It was a sweet triumph and the fans celebrated as if the FA Cup was in the bag. Alas, it wasn't.

## FA Cup Disappointment

In a final illuminated by Liam Brady, Arsenal swept into a two-goal lead by the interval and, with only four minutes remaining, they looked certain to retain it. But then a close-range poke from Gordon McQueen revived United's chances and, 120 seconds later, Sammy McIlroy danced through for a brilliant individual equalizer. Suddenly Sexton's side, having recovered from an apparently hopeless position, were the favourites to prevail in extra-time. But the additional period was not required as a cross from Graham Rix floated tantalizingly over the head of Bailey and into the path of Alan Sunderland, who supplied the conclusive strike with a minute remaining. As the onlooking Bobby Charlton put it glumly: 'It shouldn't happen to a dog.'

Now a tonic was needed urgently and it arrived in time for 1979-80 in the shape of 22-year-old Ray Wilkins, Chelsea's enormously gifted midfield general who was already an established England international. Though the deal was financed by the departures of Pearson, Brian Greenhoff and McCreery, it offered a compelling statement of United's ambition, and they headed the table by mid-September.

However, Liverpool remained the yardstick and their Boxing Day victory at Anfield left the Red Devils trailing in a two-horse dash for the title. A demoralizing 6-0 reverse at Ipswich in March appeared to signal capitulation, but United revived their cause with a stirring 2-1 home triumph over Bob Paisley's team. The winner that day was notched by a 33-year-old whose career had been written off by two specialists following serious pelvic injuries. Jimmy Greenhoff had not played a full senior game all season and was far from fully fit, but Sexton had gambled on his knowhow and he it was whose glancing header revived the Red Devils' championship dream. A further five successive wins meant that come the season's final afternoon, United were level on points with the Merseysiders, albeit well adrift on goal difference. In the end, no sums were necessary as Sexton's valiant side fell 2-0 at Leeds and Liverpool brushed aside Aston Villa 4-1.

It was a frustrating but not crushing end to a season in which the title had never quite seemed to be in reach, but which represented the club's best league finish since 1967. It had been a landmark term, too, thanks to the signing of United's first overseas player, defender cum midfielder Nikola Jovanovic of Red Star Belgrade. Though extremely talented, the £350,000 Yugoslavian star never settled in England, but it was a bold and imaginative gamble by Sexton, and one which foretold the radical change which would come over the transfer market in decades to come.

The 1979-80 campaign had a tragic overtone, too, with the death of chairman Louis Edwards, who suffered a heart attack a month after televised allegations, which he denied strenuously, of financial irregularities at the club. He was succeeded by his son, Martin, who signalled his readiness to spend heavily in

*Dave Sexton presided over a largely unsuccessful period for United but brought the likes of Joe Jordan and Gordon McQueen to Old Trafford.*

the quest for success with a reported offer of £1.5 million to lure Liam Brady from Arsenal. The Irishman chose to join Juventus, but United's grisly start to 1980-81 soon had the chairman reaching once more for his chequebook, paying Nottingham Forest £1.25 million for Garry Birtles. Supporters, growing ever more disillusioned with their side's functional style, were cheered by the recruitment of an England marksman, although many were upset by the corresponding sale of the promising Ritchie to Brighton for £500,000. At 19, he had begun 32 games and scored 13 goals, a record which, all too soon, would contrast vividly with that of the hapless Birtles.

Not that Garry was a dud, but it was galling to witness a star striker arriving in October, then failing to score a league goal for the remainder of the season and beyond. In mitigation, he enjoyed no luck and never gelled with Jordan, but that can have been scant consolation to Sexton as fans began calling for his head. A debilitating crop of injuries heightened his problems and even a run of seven successive victories to close the campaign, which lifted United to eighth place, was not enough to save his job. Dave Sexton had to leave United because four years had passed without a trophy and his team was perceived as dull by the fans, who never related to the cool, unassuming Londoner in the way they did to his brash Scottish predecessor.

## Ron Atkinson Brings Flair and Silverware

The early summer of 1981 was a time of tantalizing titillation for the Red Army as the board agonized over the appointment of a new boss. Brian Clough was among the fans' favourites, while Lawrie McMenemy, Bobby Robson and Ron Saunders were all considered, but some top-notch candidates regarded the Old Trafford challenge as a poisoned chalice. Not West Bromwich Albion's Ron Atkinson though; he didn't give a fig that he was not first choice, clearly relishing the chance to perform on the grand stage.

The bluff Merseysider was a born showman, but for all his perceived flashiness he was a sound operator who had demonstrated flair and stability in his managerial career to date with Cambridge United and the high-riding Baggies. After sweeping away most of Sexton's back-up staff and replacing them with his own, Atkinson acted swiftly, and expensively, to reshape the team. Joe Jordan,

*The flamboyant Ron Atkinson took over as manager – could his swashbuckling style bring the title back to Manchester?*

### 50 Greatest Players

**SAMMY McILROY Forward/Midfielder**

**Born:** Belfast, 2 August 1954

**Joined Manchester United:** 1969 **From:** Juniors

**Debut:** 6 November 1971 v Manchester City, League

**Appearances:** 391 (28) **Goals:** 71

**Left Manchester United:** 1982 **For:** Stoke City

**Honours won with United:** FA Cup winner 1977

Sammy McIlroy was just a few months past his 17th birthday when he was thrust into the most testing first team debut imaginable. The former Northern Ireland schoolboy international could easily have been fazed when asked to fill Denis Law's No. 10 shirt in front of 63,326 fans against City in the Manchester Derby at Maine Road, but he took to the task like a duck to water. Law was injured and unavailable for the game but he needn't have worried for the young Ulsterman deputized magnificently and even kept a cool head to claim one of the goals in a thrilling 3-3 draw. It was a baptism of fire, but McIlroy took the chance to confirm that he had what was required to make it in top class football. The next 11 years saw him become a virtual ever-present in the side.

having reached his peak at roughly the same time that his contract had expired, realized a long-standing ambition to sample Italian football by signing for AC Milan, so a new centre forward was a priority. In his place came Irishman Frank Stapleton, after much acrimony with Arsenal which culminated in a transfer tribunal fee of £900,000 for the man who had scored against United in the 1979 FA Cup final. Buccaneering full back John Gidman arrived from Everton in exchange for Mickey Thomas and other Atkinson targets included Nottingham Forest's Trevor Francis, Glenn Hoddle of Tottenham and Brighton's Mark Lawrenson.

No more deals were struck until Ron carried out a £2.4 million autumn raid on his former employers, West Bromwich Albion, to enlist two midfielders: the combative Remi Moses and the supremely inspirational Bryan Robson. Moses proved a useful if injury-plagued acquisition, while Robson emerged as the key signing of the decade, justifying Bill Shankly's advice to Atkinson that he should sign the lion-hearted north-easterner 'whatever the cost'. The October arrival of Robson created fresh momentum and subsequent steady improvement to finish third in the League, while playing attractively, was deemed acceptable by most fans. Injuries to McQueen and Buchan had opened the door for the combative one-time Gaelic footballer Kevin Moran to impress in central defence, while Lancastrian Mike Duxbury confirmed the progress started under Sexton as an invaluable utility man. Inevitably there were casualties, with Sammy McIlroy and Jimmy Nicholl proving surplus to requirements, though a fellow Ulsterman marked his full debut on the season's closing day with a goal in a 2-0 win against Stoke. He was 17-year-old Norman Whiteside and later that summer he would capture headlines across the globe by succeeding Pele, no less, as the youngest player to appear in the World Cup finals.

Back at Old Trafford it seemed that Atkinson, his side further strengthened by the delightfully fluent skills of Dutch midfielder Arnold Muhren (acquired without a fee at the end of his Ipswich contract), had established a viable platform for a meaningful tilt at the league title and, sure enough, United led the table by late September. Up front Whiteside was linking promisingly with Stapleton – Birtles was dispatched back to Forest for the staggering loss of nearly £1 million – and a midfield quartet of Coppell, Wilkins, Robson and Muhren positively oozed class; meanwhile, a rearguard comprising keeper Bailey, full backs Duxbury and Albiston and centre halves McQueen and Moran was performing solidly. However, the successful pattern was disrupted in October when Wilkins suffered a fractured cheekbone, the captaincy of both club and country passing to Robson, and Coppell began to struggle with the knee problem, emanating from an injury picked up on England duty in 1981 which would shortly signal a heartbreakingly premature end to his career. There were other fitness worries, too, and though capable deputies stepped in, including the gifted young Paul McGrath for Moran, cohesion suffered and United finished third behind Liverpool once more.

Crucially for Atkinson, both domestic knockout competitions offered welcome diversion. In the League Cup, then sponsored by the Milk Marketing Board, United reached the final via an exhilarating two-legged semi in which Arsenal were eclipsed 6-3 on aggregate. That set up a confrontation with Liverpool, which began promisingly when Whiteside turned Alan Hansen and netted with his unfavoured right foot after only 12 minutes, thus becoming the youngest man to score in a Wembley final. United held their lead until a quarter of an hour from the end when, having lost Moran to injury, they conceded an equalizer to Alan Kennedy.

Almost immediately McQueen, their other central defender, became a passenger after suffering a serious knock, so the Red Devils limped into extra-time with a bizarre back four consisting of substitute Macari, Duxbury, centre forward Stapleton and Albiston. It was unlikely that they would hold out, and they didn't, Ronnie Whelan curling a magnificent winner. Happily, Atkinson's post-match reminder that the Red Devils could be back at Wembley within six weeks proved prophetic. That was in the FA Cup, of course, and again they defeated Arsenal in the semi-final, this time producing an epic performance at Villa Park where sensational second-half goals by Robson and Whiteside negated an earlier strike by Tony Woodcock.

### FA Cup Glory

After that United were clear favourites to prevail against Brighton, who were freshly relegated from the top flight, and they were on the verge of doing so when efforts from Stapleton and Wilkins established a 2-1 lead. But Gary Stevens equalized three minutes from time and then the feisty Seagulls almost plundered an astonishing victory. Gordon Smith found himself clean through with only Gary Bailey to beat, but the keeper smothered the Scot's point-blank effort and United breathed again. As Atkinson put it with a typical touch of melodrama: 'It was the moment when we died a thousand deaths.' The replay was much more straightforward for United, with the young Welsh winger Alan Davies – who replaced Coppell for both matches – setting up early goals for Robson and Whiteside. Further strikes by Robson and Muhren (penalty) completed a 4-0 scoreline which was a little hard on Brighton.

The game remains a happy memory for the Reds, but there is one tragic footnote. Davies, who appeared to be on the brink of a golden future, soon suffered a broken leg and left Old Trafford, going on to serve five more clubs and to start a family. But in February 1992 he was found dead in his car near

*United had to take Brighton to a replay in the 1983 FA Cup final after a 2-2 draw but they put four past them in the replay, including a penalty from Arnold Muhren.*

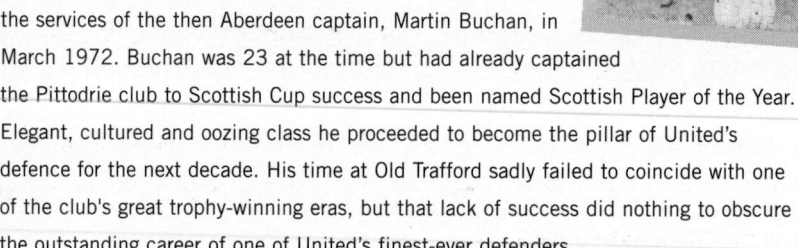

## 50 Greatest Players

**MARTIN BUCHAN Defender**

**Born:** Aberdeen, 6 March 1949

**Joined Manchester United:** 1972 **From:** Aberdeen

**Debut:** 4 March 1972 v Tottenham Hotspur, League

**Appearances:** 456 **Goals:** 4

**Left Manchester United:** 1983 **For:** Oldham Athletic

**Honours won with United:** FA Cup winner 1977

Frank O'Farrell's managerial tenure at Old Trafford, 18 months between June 1971 and December 1972, passed with few moments of triumph, but United supporters of the day were immensely grateful to the softly-spoken Irishman for securing the services of the then Aberdeen captain, Martin Buchan, in March 1972. Buchan was 23 at the time but had already captained the Pittodrie club to Scottish Cup success and been named Scottish Player of the Year. Elegant, cultured and oozing class he proceeded to become the pillar of United's defence for the next decade. His time at Old Trafford sadly failed to coincide with one of the club's great trophy-winning eras, but that lack of success did nothing to obscure the outstanding career of one of United's finest-ever defenders.

his home in South Wales, having committed suicide. But for his injury in a pre-season friendly, Davies might have cemented a future as a Red Devil; as it was, with Coppell soon to learn that he would never play again, Atkinson paid Leeds £45,000 for Scottish international Arthur Graham, who figured prominently in an uplifting start to the new term.

Liverpool were beaten twice, in the Charity Shield and the League, and Manchester United were never far from the First Division summit, topping the pile at the end of October and again in mid March. But then injuries to Robson and Muhren, added to the longer-term absence of McQueen (who was replaced by young Graeme Hogg), saw them flounder fatally on the run-in to finish in a wretchedly disappointing fourth place.

The reliance on Robson, in particular, was to become a worryingly recurrent theme in the years ahead, but at least 'Captain Marvel' furnished a host of golden memories along the way, few more vivid than his barnstorming efforts in the Cup-Winners' Cup quarter-final comeback to beat Barcelona. After that, sadly, the Reds fell to a late Juventus goal in the semi-final, their cause handicapped ruinously by the injury absences of Robson and Muhren, and Wilkins' first-leg suspension.

A major bonus of 1983-84 was the springtime emergence of the dynamic young Welsh front-runner Mark Hughes, who became a regular in 1984-85 in a radically reshaped attack. That summer saw frantic transfer activity with the arrival of striker Alan Brazil (£700,000) from Spurs, flankmen Gordon Strachan (£600,000) from Aberdeen and Jesper Olsen (£350,000) from Ajax, the influx financed by the £1.5 million departure of Ray Wilkins to AC Milan. Although Brazil didn't settle, the overall facelift produced entertaining football but precious little consistency and yet another title challenge tailed off tamely in the spring. The UEFA Cup brought more dismay, with elimination to unconsidered Hungarians Videoton by penalty shoot-out in the quarter-finals, but once again the FA Cup proved to be the Red Devils' saving grace.

## A Thrilling FA Cup Campaign

A hat-trick by Whiteside, who had made a successful transition to midfield, saw off West Ham in the quarter-final to set up a last-four meeting with Liverpool which see-sawed enthrallingly over two encounters before United won through. The teams shared four goals in the first instalment at Goodison Park, but when a stray header from Paul McGrath sneaked past Gary Bailey

### 50 Greatest Players

**STEVE COPPELL Forward**

**Born:** Liverpool, 9 July 1955

**Joined Manchester United:** 1975 **From:** Tranmere Rovers

**Debut:** 1 March 1975 v Cardiff City, League

**Appearances:** 393 (3) **Goals:** 70

**Left Manchester United:** 1983 (retired)

**Honours won with United:** FA Cup winner 1977

United supporters are as mesmerized by the tantalizing skills of a winger as any football fan, so it was with delight that they witnessed the arrival at Old Trafford of the virtually unknown Steve Coppell from Tranmere Rovers. The fact that he was born in Liverpool and had been purloined by Merseyside's 'other' club was soon forgotten as he helped to secure United's place back in the top grade after one season (1974-75) in Division Two. He was an instant hit and from then on figured regularly in United's starting line-up until he was forced to retire, aged 28, through injury in September 1983. His run of 206 consecutive league appearances, between 15 January 1977 and 7 November 1981, looks likely to stand forever as a United club record.

## Great Matches

### EUROPEAN CUP-WINNERS' CUP, QUARTER-FINAL, 2ND LEG

**Old Trafford, 21 March 1984**

**Manchester United 3** **Barcelona 0** **Attendance: 58,547**
Robson 2
Stapleton

If ever one contest summed up the indomitable dynamism of Bryan Robson, this was it. Having proclaimed that he was out to atone for two glaring misses during Barcelona's 2-0 first-leg victory, he did just that, and went desperately close to a hat-trick as United completed an unforgettable recovery against one of the world's top teams. With Diego Maradona shackled by the relentlessly attentive Moses, the Reds launched a wave of early attacks and Whiteside was unlucky when his lob bounced to safety off the top of the crossbar. Midway through the first period the Irishman set up the breakthrough, nodding on Wilkins' near-post corner to the charging Robson, who stooped to net with a powerful header. Having tasted blood, United stepped up their offensive, but the Spanish giants held out until their resistance was shattered by two goals in two minutes early in the second period. A slack back-pass by Alonso caused mayhem in his own rearguard, Moses delivered from the right and Urruti parried to Robson who stabbed home. Then Albiston crossed from the left, Whiteside headed back across goal and Stapleton struck to put the Reds ahead on aggregate. Robson continued to surge forward but his hat-trick wasn't to be, and soon Ron Atkinson was celebrating his most rousing European victory.

**Manchester United:** Bailey, Duxbury, Albiston, Wilkins, Moran, Hogg, Robson, Muhren, Stapleton, Whiteside (Hughes), Moses
**Barcelona:** Urruti, Gerardo, Moratalla, Julio Alberto, Victor, Alesanco, Alonso (Clos), Schuster, Rojo, Maradona, Marcos
**Referee:** P. Casarin

*The European Cup-Winners' Cup quarter-final second leg was a showcase for Bryan Robson who scored two goals. Even Diego Maradona couldn't conjure up any magic for the Spanish giants.*

to gift Liverpool a first-half advantage in the Maine Road replay, United's prospects looked bleak. However, explosive second-half efforts from Robson and Hughes saw their side through to a final against Everton. Howard Kendall's team, having clinched the League title with five games to spare and then added the European Cup-Winners' Cup, were targeting an historic treble. Ostensibly they had little to fear from the Reds, whom they had humiliated 5-0 at Goodison in the gala display of their championship campaign and then knocked out of the Milk Cup at Old Trafford.

But United proved dogged opponents in a woefully drab contest which sprang into tempestuous life in the 77th minute when Kevin Moran became the first man to be sent off in an FA Cup final, having sent Peter Reid somersaulting. It was a draconian punishment for an apparently honest attempt to play the ball and it left United in deep mire. Clearly lifted by a sense of perceived injustice, and with Stapleton deputizing nobly at the back, the Reds began to play their most persuasive football of the day. After forcing extra-time, they eschewed the option of digging in to force a replay, garnering sensational reward when Hughes sent Whiteside clear on the right and Belfast's answer to Roy of the Rovers curled a delicious winner past plunging keeper Neville Southall. United's celebrations were all the more joyous for the trauma that had preceded them and, although competition rules meant that poor Moran's medal was withheld temporarily, it was presented to him a few days later.

But while lifting the FA Cup was all well and good, what really mattered was ending the league title drought which stretched all the way back to 1967. That was primarily what Atkinson was employed to achieve and in the early months of 1985-86 he appeared to be on the brink of success. The Red Devils won their first ten games and did not lose until their 16th. Now, with Robson, Hughes and Whiteside in particularly rampant form, and former Manchester City and England star Peter Barnes reviving his flagging fortunes with a dazzling spell on the left flank, a lusciously entertaining United looked odds-on to claim that elusive crown. It was balm to the souls of Old Trafford fans worn down by too many years of relentless Merseyside dominance, but a cruelly debilitating anti-climax was lying in wait. Robson, the Reds' touchstone and heartbeat of the team, was lost to a hamstring tear, there was a plague of injuries to other key men and, most perplexing of all to supporters who spent vast sums of money following their heroes all over the country, rumours circulated that the lionised Hughes was to be sold to Barcelona for more than £2 million at season's end.

Against the demoralizing background of a midwinter decline in results, and with Hughes' goals drying up alarmingly, the story was denied by all concerned.

*Frank Stapleton, Norman Whiteside and Bryan Robson celebrate winning the FA Cup against Everton in 1985. United had success in the FA Cup competition in the 80s but they failed to make any significant title challenge.*

But come the spring, as United capitulated calamitously to the Anfield foe, it was revealed to be correct. Later it transpired that young 'Sparky' had not been eager to move, but had been persuaded that such an opportunity was too rare to pass up. That was of little consolation to the fans, who felt betrayed by their club, which finished fourth for the third successive term.

It was a time of reassessment for Atkinson, who had brought in strikers Terry Gibson from Coventry and Peter Davenport from Nottingham Forest in unavailing attempts to plug the gap left by Hughes, and during the close-season he considered resignation. He was talked out of it by Martin Edwards, but the cloud over Old Trafford refused to lift, and a chronic, injury-ridden start to 1986-87 saw United slump perilously close to the foot of the table by early November. A 4-1 drubbing in a League Cup replay at Southampton proved to be the final straw and the next day Ron Atkinson and United parted company.

His overall record – two FA Cup triumphs, reaching a League Cup final and never finishing outside the top four in the First Division – suggested that he had no need to hang his head, and he didn't, exiting in typically expansive style with a farewell party. Though he never truly commanded the affection of the fans, many of whom were alienated by his Champagne Charlie image, Big Ron was a genuine football man whose teams played with flair, and who went agonizingly close to giving the Red Devils their hearts' desire. Now the torch passed to a man who was tolerably well acquainted with success already, and was rather keen to taste some more.

# Chapter Eleven: 1986-92
# The Man from Govan

The task facing Alex Ferguson when he succeeded Ron Atkinson as manager of Manchester United in November 1986 was straightforward – stave off relegation, then win the league championship without undue delay. That was the stark agenda placed before the one-time apprentice toolmaker and trade union official from the tough Govan area of Glasgow when he met Martin Edwards, the Old Trafford chairman, on the day of Atkinson's dismissal. So focused was Edwards on recruiting the Aberdeen boss that within three hours of terminating one contract, he was on board a plane to the Granite City to put the final touches to another which must have been in the pipeline already. It was easy to understand why United craved the Scot's services so avidly. During a trophy-laden eight years at Pittodrie, he had shattered the crushing domestic duopoly of Celtic and Rangers and led the Dons to European glory, an astonishing story of success achieved in the face of seemingly impossible odds.

Though United were already rich and powerful, Ferguson's new challenge was as daunting as his previous one in that, once more, there was an apparently untouchable giant to be slain. If the Red Devils were to become top dogs in English football once again, as they had been during the gilded era of Sir Matt Busby, then they would have to climb over the body of the mighty Liverpool. As he set out on a long and rocky road with a dismal 2-0 defeat at the Manor Ground, Oxford, the awesome scale of his task began to sink in. Ferguson was appalled by what he found on settling in at Old Trafford. He was unimpressed by fitness levels, disturbed by what he perceived as a drinking culture among some of the team's stars, disappointed by the standard of many of the club's youngsters, and outraged by a sketchy scouting system which saw the cream of local talent disappearing in the direction of Maine Road.

Aside from the urgent business of improving the points total so that United climbed the First Division table, he knew that he must embark on radical reform which would take years to bear fruit. He recognized that there would be bloody internal battles to fight, and he was determined not to flinch from them.

On the field, the gruelling haul towards immediate safety began with a gradual upturn in results, of which the highlight was a Boxing Day victory

## 50 Greatest Players

**LOU MACARI Forward**

**Born:** Edinburgh, 4 June 1949

**Joined Manchester United:** 1973 **From:** Celtic

**Debut:** 20 January 1973 v West Ham United, League

**Appearances:** 374 (27) **Goals:** 97

**Left Manchester United:** 1984 **For:** Swindon Town

**Honours won with United:** FA Cup winner 1977

Scot Tommy Docherty became United's manager late in 1972 and seemed hell-bent on surrounding himself with his fellow countrymen. Arguably his prize capture, Lou Macari, very nearly signed for Liverpool instead. He was on the brink of moving from Celtic to Anfield when United, and Docherty, nipped in to whisk him off to Old Trafford. And what a fortuitous moment that proved to be. Macari became an instant hit with the Red hordes after he'd scored on his debut against West Ham United at Old Trafford. The fans were looking for a new hero and the Stretford End were quick to acclaim the diminutive striker who went on to give the club 11 years' splendid service.

over Liverpool at Anfield, courtesy of a 78th-minute goal by Norman Whiteside. When an even later strike by Peter Davenport settled the return encounter in April, underlining United's recovery to a safe mid-table position and virtually ending Liverpool's hopes of retaining the championship, optimism was abroad among the Red legions, who also had home wins over Manchester City in both the League and FA Cup to savour.

### Ferguson Makes an Impression

Working in harness with his former Pittodrie lieutenant Archie Knox, Ferguson had halted the slide and, it seemed to the layman, possessed the nucleus of a top-class squad. Tellingly, though, of the two dozen footballers who represented United at first-team level during 1986-87, only two – Bryan Robson and Clayton Blackmore – would linger to partake in the medal-fest which, at that point, was no more than the merest gleam in the manager's eye. What would become an inexorable weeding-out process began that summer with the departure of Frank Stapleton to Ajax and Danish international utility man Johnny Sivebaek to St Étienne, while Ferguson pondered on a raft of possible arrivals. Targets mentioned but not captured included Watford's John Barnes, Newcastle's Peter Beardsley, Gothenburg's

Glenn Hysen and a certain Mark Hughes of Barcelona. Of these Barnes, Hysen and Beardsley, who had been rejected by Ron Atkinson after being given only one senior opportunity for the Red Devils back in 1982, would all gravitate to Liverpool, while any move for Hughes was deferred because of the player's tax situation.

Ferguson professed himself well satisfied, however, with the two signings he did make. Celtic striker Brian McClair, fresh from being anointed as Scotland's Player of the Year after netting 41 times in his final campaign at Parkhead, cost £850,000, while Arsenal full back Viv Anderson was priced at £250,000, both fees being set by transfer tribunal. The two newcomers excelled in 1987-88, which proved an encouraging season, albeit one which heralded a premature dawn as United soared in the First Division table to finish as runners-up to Liverpool. McClair laid a club bogey, becoming the first Red Devil since George Best in the 1960s to score 20 league goals in a season, earning widespread plaudits for both his opportunism and his persistence. Never fazed by missing, 'Choccy' always bounced back after any disappointment, ready to make the next opportunity count.

Anderson proved similarly determined, displaying the backbone and commitment which had made him a European Cup winner and the first black player to earn a full England cap during his Nottingham Forest days. It should have proved a landmark campaign, too, for young keeper Gary Walsh, who appeared favourite to become the long-term replacement for Gary Bailey, forced into early retirement with knee trouble. Ferguson had faith in the tall Lancastrian, but the boy's progress was interrupted repeatedly by injury and he was destined to remain a peripheral figure. In the meantime Chris Turner, an Atkinson acquisition from Sunderland in 1985, stepped up and performed adequately enough, without suggesting that he would become a fixture.

*Arthur Albiston was an ever-present in the United defence for over a decade and was a three-time FA Cup winner with the Reds.*

*Irishman Paul McGrath was a reassuring and stylish presence in the defence during the 1980s.*

One man soon be a part of the club furniture was stopper Steve Bruce, who arrived from Norwich City in December following injury to Paul McGrath. He never boasted the Irishman's natural ability, and he was not Ferguson's first choice – that was Rangers' Terry Butcher, who suffered a broken leg when a deal seemed imminent – but in terms of sheer heart and durability he was a champion, as he would prove time and again over the next nine years.

Although United garnered 81 points, which would have been enough to take the title in each of the two subsequent terms, they never seriously threatened the pre-eminence of Kenny Dalglish's lovely Liverpool team, arguably the most entertaining combination ever produced at Anfield. Still, Ferguson had demanded consistency, and he had got it, with only two league defeats after Boxing Day. It was a remarkable effort, especially in the light of growing difficulties with two of the club's most popular players, McGrath and Whiteside, both of whom were labouring with knee trouble, and both of whom spent too much time in bars for their manager's peace of mind.

Their day of reckoning would arrive, but meanwhile the summer of 1988 brought dramatic developments which unfolded in an atmosphere of white-hot expectation among United fans convinced that, after more than two decades in the title wilderness, a realistic bid was about to be mounted. By far the biggest boost to their aspirations arrived with the re-signing of Mark Hughes from Barcelona for £1.6 million. 'Sparky' was adored for his spectacular goals, his compelling blend of rumbustious strength and deft skills, and a distinctly tempestuous on-field charisma which was appealingly at odds with his unassuming personality away from the fray.

In addition, Ferguson had returned to Aberdeen with a cheque for £750,000 to enlist Jim Leighton, with whom he had shared multiple triumphs at

Pittodrie and who was touted in some quarters as the finest Scottish goalkeeper of all time. Less trumpeted was the arrival of Lee Sharpe, a versatile, left-sided 17-year-old who was secured from Torquay for £200,000 after the Old Trafford boss, wary of attracting attention from rival scouts, had disguised himself in a balaclava while running the rule over the slender Brummie during an evening game at Plainmoor. There had been strenuous efforts, too, to take Paul Gascoigne from Newcastle – Ferguson believed that a deal had been struck, only for the player to change tack – and Stuart Pearce, the ferociously abrasive Nottingham Forest defender, who would surely have proved a key acquisition.

Using the exit door, meanwhile, was the faithful Arthur Albiston, viewed by some shrewd contemporary observers as still the most accomplished full back at the club, and the unfailingly brave Kevin Moran, who was destined to know some of his finest footballing hours with Blackburn. Both were described by the manager as outstanding professionals, but that didn't prevent him from sacrificing them on the altar of youth as he strove to reduce the average age of his team. After all the comings and goings, United embarked upon what turned out to be a mess of a season in which the side

## 50 Greatest Players

**ARTHUR ALBISTON Defender**

**Born:** Edinburgh, 14 July 1957

**Joined Manchester United:** 1972 **From:** Juniors

**Debut:** 9 October 1974 v Manchester City, League Cup

**Appearances:** 467 (18) **Goals:** 7

**Left Manchester United:** 1988 **For:** West Bromwich Albion

**Honours won with United:** FA Cup winner 1977, 1983, 1985

Arthur Albiston made his senior debut against Manchester City in a League Cup third round tie at Old Trafford. United were in the Second Division at the time, but they managed to put one over on City and Albiston played his part to the full. Two and a half years later, and with a limited number of first team appearances to his name, he made his FA Cup debut, as a replacement for the injured Stewart Houston, in the 1977 final against Liverpool at Wembley. United won 2-1 and from that day on Albiston rarely looked back as he went on to become a regular in the first team setup. A beautifully compact defender, he had the knack of making the job look easy when, of course, it wasn't. Primarily an accomplished full back, he was adept at joining the attack where he would make his presence felt. He was a near-fixture in the Reds' defence for the next ten years, in which time he also collected 14 caps for Scotland.

**50 Greatest Players**

**PAUL McGRATH Defender**

**Born:** Ealing, 4 December 1959

**Joined Manchester United:** 1982 **From:** St Patrick's Athletic

**Debut:** 13 November 1982 v Tottenham Hotspur, League

**Appearances:** 192 (7) **Goals:** 16

**Left Manchester United:** 1989 **For:** Aston Villa

**Honours won with United:** FA Cup winner 1985

Sadly, Manchester United supporters didn't see the very best of Paul McGrath, but he would still find a place in any Reds' top 50 list of all-time greats. Stylish, composed and richly gifted there is little doubt that had he not become a top class central defender he would have enjoyed an equally successful career in midfield. He arrived at Old Trafford from Dublin club St Patrick's Athletic for £30,000 in April 1982. He made his debut the following season and the United faithful immediately decided that he was made of the right stuff. Countless cultured displays confirmed the fans' initial impression, but as far as United were concerned it was to be a story without a happy ending. Alex Ferguson decided that United could survive without the Republic of Ireland international and in August 1989 he was sold to Aston Villa.

was decimated by injuries. Though Hughes gave plenty of terrific individual displays and was voted Player of the Year for 1989 by his peers, he took time to gel with McClair, who eventually took a midfield role, and there was a distressing lack of overall fluency.

## Ferguson Brings in the Youngsters

As he struggled to reshape his line-up Ferguson dispensed with the likes of Peter Davenport, Jesper Olsen, Chris Turner and Liam O'Brien in the autumn, then was mortified to find himself short of senior players as the casualties piled up. Thus the experienced Northern Ireland defender Mal Donaghy arrived from Luton, and Ralph Milne, once a star winger with Dundee United, was recruited from Bristol City, but the most exciting development was the sudden emergence of a crop of rookies, dubbed 'Fergie's Fledglings' by the media in reference to the Busby Babes of old, around mid-season. Lee Sharpe was already making an impact, mostly at left back but occasionally in a forward role, and now opportunity knocked for Lee Martin, another classy full back, midfielders Russell Beardsmore, Tony Gill and David Wilson, winger Jools Maiorana and strikers Mark Robins and Deiniol Graham. It constituted a wonderfully romantic mass promotion, but only Sharpe was destined to hold a long-term place, while others would sample fleeting moments of glory and the majority, notably the splendidly versatile Gill, would be lost to the game through various injuries.

The boy who seized the public imagination most vividly for a spell was the scrawnily slender, locally-born Beardsmore, who starred in a New Year's Day triumph over Liverpool at Old Trafford. With the Red Devils trailing to a John Barnes strike, the deliciously talented 19-year-old helped to create goals for McClair and Hughes, then volleyed one of his own, and his potential appeared limitless. The following term, though, he faded, seemingly too lightweight to thrive at the top level, and eventually joined Bournemouth.

That Liverpool game and its sequel, a 1-0 defeat by Middlesbrough less than 24 hours later, summed up the infuriating inconsistency of the entire season, and more mammoth frustration was lying in wait – a limp FA Cup quarter-final defeat at the hands of Nottingham Forest. Now steadily mounting public criticism about United's lack of style reached new heights and Ferguson, with the jeers of supporters ringing in his ears, decided that sweeping changes were necessary if he was not to flop for the first time in his managerial career. Within days he had dispatched Gordon Strachan to Second Division Leeds United, declaring that his former Aberdeen charge, with whom he endured a periodically strained relationship, had run out of steam and needed a change. Certainly the switch benefited the effervescent little redhead, who proved vastly influential at Elland Road as his new employers earned promotion and then, after he had passed his 35th birthday, lifted the league title at the expense of the Red Devils.

But that was some three years away. For now, with all hope of the 1988-89 crown having evaporated, Alex Ferguson opted for springtime experimentation, resulting in only three wins from 14 matches and a dismal 11th-place finish, before addressing the need for further investment. He prepared for what would prove the most turbulent year of his Old Trafford tenure to date with the summer purchase of two contrasting midfielders, the sweet-passing Neil Webb from Nottingham Forest for £1.75 million and the more mundane but endlessly industrious Mike Phelan from Norwich City for £750,000.

Come August the activity intensified with the controversial exits of crowd favourites and 'bon viveurs' McGrath and Whiteside, to Aston Villa and Everton respectively, and the £2.3 million arrival of centre half Gary Pallister from Middlesbrough. The spree continued in September when spiky young midfielder Paul Ince was secured, at the end of an on-off saga concerning his fitness, from West Ham for a pay-as-you-play £1.7 million, and a further £1.1 million was expended on Southampton forward Danny Wallace.

## 50 Greatest Players

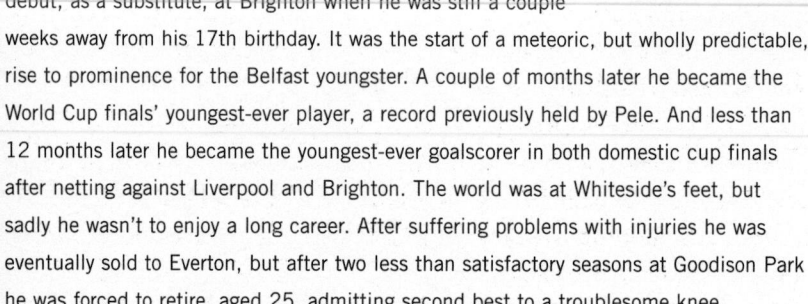

### NORMAN WHITESIDE Forward/Midfielder

**Born:** Belfast, 7 May 1965

**Joined Manchester United:** 1981 **From:** Juniors

**Debut:** 24 April 1982 v Brighton & Hove Albion, League

**Appearances:** 256 (18) **Goals:** 67

**Left Manchester United:** 1989 **For:** Everton

**Honours won with United:** FA Cup winner 1983, 1985

Almost every respected observer in the game tipped Norman Whiteside for stardom from the moment he arrived at Old Trafford in 1981 to begin his apprenticeship. A teenage giant, he already possessed the physique of a man and he was also bountifully equipped in the skill department. So it was no real surprise when manager Ron Atkinson gave him his league debut, as a substitute, at Brighton when he was still a couple weeks away from his 17th birthday. It was the start of a meteoric, but wholly predictable, rise to prominence for the Belfast youngster. A couple of months later he became the World Cup finals' youngest-ever player, a record previously held by Pele. And less than 12 months later he became the youngest-ever goalscorer in both domestic cup finals after netting against Liverpool and Brighton. The world was at Whiteside's feet, but sadly he wasn't to enjoy a long career. After suffering problems with injuries he was eventually sold to Everton, but after two less than satisfactory seasons at Goodison Park he was forced to retire, aged 25, admitting second best to a troublesome knee.

All this took place against the backdrop of an anticipated takeover of Manchester United by the businessman Michael Knighton, which was announced on the eve of the opening game, at home to Arsenal. Before kickoff, keen to bond with the supporters, Knighton strode on to the pitch decked out in full United kit and proceeded to juggle a football before lashing it into the net at the Stretford End. It was a bizarre, oddly endearing, if ultimately futile introduction – by October the financial deal was off, though Knighton joined the board – but the fans were more impressed by the Red Devils' performance that day, thrashing Arsenal 4-1 with Webb shining and contributing a fine goal. The sun illuminated a shirt-sleeved crowd and championship talk abounded – but it was all a cruel illusion.

Form declined abruptly, the new play-maker ruptured an achilles tendon while on international duty and the next wave of expensive reinforcements, understandably enough, took time to bed in. Soon the Reds' perennial fear –

a new injury to Robson – became a stark reality. There was an alarming plunge towards the foot of the table, the football was devoid of confidence and frankly awful. The fearful decline was symbolized by the most calamitous result in the club's modern history, a 5-1 defeat at Maine Road, the memory of which Manchester City fans would use as a comforter throughout their own horrendous travail over the next decade and more. In fact, it was a scoreline which thoroughly flattered the Blues on the run of play, but no matter, United were in dire straits.

By the turn of the year relegation loomed as a distinct possibility, the pressure on the manager was becoming intense and it seemed likely that only a decent FA Cup run could save his job. The theory was that undemanding third-round opponents were essential so when the draw threw up high-riding Nottingham Forest at the City Ground, the portents were doom-laden, especially when TV analyst Jimmy Hill declared that United looked a beaten team even during the kick-in! Cue Mark Robins, who raced on to a beautifully curled dispatch from Mark Hughes to nudge the only goal of an unbearably nervy encounter which reached new heights of tension near the end, when Forest had a strike ruled out.

Chairman Martin Edwards has always maintained that because the board was happy with Ferguson's behind-the-scenes reconstruction of the club, the manager would not have been dismissed even if that tie had been lost, but with more and more fans turning against him, it is almost certain that his position would have become untenable.

## Title Misery but FA Cup Joy

However, such speculation receded as the Red Devils inched past the Uniteds of Hereford, Newcastle and Sheffield, then overcame Second Division Oldham Athletic in a pulsating semi-final which needed two games (3-3 and 2-1) to reach Wembley. Crucially, too, running parallel to this exciting diversion was a gradual league recovery culminating joyfully in four straight wins in the spring which secured safety. Ferguson knew, though, that 13th place in the First Division would be scoffed at by his critics if it were not offset by silverware, so the FA Cup final against Crystal Palace, managed by former United favourite Steve

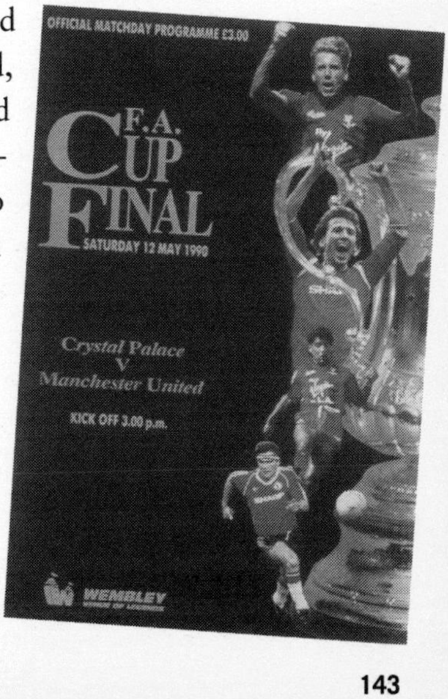

*Full back Lee Martin scored the only goal in the 1990 FA Cup replay, a crucial win for United during a period of disappointing results – a trying time for Alex Ferguson.*

Coppell, remained central to his Old Trafford future. The men on whom he was depending at Wembley were Leighton, Ince, Bruce, Pallister, Martin, Phelan, Robson, Webb, Wallace, McClair and Hughes, with Blackmore and Robins on the bench.

The game was an error-strewn six-goal thriller which went to extra-time but still couldn't produce a winner. Palace took the lead through Gary O'Reilly, then goals from Robson and Hughes saw United in the ascendancy, only for a double-strike from substitute Ian Wright to put Palace on the verge of victory. Hughes was the saviour with only seven minutes to spare, leaving Ferguson to make the most painful decision of his professional life ahead of the replay.

Jim Leighton had been experiencing a run of shaky form, and many observers, perhaps a tad harshly, found him culpable for all three Palace strikes. Now the United boss opted to drop his former Pittodrie protégé for the replay, placing the good of his club over his personal feelings and apparently alienating Leighton forever. Into the team strode Les Sealey, on loan from Luton, and he responded in typically ebullient fashion, giving a confident display which contrasted vividly with unlucky Jim's hesitancy.

It was a terrible match, ruined by Palace's spoiling tactics, but United triumphed by a solitary goal from an unlikely hero, full back Lee Martin, who chested down a sublime crossfield pass from Webb and thumped an unstoppable shot just under the crossbar. For the modest youngster it turned out to be the glittering highlight of a career sabotaged by injuries; for Alex Ferguson, it signalled sensational lift-off.

Now the whole atmosphere of the club brightened, the feeling of genuine renaissance heightened by the ending of the European ban on English participants, imposed following the Heysel disaster in 1985. Thanks to beating Palace, United would once more be blazing a trans-continental trail in the Cup-Winners' Cup, and they would be strengthened by the £650,000 signing of the unobtrusively excellent full back Denis Irwin from Oldham.

League form in 1990-91 offered a colossal improvement on the previous sorry term, though a brisk start was placed into sober context by a 4-0 drubbing at Anfield in mid September, underlining the fact that Ferguson's Reds were still off the pace of their principal rivals. This was confirmed by finishing in sixth place, though the steady progress being made by most of the players justified enormous optimism. The title was claimed for the second time in three years by Arsenal, with whom United had brawled on the pitch during a 1-0 defeat at Old Trafford. Though Alex Ferguson dismissed the fracas as 'handbags at dawn', the League took a different view, fining the Reds one point and the Gunners two.

The defence of the FA Cup ended in fifth-round defeat at Norwich, but the League Cup campaign lasted to the final, featuring memorable triumphs over Liverpool, Arsenal (6-2 at Highbury, including a brilliant hat-trick by Lee Sharpe) and Leeds along the way. At Wembley, anti-climactically, United appeared to fall prey to complacency, losing tamely 1-0 to Ron Atkinson's Sheffield Wednesday. It was a timely reminder that loftier standards were demanded and Ferguson's men responded in grand style on the European stage.

After breezing past Pecsi Munkas of Hungary and Welsh Cup holders Wrexham, Ferguson's men faced their first serious test against Montpellier in the quarter-final. It proved a tense tie, with the visitors having a man sent off following a tussle with Hughes at Old Trafford, but a second-minute free kick from Blackmore – enjoying the season of his life at left back – and a penalty from Bruce saw the Reds into the last four.

In the semi-final they were favoured by the draw, facing Legia Warsaw while Juventus took on Barcelona, but they fell behind in the away leg before goals from McClair, Hughes and Bruce put them in control, then a 1-1 draw back in Manchester ensured United's place in their first European final for nearly a quarter of a century. By this time team spirit was bubbling, the bonding of the players having been helped in no small measure by a perception that many outsiders gloried in the club's recent struggles, and a consequent determination to spit in their collective eye. It was an attitude not discouraged by the canny Ferguson, who would utilize it more than once with telling success over the ensuing decade and beyond.

Confronting the white-shirted Red Devils on a foggy, soggy night in Rotterdam were Johan Cruyff's mighty Barcelona, the contest holding special significance for Mark Hughes, who had been rejected by the Spaniards and packed back to Manchester three years earlier. He responded in typically tumultuous style with both goals in a wonderful 2-1 triumph by the underdogs, an uplifting display which had a key bearing on his election as PFA Footballer of the Year for the second time in three seasons.

## Success in Europe

As Gary Pallister recalled: 'We were the better side for at least 90 per cent of the match and when Sparky put us in front after 68 minutes, we really deserved it. Mind you, I don't think Brucie was too happy when Mark nicked his goal! He was certain that his header was going in but I don't think you could blame Sparky for poking it over the line to make sure. For sure, he'd have been blamed if a Barcelona defender had got back to clear. At least there was no shadow of doubt about the second goal. No one who saw Sparky's strike will ever forget it. Apparently the commentator had just said he'd taken it too wide when, typical of Mark, he lashed it into the back of the net with all his usual ferocity.'

Still ahead was a slight wobble when United's keeper, the late Les Sealey, was beaten by Ronald Koeman. Of the closing drama, Pally said: 'I'm sure Les was struggling a bit with the nasty leg injury he had picked up in the League

*Mark Hughes goes round the Barcelona keeper to score his second goal in the 1991 European Cup-Winners' Cup final, a turning point in United's fortunes.*

Cup final defeat by Sheffield Wednesday, which meant he couldn't get across his line as quickly as usual, but fortunately it didn't cost us in the end.' The main reason it didn't was a momentous goal-line clearance from Clayton Blackmore: 'I felt quite thankful to Clayton, but not as thankful as Brucie. He hadn't put a foot wrong all night but then he chested the ball down and tried to hit it back, probably with his weaker peg. Michael Laudrup took advantage and when I saw his effort go past Les, the horrible thought flashed across my mind that we were going to extra-time after dominating so much of the play. But then Clayton popped up to save us.'

It was the perfect ending to a term which can be viewed in retrospect as a significant turning point, one in which Manchester United proved once more that they could compete with the best. There was a telling nod towards the future, too, in two names at the tail-end of the season's appearance list, Ryan Giggs and Andrei Kanchelskis cropping up for the first time.

Still Alex Ferguson wasn't quite content with his line-up, and for 1991-92 he added giant Danish goalkeeper Peter Schmeichel, for whom Brondby banked a £550,000 fee, and adaptable England defender Paul Parker, signed for £1.7 million from Queens Park Rangers. After that the United boss, now assisted by Brian Kidd in place of the departed Archie Knox, declared that his team was ready for a title tilt. They began with four clean sheets and not losing until their 13th game as they moved smoothly to the league summit. With Welsh wunderkind Giggs and the flying Ukrainian Kanchelskis terrorizing defenders from the flanks and compensating for the early absence through injury of Sharpe, United threatened to take the First Division by storm.

Autumn brought mixed European fortunes, with Cup-Winners' Cup defeat by Atletico Madrid being mitigated by a rather fortunate European Super Cup victory against Red Star Belgrade, the final being completed in one leg at Old Trafford due to the war in Yugoslavia. The only goal of the game was scored by Brian McClair, but Red Star played the best football and were in command for long periods.

By midwinter it had become clear that United's main championship rivals would be Leeds, and Fergie's men were not helped by being drawn against the Yorkshiremen in both domestic cups. The Reds emerged triumphant from both ties, but thereafter Howard Wilkinson's fine side, in which Gordon Strachan was a leading light, appeared to benefit from having no knockout distractions. Suddenly, in the second half of the season, United began scoring fewer goals and, weighed down by the weight of expectation from fans who had been starved of the title for 25 years, began to lose momentum. As Gary Pallister put it: 'The championship had become the fans' Holy Grail and the

*Flying Ukrainian winger Andrei Kanchelskis ran rampant on the flanks in 1991-92 to boost United's chance of a title.*

players could sense their desperation. The crowds became more and more tense as the season wore on and that communicated itself to us. The manager tried to take the pressure off us, but it wasn't easy.'

After being ejected from the FA Cup in a penalty shoot-out by Southampton, the Reds made amends by lifting the League Cup for the first time, Brian McClair's goal proving too much for Nottingham Forest. With only six league games remaining, that might have provided the necessary tonic to go on and lift the main prize, and after beating Southampton and drawing with Luton, they were still the favourites. But by then they were in a nightmare sequence of five matches in ten days, and they bowed in turn to Nottingham Forest, West Ham and, most painful of all, to Liverpool at Anfield, where all hope was finally extinguished.

Gary Pallister, who gained a degree of personal consolation by succeeding Hughes as PFA Footballer of the Year, was in no doubt about where the blame lay: 'I think the main reason we lost the title was because the Football League mishandled the fixtures; they gave us no leeway. We were already suffering from loads of injuries and it was plain ridiculous to settle a championship in such a way.'

The United team was mocked mercilessly by an almost hysterical Merseyside crowd which could hardly have exhibited more glee had their own side just been crowned as champions, rather than finishing 18 points back in sixth place. Ferguson was hurt, desperately so, but even in this darkest of hours he extracted something positive. As Anfield's deafening celebrations applied salt by the bucketful to the Red Devils' gaping wounds, he told his shattered charges to soak up the sickening experience, so they would never let it happen again.

# Chapter Twelve: 1992-98
# Paradise Regained

It was the year of the first heart transplant operation, the year Muhammad Ali was stripped of his world heavyweight title for refusing to fight in Vietnam, and of Francis Chichester's historic solo yacht voyage around the globe. But to the long-suffering United faithful, 1967 represented an event of far deeper emotive significance – it was the last time their beloved club had lifted the league championship. Since then a whole generation of Red Devils had been born, passed through school and grown to adulthood without experiencing the unique joy of knowing that their team – not Liverpool, not Arsenal or Everton or Leeds, but Manchester United – had earned the right to the title of England's finest. Now, finally, driven by a fearsome Scot utterly consumed by the rage to win, and inspired by a capricious French genius, they were about to emerge from their wilderness after more than a quarter of a century.

Yet in the summer of 1992, the omens had not been hopeful. With a residue of disappointment over the previous season's letdown still hanging in the Old Trafford air, the much-coveted Southampton and England centre forward Alan Shearer chose to join Blackburn rather than the Reds, who turned instead to Dion Dublin. With all due respect to Cambridge United's shaven-headed totem, whose prowess was such an unknown quantity that his £1 million sale was conducted by circulating a videotape of his goals to possible buyers, he was not exactly the star tonic craved by jaded supporters. Apprehension heightened with defeats in the opening two games of the new campaign, then poor Dublin was sidelined for six months with a broken leg and attempts to sign centre forward David Hirst from Sheffield Wednesday were rebuffed angrily by Owls boss Trevor Francis.

Three months of vacillating form found United in eighth place come late November, but with a 26th title-less campaign seemingly inevitable, their fortunes were transformed by a touch of purest serendipity. When Leeds United director Bill Fotherby rang Martin Edwards to ask about the availability of their former full back Denis Irwin he was told immediately that the Irishman was not for sale. Then Alex Ferguson, who happened to be in his chairman's office, prompted a casual inquiry about Eric Cantona, whose springtime arrival at Elland Road had been key to the Yorkshiremen's overhauling of the Reds in the championship race. To the manager's astonishment he was

*Was Eric Cantona the catalyst that took United to the top of the Premiership? Whatever, his genius inspired the Reds to four championships in five seasons.*

not met with a flat refusal and soon the tempestuous French frontman had joined Manchester United for a mere £1.2 million.

It seemed that Leeds boss Howard Wilkinson had become disenchanted by Eric's eccentricities, but Ferguson had a hunch that the so-called maverick, whose temperamental excesses had marred his career to date, might supply the final frisson of flair and imagination that would transform his multi-talented squad into league champions.

## The Frenchman Takes Centre Stage

Unlike many fine footballers before him, Cantona was not overawed by the prospect of striding out at Old Trafford, instead welcoming the grandeur of the stage as fit for his talent and showing not the merest hint of feeling pressure. In turn, the shrewd Ferguson realized that Eric was not as other men, and he made allowances for his whims, handling him as an individual, offering the freedom he needed to flourish. And how he flourished! Cantona's visionary skills were there for all to admire, but equally significant was his supreme professionalism, turning up early for training and continuing to work when the main session was over, an example of single-minded dedication which rubbed off on his new colleagues, especially the youngsters.

Gary Pallister put the Cantona contribution into context: 'We were already a very good team, the core was very strong, as we had proved. But we needed a little more cutting edge up front, a last little touch of spice to open up opposing teams when they came to Old Trafford and defended – and that's what Eric provided. It was clear from the start that he was made for Manchester United, with his swashbuckling style and the imagination of his final pass, inspiring the fans and everybody around him. Eric was a terrific professional, too. Often he was portrayed as wayward genius, the arrogant strutting Frenchman, but he took his job very seriously and looked after himself impeccably, setting a supreme example for the Beckham and Scholes generation.' One experienced beneficiary was Mark Hughes, widely tipped as the man to make way, but Sparky showed his true mettle, scoring a brilliant goal in the home victory over Manchester City during which Eric rose from the bench to make his debut, and generally playing like a man possessed as he formed a fabulous partnership with the exotic newcomer. With Cantona both prompting and scoring, the Red Devils attained a new consistency, buttressed by a belief that, now, anything was possible. This was demonstrated compellingly on Boxing Day when, having fallen three behind to Sheffield Wednesday at Hillsborough, United roared back to claim a point with Eric snatching the late equalizer.

By the New Year they were in firm contention for the newly-constituted Premier League title along with Aston Villa, now bossed by Ron Atkinson, and Norwich City, and victory at Anfield in early March took them to the top of the table. But then a worrying spell in which only three points were gathered from a possible 12 raised the spectre of yet another chronic disappointment. A crucial triumph at Carrow Road, in which Norwich were crushed by three early goals from Giggs, Kanchelskis and Cantona, re-established equilibrium but it was after the next match, at home to Sheffield Wednesday on 10 April, that hardcore fans began to believe, truly believe, that this was the year in which the championship agony would end.

Their nerves clearly jangling, the Reds played with little fluency and midway through the second half, after a lengthy delay caused by injury to the referee, they fell behind to John Sheridan's penalty. Thereafter they pushed forward relentlessly, but it looked as if Wednesday would hold out until Steve Bruce nodded an equalizer in the 86th minute. Old Trafford rocked with relief, yet there was yet more euphoria in store, no less than eight minutes into added time, when Pallister's deflected cross was met by the head of Bruce and Ferguson's men had plundered an unlikely victory. United's joy was personified unforgettably by Brian Kidd, on his knees in ecstasy at the barely credible climax, and their soaring morale carried them to further wins over Coventry, Chelsea and Crystal Palace, leaving them on the very brink of their hearts' desire.

Now one more victory, at home to Blackburn, would be enough to clinch the prize, but in the event it wasn't necessary. When lowly Oldham shattered the formbook by winning at Villa Park on Sunday 2 May they crowned Manchester United as champions, the news being conveyed to Alex Ferguson on a Cheshire golf course where he had elected to spend the afternoon rather than endure the purgatory of watching the drama unfold.

Accordingly the following night's date with Kenny Dalglish's Rovers was turned into a coronation, perhaps the most tumultuous outpouring of joy even Old Trafford had ever witnessed. Pallister talked of emerging from the tunnel to be engulfed by a tidal wave of happiness and relief: 'It was like a huge burden had been lifted from the supporters. At last, after 26 years, United would no longer be ridiculed as the massive club that couldn't take the title. Now people could hold their heads high again. As for the game, it went by in a flash, and it was a special moment for me when I became the last of our regular outfielders to score a league goal. But it was the club's triumph which really mattered.'

## Champions at Last

Appropriately the trophy was received jointly by current captain Steve Bruce and predecessor Bryan Robson, whose appearances were now rationed by age, but who richly deserved this accolade for all his noble striving down the years. United's core players in that landmark term were goalkeeper Peter Schmeichel, full backs Paul Parker and Denis Irwin, central defenders Steve Bruce and Gary Pallister, midfielders Paul Ince and Brian McClair, wingers Ryan Giggs and Lee Sharpe with a major contribution from Andrei Kanchelskis, and frontmen Mark Hughes and Eric Cantona. Medals went also to the indomitable Robson, fellow midfielders Mike Phelan and Darren Ferguson (the manager's son) and to faithful utility man Clayton Blackmore. It was a stellar line-up, but Ferguson knew the importance of recruitment from a position of strength, so that summer he paid Nottingham Forest a British record £3.75 million for Roy Keane, a young Irish midfield dynamo, disarmingly self-deprecating about his talent, yet chillingly single-minded in pursuit of success.

Thus fortified, and with the unfortunate McClair losing his regular pace to the new arrival, United moved smoothly to the top of the league table in August. They underlined their domestic pre-eminence in September with a home triumph over Arsenal, then their nearest challengers, secured with a spectacular Cantona piledriver, and soon embarked on a remarkable sequence of 34 matches unbeaten in all competitions. Their collective ability was beyond question, but now character and resilience proved exceptional, too, as they proved in the Manchester derby at Maine Road, fighting back from a two-goal deficit with a brace from Cantona and a late winner from the powerhouse Keane. This surge could not prevent anti-climax in the renamed UEFA Champions League (formerly the European Cup), though, as they bowed out to Galatasaray on the away-goals rule after a 3-3 draw at Old Trafford. This

*By 1993 'Captain Marvel' Bryan Robson's appearances had become rationed due to age but he collected the championship cup with then captain, Steve Bruce.*

was followed by a stalemate in front of a near-hysterical Turkish crowd.

That left a hitherto unprecedented domestic treble to attempt, but the dream died when Aston Villa exacted revenge for the league disappointment of the previous term when they beat the Reds 3-1 in the Coca-Cola (League) Cup final. It was a tactical triumph for Ron Atkinson, who orchestrated a clever counter-attacking policy which flummoxed the favourites. United's Wembley preparation had hardly been ideal, having had Schmeichel dismissed during the FA Cup quarter-final win over Charlton and Cantona red-carded in successive draws with Swindon Town and Arsenal. Soon their Premiership stutter intensified when they lost at the home of their closest pursuers, Blackburn, who thus trimmed what had been a commanding lead to a mere three points.

Now, troubled by declining form and disciplinary problems, United were pilloried in the press and Alex Ferguson, for neither the first time nor the last, adopted a siege mentality, his combative utterances effectively dropping a portcullis in the faces of his media tormentors. Still his team were floundering when they faced Oldham at Wembley in an FA Cup semi-final, and as the Latics went ahead through Neil Pointon, courtesy of a rare Schmeichel fumble in the first period of extra-time, it seemed possible that a season which had promised so much might fracture beyond repair. That particular plotline had not been read by Mark Hughes. With barely a minute to go, an Oldham clearance was nodded back in by young Nicky Butt, McClair looped it on and Sparky stretched to dispatch a thunderous volley. It was more than the goal which earned a replay; it was a cathartic moment on which the campaign turned. Thereafter, sagging spirits buoyantly restored, United hammered their relegation-bound neighbours 4-1 in the

**50 Greatest Players**

**BRYAN ROBSON Midfielder**

**Born:** Chester-le-Street, 11 January 1957

**Joined Manchester United:** 1981 **From:** West Bromwich Albion

**Debut:** 7 October 1981 v Tottenham Hotspur, League Cup

**Appearances:** 437 (25) **Goals:** 99

**Left Manchester United:** 1994 **For:** Middlesbrough

**Honours won with United:** European Cup-Winners' Cup winner 1991; Premiership championship 1993, 1994; FA Cup winner 1983, 1985, 1990

United have been fortunate to have some truly great captains over the years and Bryan Robson can stand shoulder to shoulder with the best of them. Inspirational, combative and courageous to the point of recklessness, he always led by example and regularly ventured way above and beyond the call of duty in pursuance of the team's ambitions. His services cost United £1.5m when he signed from West Bromwich Albion but United manager Ron Atkinson, who'd earlier been Robson's boss at the Hawthorns, knew what he was doing. Robson was a magnificent leader, of both club and country, who demanded maximum commitment from all those around him. His career was littered with injuries and lengthy lay-offs, but he still managed to cram in more than 450 appearances for United and 90 for England.

Maine Road rematch and, after one more setback at Wimbledon, they climbed back aboard their majestic pedestal to take the title with two matches to spare.

## An Historic 'Double'

Now they were closer to their first League and FA Cup 'Double' than at any time since 1957, when their chance had been scuppered by injury to their keeper, and once again they were favourites to prevail. Standing in the way were Chelsea, who had already beaten them at home and away in the Premiership that term. Glenn Hoddle's men held their own in the first period and were unlucky not to take the lead when a shot from Gavin Peacock, whose goals had settled both league encounters, crashed against Schmeichel's bar. But on the hour mark a reckless lunge from Eddie Newton sent Denis Irwin somersaulting in the Chelsea box and up stepped PFA Player of the Year Eric Cantona to net from the spot with the iciest of aplomb, oblivious of the mischievous efforts of Dennis Wise to distract him with a bet that he would miss.

The penalty decision had been clear-cut, but six minutes later referee David Elleray was faced with a more controversial choice when Frank Sinclair appeared to collide with Andrei Kanchelskis. He came down in United's favour and Cantona sent keeper Dimitri Kharine the wrong way again with an identical finish. Chelsea folded, conceding further goals to Hughes and McClair which massaged the scoreline unduly, as Ferguson was ready to admit. For all that, his great side were worthy winners of the 'Double' and only the fourth side to do so in the 20th century, emulating Tottenham Hotspur, Arsenal and Liverpool. The Reds who graced Wembley were Schmeichel, Parker, Bruce, Pallister, Irwin, Kanchelskis, Keane, Ince, Giggs, Hughes and Cantona, with Sharpe and McClair joining the action from the bench.

The most notable absentee was the 37-year-old Bryan Robson, who ended an Old Trafford era that summer when he became player-manager of Middlesbrough. Though it was a shame that his own phenomenal peak had not coincided with an exceptional United team, at least he signed off with successive title gongs to place alongside his hat-trick of FA Cup winner's medals and his European Cup-Winners' Cup triumph. There had, however, been one unutterably poignant shadow over the Red Devils' momentous 1993-94 season, the death in January of Sir Matt Busby at the age of 84. Had he been spared, how he would have revelled in the League and FA Cup 'Double', one achievement which even he had not managed to attain. When his passing was announced, Old Trafford was transformed into a temporary shrine with flowers and mementoes, and at the next home game there was a heart-swelling tribute to the man who made the modern Manchester United. Before the players took on Everton, a lone piper gave an eerily moving rendition of 'A Scottish Soldier', then the Red Devils honoured the great man's memory in the most appropriate manner possible, by beating the Merseysiders with a display of ravishly attractive football which was far more comprehensive than the single-goal margin suggested.

Understandably happy with his senior squad and with an exciting wave of fresh talent rising through the junior ranks, Alex Ferguson contented himself with the relatively modest summer outlay of £1.2 million to sign defender David May from runners-up Blackburn. Ironically it would be Kenny Dalglish's Rovers who would stand in the way of United's title hat-trick ambitions, but the Reds, buoyed in November by the 5-0 derby demolition of Manchester City – to which the dashing Andrei Kanchelskis contributed three goals – kept in touch during the first half of a season which would nudge unimagined heights of melodrama in January.

After pondering the merits of Nottingham Forest's multi-gifted but serially turbulent Stan Collymore, Ferguson spiced up his team by enticing Newcastle to part with the free-scoring Andy Cole for £6 million plus the services of the promising Irish winger Keith Gillespie. Cole made his debut in a crucial encounter with Blackburn, which was won by a late goal from Cantona, throwing the title race wide open. Though they still trailed Rovers by two points, United were now the favourites, but three days later their equilibrium was to be shattered in well-nigh apocalyptic fashion at Selhurst Park.

## Cantona Kicks Off

During the 1-1 draw with Crystal Palace, Cantona was sent off for retaliation against Richard Shaw, which was bad enough, but as he trudged towards the dressing rooms, the Frenchman was taunted by a so-called fan, who had charged to the front of the stand to hurl verbal abuse. Eric's reaction was to launch a flying kick at the chest of his tormentor; then the two men began swinging blows at each other. When the dust had settled, Cantona was charged with assault and predictably was condemned avidly and hysterically by sections of the media, whose demands for retribution included deportation and a life ban from the game. Recognizing the seriousness of the offence, United suspended their star for the remainder of the season, but his predicament deepened when Croydon magistrates handed down a two-week prison term. It seemed a draconian sentence and Cantona's immediate appeal was upheld on grounds of provocation, his punishment being commuted to 120 hours of community service.

At the press conference after the second hearing, Eric made his famously inscrutable pronouncement: 'When the seagulls follow the trawler it's because they think sardines will be thrown into the sea.' The world was suitably mystified and, while rancorous calls for his head on a plate rumbled on, he served his sentence, earning approbation for his diligence in coaching a group of ten-year-olds from Salford schools. However, for many weeks it seemed inevitable that Cantona would never play for United again, particularly with Internazionale of Milan offering a fat contract. But Ferguson

*Andy Cole joined United in 1995 as United strove for a third successive championship. He scored five against Ipswich but United missed out to Blackburn Rovers.*

## 50 Greatest Players

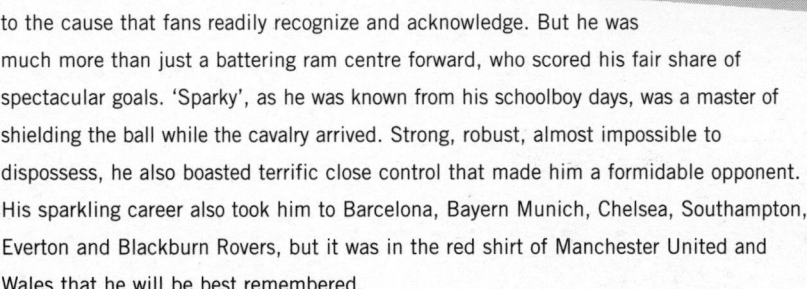

**MARK HUGHES Forward**

**Born:** Wrexham, 1 November 1963

**Joined Manchester United:** 1980, 1988 **From:** Juniors, Barcelona

**Debut:** 30 November 1983 v Oxford United, League Cup

**Appearances:** 453 (14) **Goals:** 163

**Left Manchester United:** 1986, 1995 **For:** Barcelona, Chelsea

**Honours won with United:** European Cup-Winners' Cup winner 1991; Premiership championship 1993, 1994; FA Cup winner 1985, 1990, 1994; League Cup winner 1992; PFA Player of the Year 1989, 1991

Swashbuckling Mark Hughes was idolized by supporters during his two spells at Old Trafford. The Wrexham-born striker epitomized the never-say-die-attitude and commitment to the cause that fans readily recognize and acknowledge. But he was much more than just a battering ram centre forward, who scored his fair share of spectacular goals. 'Sparky', as he was known from his schoolboy days, was a master of shielding the ball while the cavalry arrived. Strong, robust, almost impossible to dispossess, he also boasted terrific close control that made him a formidable opponent. His sparkling career also took him to Barcelona, Bayern Munich, Chelsea, Southampton, Everton and Blackburn Rovers, but it was in the red shirt of Manchester United and Wales that he will be best remembered.

pulled off the most delicate coup of his managerial reign by pursuing his tempestuous but much-needed star to Paris, persuading him that his future was at Old Trafford, where he was loved and revered as nowhere else.

Back on the pitch the Reds maintained pressure on Blackburn, notably with a 9-0 annihilation of Ipswich in March, featuring five goals from Cole, a gratifying riposte to critics of his hitherto meagre strike-rate. As United entered the final week of the season it was possible that they could retain both league title and FA Cup, but a miserable denouement awaited. Though Blackburn lost at Liverpool, United could not force the victory at West Ham which would have made them champions again, despite waves of frantic late pressure. Six days later there was more despair at Wembley where Ferguson's jaded side fell to Everton in a contest decided by a single strike from Paul Rideout. There had been no glory in Europe, either, the Reds having been ejected from the Champions League by Barcelona, having failed to come to terms with rules restricting the number of 'foreigners' in the team.

## 50 Greatest Players

**PAUL INCE Midfielder**

**Born:** Ilford, 21 October 1967

**Joined Manchester United:** 1989 **From:** West Ham United

**Debut:** 16 September 1989 v Millwall, League

**Appearances:** 276 (5) **Goals:** 29

**Left Manchester United:** 1995 **For:** Internazionale

**Honours won with United:** European Cup-Winners' Cup winner 1991; Premiership championship 1993, 1994; FA Cup winner 1990, 1994; League Cup winner 1992

The chirpy Ilford-born midfielder was one of several expensive new recruits Alex Ferguson had decided United required if they were to become capable of winning the major prizes. The years that followed proved conclusively that Ferguson's forethought had been well-founded and few of his acquisitions were more influential than Ince as United's trophy-gathering juggernaut picked up speed. Ince's midfield mastery helped United claim the FA Cup in his first season, and several subsequent trophies, but his association with United wasn't to last as long most had expected. In the summer of 1995 he was part of a shock triple departure which saw him moving to Internazionale, Andrei Kanchelskis to Everton and Mark Hughes to Chelsea.

Thus United fans faced a sombre summer, the mood growing steadily bleaker as they bade farewell to a succession of their erstwhile heroes. Paul Ince, who called himself 'The Guv'nor' and whose attitude was bothering the manager, was sold to Internazionale for £6 million; the vastly popular Mark Hughes joined Chelsea in a £1.5 million deal; and, most surprising of all, the devastatingly penetrative flankman Andrei Kanchelskis, having fallen out with Ferguson, departed to Everton for £5.5 million. The United boss was vilified misguidedly, by some of the club's own supporters as well as outsiders, especially when no star replacements materialized, and he proclaimed his faith in his latest crop of youngsters. In fact, he had ample reason for his confidence, having watched the likes of full back Gary Neville, forward Paul Scholes, and midfielders Nicky Butt and David Beckham enjoy impressive first-team sequences during 1994-95, while the even younger Phil Neville, brother of Gary and another full back, also made his entrance.

The fans were not the only people to be dumbfounded, as Pallister recalled: 'In the end Andrei Kanchelskis' exit couldn't be helped because he didn't want to play for the club any more and forced their hand. But the departures of Mark Hughes and Paul Ince shocked me; they were both major parts of the team.' After a 3-1 opening-day defeat by Aston Villa, and with Cantona's suspension having been extended by the FA until the end of September, the vultures began to gather and TV pundit Alan Hansen summed up the general opinion when he opined memorably: 'You will never win anything with kids.'

An unbeaten run of ten league games lifted the Reds into second place behind Newcastle, but an impression of fallibility was heightened by early exits from the Coca-Cola (League) and UEFA Cups at the unlikely hands of York City and Rotor Volgograd respectively, the latter knockout being tempered by a late goal from keeper Peter Schmeichel which maintained the proud record of never having lost a home game in European competition. On the positive side, Cantona marked the end of his exile by creating a goal for Butt in the second minute of his comeback match at home to Liverpool, then netting the second-half penalty which earned a point in the 2-2 draw.

## The Youngsters Triumph

Above them, meanwhile, Kevin Keegan's Newcastle were looking unstoppable, stretching their lead to ten points in January. But by early March, when the contenders collided at St. James's Park, the Reds had reeled the gap back to four points, albeit with an extra game played. The early stages of that pivotal contest were dominated by the Magpies, with only the brilliance of Schmeichel keeping Manchester United in contention. But after the interval Cantona intervened to plunder the points with an opportunistic volley, one of a devastating succession of key springtime strikes by the Frenchman as Alex Ferguson's resurgent young side gradually overhauled the tense Tynesiders to claim pole position.

As the climax approached, the Old Trafford boss used every last iota of his experience to turn the psychological screw on Keegan who duly lost his composure on live television with

*Nicky Butt was one of a crop of youngsters brought in by Ferguson from the juniors who matured swiftly to lead United to yet another championship in 1995.*

*Welsh wizard Ryan Giggs, one of United's young superstars of the 1990s who is now approaching 500 appearances for the Reds.*

his much derided 'I'd love it, really love it, if we beat them' speech. Come the last day of the campaign, the Reds needed a win at Bryan Robson's Boro to be sure of the title and, after a shaky opening, cantered home 3-0, with goals from May, Cole and Giggs.

It was a stunning achievement with such a changed team, but Old Trafford insiders were not surprised that Ferguson had relied on his youngsters, having witnessed their quality in training. Pallister again: 'They all had massive ability, but I thought that they might need more time to bed in. It seemed likely that there would be a couple of years of consolidation before we contended for the top prizes again, but they were helped to settle quickly by our group of established professionals and we ended up with a marvellous mix.'

In parallel to their third league triumph in four seasons, the Red Devils had won through to a third successive FA Cup final, and now their most intense rivals, Liverpool, stood between them and a barely dreamed-of double 'Double'. The Anfielders were suffering bad press, being dubbed 'The Spice Boys' through a perception that some of their players were more focused on being style symbols than athletes, an impression heightened when they arrived at Wembley in cream suits tailored by Giorgio Armani.

## The Double 'Double'

Sadly, the game was anything but stylish, a grim exhibition of safety-first negativity for which both sides had to take a share of the blame. But after 86 minutes, with extra-time looming, the drabness was pierced by a shaft of blinding light, courtesy of the Footballer of the Year, Eric Cantona. Beckham sent in an outswinging corner which was pushed away by keeper David James, the ball bouncing off Ian Rush and out to the edge of the box, where the predatory Frenchman was lurking. Adjusting his balance with balletic precision, he smote an exquisite waist-high volley through a thicket of defenders, whose legs flashed out unavailingly as the leather sped past into the net.

For United's Red Army of fans, it was a sequence of pure, untrammelled joy, an ultimate underlining of the 1990s shift in the balance of power from Anfield to Old Trafford. Roy Keane was crowned man of the match in recognition of the iron supremacy he wielded over a midfield which Steve McManaman and John Barnes had hoped in vain to grace, but it is Eric Cantona's coup de grace which remains deathless in the memory. United's starting line-up read: Schmeichel, Phil Neville, Irwin, May, Pallister, Beckham, Butt, Keane, Giggs, Cantona and Cole, with Scholes and Gary Neville also joining the action. All those pocketed championship medals, too, as did Sharpe and the old warrior Bruce, who had been edged out of a Wembley berth by May. Soon Steve would join Birmingham City, having devoted his great fighting heart to the Red Devils for nearly a decade.

## 50 Greatest Players

### STEVE BRUCE Defender

**Born:** Corbridge, 31 December 1960

**Joined Manchester United:** 1987 **From:** Norwich City

**Debut:** 19 December 1987 v Portsmouth, League

**Appearances:** 411 (3) **Goals:** 51

**Left Manchester United:** 1996 **For:** Birmingham City

**Honours won with United:** European Cup-Winners' Cup winner 1991; Premiership championship 1993, 1994, 1996; FA Cup winner 1990, 1994; League Cup winner 1992

When United finally ended the long wait to recapture the league title in 1993, could there have been a more appropriate pairing than Steve Bruce and Bryan Robson to collect the massive trophy? Bruce succeeded Robson as Reds' skipper and he shared so many of his predecessor's warrior-like attributes. But, again like Robson, there was much more to Bruce than just an aptitude for getting stuck in. He was a striker in his Gillingham days and he retained an eye for goal during his sojourn at Old Trafford, famously scoring twice in the closing stages against Sheffield Wednesday in April 1993 when vital title points appeared to be slipping away. United won 2-1 and went on to seal their first championship in 25 years.

With so much thrusting youth in evidence, it surprised many observers when Ferguson played the transfer market quite so robustly in the close season, but with the 'foreigners' rules for European competition being relaxed, he believed he could improve his squad significantly by an injection of overseas talent. The newcomers were flankman Karel Poborsky, who had starred for the Czech Republic during Euro '96; Dutch forward Jordi Cruyff, son of the great Johan; Norwegian defender Ronny Johnsen and his countryman Ole Gunnar Solskjaer, a rookie marksman; and goalkeeper Raimond van der Gouw, another Dutchman.

Yet the man he coveted most, Blackburn and England centre forward Alan Shearer, escaped Fergie's clutches, instead joining Newcastle with whom he was soon to endure a 4-0 thrashing from United in the Charity Shield. It was an auspicious start to the new term for the champions and an extra gloss was added in the opening Premiership game, a 3-0 victory rounded off with a strike by David Beckham from inside his own half. As with George Best and his sombrero some 30 years earlier, that was the defining moment in a young footballer's ascendancy to a celebrity which was to stretch way beyond the confines of sport.

## 50 Greatest Players

**ERIC CANTONA Forward**

**Born:** Paris, 24 May 1966

**Joined Manchester United:** 1992 **From:** Leeds United

**Debut:** 6 December 1992 v Manchester City, League

**Appearances:** 184 (1) **Goals:** 82

**Left Manchester United:** 1997 (retired)

**Honours won with United:** Premiership championship 1993, 1994, 1996, 1997; FA Cup winner 1994, 1996; PFA Player of the Year 1994; FWA Footballer of the Year 1996

If there is a single defining moment when United were transformed from being a good side to one capable of winning titles it was when Eric Cantona crossed the Pennines. Cantona's surprise transfer from Leeds United, which came about following a chance enquiry, cost a measly £1.2 million. Leeds supporters were up in arms, and no wonder, for Cantona had just helped them to pip United to the last Division One title under the old format. They surely felt that he was about to lead them into a golden era, but instead he was all set to become their fiercest rival's 'Messiah'. And their worst fears were to be dramatically realized over the next few years. Cantona stayed for four and a half seasons, in which time United claimed four FA Premier League titles and triumphed twice in the FA Cup. A football genius and singular character, he was frequently in scrapes with authority after allowing his Gallic passion to get out of control.

At that point in the new campaign it was being predicted freely that the Reds would romp away with yet another championship, and Solskjaer's emergence ahead of schedule as a goal-scoring gem – he had been viewed by Ferguson as a long-term investment – did nothing to lessen that impression. But the perspective altered dramatically with an autumn blip which encompassed successive league beatings by Newcastle (5-0), Southampton (6-3) and Chelsea (2-1), precipitating a drop to seventh place in the Premiership table, and by the loss of the 40-year undefeated home record in Europe, to Fenerbahce of Turkey, four days on from the Dell debacle.

Mounting unease was heightened by home and away Champions League defeats by Juventus, and by multiple injury problems, but United dug in to gain the Premiership summit by January. Indeed, after the Chelsea setback in early November, they did not lose again in the League until March and went a long way towards clinching another championship with a rousing 3-1 triumph at Anfield in mid April. The hero of that particular hour was Gary Pallister, who netted with two powerful headers from Beckham corners. Eventually, though the next two games were drawn, the title was claimed on a night when United weren't in action but Newcastle and Liverpool both faltered, and with two matches to spare.

The European arena, meanwhile, produced one of the performances of the season when an accomplished Porto side were humbled 4-0 at Old Trafford in the first leg of a Champions League quarter-final, but bitter anti-climax ensued in the form of two single-goal defeats by Borussia Dortmund in the semi-final. That was hard to take because the Reds played the more convincing football over the two legs, but enjoyed no luck in front of goal.

The most stunning shock of 1996-97, however, was delivered after the final ball had been kicked. Eric Cantona announced his retirement a few days before his 31st birthday. Having been the catalyst in Manchester United's return to the pinnacle of the English game, and an inspiration to a new generation of stars such as Beckham and Scholes, he had opted to leave while still at the top, before his lustre had dimmed appreciably. Only few footballers, even those who ply their trade at Old Trafford, attain genuine greatness, but none could reasonably dispute the Frenchman's fitness for such an accolade.

Some pundits reckoned that without their Gallic talisman, the Red Devils would be ordinary, but that theory was scarcely borne out by events. True, there was a stutter in 1997-98, and certainly an onerous burden was carried by the man brought in to fill the breach, Teddy Sheringham. Ferguson was at pains to stress that he was not a direct replacement for Cantona, though plainly that assertion was merely to lift the pressure on Teddy. In fact, the

*Teddy Sheringham was brought in to step in to the boots of the departing Cantona – a tall order that he eventually fulfilled to become another United hero.*

experienced £3.5 million acquisition from Tottenham was a tall, skilful and imaginative attacker who flourished most freely when playing alongside a more direct front-runner; just like Eric. Teddy made an inauspicious start, missing a penalty against his former employers on his debut, and although his lavish all-round quality was never in doubt, his form was variable during his first Old Trafford term, and he was fastened upon as a scapegoat by many disillusioned fans. His day would come.

Injuries scarred the opening to the campaign. The underrated Ronny Johnsen's absence was covered by the £5 million arrival of his fellow Norwegian Henning Berg from Blackburn, but the September loss therough injury of vastly influential skipper Roy Keane for the remainder of the season was a crushing blow. Only four days after the Irishman's exit, however, United produced a thrilling display to overcome Juventus 3-2 at Old Trafford, and by late autumn they had qualified for the Champions League quarter-finals. They shone in the Premiership, too, and when Phil Neville's first senior goal secured victory at Stamford Bridge on the last day of February, they topped the table by 11 points from Blackburn and 12 from Arsenal.

Arsène Wenger's men did have three games in hand, though, and now they hit a vein of relentless form, including a victory at Old Trafford, which carried them to a richly deserved League and FA Cup 'Double'. United didn't fall apart – far from it, they lost only two of their last 14 league games – but, hard hit by further fitness problems, they could not meet the Gunners' irresistible surge. Europe, too, brought dismay, with a tame last-eight knockout by Monaco on the away-goals regulation, and those who had forecast that Cantona's departure would presage the crumbling of Ferguson's empire trumpeted their vindication. As it turned out, their prophecies of doom proved a tad unreliable.

## Chapter Thirteen: 1998-2001 The Treble and More

Manchester United had just endured only their second trophyless term in nine years, and Alex Ferguson was not going to take it lying down, though even he could hardly have foreseen the melodramatic, controversial, incandescently unforgettable campaign that was in store. As he licked his wounds and surveyed his forces in the summer of 1998, the endlessly ambitious Old Trafford boss bade farewell to two much-decorated stalwarts of the past decade – Gary Pallister rejoining Boro for £2 million and Brian McClair departing to Motherwell – and spent a little matter of £28 million on three newcomers to freshen a squad already dripping in talent.

First to arrive was Jaap Stam, a mountainous warrior of a centre half described by his fellow Dutchman Johan Cruyff as the most complete defender in the world, and he became the most costly when United paid PSV Eindhoven £10.75 million to secure his signature. With his Goliath-like frame, rugged features and stonily imperious on-pitch demeanour, he was the epitome of an old-fashioned stopper, but he was quick, intelligent and skilful, too, and after a briefly traumatic acclimatization to the frenetic nature of the English game, he became a cult idol with the fans.

Next in was Swedish international Jesper Blomqvist, identified as ideal left-flank cover for the virtually irreplaceable Ryan Giggs, whose injury absences had proved costly during 1997-98. Blomqvist's £4.4 million acquisition from Parma was applauded by all who recalled his tormenting of poor David May when the Reds had stumbled against Gothenburg in November 1994, and though he never

*Dutchman Jaap Stam was a colossus in defence and became a huge favourite with the fans.*

## 50 Greatest Players

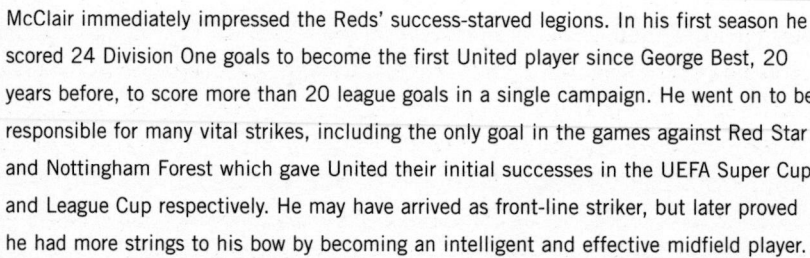

**BRIAN McCLAIR Forward**

**Born:** Airdrie, 8 December 1963

**Joined Manchester United:** 1987 **From:** Celtic

**Debut:** 15 August 1987 v Southampton, League

**Appearances:** 399 (72) **Goals:** 127

**Left Manchester United:** 1998 **For:** Motherwell

**Honours won with United:** European Cup-Winners' Cup winner 1991; Premiership championship 1993, 1994, 1996,1997; FA Cup winner 1990, 1994; League Cup winner 1992

When he arrived at United McClair had already proved himself as a top-line striker after stacking up an impressive haul of goals in Celtic's famous green hoops. When the call came to head south and try his luck at Old Trafford the lure proved irresistible. United supporters know a class act when they see one and McClair immediately impressed the Reds' success-starved legions. In his first season he scored 24 Division One goals to become the first United player since George Best, 20 years before, to score more than 20 league goals in a single campaign. He went on to be responsible for many vital strikes, including the only goal in the games against Red Star and Nottingham Forest which gave United their initial successes in the UEFA Super Cup and League Cup respectively. He may have arrived as front-line striker, but later proved he had more strings to his bow by becoming an intelligent and effective midfield player.

touched the heights of wizardry of which he was capable, he proved an admirable deputy before injury curtailed his Old Trafford future. The most expensive of the three acquisitions was also the most perplexing to many. Though Dwight Yorke was seen as a high-quality striker who had done well in his nine years with Aston Villa, United had been expected to enlist a member of the international glitterati, the likes of Patrick Kluivert or Gabriel Batistuta. The signing of the effervescent Tobagan was greeted with widespread scepticism and jibes that, at £12.6 million, he was horrendously over-priced.

Arguably more telling than any of the recent purchases, though, was the welcome return to fitness of captain Roy Keane, whose absence with knee ligament damage throughout most of the previous term had been grievously debilitating to the quest for silverware. And then there was the Beckham factor. Following his sending off for a fleeting moment of daft but scarcely malicious petulance against Argentina during the World Cup finals, he was vilified hysterically in the tabloid press and by rival fans. As the new campaign loomed, two pertinent questions hung over the wondrously gifted but tediously hyped midfielder. How would be cope with the constant denigration? And how would it affect Manchester United?

The season began a few days earlier than usual because the Reds, having been nudged from their title perch, were required to take part in a Champions League qualifying round before entering the competition proper. Duly they dispatched the Polish side LKS Lodz and set about the daunting task of re-establishing their domestic pre-eminence. On paper the opening Premiership result, a 2-2 draw at home to Leicester, looks disappointing, but on the day it felt like victory as United came from behind to claim a point with two late strikes. Satisfaction was even deeper at Old Trafford because the architect of revival was the resolute Beckham, who unloosed a piledriver which was touched in by Sheringham, then netted a trademark free kick in the third minute of stoppage time.

An immediate priority for the manager was to discover his most effective frontline pairing, perming any two from Cole, Solskjaer, Yorke and Sheringham. Initial indications favoured the Norwegian and the Tobagan, but eventually it was Cole and Yorke who gained the ascendancy, though Teddy and Ole were to contribute lavishly, too, in due course.

Autumn brought sumptuous entertainment and plenty of goals – the 3-3 Champions League draw with Barcelona at Old Trafford thrilled from first whistle to last – but a 3-0 reverse at Highbury appeared ominous, and although the Reds had risen to second place in the League behind Aston Villa by early October, there was nothing to suggest that the season of a lifetime was taking shape. Indeed, that month the team's development was shoved unceremoniously from the immediate spotlight when it was revealed that the satellite broadcasting company B-Sky-B had bid £623 million to take over Manchester United, and the board wanted to accept. The offer sparked furious controversy, with many fans and shareholders maintaining that their beloved club was being sacrificed on the altar of Mammon. A bitter debate dragged on throughout the winter until it was settled in the spring when, after the bid had been referred to the Monopolies and Mergers Commission, the Department of Trade and Industry stymied the deal.

### Peter Schmeichel Bombshell

While the financial and political brouhaha continued to rage, the players were rocked by two bombshells of far more immediate concern. In November Peter Schmeichel, widely lauded as the most accomplished goalkeeper in United's history and a colossal influence during the club's majestic march through the 1990s, announced that he was leaving at the end of the campaign. He'd had enough of the United pressure-cooker, wanted to play in a slightly lower gear and less demanding atmosphere, and saw himself winding down to retirement with a couple of seasons in climes sunnier than Manchester. Not long after that shock had been digested, another materialized shortly before Christmas with the news that assistant boss Brian Kidd was leaving to succeed Roy Hodgson as manager of Blackburn Rovers. One of the heroes of the 1968 European Cup triumph, Kidd had played a key role in United's modern rise, excelling in the coaching and all-round preparation of footballers, and proving an ideal liaison man between Alex Ferguson and the players.

Back on the field, refusing to be distracted by extraneous matters, the Reds found themselves still in touch with the Premiership leaders at the turn of the year and, having shared another six goals with Barcelona and recorded a second draw with Bayern Munich, they had advanced to the last eight in the Champions League. But it was not until January that they flexed their muscles, shook off the inconsistency which had dogged them all season, and assumed the aura of an exceptionally fine team. Middlesbrough, who had plundered

**50 Greatest Players**

**PETER SCHMEICHEL Goalkeeper**

**Born:** Gladsaxe, Denmark, 18 November 1963

**Joined Manchester United:** 1991 **From:** Brondby

**Debut:** 17 August 1991 v Notts County, League

**Appearances:** 398 **Goals:** 1

**Left Manchester United:** 1999 **For:** Sporting Lisbon

**Honours won with United:** European Cup winner 1999; Premiership championship 1993, 1994, 1996, 1997, 1999; FA Cup winner 1994, 1996, 1999; League Cup winner 1992

Peter Schmeichel, the 'Great Dane', proved time and time again that he was Manchester United's finest-ever custodian, but he also warranted a place among the ranks of the game's very best. Few people had heard of Schmeichel when he joined United from Danish club Brondby but there can be little doubting that the club's scouting network had done their work well for in no time it was apparent that United had landed a gem. He kept eight 'clean sheets' in his first ten league games for the club to set the towering standard that was to run throughout his eight years in Manchester. He played a part in all United's triumphs from that point to the pinnacle of his career when he captained United – in Roy Keane's absence – to their European Cup triumph in 1999. He subsequently played for Sporting Lisbon, Aston Villa and Manchester City.

## 50 Greatest Players

**GARY PALLISTER Defender**

**Born:** Ramsgate, 30 June 1963

**Joined Manchester United:** 1989 **From:** Middlesbrough

**Debut:** 30 August 1989 v Norwich City, League

**Appearances:** 433 (4) **Goals:** 15

**Left Manchester United:** 1998 **For:** Middlesbrough

**Honours won with United:** European Cup-Winners' Cup winner 1991; Premiership championship 1993, 1994, 1996, 1997; FA Cup winner 1990, 1994, 1996; League Cup winner 1992; PFA Player of the Year 1992

Alex Ferguson paid Middlesbrough £2.3m for giant defender Gary Pallister. He had caught the eye of several club scouts, but it was a mighty fee at the time and early indications suggested that the fans' fears may be justified. Pallister took a little time to settle, but he eventually found his feet to develop into one of the most powerful central defenders ever to play for the club. Along with Steve Bruce he formed one of the best defensive pairings to serve Manchester United. They provided a rock-solid foundation on which United began its journey to becoming the most successful club of the 20th century's final decade.

three points at Old Trafford in December, were removed comfortably from the FA Cup, then Liverpool were mugged gleefully in the same competition. West Ham and Leicester were crushed in the League, and on the last day of the month Yorke's 89th-minute winner at Charlton propelled United to the Premiership's peak, albeit with Chelsea, Villa and Arsenal in close attendance.

Early in February, Steve McClaren arrived from Derby as Kidd's replacement after spending his final game with the Rams in the Old Trafford dugout, where he witnessed another Yorke decider. The new coach's first United experience was of the euphoric variety, an 8-1 mangling of Nottingham Forest at the City Ground to which the quicksilver Ole Gunnar Solskjaer contributed four goals in 11 electrifying minutes as a late substitute. Afterwards Forest and former United boss Ron Atkinson summed up ruefully: 'Good job they didn't put him on earlier or we'd really have been in trouble!' Certainly the Reds were reaping a bountiful benefit from Solskjaer's refusal to join Tottenham earlier in the season, even though the clubs had agreed a £5 million fee.

After Kevin Keegan's Fulham, the runaway leaders of the Second Division, had been overcome in the fifth round of the FA Cup, the Reds continued to

**Great Matches**

**FA CUP, FOURTH ROUND** — **Old Trafford, 24 January 1999**

**Manchester United 2** — **Liverpool 1** — **Attendance: 54,591**

| Manchester United 2 | Liverpool 1 |
|---|---|
| Yorke | Owen |
| Solskjaer | |

Here was a contest which began for United fans in stunned dismay and ended in euphoria. Having lorded it over their Merseyside rivals in recent years, and having surged ahead of new Anfield boss Gérard Houllier's men in the latest race for the league title, the Red Devils kicked off as clear favourites to reach the fifth round of the FA Cup. But Liverpool confounded expectations by a whirlwind opening which climaxed when Heggem galloped down the right flank and delivered a deep cross which fell between three markers for Owen to nod past Schmeichel. Thereafter United took a stranglehold on proceedings, dominating possession and creating plenty of chances, but without managing to break through. Twice Keane rattled the visitors' woodwork, but both times the ball was scrambled to safety and it seemed they were fated not to score.

But with only two minutes remaining Redknapp fouled Johnsen and Beckham flighted a free kick to Cole, whose neatly-cushioned header presented the lurking Yorke with a routine tap-in. Old Trafford almost exploded with a roar of communal relief, yet it was but the merest whisper compared with the stentorian frenzy still in store. Deep in injury time Stam pumped a pass to Scholes in the Liverpool box and the ball squirted free to Solskjaer, who swerved past a challenge before unloosing a low left-footer which beat James at his near post. Cue unbridled bedlam. For United supporters, no matter how long in the tooth, there can have been few more rapturous moments.

**Manchester United:** Schmeichel, Gary Neville, Berg (Johnsen), Stam, Irwin (Solskjaer), Beckham, Keane, Butt (Scholes), Giggs, Yorke, Cole

**Liverpool:** James, Heggem, Harkness, Carragher, Matteo, Bjornebye, Ince, Redknapp (McAteer), Berger, Fowler, Owen

**Referee:** G. Poll

hold sway in the Premiership and fuelled talk of an incredible treble – the league title, FA Cup and European crown – with magnificent victories over Chelsea and Internazionale, respectively, in the quarter-finals of the two knockout competitions.

When the star-studded Italians checked in at Old Trafford for the first leg of their tie, there was added spice in the 'reunion' of Beckham with Diego Simeone, the Argentinian midfielder with whom he had sparred fatefully at St Étienne during France '98. This time it was the Englishman who emerged the happier after delivering two beautiful first-time crosses, both of which were nodded home by Yorke, while Simeone's principal contribution to his side's 2-0 reverse was netting with a powerful header which was disallowed, rather harshly, for pushing. The second leg at a simmering San Siro was a test of United's character as much as their talent, especially after falling behind on the night with half an hour to play. They were not found wanting, especially Paul Scholes, who equalized with cool precision near the end, sending the Reds through to the semi-final by the aggregate margin of 3-1.

The FA Cup clash with Chelsea ran to two encounters, United dominating the first at Old Trafford, which finished 0-0 despite a goal-attempt count of 24 to four in the host's favour. At Stamford Bridge, Yorke atoned for the profligacy with a match-winning brace, including the sweetest of first-time chips.

As March ended, Alex Ferguson's side were four points clear of Arsenal, who were also their opponents in the semi-finals of the FA Cup. Once again two games were needed, both at Villa Park, to separate the teams: the first was thunderous, but the scoresheet remained blank; the replay was utterly titanic and was graced by three goals, the first memorable, the second distinctly fortunate, and as for the third, it was one of the most spellbindingly brilliant in the history of senior football's most venerable competition.

## Giggs' Golden Goal

United snatched the lead after 17 minutes when Beckham bent a sublime 20-yarder beyond his England colleague David Seaman following a deft lay-off by Sheringham. Then the Reds missed a succession of openings and were punished on 69 minutes when a Dennis Bergkamp drive was deflected past Schmeichel by Stam. Shortly afterwards a strike by Nicolas Anelka was ruled out for offside and soon the scales appeared to tip in Arsenal's favour when Keane was dismissed for a second bookable offence. United's prospects looked bleaker still when Phil Neville tripped Ray Parlour near the end of normal time and Bergkamp stepped up to the penalty spot. Schmeichel was equal to the challenge, though, plunging to his left to save and force extra-time. Though they were facing ten men, now the north Londoners appeared deflated, and when Patrick Vieira played a loose pass after 109 minutes, substitute Giggs intercepted with alacrity before dancing at top speed towards the tightest defence of modern times. The challenges rained in, five of them, but the bewitchingly nimble Welshman evaded the lot before dispatching a ferocious drive over the diving Seaman's despairing clutch. Then he was off again, chest bared and shirt whirling around his head in exultation at scoring the goal of his life when the pressure was at its most intense.

*Roy Keane, the assured Irishman who has courted controversy but driven United as captain with unparalleled passion.*

The Champions League semi-final, the two legs of which sandwiched the meetings with Arsenal, was scarcely less dramatic. At Old Trafford Juventus had taken a first-half lead, which was not wiped out until the last minute, when Giggs popped up to lash home a loose clearance from Beckham's overhead cross. Zinedine Zidane and company, having dictated most of the action, felt robbed by the outcome, but there was even more trauma in store for them in the return at the Stadio delle Alpi in Turin. The game began perfectly for Juve as Filippo Inzaghi poached two early goals, the second following a ricochet from Jaap Stam.

Now United, 3-1 down on aggregate, might have been humiliated but Roy Keane, in particular, simply would not allow it. Marshalling his troops with a fervour that evoked the memory of Bryan Robson at his most rampant, Keane was at the heart of a succession of coherent attacks and it was supremely fitting when he scored the goal which changed the face of the contest, rising to net with a glancing header from Beckham's raking corner in the 24th minute.

Jolted from the contemplation of seemingly inevitable victory, Juve hit back and Stam cleared off his own line from Antonio Conte. Then the Reds suffered a chronic blow when Keane was yellow-carded for fouling Zidane. It meant that even if United reached the final, their inspirational captain would be banned from taking part, a hammer blow which would have left most men distraught. But Keane never even broke his stride, continuing to strive passionately for a cause which was boosted immeasurably after 34 minutes when Yorke hurled himself at a cross from Cole to head an overall equalizer, which lifted the Reds into the ascendancy thanks to the away-goals rule.

Thereafter the contest reached new heights of intensity, with Yorke and Irwin both shooting against the woodwork, and an Inzaghi strike being disallowed for offside. Finally Cole put the issue beyond doubt with six minutes remaining when he clipped home from a tight angle after the charging Yorke had been felled by keeper Angelo Peruzzi. Thus United had battled back from the brink of elimination to reach the club's second European Cup final, though their joy was tempered not only by the unavailability of Keane for the day of days, but also of Scholes, who had been booked after rising from the bench to replace Blomqvist during the second half.

Yet even those personal sporting calamities to two of the top players could not dampen a burgeoning belief in the Red Devils' camp that, now, nothing was impossible. League form, though, began to falter. There were no defeats – they remained unbeaten since December in all competitions – but several damaging draws, particularly at Anfield in early May where Paul Ince's late equalizer completed the wiping out of a two-goal lead. Understandably the 'Guv'nor' cavorted with glee, relishing the delivery of a potentially decisive blow against the title hopes of his former employers. It might have been just that, but for a slip by Arsenal in their penultimate game at Leeds, though still the Reds walked a tightrope one night later at Ewood Park, when they could manage only a goalless draw, which consigned Brian Kidd's side to relegation.

Come the final day of the league campaign, Alex Ferguson's treble-hunters were one point better off than the Gunners and with a slightly superior goal difference. As United prepared to play host to Spurs and Arsenal travelled to Villa Park, the fans toyed agonizingly with permutations of possible results. It boiled down to this: United would be champions if they beat Spurs, or if they achieved the same result as Arsenal or better, or if they lost by a single goal and the Gunners drew; but the crown would remain at Highbury if Arsenal won and United didn't, or if Arsenal drew and United lost by at least two goals.

An afternoon of unremitting drama kicked off in earnest when a fourth-minute clearance from Tottenham's Ian Walker rebounded off Yorke and against a post before the keeper grasped the spinning ball on the line. Now United began to dominate, only for Les Ferdinand to momentarily silence Old Trafford with a deftly scooped lob after 25 minutes. Still there were no goals at Villa Park, but now the outcome was on a knife edge. The tension was punctured by United strikes on either side of half-time, Beckham beating Walker with an explosive cross-shot and Cole, called on as a substitute for Sheringham, putting the Reds in front with an audacious dink over the keeper. Some 15 minutes of euphoria ensued before news of a Kanu goal some 80 miles down the M6 ratcheted up the agitation level once more.

Now one error could have scuppered United's dream and, with Spurs competing purposefully, every remaining minute felt like an eternity until referee Graham Poll blew the final whistle, signalling that United were champions for the 12th time. The manager sprinted on to the field, ecstatic for the title's sake alone, but mindful also of the incalculable psychological boost it would provide for the two finals which lay ahead in the next ten days. As he said: 'We have a great chance now of landing the treble. We are in fantastic shape. This is our 60th game of the season but we are fit and fresh and the whole place is alive.'

## Two Down, One to Go

United's FA Cup opponents were Ruud Gullit's Newcastle, who had struggled in the Premiership and were not expected to offer a significant obstacle at Wembley. That perspective altered briefly when Keane limped away from an early challenge by Gary Speed and left the action after only nine minutes, but only 96 seconds later his replacement, Sheringham, had opened the scoring following a neat one-two interchange of passes with Scholes. Shortly after the interval the two combined again and this time it was the little redhead firing past Steve Harper. The Magpies never got off the ground as an attacking force and the favourites won at a canter – two down and one to go.

Though Manchester United had now secured their third League and FA Cup 'Double', more than any other club, the squad left Wembley consumed by feelings of anticipation rather than fulfilment. Dominating their thoughts was a certain date with Bayern Munich in Barcelona, four days hence. Everyone involved, certainly Alex Ferguson, was acutely aware that they had a unique opportunity to create history and, after arriving in Spain by Concorde, he showed he was abnormally on edge by raging at fans for pestering his players, an outburst for which he duly apologized. By now Ferguson's defence and front pair virtually selected themselves if fit, but he faced a taxing midfield poser due to the suspension of Keane and Scholes. Eventually he opted for Beckham and Butt in the centre, with Giggs on the right and Blomqvist on the left, and while that didn't achieve the enchanting fluency which had become United's hallmark, no one was complaining in the wake of the fairytale triumph over Bayern on the 90th anniversary of Sir Matt Busby's birth.

How appropriate it was that Peter Schmeichel, an unmistakable symbol of the modern Reds' pre-eminence and skipper for the night in the absence of Keane, should receive the gigantic trophy at the end of his valedictory appearance for Manchester United. And how gloriously inappropriate, but vastly entertaining, when substitute David May, who took no part in the action, orchestrated the uproarious post-match celebrations, conducting the crowd in their joyous anthems and ensconcing himself as the unavoidable focal point of the subsequent group photograph. It was a barely credible climax to an epic season studded with classic team performances, staggering comebacks and exquisite individual displays. Sometimes silverware can be accumulated in a clinical manner, but that was never an accusation which could be laid at the door of Fergie's vintage 1998-99 combination.

It was a squad of awesome all-round quality, comprising keepers Peter Schmeichel and deputy Raimond van der Gouw; full backs Denis Irwin, the Neville brothers and the promising young Wes Brown, destined for a central defensive role; Jaap Stam, Ronny Johnsen, Henning Berg and occasionally May at the core of the rearguard; midfielders David Beckham, Roy Keane, Paul Scholes, Ryan Giggs, Nicky Butt and Jesper Blomqvist; and Andy Cole and Dwight Yorke sharing the striking duties with Teddy Sheringham and Ole Gunnar Solskjaer, the two substitutes whose late, late goals garnered the treble.

## European Glory and a Unique Treble

A key reason for their lavish success, according to the recently departed Pallister, was that the players knew each other so well: 'The nucleus of the side was rock solid, having been together so long. Sir Alex was able to tinker with it but he always had that core. It provided the crucial element of continuity, as at Liverpool in previous decades. Meanwhile, the young ones, Beckham and the rest, were learning and improving. It was never a question of if success would come, but when, and certainly it didn't surprise me that it snowballed into something special.'

For all that talent, newly-knighted Sir Alex faced one pressing problem as he contemplated future conquests: who would replace goalkeeper Peter Schmeichel? His eye fell on Aston Villa's Mark Bosnich, a hugely self-assured Australian who had served a brief spell at Old Trafford under Ron Atkinson, then left because of work-permit difficulties but now was available on a free transfer under the Bosman ruling.

*Peter Schmeichel, the team's rock in defence for so long and deserved captain on the night United won the 1999 European Cup.*

## Great Matches

**UEFA CHAMPIONS LEAGUE FINAL** **Nou Camp, 26 May 1999**

**Bayern Munich 1** **Manchester United 2** **Attendance: 91,000**

**Basler** **Sheringham** **Solskjaer**

Nowhere in the realm of sporting fact or fiction has a major sporting contest ended on such a melodramatic note. Despite all Alex Ferguson's careful planning, Bayern Munich had plundered a soft breakthrough after only six minutes when Basler bent a free kick – awarded for an apparently innocuous challenge on Jancker by Johnsen – just inside Schmeichel's far post. Thereafter, though, the Red Devils saw plenty of the ball, their work lacked the customary fluidity and bite provided respectively by suspended midfielders Scholes and Keane, and as time ebbed away the Germans appeared to be cruising. That impression was heightened late in the second half when Scholl chipped against an upright, then Jancker shivered the crossbar with a fulminating overhead volley.

As the clock ticked into stoppage time, United's treble dream appeared to be dead, their 11th-hour attacking sortie seemingly launched more out of habit than conviction. But then Beckham dispatched a corner from the left, the ball parted the hair of the charging Schmeichel and Yorke took a touch before a German defender sliced to the edge of the box where Giggs was waiting. The Welshman half hit a volley, but the ball fell to Sheringham, who turned it inside Kahn's post from six yards. Two minutes later, with Bayern bemused, Beckham delivered from the same quadrant, Sheringham nodded on and there was his fellow substitute, Solskjaer, to steer high into the net from three yards. Schmeichel turned cartwheels of joy and TV commentator Clive Tyldesley proclaimed: 'Manchester United have reached the promised land!'

**Bayern Munich:** Kahn, Babbel, Tarnat, Kuffour, Linke, Jeremies, Matthaus (Fink), Effenberg, Basler (Salihamidzic), Zickler (Scholl), Jancker
**Manchester United:** Schmeichel, Gary Neville, Johnsen, Stam, Irwin, Giggs, Beckham, Butt, Blomqvist (Sheringham), Yorke, Cole (Solskjaer)
**Referee:** P. Collina

Unfortunately, although the Reds romped to another title in 1999-2000 – comprehensively eclipsing the opposition, finishing 18 points ahead of runners-up Arsenal and racking up 97 league goals in the process – Bosnich failed to establish himself as Schmeichel's long-term successor. He emerged as a fabulous shot-stopper, but he proved fallible in the air, his kicking was unreliable, he was handicapped by a succession of injuries and he fell out with Ferguson. Bosnich wasn't a complete flop, having qualified for a title gong

*Wes Brown, the promising young defender who has gone on to earn several England caps.*

and starred in United's Inter-Continental Cup victory over the Brazilian side Palmeiras in Tokyo, but he was destined eventually for another free transfer, this time to Chelsea.

Doubtless his confidence had not been massaged by the August arrival of another keeper, £4.5 million Massimo Taibi from Venezia, who fared even worse than Bosnich, dropping a series of clangers and playing only four times before returning to Italy. Thus United's most consistent and popular custodian of the campaign was veteran van der Gouw who was too old to be a long-term proposition. Age was no problem for the one newcomer who bedded into the squad, Mikael Silvestre, a fleet-footed young French defender who snubbed Liverpool to join United from Internazionale for £4 million. Though inclined to lapses of concentration, he was an outstanding prospect.

## The Championships Keep Coming

Sadly, for all the Red Devils' Premiership pre-eminence, there was no chance of repeating the treble, owing to the controversial decision to withdraw from the FA Cup to join in the much maligned inaugural Club World Championship in Rio de Janeiro in January. Perhaps there was behind-the-scenes political pressure to support the FIFA-sponsored event with the aim of bolstering England's bid to host the 2006 World Cup. If so, it didn't work, and neither did the tournament, which was an overall letdown and in which United under-performed in the sapping Brazilian heat. They were not at their best, either, in their Champions League showdown with Real Madrid, being indebted to Bosnich for a goalless draw in the Bernabeu, then being taken apart by Raul and company at Old Trafford. That said, United clawed back from a humiliating three goals down to finish 3-2 against the eventual European champions.

It would be churlish, however, for the season to sink into the mists of time without due accolades to the Reds' domestic supremacy. They played some of the most rapturously fluent passing football ever witnessed on English soil,

*Mikael Silvestre, the exciting young French defender who joined United in 1999 from Internazionale.*

with the first-choice midfield quartet of Beckham, Keane (who received both major Footballer of the Year awards), Scholes and Giggs a joy to behold. The unassuming Scholes, in particular, deserves singling out, for the vision and accuracy of his distribution and his predatory eye for goal; certainly his prodigious volley direct from a Beckham corner at Bradford in March was this humble observer's strike of the season.

The 2000-01 term produced yet another tale of Premiership domination, though this time the winning margin was a mere ten points as the team slackened off visibly once the finishing line had been crossed on Easter Saturday with five weeks of the season remaining. This time the veteran Sheringham, who emulated Keane's awards double of the previous term, offered a particularly eye-catching contribution, while also it was difficult to miss Fabien Barthez, the eccentric French international goalkeeper who, in general, was as safe as he was entertaining as United's last line of defence. Sure, he caused palpitations with some of his extravagant dribbles, but for this season, at least, the flamboyant £7.8 million capture from Monaco offered the supporters thrills and pleasure in equal measure.

The highlight of the campaign was the 6-1 drubbing handed to next-best team, Arsenal, at Old Trafford in late February, the day Ferguson effectively became the first manager to claim seven English championships and the first to take three in a row. Such total command of their own league might have been less than helpful in the European arena, causing a loss of competitive edge and maybe a degree of sub-conscious complacency, as indicated by the forthright Keane in the wake of another anti-climactic quarter-final elimination, this time at the hands of Bayern Munich. A testing interlude was in prospect, but Sir Alex Ferguson's head was not in the sand; in the summer of 2001 he addressed the situation by spending more than £50 million.

## Chapter Fourteen: 2001-03
## Back to the Mountain Top

It was with a turbulent mixture of emotions that Manchester United fans returned from their summer holidays in 2001. While drooling over the arrival of world-class reinforcements Ruud van Nistelrooy and Juan Sebastian Veron they were assailed by a creeping sense of uncertainty, the like of which they had not experienced for more than a decade. Sir Alex Ferguson had announced that he would be stepping down as boss at the end of his contract in the spring of 2002 and, clearly enraged at not being allotted an appropriate post-management ambassadorial role, he had vowed to sever all connections with the club. The possible debilitating effects of a season-long lap of honour left many observers with a profound feeling of unease. Surely, they argued, given that the players' long-term futures would no longer be in thrall to Sir Alex, an erosion of his authority was inevitable.

Early indications were not conclusive. Van Nistelrooy, signed for £19 million from PSV Eindhoven a year later than originally intended because of a chronic knee injury, made an instant impact with two goals on his Premiership debut against Fulham. There was early approbation, too, for the £28.1 million Argentinian playmaker, Veron, who began his Old Trafford career in sumptuous form, being voted Premiership player of the month for September. Against that Jaap Stam, adored by the fans for his colossal presence at the heart of United's defence, was sold sensationally to Lazio, Veron's former employers, amid a fog of controversy. A

*The shaven-headed Juan Veron, left, and Fabien Barthez, above, two of the expensive foreign imports that were part of United's heady brew of talent in the new millennium.*

## 50 Greatest Players

### DENIS IRWIN Defender

**Born:** Cork, 31 October 1965

**Joined Manchester United:** 1990 **From:** Oldham Athletic

**Debut:** 19 August 1990 v Liverpool, FA Charity Shield

**Appearances:** 510 (18) **Goals:** 33

**Left Manchester United:** 2002 **For:** Wolves

**Honours won with United:** European Cup winner 1999; European Cup-Winners' Cup winner 1991; Premiership championship 1993, 1994, 1996, 1997, 1999, 2000, 2001; FA Cup winner 1994, 1996; League Cup winner 1992

Denis Irwin was in the Oldham Athletic side which took United to a replay in 1990 FA Cup semi-final. United went on to win Ferguson his first trophy as manager at Old Trafford but Irwin's contribution to Latics' exciting cup run hadn't gone unnoticed and by the start of the 1990-91 season he was at Old Trafford, his transfer costing £650,000. It was a brilliant piece of business for United as the Republic of Ireland star was to give sterling service to the club during the next 12 years. A model professional, he went on to become a permanent fixture in the United defence as the trophies began to roll in. Irwin eventually ended his Old Trafford career in 2002, but he left with a bagful of medals and trophies and an even bigger haul of wonderful memories.

popular theory was that the Dutchman's £16.5 million exit was due to the candid picture of Ferguson he had painted in his autobiography, though the manager maintained that it was purely a football decision. In his place came the timelessly classy but inescapably slow-moving French veteran Laurent Blanc, who took time to settle, while there was an unexpected change in team tactics – the use of Paul Scholes as a deep-lying striker behind van Nistelrooy, a role in which he did not immediately flourish.

Come autumn, the team was struggling and the media vultures circled, hoping to feast on the carcass of what they perceived as a fast-failing empire. There was evidence to support their ghoulish notions as the side plunged to horribly conclusive defeats against Arsenal, Liverpool and Chelsea, their three main rivals. Roy Keane's customary rants became ever more barbed, Fabien Barthez committed a succession of calamitous blunders and Veron began to look out of his depth in the Premiership maelstrom. Meanwhile, David Beckham, while thriving as England captain, became intermittently peripheral for United and briefly he was dropped. But now, demonstrating for the umpteenth time in his football life that his rage to succeed was utterly unquenchable, Sir Alex proclaimed defiantly that the foundations of his side were still solid, and duly he engineered an astonishing reversal of fortunes. Demanding and getting a simple back-to-basics approach from his players, he presided over a succession of victories which lifted the Reds from the verge of mid-table anonymity back to the heart of the title race by January.

### Sir Alex – Coming or Going?

Through it all van Nistelrooy had been unremittingly brilliant, that month setting a new Premiership record of scoring in eight successive matches, and it became increasingly unthinkable that Fergie could relinquish the Old Trafford reins while Ruud and the rest of a stellar squad were oozing such mouth-watering potential. And so it proved. Early in February the United boss announced that, with a little help from his family, he had changed his mind about retirement and that he would remain at the Old Trafford helm until the summer of 2005, at least. The team celebrated by ascending to the Premiership's pinnacle a few days later and it seemed that old order was fully restored.

**50 Greatest Players**

**RYAN GIGGS Forward**

**Born:** Cardiff, 29 November 1973

**Joined Manchester United:** 1990 **From:** Juniors

**Debut:** 2 March 1991 v Everton, League

**Appearances:** 488 (56) **Goals:** 113

Still at club

**Honours won with United:** European Cup winner 1999; Premiership championship 1993, 1994, 1996, 1997, 1999, 2000, 2001, 2003; FA Cup winner 1994, 1996, 1999; League Cup winner 1992

Who has been United's greatest-ever Welsh-born player? Along with Billy Meredith and Mark Hughes, Ryan Giggs is a likely candidate. Giggs attracted superstar status from the earliest days of his senior career. Widely tipped to be the new George Best, it was a burden which never really bothered the young winger who was born in Cardiff, but grew up in Salford. Giggs was too busy becoming the one of the most exciting players of his generation. Having said that it, was easy to see how people were thinking because Giggs, like Best, could change the course of a game on his own. His extra-time winner in the 1999 FA Cup semi-final against Arsenal at Villa Park was unforgettable. Ryan Giggs is one of United's finest-ever players and a terrifically loyal servant.

In the event it was not quite that simple as springtime injuries to Keane and Beckham disrupted the smooth-running of the Red machine, and an exceptionally fine Arsenal side won both Premier League and FA Cup. The loss of the title was especially galling, as the Gunners clinched the crown with a 1-0 triumph at Old Trafford, while there was despair on the European front, too, in the form of a Champions League semi-final exit to Bayer Leverkusen on the away-goals rule. Thus ended Fergie's dream of ultimate glory in his hometown of Glasgow, where the final was being played. Still, considering the depth of the so-called crisis a few months earlier, Manchester United were hardly in disastrous shape to confront the 2002-03 campaign. True, the stability of Keane, for so long the heartbeat of the side, was being questioned in the light of both his unedifying World Cup fall-out with Republic of Ireland manager Mick McCarthy, and controversy over his new book, but the £30 million purchase of Leeds centre half Rio Ferdinand, who had excelled for England in Japan, offered at least a partial antidote to any qualms among supporters.

With Dwight Yorke having followed Andy Cole to Blackburn, United commenced with only three recognized front-line strikers – van Nistelrooy, Solskjaer and Diego Forlan, a Uruguayan international signed for £6.9

**50 Greatest Players**

**DAVID BECKHAM Midfielder**

**Born:** Leytonstone, 2 May 1975

**Joined Manchester United:** 1991 **From:** Juniors

**Debut:** 23 September 1992 v Brighton & Hove Albion, League Cup

**Appearances:** 356 (38) **Goals:** 85

**Left Manchester United:** 2003 **For:** Real Madrid

**Honours won with United:** European Cup winner 1999; Premiership championship 1996, 1997, 1999, 2000, 2001, 2003; FA Cup winner 1996, 1999

David Beckham's links with Manchester United, which stretched back to his schooldays in Leytonstone, London, were severed in June 2003 after he agreed to join Spanish giants Real Madrid. The transfer followed months of intense media attention. The realization that United were prepared to release their most famous player split the club's supporters, but it wasn't the first time that the departure of a big name had caused a stir and it won't be the last. Beckham, a member of United's famous 1992 FA Youth Cup winning side that was dubbed the 'Dream Team', will always have a place of great affection in United fans' hearts because he was one of them: an ordinary working class lad for whom the dream of playing for his favourite team came true. The England captain was famed for his trademark free kicks, terrific stamina, mobility and boundless enthusiasm.

*After a brilliant display at the 2002 World Cup, United splashed out £30 million on defender Rio Ferdinand.*

million from Independiente of Argentina in January, still without a goal – but with both Scholes and Giggs able to fill forward positions, no further recruits were deemed necessary.

All too soon the Reds, and the rest of the Premiership, were languishing in the giant shadow cast by Arsenal, whose intoxicatingly flowing style threatened to engulf all-comers. Manager Arsène Wenger spoke portentiously of a shift in the balance of power from Manchester to north London and suggested that his side could go through the season unbeaten.

United's problems mounted during the autumn with a succession of injuries which demanded operations on eight senior players, including Keane, whose personal trauma was exacerbated by suspension for bringing the game into dispute through his autobiography. A sorry nadir was reached in November with a 3-1 reverse at Maine Road. It wasn't so much the defeat as the abject manner of United's performance which dismayed the fans, but Ferguson, ever the opportunist, turned his side's virtual humiliation to telling advantage.

In its wake he threw down the gauntlet to his apparently jaded collection of youthful millionaires, making it clear that more failures would result in sweeping changes. Countless pundits reckoned it would be impossible even for the demonically driven Scot to revive the old certainties, and once again the news columns were clogged with predictions of his impending demise. But just as he had confounded his doubters when his back had been jammed to the wall a year earlier, so Sir Alex fed them a diet of their own gloating words in the run-up to Christmas 2002. Newcastle, Liverpool and a suddenly not-so-invincible Arsenal were beaten in quick succession, convincing triumphs over Basle and Deportivo comprised a perfect start to the second phase of the Champions League campaign and a late Forlan winner over Chelsea earned a place in the last four of the League Cup.

Gratifyingly there was improvement in every area of the side which needed it, particularly in the back line, where Ferdinand was bedding in after initial

**50 Greatest Players**

**ROY KEANE Midfielder**

**Born:** Cork, 10 August 1971

**Joined Manchester United:** 1993 **From:** Nottingham Forest

**Debut:** 7 August 1993 v Arsenal, FA Charity Shield

**Appearances:** 379 (14) **Goals:** 46

Still at club

**Honours won with United:** Premiership championship 1994, 1996, 1997, 1999, 2000, 2001, 2003; FA Cup winner 1994, 1996, 1999; FWA Footballer of the Year 2000; PFA Player of the Year 2000

Roy Keane will go down as one of Manchester United's great captains. A wonderfully inspirational and fearless leader, he cost £3.75 million, a record British transfer fee, when he moved from Nottingham Forest in July 1993, but even at that lofty price it was hardly a gamble. Keane had impressed since leaving his native Cork to join Forest and it was only a matter of time before he continued to ascend the football ladder. He developed into one of United's most influential players. Like so many outstanding players he's been prone to crossing the line between fervour and recklessness, which has resulted in several brushes with disciplinary committees, most notably the suspension that saw him miss the 1999 European Cup final against Bayern Munich at the Nou Camp. It was an upsetting end to the greatest of all campaigns for a terrific competitor who had done so much to push United towards an historic treble.

problems of fitness and form, Gary Neville was consistently reliable and Wesley Brown, Mikael Silvestre and John O'Shea were excelling. They were all quick, strong and skilful, and all but Ferdinand could double as central or flank defenders, thus offering their manager plentiful options. Certainly O'Shea was a revelation, progressing as the term wore on from promising stopper to overlapping full back par excellence, one of the most dangerous attackers in the team. The delightfully unassuming Irishman showed a depth of composure which belied his callow years, and a quickness of feet remarkable for a fellow of such towering stature. Meanwhile, his versatility extended to a dominating performance in central midfield against Burnley in the League Cup and eventually that might prove to be his best position.

United's gathering momentum was jolted by yuletide reverses against Blackburn and Middlesbrough, but the New Year confirmed the generally optimistic trend. Now that footballing thoroughbred Paul Scholes, having put nagging fitness difficulties behind him, entered a vein of sumptuous form, passing like a god and scoring in six successive games, his creative influence on the team was not dissimilar to that of Eric Cantona during the previous decade. However, with Arsenal still purring ominously at the Premiership summit, it seemed that knockout competitions might offer the most realistic chance of silverware, but disillusion was in store. In the FA Cup the Gunners won with worrying ease at Old Trafford, after which Ferguson demonstrated the depth of his frustration by swinging his foot at a stray boot, sending it flying across the dressing room and cutting the eyebrow of David Beckham in the process. It was a pure accident, but that did not prevent a media hue-and-cry which elbowed the Iraq crisis off the front pages of less discriminating tabloids.

Of more concern was the Worthington Cup Final defeat to Liverpool, who enjoyed the bounce of the ball in an entertaining encounter at the Millennium Stadium, though the ultimate priority was Europe. With the Champions League final due to be staged at Old Trafford, an inevitable destiny appeared to beckon and hopes were fanned by two fine wins over Juventus, including a fabulous show in Turin where Ryan Giggs contributed a stunning individual goal, running from deep in a manner reminiscent of his 1999 FA Cup semi-final replay classic against Arsenal. For the often-inspirational

## 50 Greatest Players

**OLE GUNNAR SOLSKJAER Forward**

**Born:** Kristiansund, Norway, 26 February 1973

**Joined Manchester United:** 1996 **From:** Molde

**Debut:** 25 August 1996 v Blackburn Rovers, League

**Appearances:** 189 (121) **Goals:** 114

Still at club

**Honours won with United:** European Cup winner 1999; Premiership championship 1997, 1999, 2000, 2001, 2003; FA Cup winner 1999

Ole Gunnar Solskjaer was part of the influx of players which boosted United's staff in time for the 1996-97 season. Ronny Johnsen, Jordi Cruyff, Karel Poborsky, Raimond van der Gouw and Solskjaer arrived at Old Trafford within a few weeks of each other, but by the onset of the 2002-03 campaign 'Ollie' was the only one still on the United team roster, emphasizing the huge strides he made after transferring from Molde. He soon became one of the most highly-respected strikers in the Premiership, a goalscoring phenomenon with his four in 11 minutes against Nottingham Forest in February 1999 and his last-ditch winner against Bayern Munich in the UEFA Champions League final later that year among his most celebrated feats.

### 50 Greatest Players

**PAUL SCHOLES Forward/Midfielder**

**Born:** Salford, 16 November 1974

**Joined Manchester United:** 1991 **From:** Juniors

**Debut:** 21 September 1994 v Port Vale, League Cup

**Appearances:** 298 (77) **Goals:** 101

Still at club

**Honours won with United:** Premiership championship 1996, 1997, 1999, 2000, 2001, 2003; FA Cup 1996, 1999

Many believe that Paul Scholes has developed into one of the best midfielders in the Premiership and could comfortably hold his own with the best the world has to offer. Perhaps it was Scholes' almost retiring demeanour that deceived many into deducing that he was probably not quite top bracket material. Those closer to the massively-talented youngster were perhaps better placed to understand his unfussy and dedicated approach. Scholes has always been happy for his more flamboyant team-mates to get the headlines, while he quietly went about the business of evolving into one of the best attacking midfield players ever to come off United's famed conveyor belt. He has been involved in most of the club's triumphs in recent years but his one major regret was that he was missing, along with skipper Roy Keane, through suspension from United's European Cup triumph at Nou Camp in 1999.

Welshman, it was a timely riposte to critics who had sounded his Old Trafford death-knell a tad prematurely following a run of indifferent displays. The bell did toll for United, however, in the quarter-finals, where they bowed out 6-5 on aggregate to Real Madrid. At the Bernabeu they were substantially outplayed, but they stormed back at Old Trafford, winning 4-3 on the night and created more than enough scoring opportunities to have turned the tables. That said, every time the Reds moved back into contention, the Spaniards simply plundered another goal, and it was fitting that hat-trick man Ronaldo received a standing ovation from United fans when he left the pitch.

## An Amazing Fightback to the Title

That left only the league title at which to tilt and, as Arsenal had moved eight points clear on the same afternoon that the Red Devils had lost to Liverpool at Cardiff, their hopes appeared to be slim, especially given a run-in which included encounters with Liverpool, Newcastle and Arsenal. But the

Merseysiders were battered 4-0 after the early dismissal of defender Sami Hyypia, a Scholes hat-trick was the centrepiece of a phenomenal 6-2 raid on St. James's Park and the Gunners were outplayed in a 2-2 draw at Highbury.

The balance of power, to coin Monsieur Wenger's earlier phrase, began a decisive shift as Arsenal squandered a two-goal advantage to draw at Bolton, United saw off Spurs and van Nistelrooy plundered his third hat-trick of the season to beat Charlton. So the one-time eight-point deficit had been transformed into an eight-point advantage, albeit with the north Londoners having two games in hand. All that remained was for relegation-haunted Leeds to win at Highbury, thus presenting the title to their trans-Pennine rivals, a delicious irony on one of the most satisfying days that Sir Alex Ferguson had ever experienced, even in his marathon management stint.

Indeed, as he told a hastily-convened gathering of media after leaving his grandson's birthday party on hearing of Leeds' feat, this championship meant more than any other since his first back in 1993. The reason was the sheer scale of the challenge, after being written off so comprehensively in November. He

## 50 Greatest Players

### GARY NEVILLE Defender

**Born:** Bury, 18 February 1975

**Joined Manchester United:** 1991 **From:** Juniors

**Debut:** 29 September 1992 v Torpedo Moscow, UEFA Cup

**Appearances:** 370 (23) **Goals:** 4

Still at club

**Honours won with United:** European Cup winner 1999; Premiership championship 1996, 1997, 1999, 2000, 2001, 2003; FA Cup winner 1996, 1999

Gary Neville has been one of the Old Trafford crowd's favourites since the days when he was a member of the 1992 FA Youth Cup-winning side. His boundless enthusiasm for the club was obvious from the earliest days of his career and it has showed little sign of waning years later after he'd been part of so many trophy-winning sides. United fans are particularly fond of local lads who make it all the way to the top and Gary Neville was never frightened to nail his colours to the mast. He is best known for his appearances at full back for both United and England, but he has never looked out of place when switching to the centre of defence. He ended the 2002-03 season having made close to 400 appearances for United and with, hopefully, numerous playing years remaining he could become one the club's greatest-ever servants.

*After unprecedented media hype and controversy, England captain and midfield hero David Beckham was sold to Real Madrid. No player was bigger than the club.*

said: 'We had to overcome injuries early in the season. We bit the bullet and took the poison, deciding to get operations out of the way ready to have a go during the run-in. After that we showed great perseverance and determination. We never gave up and that's what got us the title.' The Red Devils' form and composure in the home straight was remarkable by any standards as they remained unbeaten in the League from December to May. Arsenal's perceived hubris was used cannily by the Old Trafford boss as a motivational ploy, and once the Gunners began to stumble the outcome became inevitable.

Among the 18 medal-winners, three stand out. Ruud van Nistelrooy was the star of the campaign, with his 44 goals in all competitions, including the 25 which earned him the Premiership Golden Boot. The single-minded Dutchman's power, accuracy and subtlety was melded with an almost frightening intensity, elevating him into a class of his own; he was pretty well the perfect striker. Paul Scholes, too, enjoyed a majestic term, contributing 20 goals as he moved between midfield and the front line, while his ability to spot and execute an imaginative pass was unequalled in the English game. Finally, young John O'Shea was a revelation all across the back four, but particularly on the left flank of the rearguard, giving the United attack a fresh dimension without sacrificing defensive solidity.

The others to pocket gongs were Ryan Giggs, for a record-equalling eighth time; goalkeepers Fabien Barthez, who was tipped to depart following another spell of wobbly displays, and Roy Carroll; defenders Gary Neville, Rio

## 50 Greatest Players

**RUUD VAN NISTELROOY Forward**

**Born:** Oss, Holland, 1 July 1976

**Joined Manchester United:** 2001 **From:** PSV Eindhoven

**Debut:** 12 August 2001 v Liverpool, FA Charity Shield

**Appearances:** 94 (7) **Goals:** 80

Still at club

**Honours won with United:** Premiership championship 2003; PFA Player of the Year 2003

Denis Law may not hold United's all-time goalscoring record, but he is the one who provides the benchmark by which all other Reds strikers are judged. Such is the impact van Nistelrooy has made in his early campaigns with United that it is not beyond the realms of possibility that one day he will take over as the strikers' standard-bearer. He was originally set to go to United in 2000, but a serious knee injury halted the move. Sir Alex Ferguson kept an eye on the situation and 12 months later the transfer from PSV Eindhoven was completed. A fee of £19m changed hands, but in no time it proved to be money well spent. The Dutch international was quick to display his instinctive eye in front of goal and at the end of his second season at the club had already amassed 80 goals in 101 appearances – a remarkable scoring ratio.

Ferdinand, Wes Brown, Mikael Silvestre, soon-to-retire Laurent Blanc and Phil Neville, who also excelled as a midfield enforcer; regular midfielders Roy Keane, David Beckham, Nicky Butt and the brilliant but inconsistent Juan Veron; and strikers Ole Gunnar Solskjaer and the endearing Diego Forlan, who struggled at first to settle in the English League but eventually delivered a clutch of crucially important goals, becoming a minor cult idol along the way.

### The Future Looks Bright

An eighth Premiership triumph in the space of 11 seasons was a cause for unbridled rejoicing, but while United could be proud of being the only club in Europe to reach seven successive Champions League quarter-finals, the failure to win the club game's top prize on six of those occasions rankled. However, the fans could rest assured that their club – described variously as the biggest, the best-supported and the richest in the world – would persevere with the relentless quest to merit that mighty billing, and while all sporting success is cyclical, the omens remained broadly favourable.

## Great Managers – 1986-present

### SIR ALEX FERGUSON

Ferguson arrived at Old Trafford with an impressive CV, which included a hugely-successful eight-year stint at Aberdeen, where he interrupted the Rangers/Celtic domination of Scottish football. United had recruited and dismissed several managers in an attempt to rekindle the glory years of the Busby era, but it wasn't until the Govan-born Ferguson was drafted in that the long wait was ended. And even then it wasn't immediately forthcoming. It was widely predicted that Ferguson, after more than three years in the job, was on the brink of being sacked, but he was reprieved at the 11th hour by a successful FA Cup campaign which began at Nottingham Forest and culminated in triumph over Crystal Palace at Wembley. The dam had been breached as the club, under Ferguson's incomparable stewardship, embarked on its most successful era. Eight FA Premier League titles, three further FA Cup wins, the European Cup, the European Cup-Winners' Cup, Football League Cup, Inter-Continental Cup, UEFA Super Cup and the FA Charity Shield, on five occasions, all found their way to the Old Trafford trophy room. By the end of the 2002-03 season Ferguson had been firmly installed as the most successful British manager of all time.

Even the summer sale of Beckham to Real Madrid, for a staged payment which was expected to amount to £25 million over four years, could not dent the feelgood factor, although some United insiders admitted to a tremor of disquiet over the departure after only one year of coach Carlos Queiroz, also to the Bernabeu, the technically astute Mozambiquan having been credited with recent defensive improvements. On the positive side, Old Trafford had been redeveloped sumptuously to a capacity of nearly 68,000; the Red Devils' commercial tentacles threatened to envelop the entire planet; a new raft of star signings appeared to be imminent; the lifting of the 2003 FA Youth Cup bore witness to the continued bounty of home-nurtured young talent; and Sir Alex Ferguson was committed to remain at the helm for the foreseeable future.

Back in 1986 he had accepted stewardship of an incomparably illustrious legacy laid down by the likes of Ernest Mangnall, Billy Meredith, Matt Busby, John Carey, Duncan Edwards, Bobby Charlton, George Best and the rest. He had been faithful to it; indeed, he had enhanced it immeasurably; and the desire for yet more glory still blazed insatiably within him. For Manchester United supporters from Salford to Singapore, there could have been no better news.

# THE ESSENTIAL HISTORY OF MANCHESTER UNITED

## CLUB STATISTICS

# The Manchester United Directory

## Origins

- It is widely assumed that Manchester United were formed in 1878 by the Dining Room Committee of the Carriage & Wagon Works Lancashire and Yorkshire Railway depot at Newton Heath, North Manchester. However, no documentary evidence of this has been uncovered and the precise date of the club's foundation has yet to be confirmed. The club's original title was the rather cumbersome: Newton Heath (Lancashire & Yorkshire Railway) Cricket & Football Club, or more simply Newton Heath (LYR). The (LYR) suffix was dropped in 1892. Newton Heath changed its name to Manchester United on 28 April 1902.

## Honours

- European Cup Winners: 1967-68, 1998-99
- European Cup-Winners' Cup
  Winners: 1990-91
- FA Premier League Champions: 1992-93, 1993-94, 1995-96, 1996-97, 1998-99, 1999-2000, 2000-01, 2002-03
  Runners-up: 1994-95, 1997-98
- Football League Division One Champions: 1907-08, 1910-11, 1951-52, 1955-56, 1956-57, 1964-65, 1966-67
  Runners-up: 1946-47, 1947-48, 1948-49, 1950-51, 1958-59, 1963-64, 1967-68, 1979-80, 1987-88, 1991-92
- Football League Division Two Champions: 1935-36, 1974-75
  Runners-up: 1896-97, 1905-06, 1924-25, 1937-38
- FA Cup Winners: 1908-09, 1947-48, 1962-63, 1976-77, 1982-83, 1984-85, 1989-90, 1993-94, 1995-96, 1998-99
  Finalists: 1956-57, 1957-58, 1975-76, 1978-79, 1994-95
- Football League Cup Winners: 1991-92
  Finalists: 1982-83, 1990-91, 1993-94, 2002-03
- Inter-Continental Cup Winners: 1999-2000
  Finalists: 1968-69
- UEFA Super Cup Winners: 1991-92
  Finalists: 1999-2000
- FA Charity Shield Winners: 1908-09, 1911-12, 1952-53, 1956-57, 1957-58, 1983-84, 1993-94, 1994-95, 1996-97, 1997-98
  Finalists: 1948-49, 1963-64, 1985-86, 1998-99, 1999-2000, 2000-01, 2001-02
  Joint winners: 1965-66, 1967-68, 1977-78, 1990-91

## League and Premiership Record

- Football League Division One 1892-93 to 1893-94
- Football League Division Two 1894-95 to 1905-06
- Football League Division One 1906-07 to 1921-22
- Football League Division Two 1922-23 to 1924-25
- Football League Division One 1925-26 to 1930-31
- Football League Division Two 1931-32 to 1935-36
- Football League Division One 1936-37
- Football League Division Two 1937-38
- Football League Division One 1938-39 to 1973-74
- Football League Division Two 1974-75
- Football League Division One 1975-76 to 1991-92
- FA Premier League 1992-93 to present

## Club Information

- Manchester United FC, Sir Matt Busby Way, Old Trafford, Manchester M16 0RA
- Telephone: 0161 868 8000
- Ticket & Match Information Line: 0870 757 1968
- Website: www.manutd.com
- Stadium capacity: 68,210
- Pitch dimensions: 116 yards x 76 yards
- President: C. Martin Edwards
- Chief Executive: Peter Kenyon
- Year formed: 1878
- Turned professional: 1891
- Club nickname: 'Reds' or 'Red Devils'
- Previous grounds: North Road, Newton Heath c1880-93; Bank Street, Clayton 1893-1910; Old Trafford 1910-41; Maine Road, Moss Side 1941-49; Old Trafford 1949-present
- Colours: Red shirts, white shorts, black socks
- Change colours: Black shirts, shorts and socks

## Managers

*Secretary **Player-manager ***Caretaker-manager

A.H. Albut* 1892-1900
James West* 1900-03
J. Ernest Mangnall* 1903-12
J.J. Bentley 1912-16
John Robson 1914-21
John Chapman 1921-26
Clarence Hilditch** 1926-27
Herbert Bamlett 1927-31
Walter Crickmer* 1931-32
A. Scott Duncan 1932-37
Walter Crickmer* 1937-45
Matt Busby 1945-69
Jimmy Murphy*** 1958
Wilf McGuinness 1969-70
Sir Matt Busby 1970-71
Frank O'Farrell 1971-72
Tommy Docherty 1972-77
Dave Sexton 1977-81
Ron Atkinson 1981-86
Sir Alex Ferguson 1986-present

## Records

- Highest attendances: (Stadium record) 76,692 Wolverhampton Wanderers v Grimsby Town, FA Cup semi-final, 25 March 1939
  Club record: 70,504 v Aston Villa, Division One, 27 December 1920
- Highest league position: Champions 15 times (7 Division One, 8 FA Premier League)
- Record league victory: (Newton Heath) 10-1 v Wolverhampton Wanderers (home), Division One, 15 October 1892
  (Manchester United) 9-0 v Ipswich Town (home) FA Premier League, 4 March 1995
- Record Cup victory: 10-0 v Anderlecht (home), European Cup preliminary round 2nd leg, 26 September 1956
- Most league points (2 for a win): 64, Division One, 1956-57
- Most league points (3 for a win): 92, FA Premier League, 1993-94
- Most league goals: 103, Division One, 1956-1957 & 1958-59
- Record league appearances: 606 Bobby Charlton, 1956-73
- Most league goals: 199 Bobby Charlton, 1956-73
- Most league goals in one season: 32 Dennis Viollet, 1959-60
- Most capped player: 106 England caps, Bobby Charlton
- Record transfer fee paid: £30m, Rio Ferdinand (from Leeds United), July 2002
- Record transfer fee received: £25m, David Beckham (to Real Madrid), July 2003

# 50 Greatest Players

This list is not intended to be definitive. Not many fans would agree on exactly the same choice of the greatest players ever to have donned a United shirt. The 50 listed here are our choices, taking into consideration their respective performances, their achievements as players and their dedication to the club. Whether or not you agree with our selection, it shows what a great variety of incredible talent has represented Manchester United Football Club over the years.

**No. 1 George Best (Forward)** – 470 appearances, 179 goals. One of greatest players of all-time, his brilliance was the centrepiece of United's wonderful mid-1960s side (see page 118).
**No. 2 Bobby Charlton (Forward/Midfielder)** – 759 appearances, 249 goals. Holds club records for goals and appearances – a wonderful sportsman (see page 116).
**No. 3 Denis Law (Forward)** – 404 appearances, 237 goals. The original 'King' of the Stretford End, he was an instant hit with the crowd following his £115,000 transfer from Italy (see page 115).
**No. 4 Duncan Edwards (Wing half)** – 177 appearances, 21 goals. The Munich air disaster robbed both United and England of this young giant (see page 76).
**No. 5 Eric Cantona (Forward)** – 185 appearances, 82 goals. The single most influential player in United's re-emergence as a major club during the remarkably successful 1990s (see page 162).
**No. 6 Billy Meredith (Forward)** – 335 appearances, 36 goals. United's first 'Welsh wizard', a mega-star long before the title became commonplace (see page 32).
**No. 7 Peter Schmeichel (Goalkeeper)** – 398 appearances, 1 goal. The greatest goalkeeper ever to represent United, he played a huge part in the club's enormous success during the late 20th century (see page 168).
**No. 8 Roy Keane (Midfielder)** – 393 appearances, 46 goals. Inspirational skipper who leads by example, he is a terrifically combative motivator (see page 184).
**No. 9 Stan Pearson (Inside forward)** – 346 appearances, 149 goals. Stylish inside forward who played a vital role in Busby's first great side that won the 1948 FA Cup and the league championship in 1952 (see page 57).
**No.10 Paul Scholes (Forward/Midfielder)** – 375 appearances, 101 goals. Underrated during the early years of his career he's progressed to become one of the great midfield players of his generation (see page 186).
**No.11 Ruud van Nistelrooy (Forward)** – 101 appearances, 80 goals. United's finest striker in decades who looks destined for a place high up in the club's all-time 'Hall of Fame' (see page 189).
**No.12 Tommy Taylor (Forward)** – 191 appearances, 131 goals. Strong candidate for the accolade of United's best-ever centre forward, he was the highly-effective leader of the pre-Munich forward line (see page 77).
**No. 13 Bryan Robson (Midfielder)** – 462 appearances, 99 goals. Fearless skipper who would stop at nothing to drive himself and his team (see page 154).
**No. 14 Mark Hughes (Forward)** – 467 appearances, 163 goals. Solidly-built striker, gave United marvellous service in two spells at Old Trafford (see page 157).
**No. 15 Dennis Viollet (Forward)** – 293 appearances, 179 goals. Mancunian goalscoring inside forward whose record of 32 league goals in one season still remains intact (see page 87).
**No. 16 Steve Bruce (Defender)** – 414 appearances, 51 goals. Central defender with an eye for goal, he was United's skipper in 1993 when they won their first league title in 26 years (see page 161).
**No. 17 John Carey (Defender)** – 346 appearances, 18 goals. Gentleman John was the skipper of United's 1948 FA Cup-winning side and 1952 league champions (see page 54).
**No. 18 Roger Byrne (Defender)** – 280 appearances, 20 goals. Captain of the 'Busby Babes' who was one the best full backs in the game. Died two days short of his 29th birthday, in the Munich air disaster (see page 71).
**No. 19 Ryan Giggs (Forward)** – 544 appearances, 113 goals. Another contender for the title of best Welsh-born player to play for United, he is capable of truly great feats with a football at his feet (see page 181).
**No. 20 David Beckham (Midfielder)** – 394 appearances, 85 goals. Broke the hearts of millions of United fans around the globe when he moved to Real Madrid in the 2003 close season. One of the finest free-kick exponents ever to wear a United shirt (see page 182).
**No. 21 Nobby Stiles (Half back)** – 395 appearances, 19 goals. A pocket battleship if ever there was one, proud Mancunian Nobby was an integral element of United's great mid-1960s side (see page 111).
**No. 22 Charlie Roberts (Defender)** 302 appearances, 23 goals. Captain and centre half in United's first great side in the years before the World War I, he was one third of the famous half back line which also included Dick Duckworth and Alex Bell (see page 24).
**No. 23 Harry Gregg (Goalkeeper)** – 247 appearances. Brave and spectacular goalkeeper who played in the 1958 FA Cup final barely three months after surviving the Munich air disaster (see page 93).

**No. 24 Tony Dunne (Defender)** – 535 appearances, 2 goals. Brilliant Republic of Ireland international full back who holds a top ten place in United's all-time appearances chart (see page 113).

**No. 25 Eddie Colman (Half back)** – 108 appearances, 2 goals. Salford-born midfield player who was another victim of the Munich air disaster. Hugely popular, set for a glittering career in the game (see page 73).

**No. 26 Bill Foulkes (Defender)** – 688 appearances, 9 goals. Second only to Bobby Charlton in the club's appearances list, he is another player who survived the horror of the Munich air disaster (see page 103).

**No. 27 Gary Pallister (Defender)** – 437 appearances, 15 goals. Towering defender who formed, with Steve Bruce, one of the club's greatest-ever central defensive partnerships (see page 169).

**No. 28 Jack Rowley (Forward)** – 424 appearances, 211 goals. Prolific goalscorer who played a vital role in United's trophy-winning side of the immediate post World War II period (see page 62).

**No. 29 Denis Irwin (Defender)** – 528 appearances, 33 goals. Polished full back who played a part in almost all United's triumphs under Sir Alex Ferguson (see page 180).

**No. 30 Pat Crerand (Half-back)** – 397 appearances, 15 goals. One of the best constructive midfield players in United's history, he was a member of all the club's trophy-winning sides of the 1960s (see page 106).

**No. 31 Joe Spence (Forward)** – 510 appearances, 168 goals. United didn't have many stars in the years between the two World Wars, but Spence proved the exception to the rule. (see page 37).

**No. 32 Martin Buchan (Defender)** – 456 appearances, 4 goals. Cultured, composed defender and captain, enjoyed Scottish FA Cup success in Scotland with Aberdeen and FA Cup glory with United (see page 130).

**No. 33 Ole Gunnar Solskjaer (Forward)** – 310 appearances, 114 goals. Lethal finisher who has gained a glowing reputation for scoring vital goals, such as the winner in the European Cup in 1999 (see page 185).

**No. 34 Allenby Chilton (Defender)** – 392 appearances, 3 goals. Tough centre half who gave United wonderful service during the successful years that followed the end of World War II (see page 59).

**No. 35 Alex Stepney (Goalkeeper)** – 539 appearances, 2 goals. Fantastic goalkeeper and terrific servant to the club. Collected medals for both the First and Second Division championships (see page 124).

**No. 36 Arthur Albiston (Defender)** – 485 appearances, 7 goals. Progressed through the club's ranks to become one of the most accomplished and consistent full backs ever to pull on a United shirt (see page 139).

**No. 37 Liam Whelan (Forward)** – 98 appearances, 52 goals. Had he not perished in the Munich air disaster there is every chance that Liam 'Billy' Whelan would have gone on to become one of United's truly great goalscorers (see page 78).

**No. 38 Brian McClair (Forward)** – 471 appearances, 127 goals. Followed several players in successful moves from Celtic to United. Prolific goalscorer who later moved back into midfield (see page 166).

**No. 39 Charlie Mitten (Forward)** – 162 appearances, 61 goals. Accomplished winger who won an FA Cup medal with the club in 1948 and later left to seek his fortune with Santa Fe in Bogota (see page 51).

**No. 40 Gary Neville (Defender)** – 393 appearances, 4 goals. Member of United's 1992 FA Youth Cup 'Dream Team' who went on to become a top class full back for club and country (see page 187).

**No. 41 John Berry (Forward)** – 276 appearances, 45 goals. Nippy winger, won three league championship medals and played in the 1957 FA Cup final before surviving the Munich air disaster (see page 70).

**No. 42 Steve Coppell (Forward)** – 396 appearances, 70 goals. Raiding winger who moved from Tranmere to United during their one-year Division Two sojourn in 1975 and developed into a class act of international repute (see page 131).

**No. 43 Paul McGrath (Defender)** – 199 appearances, 16 goals. Comparatively short career at Old Trafford to many in this selection, but he was still considered by many to being one of the finest defenders the club has ever had (see page 140).

**No. 44 Norman Whiteside (Forward/Midfielder)** – 274 appearances, 67 goals. Robust striker who later developed into an accomplished midfield player, but sadly had his career curtailed by injury (see page 142).

**No. 45 David Herd (Forward)** – 265 appearances, 145 goals. May not have received the accolades enjoyed by some 1960s team-mates but his goalscoring played a vital role in United's success (see page 101).

**No. 46 Jack Silcock (Defender)** – 449 appearances, 2 goals. Another great United player whose name isn't familiar to modern fans of the club (see page 40).

**No. 47 Paul Ince (Midfielder)** – 281 appearances, 29 goals. Self-styled 'Guv'nor', who joined United from West Ham and contributed enormously in the process that transformed the club into the most successful of the 1990s (see page 158).

**No. 48 Sammy McIlroy (Forward/Midfielder)** – 419 appearances, 71 goals. Great favourite with United supporters from the moment he scored on his league debut (see page 127).

**No. 49 Lou Macari (Forward)** – 401 appearances, 97 goals. Busy striker, who made an instant impression when he scored on his United debut (see page 136).

**No. 50 Noel Cantwell (Defender)** – 146 appearances, 8 goals. Elegant full back, captained United when they won the 1963 FA Cup (see page 95).

# Results and Tables 1886-2003

The following pages include details of every official match played by Manchester United. Each season has its own page and is dated at the top. The opponents played at home are written in capital letters and appear in upper and lower case for away fixtures. The date of the match, the result, score and Manchester United's goalscorers and the match attendance are also included. Individual appearance and goalscoring details for each player are shown in a separate chart. The final league table is included at the foot of the page as is a Fact File, which provides further information from that particular season's records.

The results of matches played during the war years, 1914-1918 and 1939-1945, are not included. During these years the official Football League fixture programme was suspended and replaced by regional competitions. There is also a page dedicated to pre-league FA Cup fixtures and the 1939-1940 Football League Division One season, which was abandoned following the outbreak of World War II.

In both League & Cup Appearances and Goalscorers tables the column that is headed 'others' includes matches from the following competitions: the FIFA Club World Championship, Inter-Continental Cup (Europe/South America), UEFA Super Cup, FA Charity Shield and Football League Test Matches.

**Key:** Rd – round; Q – qualifying round; P – preliminary; I – intermediate; R – replay; 2R – second replay; 1L – first leg; 2L – second leg; QF – quarter-final; SF – semi-final; F – final; PO – play-off; Grp – Group

## Pre-League FA Cup

## Season1886-87

### FA Cup 1886-87

| DATE | OPPONENTS | | SCORE | GOALSCORERS | ATTENDANCE |
|---|---|---|---|---|---|
| Oct 30 | Fleetwood Rangers | (Rd1) | D 2-2* | Doughty 2 | 2,000 |

*Newton Heath refused to play extra-time and the tie was awarded to Fleetwood Rangers.

### FA Cup Appearances & Goalscorers

| PLAYER | APPEARANCES | GOALSCORERS |
|---|---|---|
| Beckett R. | 1 | |
| Burke T. | 1 | |
| Davies J. | 1 | |
| Davies L. | 1 | |
| Doughty J. | 1 | 2 |
| Earp J. | 1 | |
| Gotheridge J. | 1 | |
| Howells E. | 1 | |
| Longton | 1 | |
| Mitchell J. | 1 | |
| Powell J. | 1 | |

## Season 1889-90

### FA Cup

| DATE | OPPONENTS | | SCORE | GOALSCORERS | ATTENDANCE |
|---|---|---|---|---|---|
| Jan 18 | Preston North End | (Rd1) | L 1-6 | Craig | 7,900 |

### FA Cup Appearances & Goalscorers

| PLAYER | APPEARANCES | GOALSCORERS |
|---|---|---|
| Craig T. | 1 | 1 |
| Davies J. | 1 | |
| Doughty J. | 1 | |
| Doughty R. | 1 | |
| Farman A. | 1 | |
| Harrison C. | 1 | |
| Hay T. | 1 | |
| Owen G. | 1 | |
| Owen J. | 1 | |
| Powell J. | 1 | |
| Wilson E. | 1 | |

# Season 1890-91

## FA Cup

| DATE | OPPONENTS | SCORE | GOALSCORERS | ATTENDANCE |
|---|---|---|---|---|
| Oct 4 | HIGHER WALTON* | W 2-0 | Farman, Evans | 3,000 |
| Oct 25 | Bootle** | L 0-1 | | 500 |

*Higher Walton drawn at home but agreed to game being switched to North Road.
**Both Newton Heath and Bootle fielded reserve 11s.

## FA Cup Appearances & Goalscorers

| PLAYER | APPEARANCES | GOALSCORERS |
|---|---|---|
| Craig T. | 1 | |
| Dale H. | 1 | |
| Donnelly | 1 | |
| Doughty R. | 1 | |
| Evans G. | 1 | 1 |
| Farman A. | 1 | 1 |
| Felton G. | 1 | |
| Gyves W. | 1 | |
| Milarvie R. | 1 | |
| Mitchell J. | 2 | |
| O'Shaughnessey T. | 1 | |
| Owen J. | 2 | |
| Powell J. | 2 | |
| Ramsey R. | 1 | |
| Rattigan | 1 | |
| Sharpe W. | 1 | |
| Slater J. | 1 | |
| Stewart W. | 1 | |
| Turner | 1 | |

# Season 1891-92

## FA Cup

| DATE | OPPONENTS | SCORE | GOALSCORERS | ATTENDANCE |
|---|---|---|---|---|
| Oct 3 | ARDWICK | (Q1) W 5-1 | Farman 2, Doughty R. 1, Sneddon, Edge | 11,000 |
| Oct 24 | HEYWOOD* | (Q2) | | |
| Nov 14 | South Shore | (Q3) W 2-0 | Farman, Doughty J. | 2,000 |
| Dec 5 | BLACKPOOL | (Q4) L 3-4 | Edge 2, Farman | 4,000 |

*Heywood scratched, Newton Heath walk-over.

## FA Cup Appearances & Goalscorers

| PLAYER | APPEARANCES | GOALSCORERS |
|---|---|---|
| Clements J. | 3 | |
| Denman J. | 1 | |
| Doughty J. | 1 | 1 |
| Doughty R. | 3 | 1 |
| Edge A. | 3 | 3 |
| Farman A. | 3 | 4 |
| Henrys A. | 3 | |
| McFarlane R. | 3 | |
| Owen J. | 3 | |
| Sharpe W. | 1 | |
| Slater J. | 3 | |
| Sneddon J. | 3 | 1 |
| Stewart W. | 3 | |

# Season 1939-40

## Football League Division One

| DATE | OPPONENTS | SCORE | GOALSCORERS | ATTENDANCE |
|---|---|---|---|---|
| Aug 26 | GRIMSBY TOWN | W 4-0 | Bryant, Carey, Pearson, Wrigglesworth | 22,537 |
| Aug 30 | Chelsea | D 1-1 | Bryant | 15,157 |
| Sep 2 | Charlton Athletic | L 0-2 | | 8,608 |

### Division One table
(Up to and including 2 September 1939)

| | | P | W | D | L | F | A | Pts |
|---|---|---|---|---|---|---|---|---|
| 1 | Blackpool | 3 | 3 | 0 | 0 | 5 | 2 | 6 |
| 2 | Sheffield United | 3 | 2 | 1 | 0 | 3 | 1 | 5 |
| 3 | Arsenal | 3 | 2 | 1 | 0 | 8 | 4 | 5 |
| 4 | Liverpool | 3 | 2 | 0 | 1 | 6 | 3 | 4 |
| 5 | Everton | 3 | 1 | 2 | 0 | 5 | 4 | 4 |
| 6 | Bolton Wanderers | 3 | 2 | 0 | 1 | 6 | 5 | 4 |
| 7 | Derby County | 3 | 2 | 0 | 1 | 3 | 3 | 4 |
| 8 | Charlton Athletic | 3 | 2 | 0 | 1 | 3 | 4 | 4 |
| 9 | Stoke City | 3 | 1 | 1 | 1 | 7 | 4 | 3 |
| 10 | Manchester United | 3 | 1 | 1 | 1 | 5 | 3 | 3 |
| 11 | Brentford | 3 | 1 | 1 | 1 | 3 | 3 | 3 |
| 12 | Chelsea | 3 | 1 | 1 | 1 | 4 | 4 | 3 |
| 13 | Grimsby Town | 3 | 1 | 1 | 1 | 2 | 4 | 3 |
| 14 | Aston Villa | 3 | 1 | 0 | 2 | 3 | 3 | 2 |
| 15 | Sunderland | 3 | 1 | 0 | 2 | 6 | 7 | 2 |
| 16 | Wolverhampton W | 3 | 0 | 2 | 1 | 3 | 4 | 2 |
| 17 | Huddersfield Town | 3 | 1 | 0 | 2 | 2 | 3 | 2 |
| 18 | Portsmouth | 3 | 1 | 0 | 2 | 3 | 5 | 2 |
| 19 | Preston North End | 3 | 0 | 2 | 1 | 0 | 2 | 2 |
| 20 | Blackburn Rovers | 3 | 0 | 1 | 2 | 3 | 5 | 1 |
| 21 | Middlesbrough | 3 | 0 | 1 | 2 | 3 | 8 | 1 |
| 22 | Leeds United | 3 | 0 | 1 | 2 | 0 | 2 | 1 |

## League Appearances & Goalscorers

| PLAYER | APPEARANCES | GOALSCORERS |
|---|---|---|
| Asquith B. | 1 | |
| Breedon J. | 3 | |
| Bryant W. | 3 | 2 |
| Carey J. | 2 | 1 |
| Chilton A. | 1 | |
| Griffiths J. | 3 | |
| Hanlon J. | 1 | |
| McKay W. | 2 | |
| Pearson S. | 3 | 1 |
| Redwood H. | 3 | |
| Smith J. | 1 | |
| Vose G. | 2 | |
| Warner J. | 3 | |
| Wassall J. | 1 | |
| Whalley H. | 1 | |
| Wrigglesworth W. | 3 | 1 |

# Season 1892-1893

## Football League Division One

| DATE | OPPONENTS | SCORE | GOALSCORERS | ATTENDANCE |
|---|---|---|---|---|
| Sep 3 | Blackburn Rovers | L 3-4 | Coupar, Donaldson, Farman | 8,000 |
| Sep 10 | BURNLEY | D 1-1 | Donaldson | 10,000 |
| Sep 17 | Burnley | L 1-4 | Donaldson | 7,000 |
| Sep 24 | Everton | L 0-6 | | 10,000 |
| Oct 1 | West Bromwich Albion | D 0-0 | | 4,000 |
| Oct 8 | WEST BROMWICH ALBION | L 2-4 | Donaldson, Hood | 9,000 |
| Oct 15 | WOLVERHAMPTON WANDERERS | W10-1 | Donaldson 3, Stewart 3, Carson, Farman, Hendry, Hood | 4,000 |
| Oct 19 | EVERTON | L 3-4 | Donaldson, Farman, Hood | 4,000 |
| Oct 22 | Sheffield Wednesday | L 0-1 | | 6,000 |
| Oct 29 | Nottingham Forest | D 1-1 | Farman | 6,000 |
| Nov 5 | BLACKBURN ROVERS | D 4-4 | Farman 2, Carson, Hood | 12,000 |
| Nov 12 | NOTTS COUNTY | L 1-3 | Carson | 8,000 |
| Nov 19 | ASTON VILLA | W 2-0 | Coupar, Fitzsimmons | 7,000 |
| Nov 26 | Accrington | D 2-2 | Colville, Fitzsimmons | 3,000 |
| Dec 3 | Bolton Wanderers | L 1-4 | Coupar | 3,000 |
| Dec 10 | BOLTON WANDERERS | W 1-0 | Donaldson | 4,000 |
| Dec 17 | Wolverhampton Wanderers | L 0-2 | | 5,000 |
| Dec 24 | SHEFFIELD WEDNESDAY | L 1-5 | Hood | 4,000 |
| Dec 26 | Preston North End | L 1-2 | Coupar | 4,000 |
| Dec 31 | DERBY COUNTY | W 7-1 | Donaldson 3, Farman 3, Fitzsimmons | 3,000 |
| Jan 7 | Stoke | L 1-7 | Coupar | 1,000 |
| Jan 14 | NOTTINGHAM FOREST | L 1-3 | Donaldson | 8,000 |
| Jan 26 | Notts County | L 0-4 | | 1,000 |
| Feb 11 | Derby County | L 1-5 | Fitzsimmons | 5,000 |
| Mar 4 | SUNDERLAND | L 0-5 | | 15,000 |
| Mar 6 | Aston Villa | L 0-2 | | 4,000 |
| Mar 31 | STOKE | W 1-0 | Farman | 10,000 |
| Apr 1 | PRESTON NORTH END | W 2-1 | Donaldson 2 | 9,000 |
| Apr 4 | Sunderland | L 0-6 | | 3,500 |
| Apr 8 | ACCRINGTON | D 3-3 | Donaldson, Fitzsimmons, Stewart | 3,000 |

## FA Cup

| | | | | |
|---|---|---|---|---|
| Jan 2 | Blackburn Rovers | L 0-4 | | 7,000 |

## Test Matches

| | | | | |
|---|---|---|---|---|
| Apr 22 | Small Heath* | D 1-1 | Farman | 4,000 |
| Apr 27 | Small Heath** | W 5-2 | Farman 3, Cassidy, Coupar | 6,000 |

*Played at Victoria Ground, Stoke. **Played at Bramall Lane, Sheffield.

## League & Cup Appearances

| PLAYER | LEAGUE | CUP COMPETITION FA CUP | OTHER | TOTAL |
|---|---|---|---|---|
| Brown | 7 | | | 7 |
| Carson | 13 | | | 13 |
| Cassidy | 4 | | 2 | 6 |
| Clements | 24 | 1 | 2 | 27 |
| Colville | 9 | 1 | | 10 |
| Coupar | 21 | | 2 | 23 |
| Davies | 7 | 1 | 2 | 10 |
| Donaldson | 25 | 1 | 2 | 29 |
| Erentz | 29 | 1 | 2 | 32 |
| Farman | 28 | 1 | 2 | 31 |
| Fitzsimmons | 18 | 1 | 2 | 21 |
| Hendry | 2 | | | 2 |
| Henrys | 5 | | | 3 |
| Hood | 21 | 1 | 1 | 23 |
| Kinloch | 1 | | | 1 |
| Mathieson | 8 | | | 8 |
| Mitchell | 29 | 1 | 2 | 32 |
| Perrins | 28 | 1 | 2 | 31 |
| Stewart | 28 | 1 | 1 | 31 |
| Warner | 22 | | | 22 |

## Goalscorers

| PLAYER | LEAGUE | CUP COMPETITION FA CUP | OTHER | TOTAL |
|---|---|---|---|---|
| Donaldson | 16 | | | 16 |
| Farman | 10 | | 4 | 14 |
| Coupar | 5 | | 1 | 6 |
| Fitzsimmons | 5 | | | 5 |
| Stewart | 4 | | | 4 |
| Carson | 3 | | | 3 |
| Cassidy | | | 1 | 1 |
| Colville | 1 | | | 1 |
| Hendry | 1 | | | 1 |
| Hood | 5 | | | 1 |

## Fact File

The 10-1 win over Wolverhampton Wanderers on Saturday 15 October 1892 remained – up to the end of season 2002-03 – the club's biggest-ever league victory.

**SECRETARY:** A.H. Albut

**MOST APPEARANCES:** Fred Erentz, Andrew Mitchell 32

**TOP GOALSCORER:** Bob Donaldson 16 (all League)

**BIGGEST WIN:** 10-1 v Wolverhampton Wanderers, 15 October 1892, League

**HIGHEST ATTENDANCE:** 15,000 v Sunderland, 4 March 1893, League

## Final Division One Table

| | | P | W | D | L | F | A | Pts |
|---|---|---|---|---|---|---|---|---|
| 1 | Sunderland | 30 | 22 | 4 | 4 | 100 | 36 | 48 |
| 2 | Preston North End | 30 | 17 | 3 | 10 | 57 | 39 | 37 |
| 3 | Everton | 30 | 16 | 4 | 10 | 74 | 51 | 36 |
| 4 | Aston Villa | 30 | 16 | 3 | 11 | 73 | 62 | 35 |
| 5 | Bolton Wanderers | 30 | 13 | 6 | 11 | 56 | 55 | 32 |
| 6 | Burnley | 30 | 13 | 4 | 13 | 51 | 44 | 30 |
| 7 | Stoke | 30 | 12 | 5 | 13 | 58 | 48 | 29 |
| 8 | WBA | 30 | 12 | 5 | 13 | 58 | 69 | 29 |
| 9 | Blackburn Rovers | 30 | 8 | 13 | 9 | 47 | 56 | 29 |
| 10 | Nottingham Forest | 30 | 10 | 8 | 12 | 48 | 52 | 28 |
| 11 | Wolverhampton W | 30 | 12 | 4 | 14 | 47 | 68 | 28 |
| 12 | Sheffield Wednesday | 30 | 12 | 3 | 15 | 55 | 65 | 27 |
| 13 | Derby County | 30 | 9 | 9 | 16 | 53 | 61 | 27 |
| 14 | Accrington | 30 | 6 | 11 | 13 | 57 | 81 | 23 |
| 15 | Newton Heath | 30 | 6 | 6 | 18 | 50 | 85 | 18 |

# Season 1893-94

## Football League Division One

| DATE | OPPONENTS | SCORE | GOALSCORERS | ATTENDANCE |
|---|---|---|---|---|
| Sep 2 | BURNLEY | W 3-2 | Farman 3 | 10,000 |
| Sep 9 | West Bromwich Albion | L 1-3 | Donaldson | 4,500 |
| Sep 16 | The Wednesday | W 1-0 | Farman | 7,000 |
| Sep 23 | NOTTINGHAM FOREST | D 1-1 | Donaldson | 10,000 |
| Sep 30 | Darwen | L 0-1 | | 4,000 |
| Oct 7 | Derby County | L 0-2 | | 7,000 |
| Oct 14 | WEST BROMWICH ALBION | W 4-1 | Peden 2, Donaldson, Erentz | 8,000 |
| Oct 21 | Burnley | L 1-4 | Hood | 7,000 |
| Oct 28 | Wolverhampton Wanderers | L 0-2 | | 4,000 |
| Nov 4 | DARWEN | L 0-1 | | 8,000 |
| Nov 11 | WOLVERHAMPTON WANDERERS | W 1-0 | Davidson | 5,000 |
| Nov 25 | Sheffield United | L 1-3 | Fitzsimmons | 2,000 |
| Dec 2 | EVERTON | L 0-3 | | 6,000 |
| Dec 6 | Sunderland | L 1-4 | Campbell | 5,000 |
| Dec 9 | Bolton Wanderers | L 0-2 | | 5,000 |
| Dec 16 | ASTON VILLA | L 1-3 | Peden | 8,000 |
| Dec 23 | Preston North End | L 0-2 | | 5,000 |
| Jan 6 | Everton | L 0-2 | | 8,000 |
| Jan 13 | THE WEDNESDAY | L 1-2 | Peden | 9,000 |
| Feb 3 | Aston Villa | L 1-5 | Mathieson | 5,000 |
| Mar 3 | SUNDERLAND | L 2-4 | McNaught, Peden | 10,000 |
| Mar 10 | SHEFFIELD UNITED | L 0-2 | | 5,000 |
| Mar 12 | BLACKBURN ROVERS | W 5-1 | Donaldson 3, Clarkin, Farman | 5,000 |
| Mar 17 | DERBY COUNTY | L 2-6 | Clarkin 2 | 7,000 |
| Mar 23 | STOKE CITY | W 6-2 | Farman 2, Peden 2, Clarkin, Erentz | 8,000 |
| Mar 24 | BOLTON WANDERERS | D 2-2 | Donaldson, Farman | 10,000 |
| Mar 26 | Blackburn Rovers | L 0-4 | | 5,000 |
| Mar 31 | Stoke City | L 1-3 | Clarkin | 4,000 |
| Apr 7 | Nottingham Forest | L 0-2 | | 4,000 |
| Apr 14 | PRESTON NORTH END | L 1-3 | Mathieson | 4,000 |

## FA Cup

| | | | | |
|---|---|---|---|---|
| Jan 27 | MIDDLESBROUGH | (Rd1) W 4-0 | Donaldson 2, Farman, Peden | 5,000 |
| Feb 10 | BLACKBURN ROVERS | (Rd2) D 0-0* | | 18,000 |
| Feb 17 | Blackburn Rovers | (R) L 1-5 | Donaldson | 5,000 |

*After extra-time.

## Test Match

| | | | | |
|---|---|---|---|---|
| Apr 28 | Liverpool** | L 0-2 | | 3,000 |

**Played at Ewood Park, Blackburn.

## League & Cup Appearances

| PLAYER | LEAGUE | CUP COMPETITION FA CUP | OTHER | TOTAL |
|---|---|---|---|---|
| Campbell | 5 | | | 5 |
| Clarkin | 12 | 2 | 1 | 15 |
| Clements | 12 | | | 12 |
| Davidson | 28 | 3 | 1 | 32 |
| Donaldson | 24 | 3 | 1 | 2 |
| Douglas | 7 | | | 7 |
| Dow | 2 | | | 2 |
| Erentz | 22 | 3 | 1 | 26 |
| Fall | 23 | 3 | 1 | 27 |
| Farman | 18 | 1 | 1 | 20 |
| Fitzsimmons | 9 | | | 9 |
| Graham | 4 | | | 4 |
| Hood | 12 | 3 | 1 | 16 |
| McNaught | 26 | 3 | 1 | 30 |
| Mathieson | 2 | | | 2 |
| Mitchell | 25 | 3 | 1 | 29 |
| Parker | 11 | | | 11 |
| Peden | 28 | 3 | 1 | 32 |
| Perrins | 27 | 3 | 1 | 31 |
| Prince | 2 | | | 2 |
| Rothwell | 1 | | | 1 |
| Stewart | 25 | 3 | | 28 |
| Stone | 2 | | | 2 |
| Thompson | 3 | | | 3 |

## Goalscorers

| PLAYER | LEAGUE | CUP COMPETITION FA CUP | OTHER | TOTAL |
|---|---|---|---|---|
| Donaldson | 7 | 3 | | 10 |
| Farman | 8 | 1 | | 9 |
| Peden | 7 | 1 | | 8 |
| Clarkin | 5 | | | 5 |
| Erentz | 2 | | | 2 |
| Campbell | 1 | | | 1 |
| Davidson | 1 | | | 1 |
| Fitzsimmons | 1 | | | 1 |
| Hood | 1 | | | 1 |
| Mathieson | 2 | | | 1 |
| McNaught | 1 | | | 1 |

## Fact File

Newton Heath lost the end of season 'Test Match' against Division Two champions Liverpool and were relegated just two seasons after being elected to Division One.

**SECRETARY:** A.H. Albut
**MOST APPEARANCES:** William Davidson, John Peden 32
**TOP GOALSCORER:** Bob Donaldson 10 (7 League)
**BIGGEST WIN:** 6-2 v Stoke City, 23 March 1894, League
**HIGHEST ATTENDANCE:** 18,000 v Blackburn Rovers, 10 February 1894, FA Cup

## Final Division One Table

| | | P | W | D | L | F | A | Pts |
|---|---|---|---|---|---|---|---|---|
| 1 | Aston Villa | 30 | 19 | 6 | 5 | 84 | 42 | 44 |
| 2 | Sunderland | 30 | 17 | 4 | 9 | 72 | 44 | 38 |
| 3 | Derby County | 30 | 16 | 4 | 10 | 73 | 62 | 36 |
| 4 | Blackburn Rovers | 30 | 16 | 2 | 12 | 69 | 53 | 34 |
| 5 | Burnley | 30 | 15 | 4 | 11 | 61 | 51 | 34 |
| 6 | Everton | 30 | 15 | 3 | 12 | 90 | 57 | 33 |
| 7 | Nottingham Forest | 30 | 14 | 4 | 12 | 57 | 48 | 32 |
| 8 | WBA | 30 | 14 | 4 | 12 | 66 | 59 | 32 |
| 9 | Wolverhampton W | 30 | 14 | 3 | 13 | 52 | 63 | 31 |
| 10 | Sheffield United | 30 | 13 | 5 | 12 | 47 | 61 | 31 |
| 11 | Stoke City | 30 | 13 | 3 | 14 | 65 | 79 | 29 |
| 12 | The Wednesday | 30 | 9 | 8 | 13 | 48 | 57 | 26 |
| 13 | Bolton Wanderers | 30 | 10 | 4 | 16 | 38 | 52 | 24 |
| 14 | Preston North End | 30 | 10 | 3 | 17 | 44 | 56 | 23 |
| 15 | Darwen | 30 | 7 | 5 | 18 | 37 | 83 | 19 |
| 16 | Newton Heath | 30 | 6 | 2 | 22 | 36 | 72 | 14 |

## Season 1894-95

### Football League Division Two

| DATE | OPPONENTS | SCORE | GOALSCORERS | ATTENDANCE |
|---|---|---|---|---|
| Sep 8 | Burton Wanderers | L 0-1 | | 3,000 |
| Sep 15 | CREWE ALEXANDRA | W 6-1 | Dow 2, Smith 2, Clarkin, McCartney | 6,000 |
| Sep 22 | Leicester Fosse | W 3-2 | Dow 2, Smith | 6,000 |
| Oct 6 | Darwen | D 1-1 | Donaldson | 6,000 |
| Oct 13 | WOOLWICH ARSENAL | D 3-3 | Donaldson 2, Clarkin | 4,000 |
| Oct 20 | Burton Swifts | W 2-1 | Donaldson 2 | 5,000 |
| Oct 27 | LEICESTER FOSSE | D 2-2 | McNaught, Smith | 3,000 |
| Nov 3 | Manchester City | W 5-2 | Smith 4, Clarkin | 14,000 |
| Nov 10 | ROTHERHAM TOWN | W 3-2 | Davidson, Donaldson, Peters | 4,000 |
| Nov 17 | Grimsby Town | L 1-2 | Clarkin | 3,000 |
| Nov 24 | DARWEN | D 1-1 | Donaldson | 5,000 |
| Dec 1 | Crewe Alexandra | W 2-0 | Clarkin, Smith | 600 |
| Dec 8 | BURTON SWIFTS | W 5-1 | Peters 2, Smith 2, Dow | 4,000 |
| Nov 15 | Notts County | D 1-1 | Donaldson | 3,000 |
| Dec 22 | LINCOLN CITY | W 3-0 | Donaldson, Millar, Smith | 2,000 |
| Dec 24 | Burslem Port Vale | W 5-2 | Clarkin, Donaldson, McNaught, Millar, Smith | 1,000 |
| Dec 26 | Walsall Town Swifts | W 2-1 | Millar, Stewart | 1,000 |
| Dec 29 | Lincoln City | L 0-3 | | 3,000 |
| Jan 1 | BURSLEM PORT VALE | W 3-0 | Millar 2, Rothwell | 5,000 |
| Jan 5 | MANCHESTER CITY | W 4-1 | Clarkin 2, Donaldson, Smith | 12,000 |
| Jan 12 | Rotherham Town | L 1-2 | Erentz | 2,000 |
| Mar 2 | BURTON WANDERERS | D 1-1 | Peters | 6,000 |
| Mar 23 | GRIMSBY TOWN | W 2-0 | Cassidy 2 | 9,000 |
| Mar 30 | Woolwich Arsenal | L 2-3 | Clarkin, Donaldson | 6,000 |
| Apr 3 | WALSALL TOWN SWIFTS | W 9-0 | Cassidy 2, Donaldson 2, Peters 2, Smith 2, Clarkin | 6,000 |
| Apr 6 | NEWCASTLE UNITED | W 5-1 | Cassidy 2, Smith 2, McDermid o.g. | 5,000 |
| Apr 12 | BURY | D 2-2 | Cassidy, Donaldson | 15,000 |
| Apr 13 | Newcastle United | L 0-3 | | 4,000 |
| Apr 15 | Bury | L 1-2 | Peters | 10,000 |
| Apr 20 | NOTTS COUNTY | D 3-3 | Cassidy, Clarkin, Smith | 12,000 |

### FA Cup

| | | | | |
|---|---|---|---|---|
| Feb 2 | STOKE CITY | (Rd1) L 2-3 | Smith, Peters | 7,000 |

### Test Match

| | | | | |
|---|---|---|---|---|
| Apr 27 | Stoke City* | L 0-3 | | 10,000 |

*Played at Cobridge Athletic Ground, Burslem.

### League & Cup Appearances

| PLAYER | LEAGUE | CUP COMPETITION FA CUP | OTHER | TOTAL |
|---|---|---|---|---|
| Cairns | 1 | | | 1 |
| Cassidy | 8 | | 1 | 9 |
| Clarkin | 29 | 1 | 1 | 31 |
| Davidson | 12 | | | 12 |
| Donaldson | 27 | 1 | 1 | 29 |
| Douglas | 30 | 1 | 1 | 32 |
| Dow | 26 | | 1 | 27 |
| Erentz | 28 | 1 | | 29 |
| Farman | 5 | | | 5 |
| Longair | 1 | | | 1 |
| McCartney | 19 | 1 | 1 | 21 |
| McFetteridge | 1 | | | 1 |
| McNaught | 26 | 1 | | 27 |
| Millar | 6 | 1 | | 7 |
| Perrins | 26 | 1 | 1 | 28 |
| Peters | 30 | 1 | 1 | 32 |
| Rothwell | 1 | | | 1 |
| Smith | 29 | 1 | 1 | 31 |
| Stewart | 21 | 1 | 1 | 23 |
| Stone | 4 | | 1 | 5 |

### Goalscorers

| PLAYER | LEAGUE | CUP COMPETITION FA CUP | OTHER | TOTAL |
|---|---|---|---|---|
| Smith | 19 | 1 | | 20 |
| Donaldson | 15 | | | 15 |
| Clarkin | 11 | | | 11 |
| Cassidy | 8 | | | 8 |
| Peters | 7 | 1 | | 8 |
| Dow | 5 | | | 5 |
| Millar | 5 | | | 5 |
| McNaught | 2 | | | 2 |
| Davidson | 1 | | | 1 |
| Erentz | 1 | | | 1 |
| McCartney | 1 | | | 1 |
| Rothwell | 1 | | | 1 |
| Stewart | 1 | | | 1 |
| Opps' o.gs. | 1 | | | 1 |

### Fact File

The initial Manchester league 'Derby' matches both ended in success for Newton Heath, 5-2 at Hyde Road, Ardwick and 4-1 at Bank Street, Clayton.

**SECRETARY:** A.H. Albut
**MOST APPEARANCES:** William Douglas, James Peters 32
**TOP GOALSCORER:** Richard Smith 20 (19 League)
**BIGGEST WIN:** 9-0 v Walsall Town Swifts, 3 April 1895, League
**HIGHEST ATTENDANCE:** 15,000 v Bury, 12 April 1895, League

### Final Division Two Table

| | | P | W | D | L | F | A | PTS |
|---|---|---|---|---|---|---|---|---|
| 1 | Bury | 30 | 23 | 2 | 5 | 78 | 33 | 48 |
| 2 | Notts County | 30 | 17 | 5 | 8 | 75 | 45 | 39 |
| 3 | Newton Heath | 30 | 15 | 8 | 7 | 78 | 44 | 38 |
| 4 | Leicester Fosse | 30 | 15 | 8 | 7 | 72 | 53 | 38 |
| 5 | Grimsby Town | 30 | 18 | 1 | 11 | 79 | 52 | 38 |
| 6 | Darwen | 30 | 16 | 4 | 10 | 74 | 43 | 36 |
| 7 | Burton Wanderers | 30 | 14 | 7 | 9 | 67 | 39 | 35 |
| 8 | Woolwich Arsenal | 30 | 14 | 6 | 10 | 75 | 58 | 34 |
| 9 | Manchester City | 30 | 14 | 3 | 13 | 82 | 72 | 31 |
| 10 | Newcastle United | 30 | 12 | 3 | 15 | 72 | 84 | 27 |
| 11 | Burton Swifts | 30 | 11 | 3 | 16 | 52 | 74 | 25 |
| 12 | Rotherham Town | 30 | 11 | 2 | 17 | 55 | 62 | 24 |
| 13 | Lincoln City | 30 | 10 | 0 | 20 | 47 | 92 | 20 |
| 14 | Walsall Town Swifts | 30 | 10 | 0 | 20 | 39 | 77 | 18 |
| 15 | Burslem Port Vale | 30 | 7 | 4 | 19 | 39 | 77 | 18 |
| 16 | Crewe Alexandra | 30 | 3 | 4 | 23 | 26 | 103 | 10 |

# Season 1895-96

## Football League Division Two

| DATE | OPPONENTS | SCORE | GOALSCORERS | ATTENDANCE |
|---|---|---|---|---|
| Sep 7 | CREWE ALEXANDRA | W 5-0 | Cassidy 2, Aitken, Kennedy, Smith | 8,000 |
| Sep 14 | Loughborough Town | D 3-3 | Cassidy 2, McNaught | 3,000 |
| Sep 21 | BURTON SWIFTS | W 5-0 | Cassidy 2, Donaldson 2, Kennedy | 9,000 |
| Sep 28 | Crewe Alexandra | W 2-0 | Smith 2 | 2,000 |
| Oct 5 | MANCHESTER CITY | D 1-1 | Clarkin | 12,000 |
| Oct 12 | Liverpool | L 1-7 | Cassidy | 7,000 |
| Oct 19 | NEWCASTLE UNITED | W 2-1 | Cassidy, Peters | 8,000 |
| Oct 26 | Newcastle United | L 1-2 | Kennedy | 8,000 |
| Nov 2 | LIVERPOOL | W 5-2 | Peters 3, Clarkin, Smith | 10,000 |
| Nov 9 | Woolwich Arsenal | L 1-2 | Cassidy | 9,000 |
| Nov 16 | LINCOLN CITY | D 5-5 | Clarkin 2, Cassidy, Collinson, Peters | 8,000 |
| Nov 23 | Notts County | W 2-0 | Cassidy, Kennedy | 3,000 |
| Nov 30 | WOOLWICH ARSENAL | W 5-1 | Cartwright 2, Clarkin, Kennedy, Peters | 6,000 |
| Dec 7 | Manchester City | L 1-2 | Cassidy | 18,000 |
| Dec 14 | NOTTS COUNTY | W 3-0 | Cassidy, Clarkin, Donaldson | 3,000 |
| Dec 21 | Darwen | L 0-3 | | 3,000 |
| Jan 1 | GRIMSBY TOWN | W 3-2 | Cassidy 3 (1pen) | 8,000 |
| Jan 4 | Leicester Fosse | L 0-3 | | 7,000 |
| Jan 11 | ROTHERHAM TOWN | W 3-0 | Donaldson 2, Stephenson | 3,000 |
| Feb 3 | LEICESTER FOSSE | W 2-0 | Kennedy, Smith | 1,000 |
| Feb 8 | Burton Swifts | L 1-4 | Vance | 2,000 |
| Feb 29 | BURTON WANDERERS | L 1-2 | McNaught | 1,000 |
| Mar 7 | Rotherham Town | W 3-2 | Donaldson, Kennedy, Smith | 1,500 |
| Mar 14 | Grimsby Town | L 2-4 | Kennedy, Smith | 2,000 |
| Mar 18 | Burton Wanderers | L 1-5 | Dow | 2,000 |
| Mar 23 | Burslem Port Vale | L 0-3 | | 3,000 |
| Apr 3 | DARWEN | W 4-0 | Kennedy 3, McNaught | 1,000 |
| Apr 4 | LOUGHBOROUGH TOWN | W 2-0 | Donaldson, Smith | 4,000 |
| Apr 6 | BURSLEM PORT VALE | W 2-1 | Clarkin, Smith | 5,000 |
| Apr 11 | Lincoln City | L 0-2 | | 2,000 |

## FA Cup

| | | | | | |
|---|---|---|---|---|---|
| Feb 1 | KETTERING TOWN | (Rd1) | W 2-1 | Donaldson, Smith | 6,000 |
| Feb 15 | DERBY COUNTY | (Rd2) | D 1-1 | Kennedy | 20,000 |
| Feb 19 | Derby County | (R) | L 1-5 | Donaldson | 6,000 |

## League & Cup Appearances

| PLAYER | LEAGUE | CUP COMPETITION FA CUP | TOTAL |
|---|---|---|---|
| Aitken | 2 | | 2 |
| Cartwright | 27 | 3 | 30 |
| Cassidy | 19 | 1 | 20 |
| Clarkin | 26 | 2 | 2 |
| Collinson | 13 | 3 | 16 |
| Donaldson | 17 | 3 | 20 |
| Douglas | 18 | | 18 |
| Dow | 19 | 1 | 20 |
| Erentz | 24 | 2 | 26 |
| Fitzsimmons | 27 | 3 | 30 |
| Kennedy | 29 | 3 | 32 |
| McNaught | 29 | 2 | 31 |
| Perrins | 11 | 1 | 12 |
| Peters | 15 | 3 | 18 |
| Ridgway | 6 | 3 | 9 |
| Smith | 28 | 3 | 31 |
| Stafford | 4 | | 4 |
| Stephenson | 1 | | 1 |
| Vance | 10 | | 10 |
| Whitney | 2 | | 2 |
| Whittaker | 3 | | 3 |

## Goalscorers

| PLAYER | LEAGUE | CUP COMPETITION FA CUP | TOTAL |
|---|---|---|---|
| Cassidy | 16 | | 16 |
| Kennedy | 11 | 1 | 12 |
| Smith | 9 | 1 | 10 |
| Donaldson | 7 | 2 | 9 |
| Clarkin | 7 | | 7 |
| Peters | 6 | | 6 |
| McNaught | 3 | | 3 |
| Cartwright | 2 | | 2 |
| Aitken | 1 | | 1 |
| Collinson | 1 | | 1 |
| Dow | 1 | | 1 |
| Stephenson | 1 | | 1 |
| Vance | 1 | | 1 |

### Fact File

The club's first-ever league meetings with Liverpool provided two high-scoring games. Liverpool won 7-1 at Anfield, while Newton Heath gained some revenge with a 5-2 success at Bank Street, Clayton.

**SECRETARY:** A.H. Albut

**MOST APPEARANCES:** William Kennedy 32

**TOP GOALSCORER:** Joe Cassidy 16 (all League)

**BIGGEST WIN:** 5-0 v Crewe Alexandra, 7 September 1895, League; 5-0 v Burton Swifts, 21 September 1895, League

**HIGHEST ATTENDANCE:** 20,000 v Derby County, 15 February 1896, FA Cup

### Final Division Two Table

| | | P | W | D | L | F | A | Pts |
|---|---|---|---|---|---|---|---|---|
| 1 | Liverpool | 30 | 22 | 2 | 6 | 106 | 32 | 46 |
| 2 | Manchester City | 30 | 21 | 4 | 5 | 63 | 38 | 46 |
| 3 | Grimsby Town | 30 | 20 | 2 | 8 | 82 | 38 | 42 |
| 4 | Burton Wanderers | 30 | 19 | 4 | 7 | 69 | 40 | 42 |
| 5 | Newcastle United | 30 | 16 | 2 | 12 | 73 | 50 | 34 |
| 6 | Newton Heath | 30 | 15 | 3 | 12 | 66 | 57 | 33 |
| 7 | Woolwich Arsenal | 30 | 14 | 4 | 12 | 59 | 42 | 32 |
| 8 | Leicester Fosse | 30 | 14 | 4 | 12 | 57 | 44 | 32 |
| 9 | Darwen | 30 | 12 | 6 | 12 | 72 | 67 | 30 |
| 10 | Notts County | 30 | 12 | 2 | 16 | 57 | 54 | 26 |
| 11 | Burton Swifts | 30 | 10 | 4 | 16 | 39 | 69 | 24 |
| 12 | Loughborough Town | 30 | 9 | 5 | 16 | 40 | 67 | 23 |
| 13 | Lincoln City | 30 | 9 | 4 | 17 | 53 | 75 | 22 |
| 14 | Burslem Port Vale | 30 | 7 | 4 | 19 | 43 | 78 | 18 |
| 15 | Rotherham Town | 30 | 7 | 3 | 20 | 34 | 97 | 17 |
| 16 | Crewe Alexandra | 30 | 5 | 3 | 22 | 30 | 95 | 13 |

# Season 1896-97

## Football League Division Two

| DATE | OPPONENTS | SCORE | GOALSCORERS | ATTENDANCE |
|---|---|---|---|---|
| Sep 1 | GAINSBOROUGH TRINITY | W 2-0 | McNaught 2 | 4,000 |
| Sep 5 | Burton Swifts | W 5-3 | Brown, Bryant, Cassidy, Draycott, McNaught | 3,000 |
| Sep 7 | WALSALL | W 2-0 | Cassidy, Donaldson | 7,000 |
| Sep 12 | LINCOLN CITY | W 3-1 | Cassidy 2, Donaldson | 7,000 |
| Sep 19 | Grimsby Town | L 0-2 | | 3,000 |
| Sep 21 | Walsall | W 3-2 | Brown, Draycott, McNaught | 7,000 |
| Sep 26 | NEWCASTLE UNITED | W 4-0 | Cassidy 3, Donaldson | 7,000 |
| Oct 3 | Manchester City | D 0-0 | | 20,000 |
| Oct 10 | SMALL HEATH | D 1-1 | Draycott | 7,000 |
| Oct 17 | Blackpool | L 2-4 | Bryant, Draycott | 5,000 |
| Oct 21 | Gainsborough Trinity | L 0-2 | | 4,000 |
| Oct 24 | BURTON WANDERERS | W 3-0 | Cassidy 3 | 4,000 |
| Nov 7 | GRIMSBY TOWN | W 4-2 | Cassidy 2, Donaldson, Jenkyns | 5,000 |
| Nov 28 | Small Heath | L 0-1 | | 4,000 |
| Nov 19 | Notts County | L 0-3 | | 5,000 |
| Dec 25 | MANCHESTER CITY | W 2-1 | Donaldson, Smith | 18,000 |
| Dec 26 | BLACKPOOL | W 2-0 | Cassidy 2 | 9,000 |
| Dec 28 | Leicester Fosse | L 0-1 | | 8,000 |
| Jan 1 | Newcastle United | L 0-2 | | 17,000 |
| Jan 9 | BURTON SWIFTS | D 1-1 | Donaldson | 3,000 |
| Feb 6 | LOUGHBOROUGH TOWN | W 6-0 | Smith 2, Boyd, Donaldson, Draycott, Jenkyns | 5,000 |
| Feb 20 | LEICESTER FOSSE | W 2-1 | Boyd, Donaldson | 8,000 |
| Mar 2 | DARWEN | W 3-1 | Cassidy 2, Boyd | 3,000 |
| Mar 13 | Darwen | W 2-0 | Cassidy, Gillespie | 2,000 |
| Mar 20 | Burton Wanderers | W 2-1 | Gillespie, Lowe o.g. | 3,000 |
| Mar 22 | WOOLWICH ARSENAL | D 1-1 | Boyd | 3,000 |
| Mar 27 | NOTTS COUNTY | D 1-1 | Bryant | 10,000 |
| Apr 1 | Lincoln City | W 3-1 | Jenkyns 3 | 1,000 |
| Apr 3 | Woolwich Arsenal | W 2-0 | Boyd, Donaldson | 6,000 |
| Apr 10 | Loughborough Town | L 0-2 | | 3,000 |

## FA Cup

| | | | | | |
|---|---|---|---|---|---|
| Dec 12 | WEST MANCHESTER | (Q1) | W 7-0 | Cassidy 2, Gillespie 2, Rothwell 2, Bryant | 6,000 |
| Jan 2 | NELSON | (Q2) | W 3-0 | Stephenson, Bryant, untraced | 5,000 |
| Jan 16 | BLACKPOOL | (Q3) | D 2-2 | Gillespie, Donaldson | 1,500 |
| Jan 20 | Blackpool | (R) | W 2-1 | Bryant, Cassidy | 1,500 |
| Jan 30 | KETTERING TOWN | (Rd1) | W 5-1 | Cassidy 2, Donaldson 2, Bryant | 5,000 |
| Feb 13 | Southampton | (Rd2) | D 1-1 | Donaldson | 8,000 |
| Feb 17 | SOUTHAMPTON | (R) | W 3-1 | Bryant 2, Cassidy | 7,000 |
| Feb 27 | Derby County | (Rd3) | L 0-2 | | 12,000 |

## Test Matches

| | | | | |
|---|---|---|---|---|
| Apr 19 | Burnley | L 0-2 | | 10,000 |
| Apr 21 | BURNLEY | W 2-0 | Boyd, Jenkyns | 7,000 |
| Apr 24 | SUNDERLAND | D 1-1 | Boyd | 18,000 |
| Apr 26 | Sunderland | L 0-2 | | 6,000 |

## League & Cup Appearances

| PLAYER | LEAGUE | CUP COMPETITION | OTHER | TOTAL |
|---|---|---|---|---|
| | | FA CUP | | |
| Barrett | 23 | 8 | 4 | 35 |
| Boyd | 10 | 3 | 3 | 16 |
| Brown | 7 | | | 7 |
| Bryant | 29 | 8 | 4 | 41 |
| Cartwright | 24 | 5 | 2 | 31 |
| Cassidy | 28 | 8 | 4 | 40 |
| Donaldson | 29 | 8 | 4 | 41 |
| Doughty | | | 3 | 3 |
| Draycott | 29 | 3 | 4 | 36 |
| Erentz | 27 | 6 | 4 | 37 |
| Gillespie | 17 | 8 | 4 | 29 |
| Jenkyns | 27 | 8 | 4 | 39 |
| Kennedy | 1 | | | 1 |
| McNaught | 30 | 8 | 4 | 42 |
| Morgan | 2 | | | 1 |
| Ridgeway | 5 | | | 5 |
| Rothwell | | 1 | | 1 |
| Smith | 15 | 5 | | 20 |
| Stafford | 24 | 8 | | 32 |
| Stephenson | | 1 | | 1 |
| Vance | 1 | | | 1 |
| Wetherell | 2 | | | 2 |

## Goalscorers

| PLAYER | LEAGUE | CUP COMPETITION | OTHER | TOTAL |
|---|---|---|---|---|
| | | FA CUP | | |
| Cassidy | 17 | 6 | | 23 |
| Donaldson | 9 | 4 | | 13 |
| Boyd | 5 | 1 | 2 | 8 |
| Bryant | 3 | 6 | | 6 |
| Jenkyns | 5 | | 1 | 6 |
| Draycott | 5 | | | 5 |
| Gillespie | 2 | 3 | | 5 |
| McNaught | 4 | | | 4 |
| Smith | 3 | | | 3 |
| Brown | 2 | | | 2 |
| Rothwell | | 2 | | 2 |
| Stephenson | | 1 | | 1 |
| Opps' o.gs. | 1 | | | 1 |

### Fact File

The end of season 'Test Matches' thwarted Newton Heath's promotion aspirations despite finishing the campaign as Division Two runners-up to champions Notts County.

**SECRETARY:** A.H. Albut
**MOST APPEARANCES:** James McNaught 42
**TOP GOALSCORER:** Joe Cassidy 23 (17 League)
**BIGGEST WIN:** 7-0 v West Manchester, 12 December 1896, FA Cup
**HIGHEST ATTENDANCE:** 20,000 v Manchester City, 3 October 1896, League

### Final Division Two Table

| | | P | W | D | L | F | A | Pts |
|---|---|---|---|---|---|---|---|---|
| 1 | Notts County | 30 | 19 | 4 | 7 | 92 | 43 | 42 |
| 2 | Newton Heath | 30 | 17 | 5 | 8 | 56 | 34 | 39 |
| 3 | Grimsby Town | 30 | 17 | 4 | 9 | 66 | 45 | 38 |
| 4 | Small Heath | 30 | 16 | 5 | 9 | 69 | 47 | 37 |
| 5 | Newcastle United | 30 | 17 | 1 | 12 | 56 | 52 | 35 |
| 6 | Manchester City | 30 | 12 | 8 | 10 | 58 | 50 | 32 |
| 7 | Gainsborough Trinity | 30 | 12 | 7 | 11 | 50 | 47 | 31 |
| 8 | Blackpool | 30 | 13 | 5 | 12 | 59 | 56 | 31 |
| 9 | Leicester Fosse | 30 | 13 | 4 | 13 | 59 | 56 | 30 |
| 10 | Woolwich Arsenal | 30 | 13 | 4 | 13 | 68 | 70 | 30 |
| 11 | Darwen | 30 | 14 | 0 | 16 | 67 | 61 | 28 |
| 12 | Walsall | 30 | 11 | 4 | 15 | 53 | 69 | 26 |
| 13 | Loughborough Town | 30 | 12 | 1 | 17 | 50 | 64 | 25 |
| 14 | Burton Swifts | 30 | 9 | 6 | 15 | 46 | 61 | 24 |
| 15 | Burton Wanderers | 30 | 9 | 2 | 19 | 31 | 67 | 20 |
| 16 | Lincoln City | 30 | 5 | 2 | 23 | 27 | 85 | 12 |

## Season 1897-98

### Football League Division Two

| DATE | OPPONENTS | SCORE | GOALSCORERS | ATTENDANCE |
|---|---|---|---|---|
| Sep 4 | LINCOLN CITY | W 5-0 | Boyd 3, Cassidy, Bryant | 5,000 |
| Sep 11 | Burton Swifts | W 4-0 | Boyd 3, Cassidy | 2,000 |
| Sep 18 | LUTON TOWN | L 1-2 | Cassidy | 8,000 |
| Sep 25 | Blackpool | W 1-0 | Smith | 2,000 |
| Oct 2 | LEICESTER FOSSE | W 2-0 | Boyd 2 | 6,000 |
| Oct 9 | Newcastle United | L 0-2 | | 12,000 |
| Oct 16 | MANCHESTER CITY | D 1-1 | Gillespie | 20,000 |
| Oct 23 | Small Heath | L 1-1 | Bryant | 6,000 |
| Oct 30 | WALSALL | W 6-0 | Cassidy 2, Donaldson 2, Bryant, Gillespie | 6,000 |
| Nov 6 | Lincoln City | L 0-1 | | 2,000 |
| Nov 13 | NEWCASTLE UNITED | L 0-1 | | 7,000 |
| Nov 20 | Leicester Fosse | D 1-1 | Wedge | 6,000 |
| Nov 27 | GRIMSBY TOWN | W 2-1 | Bryant, o.g. | 5,000 |
| Dec 11 | Walsall | D 1-1 | Boyd | 2,000 |
| Dec 25 | Manchester City | W 1-0 | Cassidy | 16,000 |
| Dec 27 | Gainsborough Trinity | L 1-2 | Carman | 3,000 |
| Jan 1 | BURTON SWIFTS | W 4-0 | Boyd, Bryant, Carman, McNaught | 6,000 |
| Jan 8 | Woolwich Arsenal | L 1-5 | Erentz F | 8,000 |
| Jan 12 | BURNLEY | D 0-0 | | 7,000 |
| Jan 15 | BLACKPOOL | W 4-0 | Boyd 2, Cartwright, Cassidy | 4,000 |
| Feb 26 | WOOLWICH ARSENAL | W 5-1 | Bryant, Cassidy 2, Collinson, Ord o.g. | 6,000 |
| Mar 7 | Burnley | L 3-6 | Bryant 2, Collinson | 3,000 |
| Mar 19 | Darwen | W 3-2 | Boyd 2, McNaught | 2,000 |
| Mar 21 | Luton Town | D 2-2 | Boyd, Cassidy | 2,000 |
| Mar 29 | LOUGHBOROUGH TOWN | W 5-1 | Boyd 3, Cassidy 2 | 2,000 |
| Apr 2 | Grimsby Town | W 3-1 | Cassidy 2, Boyd | 2,000 |
| Apr 8 | GAINSBOROUGH TRINITY | W 1-0 | Cassidy | 5,000 |
| Apr 9 | SMALL HEATH | W 3-1 | Boyd, Gillespie, Morgan | 4,000 |
| Apr 16 | Loughborough Trinity | D 0-0 | | 1,200 |
| Apr 23 | DARWEN | W 3-2 | Collinson 2, Bryant | 4,000 |

### FA Cup

| DATE | OPPONENTS | SCORE | GOALSCORERS | ATTENDANCE |
|---|---|---|---|---|
| Jan 29 | WALSALL | W 1-0 | Pears o.g. | 6,000 |
| Feb 12 | LIVERPOOL | D 0-0 | | 12,000 |
| Feb 16 | Liverpool | L 1-2 | Collinson | 6,000 |

### League & Cup Appearances

| PLAYER | LEAGUE | CUP COMPETITION FA CUP | TOTAL |
|---|---|---|---|
| Barrett | 27 | 3 | 30 |
| Boyd | 30 | 3 | 33 |
| Bryant | 28 | | 31 |
| Carman | 4 | | 4 |
| Cartwright | 27 | 3 | 30 |
| Cassidy | 30 | 3 | 33 |
| Collinson | 10 | 3 | 13 |
| Donaldson | 8 | | 8 |
| Draycott | 21 | 3 | 24 |
| Dunn | 10 | 2 | 12 |
| Erentz F. | 28 | 3 | 31 |
| Erentz H. | 6 | 3 | 9 |
| Gillespie | 19 | 1 | 20 |
| Jenkyns | 8 | | 8 |
| McNaught | 30 | 3 | 33 |
| Morgan | 9 | | 9 |
| Ridgway | 3 | | 3 |
| Smith | 5 | | 5 |
| Stafford | 25 | | 25 |
| Wedge | 2 | | 2 |

### Goalscorers

| PLAYER | LEAGUE | CUP COMPETITION FA CUP | TOTAL |
|---|---|---|---|
| Boyd | 20 | | 20 |
| Cassidy | 15 | | 15 |
| Bryant | 9 | | 9 |
| Collinson | 4 | 1 | 5 |
| Gillespie | 3 | | 3 |
| Carman | 2 | | 2 |
| Donaldson | 2 | | 2 |
| McNaught | 2 | | 2 |
| Cartwright | 1 | | 1 |
| Erentz F | 1 | | 1 |
| Morgan | 1 | | 1 |
| Smith | 1 | | 1 |
| Wedge | 1 | | 1 |
| Opps' o.gs. | 2 | 1 | 3 |

### Fact File

Brothers Fred and Harry Erentz appeared together for the first time in the same Newton Heath side against Woolwich Arsenal on 8 January 1898. Fred, the older of the two, scored the Heathens' only goal in a 5-1 defeat.

**SECRETARY:** A.H. Albut

**MOST APPEARANCES:** Joe Cassidy, James McNaught, Henry Boyd 33

**TOP GOALSCORER:** Henry Boyd 20 (all League)

**BIGGEST WIN:** 6-0 v Walsall, 30 October 1897, League

**HIGHEST ATTENDANCE:** 20,000 v Manchester City, 16 October 1897, League

### Final Division Two Table

| | | P | W | D | L | F | A | Pts |
|---|---|---|---|---|---|---|---|---|
| 1 | Burnley | 30 | 20 | 8 | 2 | 80 | 24 | 48 |
| 2 | Newcastle United | 30 | 21 | 3 | 6 | 64 | 32 | 45 |
| 3 | Manchester City | 30 | 15 | 9 | 6 | 66 | 36 | 39 |
| 4 | Newton Heath | 30 | 16 | 6 | 8 | 64 | 35 | 38 |
| 5 | Woolwich Arsenal | 30 | 16 | 5 | 9 | 69 | 49 | 37 |
| 6 | Small Heath | 30 | 16 | 4 | 10 | 58 | 50 | 36 |
| 7 | Leicester Fosse | 30 | 13 | 7 | 10 | 46 | 35 | 33 |
| 8 | Luton Town | 30 | 13 | 4 | 13 | 68 | 50 | 30 |
| 9 | Gainsborough Trinity | 30 | 12 | 6 | 12 | 50 | 54 | 30 |
| 10 | Walsall | 30 | 12 | 5 | 13 | 58 | 58 | 29 |
| 11 | Blackpool | 30 | 10 | 5 | 15 | 49 | 61 | 25 |
| 12 | Grimsby Town | 30 | 10 | 4 | 16 | 52 | 62 | 24 |
| 13 | Burton Swifts | 30 | 8 | 5 | 17 | 38 | 69 | 21 |
| 14 | Lincoln City | 30 | 6 | 5 | 19 | 43 | 82 | 17 |
| 15 | Darwen | 30 | 6 | 2 | 22 | 31 | 76 | 14 |
| 16 | Loughborough Town | 30 | 6 | 2 | 22 | 24 | 87 | 14 |

# Season 1898-99

## Football League Division Two

| DATE | OPPONENTS | SCORE | GOALSCORERS | ATTENDANCE |
|---|---|---|---|---|
| Sep 3 | Gainsborough Trinity | W 2-0 | Bryant, Cassidy | 2,000 |
| Sep 10 | MANCHESTER CITY | W 3-0 | Boyd, Cassidy 2 (1 pen) | 20,000 |
| Sep 17 | Glossop North End | W 2-1 | Bryant, Cassidy | 6,000 |
| Sep 24 | WALSALL | W 1-0 | Gillespie | 8,000 |
| Oct 1 | Burton Swifts | L 1-5 | Boyd | 2,000 |
| Oct 8 | BURSLEM PORT VALE | W 2-1 | Bryant, Cassidy | 10,000 |
| Oct 15 | Small Heath | L 1-4 | Cassidy | 5,000 |
| Oct 22 | LOUGHBOROUGH TOWN | W 6-1 | Brooks 2, Cassidy 2, Collinson 2 | 2,000 |
| Nov 5 | GRIMSBY TOWN | W 3-2 | Brooks, Cassidy, Gillespie | 5,000 |
| Nov 12 | BARNSLEY | D 0-0 | | 6,000 |
| Nov 19 | New Brighton Tower | W 3-0 | Collinson 2, Cunningham | 5,000 |
| Nov 26 | LINCOLN CITY | W 1-0 | Bryant | 4,000 |
| Dec 3 | Woolwich Arsenal | L 1-5 | Collinson | 6,000 |
| Dec 10 | BLACKPOOL | W 3-1 | Cassidy, Collinson, Cunningham | 5,000 |
| Dec 17 | Leicester Fosse | L 0-1 | | 8,000 |
| Dec 24 | DARWEN | W 9-0 | Bryant 3, Cassidy 3, Gillespie 2, Radcliffe o.g. | 2,000 |
| Dec 26 | Manchester City | L 0-4 | | 25,000 |
| Dec 31 | GAINSBOROUGH TRINITY | W 6-1 | Collinson 2, Bryant, Boyd, Cartwright, Draycott | 2,000 |
| Jan 2 | BURTON SWIFTS | D 2-2 | Boyd, Cassidy | 6,000 |
| Jan 14 | GLOSSOP NORTH END | W 3-0 | Cunningham, Erentz, Gillespie | 12,000 |
| Jan 21 | Walsall | L 0-1 | | 3,000 |
| Feb 4 | Burslem Port Vale | L 0-1 | | 6,000 |
| Feb 18 | Loughborough Town | W 1-0 | Bryant | 1,500 |
| Feb 25 | SMALL HEATH | W 2-0 | Boyd, Roberts | 12,000 |
| Mar 4 | Grimsby Town | L 0-3 | | 4,000 |
| Mar 18 | NEW BRIGHTON TOWER | L 1-2 | Cassidy | 20,000 |
| Mar 25 | Lincoln City | L 0-2 | | 3,000 |
| Apr 1 | WOOLWICH ARSENAL | D 2-2 | Bryant, Cassidy | 5,000 |
| Apr 3 | Blackpool | W 1-0 | Cassidy | 3,000 |
| Apr 4 | Barnsley | W 2-0 | Lee 2 | 4,000 |
| Apr 8 | Luton Town | W 1-0 | Lee | 1,500 |
| Apr 12 | LUTON TOWN | W 5-0 | Cartwright, Cassidy, Gillespie, Lee, Morgan | 3,000 |
| Apr 15 | LEICESTER FOSSE | D 2-2 | Cassidy, Gillespie | 7,000 |
| Apr 22 | Darwen | D 1-1 | Morgan | 1,000 |

## FA Cup

| | | | | |
|---|---|---|---|---|
| Jan 28 | Tottenham Hotspur | (Rd1) D 1-1 | Cassidy | 15,000 |
| Feb 1 | TOTTENHAM HOTSPUR | (R) L 3-5 | Bryant 3 | 6,000 |

## League & Cup Appearances

| PLAYER | LEAGUE | CUP COMPETITION FA CUP | TOTAL |
|---|---|---|---|
| Barratt | 34 | 2 | 36 |
| Boyd | 11 | | 11 |
| Brooks | 3 | | 3 |
| Bryant | 32 | 2 | 34 |
| Cairns | 1 | | 1 |
| Cartwright | 33 | 1 | 34 |
| Cassidy | 34 | 2 | 36 |
| Collinson | 21 | 2 | 23 |
| Connachan | 4 | | 4 |
| Cunningham | 15 | 2 | 17 |
| Draycott | 31 | 2 | 33 |
| Erentz | 32 | 2 | 34 |
| Gillespie | 28 | 2 | 30 |
| Gourlay | 1 | | 1 |
| Griffiths | 7 | | 7 |
| Hopkins | 1 | | 1 |
| Jones | 3 | | 3 |
| Lee | 7 | | 7 |
| Morgan | 24 | 2 | 26 |
| Owen | 1 | | 1 |
| Pepper | 7 | 1 | 8 |
| Radcliffe | 1 | | 1 |
| Roberts | 3 | | 3 |
| Stafford | 33 | 2 | 35 |
| Turner J. | 3 | 1 | 4 |
| Turner R. | 2 | | 3 |
| Walker | 2 | | 2 |

## Goalscorers

| PLAYER | LEAGUE | CUP COMPETITION FA CUP | TOTAL |
|---|---|---|---|
| Cassidy | 19 | 1 | 20 |
| Bryant | 10 | 3 | 13 |
| Collinson | 8 | | 8 |
| Gillespie | 7 | | 7 |
| Boyd | 5 | | 5 |
| Lee | 4 | | 4 |
| Brooks | 3 | | 3 |
| Cunningham | 3 | | 3 |
| Cartwright | 2 | | 2 |
| Morgan | 2 | | 2 |
| Draycott | 1 | | 1 |
| Erentz | 1 | | 1 |
| Roberts | 1 | | 1 |
| Opps' o.gs. | 1 | | 1 |

## Fact File

Newton Heath were beaten only once at home all season, against New Brighton Tower on 18 March, but they still failed to secure promotion to Division One.

**SECRETARY:** A.H. Albut

**MOST APPEARANCES:** Frank Barratt, Joe Cassidy 36

**TOP GOALSCORER:** Joe Cassidy 20 (19 League)

**BIGGEST WIN:** 9-0 v Darwen, 24 December 1898, League

**HIGHEST ATTENDANCE:** 25,000 v Manchester City, 26 December 1898, League

## Final Division Two Table

| | | P | W | D | L | F | A | Pts |
|---|---|---|---|---|---|---|---|---|
| 1 | Manchester City | 34 | 23 | 5 | 6 | 92 | 35 | 52 |
| 2 | Glossop North End | 34 | 20 | 6 | 8 | 76 | 38 | 46 |
| 3 | Leicester Fosse | 34 | 18 | 9 | 7 | 64 | 42 | 45 |
| 4 | Newton Heath | 34 | 19 | 5 | 10 | 67 | 43 | 43 |
| 5 | New Brighton | 34 | 18 | 7 | 9 | 71 | 52 | 43 |
| 6 | Walsall | 34 | 15 | 12 | 7 | 79 | 36 | 42 |
| 7 | Woolwich Arsenal | 34 | 18 | 5 | 11 | 72 | 41 | 41 |
| 8 | Small Heath | 34 | 17 | 7 | 10 | 85 | 50 | 41 |
| 9 | Burslem Port Vale | 34 | 17 | 5 | 12 | 56 | 34 | 39 |
| 10 | Grimsby Town | 34 | 15 | 5 | 14 | 71 | 60 | 35 |
| 11 | Barnsley | 34 | 12 | 7 | 15 | 52 | 56 | 31 |
| 12 | Lincoln City | 34 | 12 | 7 | 15 | 51 | 56 | 31 |
| 13 | Burton Swifts | 34 | 10 | 8 | 16 | 51 | 70 | 28 |
| 14 | Gainsborough Trinity | 34 | 10 | 5 | 19 | 56 | 72 | 25 |
| 15 | Luton Town | 34 | 10 | 3 | 21 | 51 | 95 | 23 |
| 16 | Blackpool | 34 | 8 | 4 | 22 | 49 | 90 | 20 |
| 17 | Loughborough Town | 34 | 6 | 6 | 22 | 38 | 92 | 18 |
| 18 | Darwen | 34 | 2 | 5 | 27 | 22 | 141 | 11 |

# Season 1899-1900

## Football League Division Two

| DATE | OPPONENTS | SCORE | GOALSCORERS | ATTENDANCE |
|---|---|---|---|---|
| Sep 2 | GAINSBOROUGH TRINITY | D 2-2 | Cassidy, Lee | 8,000 |
| Sep 9 | Bolton Wanderers | L 1-2 | Ambler | 5,000 |
| Sep 16 | LOUGHBOROUGH TOWN | W 4-0 | Bain, Cassidy, Griffiths, o.g. | 6,000 |
| Sep 23 | Burton Swifts | D 0-0 | | 2,000 |
| Sep 30 | The Wednesday | L 1-2 | Bryant | 8,000 |
| Oct 7 | LINCOLN CITY | W 1-0 | Cassidy | 5,000 |
| Oct 14 | Small Heath | L 0-1 | | 10,000 |
| Oct 21 | NEW BRIGHTON TOWER | W 2-1 | Cassidy 2 | 5,000 |
| Nov 4 | WOOLWICH ARSENAL | W 2-0 | Jackson, Roberts | 5,000 |
| Nov 11 | Barnsley | D 0-0 | | 3,000 |
| Nov 25 | Luton Town | W 1-0 | Jackson | 3,000 |
| Dec 2 | BURSLEM PORT VALE | W 3-0 | Cassidy 2, Jackson | 5,000 |
| Dec 16 | MIDDLESBROUGH | W 2-1 | Erentz (pen), Parkinson | 5,000 |
| Dec 23 | Chesterfield | L 1-2 | Griffiths | 2,000 |
| Dec 26 | Grimsby Town | W 7-0 | Bryant 2, Cassidy 2, Jackson, Parkinson, o.g. | 2,000 |
| Dec 30 | Gainsborough Trinity | W 1-0 | Parkinson | 2,000 |
| Jan 6 | BOLTON WANDERERS | L 1-2 | Parkinson | 5,000 |
| Jan 13 | Loughborough Town | W 2-0 | Jackson, Parkinson | 800 |
| Jan 20 | BURTON SWIFTS | W 4-0 | Gillespie 3, Parkinson | 5,000 |
| Feb 3 | THE WEDNESDAY | W 1-0 | Bryant | 10,000 |
| Feb 10 | Lincoln City | L 0-1 | | 3,000 |
| Feb 17 | SMALL HEATH | W 3-2 | Cassidy, Godsmark, Parkinson | 12,000 |
| Feb 24 | New Brighton Tower | W 4-1 | Collinson 2, Godsmark, Smith | 8,000 |
| Mar 3 | GRIMSBY TOWN | W 1-0 | Smith | 12,000 |
| Mar 10 | Woolwich Arsenal | L 1-2 | Cassidy | 3,000 |
| Mar 17 | BARNSLEY | W 3-0 | Cassidy 2, Leigh | 6,000 |
| Mar 24 | Leicester Fosse | L 0-2 | | 8,000 |
| Mar 31 | LUTON TOWN | W 5-0 | Cassidy 3, Godsmark 2 | 6,000 |
| Apr 7 | Burslem Port Vale | L 0-1 | | 3,000 |
| Apr 13 | LEICESTER FOSSE | W 3-2 | Gillespie, Griffiths, unknown | 10,000 |
| Apr 14 | WALSALL | W 5-0 | Jackson 2, Erentz, Foley, Gillespie | 5,000 |
| Apr 17 | Walsall | D 0-0 | | 3,000 |
| Apr 21 | Middlesbrough | L 0-2 | | 8,000 |
| Apr 28 | CHESTERFIELD | W 2-1 | Holt, Grundy | 6,000 |

## FA Cup

| | | | | |
|---|---|---|---|---|
| Oct 28 | South Shore | (Q1) L 1-3 | Jackson | 3,000 |

## League & Cup Appearances

| PLAYER | LEAGUE | CUP COMPETITION FA CUP | TOTAL |
|---|---|---|---|
| Ambler | 6 | | 6 |
| Bain | 2 | | 2 |
| Barrett | 34 | 1 | 35 |
| Blackmore | 1 | 1 | 2 |
| Bryant | 19 | 1 | 20 |
| Cartwright | 25 | 1 | 26 |
| Cassidy | 29 | 1 | 30 |
| Clark | 8 | | 8 |
| Collinson | 8 | | 8 |
| Erentz | 34 | 1 | 35 |
| Fitzsimmons | 2 | | 2 |
| Foley | 7 | | 7 |
| Gillespie | 10 | | 10 |
| Godsmark | 9 | | 9 |
| Griffiths | 33 | 1 | 34 |
| Grundy | 1 | | 1 |
| Heathcote | 1 | | 1 |
| Holt | 1 | | 1 |
| Jackson | 32 | 1 | 33 |
| Lee | 4 | | 4 |
| Leigh | 9 | | 9 |
| Morgan | 30 | 1 | 31 |
| Parkinson | 15 | | 15 |
| Roberts | 6 | 1 | 7 |
| Sawyer | 2 | | 2 |
| Smith | 12 | | 12 |
| Stafford | 31 | 1 | 32 |

## Goalscorers

| PLAYER | LEAGUE | CUP COMPETITION FA CUP | TOTAL |
|---|---|---|---|
| Cassidy | 16 | | 16 |
| Jackson | 7 | 1 | 8 |
| Parkinson | 7 | | 7 |
| Gillespie | 5 | | 5 |
| Bryant | 4 | | 4 |
| Godsmark | 4 | | 4 |
| Griffiths | 3 | | 3 |
| Collinson | 2 | | 2 |
| Erentz | 2 | | 2 |
| Smith | 2 | | 2 |
| Ambler | 1 | | 1 |
| Bain | 1 | | 1 |
| Foley | 1 | | 1 |
| Grundy | 1 | | 1 |
| Holt | 1 | | 1 |
| Lee | 1 | | 1 |
| Leigh | 1 | | 1 |
| Roberts | 1 | | 1 |
| Unknown | 1 | | 1 |
| Opps' o.gs. | 2 | | 2 |

## Fact File

Another fantastic home campaign concluded with only Bolton Wanderers, 6 January, having taken both points away from Bank Street, but promotion remained elusive as Newton Heath finished in fourth place again.

**SECRETARY:** A.H. Albut
**MOST APPEARANCES:** Frank Barratt, Fred Erentz 35
**TOP GOALSCORER:** Joe Cassidy 16 (all League)
**BIGGEST WIN:** 7-0 v Grimsby Town, 26 December 1899, League
**HIGHEST ATTENDANCE:** 12,000 v Small Heath, 17 February 1900, League; 12,000 v Grimsby Town, 3 March 1900, League

## Final Division Two Table

| | | P | W | D | L | F | A | Pts |
|---|---|---|---|---|---|---|---|---|
| 1 | The Wednesday | 34 | 25 | 4 | 5 | 84 | 22 | 54 |
| 2 | Bolton Wanderers | 34 | 22 | 8 | 4 | 79 | 25 | 52 |
| 3 | Small Heath | 34 | 20 | 6 | 8 | 78 | 38 | 46 |
| 4 | Newton Heath | 34 | 20 | 4 | 10 | 63 | 27 | 44 |
| 5 | Leicester Fosse | 34 | 17 | 9 | 8 | 53 | 36 | 43 |
| 6 | Grimsby Town | 34 | 17 | 6 | 11 | 67 | 46 | 40 |
| 7 | Chesterfield | 34 | 16 | 6 | 12 | 65 | 60 | 38 |
| 8 | Woolwich Arsenal | 34 | 16 | 4 | 14 | 61 | 43 | 36 |
| 9 | Lincoln City | 34 | 14 | 8 | 12 | 46 | 43 | 36 |
| 10 | New Brighton | 34 | 13 | 9 | 12 | 66 | 58 | 35 |
| 11 | Burslem Port Vale | 34 | 14 | 6 | 14 | 39 | 49 | 34 |
| 12 | Walsall | 34 | 12 | 8 | 14 | 50 | 55 | 32 |
| 13 | Gainsborough Trinity | 34 | 9 | 7 | 18 | 47 | 75 | 25 |
| 14 | Middlesbrough | 34 | 8 | 8 | 18 | 39 | 69 | 24 |
| 15 | Burton Swifts | 34 | 9 | 6 | 19 | 43 | 84 | 24 |
| 16 | Barnsley | 34 | 8 | 7 | 19 | 46 | 79 | 23 |
| 17 | Luton Town | 34 | 5 | 8 | 21 | 40 | 75 | 18 |
| 18 | Loughborough Town | 34 | 1 | 6 | 27 | 18 | 100 | 8 |

## Season 1900-01

### Football League Division Two

| DATE | OPPONENTS | SCORE | GOALSCORERS | ATTENDANCE |
|---|---|---|---|---|
| Sep 1 | Glossop North End | L 0-1 | | 2,000 |
| Sep 8 | MIDDLESBROUGH | W 4-0 | Griffiths, Grundy, Jackson, Leigh | 8,000 |
| Sep 15 | Burnley | L 0-1 | | 2,000 |
| Sep 22 | BURSLEM PORT VALE | W 4-0 | Grundy, Leigh, Schofield 2 | 6,000 |
| Sep 29 | Leicester Fosse | L 0-1 | | 6,000 |
| Oct 6 | NEW BRIGHTON TOWER | W 1-0 | Jackson | 5,000 |
| Oct 13 | Gainsborough Trinity | W 1-0 | Leigh | 2,000 |
| Oct 20 | WALSALL | D 1-1 | Schofield | 8,000 |
| Oct 27 | Burton Swifts | L 1-3 | Leigh | 2,000 |
| Nov 10 | Woolwich Arsenal | L 1-2 | Jackson | 8,000 |
| Nov 24 | Stockport County | L 0-1 | | 5,000 |
| Dec 1 | SMALL HEATH | L 0-1 | | 5,000 |
| Dec 8 | Grimsby Town | L 0-2 | | 4,000 |
| Dec 15 | LINCOLN CITY | W 4-1 | Leigh 3, Morgan H. | 4,000 |
| Dec 22 | Chesterfield | L 1-2 | Hancock o.g. | 4,000 |
| Dec 26 | BLACKPOOL | W 4-0 | Griffiths, Leigh, Morgan W., Schofield | 10,000 |
| Dec 29 | GLOSSOP NORTH END | W 3-0 | Leigh 2, Morgan H., (pen) | 8,000 |
| Jan 1 | Middlesbrough | W 2-1 | Schofield 2 | 12,000 |
| Jan 12 | BURNLEY | L 0-1 | | 10,000 |
| Jan 19 | Burslem Port Vale | L 0-2 | | 1,000 |
| Feb 16 | GAINSBOROUGH TRINITY | D 0-0 | | 3,000 |
| Feb 19 | New Brighton Tower | L 0-2 | | 2,000 |
| Feb 25 | Walsall | D 1-1 | Morgan W. | 2,000 |
| Mar 2 | BURTON SWIFTS | D 1-1 | Leigh | 5,000 |
| Mar 13 | BARNSLEY | W 1-0 | Leigh | 6,000 |
| Mar 16 | WOOLWICH ARSENAL | W 1-0 | Leigh | 5,000 |
| Mar 20 | LEICESTER FOSSE | L 2-3 | Fisher 2 | 2,000 |
| Mar 23 | Blackpool | W 2-1 | Griffiths 2 | 2,000 |
| Mar 30 | STOCKPORT COUNTY | W 3-1 | Leigh, Morgan H., Schofield | 4,000 |
| Apr 5 | Lincoln City | L 0-2 | | 5,000 |
| Apr 6 | Small Heath | L 0-1 | | 6,000 |
| Apr 9 | Barnsley | L 2-6 | Jackson, Morgan W. | 3,000 |
| Apr 13 | GRIMSBY TOWN | W 1-0 | Morgan H. | 3,000 |
| Apr 27 | CHESTERFIELD | W 1-0 | Leigh | 1,000 |

### FA Cup

| | | | | |
|---|---|---|---|---|
| Jan 5 | PORTSMOUTH | (IR) W 3-0 | Griffiths, Stafford, Jackson | 5,000 |
| Feb 9 | BURNLEY | (Rd1) D 0-0 | | 10,000 |
| Feb 13 | Burnley | (R) L 1-7 | Schofield | 4,000 |

### League & Cup Appearances

| PLAYER | LEAGUE | CUP COMPETITION FA CUP | OTHER | TOTAL |
|---|---|---|---|---|
| Cairns | 1 | | | 1 |
| Booth | 2 | | | 2 |
| Cartwright | 32 | 3 | | 35 |
| Collinson | 11 | 1 | | 12 |
| Erentz | 31 | 3 | | 34 |
| Fisher | 25 | 3 | | 28 |
| Garvey | 6 | | | 6 |
| Greenwood | 3 | | | 3 |
| Griffiths | 31 | 2 | | 33 |
| Grundy | 10 | | | 10 |
| Hayes | 1 | | | 1 |
| Heathcote | 3 | 1 | | 4 |
| Jackson | 29 | 2 | | 31 |
| Johnson | 1 | | | 1 |
| Lappin | 1 | | | 1 |
| Lawson | 3 | | | 3 |
| Leigh | 34 | 3 | | 37 |
| Morgan H. | 20 | 3 | | 23 |
| Morgan W. | 33 | 3 | | 36 |
| Sawyer | 4 | | | 4 |
| Schofield | 29 | 3 | | 32 |
| Smith | 5 | | | 5 |
| Stafford | 30 | 3 | | 33 |
| Whitehouse | 29 | 3 | | 32 |
| Whitney | 1 | | | 1 |

### Goalscorers

| PLAYER | LEAGUE | CUP COMPETITION FA CUP | OTHER | TOTAL |
|---|---|---|---|---|
| Leigh | 15 | | | 15 |
| Schofield | 7 | 1 | | 8 |
| Griffiths | 4 | 1 | | 5 |
| Jackson | 4 | 1 | | 5 |
| Morgan H. | 4 | | | 4 |
| Morgan W. | 3 | | | 3 |
| Fisher | 2 | | | 2 |
| Grundy | 2 | | | 2 |
| Stafford | | 1 | | 1 |
| Opps' o.gs. | 1 | | | 1 |

### Fact File

Newton Heath were dumped out of the FA Cup 7-1 in a replayed first round tie against Burnley at Turf Moor following a goalless draw in the original tie at Bank Street.

**SECRETARY:** James West

**MOST APPEARANCES:** Tom Leigh 37

**TOP GOALSCORER:** Tom Leigh 15 (all League)

**BIGGEST WIN:** 4-0 v Middlesbrough, 8 September 1900, League;
4-0 v Burslem Port Vale, 22 September 1900, League;
4-0 v Blackpool 26 December 1900, League

**HIGHEST ATTENDANCE:** 12,000 v Middlesbrough, 1 January 1901, League

### Final Division Two Table

| | | P | W | D | L | F | A | Pts |
|---|---|---|---|---|---|---|---|---|
| 1 | Grimsby Town | 34 | 20 | 9 | 5 | 60 | 33 | 49 |
| 2 | Small Heath | 34 | 19 | 10 | 5 | 57 | 24 | 48 |
| 3 | Burnley | 34 | 20 | 4 | 10 | 53 | 29 | 44 |
| 4 | New Brighton Tower | 34 | 17 | 8 | 9 | 57 | 38 | 42 |
| 5 | Glossop North End | 34 | 15 | 8 | 11 | 51 | 33 | 38 |
| 6 | Middlesbrough | 34 | 15 | 7 | 12 | 50 | 40 | 37 |
| 7 | Woolwich Arsenal | 34 | 15 | 6 | 13 | 39 | 35 | 36 |
| 8 | Lincoln City | 34 | 13 | 7 | 14 | 43 | 39 | 33 |
| 9 | Burslem Port Vale | 34 | 11 | 11 | 12 | 45 | 47 | 33 |
| 10 | Newton Heath | 34 | 14 | 4 | 16 | 42 | 38 | 32 |
| 11 | Leicester Fosse | 34 | 11 | 10 | 13 | 39 | 37 | 32 |
| 12 | Blackpool | 34 | 12 | 7 | 15 | 33 | 58 | 31 |
| 13 | Gainsborough Trinity | 34 | 10 | 10 | 14 | 45 | 60 | 30 |
| 14 | Chesterfield | 34 | 9 | 10 | 15 | 46 | 58 | 28 |
| 15 | Barnsley | 34 | 11 | 5 | 18 | 47 | 60 | 27 |
| 16 | Walsall | 34 | 7 | 13 | 14 | 40 | 56 | 27 |
| 17 | Stockport County | 34 | 11 | 3 | 20 | 38 | 68 | 25 |
| 18 | Burton Swifts | 34 | 8 | 4 | 22 | 34 | 66 | 20 |

## Season 1901-02

### Football League Division Two

| DATE | OPPONENTS | SCORE | GOALSCORERS | ATTENDANCE |
|---|---|---|---|---|
| Sep 7 | GAINSBOROUGH TRINITY | W 3-0 | Preston 2, Lappin | 10,000 |
| Sep 14 | Middlesbrough | L 0-5 | | 12,000 |
| Sep 21 | BRISTOL CITY | W 1-0 | Griffiths | 6,000 |
| Sep 28 | Blackpool | W 4-2 | Preston 2, Schofield, o.g. | 4,000 |
| Oct 5 | STOCKPORT COUNTY | D 3-3 | Schofield, Smith, Preston | 5,000 |
| Oct 12 | Burton United | D 0-0 | | 3,000 |
| Oct 19 | Glossop North End | D 0-0 | | 5,000 |
| Oct 26 | DONCASTER ROVERS | W 6-0 | Coupar 2, Schofield, Griffiths, Preston, o.g. | 7,000 |
| Nov 9 | WEST BROMWICH ALBION | L 1-2 | Fisher | 13,000 |
| Nov 16 | Woolwich Arsenal | L 0-2 | | 3,000 |
| Nov 23 | BARNSLEY | W 1-0 | Griffiths | 4,000 |
| Nov 30 | Leicester Fosse | L 2-3 | Cartwright 2 | 4,000 |
| Dec 7 | Preston North End | L 1-5 | Preston | 3,000 |
| Dec 21 | BURSLEM PORT VALE | W 1-0 | Richards | 3,000 |
| Dec 26 | Lincoln City | L 0-2 | | 4,000 |
| Jan 1 | PRESTON NORTH END | L 0-2 | | 10,000 |
| Jan 4 | Gainsborough Trinity | D 1-1 | Lappin | 2,000 |
| Jan 18 | Bristol City | L 0-4 | | 6,000 |
| Jan 25 | BLACKPOOL | L 0-1 | | 3,000 |
| Feb 1 | Stockport County | L 0-1 | | 3,000 |
| Feb 11 | BURNLEY | W 2-0 | Lappin, Preston | 1,000 |
| Feb 15 | GLOSSOP NORTH END | W 1-0 | Erentz | 4,000 |
| Feb 22 | Doncaster Rovers | L 0-4 | | 3,000 |
| Mar 1 | LINCOLN CITY | D 0-0 | | 6,000 |
| Mar 8 | West Bromwich Albion | L 0-4 | | 8,000 |
| Mar 15 | WOOLWICH ARSENAL | L 0-1 | | 3,000 |
| Mar 17 | Chesterfield | L 0-3 | | 2,000 |
| Mar 22 | Barnsley | L 2-3 | Cartwright, Higson | 2,500 |
| Mar 28 | Burnley | L 0-1 | | 3,000 |
| Mar 29 | LEICESTER FOSSE | W 2-0 | Griffiths, Hayes | 2,000 |
| Apr 7 | MIDDLESBROUGH | L 1-2 | Erentz (pen) | 2,000 |
| Apr 19 | Burslem Port Vale | D 1-1 | Coupar | 2,000 |
| Apr 21 | BURTON UNITED | W 3-1 | Cartwright, Griffiths, Preston | 500 |
| Apr 23 | CHESTERFIELD | W 2-0 | Coupar, Preston | 2,000 |

### FA Cup

| | | | | |
|---|---|---|---|---|
| Dec 14 | LINCOLN CITY | (Rd1) L 1-2 | Fisher | 4,000 |

### League & Cup Appearances

| PLAYER | LEAGUE | CUP COMPETITION FA CUP | TOTAL |
|---|---|---|---|
| Banks | 27 | 1 | 28 |
| Cartwright | 29 | 1 | 30 |
| Coupar | 11 | | 11 |
| Erentz | 25 | 1 | 26 |
| Fisher | 17 | 1 | 18 |
| Griffiths | 29 | 1 | 30 |
| Hayes | 16 | | 16 |
| Heathcote | 3 | | 3 |
| Higgins | 10 | | 10 |
| Higson | 5 | | 5 |
| Lappin | 21 | | 21 |
| Morgan | 33 | 1 | 34 |
| O'Brien | 1 | | 1 |
| Preston | 29 | 1 | 30 |
| Richards | 9 | | 9 |
| Saunders | 11 | | 11 |
| Schofield | 29 | 1 | 30 |
| Smith | 16 | 1 | 17 |
| Stafford | 26 | 1 | 27 |
| Whitehouse | 23 | 1 | 24 |
| Williams | 4 | | 4 |

### Goalscorers

| PLAYER | LEAGUE | CUP COMPETITION FA CUP | TOTAL |
|---|---|---|---|
| Preston | 10 | | 10 |
| Griffiths | 5 | | 5 |
| Cartwright | 4 | | 4 |
| Coupar | 4 | | 4 |
| Lappin | 3 | | 3 |
| Schofield | 3 | | 3 |
| Erentz | 2 | | 2 |
| Fisher | 1 | 1 | 2 |
| Hayes | 1 | | 1 |
| Higson | 1 | | 1 |
| Richards | 1 | | 1 |
| Smith | 1 | | 1 |
| Opps' o.gs. | 2 | | 2 |

### Fact File

There was no change of fortune for the club in its last season under the Newton Heath banner. They finished fourth from bottom of the Division Two table and failed to make their mark in the FA Cup.

**SECRETARY:** James West
**MOST APPEARANCES:** William Morgan 34
**TOP GOALSCORER:** Steve Preston 10 (all League)
**BIGGEST WIN:** 6-0 v Doncaster Rovers, 26 October 1901, League
**HIGHEST ATTENDANCE:** 13,000 v West Bromwich Albion, 9 November 1901, League

### Final Division Two Table

| | | P | W | D | L | F | A | PTS |
|---|---|---|---|---|---|---|---|---|
| 1 | West Bromwich Albion | 34 | 25 | 5 | 4 | 82 | 29 | 55 |
| 2 | Middlesbrough | 34 | 23 | 5 | 6 | 90 | 24 | 51 |
| 3 | Preston North End | 34 | 18 | 6 | 10 | 71 | 32 | 42 |
| 4 | Woolwich Arsenal | 34 | 18 | 6 | 10 | 50 | 26 | 42 |
| 5 | Lincoln City | 34 | 14 | 13 | 7 | 45 | 35 | 41 |
| 6 | Bristol City | 34 | 17 | 6 | 11 | 52 | 35 | 40 |
| 7 | Doncaster Rovers | 34 | 13 | 8 | 13 | 49 | 58 | 34 |
| 8 | Glossop North End | 34 | 10 | 12 | 12 | 36 | 40 | 32 |
| 9 | Burnley | 34 | 10 | 10 | 14 | 41 | 45 | 30 |
| 10 | Burton United | 34 | 11 | 8 | 15 | 46 | 54 | 30 |
| 11 | Barnsley | 34 | 12 | 6 | 16 | 51 | 63 | 30 |
| 12 | Blackpool | 34 | 11 | 7 | 16 | 40 | 56 | 29 |
| 13 | Burslem Port Vale | 34 | 10 | 9 | 15 | 43 | 59 | 29 |
| 14 | Leicester Fosse | 34 | 12 | 5 | 17 | 38 | 56 | 29 |
| 15 | Newton Heath | 34 | 11 | 6 | 17 | 38 | 53 | 28 |
| 16 | Chesterfield | 34 | 11 | 6 | 17 | 47 | 68 | 28 |
| 17 | Stockport County | 34 | 8 | 7 | 19 | 36 | 72 | 23 |
| 18 | Gainsborough Trinity | 34 | 4 | 11 | 19 | 30 | 80 | 19 |

# Season 1902-03

## Football League Division Two

| DATE | OPPONENTS | SCORE | GOALSCORERS | ATTENDANCE |
|---|---|---|---|---|
| Sep 6 | Gainsborough Trinity | W 1-0 | Richards | 4,000 |
| Sep 13 | BURTON UNITED | W 1-0 | Hurst | 15,000 |
| Sep 20 | Bristol City | L 1-3 | Hurst | 6,000 |
| Sep 27 | GLOSSOP NORTH END | D 1-1 | Hurst | 12,000 |
| Oct 4 | CHESTERFIELD | W 2-1 | Preston 2 | 12,000 |
| Oct 11 | Stockport County | L 1-2 | Pegg | 6,000 |
| Oct 25 | Woolwich Arsenal | W 1-0 | Beadsworth | 12,000 |
| Nov 8 | Lincoln City | W 3-1 | Peddie 2, Hurst | 3,000 |
| Nov 15 | SMALL HEATH | L 0-1 | | 25,000 |
| Nov 22 | Leicester Fosse | D 1-1 | Downie | 5,000 |
| Dec 6 | Burnley | W 2-0 | Pegg, Lockhart o.g. | 4,000 |
| Dec 20 | Burslem Port Vale | D 1-1 | Peddie | 1,000 |
| Dec 25 | MANCHESTER CITY | D 1-1 | Pegg | 40,000 |
| Dec 26 | BLACKPOOL | D 2-2 | Downie, Morrison | 10,000 |
| Dec 27 | BARNSLEY | W 2-1 | Peddie, Lappin | 9,000 |
| Jan 3 | GAINSBOROUGH TRINITY | W 3-1 | Downie, Peddie, Pegg | 8,000 |
| Jan 10 | Burton United | L 1-3 | Peddie | 3,000 |
| Jan 17 | BRISTOL CITY | L 1-2 | Preston | 12,000 |
| Jan 24 | Glossop North End | W 3-1 | Downie, Griffiths, Morrison | 5,000 |
| Jan 31 | Chesterfield | L 0-2 | | 6,000 |
| Feb 14 | Blackpool | L 0-2 | | 3,000 |
| Feb 28 | Doncaster Rovers | D 2-2 | Morrison 2 | 4,000 |
| Mar 7 | LINCOLN CITY | L 1-2 | Downie | 4,000 |
| Mar 9 | WOOLWICH ARSENAL | W 3-0 | Arkesden, Peddie, Pegg | 5,000 |
| Mar 21 | LEICESTER FOSSE | W 5-1 | Fitchett, Griffiths, Morrison, Pegg, Smith | 8,000 |
| Mar 23 | STOCKPORT COUNTY | D 0-0 | | 2,000 |
| Mar 30 | PRESTON NORTH END | L 0-1 | | 3,000 |
| Apr 4 | BURNLEY | W 4-0 | Peddie 2, Griffiths, Morrison | 5,000 |
| Apr 10 | Manchester City | W 2-0 | Peddie, Schofield | 30,000 |
| Apr 11 | Preston North End | L 1-3 | Pegg | 7,000 |
| Apr 13 | DONCASTER ROVERS | W 4-0 | Arkesden, Bell, Griffiths, Morrison | 6,000 |
| Apr 18 | BURSLEM PORT VALE | W 2-1 | Schofield 2 | 8,000 |
| Apr 20 | Small Heath | L 1-2 | Peddie | 6,000 |
| Apr 25 | Barnsley | D 0-0 | | 2,000 |

## FA Cup

| | | | | |
|---|---|---|---|---|
| Nov 1 | ACCRINGTON STANLEY | (3Q) W 7-0 | Williams 3, Peddie, Richards, Pegg, Morgan | 6,000 |
| Nov 13 | OSWALDTWISTLE ROVERS | (4Q) W 3-2 | Pegg, Beadsworth, Williams | 5,000 |
| Nov 29 | SOUTHPORT CENTRAL | (5Q) W 4-1 | Pegg 3, Banks | 6,000 |
| Dec 13 | BURTON UNITED | (IRd) D 1-1 | Griffiths | 6,000 |
| Dec 17 | Burton United | (R) W 3-1 | Schofield, Pegg, Peddie | 7,000 |
| Feb 7 | LIVERPOOL | (Rd1) W 2-1 | Peddie | 15,000 |
| Feb 21 | Everton | (Rd2) L 1-3 | Griffiths | 15,000 |

## League & Cup Appearances

| PLAYER | LEAGUE | CUP COMPETITION FA CUP | TOTAL |
|---|---|---|---|
| Arkesden | 9 | | 9 |
| Ball | 4 | | 4 |
| Banks | 13 | 3 | 16 |
| Beadsworth | 9 | 3 | 12 |
| Bell | 5 | | 5 |
| Birchenough | 25 | 5 | 30 |
| Bunce | 2 | | 2 |
| Cartwright | 22 | 4 | 26 |
| Christie | 1 | | 1 |
| Cleaver | 1 | | 1 |
| Fitchett | 5 | | 5 |
| Griffiths | 25 | 7 | 32 |
| Downie | 22 | 5 | 27 |
| Hayes | 2 | | 2 |
| Hurst | 16 | 5 | 21 |
| Lappin | 5 | | 5 |
| Marshall | 6 | | 6 |
| Morgan | 12 | 2 | 14 |
| Morrison | 20 | | 20 |
| Peddie | 30 | 6 | 36 |
| Pegg | 28 | 7 | 35 |
| Preston | 4 | | 4 |
| Read | 27 | 6 | 33 |
| Richards | 8 | 3 | 11 |
| Rothwell | 22 | 6 | 28 |
| Saunders | 1 | 1 | 2 |
| Schofield | 16 | 4 | 20 |
| Smith | 8 | 2 | 6 |
| Stafford | 10 | 2 | 12 |
| Street | 1 | 2 | 3 |
| Turner | 1 | | 1 |
| Whitehouse | 7 | 1 | 8 |
| Williams | 8 | 2 | 10 |

## Goalscorers

| PLAYER | LEAGUE | CUP COMPETITION FA CUP | TOTAL |
|---|---|---|---|
| Peddie | 11 | 4 | 15 |
| Pegg | 7 | 6 | 13 |
| Morrison | 7 | | 7 |
| Griffiths | 4 | 2 | 6 |
| Downie | 5 | | 5 |
| Hurst | 4 | | 4 |
| Schofield | 3 | 1 | 4 |
| Williams | | 4 | 4 |
| Preston | 3 | | 3 |
| Arkesden | 2 | | 2 |
| Beadsworth | 1 | 1 | 2 |
| Richards | 1 | 1 | 2 |
| Bell | 1 | | 1 |
| Fitchett | 1 | | 1 |
| Lappin | 1 | | 1 |
| Smith | 1 | | 1 |
| Banks | | 1 | 1 |
| Morgan | | 1 | 1 |
| Opps' o.gs. | 1 | | 1 |

## Fact File

The club's first season after its metamorphosis from Newton Heath to Manchester United in April 1902.

**SECRETARY:** James West
**MOST APPEARANCES:** John Peddie 36
**TOP GOALSCORER:** John Peddie 15 (11 League)
**BIGGEST WIN:** 7-0 v Accrington Stanley, 1 November 1902, FA Cup
**HIGHEST ATTENDANCE:** 40,000 v Manchester City, 25 December 1902, League

## Final Division Two Table

| | | P | W | D | L | F | A | Pts |
|---|---|---|---|---|---|---|---|---|
| 1 | Manchester City | 34 | 25 | 4 | 5 | 95 | 29 | 54 |
| 2 | Small Heath | 34 | 24 | 3 | 7 | 74 | 36 | 51 |
| 3 | Woolwich Arsenal | 34 | 20 | 8 | 6 | 66 | 30 | 48 |
| 4 | Bristol City | 34 | 17 | 8 | 9 | 59 | 38 | 42 |
| 5 | Manchester United | 34 | 15 | 8 | 11 | 53 | 38 | 38 |
| 6 | Chesterfield | 34 | 14 | 9 | 11 | 67 | 40 | 37 |
| 7 | Preston North End | 34 | 13 | 10 | 11 | 56 | 40 | 36 |
| 8 | Barnsley | 34 | 13 | 8 | 13 | 55 | 51 | 34 |
| 9 | Burslem Port Vale | 34 | 13 | 8 | 13 | 57 | 62 | 34 |
| 10 | Lincoln City | 34 | 12 | 6 | 16 | 46 | 53 | 30 |
| 11 | Glossop North End | 34 | 11 | 7 | 16 | 43 | 58 | 29 |
| 12 | Gainsborough Trinity | 34 | 11 | 7 | 16 | 41 | 59 | 29 |
| 13 | Burton United | 34 | 11 | 7 | 16 | 39 | 59 | 29 |
| 14 | Blackpool | 34 | 9 | 10 | 15 | 44 | 59 | 28 |
| 15 | Leicester Fosse | 34 | 10 | 8 | 16 | 41 | 65 | 28 |
| 16 | Doncaster Rovers | 34 | 9 | 7 | 18 | 35 | 72 | 25 |
| 17 | Stockport County | 34 | 7 | 6 | 21 | 39 | 74 | 20 |
| 18 | Burnley | 34 | 6 | 8 | 20 | 30 | 77 | 20 |

# Season 1903-04

## Football League Division Two

| DATE | OPPONENTS | SCORE | GOALSCORERS | ATTENDANCE |
|---|---|---|---|---|
| Sep 5 | BRISTOL CITY | D 2-2 | Griffiths 2 | 40,000 |
| Sep 7 | Burnley | L 0-3 | | 5,000 |
| Sep 12 | Burslem Port Vale | L 0-1 | | 3,000 |
| Sep 19 | Glossop North End | W 5-0 | Griffiths 2, Robertson A., Downie, Arkesden | 3,000 |
| Sep 26 | BRADFORD CITY | W 3-1 | Pegg 3 | 30,000 |
| Oct 3 | Woolwich Arsenal | L 0-4 | | 20,000 |
| Oct 10 | BARNSLEY | W 4-0 | Pegg 2, Griffiths, Robertson A. | 20,000 |
| Oct 17 | Lincoln City | D 0-0 | | 5,000 |
| Oct 24 | STOCKPORT COUNTY | W 3-1 | Arkesden, Grassam, Schofield A.J. | 15,000 |
| Nov 7 | BOLTON WANDERERS | D 0-0 | | 30,000 |
| Nov 21 | PRESTON NORTH END | L 0-2 | | 15,000 |
| Dec 19 | Gainsborough Trinity | W 4-2 | Arkesden, Duckworth, Grassam, Robertson A. | 6,000 |
| Dec 25 | CHESTERFIELD | W 3-1 | Arkesden 2, Robertson A. | 15,000 |
| Dec 26 | Burton United | D 2-2 | Arkesden 2 | 4,000 |
| Jan 2 | Bristol City | D 1-1 | Griffiths | 8,000 |
| Jan 9 | BURSLEM PORT VALE | W 2-0 | Arkesden, Grassam | 10,000 |
| Jan 16 | GLOSSOP NORTH END | W 3-1 | Arkesden 2, Downie | 10,000 |
| Jan 23 | Bradford City | D 3-3 | Griffiths 2, Downie | 12,000 |
| Jan 30 | WOOLWICH ARSENAL | W 1-0 | Roberston A. | 40,000 |
| Feb 13 | LINCOLN CITY | W 2-0 | Downie, Griffiths | 8,000 |
| Mar 9 | Blackpool | L 1-2 | Grassam | 3,000 |
| Mar 12 | BURNLEY | W 3-1 | Grassam 2, Griffiths | 14,000 |
| Mar 19 | Preston North End | D 1-1 | Arkesden | 7,000 |
| Mar 26 | GRIMSBY TOWN | W 2-0 | Robertson A. 2 | 12,000 |
| Sep 28 | Stockport County | W 3-0 | Hall, Pegg, Schofield A.J. | 2,500 |
| Apr 1 | Chesterfield | W 2-0 | Bell, Hall | 5,000 |
| Apr 2 | Leicester Fosse | W 1-0 | McCartney | 4,000 |
| Apr 5 | Barnsley | W 2-0 | Grassam, Schofield A.J. | 5,000 |
| Apr 9 | BLACKPOOL | W 3-1 | Grassam 2, Schofield A.J. | 10,000 |
| Apr 12 | Grimsby Town | L 1-3 | Grassam | 8,000 |
| Apr 16 | Gainsborough Trinity | W 1-0 | Robertson A. | 4,000 |
| Apr 23 | BURTON UNITED | W 2-0 | Grassam, Robertson A. | 8,000 |
| Apr 25 | Bolton Wanderers | D 0-0 | | 10,000 |
| Apr 30 | LEICESTER FOSSE | W 5-2 | Schofield A.J. 2, Bonthron, Griffiths, Robertson A. | 7,000 |

## FA Cup

| | | | | | |
|---|---|---|---|---|---|
| Dec 12 | SMALL HEATH | (IR) D 1-1 | Schofield A.J. | 10,000 |
| Dec 16 | Small Heath | (R) D 1-1* | Arkesden | 5,000 |
| Dec 21 | Small Heath | (2R) D 1-1* | Schofield A.J. | 3,000 |
| Jan 11 | Small Heath | (3R) W 3-1 | Arkesden 2, Grassam | 9,372 |
| Feb 6 | Notts County | (Rd1) D 3-3 | Downie, Schofield A.J., Arkesden | 12,000 |
| Feb 10 | NOTTS COUNTY | (R) W 2-1 | Morrison, Pegg | 18,000 |
| Feb 20 | The Wednesday | (Rd2) L 0-6 | | 22,051 |

*After extra-time.

## League & Cup Appearances

| PLAYER | LEAGUE | CUP COMPETITION FA CUP | TOTAL |
|---|---|---|---|
| Arkesden | 26 | 6 | 32 |
| Bell | 6 | | 6 |
| Blackstock | 7 | 3 | 10 |
| Bonthron | 33 | 7 | 40 |
| Cartwright | 9 | 6 | 15 |
| Downie | 29 | 6 | 35 |
| Duckworth | 1 | | 1 |
| Gaudie | 7 | 1 | 8 |
| Grassam | 23 | 5 | 28 |
| Griffiths | 30 | 7 | 37 |
| Hall | 8 | | 8 |
| Hartwell | 1 | | 1 |
| Hayes | 21 | 3 | 24 |
| Kerr | 2 | | 2 |
| Lyons | 2 | | 2 |
| McCartney | 13 | | 13 |
| Moger | 13 | | 13 |
| Morrison | 9 | 7 | 16 |
| Pegg | 13 | 3 | 16 |
| Read | 8 | 1 | 9 |
| Roberts | 2 | | 2 |
| Robertson A. | 24 | 1 | 25 |
| Robertson S. | 27 | 6 | 33 |
| Robertson T. | 3 | | 3 |
| Schofield A.J. | 26 | 7 | 33 |
| Schofield J. | 2 | | 2 |
| Sutcliffe | 21 | 7 | 28 |
| Wilkinson | 8 | 1 | 9 |

## Goalscorers

| PLAYER | LEAGUE | CUP COMPETITION FA CUP | TOTAL |
|---|---|---|---|
| Arkesden | 11 | 4 | 15 |
| Grassam | 11 | 1 | 12 |
| Griffiths | 11 | | 11 |
| Robertson A. | 10 | | 10 |
| Schofield A.J. | 6 | 3 | 9 |
| Pegg | 6 | 1 | 7 |
| Downie | 4 | 1 | 5 |
| Hall | 2 | | 2 |
| Bell | 1 | | 1 |
| Bonthron | 1 | | 1 |
| Duckworth | 1 | | 1 |
| McCartney | 1 | | 1 |
| Morrison | | 1 | 1 |

## Fact File

Three players named Robertson, two Alexanders and Tom, made their league debut for United against Bristol City on the opening day of the season.

**SECRETARY:** Ernest Mangnall
**MOST APPEARANCES:** Robert Bonthron 40
**TOP GOALSCORER:** Tommy Arkesden 15 (11 League)
**BIGGEST WIN:** 5-0 v Glossop North End, 19 September 1903, League
**HIGHEST ATTENDANCE:** 40,000 v Bristol City, 5 September 1903, League; 40,000 v Woolwich Arsenal, 30 January 1904, League

## Final Division Two Table

| | | P | W | D | L | F | A | PTS |
|---|---|---|---|---|---|---|---|---|
| 1 | Preston North End | 34 | 20 | 10 | 4 | 62 | 24 | 50 |
| 2 | Woolwich Arsenal | 34 | 21 | 7 | 6 | 91 | 22 | 49 |
| 3 | Manchester United | 34 | 20 | 8 | 6 | 65 | 33 | 48 |
| 4 | Bristol City | 34 | 18 | 6 | 10 | 73 | 41 | 42 |
| 5 | Burnley | 34 | 15 | 9 | 10 | 50 | 55 | 39 |
| 6 | Grimsby Town | 34 | 14 | 8 | 12 | 50 | 49 | 36 |
| 7 | Bolton Wanderers | 34 | 12 | 10 | 12 | 59 | 41 | 34 |
| 8 | Barnsley | 34 | 11 | 10 | 13 | 38 | 57 | 32 |
| 9 | Gainsborough Trinity | 34 | 14 | 3 | 17 | 53 | 60 | 31 |
| 10 | Bradford City | 34 | 12 | 7 | 15 | 45 | 59 | 31 |
| 11 | Chesterfield | 34 | 11 | 8 | 15 | 37 | 45 | 30 |
| 12 | Lincoln City | 34 | 11 | 8 | 15 | 41 | 58 | 30 |
| 13 | Burslem Port Vale | 34 | 10 | 9 | 15 | 54 | 52 | 29 |
| 14 | Burton United | 34 | 11 | 7 | 16 | 45 | 61 | 29 |
| 15 | Blackpool | 34 | 11 | 5 | 18 | 40 | 67 | 27 |
| 16 | Stockport County | 34 | 8 | 11 | 15 | 40 | 72 | 27 |
| 17 | Glossop North End | 34 | 10 | 6 | 18 | 57 | 64 | 26 |
| 18 | Leicester Fosse | 34 | 6 | 10 | 18 | 42 | 82 | 22 |

# Season 1904-05

## Football League Division Two

| DATE | OPPONENTS | SCORE | GOALSCORERS | ATTENDANCE |
|---|---|---|---|---|
| Sep 3 | Burslem Port Vale | D 2-2 | Allan 2 | 4,000 |
| Sep 10 | BRISTOL CITY | W 4-1 | Peddie, Robertson A., Schofield, Williams | 20,000 |
| Sep 17 | BOLTON WANDERERS | L 1-2 | Mackie | 25,000 |
| Sep 24 | Glossop North End | W 2-1 | Allan, Roberts | 6,000 |
| Oct 8 | Bradford City | D 1-1 | Arkesden | 12,000 |
| Oct 15 | LINCOLN CITY | W 2-0 | Arkesden, Schofield | 15,000 |
| Oct 22 | Leicester Fosse | W 3-0 | Arkesden, Peddie, Schofield | 7,000 |
| Oct 29 | BARNSLEY | W 4-0 | Allan, Downie, Peddie, Schofield | 15,000 |
| Nov 5 | West Bromwich Albion | W 2-0 | Arkesden, Williams | 5,000 |
| Nov 12 | BURNLEY | W 1-0 | Arkesden | 15,000 |
| Nov 19 | Grimsby Town | W 1-0 | Bell | 4,000 |
| Dec 3 | Doncaster Rovers | W 1-0 | Peddie | 10,000 |
| Dec 10 | GAINSBOROUGH TRINITY | W 3-1 | Arkesden 2, Allan | 12,000 |
| Dec 17 | Burton United | W 3-2 | Peddie 3 | 3,000 |
| Dec 24 | LIVERPOOL | W 3-1 | Arkesden, Roberts, Williams | 40,000 |
| Dec 26 | CHESTERFIELD | W 3-0 | Allan 2, Williams | 20,000 |
| Dec 31 | BURSLEM PORT VALE | W 6-1 | Allan 3, Arkesden, Hayes, Roberts | 8,000 |
| Jan 2 | BRADFORD CITY | W 7-0 | Arkesden 2, Roberts 2, Allan, Peddie, Robinson o.g. | 10,000 |
| Jan 3 | Bolton Wanderers | W 4-2 | Allan 2, Peddie, Williams | 35,000 |
| Jan 7 | Bristol City | D 1-1 | Arkesden | 12,000 |
| Jan 21 | GLOSSOP NORTH END | W 4-1 | Mackie 2, Arkesden, Grassam | 20,000 |
| Feb 11 | Lincoln City | L 0-3 | | 2,000 |
| Feb 18 | LEICESTER FOSSE | W 4-1 | Peddie 3, Allan | 7,000 |
| Feb 25 | Barnsley | D 0-0 | | 5,000 |
| Mar 4 | WEST BROMWICH ALBION | W 2-0 | Peddie, Williams | 8,000 |
| Mar 11 | Burnley | L 0-2 | | 7,000 |
| Mar 18 | GRIMSBY TOWN | W 2-1 | Allan, Duckworth | 12,000 |
| Mar 25 | Blackpool | W 1-0 | Grassam | 6,000 |
| Apr 1 | DONCASTER ROVERS | W 6-0 | Duckworth 3, Beddow, Peddie, Wombwell | 6,000 |
| Apr 8 | Gainsborough Trinity | D 0-0 | | 6,000 |
| Apr 15 | BURTON UNITED | W 5-0 | Duckworth 2, Peddie 2, Arkesden | 16,000 |
| Apr 21 | Chesterfield | L 0-2 | | 10,000 |
| Apr 22 | Liverpool | L 0-4 | | 28,000 |
| Apr 24 | BLACKPOOL | W 3-1 | Allan, Arkesden, Peddie | 4,000 |

## FA Cup

| | | | | |
|---|---|---|---|---|
| Jan 14 | FULHAM | (Rd1) D 2-2 | Mackie, Arkesden | 17,000 |
| Jan 18 | Fulham | (R) D 0-0* | | 15,000 |
| Jan 23 | Fulham† | (2R) L 0-1 | | 6,000 |

*After extra-time. †Played at Villa Park.

## League & Cup Appearances

| PLAYER | LEAGUE | CUP COMPETITION FA CUP | TOTAL |
|---|---|---|---|
| Allan | 27 | | 27 |
| Arkesden | 28 | 3 | 31 |
| Beddow | 9 | | 9 |
| Bell | 29 | 3 | 32 |
| Blackstock | 3 | | 3 |
| Bonthron | 32 | 3 | 35 |
| Downie | 32 | 3 | 35 |
| Duckworth | 8 | | 8 |
| Fitchett | 11 | 2 | 13 |
| Grassam | 6 | 3 | 9 |
| Griffiths | 2 | | 2 |
| Hartwell | 2 | 1 | 3 |
| Hayes | 22 | 3 | 25 |
| Holden | 1 | | 1 |
| Lyons | 0 | 1 | 1 |
| Mackie | 5 | 2 | 7 |
| Moger | 32 | 3 | 35 |
| Peddie | 32 | | 32 |
| Roberts | 28 | | 28 |
| Robertson A. | 8 | 1 | 9 |
| Robertson S. | 1 | | 1 |
| Schofield | 24 | 3 | 27 |
| Valentine | 2 | | 2 |
| Williams | 22 | 2 | 24 |
| Wombwell | 8 | | 8 |

## Goalscorers

| PLAYER | LEAGUE | CUP COMPETITION FA CUP | TOTAL |
|---|---|---|---|
| Peddie | 17 | | 17 |
| Allan | 16 | | 16 |
| Arkesden | 15 | 1 | 16 |
| Duckworth | 6 | | 6 |
| Williams | 6 | | 6 |
| Roberts | 5 | | 5 |
| Schofield | 4 | | 4 |
| Mackie | 3 | 1 | 4 |
| Grassam | 2 | | 2 |
| Beddow | 1 | | 1 |
| Bell | 1 | | 1 |
| Downie | 1 | | 1 |
| Hayes | 1 | | 1 |
| Robertson A. | 1 | | 1 |
| Wombwell | 1 | | 1 |
| Opp's o.gs. | 1 | | 1 |

## Fact File

United failed to secure promotion from Division Two despite putting together a record 14 straight wins between 15 October and 3 January.

**SECRETARY:** Ernest Mangnall
**MOST APPEARANCES:** Robert Bonthron, Alex Downie, Harry Moger 35
**TOP GOALSCORER:** John Peddie 17 (all League)
**BIGGEST WIN:** 7-0 v Bradford City, 2 January 1905, League
**HIGHEST ATTENDANCE:** 40,000 v Liverpool, 24 December 1904, League

## Final Division Two Table

| | | P | W | D | L | F | A | Pts |
|---|---|---|---|---|---|---|---|---|
| 1 | Liverpool | 34 | 27 | 4 | 3 | 93 | 25 | 58 |
| 2 | Bolton Wanderers | 34 | 27 | 2 | 5 | 87 | 32 | 56 |
| 3 | Manchester United | 34 | 24 | 5 | 5 | 81 | 30 | 53 |
| 4 | Bristol City | 34 | 19 | 4 | 11 | 66 | 45 | 42 |
| 5 | Chesterfield Town | 34 | 14 | 11 | 9 | 44 | 35 | 39 |
| 6 | Gainsborough Trinity | 34 | 14 | 8 | 12 | 61 | 58 | 36 |
| 7 | Barnsley | 34 | 14 | 5 | 15 | 38 | 56 | 33 |
| 8 | Bradford City | 34 | 12 | 8 | 14 | 45 | 49 | 32 |
| 9 | Lincoln City | 34 | 12 | 7 | 15 | 42 | 40 | 31 |
| 10 | West Bromwich Al | 34 | 13 | 4 | 17 | 56 | 48 | 30 |
| 11 | Burnley | 34 | 12 | 6 | 16 | 43 | 52 | 30 |
| 12 | Glossop North End | 34 | 10 | 10 | 14 | 37 | 46 | 30 |
| 13 | Grimsby Town | 34 | 11 | 8 | 15 | 33 | 46 | 30 |
| 14 | Leicester Fosse | 34 | 11 | 7 | 16 | 40 | 55 | 29 |
| 15 | Blackpool | 34 | 9 | 10 | 15 | 36 | 48 | 28 |
| 16 | Burslem Port Vale | 34 | 10 | 7 | 17 | 47 | 72 | 27 |
| 17 | Burton United | 34 | 8 | 4 | 22 | 30 | 84 | 20 |
| 18 | Doncaster Rovers | 34 | 3 | 2 | 29 | 23 | 81 | 8 |

# Season 1905-06

## Football League Division Two

| DATE | OPPONENTS | SCORE | GOALSCORERS | ATTENDANCE |
|---|---|---|---|---|
| Sep 2 | BRISTOL CITY | W 5-1 | Sagar 3, Beddow, Picken | 25,000 |
| Sep 4 | BLACKPOOL | W 2-1 | Peddie 2 | 7,000 |
| Sep 9 | Grimsby Town | W 1-0 | Sagar | 6,000 |
| Sep 16 | Glossop North End | W 2-1 | Bell, Beddow | 7,000 |
| Sep 23 | STOCKPORT COUNTY | W 3-1 | Peddie 2, Sagar | 15,000 |
| Sep 30 | Blackpool | W 1-0 | Roberts | 7,000 |
| Oct 7 | BRADFORD CITY | D 0-0 | | 17,000 |
| Oct 14 | West Bromwich Albion | L 0-1 | | 15,000 |
| Oct 21 | LEICESTER FOSSE | W 3-2 | Peddie 2, Sagar | 12,000 |
| Oct 25 | Gainsborough Trinity | D 2-2 | Bonthron 2 | 4,000 |
| Oct 28 | Hull City | W 1-0 | Picken | 14,000 |
| Nov 4 | LINCOLN CITY | W 2-1 | Picken, Roberts | 15,000 |
| Nov 11 | Chesterfield | L 0-1 | | 3,000 |
| Nov 18 | BURSLEM PORT VALE | W 3-0 | Beddow, Peddie, Hamilton o.g. | 8,000 |
| Nov 25 | Barnsley | W 3-0 | Beddow, Picken, Silto o.g. | 3,000 |
| Dec 2 | CLAPTON ORIENT | W 4-0 | Peddie 2, Picken 2 | 12,000 |
| Dec 9 | Burnley | W 3-1 | Beddow, Peddie, Picken | 8,000 |
| Dec 23 | Burton United | W 2-0 | Schofield 2 | 5,000 |
| Dec 25 | CHELSEA | D 0-0 | | 35,000 |
| Dec 30 | Bristol City | D 1-1 | Roberts | 18,000 |
| Jan 6 | GRIMSBY TOWN | W 5-0 | Beddow 3, Picken 2 | 10,000 |
| Jan 15 | LEEDS CITY | L 0-3 | | 6,000 |
| Jan 20 | GLOSSOP NORTH END | W 5-2 | Picken 2, Beddow, Peddie, Williams | 7,000 |
| Jan 27 | Stockport County | W 1-0 | Peddie | 15,000 |
| Feb 10 | Bradford City | W 5-1 | Beddow 2, Roberts, Schofield, Wombwell | 8,000 |
| Feb 17 | WEST BROMWICH ALBION | D 0-0 | | 30,000 |
| Mar 3 | HULL CITY | W 5-0 | Picken 2, Peddie, Sagar, Schofield | 16,000 |
| Mar 17 | CHESTERFIELD | W 4-1 | Picken 3, Sagar | 16,000 |
| Mar 24 | Burslem Port Vale | L 0-1 | | 3,000 |
| Mar 29 | Leicester Fosse | W 5-2 | Peddie 3, Picken, Sagar | 5,000 |
| Mar 31 | BARNSLEY | W 5-1 | Sagar 3, Bell, Picken | 15,000 |
| Apr 7 | Clapton Orient | W 1-0 | Wall | 8,000 |
| Apr 13 | Chelsea | D 1-1 | Sagar | 60,000 |
| Apr 14 | BURNLEY | W 1-0 | Sagar | 12,000 |
| Apr 16 | GAINSBOROUGH TRINITY | W 2-0 | Allan 2 | 20,000 |
| Apr 21 | Leeds City | W 3-1 | Allan, Peddie, Wombwell | 15,000 |
| Apr 25 | Lincoln City | W 3-2 | Allan 2, Wall | 1,500 |
| Apr 28 | BURTON UNITED | W 6-0 | Sagar 2, Picken 2, Peddie, Wall | 16,000 |

## FA Cup

| | | | | | |
|---|---|---|---|---|---|
| Jan 13 | STAPLE HILL | (Rd1) | W 7-2 | Beddow 3, Picken 2, Allan, Williams | 7,560 |
| Feb 3 | NORWICH CITY | (Rd2) | W 3-0 | Downie, Peddie, Sagar | 10,000 |
| Feb 24 | ASTON VILLA | (Rd3) | W 5-1 | Picken 3, Sagar 2 | 35,500 |
| Mar 10 | WOOLWICH ARSENAL | (Rd4) | L 2-3 | Peddie, Sagar | 26,500 |

## League & Cup Appearances

| PLAYER | LEAGUE | CUP COMPETITION FA CUP | TOTAL |
|---|---|---|---|
| Allan | 5 | 1 | 6 |
| Arkesden | 7 | | 7 |
| Bell | 36 | 4 | 40 |
| Beddow | 21 | 1 | 22 |
| Blackstock | 21 | | 21 |
| Blew | 1 | 1 | 1 |
| Bonthron | 26 | 4 | 30 |
| Donaghy | 3 | | 3 |
| Downie | 34 | 4 | 38 |
| Duckworth | 10 | | 10 |
| Dyer | 1 | | 1 |
| Holden | 27 | 4 | 31 |
| Lyons | 2 | | 2 |
| Moger | 27 | 4 | 31 |
| Montgomery | 3 | | 3 |
| Peddie | 34 | 3 | 37 |
| Picken | 33 | 4 | 37 |
| Roberts | 34 | 4 | 38 |
| Robertson | 1 | | 1 |
| Sagar | 20 | 3 | 23 |
| Schofield | 23 | 4 | 27 |
| Valentine | 8 | | 8 |
| Wall | 6 | | 6 |
| Williams | 10 | 2 | 12 |
| Wombwell | 25 | 2 | 27 |

## Goalscorers

| PLAYER | LEAGUE | CUP COMPETITION FA CUP | TOTAL |
|---|---|---|---|
| Picken | 20 | 5 | 25 |
| Peddie | 18 | 2 | 20 |
| Sagar | 16 | 4 | 20 |
| Beddow | 11 | 3 | 14 |
| Allan | 5 | 1 | 6 |
| Roberts | 4 | | 4 |
| Schofield | 4 | | 4 |
| Wall | 3 | | 3 |
| Bell | 2 | | 2 |
| Bonthron | 2 | | 2 |
| Wombwell | 2 | | 2 |
| Williams | 1 | 1 | 2 |
| Downie | | 1 | 1 |
| Opps' o.gs. | 2 | | 2 |

## Fact File

The club claimed top-flight status for the first time since becoming Manchester United when they were promoted after finishing as runners-up to Bristol City. Only Leeds City claimed a victory against United at Bank Street.

**SECRETARY:** Ernest Mangnall

**MOST APPEARANCES:** Alex Bell 40

**TOP GOALSCORER:** John Picken 25 (20 League)

**BIGGEST WIN:** 6-0 v Burton United, 28 April 1906, League

**HIGHEST ATTENDANCE:** 60,000 v Chelsea, 13 April 1906, League

## Final Division Two Table

| | | P | W | D | L | F | A | PTS |
|---|---|---|---|---|---|---|---|---|
| 1 | BRISTOL CITY | 38 | 30 | 6 | 2 | 83 | 28 | 66 |
| 2 | MANCHESTER UNITED | 38 | 28 | 6 | 4 | 90 | 28 | 62 |
| 3 | CHELSEA | 38 | 22 | 9 | 7 | 90 | 37 | 53 |
| 4 | WBA | 38 | 22 | 8 | 8 | 79 | 36 | 52 |
| 5 | HULL CITY | 38 | 19 | 6 | 13 | 67 | 54 | 44 |
| 6 | LEEDS CITY | 38 | 17 | 9 | 12 | 59 | 47 | 43 |
| 7 | LEICESTER FOSSE | 38 | 15 | 12 | 11 | 53 | 48 | 42 |
| 8 | GRIMSBY TOWN | 38 | 15 | 10 | 13 | 46 | 46 | 40 |
| 9 | BURNLEY | 38 | 15 | 8 | 15 | 42 | 53 | 38 |
| 10 | STOCKPORT COUNTY | 38 | 13 | 9 | 16 | 44 | 56 | 35 |
| 11 | BRADFORD CITY | 38 | 13 | 8 | 17 | 46 | 60 | 34 |
| 12 | BARNSLEY | 38 | 12 | 9 | 17 | 60 | 62 | 33 |
| 13 | LINCOLN CITY | 38 | 12 | 6 | 20 | 69 | 72 | 30 |
| 14 | BLACKPOOL | 38 | 10 | 9 | 19 | 37 | 62 | 29 |
| 15 | GAINSBOROUGH TRINITY | 38 | 12 | 4 | 22 | 44 | 57 | 28 |
| 16 | GLOSSOP NORTH END | 38 | 10 | 8 | 20 | 49 | 71 | 28 |
| 17 | BURSLEM PORT VALE | 38 | 12 | 4 | 22 | 49 | 82 | 28 |
| 18 | CHESTERFIELD TOWN | 38 | 10 | 8 | 20 | 40 | 72 | 28 |
| 19 | BURTON UNITED | 38 | 10 | 6 | 22 | 34 | 67 | 26 |
| 20 | CLAPTON ORIENT | 38 | 7 | 7 | 24 | 35 | 78 | 21 |

# Season 1906-07

## Football League Division One

| DATE | OPPONENTS | SCORE | GOALSCORERS | ATTENDANCE |
|---|---|---|---|---|
| Sep 1 | Bristol City | W 2-1 | Picken, Roberts | 5,000 |
| Sep 3 | Derby County | D 2-2 | Schofield 2 | 5,000 |
| Sep 8 | NOTTS COUNTY | D 0-0 | | 30,000 |
| Sep 15 | Sheffield United | W 2-0 | Bell, Downie | 12,000 |
| Sep 22 | BOLTON WANDERERS | L 1-2 | Peddie | 45,000 |
| Sep 29 | DERBY COUNTY | D 1-1 | Bell | 25,000 |
| Oct 6 | Stoke City | W 2-1 | Duckworth 2 | 7,000 |
| Oct 13 | BLACKBURN ROVERS | D 1-1 | Wall | 20,000 |
| Oct 20 | Sunderland | L 1-4 | Peddie | 18,000 |
| Oct 27 | BIRMINGHAM | W 2-1 | Peddie 2 | 14,000 |
| Nov 3 | Everton | L 0-3 | | 20,000 |
| Nov 10 | WOOLWICH ARSENAL | W 1-0 | Downie | 20,000 |
| Nov 17 | The Wednesday | L 2-5 | Menzies, Peddie | 7,000 |
| Nov 24 | BURY | L 2-4 | Peddie, Wall | 30,000 |
| Dec 1 | Manchester City | L 0-3 | | 40,000 |
| Dec 8 | MIDDLESBROUGH | W 3-1 | Wall 2, Sagar | 12,000 |
| Dec 15 | Preston North End | L 0-2 | | 9,000 |
| Dec 22 | NEWCASTLE UNITED | L 1-3 | Menzies | 18,000 |
| Dec 25 | LIVERPOOL | D 0-0 | | 20,000 |
| Dec 26 | Aston Villa | L 0-2 | | 20,000 |
| Dec 29 | BRISTOL CITY | D 0-0 | | 10,000 |
| Jan 1 | ASTON VILLA | W 1-0 | Turnbull | 40,000 |
| Jan 5 | Notts County | L 0-3 | | 10,000 |
| Jan 19 | SHEFFIELD UNITED | W 2-0 | Turnbull, Wall | 15,000 |
| Jan 26 | Bolton Wanderers | W 1-0 | Turnbull | 25,000 |
| Feb 2 | Newcastle United | L 0-5 | | 30,000 |
| Feb 9 | STOKE CITY | W 4-1 | Picken 2, Meredith, Holford o.g. | 15,000 |
| Feb 16 | Blackburn Rovers | W 4-2 | Meredith 2, Sagar, Wall | 5,000 |
| Feb 23 | PRESTON NORTH END | W 3-0 | Wall 2, Sagar | 16,000 |
| Mar 2 | Birmingham | D 1-1 | Menzies | 20,000 |
| Mar 16 | Woolwich Arsenal | L 0-4 | | 6,000 |
| Mar 25 | SUNDERLAND | W 2-0 | Turnbull, Williams | 12,000 |
| Mar 30 | Bury | W 2-1 | Menzies, Meredith | 25,000 |
| Apr 1 | Liverpool | W 1-0 | Turnbull | 20,000 |
| Apr 6 | MANCHESTER CITY | D 1-1 | Roberts | 40,000 |
| Apr 10 | THE WEDNESDAY | W 5-0 | Wall 3, Picken, Sagar | 10,000 |
| Apr 13 | Middlesbrough | L 0-2 | | 15,000 |
| Apr 22 | EVERTON | W 3-0 | Bannister, Meredith, Turnbull | 10,000 |

## FA Cup

| | | | | |
|---|---|---|---|---|
| Jan 12 | Portsmouth | (Rd1) D 2-2 | Picken, Wall | 24,329 |
| Jan 16 | PORTSMOUTH | (R) L 1-2 | Wall | 8,000 |

## League & Cup Appearances

| PLAYER | LEAGUE | CUP COMPETITION FA CUP | TOTAL |
|---|---|---|---|
| Allan | 3 | | 3 |
| Bannister | 4 | | 4 |
| Beddow | 3 | | 3 |
| Bell | 35 | 2 | 37 |
| Berry | 9 | | 9 |
| Blackstock | 3 | 1 | 4 |
| Bonthron | 28 | 1 | 29 |
| Buckley | 3 | | 3 |
| Burgess | 17 | | 17 |
| Downie | 19 | 1 | 20 |
| Duckworth | 28 | 2 | 30 |
| Holden | 27 | 2 | 29 |
| Menzies | 17 | 2 | 19 |
| Meredith | 16 | 2 | 18 |
| Moger | 38 | 2 | 40 |
| Peddie | 16 | | 16 |
| Picken | 26 | 2 | 28 |
| Roberts | 31 | 1 | 32 |
| Sagar | 10 | | 10 |
| Schofield | 10 | | 10 |
| Turnbull | 15 | | 15 |
| Wall | 38 | 2 | 40 |
| Williams | 3 | | 3 |
| Wombwell | 14 | 2 | 16 |
| Yates | 3 | | 3 |
| Young | 2 | | 2 |

## Goalscorers

| PLAYER | LEAGUE | CUP COMPETITION FA CUP | TOTAL |
|---|---|---|---|
| Wall | 11 | 2 | 13 |
| Peddie | 6 | | 6 |
| Turnbull | 6 | | 6 |
| Meredith | 5 | | 5 |
| Picken | 4 | 1 | 5 |
| Menzies | 4 | | 4 |
| Sagar | 4 | | 4 |
| Bell | 2 | | 2 |
| Downie | 2 | | 2 |
| Duckworth | 2 | | 2 |
| Roberts | 2 | | 2 |
| Schofield | 2 | | 2 |
| Bannister | 1 | | 1 |
| Williams | 1 | | 1 |
| Opps' o.gs. | 1 | | 1 |

## Fact File

Billy Meredith, the original Welsh wizard, made his league debut for United against Aston Villa on New Year's Day 1907.

**SECRETARY:** Ernest Mangnall
**MOST APPEARANCES:** Harry Moger, George Wall 40
**TOP GOALSCORER:** George Wall 13 (11 League)
**BIGGEST WIN:** 5-0 v The Wednesday, 10 April 1907, League
**HIGHEST ATTENDANCE:** 45,000 v Bolton Wanderers, 22 September 1906, League

## Final Division One Table

| | | P | W | D | L | F | A | Pts |
|---|---|---|---|---|---|---|---|---|
| 1 | Newcastle United | 38 | 22 | 7 | 9 | 74 | 46 | 51 |
| 2 | Bristol City | 38 | 20 | 8 | 10 | 66 | 47 | 48 |
| 3 | Everton | 38 | 20 | 5 | 13 | 70 | 46 | 45 |
| 4 | Sheffield United | 38 | 17 | 11 | 10 | 57 | 55 | 45 |
| 5 | Aston Villa | 38 | 19 | 6 | 13 | 78 | 52 | 44 |
| 6 | Bolton Wanderers | 38 | 18 | 8 | 12 | 59 | 47 | 44 |
| 7 | Woolwich Arsenal | 38 | 20 | 4 | 14 | 66 | 59 | 44 |
| 8 | Manchester United | 38 | 17 | 8 | 13 | 53 | 56 | 42 |
| 9 | Birmingham | 38 | 15 | 8 | 15 | 52 | 52 | 38 |
| 10 | Sunderland | 38 | 14 | 9 | 15 | 65 | 66 | 37 |
| 11 | Middlesbrough | 38 | 15 | 6 | 17 | 56 | 63 | 36 |
| 12 | Blackburn Rovers | 38 | 14 | 7 | 17 | 56 | 59 | 35 |
| 13 | The Wednesday | 38 | 12 | 11 | 15 | 49 | 60 | 35 |
| 14 | Preston North End | 38 | 14 | 7 | 17 | 44 | 57 | 35 |
| 15 | Liverpool | 38 | 13 | 7 | 18 | 64 | 65 | 33 |
| 16 | Bury | 38 | 13 | 6 | 19 | 58 | 68 | 32 |
| 17 | Manchester City | 38 | 10 | 12 | 16 | 53 | 77 | 32 |
| 18 | Notts County | 38 | 8 | 15 | 15 | 46 | 50 | 31 |
| 19 | Derby County | 38 | 9 | 9 | 20 | 41 | 59 | 27 |
| 20 | Stoke City | 38 | 8 | 10 | 20 | 41 | 64 | 26 |

# Season 1907-08

## Football League Division One

| DATE | OPPONENTS | SCORE | GOALSCORERS | ATTENDANCE |
|---|---|---|---|---|
| Sep 2 | Aston Villa | W 4-1 | Meredith 2, Bannister, Wall | 20,000 |
| Sep 7 | LIVERPOOL | W 4-0 | Turnbull A. 3, Wall | 24,000 |
| Sep 9 | MIDDLESBROUGH | W 2-1 | Turnbull A. 2 | 20,000 |
| Sep 14 | Middlesbrough | L 1-2 | Bannister | 18,000 |
| Sep 21 | SHEFFIELD UNITED | W 2-1 | Turnbull A. 2 | 25,000 |
| Sep 28 | Chelsea | W 4-1 | Meredith 2, Bannister, Turnbull A. | 40,000 |
| Oct 5 | NOTTINGHAM FOREST | W 4-0 | Bannister, Turnbull J., Wall, Maltby o.g. | 20,000 |
| Oct 12 | Newcastle United | W 6-1 | Wall 2, Meredith, Roberts, Turnbull A., Turnbull J. | 25,000 |
| Oct 19 | Blackburn Rovers | W 5-1 | Turnbull A. 3, Turnbull J. 2 | 30,000 |
| Oct 26 | BOLTON WANDERERS | W 2-1 | Turnbull A., Turnbull J. | 35,000 |
| Nov 2 | BIRMINGHAM | W 4-3 | Meredith 2, Turnbull J., Wall | 20,000 |
| Nov 9 | EVERTON | W 4-3 | Wall 2, Meredith, Roberts | 30,000 |
| Nov 16 | Sunderland | W 2-1 | Turnbull A. 2 | 30,000 |
| Nov 24 | WOOLWICH ARSENAL | W 4-2 | Turnbull A. 4 | 10,000 |
| Nov 30 | The Wednesday | L 0-2 | | 40,000 |
| Dec 7 | BRISTOL CITY | W 2-1 | Wall 2 | 20,000 |
| Dec 14 | Notts County | D 1-1 | Meredith | 11,000 |
| Dec 21 | MANCHESTER CITY | W 3-1 | Turnbull A. 2, Wall | 35,000 |
| Dec 25 | BURY | W 2-1 | Meredith, Turnbull J. | 45,000 |
| Dec 28 | Preston North End | D 0-0 | | 12,000 |
| Jan 11 | Bury | W 1-0 | Wall | 29,500 |
| Jan 18 | Sheffield United | L 0-2 | | 17,000 |
| Jan 25 | CHELSEA | W 1-0 | Turnbull J. | 20,000 |
| Feb 8 | NEWCASTLE UNITED | D 1-1 | Turnbull J. | 50,000 |
| Feb 15 | BLACKBURN ROVERS | L 1-2 | Turnbull A. | 15,000 |
| Feb 29 | BIRMINGHAM | W 1-0 | Turnbull A. | 12,000 |
| Mar 14 | SUNDERLAND | W 3-0 | Bell, Berry, Wall | 15,000 |
| Mar 21 | Woolwich Arsenal | L 0-1 | | 20,000 |
| Mar 25 | Liverpool | L 4-7 | Wall 2, Bannister, Turnbull J. | 10,000 |
| Mar 28 | THE WEDNESDAY | W 4-1 | Wall 2, Halse, Turnbull A. | 30,000 |
| Apr 4 | Bristol City | D 1-1 | Wall | 12,000 |
| Apr 8 | Everton | W 3-1 | Halse, Turnbull A., Wall | 17,000 |
| Apr 11 | NOTTS COUNTY | L 0-1 | | 20,000 |
| Apr 17 | Nottingham Forest | L 0-2 | | 22,000 |
| Apr 18 | Manchester City | D 0-0 | | 40,000 |
| Apr 20 | ASTON VILLA | L 1-2 | Picken | 10,000 |
| Apr 22 | Bolton Wanderers | D 2-2 | Halse, Stacey | 18,000 |
| Apr 25 | PRESTON NORTH END | W 2-1 | Halse, Rodway o.g. | 8,000 |

## FA Cup

| | | | | |
|---|---|---|---|---|
| Jan 11 | BLACKPOOL | W 3-1 | Wall 2, Bannister | 11,747 |
| Feb 1 | CHELSEA | W 1-0 | Turnbull A. | 25,184 |
| Feb 22 | Aston Villa | W 2-0 | Turnbull A., Wall | 12,777 |
| Mar 7 | Fulham | L 1-2 | Turnbull J. | 41,000 |

## FA Charity Shield

| | | | | |
|---|---|---|---|---|
| Apr 27 | Queens Park Rangers* | D 1-1 | Meredith | 12,000 |
| Aug 29 | Queens Park Rangers** | (R) W 4-0 | Turnbull J. 3, Wall | 10,000 |

*Played at Stamford Bridge, London. **Replay held over to following pre-season.

## League & Cup Appearances

| PLAYER | LEAGUE | CUP COMPETITION | OTHER | TOTAL |
|---|---|---|---|---|
| | | FA CUP | | |
| Bannister | 36 | 4 | 2 | 42 |
| Bell | 35 | 4 | 2 | 41 |
| Berry | 3 | 1 | | 4 |
| Broomfield | 9 | | | 9 |
| Burgess | 27 | 3 | 2 | 32 |
| Dalton | 1 | | | 1 |
| Downie | 10 | | | 10 |
| Duckworth | 35 | 3 | 2 | 40 |
| Halse | 6 | | | 6 |
| Holden | 26 | 3 | | 29 |
| Hulme | 1 | | | 1 |
| McGillivray | 1 | 1 | | 2 |
| Menzies | 6 | | | 6 |
| Meredith | 37 | 4 | 2 | 43 |
| Moger | 29 | 4 | 2 | 35 |
| Picken | 8 | | 1 | 9 |
| Roberts | 32 | 3 | 2 | 37 |
| Stacey | 18 | 3 | 2 | 23 |
| Thomson | 3 | | | 3 |
| Turnbull A. | 30 | 4 | 1 | 35 |
| Turnbull J. | 26 | 3 | 2 | 31 |
| Wall | 36 | 4 | 2 | 42 |
| Whiteside | 1 | | | 1 |
| Williams | 1 | | | 1 |
| Wilson | 1 | | | 1 |

## Goalscorers

| PLAYER | LEAGUE | CUP COMPETITION | OTHER | TOTAL |
|---|---|---|---|---|
| | | FA CUP | | |
| Turnbull A | 25 | 2 | | 27 |
| Wall | 19 | 3 | 1 | 23 |
| Meredith | 10 | | 1 | 11 |
| Bannister | 5 | 1 | | 6 |
| Halse | 4 | | | 4 |
| Turnbull J. | 10 | 1 | 3 | 4 |
| Roberts | 2 | | | 2 |
| Bell | 1 | | | 1 |
| Berry | 1 | | | 1 |
| Picken | 1 | | | 1 |
| Stacey | 1 | | | 1 |
| Opps' o.gs. | 2 | | | 2 |

### Fact File

A fantastic opening to the season – 13 wins and just one defeat in the opening 14 games – put United well on course for their first-ever league championship.

**SECRETARY:** Ernest Mangnall
**MOST APPEARANCES:** Billy Meredith 43
**TOP GOALSCORER:** Alex 'Sandy' Turnbull 27 (25 League)
**BIGGEST WIN:** 6-1 v Newcastle United, 12 October 1907, League
**HIGHEST ATTENDANCE:** 50,000 v Newcastle United, 8 February 1908, League

### Final Division One Table

| | | P | W | D | L | F | A | Pts |
|---|---|---|---|---|---|---|---|---|
| 1 | Manchester United | 38 | 23 | 6 | 9 | 81 | 48 | 52 |
| 2 | Aston Villa | 38 | 17 | 9 | 12 | 77 | 59 | 43 |
| 3 | Manchester City | 38 | 16 | 11 | 11 | 62 | 54 | 43 |
| 4 | Newcastle United | 38 | 15 | 12 | 11 | 65 | 54 | 42 |
| 5 | The Wednesday | 38 | 19 | 4 | 15 | 73 | 64 | 42 |
| 6 | Middlesbrough | 38 | 17 | 7 | 14 | 54 | 45 | 41 |
| 7 | Bury | 38 | 14 | 11 | 13 | 58 | 61 | 39 |
| 8 | Liverpool | 38 | 16 | 6 | 16 | 68 | 61 | 38 |
| 9 | Nottingham Forest | 38 | 13 | 11 | 14 | 59 | 62 | 37 |
| 10 | Bristol City | 38 | 12 | 12 | 14 | 58 | 61 | 36 |
| 11 | Everton | 38 | 15 | 6 | 17 | 58 | 64 | 36 |
| 12 | Preston North End | 38 | 12 | 12 | 14 | 47 | 53 | 36 |
| 13 | Chelsea | 38 | 14 | 8 | 16 | 53 | 62 | 36 |
| 14 | Blackburn Rovers | 38 | 12 | 12 | 14 | 51 | 63 | 36 |
| 15 | Woolwich Arsenal | 38 | 12 | 12 | 14 | 51 | 63 | 36 |
| 16 | Sunderland | 38 | 16 | 3 | 19 | 78 | 75 | 35 |
| 17 | Sheffield United | 38 | 12 | 11 | 15 | 52 | 58 | 35 |
| 18 | Notts County | 38 | 13 | 8 | 17 | 39 | 51 | 34 |
| 19 | Bolton Wanderers | 38 | 14 | 5 | 19 | 52 | 58 | 33 |
| 20 | Birmingham | 38 | 9 | 12 | 17 | 40 | 60 | 30 |

# Season 1908-09

## Football League Division One

| DATE | OPPONENTS | SCORE | GOALSCORERS | ATTENDANCE |
|---|---|---|---|---|
| Sep 5 | Preston North End | W 3-0 | Turnbull J. 2, Halse | 18,000 |
| Sep 7 | BURY | W 2-1 | Turnbull J. 2 | 16,000 |
| Sep 12 | MIDDLESBROUGH | W 6-3 | Turnbull J. 4, Halse, Wall | 25,000 |
| Sep 19 | Manchester City | W 2-1 | Halse, Turnbull J. | 40,000 |
| Sep 26 | LIVERPOOL | W 3-2 | Halse 2, Turnbull J. | 25,000 |
| Oct 3 | Bury | D 2-2 | Halse, Wall | 25,000 |
| Oct 10 | SHEFFIELD UNITED | W 2-1 | Bell 2 | 14,000 |
| Oct 17 | Aston Villa | L 1-3 | Halse | 40,000 |
| Oct 24 | NOTTINGHAM FOREST | D 2-2 | Turnbull A. 2 | 20,000 |
| Oct 31 | Sunderland | L 1-6 | Turnbull A. | 30,000 |
| Nov 7 | CHELSEA | L 0-1 | | 15,000 |
| Nov 14 | Blackburn Rovers | W 3-1 | Halse, Turnbull J., Wall | 25,000 |
| Nov 21 | BRADFORD CITY | W 2-0 | Picken, Wall | 15,000 |
| Nov 28 | THE WEDNESDAY | W 3-1 | Halse, Picken, Turnbull J. | 20,000 |
| Dec 5 | Everton | L 2-3 | Bannister, Halse | 35,000 |
| Dec 12 | LEICESTER FOSSE | W 4-2 | Wall 3, Picken | 10,000 |
| Dec 19 | Woolwich Arsenal | W 1-0 | Halse | 10,000 |
| Dec 25 | Newcastle United | L 1-2 | Wall | 35,000 |
| Dec 26 | NEWCASTLE UNITED | W 1-0 | Halse | 40,000 |
| Jan 1 | NOTTS COUNTY | W 4-3 | Halse 2, Roberts, Turnbull A. | 15,000 |
| Jan 2 | PRESTON NORTH END | L 0-2 | | 18,000 |
| Jan 9 | Middlesbrough | L 0-5 | | 15,000 |
| Jan 23 | MANCHESTER CITY | W 3-1 | Livingstone 2, Wall | 40,000 |
| Jan 30 | Liverpool | L 1-3 | Turnbull A. | 30,000 |
| Feb 13 | Sheffield United | D 0-0 | | 12,000 |
| Feb 27 | Nottingham Forest | L 0-2 | | 7,000 |
| Mar 13 | Chelsea | D 1-1 | Wall | 30,000 |
| Mar 15 | SUNDERLAND | D 2-2 | Payne, Turnbull J. | 10,000 |
| Mar 20 | BLACKBURN ROVERS | L 0-3 | | 11,000 |
| Mar 31 | ASTON VILLA | L 0-2 | | 10,000 |
| Apr 3 | The Wednesday | L 0-2 | | 15,000 |
| Apr 9 | BRISTOL CITY | L 0-1 | | 18,000 |
| Apr 10 | EVERTON | D 2-2 | Turnbull J. 2 | 8,000 |
| Apr 12 | Bristol City | D 0-0 | | 18,000 |
| Apr 13 | Notts County | W 1-0 | Livingstone | 7,000 |
| Apr 17 | Leicester Fosse | L 2-3 | Turnbull J., Wall | 8,000 |
| Apr 27 | WOOLWICH ARSENAL | L 1-4 | Turnbull J. | 10,000 |
| Apr 29 | Bradford City | L 0-1 | | 30,000 |

## FA Cup

| | | | | | |
|---|---|---|---|---|---|
| Jan 16 | BRIGHTON & HOVE ALBION | (Rd1) | W 1-0 | Halse | 8,300 |
| Feb 6 | EVERTON | (Rd2) | W 1-0 | Halse | 35,217 |
| Feb 20 | BLACKBURN ROVERS | (Rd3) | W 6-1 | Turnbull A. 3, Turnbull J. 3 | 38,500 |
| Mar 10 | Burnley* | (Rd4) | W 3-2 | Turnbull J. 2, Halse | 16,850 |
| Mar 27 | Newcastle United** | (SF) | W 1-0 | Halse | 40,118 |
| Apr 24 | Bristol City† | (F) | W 1-0 | Turnbull A. | 71,401 |

*Original match postponed after 72 minutes, Burnley winning 1-0.
**Played at Bramall Lane, Sheffield. †Played at Crystal Palace, London.

## League & Cup Appearances

| PLAYER | LEAGUE | CUP COMPETITION FA CUP | TOTAL |
|---|---|---|---|
| Bannister | 16 | | 16 |
| Bell | 20 | 6 | 26 |
| Berry | 1 | | 1 |
| Burgess | 4 | | 4 |
| Christie | 2 | | 2 |
| Curry | 8 | | 8 |
| Donnelly | 1 | | 1 |
| Downie | 23 | | 23 |
| Duckworth | 33 | 6 | 39 |
| Ford | 4 | | 4 |
| Halse | 29 | 6 | 35 |
| Hardman | 4 | | 4 |
| Hayes | 22 | 6 | 28 |
| Holden | 2 | | 2 |
| Hulme | 3 | | 3 |
| Linkson | 10 | | 10 |
| Livingstone | 11 | 2 | 13 |
| McGillivray | 2 | | 2 |
| Meredith | 34 | 4 | 38 |
| Moger | 36 | 6 | 42 |
| Payne | 2 | | 2 |
| Picken | 13 | | 13 |
| Quin | 1 | | 1 |
| Roberts | 27 | 6 | 33 |
| Stacey | 32 | 6 | 38 |
| Thomson | 1 | | 1 |
| Turnbull A. | 19 | 6 | 25 |
| Turnbull J. | 22 | 6 | 28 |
| Wall | 34 | 6 | 40 |
| Wilcox | 2 | | 2 |

## Goalscorers

| PLAYER | LEAGUE | CUP COMPETITION FA CUP | TOTAL |
|---|---|---|---|
| Turnbull J. | 17 | 5 | 22 |
| Halse | 14 | 4 | 18 |
| Wall | 11 | | 11 |
| Turnbull A. | 5 | 4 | 9 |
| Livingstone | 3 | | 3 |
| Picken | 3 | | 3 |
| Bell | 2 | | 2 |
| Bannister | 1 | | 1 |
| Payne | 1 | | 1 |
| Roberts | 1 | | 1 |

## Final Division One Table

| | P | W | D | L | F | A | Pts |
|---|---|---|---|---|---|---|---|
| 1 Newcastle United | 38 | 24 | 5 | 9 | 65 | 41 | 53 |
| 2 Everton | 38 | 18 | 10 | 10 | 82 | 57 | 46 |
| 3 Sunderland | 38 | 21 | 2 | 15 | 78 | 63 | 44 |
| 4 Blackburn Rovers | 38 | 14 | 13 | 11 | 61 | 50 | 41 |
| 5 The Wednesday | 38 | 17 | 6 | 15 | 67 | 61 | 40 |
| 6 Woolwich Arsenal | 38 | 14 | 10 | 14 | 52 | 49 | 38 |
| 7 Aston Villa | 38 | 14 | 10 | 14 | 58 | 56 | 38 |
| 8 Bristol City | 38 | 13 | 12 | 13 | 45 | 58 | 38 |
| 9 Middlesbrough | 38 | 14 | 9 | 15 | 59 | 53 | 37 |
| 10 Preston North End | 38 | 13 | 11 | 14 | 48 | 44 | 37 |
| 11 Chelsea | 38 | 14 | 9 | 15 | 56 | 61 | 37 |
| 12 Sheffield United | 38 | 14 | 9 | 15 | 51 | 59 | 37 |
| 13 Manchester United | 38 | 15 | 7 | 16 | 58 | 68 | 37 |
| 14 Nottingham Forest | 38 | 14 | 8 | 16 | 66 | 57 | 36 |
| 15 Notts County | 38 | 14 | 8 | 16 | 51 | 48 | 36 |
| 16 Liverpool | 38 | 15 | 6 | 17 | 57 | 65 | 36 |
| 17 Bury | 38 | 14 | 8 | 16 | 63 | 77 | 36 |
| 18 Bradford City | 38 | 12 | 10 | 16 | 47 | 47 | 34 |
| 19 Manchester City | 38 | 15 | 4 | 19 | 67 | 69 | 34 |
| 20 Leicester Fosse | 38 | 8 | 9 | 21 | 54 | 102 | 25 |

### Fact File

Alex 'Sandy' Turnbull's 22nd-minute goal against Bristol City at the old Crystal Palace was enough to give United their inaugural FA Cup triumph.

**SECRETARY:** Ernest Mangnall
**MOST APPEARANCES:** Harry Moger 42
**TOP GOALSCORER:** Jimmy Turnbull 22 (17 League)
**BIGGEST WIN:** 6-1 v Blackburn Rovers, 20 February 1909, FA Cup
**HIGHEST ATTENDANCE:** 71,401 v Bristol City, 24 April 1909, FA Cup

## Season 1909-10

### Football League Division One

| DATE | OPPONENTS | SCORE | GOALSCORERS | ATTENDANCE |
|---|---|---|---|---|
| Sep 1 | BRADFORD CITY | W 1-0 | Wall | 12,000 |
| Sep 4 | BURY | W 2-0 | Turnbull J. 2 | 12,000 |
| Sep 6 | NOTTS COUNTY | W 2-1 | Turnbull J., Wall | 6,000 |
| Sep 11 | Tottenham Hotspur | D 2-2 | Turnbull J., Wall | 40,000 |
| Sep 18 | PRESTON NORTH END | D 1-1 | Roberts | 13,000 |
| Sep 25 | Notts County | L 2-3 | Turnbull A. 2 | 11,000 |
| Oct 2 | NEWCASTLE UNITED | D 1-1 | Wall | 30,000 |
| Oct 9 | Liverpool | L 2-3 | Turnbull A. 2 | 30,000 |
| Oct 16 | ASTON VILLA | W 2-0 | Halse, Turnbull A. | 20,000 |
| Oct 23 | Sheffield United | W 1-0 | Wall | 30,000 |
| Oct 30 | WOOLWICH ARSENAL | W 1-0 | Wall | 20,000 |
| Nov 6 | Bolton Wanderers | W 3-2 | Homer 2, Halse | 20,000 |
| Nov 13 | CHELSEA | W 2-0 | Turnbull A., Wall | 10,000 |
| Nov 20 | Blackburn Rovers | L 2-3 | Homer 2 | 40,000 |
| Nov 27 | NOTTINGHAM FOREST | L 2-6 | Halse, Wall | 12,000 |
| Dec 4 | Sunderland | L 0-3 | | 12,000 |
| Dec 18 | Middlesbrough | W 2-1 | Homer, Turnbull A. | 10,000 |
| Dec 25 | THE WEDNESDAY | L 0-3 | | 25,000 |
| Dec 27 | The Wednesday | L 1-4 | Wall | 37,000 |
| Jan 1 | Bradford City | W 2-0 | Turnbull A., Wall | 25,000 |
| Jan 8 | Bury | D 1-1 | Homer | 10,000 |
| Jan 22 | TOTTENHAM HOTSPUR | W 5-0 | Roberts 2, Connor, Hooper, Meredith | 7,000 |
| Feb 5 | Preston North End | L 0-1 | | 4,000 |
| Feb 12 | Newcastle United | W 4-3 | Turnbull A. 2, Blott, Roberts | 20,000 |
| Feb 19 | LIVERPOOL | L 3-4 | Homer, Turnbull A., Wall | 45,000 |
| Feb 26 | Aston Villa | L 1-7 | Meredith | 20,000 |
| Mar 5 | SHEFFIELD UNITED | W 1-0 | Picken | 40,000 |
| Mar 12 | Woolwich Arsenal | D 0-0 | | 4,000 |
| Mar 19 | BOLTON WANDERERS | W 5-0 | Halse, Meredith, Picken, Turnbull J., Wall | 20,000 |
| Mar 25 | BRISTOL CITY | W 2-1 | Picken, Turnbull J. | 50,000 |
| Mar 26 | Chelsea | D 1-1 | Turnbull J. | 25,000 |
| Mar 28 | Bristol City | L 1-2 | Meredith | 18,000 |
| Apr 2 | BLACKBURN ROVERS | W 2-0 | Halse 2 | 20,000 |
| Apr 6 | EVERTON | W 3-2 | Turnbull J., 2, Meredith | 5,500 |
| Apr 9 | Nottingham Forest | L 0-2 | | 7,000 |
| Apr 16 | SUNDERLAND | W 2-0 | Turnbull A., Wall | 12,000 |
| Apr 23 | Everton | D 3-3 | Homer, Turnbull A., Wall | 10,000 |
| Apr 30 | MIDDLESBROUGH | W 4-1 | Picken 4 | 10,000 |

### FA Cup

| | | | | |
|---|---|---|---|---|
| Jan 15 | Burnley | (Rd1) L 0-2 | | 16,628 |

### League & Cup Appearances

| PLAYER | LEAGUE | CUP COMPETITION FA CUP | TOTAL |
|---|---|---|---|
| Bannister | 1 | | 1 |
| Bell | 27 | 1 | 28 |
| Blott | 10 | | 10 |
| Burgess | 1 | | 1 |
| Connor | 8 | | 8 |
| Donnelly | 4 | | 4 |
| Downie | 3 | | 3 |
| Duckworth | 29 | 1 | 30 |
| Ford | 1 | | 1 |
| Halse | 27 | 1 | 28 |
| Hayes | 30 | 1 | 31 |
| Holden | 7 | | 7 |
| Homer | 17 | | 17 |
| Hooper | 2 | | 2 |
| Livingstone | 16 | | 16 |
| Meredith | 31 | 1 | 32 |
| Moger | 36 | 1 | 37 |
| Picken | 19 | | 19 |
| Quin | 1 | | 1 |
| Roberts | 28 | 1 | 29 |
| Rounds | 2 | | 2 |
| Stacey | 32 | 1 | 33 |
| Turnbull A. | 26 | 1 | 27 |
| Turnbull J. | 19 | 1 | 20 |
| Wall | 32 | 1 | 33 |
| Whalley | 9 | | 9 |

### Goalscorers

| PLAYER | LEAGUE | CUP COMPETITION FA CUP | TOTAL |
|---|---|---|---|
| Wall | 14 | | 14 |
| Turnbull A. | 13 | | 13 |
| Turnbull J. | 9 | | 9 |
| Homer | 8 | | 8 |
| Picken | 7 | | 7 |
| Halse | 6 | | 6 |
| Meredith | 5 | | 5 |
| Roberts | 4 | | 4 |
| Blott | 1 | | 1 |
| Connor | 1 | | 1 |
| Hooper | 1 | | 1 |

### Fact File

The club moved from Bank Street, Clayton to their newly-built 80,000 capacity home ground at Old Trafford. Liverpool provided the first league opponents on 19 February 1910 and spoiled the party with a 4-3 win.

**SECRETARY:** Ernest Mangnall
**MOST APPEARANCES:** Harry Moger 37
**TOP GOALSCORER:** George Wall 14 (all League)
**BIGGEST WIN:** 5-0 v Tottenham Hotspur, 22 January 1910, League; 5-0 v Bolton Wanderers, 19 March 1910, League
**HIGHEST ATTENDANCE:** 50,000 v Bristol City, 25 March 1910, League

### Final Division One Table

| | | P | W | D | L | F | A | Pts |
|---|---|---|---|---|---|---|---|---|
| 1 | Aston Villa | 38 | 23 | 7 | 8 | 84 | 42 | 53 |
| 2 | Liverpool | 38 | 21 | 6 | 11 | 78 | 57 | 48 |
| 3 | Blackburn Rovers | 38 | 18 | 9 | 11 | 73 | 55 | 45 |
| 4 | Newcastle United | 38 | 19 | 7 | 12 | 70 | 56 | 45 |
| 5 | Manchester United | 38 | 19 | 7 | 12 | 69 | 61 | 45 |
| 6 | Sheffield United | 38 | 16 | 10 | 12 | 62 | 41 | 42 |
| 7 | Bradford City | 38 | 17 | 8 | 13 | 64 | 47 | 42 |
| 8 | Sunderland | 38 | 18 | 5 | 15 | 66 | 51 | 41 |
| 9 | Notts County | 38 | 15 | 10 | 13 | 67 | 59 | 40 |
| 10 | Everton | 38 | 16 | 8 | 14 | 51 | 56 | 40 |
| 11 | The Wednesday | 38 | 15 | 9 | 14 | 60 | 63 | 39 |
| 12 | Preston North End | 38 | 15 | 5 | 18 | 52 | 58 | 35 |
| 13 | Bury | 38 | 12 | 9 | 17 | 62 | 66 | 33 |
| 14 | Nottingham Forest | 38 | 11 | 11 | 16 | 54 | 72 | 33 |
| 15 | Tottenham Hotspur | 38 | 11 | 10 | 17 | 53 | 69 | 32 |
| 16 | Bristol City | 38 | 12 | 8 | 18 | 45 | 60 | 32 |
| 17 | Middlesbrough | 38 | 11 | 9 | 18 | 56 | 73 | 31 |
| 18 | Woolwich Arsenal | 38 | 11 | 9 | 18 | 37 | 67 | 31 |
| 19 | Chelsea | 38 | 11 | 7 | 20 | 47 | 70 | 29 |
| 20 | Bolton Wanderers | 38 | 9 | 6 | 23 | 44 | 71 | 24 |

# Season 1910-11

## Football League Division One

| DATE | OPPONENTS | SCORE | GOALSCORERS | ATTENDANCE |
|---|---|---|---|---|
| Sep 1 | Woolwich Arsenal | W 2-1 | Halse, West | 15,000 |
| Sep 3 | BLACKBURN ROVERS | W 3-2 | Meredith, Halse, West | 40,000 |
| Sep 10 | Nottingham Forest | L 1-2 | Turnbull | 20,000 |
| Sep 17 | MANCHESTER CITY | W 2-1 | Turnbull, West | 60,000 |
| Sep 24 | Everton | W 1-0 | Turnbull | 25,000 |
| Oct 1 | THE WEDNESDAY | W 3-2 | Wall 2, West | 20,000 |
| Oct 8 | Bristol City | W 1-0 | Halse | 20,000 |
| Oct 15 | NEWCASTLE UNITED | W 2-0 | Halse, Turnbull | 50,000 |
| Oct 22 | Tottenham Hotspur | D 2-2 | West 2 | 30,000 |
| Oct 29 | MIDDLESBROUGH | L 1-2 | Turnbull | 35,000 |
| Nov 5 | Preston North End | W 2-0 | Turnbull, West | 13,000 |
| Nov 12 | NOTTS COUNTY | D 0-0 | | 13,000 |
| Nov 19 | Oldham Athletic | W 3-1 | Turnbull 2, Wall | 25,000 |
| Nov 26 | Liverpool | L 2-3 | Roberts, Turnbull | 8,000 |
| Dec 3 | BURY | W 3-2 | Homer 2, Turnbull | 7,000 |
| Dec 10 | Sheffield United | L 0-2 | | 8,000 |
| Dec 17 | ASTON VILLA | W 2-0 | Turnbull, West | 20,000 |
| Dec 24 | Sunderland | W 2-1 | Meredith, Turnbull | 30,000 |
| Dec 26 | WOOLWICH ARSENAL | W 5-0 | Picken 2, West 2, Meredith | 40,000 |
| Dec 27 | Bradford City | L 0-1 | | 35,000 |
| Dec 31 | Blackburn Rovers | L 0-1 | | 20,000 |
| Jan 2 | BRADFORD CITY | W 1-0 | Meredith | 40,000 |
| Jan 7 | NOTTINGHAM FOREST | W 4-2 | Homer, Picken, Wall, Needham o.g. | 10,000 |
| Jan 21 | Manchester City | D 1-1 | Turnbull | 40,000 |
| Jan 28 | EVERTON | D 2-2 | Duckworth, Wall | 45,000 |
| Feb 11 | BRISTOL CITY | W 3-1 | Homer, Picken, West | 14,000 |
| Feb 18 | Newcastle United | W 1-0 | Halse | 45,000 |
| Mar 4 | Middlesbrough | D 2-2 | Turnbull, West | 8,000 |
| Mar 11 | PRESTON NORTH END | W 5-0 | West 2, Connor, Duckworth, Turnbull | 25,000 |
| Mar 15 | TOTTENHAM HOTSPUR | W 3-2 | Meredith, Turnbull, West | 10,000 |
| Mar 18 | Notts County | L 0-1 | | 12,000 |
| Mar 25 | OLDHAM ATHLETIC | D 0-0 | | 35,000 |
| Apr 1 | LIVERPOOL | W 2-0 | West 2 | 20,000 |
| Apr 8 | Bury | W 3-0 | Homer 2, Halse | 20,000 |
| Apr 15 | SHEFFIELD UNITED | D 1-1 | West | 22,000 |
| Apr 17 | The Wednesday | D 0-0 | | 25,000 |
| Apr 22 | Aston Villa | L 2-4 | Halse 2 | 50,000 |
| Apr 29 | SUNDERLAND | W 5-1 | Halse 2, Turnbull, West, Milton o.g. | 10,000 |

## FA Cup

| | | | | | |
|---|---|---|---|---|---|
| Jan 14 | Blackpool | (Rd1) | W 2-1 | Picken, West | 12,000 |
| Feb 4 | ASTON VILLA | (Rd2) | W 2-1 | Halse, Wall | 65,101 |
| Feb 25 | West Ham United | (Rd3) | L 1-2 | Turnbull | 26,000 |

## League & Cup Appearances

| PLAYER | LEAGUE | CUP COMPETITION<br>FA CUP | TOTAL |
|---|---|---|---|
| Bell | 27 | 3 | 30 |
| Blott | 1 | | 1 |
| Connor | 7 | | 7 |
| Curry | 5 | | 5 |
| Donnelly | 15 | 3 | 18 |
| Duckworth | 22 | 3 | 25 |
| Edmonds | 13 | 1 | 14 |
| Halse | 23 | 2 | 25 |
| Hayes | 1 | | 1 |
| Hodge | 2 | | 2 |
| Hofton | 9 | | 9 |
| Holden | 8 | | 8 |
| Homer | 7 | | 7 |
| Hooper | 2 | | 2 |
| Linkson | 7 | | 7 |
| Livingstone | 10 | | 10 |
| Meredith | 35 | 3 | 38 |
| Moger | 25 | 2 | 27 |
| Picken | 14 | 1 | 15 |
| Roberts | 33 | 3 | 36 |
| Sheldon | 5 | | 5 |
| Stacey | 36 | 3 | 39 |
| Turnbull | 35 | 3 | 38 |
| Wall | 26 | 3 | 29 |
| Whalley | 15 | | 15 |
| West | 35 | 3 | 38 |

## Goalscorers

| PLAYER | LEAGUE | CUP COMPETITION<br>FA CUP | TOTAL |
|---|---|---|---|
| West | 19 | 1 | 20 |
| Turnbull | 18 | 1 | 19 |
| Halse | 9 | 1 | 10 |
| Homer | 6 | | 6 |
| Wall | 5 | 1 | 6 |
| Meredith | 5 | | 5 |
| Picken | 4 | 1 | 5 |
| Duckworth | 2 | | 2 |
| Connor | 1 | | 1 |
| Roberts | 1 | | 1 |
| Opps' o.gs. | 2 | | 2 |

## Fact File

Enoch 'Knocker' West and Alex 'Sandy' Turnbull combined to supply more than half (37) of the team's league goals (72) as United won the title for the second time in three years.

**SECRETARY:** Ernest Mangnall

**MOST APPEARANCES:** George Stacey 39

**TOP GOALSCORER:** Enoch 'Knocker' West 20 (19 League)

**BIGGEST WIN:** 5-0 v Woolwich Arsenal, 26 December 1910, League; 5-0 v Preston North End, 11 March 1911, League

**HIGHEST ATTENDANCE:** 65,10 v Aston Villa, 14 February 1911, FA Cup

## Final Division One Table

| | | P | W | D | L | F | A | Pts |
|---|---|---|---|---|---|---|---|---|
| 1 | Manchester United | 38 | 22 | 8 | 8 | 72 | 40 | 52 |
| 2 | Aston Villa | 38 | 22 | 7 | 9 | 69 | 41 | 51 |
| 3 | Sunderland | 38 | 15 | 15 | 8 | 67 | 48 | 45 |
| 4 | Everton | 38 | 19 | 7 | 12 | 50 | 36 | 45 |
| 5 | Bradford City | 38 | 20 | 5 | 13 | 51 | 42 | 45 |
| 6 | The Wednesday | 38 | 17 | 8 | 13 | 47 | 48 | 42 |
| 7 | Oldham Athletic | 38 | 16 | 9 | 13 | 44 | 41 | 41 |
| 8 | Newcastle United | 38 | 15 | 10 | 13 | 61 | 43 | 40 |
| 9 | Sheffield United | 38 | 15 | 8 | 15 | 49 | 43 | 38 |
| 10 | Woolwich Arsenal | 38 | 13 | 12 | 13 | 41 | 49 | 38 |
| 11 | Notts County | 38 | 14 | 10 | 14 | 37 | 45 | 38 |
| 12 | Blackburn Rovers | 38 | 13 | 11 | 14 | 62 | 54 | 37 |
| 13 | Liverpool | 38 | 15 | 7 | 16 | 62 | 54 | 37 |
| 14 | Preston North End | 38 | 12 | 11 | 15 | 40 | 49 | 35 |
| 15 | Tottenham Hotspur | 38 | 13 | 6 | 19 | 52 | 63 | 32 |
| 16 | Middlesbrough | 38 | 11 | 10 | 17 | 49 | 63 | 32 |
| 17 | Manchester City | 38 | 9 | 13 | 16 | 43 | 58 | 31 |
| 18 | Bury | 38 | 9 | 11 | 18 | 43 | 71 | 29 |
| 19 | Bristol City | 38 | 11 | 5 | 22 | 43 | 66 | 27 |
| 20 | Nottingham Forest | 38 | 9 | 7 | 22 | 55 | 75 | 25 |

# Season 1911-12

## Football League Division One

| DATE | OPPONENTS | SCORE | GOALSCORERS | ATTENDANCE |
|---|---|---|---|---|
| Sep 2 | Manchester City | D 0-0 | | 35,000 |
| Sep 9 | EVERTON | W 2-1 | Halse, Turnbull | 20,000 |
| Sep 16 | West Bromwich Albion | L 0-1 | | 35,000 |
| Sep 23 | SUNDERLAND | D 2-2 | Stacey 2 | 20,000 |
| Sep 30 | Blackburn Rovers | D 2-2 | West 2 | 30,000 |
| Oct 7 | THE WEDNESDAY | W 3-1 | Halse 2, West | 30,000 |
| Oct 14 | Bury | W 1-0 | Turnbull | 18,000 |
| Oct 21 | MIDDLESBROUGH | L 3-4 | Halse, Turnbull, West | 20,000 |
| Oct 28 | Notts County | W 1-0 | Turnbull | 15,000 |
| Nov 4 | TOTTENHAM HOTSPUR | L 1-2 | Halse | 20,000 |
| Nov 11 | PRESTON NORTH END | D 0-0 | | 10,000 |
| Nov 18 | Liverpool | L 2-3 | Roberts, West | 15,000 |
| Nov 25 | ASTON VILLA | W 3-1 | West 2, Roberts | 20,000 |
| Dec 2 | Newcastle United | W 3-2 | West 2, Halse | 40,000 |
| Dec 9 | SHEFFIELD UNITED | W 1-0 | Halse | 12,000 |
| Dec 16 | Oldham Athletic | D 2-2 | Turnbull, West | 20,000 |
| Dec 23 | BOLTON WANDERERS | W 2-0 | Halse, Turnbull | 20,000 |
| Dec 25 | BRADFORD CITY | L 0-1 | | 50,000 |
| Dec 26 | Bradford City | W 1-0 | West | 40,000 |
| Dec 30 | MANCHESTER CITY | D 0-0 | | 50,000 |
| Jan 1 | WOOLWICH ARSENAL | W 2-0 | Meredith, West | 20,000 |
| Jan 6 | Everton | L 0-4 | | 12,000 |
| Jan 20 | WEST BROMWICH ALBION | L 1-2 | Wall | 8,000 |
| Jan 27 | Sunderland | L 0-5 | | 12,000 |
| Feb 10 | The Wednesday | L 0-3 | | 25,000 |
| Feb 17 | BURY | D 0-0 | | 6,000 |
| Mar 2 | NOTTS COUNTY | W 2-0 | West 2 | 10,000 |
| Mar 16 | Preston North End | D 0-0 | | 7,000 |
| Mar 23 | LIVERPOOL | D 1-1 | | 10,000 |
| Mar 30 | Aston Villa | L 0-6 | | 15,000 |
| Apr 5 | Woolwich Arsenal | L 1-2 | Turnbull | 14,000 |
| Apr 6 | NEWCASTLE UNITED | L 0-2 | | 14,000 |
| Apr 9 | Tottenham Hotspur | D 1-1 | Wall | 20,000 |
| Apr 13 | Sheffield United | L 1-6 | Nuttall | 7,000 |
| Apr 17 | Middlesbrough | L 0-3 | | 5,000 |
| Apr 20 | OLDHAM ATHLETIC | W 3-1 | West 2, Wall | 15,000 |
| Apr 27 | Bolton Wanderers | D 1-1 | Meredith | 20,000 |
| Apr 29 | BLACKBURN ROVERS | W 3-1 | Hamill, Meredith, West | 20,000 |

## FA Cup

| | | | | |
|---|---|---|---|---|
| Jan 13 | HUDDERSFIELD TOWN | (Rd1) W 3-1 | West 2, Halse | 19,579 |
| Feb 3 | Coventry City | (Rd2) W 5-1 | Halse 2, West, Turnbull, Wall | 17,130 |
| Feb 24 | Reading | (Rd3) D 1-1 | West | 24,069 |
| Feb 29 | READING | (R) W 3-0 | Turnbull 2, Halse | 29,511 |
| Mar 9 | BLACKBURN ROVERS | (Rd4) D 1-1 | Own-goal | 59,300 |
| Mar 14 | Blackburn Rovers | (R) L 2-4* | West 2 | 39,296 |

*After extra-time.

## FA Charity Shield

| | | | | |
|---|---|---|---|---|
| Sep 25 | Swindon Town** | W 8-4 | Halse 6, Turnbull, Wall | 10,000 |

**Played at Stamford Bridge, London.

### Fact File

Harold Halse scored six goals as United won the FA Charity Shield for the second time with an 8-4 win over Southern League champions Swindon Town at Stamford Bridge, London.

**SECRETARY:** Ernest Mangnall
**MOST APPEARANCES:** Billy Meredith 42
**TOP GOALSCORER:** Enoch 'Knocker' West 23 (17 League)
**BIGGEST WIN:** 8-4 v Swindon Town, 25 September 1911, FA Charity Shield; 5-1 v Coventry City, 3 February 1912, FA Cup
**HIGHEST ATTENDANCE:** 59,300 v Blackburn Rovers, 9 March 1912, FA Cup

## League & Cup Appearances

| PLAYER | LEAGUE | CUP COMPETITION FA CUP | OTHER | TOTAL |
|---|---|---|---|---|
| Anderson | 1 | | | 1 |
| Bell | 32 | 6 | 1 | 39 |
| Blott | 6 | | | 6 |
| Capper | 1 | | | 1 |
| Donnelly | 13 | | | 13 |
| Duckworth | 26 | 6 | 1 | 33 |
| Edmonds | 30 | 6 | 1 | 37 |
| Halse | 24 | 6 | 1 | 31 |
| Hamill | 16 | | 1 | 17 |
| Hodge | 10 | | | 10 |
| Hofton | 7 | | 1 | 8 |
| Holden | 6 | 2 | | 8 |
| Homer | 1 | | | 1 |
| Knowles | 7 | | | 7 |
| Linkson | 21 | 4 | | 25 |
| Livingstone | 1 | | | 1 |
| McCarthy | 1 | | | 1 |
| Meredith | 35 | 6 | 1 | 42 |
| Moger | 6 | | | 6 |
| Nuttall | 6 | | | 6 |
| Roberts | 32 | 5 | 1 | 38 |
| Royals | 2 | | | 2 |
| Sheldon | 5 | | | 5 |
| Stacey | 29 | 6 | 1 | 36 |
| Turnbull | 30 | 6 | 1 | 37 |
| Wall | 33 | 6 | 1 | 40 |
| Whalley | 5 | 1 | | 38 |
| West | 32 | 6 | | 38 |

## Goalscorers

| PLAYER | LEAGUE | CUP COMPETITION FA CUP | OTHER | TOTAL |
|---|---|---|---|---|
| West | 17 | 6 | | 23 |
| Halse | 8 | 4 | 6 | 18 |
| Turnbull | 7 | 3 | 1 | 11 |
| Wall | 3 | 1 | 1 | 5 |
| Meredith | 3 | | | 3 |
| Roberts | 2 | | | 2 |
| Stacey | 2 | | | 2 |
| Nuttall | 2 | | | 2 |
| Hamill | 1 | | | 1 |
| Opps' o.gs. | | 1 | | 1 |

## Final Division One Table

| | | P | W | D | L | F | A | Pts |
|---|---|---|---|---|---|---|---|---|
| 1 | Blackburn Rovers | 38 | 20 | 9 | 9 | 60 | 43 | 49 |
| 2 | Everton | 38 | 20 | 6 | 12 | 46 | 42 | 46 |
| 3 | Newcastle United | 38 | 18 | 8 | 12 | 64 | 50 | 44 |
| 4 | Bolton Wanderers | 38 | 20 | 3 | 12 | 54 | 43 | 43 |
| 5 | The Wednesday | 38 | 16 | 9 | 13 | 69 | 49 | 41 |
| 6 | Aston Villa | 38 | 17 | 7 | 14 | 76 | 63 | 41 |
| 7 | Middlesbrough | 38 | 16 | 8 | 14 | 56 | 45 | 40 |
| 8 | Sunderland | 38 | 14 | 11 | 13 | 58 | 51 | 39 |
| 9 | WBA | 38 | 15 | 9 | 14 | 43 | 47 | 39 |
| 10 | Woolwich Arsenal | 38 | 15 | 8 | 15 | 55 | 59 | 38 |
| 11 | Bradford City | 38 | 15 | 8 | 15 | 46 | 50 | 38 |
| 12 | Tottenham Hotspur | 38 | 14 | 9 | 15 | 53 | 53 | 37 |
| 13 | Manchester United | 38 | 13 | 11 | 14 | 45 | 60 | 37 |
| 14 | Sheffield United | 38 | 13 | 10 | 15 | 63 | 56 | 36 |
| 15 | Manchester City | 38 | 13 | 9 | 16 | 56 | 58 | 35 |
| 16 | Notts County | 38 | 14 | 7 | 17 | 46 | 63 | 35 |
| 17 | Liverpool | 38 | 12 | 10 | 16 | 49 | 55 | 34 |
| 18 | Oldham Athletic | 38 | 12 | 10 | 16 | 46 | 54 | 34 |
| 19 | Preston North End | 38 | 13 | 7 | 18 | 40 | 57 | 33 |
| 20 | Bury | 38 | 6 | 9 | 23 | 32 | 59 | 21 |

# Season 1912-13

## Football League Division One

| DATE | OPPONENTS | SCORE | GOALSCORERS | ATTENDANCE |
|---|---|---|---|---|
| Sep 2 | Woolwich Arsenal | D 0-0 | | 11,000 |
| Sep 7 | MANCHESTER CITY | L 0-1 | | 39,911 |
| Sep 14 | West Bromwich Albion | W 2-1 | Livingstone, Turnbull | 25,000 |
| Sep 21 | EVERTON | W 2-0 | West 2 | 40,000 |
| Sep 28 | The Wednesday | D 3-3 | West 2, Turnbull | 30,000 |
| Oct 5 | BLACKBURN ROVERS | D 1-1 | Wall | 45,000 |
| Oct 12 | Derby County | L 1-2 | Turnbull | 15,000 |
| Oct 19 | TOTTENHAM HOTSPUR | W 2-0 | Turnbull, West | 12,000 |
| Oct 26 | Middlesbrough | L 2-3 | Nuttall 2 | 10,000 |
| Nov 2 | NOTTS COUNTY | W 2-1 | Anderson, Meredith | 12,000 |
| Nov 9 | Sunderland | L 1-3 | West | 20,000 |
| Nov 16 | Aston Villa | L 2-4 | Wall, West | 20,000 |
| Nov 23 | LIVERPOOL | W 3-1 | Anderson 2, Wall | 8,000 |
| Nov 30 | Bolton Wanderers | L 1-2 | Wall | 25,000 |
| Dec 7 | SHEFFIELD UNITED | W 4-0 | Anderson, Turnbull, Wall, West | 12,000 |
| Dec 14 | Newcastle United | W 3-1 | West 3 | 20,000 |
| Dec 21 | OLDHAM ATHLETIC | D 0-0 | | 30,000 |
| Dec 25 | Chelsea | W 4-1 | West 2, Anderson, Whalley | 33,000 |
| Dec 26 | CHELSEA | W 4-2 | Turnbull 2, Anderson, Wall | 20,000 |
| Dec 28 | Manchester City | W 2-0 | West 2 | 38,000 |
| Jan 1 | BRADFORD CITY | W 2-0 | Anderson 2 | 30,000 |
| Jan 4 | WEST BROMWICH ALBION | D 1-1 | Roberts | 25,000 |
| Jan 18 | Everton | L 1-4 | Hamill | 20,000 |
| Jan 25 | THE WEDNESDAY | W 2-0 | West, Whalley | 45,000 |
| Feb 8 | Blackburn Rovers | D 0-0 | | 38,000 |
| Feb 15 | DERBY COUNTY | W 4-0 | West 2, Anderson, Turnbull | 30,000 |
| Mar 1 | MIDDLESBROUGH | L 2-3 | Meredith, Whalley | 15,000 |
| Mar 8 | Notts County | W 2-1 | Anderson, Turnbull | 10,000 |
| Mar 15 | SUNDERLAND | L 1-3 | Sheldon | 15,000 |
| Mar 21 | WOOLWICH ARSENAL | W 2-0 | Anderson, Whalley | 20,000 |
| Mar 22 | ASTON VILLA | W 4-0 | Turnbull, Stacey, Wall, West | 30,000 |
| Mar 25 | Bradford City | L 0-1 | | 25,000 |
| Mar 29 | Liverpool | W 2-0 | Wall, West | 12,000 |
| Mar 31 | Tottenham Hotspur | D 1-1 | Blott | 12,762 |
| Apr 5 | BOLTON WANDERERS | W 2-1 | Anderson, Wall | 30,000 |
| Apr 12 | Sheffield United | L 1-2 | Wall | 12,000 |
| Apr 19 | NEWCASTLE UNITED | W 3-0 | Hunter 2, West | 10,000 |
| Apr 26 | Oldham Athletic | D 0-0 | | 3,000 |

## FA Cup

| | | | | | |
|---|---|---|---|---|---|
| Jan 11 | COVENTRY CITY | (Rd1) | D 1-1 | Wall | 11,500 |
| Jan 16 | Coventry City | (R) | W 2-1 | Anderson, Roberts | 20,042 |
| Feb 1 | Plymouth Argyle | (Rd2) | W 2-0 | Anderson, Wall | 21,700 |
| Feb 22 | Oldham Athletic | (Rd3) | D 0-0 | | 26,932 |
| Feb 26 | OLDHAM ATHLETIC | (R) | L 1-2 | West | 31,180 |

## League & Cup Appearances

| PLAYER | LEAGUE | CUP COMPETITION FA CUP | TOTAL |
|---|---|---|---|
| Anderson | 24 | 5 | 29 |
| Beale | 37 | 5 | 42 |
| Bell | 26 | | 26 |
| Blott | 2 | | 2 |
| Donnelly | 1 | | 1 |
| Duckworth | 24 | 5 | 29 |
| Gipps | 2 | | 2 |
| Hamill | 15 | 2 | 17 |
| Hodge | 19 | 5 | 24 |
| Holden | 2 | | 2 |
| Hunter | 3 | | 3 |
| Knowles | 2 | | 2 |
| Linkson | 17 | | 17 |
| Livingstone | 2 | | 2 |
| Meredith | 22 | 5 | 27 |
| Mew | 1 | | 1 |
| Nuttall | 10 | | 10 |
| Roberts | 24 | 5 | 29 |
| Sheldon | 16 | | 16 |
| Stacey | 36 | 5 | 41 |
| Turnbull | 35 | 4 | 39 |
| Wall | 36 | 5 | 41 |
| Whalley | 26 | 5 | 31 |
| West | 36 | 4 | 40 |

## Goalscorers

| PLAYER | LEAGUE | CUP COMPETITION FA CUP | TOTAL |
|---|---|---|---|
| West | 21 | 1 | 22 |
| Anderson | 12 | 2 | 14 |
| Wall | 10 | 2 | 12 |
| Turnbull | 10 | | 10 |
| Whalley | 4 | | 4 |
| Hunter | 2 | | 2 |
| Meredith | 2 | | 2 |
| Nuttall | 2 | | 2 |
| Roberts | 1 | 1 | 2 |
| Blott | 1 | | 1 |
| Hamill | 1 | | 1 |
| Livingstone | 1 | | 1 |
| Sheldon | 1 | | 1 |
| Stacey | 1 | | 1 |

### Fact File

A crowd of 39,911 attended United's first home game of the season against Manchester City which doubled as a testimonial for the great Welsh star, Billy Meredith.

**SECRETARY:** J.J. Bentley
**MOST APPEARANCES:** Robert Beale 42
**TOP SCORER:** Enoch West 22 (21 League)
**BIGGEST WIN:** 4-0 v Sheffield United, 7 December 1912, League; 4-0 v Derby County, 15 February 1913, League; 4-0 v Aston Villa, 22 March 1913, League
**HIGHEST ATTENDANCE:** 45,000 v Blackburn Rovers, 5 October 1912, League; 45,000 v The Wednesday, 25 January 1913, League

### Final Division One Table

| | | P | W | D | L | F | A | PTS |
|---|---|---|---|---|---|---|---|---|
| 1 | Sunderland | 38 | 25 | 4 | 9 | 86 | 43 | 54 |
| 2 | Aston Villa | 38 | 19 | 12 | 7 | 86 | 52 | 50 |
| 3 | The Wednesday | 38 | 21 | 7 | 10 | 75 | 55 | 49 |
| 4 | Manchester United | 38 | 19 | 8 | 11 | 69 | 43 | 46 |
| 5 | Blackburn Rovers | 38 | 16 | 13 | 9 | 79 | 43 | 45 |
| 6 | Manchester City | 38 | 18 | 8 | 12 | 53 | 37 | 44 |
| 7 | Derby County | 38 | 17 | 8 | 13 | 69 | 66 | 42 |
| 8 | Bolton Wanderers | 38 | 16 | 10 | 12 | 62 | 63 | 42 |
| 9 | Oldham Athletic | 38 | 14 | 14 | 10 | 50 | 55 | 42 |
| 10 | WBA | 38 | 13 | 12 | 13 | 57 | 50 | 38 |
| 11 | Everton | 38 | 15 | 7 | 16 | 48 | 54 | 37 |
| 12 | Liverpool | 38 | 16 | 5 | 17 | 61 | 71 | 37 |
| 13 | Bradford City | 38 | 12 | 11 | 15 | 50 | 60 | 35 |
| 14 | Newcastle United | 38 | 13 | 8 | 17 | 47 | 47 | 34 |
| 15 | Sheffield United | 38 | 14 | 6 | 18 | 56 | 70 | 34 |
| 16 | Middlesbrough | 38 | 11 | 10 | 17 | 55 | 69 | 32 |
| 17 | Tottenham Hotspur | 38 | 12 | 6 | 20 | 45 | 72 | 30 |
| 18 | Chelsea | 38 | 11 | 6 | 21 | 51 | 73 | 28 |
| 19 | Notts County | 38 | 7 | 9 | 22 | 28 | 56 | 23 |
| 20 | Woolwich Arsenal | 38 | 3 | 12 | 23 | 26 | 74 | 18 |

# Season 1913-14

## Football League Division One

| DATE | OPPONENTS | SCORE | GOALSCORERS | ATTENDANCE |
|---|---|---|---|---|
| Sep 6 | The Wednesday | W 3-1 | Turnbull, West, Spoors o.g. | 32,000 |
| Sep 8 | SUNDERLAND | W 3-1 | Anderson, Turnbull, Whalley | 25,000 |
| Sep 13 | BOLTON WANDERERS | L 0-1 | | 45,000 |
| Sep 20 | Chelsea | W 2-0 | Anderson, Wall | 40,000 |
| Sep 27 | OLDHAM ATHLETIC | W 4-1 | West 2, Anderson, Wall | 55,000 |
| Oct 4 | TOTTENHAM HOTSPUR | W 3-1 | Stacey, Wall, Whalley | 25,000 |
| Oct 11 | Burnley | W 2-1 | Anderson 2 | 30,000 |
| Oct 18 | PRESTON NORTH END | W 3-0 | Anderson 3 | 30,000 |
| Oct 25 | Newcastle United | W 1-0 | West | 35,000 |
| Nov 1 | LIVERPOOL | W 3-0 | Wall 2, West | 30,000 |
| Nov 8 | Aston Villa | L 1-3 | Woodcock | 20,000 |
| Nov 15 | MIDDLESBROUGH | L 0-1 | | 15,000 |
| Nov 22 | Sheffield United | L 0-2 | | 27,249 |
| Nov 29 | DERBY COUNTY | D 3-3 | Turnbull 2, Meredith | 20,000 |
| Dec 6 | Manchester City | W 2-0 | Anderson 2 | 40,000 |
| Dec 13 | BRADFORD CITY | D 1-1 | Knowles | 18,000 |
| Dec 20 | Blackburn Rovers | W 1-0 | Crompton o.g. | 35,000 |
| Dec 25 | EVERTON | L 0-1 | | 25,000 |
| Dec 26 | Everton | L 0-5 | | 40,000 |
| Dec 26 | THE WEDNESDAY | W 2-1 | Meredith, Wall | 10,000 |
| Jan 1 | WEST BROMWICH ALBION | W 1-0 | Wall | 16,400 |
| Jan 3 | Bolton Wanderers | L 1-6 | West | 35,000 |
| Jan 17 | CHELSEA | L 0-1 | | 20,000 |
| Jan 24 | Oldham Athletic | D 2-2 | Wall, Woodcock | 10,000 |
| Feb 7 | Tottenham Hotspur | L 1-2 | Wall | 22,000 |
| Feb 14 | BURNLEY | L 0-1 | | 35,000 |
| Feb 21 | Middlesbrough | L 1-3 | Anderson | 12,000 |
| Feb 28 | NEWCASTLE UNITED | D 2-2 | Anderson, Potts | 30,000 |
| Mar 5 | Preston North End | L 2-4 | Travers, Wall | 12,000 |
| Mar 14 | ASTON VILLA | L 0-6 | | 30,000 |
| Apr 4 | Derby County | L 2-4 | Anderson, Travers | 7,000 |
| Apr 10 | Sunderland | L 0-2 | | 20,000 |
| Apr 11 | MANCHESTER CITY | L 0-1 | | 36,440 |
| Apr 13 | West Bromwich Albion | L 1-2 | Travers | 16,907 |
| Apr 15 | Liverpool | W 2-1 | Travers, Wall | 28,000 |
| Apr 18 | Bradford City | D 1-1 | Thomson | 10,000 |
| Apr 22 | SHEFFIELD UNITED | W 2-1 | Anderson 2 | 4,500 |
| Apr 25 | BLACKBURN ROVERS | D 0-0 | | 20,000 |

## FA Cup

| | | | | |
|---|---|---|---|---|
| Jan 10 | Swindon Town | (Rd1) L 0-1 | | 18,187 |

## League & Cup Appearances

| PLAYER | LEAGUE | CUP COMPETITION<br>FA CUP | TOTAL |
|---|---|---|---|
| Anderson | 32 | | 32 |
| Beale | 31 | 1 | 32 |
| Cashmore | 3 | | 3 |
| Chorlton | 4 | | 4 |
| Duckworth | 9 | | 9 |
| Gipps | 11 | | 11 |
| Hamill | 26 | | 26 |
| Haywood | 14 | | 14 |
| Hodge, James | 28 | 1 | 29 |
| Hodge, John | 4 | | 4 |
| Hudson | 9 | | 9 |
| Hunter | 7 | | 7 |
| Hooper | 3 | | 3 |
| Knowles | 18 | 1 | 19 |
| Livingstone | 3 | 1 | 4 |
| Meredith | 34 | 1 | 35 |
| Mew | 2 | | 2 |
| Norton | 8 | | 8 |
| Potts | 6 | | 6 |
| Roberts | 2 | | 2 |
| Rowe | 1 | | 1 |
| Royals | 5 | | 5 |
| Stacey | 34 | 1 | 35 |
| Thomson | 6 | | 6 |
| Travers | 13 | | 13 |
| Turnbull | 17 | 1 | 18 |
| Wall | 29 | 1 | 30 |
| West | 30 | 1 | 31 |
| Whalley | 18 | 1 | 19 |
| Woodcock | 11 | 1 | 12 |

## Goalscorers

| PLAYER | LEAGUE | CUP COMPETITION<br>FA CUP | TOTAL |
|---|---|---|---|
| Anderson | 15 | | 15 |
| Wall | 11 | | 11 |
| West | 6 | | 6 |
| Turnbull | 4 | | 4 |
| Travers | 4 | | 4 |
| Meredith | 2 | | 2 |
| Whalley | 2 | | 2 |
| Woodcock | 2 | | 2 |
| Stacey | 1 | | 1 |
| Knowles | 1 | | 1 |
| Potts | 1 | | 1 |
| Thomson | 1 | | 1 |
| Opps' o.gs. | 2 | | 2 |

### Fact File

Scotsman John Hodge made four league appearances for United after moving south to join older brother James at Old Trafford.

**SECRETARY:** J.J. Bentley

**MOST APPEARANCES:** George Stacey, Billy Meredith 35

**TOP SCORER:** George Anderson 15 (all League)

**BIGGEST WIN:** 4-1 v Oldham Athletic, 27 September 1913, League

**HIGHEST ATTENDANCE:** 55,000 v Oldham Athletic, 27 September 1913, League

### Final Division One Table

| | | P | W | D | L | F | A | Pts |
|---|---|---|---|---|---|---|---|---|
| 1 | Blackburn Rovers | 38 | 20 | 11 | 7 | 78 | 42 | 51 |
| 2 | Aston Villa | 38 | 19 | 6 | 13 | 65 | 50 | 44 |
| 3 | Oldham Athletic | 38 | 17 | 9 | 12 | 55 | 45 | 43 |
| 4 | Middlesbrough | 38 | 19 | 5 | 14 | 77 | 60 | 43 |
| 5 | WBA | 38 | 15 | 13 | 10 | 46 | 42 | 43 |
| 6 | Bolton Wanderers | 38 | 16 | 10 | 12 | 65 | 52 | 42 |
| 7 | Sunderland | 38 | 17 | 6 | 15 | 63 | 52 | 40 |
| 8 | Chelsea | 38 | 16 | 7 | 15 | 46 | 55 | 39 |
| 9 | Bradford City | 38 | 12 | 14 | 12 | 40 | 40 | 38 |
| 10 | Sheffield United | 38 | 16 | 5 | 17 | 63 | 60 | 37 |
| 11 | Newcastle United | 38 | 13 | 11 | 14 | 39 | 48 | 37 |
| 12 | Burnley | 38 | 12 | 12 | 14 | 61 | 53 | 36 |
| 13 | Manchester City | 38 | 14 | 8 | 16 | 51 | 53 | 36 |
| 14 | Manchester United | 38 | 15 | 6 | 17 | 52 | 62 | 36 |
| 15 | Everton | 38 | 12 | 11 | 15 | 46 | 62 | 35 |
| 16 | Liverpool | 38 | 14 | 7 | 17 | 46 | 62 | 35 |
| 17 | Tottenham Hotspur | 38 | 12 | 10 | 16 | 50 | 62 | 34 |
| 18 | The Wednesday | 38 | 13 | 8 | 17 | 53 | 70 | 34 |
| 19 | Preston North End | 38 | 12 | 6 | 20 | 52 | 69 | 30 |
| 20 | Derby County | 38 | 8 | 11 | 19 | 55 | 71 | 27 |

# Season 1914-15

## Football League Division One

| DATE | OPPONENTS | SCORE | GOALSCORERS | ATTENDANCE |
|---|---|---|---|---|
| Sep 2 | OLDHAM ATHLETIC | L 1-3 | O'Connell | 13,000 |
| Sep 5 | MANCHESTER CITY | D 0-0 | | 20,000 |
| Sep 12 | Bolton Wanderers | L 0-3 | | 10,000 |
| Sep 19 | BLACKBURN ROVERS | W 2-0 | West 2 | 15,000 |
| Sep 26 | Notts County | L 2-4 | Turnbull, Wall | 12,000 |
| Oct 3 | SUNDERLAND | W 3-0 | Anderson, Stacey, West | 16,000 |
| Oct 10 | The Wednesday | L 0-1 | | 19,000 |
| Oct 17 | WEST BROMWICH ALBION | D 0-0 | | 13,200 |
| Oct 24 | Everton | L 2-4 | Anderson, Wall | 15,000 |
| Oct 31 | CHELSEA | D 2-2 | Anderson, Hunter | 15,000 |
| Nov 7 | Bradford City | L 2-4 | Hunter, West | 12,000 |
| Nov 14 | BURNLEY | L 0-2 | | 12,000 |
| Nov 21 | Tottenham Hotspur | L 0-2 | | 12,000 |
| Nov 28 | NEWCASTLE UNITED | W 1-0 | West | 5,000 |
| Dec 5 | Middlesbrough | D 1-1 | Anderson | 7,000 |
| Dec 12 | SHEFFIELD UNITED | L 1-2 | Anderson | 8,000 |
| Dec 19 | Aston Villa | D 3-3 | Norton 2, Anderson | 10,000 |
| Dec 26 | Liverpool | D 1-1 | Stacey | 25,000 |
| Jan 1 | BRADFORD PARK AVENUE | L 1-2 | Anderson | 8,000 |
| Jan 2 | Manchester City | D 1-1 | West | 30,000 |
| Jan 16 | BOLTON WANDERERS | W 4-1 | Potts 2, Stacey, Woodcock | 8,000 |
| Jan 23 | Blackburn Rovers | D 3-3 | Woodcock 2, Robinson o.g. | 7,000 |
| Jan 30 | NOTTS COUNTY | D 2-2 | Potts, Stacey | 7,000 |
| Feb 6 | Sunderland | L 0-1 | | 5,000 |
| Feb 13 | THE WEDNESDAY | W 2-0 | West, Woodcock | 7,000 |
| Feb 20 | West Bromwich Albion | D 0-0 | | 10,169 |
| Feb 27 | EVERTON | L 1-2 | Woodcock | 10,000 |
| Mar 13 | BRADFORD CITY | W 1-0 | Potts | 14,000 |
| Mar 20 | Burnley | L 0-3 | | 12,000 |
| Mar 27 | TOTTENHAM HOTSPUR | D 1-1 | Woodcock | 15,000 |
| Apr 2 | LIVERPOOL | W 2-0 | Anderson 2 | 18,000 |
| Apr 3 | Newcastle United | L 0-2 | | 12,000 |
| Apr 5 | Bradford Park Avenue | L 0-5 | | 15,000 |
| Apr 6 | Oldham Athletic | L 0-1 | | 2,000 |
| Apr 10 | MIDDLESBROUGH | D 2-2 | O'Connell, Turnbull | 15,000 |
| Apr 17 | Sheffield United | L 1-3 | West | 14,000 |
| Apr 19 | Chelsea | W 3-1 | Norton, West, Woodcock | 13,000 |
| Apr 26 | ASTON VILLA | W 1-0 | Anderson | 8,000 |

## FA Cup

| | | | | |
|---|---|---|---|---|
| Jan 9 | The Wednesday | (Rd1) L 0-1 | | 23,248 |

## League & Cup Appearances

| PLAYER | LEAGUE | CUP COMPETITION FA CUP | TOTAL |
|---|---|---|---|
| Allman | 12 | | 12 |
| Anderson | 23 | 1 | 24 |
| Beale | 37 | 1 | 38 |
| Cookson | 12 | 1 | 13 |
| Fox | | 1 | 1 |
| Gipps | 10 | | 10 |
| Haywood | 12 | | 12 |
| Hodge, James | 4 | 1 | 5 |
| Hodge, John | 26 | | 26 |
| Hudson | 2 | | 2 |
| Hunter | 15 | 1 | 16 |
| Knowles | 19 | | 19 |
| Meredith | 26 | 1 | 27 |
| Mew | 1 | | 1 |
| Montgomery | 11 | | 11 |
| Norton | 29 | | 29 |
| O'Connell | 34 | 1 | 35 |
| Potts | 17 | | 17 |
| Prince | 1 | | 1 |
| Spratt | 12 | | 12 |
| Stacey | 24 | 1 | 25 |
| Travers | 8 | | 8 |
| Turnbull | 13 | | 13 |
| Wall | 17 | 1 | 18 |
| Whalley | 1 | | 1 |
| West | 33 | 1 | 34 |
| Woodcock | 19 | | 19 |

## Goalscorers

| PLAYER | LEAGUE | CUP COMPETITION FA CUP | TOTAL |
|---|---|---|---|
| Anderson | 10 | | 10 |
| West | 9 | | 9 |
| Woodcock | 7 | | 7 |
| Potts | 4 | | 4 |
| Stacey | 4 | | 4 |
| Norton | 3 | | 3 |
| Hunter | 2 | | 2 |
| O'Connell | 2 | | 2 |
| Turnbull | 2 | | 2 |
| Wall | 2 | | 2 |
| Opps' o.gs. | 1 | | 1 |

## Fact File

Old Trafford staged the FA Cup final between Chelsea and Sheffield United. The Blades took the trophy after winning 3-0 before a crowd of 49,557.

**MANAGER:** John Robson

**MOST APPEARANCES:** Robert Beale 38

**TOP SCORER:** George Anderson 10 (all League)

**BIGGEST WIN:** 4-1 v Bolton Wanderers, 16 January 1915, League

**HIGHEST ATTENDANCE:** 30,000 v Manchester City, 2 January 1915, League

## Final Division One Table

| | | P | W | D | L | F | A | Pts |
|---|---|---|---|---|---|---|---|---|
| 1 | Everton | 38 | 19 | 8 | 11 | 76 | 47 | 46 |
| 2 | Oldham Athletic | 38 | 17 | 11 | 10 | 70 | 56 | 45 |
| 3 | Blackburn Rovers | 38 | 18 | 7 | 13 | 83 | 61 | 43 |
| 4 | Burnley | 38 | 18 | 7 | 13 | 61 | 47 | 43 |
| 5 | Manchester City | 38 | 15 | 13 | 10 | 49 | 39 | 43 |
| 6 | Sheffield United | 38 | 15 | 13 | 10 | 49 | 41 | 43 |
| 7 | The Wednesday | 38 | 15 | 13 | 10 | 61 | 54 | 43 |
| 8 | Sunderland | 38 | 18 | 5 | 15 | 81 | 72 | 41 |
| 9 | Bradford Park Avenue | 38 | 17 | 7 | 14 | 69 | 65 | 41 |
| 10 | Bradford City | 38 | 13 | 14 | 11 | 55 | 49 | 40 |
| 11 | WBA | 38 | 15 | 10 | 13 | 49 | 43 | 40 |
| 12 | Middlesbrough | 38 | 13 | 12 | 13 | 62 | 74 | 38 |
| 13 | Aston Villa | 38 | 13 | 11 | 14 | 62 | 72 | 37 |
| 14 | Liverpool | 38 | 14 | 9 | 15 | 65 | 75 | 37 |
| 15 | Newcastle United | 38 | 11 | 10 | 17 | 46 | 48 | 32 |
| 16 | Notts County | 38 | 9 | 13 | 16 | 41 | 57 | 31 |
| 17 | Bolton Wanderers | 38 | 11 | 8 | 19 | 68 | 84 | 30 |
| 18 | Manchester United | 38 | 9 | 12 | 17 | 46 | 62 | 30 |
| 19 | Chelsea | 38 | 8 | 13 | 17 | 51 | 65 | 29 |
| 20 | Tottenham Hotspur | 38 | 8 | 12 | 18 | 57 | 90 | 28 |

## Season 1919-20

### Football League Division One

| DATE | OPPONENTS | SCORE | GOALSCORERS | ATTENDANCE |
|---|---|---|---|---|
| Aug 30 | Derby County | D 1-1 | Woodcock | 12,000 |
| Sep 1 | THE WEDNESDAY | D 0-0 | | 13,000 |
| Sep 6 | DERBY COUNTY | L 0-2 | | 15,000 |
| Sep 8 | The Wednesday | W 3-1 | Meehan, Spence, Woodcock | 10,000 |
| Sep 13 | Preston North End | W 3-2 | Spence 2, Meehan | 15,000 |
| Sep 20 | PRESTON NORTH END | W 5-1 | Spence 2, Woodcock 2, Montgomery | 18,000 |
| Sep 27 | Middlesbrough | D 1-1 | Woodcock | 20,000 |
| Oct 4 | MIDDLESBROUGH | D 1-1 | Woodcock | 28,000 |
| Oct 11 | Manchester City | D 3-3 | Hodge, Hopkin, Spence | 30,000 |
| Oct 18 | MANCHESTER CITY | W 1-0 | Spence | 49,360 |
| Oct 25 | Sheffield United | D 2-2 | Hopkin, Woodcock | 18,000 |
| Nov 1 | SHEFFIELD UNITED | W 3-0 | Hodges, Spence, Woodcock | 24,500 |
| Nov 8 | Burnley | L 1-2 | Hodge | 15,000 |
| Nov 15 | BURNLEY | L 0-1 | | 25,000 |
| Nov 22 | Oldham Athletic | W 3-0 | Hodges, Hopkin, Spence | 15,000 |
| Dec 6 | Aston Villa | L 0-2 | | 40,000 |
| Dec 13 | ASTON VILLA | L 1-2 | Hilditch | 30,000 |
| Dec 20 | NEWCASTLE UNITED | W 2-1 | Hodges, Spence | 20,000 |
| Dec 26 | LIVERPOOL | D 0-0 | | 45,000 |
| Dec 27 | Newcastle United | L 1-2 | Hilditch | 45,000 |
| Jan 1 | Liverpool | D 0-0 | | 30,000 |
| Jan 3 | CHELSEA | L 0-2 | | 25,000 |
| Jan 17 | Chelsea | L 0-1 | | 40,000 |
| Jan 24 | West Bromwich Albion | L 1-2 | Woodcock | 30,192 |
| Feb 7 | Sunderland | L 0-3 | | 25,000 |
| Feb 11 | OLDHAM ATHLETIC | D 1-1 | Bissett | 15,000 |
| Feb 14 | SUNDERLAND | W 2-0 | Harris, Hodges | 58,661 |
| Feb 21 | Arsenal | W 3-0 | Spence 2, Hopkin | 25,000 |
| Feb 25 | WEST BROMWICH ALBION | L 1-2 | Spence | 21,000 |
| Feb 28 | ARSENAL | L 0-1 | | 20,000 |
| Mar 6 | EVERTON | W 1-0 | | 25,000 |
| Mar 13 | Everton | D 0-0 | | 30,000 |
| Mar 20 | BRADFORD CITY | D 0-0 | | 25,000 |
| Mar 27 | Bradford City | L 1-2 | | 18,000 |
| Apr 2 | BRADFORD PARK AVENUE | L 0-1 | | 30,000 |
| Apr 3 | BOLTON WANDERERS | D 1-1 | Toms | 39,000 |
| Apr 6 | Bradford Park Avenue | W 4-1 | Bissett, Grimwood, Toms, Woodcock | 14,000 |
| Apr 10 | Bolton Wanderers | W 5-1 | Bissett 2, Meredith, Toms, Woodcock | 25,000 |
| Apr 17 | BLACKBURN ROVERS | D 1-1 | Hopkin | 40,000 |
| Apr 24 | Blackburn Rovers | L 0-5 | | 30,000 |
| Apr 26 | NOTTS COUNTY | D 0-0 | | 30,000 |
| May 1 | Notts County | W 2-0 | Meredith, Spence | 20,000 |

### FA Cup

| | | | | |
|---|---|---|---|---|
| Jan 10 | Port Vale | (Rd1) W 1-0 | Toms | 14,549 |
| Jan 31 | ASTON VILLA | (Rd2) L 1-2 | Woodcock | 48,600 |

### League & Cup Appearances

| PLAYER | LEAGUE | CUP COMPETITION FA CUP | TOTAL |
|---|---|---|---|
| Barlow | 7 | | 7 |
| Bissett | 22 | | 22 |
| Forster | 5 | | 5 |
| Grimwood | 22 | 2 | 24 |
| Harris | 7 | | 7 |
| Hilditch | 32 | 2 | 34 |
| Hodge | 16 | | 16 |
| Hodges | 18 | | 18 |
| Hopkin | 39 | 2 | 41 |
| Meehan | 36 | 2 | 37 |
| Meredith | 19 | 2 | 21 |
| Mew | 42 | 2 | 44 |
| Montgomery | 14 | | 14 |
| Moore | 36 | 2 | 38 |
| Potts | 4 | 1 | 5 |
| Prentice | 1 | | 1 |
| Robinson | 2 | | 2 |
| Sapsford | 2 | | 2 |
| Silcock | 40 | 1 | 41 |
| Spence | 32 | 1 | 33 |
| Spratt | 1 | | 1 |
| Toms | 12 | 1 | 13 |
| Whalley | 23 | 2 | 25 |
| Williamson | 2 | | 2 |
| Woodcock | 28 | 2 | 30 |

### Goalscorers

| PLAYER | LEAGUE | CUP COMPETITION FA CUP | TOTAL |
|---|---|---|---|
| Spence | 14 | | 14 |
| Woodcock | 11 | 1 | 12 |
| Bissett | 6 | | 6 |
| Hopkins | 5 | | 5 |
| Hodges | 4 | | 4 |
| Toms | 3 | 1 | 4 |
| Hilditch | 2 | | 2 |
| Hodge | 2 | | 2 |
| Meehan | 2 | | 2 |
| Meredith | 2 | | 2 |
| Grimwood | 1 | | 1 |
| Harris | 1 | | 1 |
| Montgomery | 1 | | 1 |

### Final Division One Table

| | | P | W | D | L | F | A | Pts |
|---|---|---|---|---|---|---|---|---|
| 1 | WBA | 42 | 28 | 4 | 10 | 104 | 47 | 60 |
| 2 | Burnley | 42 | 21 | 9 | 12 | 65 | 59 | 51 |
| 3 | Chelsea | 42 | 22 | 5 | 15 | 56 | 51 | 49 |
| 4 | Liverpool | 42 | 19 | 10 | 13 | 59 | 44 | 48 |
| 5 | Sunderland | 42 | 22 | 4 | 16 | 72 | 59 | 48 |
| 6 | Bolton Wanderers | 42 | 19 | 9 | 14 | 72 | 65 | 47 |
| 7 | Manchester City | 42 | 18 | 9 | 15 | 71 | 62 | 45 |
| 8 | Newcastle United | 42 | 17 | 9 | 16 | 44 | 39 | 43 |
| 9 | Aston Villa | 42 | 18 | 6 | 18 | 75 | 73 | 42 |
| 10 | Arsenal | 42 | 15 | 12 | 15 | 56 | 58 | 42 |
| 11 | Bradford Park Avenue | 42 | 15 | 12 | 15 | 60 | 63 | 42 |
| 12 | Manchester United | 42 | 13 | 14 | 15 | 54 | 50 | 40 |
| 13 | Middlesbrough | 42 | 15 | 10 | 17 | 61 | 65 | 40 |
| 14 | Sheffield United | 42 | 16 | 8 | 18 | 59 | 69 | 40 |
| 15 | Bradford City | 42 | 14 | 11 | 17 | 54 | 63 | 39 |
| 16 | Everton | 42 | 12 | 14 | 16 | 69 | 68 | 38 |
| 17 | Oldham Athletic | 42 | 15 | 8 | 19 | 49 | 52 | 38 |
| 18 | Derby County | 42 | 13 | 12 | 17 | 47 | 57 | 38 |
| 19 | Preston North End | 42 | 14 | 10 | 18 | 57 | 73 | 38 |
| 20 | Blackburn Rovers | 42 | 13 | 11 | 18 | 64 | 77 | 37 |
| 21 | Notts County | 42 | 12 | 12 | 18 | 56 | 74 | 36 |
| 22 | The Wednesday | 42 | 7 | 9 | 26 | 28 | 64 | 23 |

### Fact File

Joe Spence, probably United's greatest player between the two World Wars, makes his debut on the opening day of the season.

**MANAGER:** John Robson

**MOST APPEARANCES:** Jack Mew 44

**TOP SCORER:** Joe Spence 14 (all League)

**BIGGEST WIN:** 5-1 v Preston North End, 20 September 1919, League; 5-1 v Bolton Wanderers, 10 April 1920, League

**HIGHEST ATTENDANCE:** 58,661 v Sunderland, 14 February 1920, League

# Season 1920-21

## Football League Division One

| DATE | OPPONENTS | SCORE | GOALSCORERS | ATTENDANCE |
|---|---|---|---|---|
| Aug 28 | BOLTON WANDERERS | L 2-3 | Hopkin, Meehan | 50,000 |
| Aug 30 | Arsenal | L 0-2 | | 40,000 |
| Sep 4 | Bolton Wanderers | D 1-1 | Sapsford | 35,000 |
| Sep 6 | ARSENAL | D 1-1 | Spence | 45,000 |
| Sep 11 | CHELSEA | W 3-1 | Meehan 2, Leonard | 40,000 |
| Sep 18 | Chelsea | W 2-1 | Leonard 2 | 35,000 |
| Sep 25 | TOTTENHAM HOTSPUR | L 0-1 | | 50,000 |
| Oct 2 | Tottenham Hotspur | L 1-4 | Spence | 45,000 |
| Oct 9 | OLDHAM ATHLETIC | W 4-1 | Sapsford 2, Meehan, Miller | 50,000 |
| Oct 16 | Oldham Athletic | D 2-2 | Spence, Hemsley o.g. | 20,000 |
| Oct 23 | PRESTON NORTH END | W 1-0 | Miller | 42,000 |
| Oct 30 | Preston North End | D 0-0 | | 25,000 |
| Nov 6 | SHEFFIELD UNITED | W 2-1 | Leonard 2 | 30,000 |
| Nov 13 | Sheffield United | D 0-0 | | 18,000 |
| Nov 20 | MANCHESTER CITY | D 1-1 | Miller | 63,000 |
| Nov 27 | Manchester City | L 0-3 | | 35,000 |
| Dec 4 | BRADFORD PARK AVENUE | W 5-1 | Miller 2, Myerscough 2, Partridge | 25,000 |
| Dec 11 | Bradford Park Avenue | W 4-2 | Myerscough 2, Miller, Partridge | 10,000 |
| Dec 18 | NEWCASTLE UNITED | W 2-0 | Hopkin, Miller | 40,000 |
| Dec 25 | Aston Villa | W 4-3 | Grimwood 2, Harrison, Partridge | 38,000 |
| Dec 27 | ASTON VILLA | L 1-3 | Harrison | 70,504 |
| Jan 1 | Newcastle United | L 3-6 | Hopkin, Partridge, Silcock | 40,000 |
| Jan 15 | WEST BROMWICH ALBION | L 1-4 | Partridge | 40,104 |
| Jan 22 | West Bromwich Albion | W 2-0 | Myerscough, Partridge | 26,826 |
| Feb 5 | LIVERPOOL | D 1-1 | Grimwood | 30,000 |
| Feb 9 | Liverpool | L 0-2 | | 35,000 |
| Feb 12 | EVERTON | L 1-2 | Meredith | 30,000 |
| Feb 20 | SUNDERLAND | W 3-0 | Harrison, Hilditch, Robinson | 40,000 |
| Mar 5 | Sunderland | W 3-2 | Sapsford 2, Goodwin | 25,000 |
| Mar 9 | Everton | L 0-2 | | 38,000 |
| Mar 12 | BRADFORD CITY | D 1-1 | Robinson | 30,000 |
| Mar 19 | Bradford City | D 1-1 | Sapsford | 25,000 |
| Mar 25 | Burnley | L 0-1 | | 20,000 |
| Mar 26 | Huddersfield Town | L 2-5 | Harris, Partridge | 17,000 |
| Mar 28 | BURNLEY | L 0-3 | | 28,000 |
| Apr 2 | HUDDERSFIELD TOWN | W 2-0 | Bissett 2 | 30,000 |
| Apr 9 | Middlesbrough | W 4-2 | Spence 2, Bissett, Grimwood | 15,000 |
| Apr 16 | MIDDLESBROUGH | L 0-1 | | 25,000 |
| Apr 23 | Blackburn Rovers | L 0-2 | | 18,000 |
| Apr 30 | BLACKBURN ROVERS | L 0-1 | | 20,000 |
| May 2 | Derby County | D 1-1 | Bissett | 8,000 |
| May 7 | DERBY COUNTY | W 3-0 | Spence 2, Sapsford | 10,000 |

## FA Cup

| | | | | | |
|---|---|---|---|---|---|
| Jan 8 | Liverpool | (Rd1) | D 1-1 | Miller | 40,000 |
| Jan 12 | LIVERPOOL | (R) | L 1-2 | Partridge | 30,000 |

## League & Cup Appearances

| PLAYER | LEAGUE | CUP COMPETITION FA CUP | TOTAL |
|---|---|---|---|
| Albinson | | 1 | 1 |
| Barlow | 19 | 1 | 20 |
| Bissett | 12 | 2 | 14 |
| Forster | 26 | 1 | 27 |
| Goodwin | 5 | | 5 |
| Grimwood | 25 | 2 | 27 |
| Harris | 26 | 2 | 28 |
| Harrison | 23 | 2 | 25 |
| Hilditch | 34 | | 34 |
| Hodges | 2 | | 2 |
| Hofton | 1 | 1 | 2 |
| Hopkin | 31 | 2 | 33 |
| Leonard | 10 | | 10 |
| Meehan | 15 | | 15 |
| Meredith | 14 | | 14 |
| Mew | 40 | 2 | 42 |
| Miller | 25 | 2 | 27 |
| Montgomery | 2 | | 2 |
| Moore | 26 | | 26 |
| Myerscough | 13 | | 13 |
| Partridge | 28 | 2 | 30 |
| Radford | 1 | | 1 |
| Robinson | 7 | | 7 |
| Sapsford | 21 | | 21 |
| Schofield | 1 | | 1 |
| Silcock | 37 | 2 | 39 |
| Spence | 15 | | 15 |
| Steward | 2 | | 2 |
| Toms | 1 | | 1 |

## Goalscorers

| PLAYER | LEAGUE | CUP COMPETITION FA CUP | TOTAL |
|---|---|---|---|
| Miller | 7 | 1 | 8 |
| Partridge | 7 | 1 | 8 |
| Sapsford | 7 | | 7 |
| Spence | 7 | | 7 |
| Leonard | 5 | | 5 |
| Myerscough | 5 | | 5 |
| Bissett | 4 | | 4 |
| Grimwood | 4 | | 4 |
| Meehan | 4 | | 4 |
| Harrison | 3 | | 3 |
| Hopkin | 3 | | 3 |
| Robinson | 2 | | 2 |
| Harris | 1 | | 1 |
| Hilditch | 1 | | 1 |
| Goodwin | 1 | | 1 |
| Meredith | 1 | | 1 |
| Silcock | 1 | | 1 |
| Opps' o.gs. | 1 | | 1 |

## Fact File

A huge crowd of 70,504 watched United's festive holiday home game with Aston Villa. It remained Old Trafford's biggest league attendance at the onset of the 2003-04 season.

**MANAGER:** John Robson

**MOST APPEARANCES:** Jack Mew 42

**TOP SCORER:** Tom Miller 8 (7 League)

**BIGGEST WIN:** 5-1 v Bradford Park Avenue, 4 December 1920, League

**HIGHEST ATTENDANCE:** 70,504 v Aston Villa, 27 December 1920, League

## Final Division One Table

| | | P | W | D | L | F | A | Pts |
|---|---|---|---|---|---|---|---|---|
| 1 | Burnley | 42 | 23 | 13 | 6 | 79 | 36 | 59 |
| 2 | Manchester City | 42 | 24 | 6 | 12 | 70 | 50 | 54 |
| 3 | Bolton Wanderers | 42 | 19 | 14 | 9 | 77 | 53 | 52 |
| 4 | Liverpool | 42 | 18 | 15 | 9 | 63 | 35 | 51 |
| 5 | Newcastle United | 42 | 20 | 10 | 12 | 66 | 45 | 50 |
| 6 | Tottenham Hotspur | 42 | 19 | 9 | 14 | 70 | 48 | 47 |
| 7 | Everton | 42 | 17 | 13 | 12 | 66 | 55 | 47 |
| 8 | Middlesbrough | 42 | 17 | 12 | 13 | 53 | 53 | 46 |
| 9 | Arsenal | 42 | 15 | 14 | 13 | 59 | 63 | 44 |
| 10 | Aston Villa | 42 | 18 | 7 | 17 | 63 | 70 | 43 |
| 11 | Blackburn Rovers | 42 | 13 | 15 | 14 | 57 | 59 | 41 |
| 12 | Sunderland | 42 | 14 | 13 | 15 | 57 | 60 | 41 |
| 13 | Manchester United | 42 | 15 | 10 | 17 | 64 | 68 | 40 |
| 14 | WBA | 42 | 13 | 14 | 15 | 54 | 58 | 40 |
| 15 | Bradford City | 42 | 12 | 15 | 15 | 61 | 63 | 39 |
| 16 | Preston North End | 42 | 15 | 9 | 18 | 61 | 65 | 39 |
| 17 | Huddersfield Town | 42 | 15 | 9 | 18 | 42 | 49 | 39 |
| 18 | Chelsea | 42 | 13 | 13 | 16 | 48 | 58 | 39 |
| 19 | Oldham Athletic | 42 | 9 | 15 | 18 | 49 | 86 | 33 |
| 20 | Sheffield United | 42 | 6 | 18 | 18 | 42 | 68 | 30 |
| 21 | Derby County | 42 | 5 | 16 | 21 | 32 | 58 | 26 |
| 22 | Bradford Park Avenue | 42 | 8 | 8 | 26 | 43 | 76 | 24 |

## Season 1921-22

### Football League Division One

| DATE | OPPONENTS | SCORE | GOALSCORERS | ATTENDANCE |
|---|---|---|---|---|
| Aug 27 | Everton | L 0-5 | | 30,000 |
| Aug 29 | WEST BROMWICH ALBION | L 2-3 | Partridge, Robinson | 20,000 |
| Sep 3 | EVERTON | W 2-1 | Harrison, Spence | 25,000 |
| Sep 7 | West Bromwich Albion | D 0-0 | | 20,557 |
| Sep 10 | Chelsea | D 0-0 | | 35,000 |
| Sep 17 | CHELSEA | D 0-0 | | 28,000 |
| Sep 24 | Preston North End | L 2-3 | Lochhead, Partridge | 25,000 |
| Oct 1 | PRESTON NORTH END | D 1-1 | Spence | 30,000 |
| Oct 8 | Tottenham Hotspur | D 2-2 | Sapsford, Spence | 36,113 |
| Oct 15 | TOTTENHAM HOTSPUR | W 2-1 | Sapsford, Spence | 30,000 |
| Oct 22 | Manchester City | L 1-4 | Spence | 24,000 |
| Oct 29 | MANCHESTER CITY | W 3-1 | Spence 3 | 56,000 |
| Nov 5 | MIDDLESBROUGH | L 3-5 | Lochhead, Sapsford, Spence | 30,000 |
| Nov 12 | Middlesbrough | L 0-2 | | 18,000 |
| Nov 19 | Aston Villa | L 1-3 | Spence | 30,000 |
| Nov 26 | ASTON VILLA | W 1-0 | Henderson | 33,000 |
| Dec 3 | Bradford City | L 1-2 | Spence | 15,000 |
| Dec 10 | BRADFORD CITY | D 1-1 | Henderson | 9,000 |
| Dec 17 | Liverpool | L 1-2 | Sapsford | 40,000 |
| Dec 24 | LIVERPOOL | D 0-0 | | 30,000 |
| Dec 26 | BURNLEY | L 0-1 | | 15,000 |
| Dec 27 | Burnley | L 2-4 | Lochhead, Sapsford | 10,000 |
| Dec 31 | Newcastle United | L 0-3 | | 20,000 |
| Jan 2 | Sheffield United | L 0-3 | | 18,000 |
| Jan 14 | NEWCASTLE UNITED | L 0-1 | | 20,000 |
| Jan 21 | Sunderland | L 1-2 | Sapsford | 10,000 |
| Jan 28 | SUNDERLAND | W 3-1 | Lochhead, Sapsford, Spence | 18,000 |
| Feb 11 | HUDDERSFIELD TOWN | D 1-1 | Spence | 30,000 |
| Feb 18 | Birmingham | W 1-0 | Spence | 20,000 |
| Feb 25 | BIRMINGHAM | D 1-1 | Sapsford | 35,000 |
| Feb 27 | Huddersfield Town | D 1-1 | Sapsford | 30,000 |
| Mar 11 | ARSENAL | W 1-0 | Spence | 30,000 |
| Mar 18 | BLACKBURN ROVERS | L 0-1 | | 30,000 |
| Mar 25 | Blackburn Rovers | L 0-3 | | 15,000 |
| Apr 1 | BOLTON WANDERERS | L 0-1 | | 28,000 |
| Apr 5 | Arsenal | L 1-3 | Lochhead | 25,000 |
| Apr 8 | Bolton Wanderers | L 0-1 | | 28,000 |
| Apr 15 | OLDHAM ATHLETIC | L 0-3 | | 30,000 |
| Apr 17 | SHEFFIELD UNITED | W 3-2 | Harrison, Lochhead, Partridge | 28,000 |
| Apr 22 | Oldham Athletic | D 1-1 | Lochhead | 30,000 |
| Apr 29 | CARDIFF CITY | D 1-1 | Partridge | 18,000 |
| May 6 | Cardiff City | L 1-3 | Lochhead | 16,000 |

### FA Cup

| | | | | | |
|---|---|---|---|---|---|
| Jan 7 | CARDIFF CITY | (Rd1) | L 1-4 | Sapsford | 25,726 |

### League & Cup Appearances

| PLAYER | LEAGUE | CUP COMPETITION FA CUP | TOTAL |
|---|---|---|---|
| Barlow | 3 | | 3 |
| Bennion | 15 | | 15 |
| Bissett | 6 | | 6 |
| Brett | 10 | | 10 |
| Forster | 4 | | 4 |
| Gibson | 11 | 1 | 12 |
| Goodwin | 2 | | 2 |
| Grimwood | 28 | | 28 |
| Harris | 13 | 1 | 14 |
| Harrison | 21 | | 21 |
| Haslam | 1 | | 1 |
| Henderson | 10 | | 10 |
| Hilditch | 29 | 1 | 30 |
| Howarth | 4 | | 4 |
| Lochhead | 31 | 1 | 32 |
| McBain | 21 | 1 | 22 |
| Mew | 41 | 1 | 42 |
| Myerscough | 7 | | 7 |
| Partridge | 37 | 1 | 38 |
| Pugh | 1 | | 1 |
| Radford | 26 | 1 | 27 |
| Robinson | 12 | | 12 |
| Sapsford | 29 | 1 | 30 |
| Schofield | 1 | | 1 |
| Scott | 23 | 1 | 24 |
| Silcock | 36 | | 36 |
| Spence | 35 | 1 | 36 |
| Steward | 1 | | 1 |
| Taylor | 1 | | 1 |
| Thomas | 3 | | 3 |

### Goalscorers

| PLAYER | LEAGUE | CUP COMPETITION FA CUP | TOTAL |
|---|---|---|---|
| Spence | 15 | | 15 |
| Sapsford | 9 | 1 | 9 |
| Lochhead | 8 | | 8 |
| Partridge | 4 | | 4 |
| Harrison | 2 | | 2 |
| Henderson | 2 | | 2 |
| Robinson | 1 | | 1 |

### Final Division One Table

| | P | W | D | L | F | A | Pts |
|---|---|---|---|---|---|---|---|
| 1 Liverpool | 42 | 22 | 13 | 7 | 63 | 36 | 57 |
| 2 Tottenham Hotspur | 42 | 21 | 9 | 12 | 65 | 39 | 51 |
| 3 Burnley | 42 | 22 | 5 | 15 | 72 | 54 | 49 |
| 4 Cardiff City | 42 | 19 | 10 | 13 | 61 | 53 | 48 |
| 5 Aston Villa | 42 | 22 | 3 | 17 | 74 | 55 | 47 |
| 6 Bolton Wanderers | 42 | 20 | 7 | 15 | 68 | 59 | 47 |
| 7 Newcastle United | 42 | 18 | 10 | 14 | 59 | 45 | 46 |
| 8 Middlesbrough | 42 | 16 | 14 | 12 | 79 | 69 | 46 |
| 9 Chelsea | 42 | 17 | 12 | 13 | 40 | 43 | 46 |
| 10 Manchester City | 42 | 18 | 9 | 15 | 65 | 70 | 45 |
| 11 Sheffield United | 42 | 15 | 10 | 17 | 59 | 54 | 40 |
| 12 Sunderland | 42 | 16 | 8 | 18 | 60 | 62 | 40 |
| 13 WBA | 42 | 15 | 10 | 17 | 51 | 63 | 40 |
| 14 Huddersfield Town | 42 | 15 | 9 | 18 | 53 | 54 | 39 |
| 15 Blackburn Rovers | 42 | 13 | 12 | 17 | 54 | 57 | 38 |
| 16 Preston North End | 42 | 13 | 12 | 17 | 42 | 65 | 38 |
| 17 Arsenal | 42 | 15 | 7 | 20 | 47 | 56 | 37 |
| 18 Birmingham | 42 | 15 | 7 | 20 | 48 | 60 | 37 |
| 19 Oldham Athletic | 42 | 13 | 11 | 18 | 38 | 50 | 37 |
| 20 Everton | 42 | 12 | 12 | 18 | 57 | 55 | 36 |
| 21 Bradford City | 42 | 11 | 10 | 21 | 48 | 72 | 32 |
| 22 Manchester United | 42 | 8 | 12 | 22 | 41 | 73 | 28 |

### Fact File

United finished the season at the foot of the table and were relegated to Division Two for the first time since their Newton Heath days.

**MANAGER:** John Robson/John Chapman
**MOST APPEARANCES:** Jack Mew 42
**TOP SCORER:** Joe Spence 15 (all League)
**BIGGEST WIN:** 3-1 v Manchester City, 29 October 1921, League; 3-1 v Sunderland, 28 January 1922, League
**HIGHEST ATTENDANCE:** 56,000 v Manchester City , 29 October 1921, League

## Season 1922-23

### Football League Division Two

| DATE | OPPONENTS | SCORE | GOALSCORERS | ATTENDANCE |
|---|---|---|---|---|
| Aug 26 | CRYSTAL PALACE | W 2-1 | Spence, Wood | 30,000 |
| Aug 28 | The Wednesday | L 0-1 | | 12,500 |
| Sep 2 | Crystal Palace | W 3-2 | Spence 2, Williams | 8,500 |
| Sep 4 | THE WEDNESDAY | W 1-0 | Spence | 22,000 |
| Sep 9 | Wolverhampton Wanderers | W 1-0 | Williams | 18,000 |
| Sep 16 | WOLVERHAMPTON WANDERERS | W 1-0 | Spence | 28,000 |
| Sep 23 | Coventry City | L 0-2 | | 19,000 |
| Sep 30 | COVENTRY CITY | W 2-1 | Henderson, Spence | 25,000 |
| Oct 7 | PORT VALE | L 1-2 | Spence | 25,000 |
| Oct 14 | Port Vale | L 0-1 | | 16,000 |
| Oct 21 | FULHAM | D 1-1 | Myerscough | 18,000 |
| Oct 28 | Fulham | D 0-0 | | 20,000 |
| Nov 4 | CLAPTON ORIENT | D 0-0 | | 16,500 |
| Nov 11 | Clapton Orient | D 1-1 | Goldthorpe | 11,000 |
| Nov 18 | Bury | D 2-2 | Goldthorpe 2 | 21,000 |
| Nov 25 | BURY | L 0-1 | | 28,000 |
| Dec 2 | ROTHERHAM COUNTY | W 3-0 | Lochhead, McBain, Spence | 13,500 |
| Dec 9 | Rotherham County | D 1-1 | Goldthorpe | 7,500 |
| Dec 16 | STOCKPORT COUNTY | W 1-0 | McBain | 24,000 |
| Dec 23 | Stockport County | L 0-1 | | 15,500 |
| Dec 25 | WEST HAM UNITED | L 1-2 | Lochhead | 17,500 |
| Dec 26 | West Ham United | W 2-0 | Lochhead 2 | 25,000 |
| Dec 30 | Hull City | L 1-2 | Lochhead | 6,750 |
| Jan 1 | BARNSLEY | W 1-0 | Lochhead | 29,000 |
| Jan 6 | HULL CITY | W 3-2 | Goldthorpe, Lochhead, Bell o.g. | 15,000 |
| Jan 20 | LEEDS UNITED | D 0-0 | | 25,000 |
| Jan 27 | Leeds United | W 1-0 | Lochhead | 24,745 |
| Feb 10 | Notts County | W 6-1 | Goldthorpe 4, Myerscough 2 | 10,000 |
| Feb 17 | DERBY COUNTY | D 0-0 | | 27,500 |
| Feb 21 | NOTTS COUNTY | D 1-1 | Lochhead | 12,100 |
| Mar 3 | SOUTHAMPTON | L 1-2 | Lochhead | 30,000 |
| Mar 14 | Derby County | D 1-1 | MacDonald | 12,000 |
| Mar 17 | Bradford City | D 1-1 | Goldthorpe | 10,000 |
| Mar 21 | BRADFORD CITY | D 1-1 | Spence | 15,000 |
| Mar 30 | SOUTH SHIELDS | W 3-0 | Goldthorpe 2, Lochhead | 26,000 |
| Mar 31 | Blackpool | L 0-1 | | 21,000 |
| Apr 2 | South Shields | W 3-0 | Goldthorpe, Hilditch, Spence | 6,500 |
| Apr 7 | BLACKPOOL | W 2-1 | Lochhead, Radford | 20,000 |
| Apr 11 | Southampton | D 0-0 | | 5,500 |
| Apr 14 | Leicester City | W 1-0 | Bain | 25,000 |
| Apr 21 | LEICESTER CITY | L 0-2 | | 30,000 |
| Apr 28 | Barnsley | D 2-2 | Lochhead, Spence | 8,000 |

### FA Cup

| | | | | | |
|---|---|---|---|---|---|
| Jan 13 | Bradford City | (Rd1) | D 1-1 | Partridge | 27,000 |
| Jan 17 | BRADFORD CITY | (R) | W 2-0 | Barber, Goldthorpe | 27,791 |
| Feb 3 | Tottenham Hotspur | (Rd2) | L 0-4 | | 38,333 |

### League & Cup Appearances

| PLAYER | LEAGUE | CUP COMPETITION FA CUP | TOTAL |
|---|---|---|---|
| Bain | 4 | | 4 |
| Barber | 2 | 1 | 3 |
| Barson | 31 | 3 | 34 |
| Bennion | 14 | | 14 |
| Broome | 1 | | 1 |
| Cartman | 3 | | 3 |
| Goldthorpe | 22 | 3 | 25 |
| Grimwood | 36 | 3 | 39 |
| Henderson | 2 | | 2 |
| Hilditch | 32 | 3 | 35 |
| Lievesley | 2 | 1 | 3 |
| Lochhead | 34 | 3 | 37 |
| Lyner | 3 | | 3 |
| McBain | 21 | | 21 |
| MacDonald | 2 | | 2 |
| Mann | 10 | | 10 |
| Mew | 41 | 3 | 44 |
| Moore | 12 | | 12 |
| Myerscough | 13 | 1 | 14 |
| Partridge | 30 | 3 | 33 |
| Pugh | 1 | | 1 |
| Radford | 34 | 3 | 37 |
| Sarvis | 1 | | 1 |
| Silcock | 37 | 3 | 40 |
| Spence | 35 | 2 | 37 |
| Steward | 1 | | 1 |
| Thomas | 18 | | 18 |
| Williams | 5 | | 5 |
| Wood | 15 | 1 | 16 |

### Goalscorers

| PLAYER | LEAGUE | CUP COMPETITION FA CUP | TOTAL |
|---|---|---|---|
| Goldthorpe | 13 | 2 | 15 |
| Lochhead | 13 | | 13 |
| Spence | 11 | | 11 |
| Myerscough | 3 | | 3 |
| McBain | 2 | | 2 |
| Williams | 2 | | 2 |
| Bain | 1 | | 1 |
| Henderson | 1 | | 1 |
| Hilditch | 1 | | 1 |
| MacDonald | 1 | | 1 |
| Partridge | | 1 | 1 |
| Radford | 1 | | 1 |
| Wood | 1 | | 1 |
| Opps' o.gs. | 1 | | 1 |

### Fact File

Frank Barson, one of the stalwarts of United's defence during mid-1920s, made his debut for the club against Wolverhampton Wanderers in early September.

**MANAGER:** John Chapman
**MOST APPEARANCES:** Jack Mew 44
**TOP SCORER:** Ernie Goldthorpe 15 (13 League)
**BIGGEST WIN:** 6-1 v Notts County, 10 February 1923, League
**HIGHEST ATTENDANCE:** 38,333 v Tottenham Hotspur, 3 February 1923, FA Cup

### Final Division Two Table

| | | P | W | D | L | F | A | Pts |
|---|---|---|---|---|---|---|---|---|
| 1 | Notts County | 42 | 23 | 7 | 12 | 46 | 34 | 53 |
| 2 | West Ham United | 42 | 20 | 11 | 11 | 63 | 38 | 51 |
| 3 | Leicester City | 42 | 21 | 9 | 12 | 65 | 44 | 51 |
| 4 | Manchester United | 42 | 17 | 14 | 11 | 51 | 36 | 48 |
| 5 | Blackpool | 42 | 18 | 11 | 13 | 60 | 43 | 47 |
| 6 | Bury | 42 | 18 | 11 | 13 | 55 | 46 | 47 |
| 7 | Leeds United | 42 | 18 | 11 | 13 | 43 | 36 | 47 |
| 8 | The Wednesday | 42 | 17 | 12 | 13 | 54 | 47 | 46 |
| 9 | Barnsley | 42 | 17 | 11 | 14 | 62 | 51 | 45 |
| 10 | Fulham | 42 | 16 | 12 | 14 | 43 | 32 | 44 |
| 11 | Southampton | 42 | 14 | 14 | 14 | 40 | 40 | 42 |
| 12 | Hull City | 42 | 14 | 14 | 14 | 43 | 45 | 42 |
| 13 | South Shields | 42 | 15 | 10 | 17 | 35 | 44 | 40 |
| 14 | Derby County | 42 | 14 | 11 | 17 | 46 | 50 | 39 |
| 15 | Bradford City | 42 | 12 | 13 | 17 | 41 | 45 | 37 |
| 16 | Crystal Palace | 42 | 13 | 11 | 18 | 54 | 62 | 37 |
| 17 | Port Vale | 42 | 14 | 9 | 19 | 39 | 51 | 37 |
| 18 | Coventry City | 42 | 15 | 7 | 20 | 46 | 63 | 37 |
| 19 | Clapton Orient | 42 | 12 | 12 | 18 | 40 | 50 | 36 |
| 20 | Stockport County | 42 | 14 | 8 | 20 | 43 | 58 | 36 |
| 21 | Rotherham County | 42 | 13 | 9 | 20 | 44 | 63 | 35 |
| 22 | Wolverhampton W | 42 | 9 | 9 | 24 | 42 | 77 | 27 |

# Season 1923-24

## Football League Division Two

| DATE | OPPONENTS | SCORE | GOALSCORERS | ATTENDANCE |
|---|---|---|---|---|
| Aug 25 | Bristol City | W 2-1 | Lochhead, MacDonald | 20,500 |
| Aug 27 | SOUTHAMPTON | W 1-0 | Goldthorpe | 21,750 |
| Sep 1 | BRISTOL CITY | W 2-1 | Lochhead, Spence | 21,000 |
| Sep 3 | Southampton | D 0-0 | | 11,500 |
| Sep 8 | Bury | L 0-2 | | 19,000 |
| Sep 15 | BURY | L 0-1 | | 43,000 |
| Sep 22 | South Shields | L 0-1 | | 9,750 |
| Sep 29 | SOUTH SHIELDS | D 1-1 | Lochhead | 22,250 |
| Oct 6 | Oldham Athletic | L 2-3 | Wynne 2 o.gs. | 12,250 |
| Oct 13 | OLDHAM ATHLETIC | W 2-0 | Bain 2 | 26,000 |
| Oct 20 | STOCKPORT COUNTY | W 3-0 | Mann 2, Bain | 31,500 |
| Oct 27 | Stockport County | L 2-3 | Barber, Lochhead | 16,500 |
| Nov 3 | Leicester City | D 2-2 | Lochhead 2 | 17,000 |
| Nov 10 | LEICESTER CITY | W 3-0 | Lochhead, Mann, Spence | 20,000 |
| Nov 17 | Coventry City | D 1-1 | Randle o.g. | 13,580 |
| Dec 1 | Leeds United | D 0-0 | | 20,000 |
| Dec 8 | LEEDS UNITED | W 3-1 | Lochhead 2, Spence | 22,250 |
| Dec 15 | Port Vale | W 1-0 | Grimwood | 7,500 |
| Dec 22 | PORT VALE | W 5-0 | Bain 3, Lochhead, Spence | 11,750 |
| Dec 25 | BARNSLEY | L 1-2 | Grimwood | 34,000 |
| Dec 26 | Barnsley | L 0-1 | | 12,000 |
| Dec 29 | Bradford City | D 0-0 | | 11,500 |
| Jan 2 | COVENTRY CITY | L 1-2 | Bain | 7,000 |
| Jan 5 | BRADFORD CITY | W 3-0 | Bain, Lochhead, McPherson | 18,000 |
| Jan 19 | Fulham | L 1-3 | Lochhead | 15,500 |
| Jan 26 | FULHAM | D 0-0 | | 25,000 |
| Feb 6 | Blackpool | L 0-1 | | 6,000 |
| Feb 9 | BLACKPOOL | D 0-0 | | 13,000 |
| Feb 16 | Derby County | L 0-3 | | 12,000 |
| Feb 23 | DERBY COUNTY | D 0-0 | | 25,000 |
| Mar 1 | Nelson | W 2-0 | Kennedy, Spence | 2,750 |
| Mar 8 | NELSON | L 0-1 | | 8,500 |
| Mar 15 | HULL CITY | D 1-1 | Lochhead | 13,000 |
| Mar 22 | Hull City | D 1-1 | Miller | 6,250 |
| Mar 29 | STOKE | D 2-2 | Smith 2 | 13,000 |
| Apr 5 | Stoke | L 0-3 | | 11,000 |
| Apr 12 | CRYSTAL PALACE | W 5-1 | Spence 4, Smith | 8,000 |
| Apr 18 | Clapton Orient | L 0-1 | | 18,000 |
| Apr 19 | CRYSTAL PALACE | D 1-1 | Spence | 7,000 |
| Apr 21 | CLAPTON ORIENT | D 2-2 | Evans 2 | 11,000 |
| Apr 26 | THE WEDNESDAY | W 2-0 | Lochhead, Smith | 7,500 |
| May 3 | The Wednesday | L 0-2 | | 7,250 |

## FA Cup

| | | | | |
|---|---|---|---|---|
| Jan 12 | Plymouth Argyle | (Rd1) W 1-0 | McPherson | 35,700 |
| Feb 2 | HUDDERSFIELD TOWN | (Rd2) L 0-3 | | 66,673 |

## League & Cup Appearances

| PLAYER | LEAGUE | CUP COMPETITION FA CUP | TOTAL |
|---|---|---|---|
| Bain | 18 | 1 | 19 |
| Barber | 1 | | 1 |
| Barson | 17 | 2 | 19 |
| Bennion | 34 | 2 | 36 |
| Dennis | 3 | | 3 |
| Ellis | 11 | | 11 |
| Evans | 6 | | 6 |
| Goldthorpe | 4 | | 4 |
| Grimwood | 22 | | 22 |
| Haslam | 7 | | 7 |
| Henderson | | 1 | 1 |
| Hilditch | 41 | 2 | 43 |
| Kennedy | 6 | | 6 |
| Lochhead | 40 | 2 | 42 |
| MacDonald | 7 | | 7 |
| McPherson | 34 | 2 | 36 |
| Mann | 25 | 2 | 27 |
| Mew | 12 | | 12 |
| Miller | 4 | | 4 |
| Moore | 42 | 2 | 44 |
| Partridge | 5 | | 5 |
| Radford | 30 | 1 | 31 |
| Silcock | 8 | 1 | 9 |
| Smith | 12 | | 12 |
| Steward | 30 | 2 | 32 |
| Spence | 36 | 2 | 38 |
| Thomas | 6 | | 6 |
| Tyler | 1 | | 1 |

## Goalscorers

| PLAYER | LEAGUE | CUP COMPETITION FA CUP | TOTAL |
|---|---|---|---|
| Lochhead | 14 | | 14 |
| Spence | 10 | | 10 |
| Bain | 8 | | 8 |
| Smith | 4 | | 4 |
| Mann | 3 | | 3 |
| Evans | 2 | | 2 |
| Grimwood | 2 | | 2 |
| McPherson | 1 | 1 | 2 |
| Barber | 1 | | 1 |
| Goldthorpe | 1 | | 1 |
| Kennedy | 1 | | 1 |
| MacDonald | 1 | | 1 |
| Miller | 1 | | 1 |
| Opps' o.gs. | 3 | | 3 |

## Fact File

Sam Wynne, playing for Oldham Athletic against United at Boundary Park, encountered the unusual experience of scoring two goals for both sides. Latics won the game 3-2.

**MANAGER:** John Chapman
**MOST APPEARANCES:** Charlie Moore 44
**TOP SCORER:** Arthur Lochhead 14 (all League)
**BIGGEST WIN:** 5-0 v Port Vale, 22 December 1923, League
**HIGHEST ATTENDANCE:** 66,673 v Huddersfield Town, 2 February 1924, FA Cup

## Final Division Two Table

| | | P | W | D | L | F | A | Pts |
|---|---|---|---|---|---|---|---|---|
| 1 | Leeds United | 42 | 21 | 12 | 9 | 61 | 35 | 54 |
| 2 | Bury | 42 | 21 | 9 | 12 | 63 | 35 | 51 |
| 3 | Derby County | 42 | 21 | 9 | 12 | 75 | 42 | 51 |
| 4 | Blackpool | 42 | 18 | 13 | 11 | 72 | 47 | 49 |
| 5 | Southampton | 42 | 17 | 14 | 11 | 52 | 31 | 48 |
| 6 | Stoke | 42 | 14 | 18 | 10 | 44 | 42 | 46 |
| 7 | Oldham Athletic | 42 | 14 | 17 | 11 | 45 | 52 | 45 |
| 8 | The Wednesday | 42 | 16 | 12 | 14 | 54 | 51 | 44 |
| 9 | South Shields | 42 | 17 | 10 | 15 | 49 | 50 | 44 |
| 10 | Clapton Orient | 42 | 14 | 15 | 13 | 40 | 36 | 43 |
| 11 | Barnsley | 42 | 16 | 11 | 15 | 57 | 61 | 43 |
| 12 | Leicester City | 42 | 17 | 8 | 17 | 64 | 54 | 42 |
| 13 | Stockport County | 42 | 13 | 16 | 13 | 44 | 52 | 42 |
| 14 | Manchester United | 42 | 13 | 14 | 15 | 52 | 44 | 40 |
| 15 | Crystal Palace | 42 | 13 | 13 | 16 | 53 | 65 | 39 |
| 16 | Port Vale | 42 | 13 | 12 | 17 | 50 | 66 | 38 |
| 17 | Hull City | 42 | 10 | 17 | 15 | 46 | 51 | 37 |
| 18 | Bradford City | 42 | 11 | 15 | 16 | 35 | 48 | 37 |
| 19 | Coventry City | 42 | 11 | 13 | 18 | 52 | 68 | 35 |
| 20 | Fulham | 42 | 10 | 14 | 18 | 45 | 56 | 34 |
| 21 | Nelson | 42 | 10 | 13 | 19 | 40 | 74 | 33 |
| 22 | Bristol City | 42 | 7 | 15 | 20 | 32 | 65 | 29 |

# Season 1924-25

## Football League Division Two

| DATE | OPPONENTS | SCORE | GOALSCORERS | ATTENDANCE |
|---|---|---|---|---|
| Aug 30 | LEICESTER CITY | W 1-0 | Goldthorpe | 21,250 |
| Sep 1 | Stockport County | L 1-2 | Lochhead | 12,500 |
| Sep 6 | Stoke | D 0-0 | | 15,250 |
| Sep 8 | BARNSLEY | W 1-0 | Henderson | 9,500 |
| Sep 13 | COVENTRY CITY | W 5-1 | Henderson 2, Lochhead, McPherson, Spence | 12,000 |
| Sep 20 | Oldham Athletic | W 3-0 | Henderson 3 | 14,500 |
| Sep 27 | THE WEDNESDAY | W 2-0 | McPherson, Smith | 29,500 |
| Oct 4 | Clapton Orient | W 1-0 | Lochhead | 15,000 |
| Oct 11 | CRYSTAL PALACE | W 1-0 | Lochhead | 27,750 |
| Oct 18 | Southampton | W 2-0 | Lochhead 2 | 10,000 |
| Oct 25 | Wolverhampton Wanderers | D 0-0 | | 17,500 |
| Nov 1 | FULHAM | W 2-0 | Henderson, Lochhead | 24,000 |
| Nov 8 | Portsmouth | D 1-1 | Smith | 19,500 |
| Nov 15 | HULL CITY | W 2-0 | Hanson, McPherson | 29,750 |
| Nov 22 | Blackpool | D 1-1 | Hanson | 9,500 |
| Nov 29 | DERBY COUNTY | D 1-1 | Hanson | 59,448 |
| Dec 6 | South Shields | W 2-1 | Henderson, McPherson | 6,500 |
| Dec 13 | BRADFORD CITY | W 3-0 | Henderson 2, McPherson | 18,250 |
| Dec 20 | Port Vale | L 1-2 | Lochhead | 11,000 |
| Dec 25 | Middlesbrough | D 1-1 | Henderson | 18,500 |
| Dec 26 | MIDDLESBROUGH | W 2-0 | Henderson, Smith | 44,000 |
| Dec 27 | Leicester City | L 0-3 | | 18,250 |
| Jan 1 | CHELSEA | W 1-0 | Grimwood | 30,500 |
| Jan 3 | STOKE | W 2-0 | Henderson 2 | 24,500 |
| Jan 17 | Coventry City | L 0-1 | | 9,000 |
| Jan 24 | OLDHAM ATHLETIC | L 0-1 | | 20,000 |
| Feb 7 | CLAPTON ORIENT | W 4-2 | Kennedy 2, McPherson, Pape | 18,250 |
| Feb 14 | Crystal Palace | L 1-2 | Lochhead | 11,250 |
| Feb 23 | The Wednesday | D 1-1 | Pape | 3,000 |
| Feb 28 | WOLVERHAMPTON WANDERERS | W 3-0 | Spence 2, Kennedy | 21,250 |
| Feb 31 | Fulham | L 0-1 | | 16,000 |
| Mar 14 | PORTSMOUTH | W 2-0 | Lochhead, Spence | 27,525 |
| Mar 21 | Hull City | W 1-0 | Lochhead | 6,250 |
| Mar 28 | BLACKPOOL | D 0-0 | | 26,250 |
| Apr 4 | Derby County | L 0-1 | | 24,438 |
| Apr 10 | STOCKPORT COUNTY | W 2-0 | Pape 2 | 43,500 |
| Apr 11 | SOUTH SHIELDS | W 1-0 | Lochhead | 24,000 |
| Apr 13 | Chelsea | D 0-0 | | 16,500 |
| Apr 18 | Bradford City | W 1-0 | Smith | 13,250 |
| Apr 22 | SOUTHAMPTON | D 1-1 | Pape | 26,500 |
| Apr 25 | PORT VALE | W 4-0 | Lochhead, McPherson, Smith, Spence | 33,500 |
| May 2 | Barnsley | D 0-0 | | 11,250 |

## FA Cup

| | | | | |
|---|---|---|---|---|
| Jan 10 | The Wednesday | (Rd1) L 0-2 | | 35,079 |

## League & Cup Appearances

| PLAYER | LEAGUE | CUP COMPETITION FA CUP | TOTAL |
|---|---|---|---|
| Bain | 1 | | 1 |
| Barson | 32 | | 32 |
| Bennion | 17 | | 17 |
| Goldthorpe | 1 | | 1 |
| Grimwood | 39 | 1 | 40 |
| Hanson | 3 | | 3 |
| Haslam | 1 | | 1 |
| Henderson | 22 | 1 | 23 |
| Hilditch | 4 | 1 | 5 |
| Jones | 15 | 1 | 16 |
| Kennedy | 11 | 1 | 12 |
| Lochhead | 37 | | 37 |
| McPherson | 38 | 1 | 39 |
| Mann | 32 | 1 | 33 |
| Moore | 40 | 1 | 41 |
| Pape | 16 | | 16 |
| Partridge | 1 | | 1 |
| Rennox | 4 | | 4 |
| Silcock | 29 | | 29 |
| Smith | 31 | 1 | 32 |
| Spence | 42 | 1 | 43 |
| Steward | 42 | 1 | 43 |
| Taylor | 1 | | 1 |
| Thomas | 3 | | 3 |

## Goalscorers

| PLAYER | LEAGUE | CUP COMPETITION FA CUP | TOTAL |
|---|---|---|---|
| Henderson | 14 | | 14 |
| Lochhead | 13 | | 13 |
| McPherson | 7 | | 7 |
| Pape | 5 | | 5 |
| Smith | 5 | | 5 |
| Spence | 5 | | 5 |
| Hanson | 3 | | 3 |
| Kennedy | 3 | | 3 |
| Goldthorpe | 1 | | 1 |
| Grimwood | 1 | | 1 |

### Fact File

United regained their place in the top flight after three seasons in Division Two. They lost just one home fixture, against Oldham Athletic in January, on their way to securing promotion.

**MANAGER:** John Chapman

**MOST APPEARANCES:** Joe Spence, Alf Steward 43

**TOP SCORER:** William Henderson 14 (all League)

**BIGGEST WIN:** 5-1 v Coventry City, 13 September 1924, League

**HIGHEST ATTENDANCE:** 59,448 v Derby County, 29 November 1924, League

### Final Division Two Table

| | | P | W | D | L | F | A | Pts |
|---|---|---|---|---|---|---|---|---|
| 1 | Leicester City | 42 | 24 | 11 | 7 | 90 | 32 | 59 |
| 2 | Manchester United | 42 | 23 | 11 | 8 | 57 | 23 | 57 |
| 3 | Derby County | 42 | 22 | 11 | 9 | 71 | 36 | 55 |
| 4 | Portsmouth | 42 | 15 | 18 | 9 | 58 | 50 | 48 |
| 5 | Chelsea | 42 | 16 | 15 | 11 | 51 | 37 | 47 |
| 6 | Wolverhampton W | 42 | 20 | 6 | 16 | 55 | 51 | 46 |
| 7 | Southampton | 42 | 13 | 18 | 11 | 40 | 36 | 44 |
| 8 | Port Vale | 42 | 17 | 8 | 17 | 48 | 56 | 42 |
| 9 | South Shields | 42 | 12 | 17 | 13 | 42 | 38 | 41 |
| 10 | Hull City | 42 | 15 | 11 | 16 | 50 | 49 | 41 |
| 11 | Clapton Orient | 42 | 14 | 12 | 16 | 42 | 42 | 40 |
| 12 | Fulham | 42 | 15 | 10 | 17 | 41 | 56 | 40 |
| 13 | Middlesbrough | 42 | 10 | 19 | 13 | 36 | 44 | 39 |
| 14 | The Wednesday | 42 | 15 | 8 | 19 | 50 | 56 | 38 |
| 15 | Barnsley | 42 | 13 | 12 | 17 | 46 | 59 | 38 |
| 16 | Bradford City | 42 | 13 | 12 | 17 | 37 | 50 | 38 |
| 17 | Blackpool | 42 | 14 | 9 | 19 | 65 | 61 | 37 |
| 18 | Oldham Athletic | 42 | 13 | 11 | 18 | 35 | 51 | 37 |
| 19 | Stockport County | 42 | 13 | 11 | 18 | 37 | 57 | 37 |
| 20 | Stoke | 42 | 12 | 11 | 19 | 34 | 46 | 35 |
| 21 | Crystal Palace | 42 | 12 | 10 | 20 | 38 | 54 | 34 |
| 22 | Coventry City | 42 | 11 | 9 | 22 | 45 | 84 | 31 |

## Season 1925-26

### Football League Division One

| DATE | OPPONENTS | SCORE | GOALSCORERS | ATTENDANCE |
|---|---|---|---|---|
| Aug 29 | West Ham United | L 0-1 | | 25,630 |
| Sep 2 | ASTON VILLA | W 3-0 | Barson, Lochhead, Spence | 41,717 |
| Sep 5 | ARSENAL | L 0-1 | | 32,288 |
| Sep 7 | Aston Villa | D 2-2 | Hanson, Rennox | 27,701 |
| Sep 12 | Manchester City | D 1-1 | Rennox | 62,994 |
| Sep 16 | LEICESTER CITY | W 3-2 | Rennox 2, Lochhead | 21,275 |
| Sep 19 | Liverpool | L 0-5 | | 18,824 |
| Sep 26 | BURNLEY | W 6-1 | Rennox 3, Hanson, Hilditch, Smith | 17,259 |
| Oct 3 | Leeds United | L 0-2 | | 26,265 |
| Oct 10 | NEWCASTLE UNITED | W 2-1 | Rennox, Thomas | 39,651 |
| Oct 17 | TOTTENHAM HOTSPUR | D 0-0 | | 26,496 |
| Oct 24 | Cardiff City | W 2-0 | McPherson 2 | 15,846 |
| Oct 31 | HUDDERSFIELD TOWN | D 1-1 | Thomas | 37,213 |
| Nov 7 | Everton | W 3-1 | McPherson, Rennox, Spence | 12,387 |
| Nov 14 | BIRMINGHAM | W 3-1 | Barson, Spence, Thomas | 23,559 |
| Nov 21 | Bury | W 3-1 | McPherson 2, Spence | 16,591 |
| Nov 28 | BLACKBURN ROVERS | W 2-0 | McPherson, Thomas | 33,660 |
| Dec 5 | Sunderland | L 1-2 | Rennox | 25,507 |
| Dec 12 | SHEFFIELD UNITED | L 1-2 | McPherson | 31,132 |
| Dec 19 | West Bromwich Albion | L 1-5 | McPherson | 17,651 |
| Dec 25 | BOLTON WANDERERS | W 2-1 | Hanson, Spence | 38,503 |
| Dec 28 | Leicester City | W 3-1 | McPherson 3 | 28,367 |
| Jan 2 | WEST HAM UNITED | W 2-1 | Rennox 2 | 29,612 |
| Jan 16 | Arsenal | L 2-3 | McPherson, Spence | 25,252 |
| Jan 23 | MANCHESTER CITY | L 1-6 | Rennox | 48,657 |
| Feb 6 | Burnley | W 1-0 | McPherson | 17,141 |
| Feb 13 | LEEDS UNITED | W 2-1 | McPherson, Sweeney | 29,584 |
| Feb 27 | Tottenham Hotspur | W 1-0 | Smith | 25,466 |
| Mar 10 | LIVERPOOL | D 3-3 | Hanson, Rennox, Spence | 9,214 |
| Mar 13 | Huddersfield Town | L 0-5 | | 27,842 |
| Mar 17 | Bolton Wanderers | L 1-3 | McPherson | 10,794 |
| Mar 20 | EVERTON | D 0-0 | | 30,058 |
| Apr 2 | Notts County | W 3-0 | Rennox 2, McPherson | 18,453 |
| Apr 3 | BURY | L 0-1 | | 41,085 |
| Apr 5 | NOTTS COUNTY | L 0-1 | | 19,606 |
| Apr 10 | Blackburn Rovers | L 0-7 | | 15,870 |
| Apr 14 | Newcastle United | L 1-4 | Hanson | 9,829 |
| Apr 19 | Birmingham | L 1-2 | Rennox | 8,948 |
| Apr 21 | SUNDERLAND | W 5-1 | Taylor 3, Smith, Thomas | 10,918 |
| Apr 24 | Sheffield United | L 0-2 | | 15,571 |
| Apr 28 | CARDIFF CITY | W 1-0 | Inglis | 9,116 |
| May 1 | WEST BROMWICH ALBION | W 3-2 | Taylor 3 | 9,974 |

### FA Cup

| | | | | | |
|---|---|---|---|---|---|
| Jan 9 | Port Vale | (Rd3) | W 3-2 | Spence 2, McPherson | 14,841 |
| Jan 30 | Tottenham Hotspur | (Rd4) | D 2-2 | Spence, Thomas | 40,000 |
| Feb 3 | TOTTENHAM HOTSPUR | (R) | W 2-0 | Spence, Rennox | 45,000 |
| Feb 20 | Sunderland | (Rd5) | D 3-3 | Smith 2, McPherson | 50,500 |
| Feb 24 | SUNDERLAND | (R) | W 2-1 | Smith, McPherson | 58,661 |
| Mar 6 | Fulham | (Rd6) | W 2-1 | Smith McPherson | 28,699 |
| Mar 27 | Manchester City* | (SF) | L 0-3 | | 46,450 |

*Played at Bramall Lane, Sheffield.

### League & Cup Appearances

| PLAYER | LEAGUE | CUP COMPETITION FA CUP | TOTAL |
|---|---|---|---|
| Astley | 1 | | 1 |
| Bain | 2 | | 2 |
| Barson | 28 | 4 | 32 |
| Bennion | 7 | | 7 |
| Grimwood | 7 | 1 | 8 |
| Hall | 3 | | 3 |
| Hannaford | 4 | 1 | 5 |
| Hanson | 24 | 2 | 26 |
| Haslam | 9 | 2 | 11 |
| Hilditch | 28 | 3 | 31 |
| Iddon | 1 | | 1 |
| Inglis | 7 | | 7 |
| Jones | 10 | | 10 |
| Lochhead | 5 | | 5 |
| McCrae | 9 | 4 | 13 |
| McPherson | 29 | 7 | 36 |
| Mew | 6 | 5 | 11 |
| Moore | 33 | 7 | 40 |
| Mann | 34 | 7 | 41 |
| Pape | 2 | | 2 |
| Partridge | 3 | | 3 |
| Rennox | 34 | 7 | 41 |
| Richardson | 1 | | 1 |
| Silcock | 33 | 7 | 40 |
| Smith | 30 | 5 | 35 |
| Spence | 39 | 7 | 46 |
| Steward | 35 | 2 | 37 |
| Sweeney | 3 | | 3 |
| Taylor | 6 | | 6 |
| Thomas | 29 | 6 | 35 |

### Goalscorers

| PLAYER | LEAGUE | CUP COMPETITION FA CUP | TOTAL |
|---|---|---|---|
| McPherson | 16 | 4 | 20 |
| Rennox | 17 | 1 | 18 |
| Spence | 7 | 4 | 11 |
| Smith | 3 | 4 | 7 |
| Taylor | 6 | | 6 |
| Thomas | 5 | 1 | 6 |
| Hanson | 5 | | 5 |
| Barson | 2 | | 2 |
| Lochhead | 2 | | 2 |
| Hilditch | 1 | | 1 |
| Inglis | 1 | | 1 |
| Sweeney | 1 | | 1 |

### Fact File

United's only appearance in the FA Cup semi-final between the two World Wars ended in defeat and disappointment against Manchester City at Bramall Lane.

**MANAGER:** John Chapman

**MOST APPEARANCES:** Joe Spence 46

**TOP SCORER:** Frank McPherson 20 (16 League)

**BIGGEST WIN:** 6-1 v Burnley, 26 September 1925, League

**HIGHEST ATTENDANCE:** 62,994 v Manchester City, 12 September 1925, League

### Final Division One Table

| | | P | W | D | L | F | A | Pts |
|---|---|---|---|---|---|---|---|---|
| 1 | Huddersfield Town | 42 | 23 | 11 | 8 | 92 | 60 | 57 |
| 2 | Arsenal | 42 | 22 | 8 | 12 | 87 | 63 | 52 |
| 3 | Sunderland | 42 | 21 | 6 | 15 | 96 | 80 | 48 |
| 4 | Bury | 42 | 20 | 7 | 15 | 85 | 77 | 47 |
| 5 | Sheffield United | 42 | 19 | 8 | 15 | 102 | 82 | 46 |
| 6 | Aston Villa | 42 | 16 | 12 | 14 | 86 | 76 | 44 |
| 7 | Liverpool | 42 | 14 | 16 | 12 | 70 | 63 | 44 |
| 8 | Bolton Wanderers | 42 | 17 | 10 | 15 | 75 | 76 | 44 |
| 9 | Manchester United | 42 | 19 | 6 | 17 | 66 | 73 | 44 |
| 10 | Newcastle United | 42 | 16 | 10 | 16 | 84 | 75 | 42 |
| 11 | Everton | 42 | 12 | 18 | 12 | 72 | 70 | 42 |
| 12 | Blackburn Rovers | 42 | 15 | 11 | 16 | 91 | 80 | 41 |
| 13 | WBA | 42 | 16 | 8 | 18 | 79 | 78 | 40 |
| 14 | Birmingham | 42 | 16 | 8 | 18 | 66 | 81 | 40 |
| 15 | Tottenham Hotspur | 42 | 15 | 9 | 18 | 66 | 79 | 39 |
| 16 | Cardiff City | 42 | 16 | 7 | 19 | 61 | 76 | 39 |
| 17 | Leicester City | 42 | 14 | 10 | 18 | 70 | 80 | 38 |
| 18 | West Ham United | 42 | 15 | 7 | 20 | 63 | 76 | 37 |
| 19 | Leeds United | 42 | 14 | 8 | 20 | 64 | 76 | 36 |
| 20 | Burnley | 42 | 13 | 10 | 19 | 85 | 108 | 36 |
| 21 | Manchester City | 42 | 12 | 11 | 19 | 89 | 100 | 35 |
| 22 | Notts County | 42 | 13 | 7 | 22 | 54 | 74 | 33 |

# Season 1926-27

## Football League Division One

| DATE | OPPONENTS | SCORE | GOALSCORERS | ATTENDANCE |
|---|---|---|---|---|
| Aug 28 | Liverpool | L 2-4 | McPherson 2 | 34,795 |
| Aug 30 | Sheffield United | D 2-2 | McPherson 2 | 14,844 |
| Sep 4 | LEEDS UNITED | D 2-2 | McPherson 2 | 26,338 |
| Sep 11 | Newcastle United | L 2-4 | McPherson, Spence | 28,050 |
| Sep 15 | ARSENAL | D 2-2 | Hanson, Spence | 15,259 |
| Sep 18 | BURNLEY | W 2-1 | Spence 2 | 32,593 |
| Sep 25 | Cardiff City | W 2-0 | Rennox, Spence | 17,267 |
| Oct 2 | ASTON VILLA | W 2-1 | Barson, Rennox | 31,234 |
| Oct 9 | Bolton Wanderers | L 0-4 | | 17,869 |
| Oct 16 | Bury | W 3-0 | Spence 2, McPherson | 22,728 |
| Sep 23 | BIRMINGHAM | L 0-1 | | 32,010 |
| Oct 30 | West Ham United | L 0-4 | | 19,733 |
| Nov 6 | THE WEDNESDAY | D 0-0 | | 16,166 |
| Nov 13 | Leicester City | W 3-2 | McPherson 2, Rennox | 18,521 |
| Nov 20 | EVERTON | W 2-1 | Rennox 2 | 24,361 |
| Nov 27 | Blackburn Rovers | L 1-2 | Spence | 17,280 |
| Dec 4 | HUDDERSFIELD TOWN | D 0-0 | | 33,135 |
| Dec 11 | Sunderland | L 0-6 | | 15,385 |
| Dec 18 | WEST BROMWICH ALBION | W 2-0 | Sweeney 2 | 18,585 |
| Dec 25 | Tottenham Hotspur | D 1-1 | Spence | 37,287 |
| Dec 27 | TOTTENHAM HOTSPUR | W 2-1 | McPherson | 50,665 |
| Dec 28 | Arsenal | L 0-1 | | 30,111 |
| Jan 1 | SHEFFIELD UNITED | W 5-0 | McPherson 2, Barson, Rennox, Sweeney | 33,593 |
| Jan 15 | LIVERPOOL | L 0-1 | | 30,304 |
| Jan 22 | Leeds United | W 3-2 | McPherson, Rennox, Spence | 16,816 |
| Feb 5 | Burnley | L 0-1 | | 22,010 |
| Feb 9 | NEWCASTLE UNITED | W 3-1 | Hanson, Harris, Spence | 25,402 |
| Feb 12 | CARDIFF CITY | D 1-1 | Hanson | 26,213 |
| Feb 19 | Aston Villa | L 0-2 | | 32,467 |
| Feb 26 | BOLTON WANDERERS | D 0-0 | | 29,618 |
| Mar 5 | BURY | L 1-2 | Smith A. | 14,709 |
| Mar 12 | Birmingham | L 0-4 | | 14,392 |
| Mar 19 | WEST HAM UNITED | L 0-3 | | 18,347 |
| Mar 26 | The Wednesday | L 0-2 | | 11,997 |
| Apr 2 | LEICESTER CITY | W 1-0 | Spence | 17,119 |
| Apr 9 | Everton | D 0-0 | | 22,564 |
| Apr 15 | DERBY COUNTY | D 2-2 | Spence 2 | 31,110 |
| Apr 16 | BLACKBURN ROVERS | W 2-0 | Hanson, Spence | 24,845 |
| Apr 18 | Derby County | D 2-2 | Spence 2 | 17,306 |
| Apr 23 | Huddersfield Town | D 0-0 | | 13,870 |
| Apr 30 | SUNDERLAND | D 0-0 | | 17,300 |
| May 7 | West Bromwich Albion | D 2-2 | Hanson, Spence | 6,668 |

## FA Cup

| | | | | | |
|---|---|---|---|---|---|
| Jan 8 | Reading | (Rd3) | D 1-1 | Bennion | 28,918 |
| Jan 12 | READING | (R) | D 2-2* | Spence, Sweeney | 29,122 |
| Jan 17 | Reading** | (2R) | L 1-2 | McPherson | 16,500 |

*After extra-time. **Played at Villa Park, Birmingham.

## League & Cup Appearances

| PLAYER | LEAGUE | CUP COMPETITION | TOTAL |
|---|---|---|---|
| | | FA CUP | |
| Astley | 1 | 1 | 2 |
| Barson | 21 | 3 | 24 |
| Bennion | 37 | 3 | 40 |
| Chapman | 17 | | 17 |
| Grimwood | 17 | | 17 |
| Hannaford | 7 | | 7 |
| Hanson | 21 | 1 | 22 |
| Harris | 4 | | 4 |
| Haslam | 4 | | 4 |
| Haworth | 2 | | 2 |
| Hilditch | 16 | 3 | 19 |
| Iddon | 1 | | 1 |
| Inglis | 6 | | 6 |
| Jones | 21 | | 21 |
| McPherson | 32 | 3 | 35 |
| Mann | 14 | | 14 |
| Moore | 30 | 3 | 33 |
| Partridge | 16 | 3 | 19 |
| Rennox | 22 | 1 | 23 |
| Silcock | 26 | 3 | 29 |
| Steward | 42 | 3 | 45 |
| Smith A. | 5 | | 5 |
| Smith T. | 10 | 1 | 11 |
| Spence | 40 | 3 | 43 |
| Sweeney | 13 | 3 | 16 |
| Thomas | 16 | | 16 |
| Wilson | 21 | | 21 |

## Goalscorers

| PLAYER | LEAGUE | CUP COMPETITION | TOTAL |
|---|---|---|---|
| | | FA CUP | |
| Spence | 18 | 1 | 19 |
| McPherson | 15 | 1 | 16 |
| Rennox | 7 | | 7 |
| Hanson | 5 | | 5 |
| Sweeney | 3 | 1 | 4 |
| Barson | 2 | | 2 |
| Bennion | | 1 | 1 |
| Harris | 1 | | 1 |
| Smith A. | 1 | | 1 |

## Final Division One Table

| | P | W | D | L | F | A | Pts |
|---|---|---|---|---|---|---|---|
| 1 Newcastle United | 42 | 25 | 6 | 11 | 96 | 58 | 56 |
| 2 Huddersfield Town | 42 | 17 | 17 | 8 | 76 | 60 | 51 |
| 3 Sunderland | 42 | 21 | 7 | 14 | 98 | 70 | 49 |
| 4 Bolton Wanderers | 42 | 19 | 10 | 13 | 84 | 62 | 48 |
| 5 Burnley | 42 | 19 | 9 | 14 | 91 | 80 | 47 |
| 6 West Ham United | 42 | 19 | 8 | 15 | 86 | 70 | 46 |
| 7 Leicester City | 42 | 17 | 12 | 13 | 85 | 70 | 46 |
| 8 Sheffield United | 42 | 17 | 10 | 15 | 74 | 86 | 44 |
| 9 Liverpool | 42 | 18 | 7 | 17 | 69 | 61 | 43 |
| 10 Aston Villa | 42 | 18 | 7 | 17 | 81 | 83 | 43 |
| 11 Arsenal | 42 | 17 | 9 | 16 | 77 | 86 | 43 |
| 12 Derby County | 42 | 17 | 7 | 18 | 86 | 73 | 41 |
| 13 Tottenham Hotspur | 42 | 16 | 9 | 17 | 76 | 78 | 41 |
| 14 Cardiff City | 42 | 16 | 9 | 17 | 55 | 65 | 41 |
| 15 Manchester United | 42 | 13 | 14 | 15 | 52 | 64 | 40 |
| 16 The Wednesday | 42 | 15 | 9 | 18 | 75 | 92 | 39 |
| 17 Birmingham | 42 | 17 | 4 | 21 | 64 | 73 | 38 |
| 18 Blackburn Rovers | 42 | 15 | 8 | 19 | 77 | 96 | 38 |
| 19 Bury | 42 | 12 | 12 | 18 | 68 | 77 | 36 |
| 20 Everton | 42 | 12 | 10 | 20 | 64 | 90 | 34 |
| 21 Leeds United | 42 | 11 | 8 | 23 | 69 | 88 | 30 |
| 22 WBA | 42 | 11 | 8 | 23 | 65 | 86 | 30 |

## Fact File

Defender Clarence Hilditch was appointed temporary player-manager after the FA suspended John Chapman for alleged management irregularities. Herbert Bamlett became United's permanent boss later in the season.

**MANAGER:** John Chapman, Clarence Hilditch, Herbert Bamlett

**MOST APPEARANCES:** Alf Steward 45

**TOP SCORER:** Joe Spence 19 (18 League)

**BIGGEST WIN:** 5-0 v Sheffield United, 1 January 1927, League

**HIGHEST ATTENDANCE:** 50,665 v Tottenham Hotspur, 27 December 1926, League

## Season 1927-28

### Football League Division One

| DATE | OPPONENTS | SCORE | GOALSCORERS | ATTENDANCE |
|---|---|---|---|---|
| Aug 27 | MIDDLESBROUGH | W 3-0 | Spence 2, Hanson | 44,957 |
| Aug 29 | The Wednesday | W 2-0 | Hanson, Partridge | 17,944 |
| Sep 3 | Birmingham | D 0-0 | | 25,863 |
| Sep 7 | THE WEDNESDAY | D 1-1 | McPherson | 18,759 |
| Sep 10 | NEWCASTLE UNITED | L 1-7 | Spence | 50,217 |
| Sep 17 | Huddersfield Town | L 2-4 | Spence 2 | 17,307 |
| Sep 19 | Blackburn Rovers | L 0-3 | | 18,243 |
| Sep 24 | TOTTENHAM HOTSPUR | W 3-0 | Hanson 2, Spence | 13,952 |
| Oct 1 | Leicester City | L 0-1 | | 22,385 |
| Oct 8 | Everton | L 2-5 | Bennion, Spence | 40,080 |
| Oct 15 | CARDIFF CITY | D 2-2 | Spence, Sweeney | 31,090 |
| Oct 22 | DERBY COUNTY | W 5-0 | Spence 3, Johnston, McPherson | 18,304 |
| Oct 29 | West Ham United | W 2-1 | McPherson, Barrett o.g. | 21,972 |
| Nov 5 | PORTSMOUTH | W 2-0 | McPherson, Clifford o.g. | 13,119 |
| Nov 12 | Sunderland | L 1-4 | Spence | 13,319 |
| Nov 19 | ASTON VILLA | W 5-1 | Partridge 2, Johnston, McPherson, Spence | 25,991 |
| Nov 26 | Burnley | L 0-4 | | 18,509 |
| Dec 3 | BURY | L 0-1 | | 23,581 |
| Dec 10 | Sheffield United | L 1-2 | Spence | 11,984 |
| Dec 17 | ARSENAL | W 4-1 | Hanson, McPherson, Partridge, Spence | 18,120 |
| Dec 24 | Liverpool | L 0-2 | | 14,971 |
| Dec 26 | BLACKBURN ROVERS | D 1-1 | Spence | 31,131 |
| Dec 31 | Middlesbrough | W 2-1 | Hanson, Johnston | 19,652 |
| Jan 7 | BIRMINGHAM | D 1-1 | Hanson | 16,853 |
| Jan 21 | Newcastle United | L 1-4 | Partridge | 25,912 |
| Feb 4 | Tottenham Hotspur | L 1-4 | Johnston | 23,545 |
| Feb 11 | LEICESTER CITY | W 5-2 | Nicol 2, Spence 2, Hanson | 16,640 |
| Feb 25 | Cardiff City | L 0-2 | | 15,579 |
| Mar 7 | HUDDERSFIELD TOWN | D 0-0 | | 35,413 |
| Mar 10 | WEST HAM UNITED | D 1-1 | Johnston | 21,577 |
| Mar 14 | EVERTON | W 1-0 | Rawlings | 25,667 |
| Mar 17 | Portsmouth | L 0-1 | | 25,400 |
| Mar 28 | Derby County | L 0-5 | | 8,323 |
| Mar 31 | Aston Villa | L 1-3 | Rawlings | 24,691 |
| Apr 6 | Bolton Wanderers | L 2-3 | Spence, Thomas | 23,795 |
| Apr 7 | BURNLEY | W 4-3 | Rawlings 3, Williams | 28,311 |
| Apr 9 | BOLTON WANDERERS | W 2-1 | Johnston, Rawlings | 28,590 |
| Apr 14 | Bury | L 3-4 | Johnston, McLenahan, Williams | 17,440 |
| Apr 21 | SHEFFIELD UNITED | L 2-3 | Rawlings, Thomas | 27,137 |
| Apr 25 | SUNDERLAND | W 2-1 | Hanson, Johnston | 9,545 |
| Apr 28 | Arsenal | W 1-0 | Rawlings | 22,452 |
| May 5 | LIVERPOOL | W 6-1 | Spence 3, Rawlings 2, Hanson | 30,625 |

### FA Cup

| | | | | | |
|---|---|---|---|---|---|
| Jan 14 | BRENTFORD | (Rd3) W 7-1 | Hanson 4, Spence, McPherson, Johnston | 18,538 |
| Jan 28 | Bury | (Rd4) D 1-1 | Johnston | 25,000 |
| Feb 1 | BURY | (R) W 1-0 | Spence | 48,001 |
| Feb 18 | BIRMINGHAM | (Rd5) W 1-0 | Johnston | 52,568 |
| Mar 3 | Blackburn Rovers | (Rd6) L 0-2 | | 42,312 |

### League & Cup Appearances

| PLAYER | LEAGUE | CUP COMPETITION FA CUP | TOTAL |
|---|---|---|---|
| Bain | 1 | | 1 |
| Barson | 11 | | 11 |
| Bennion | 36 | 5 | 41 |
| Chapman | 9 | | 9 |
| Ferguson | 4 | | 4 |
| Hanson | 30 | 5 | 35 |
| Haslam | 3 | | 3 |
| Hilditch | 5 | | 5 |
| Johnston | 31 | 5 | 36 |
| Jones | 33 | 5 | 38 |
| Mann | 26 | 5 | 31 |
| McLenahan | 10 | | 10 |
| McPherson | 26 | 3 | 29 |
| Moore | 25 | 1 | 26 |
| Nicol | 4 | 1 | 5 |
| Partridge | 23 | 3 | 26 |
| Ramsden | 2 | | 2 |
| Rawlings | 12 | | 12 |
| Richardson | 32 | 4 | 36 |
| Silcock | 26 | 4 | 30 |
| Spence | 38 | 5 | 43 |
| Steward | 10 | 1 | 11 |
| Sweeney | 4 | | 4 |
| Taylor | 2 | | 2 |
| Thomas | 13 | | 13 |
| Williams | 13 | 3 | 16 |
| Wilson | 33 | 5 | 38 |

### Goalscorers

| PLAYER | LEAGUE | CUP COMPETITION FA CUP | TOTAL |
|---|---|---|---|
| Spence | 22 | 2 | 24 |
| Hanson | 10 | 4 | 14 |
| Johnston | 8 | 3 | 11 |
| Rawlings | 10 | | 10 |
| McPherson | 6 | 1 | 7 |
| Partridge | 5 | | 5 |
| Nicol | 2 | | 2 |
| Thomas | 2 | | 2 |
| Williams | 2 | | 2 |
| Bennion | 1 | | 1 |
| McLenahan | 1 | | 1 |
| Sweeney | 1 | | 1 |
| Opps' o.gs. | 2 | | 2 |

### Fact File

United dipped perilously close to the relegation zone, finishing just one point above Tottenham Hotspur who tumbled into Division Two with bottom-placed club Middlesbrough

**MANAGER:** Herbert Bamlett
**MOST APPEARANCES:** Joe Spence 43
**TOP SCORER:** Joe Spence 24 (22 League)
**BIGGEST WIN:** 7-1 v Brentford, 14 January 1928, FA Cup
**HIGHEST ATTENDANCE:** 52,568 v Birmingham, 18 February 1928, FA Cup

### Final Division One Table

| | | P | W | D | L | F | A | Pts |
|---|---|---|---|---|---|---|---|---|
| 1 | Everton | 42 | 20 | 13 | 9 | 102 | 66 | 53 |
| 2 | Huddersfield Town | 42 | 22 | 7 | 13 | 91 | 68 | 51 |
| 3 | Leicester City | 42 | 18 | 12 | 12 | 86 | 72 | 48 |
| 4 | Derby County | 42 | 17 | 10 | 15 | 96 | 83 | 44 |
| 5 | Bury | 42 | 20 | 4 | 18 | 80 | 80 | 44 |
| 6 | Cardiff City | 42 | 17 | 10 | 15 | 81 | 66 | 43 |
| 7 | Bolton Wanderers | 42 | 16 | 11 | 15 | 81 | 66 | 43 |
| 8 | Aston Villa | 42 | 17 | 9 | 16 | 78 | 73 | 43 |
| 9 | Newcastle United | 42 | 15 | 13 | 14 | 79 | 81 | 43 |
| 10 | Arsenal | 42 | 13 | 15 | 14 | 82 | 86 | 41 |
| 11 | Birmingham | 42 | 13 | 15 | 14 | 70 | 75 | 41 |
| 12 | Blackburn Rovers | 42 | 16 | 9 | 17 | 66 | 78 | 41 |
| 13 | Sheffield United | 42 | 15 | 10 | 17 | 79 | 86 | 40 |
| 14 | The Wednesday | 42 | 13 | 13 | 16 | 81 | 78 | 39 |
| 15 | Sunderland | 42 | 15 | 9 | 18 | 74 | 76 | 39 |
| 16 | Liverpool | 42 | 13 | 13 | 16 | 84 | 87 | 39 |
| 17 | West Ham United | 42 | 14 | 11 | 17 | 81 | 88 | 39 |
| 18 | Manchester United | 42 | 16 | 7 | 19 | 72 | 80 | 39 |
| 19 | Burnley | 42 | 16 | 7 | 19 | 82 | 98 | 39 |
| 20 | Portsmouth | 42 | 16 | 7 | 19 | 66 | 90 | 39 |
| 21 | Tottenham Hotspur | 42 | 15 | 8 | 19 | 74 | 86 | 38 |
| 22 | Middlesbrough | 42 | 11 | 15 | 16 | 81 | 88 | 37 |

# Season 1928-29

## Football League Division One

| DATE | OPPONENTS | SCORE | GOALSCORERS | ATTENDANCE |
|---|---|---|---|---|
| Aug 25 | LEICESTER CITY | D 1-1 | Rawlings | 20,129 |
| Aug 27 | Aston Villa | D 0-0 | | 30,356 |
| Sep 1 | Manchester City | D 2-2 | Johnston, Wilson | 61,007 |
| Sep 8 | Leeds United | L 2-3 | Johnston, Spence | 28,723 |
| Sep 15 | LIVERPOOL | D 2-2 | Hanson, Silcock | 24,077 |
| Sep 22 | West Ham United | L 1-3 | Rawlings | 20,788 |
| Sep 29 | NEWCASTLE UNITED | W 5-0 | Rawlings 2, Hanson, Johnston, Spence | 25,243 |
| Oct 6 | Burnley | W 4-3 | Hanson 2, Spence 2 | 17,493 |
| Oct 13 | CARDIFF CITY | D 1-1 | Johnston | 26,010 |
| Oct 20 | BIRMINGHAM | W 1-0 | Johnston | 17,522 |
| Oct 27 | Huddersfield Town | W 2-1 | Hanson, Spence | 13,648 |
| Nov 3 | BOLTON WANDERERS | D 1-1 | Hanson | 31,185 |
| Nov 10 | The Wednesday | L 1-2 | Hanson | 18,113 |
| Nov 17 | DERBY COUNTY | L 0-1 | | 26,122 |
| Nov 24 | Sunderland | L 1-5 | Rowley | 15,932 |
| Dec 1 | BLACKBURN ROVERS | L 1-4 | Ramsden | 19,589 |
| Dec 8 | Arsenal | L 1-3 | Hanson | 18,923 |
| Dec 15 | EVERTON | D 1-1 | Hanson | 17,080 |
| Dec 22 | Portsmouth | L 0-3 | | 12,836 |
| Dec 25 | SHEFFIELD UNITED | D 1-1 | Ramsden | 22,202 |
| Dec 26 | Sheffield United | L 1-6 | Rawlings | 34,696 |
| Dec 29 | Leicester City | L 1-2 | Hanson | 21,535 |
| Jan 1 | ASTON VILLA | D 2-2 | Hilditch, Rowley | 25,935 |
| Jan 5 | MANCHESTER CITY | L 1-2 | Rawlings | 42,555 |
| Jan 19 | LEEDS UNITED | L 1-2 | Sweeney | 21,995 |
| Feb 2 | WEST HAM UNITED | L 2-3 | Reid, Rowley | 12,020 |
| Feb 9 | Newcastle United | L 0-5 | | 34,134 |
| Feb 13 | Liverpool | W 3-2 | Reid 2, Thomas | 8,852 |
| Feb 16 | BURNLEY | W 1-0 | Rowley | 12,516 |
| Feb 23 | Cardiff City | D 2-2 | Hanson, Reid | 13,070 |
| Mar 2 | Birmingham | D 1-1 | Hanson | 16,738 |
| Mar 9 | HUDDERSFIELD TOWN | W 1-0 | Hanson | 28,183 |
| Mar 16 | Bolton Wanderers | D 1-1 | Hanson | 17,354 |
| Mar 23 | THE WEDNESDAY | W 2-1 | Reid, Rowley | 27,095 |
| Mar 29 | Bury | W 3-1 | Reid 2, Thomas | 27,167 |
| Mar 30 | Derby County | L 1-6 | Hanson | 14,319 |
| Apr 1 | BURY | W 1-0 | Thomas | 29,742 |
| Apr 6 | SUNDERLAND | W 3-0 | Hanson, Mann, Reid | 27,772 |
| Apr 13 | Blackburn Rovers | W 3-0 | Reid 2, Ramsden | 8,193 |
| Apr 20 | ARSENAL | W 4-1 | Reid 2, Hanson, Thomas | 22,858 |
| Apr 27 | Everton | W 4-2 | Hanson 2, Reid 2 | 19,442 |
| May 4 | PORTSMOUTH | D 0-0 | | 17,728 |

## FA Cup

| | | | | | |
|---|---|---|---|---|---|
| Jan 12 | Port Vale | (Rd3) | W 3-0 | Spence, Hanson, Taylor | 17,519 |
| Jan 26 | BURY | (Rd4) | L 0-1 | | 40,558 |

## League & Cup Appearances

| PLAYER | LEAGUE | CUP COMPETITION FA CUP | TOTAL |
|---|---|---|---|
| Bennion | 34 | | 34 |
| Boyle | 1 | | 1 |
| Dale | 19 | | 19 |
| Hanson | 42 | 1 | 43 |
| Hilditch | 11 | | 11 |
| Inglis | 1 | | 1 |
| Johnston | 12 | | 12 |
| McLenahan | 1 | | 1 |
| Mann | 25 | 2 | 27 |
| Moore | 37 | 2 | 39 |
| Nicol | 2 | | 2 |
| Partridge | 5 | | 5 |
| Ramsden | 5 | | 5 |
| Rawlings | 19 | 1 | 20 |
| Reid | 17 | | 17 |
| Richardson | 5 | | 5 |
| Rowley | 25 | | 25 |
| Silcock | 27 | 2 | 29 |
| Spence | 36 | 2 | 38 |
| Spencer | 36 | 2 | 38 |
| Steward | 37 | 2 | 39 |
| Sweeney | 6 | 2 | 8 |
| Taylor | 3 | 1 | 4 |
| Thomas | 19 | 1 | 20 |
| Thomson | | 1 | 1 |
| Williams | 18 | 1 | 19 |
| Wilson | 19 | 2 | 21 |

## Goalscorers

| PLAYER | LEAGUE | CUP COMPETITION FA CUP | TOTAL |
|---|---|---|---|
| Hanson | 19 | 1 | 20 |
| Reid | 14 | | 14 |
| Rawlings | 6 | | 6 |
| Spence | 5 | 1 | 6 |
| Johnston | 5 | | 5 |
| Rowley | 5 | | 5 |
| Thomas | 4 | | 4 |
| Ramsden | 3 | | 3 |
| Hilditch | 1 | | 1 |
| Mann | 1 | | 1 |
| Silcock | 1 | | 1 |
| Sweeney | 1 | | 1 |
| Taylor | | 1 | 1 |
| Wilson | 1 | | 1 |

## Fact File

United finished in a respectable 12th place in the table despite struggling through a 16-match mid term sequence without winning a single game.

**MANAGER:** Herbert Bamlett

**MOST APPEARANCES:** Jimmy Hanson 43

**TOP SCORER:** Jimmy Hanson 20 (19 League)

**BIGGEST WIN:** 5-0 v Newcastle United, 29 September 1928, League

**HIGHEST ATTENDANCE:** 61,007 v Manchester City, 1 September 1928, League

## Final Division One Table

| | | P | W | D | L | F | A | Pts |
|---|---|---|---|---|---|---|---|---|
| 1 | The Wednesday | 42 | 21 | 10 | 11 | 86 | 62 | 52 |
| 2 | Leicester City | 42 | 21 | 9 | 12 | 96 | 67 | 51 |
| 3 | Aston Villa | 42 | 23 | 4 | 15 | 98 | 81 | 50 |
| 4 | Sunderland | 42 | 20 | 7 | 15 | 93 | 75 | 47 |
| 5 | Liverpool | 42 | 17 | 12 | 13 | 90 | 64 | 46 |
| 6 | Derby County | 42 | 18 | 10 | 14 | 86 | 71 | 46 |
| 7 | Blackburn Rovers | 42 | 17 | 11 | 14 | 72 | 63 | 45 |
| 8 | Manchester City | 42 | 18 | 9 | 15 | 95 | 86 | 45 |
| 9 | Arsenal | 42 | 16 | 13 | 13 | 77 | 72 | 45 |
| 10 | Newcastle United | 42 | 19 | 6 | 17 | 70 | 72 | 44 |
| 11 | Sheffield United | 42 | 15 | 11 | 16 | 86 | 85 | 41 |
| 12 | Manchester United | 42 | 14 | 13 | 15 | 66 | 76 | 41 |
| 13 | Leeds United | 42 | 16 | 9 | 17 | 71 | 84 | 41 |
| 14 | Bolton Wanderers | 42 | 14 | 12 | 16 | 73 | 80 | 40 |
| 15 | Birmingham | 42 | 15 | 10 | 17 | 68 | 77 | 40 |
| 16 | Huddersfield Town | 42 | 14 | 11 | 17 | 70 | 61 | 39 |
| 17 | West Ham United | 42 | 15 | 9 | 18 | 86 | 96 | 39 |
| 18 | Everton | 42 | 17 | 4 | 21 | 63 | 75 | 38 |
| 19 | Burnley | 42 | 15 | 8 | 19 | 81 | 103 | 38 |
| 20 | Portsmouth | 42 | 15 | 6 | 21 | 56 | 80 | 36 |
| 21 | Bury | 42 | 12 | 7 | 23 | 62 | 99 | 31 |
| 22 | Cardiff City | 42 | 8 | 13 | 21 | 43 | 59 | 29 |

# Season 1929-30

## Football League Division One

| DATE | OPPONENTS | SCORE | GOALSCORERS | ATTENDANCE |
|---|---|---|---|---|
| Aug 31 | Newcastle United | L 1-4 | Spence | 43,489 |
| Sep 2 | Leicester City | L 1-4 | Rowley | 20,490 |
| Sep 7 | BLACKBURN ROVERS | W 1-0 | Mann | 22,362 |
| Sep 11 | LEICESTER CITY | W 2-1 | Ball, Spence | 16,445 |
| Sep 14 | Middlesbrough | W 3-2 | Rawlings 3 | 26,428 |
| Sep 21 | LIVERPOOL | L 1-2 | Spence | 20,788 |
| Sep 28 | West Ham United | L 1-2 | Hanson | 20,695 |
| Oct 5 | MANCHESTER CITY | L 1-3 | Thomas | 57,201 |
| Oct 7 | Sheffield United | L 1-3 | Boyle | 7,987 |
| Oct 12 | GRIMSBY TOWN | L 2-5 | Ball, Rowley | 21,494 |
| Oct 19 | Portsmouth | L 0-3 | | 18,070 |
| Oct 26 | ARSENAL | W 1-0 | Ball | 12,662 |
| Nov 2 | Aston Villa | L 0-1 | | 24,292 |
| Nov 9 | DERBY COUNTY | W 3-2 | Ball, Hanson, Rowley | 15,174 |
| Nov 16 | Sheffield Wednesday | L 2-7 | Ball, Hanson | 14,264 |
| Nov 23 | BURNLEY | W 1-0 | Rowley | 9,060 |
| Nov 30 | Sunderland | W 4-2 | Spence 2, Ball, Hanson | 11,508 |
| Dec 7 | BOLTON WANDERERS | D 1-1 | Ball | 5,656 |
| Dec 14 | Everton | D 0-0 | | 18,182 |
| Dec 21 | LEEDS UNITED | W 3-1 | Ball 2, Hanson | 15,054 |
| Dec 25 | BIRMINGHAM | D 0-0 | | 18,626 |
| Dec 26 | Birmingham | W 1-0 | Rowley | 35,682 |
| Dec 28 | NEWCASTLE UNITED | W 5-0 | Boyle 2, McLachlan, Rowley, Spence | 14,862 |
| Jan 4 | Blackburn Rovers | L 4-5 | Boyle 2, Ball, Rowley | 23,923 |
| Jan 18 | MIDDLESBROUGH | L 0-3 | | 21,028 |
| Jan 25 | Liverpool | L 0-1 | | 28,592 |
| Feb 1 | WEST HAM UNITED | W 4-2 | Spence 4 | 15,424 |
| Feb 8 | Manchester City | W 1-0 | Reid | 64,472 |
| Feb 15 | Grimsby Town | D 2-2 | Reid, Rowley | 9,337 |
| Feb 22 | PORTSMOUTH | W 3-0 | Reid 2, Boyle | 17,317 |
| Mar 1 | Bolton Wanderers | L 1-4 | Reid | 17,714 |
| Mar 8 | ASTON VILLA | L 2-3 | McLachlan, Warburton | 25,407 |
| Mar 12 | Arsenal | L 2-4 | Ball, Wilson | 18,082 |
| Mar 15 | Derby County | D 1-1 | Rowley | 9,102 |
| Mar 29 | Burnley | L 0-4 | | 11,659 |
| Apr 5 | SUNDERLAND | W 2-1 | McLenahan 2 | 13,230 |
| Apr 14 | SHEFFIELD WEDNESDAY | D 2-2 | McLenahan, Rowley | 12,806 |
| Apr 18 | HUDDERSFIELD TOWN | W 1-0 | McLenahan | 26,496 |
| Apr 19 | EVERTON | D 3-3 | Mclenahan, Rowley, Spence | 13,320 |
| Apr 22 | Huddersfield Town | D 2-2 | Hilditch, McLenahan | 20,716 |
| Apr 26 | Leeds United | L 1-3 | Spence | 10,596 |
| May 3 | SHEFFIELD UNITED | L 1-5 | Rowley | 15,268 |

## FA Cup

| | | | | |
|---|---|---|---|---|
| Jan 11 | SWINDON TOWN | (Rd3) L 0-2 | | 33,226 |

## League & Cup Appearances

| PLAYER | LEAGUE | CUP COMPETITION FA CUP | OTHER | TOTAL |
|---|---|---|---|---|
| Ball | 23 | 1 | | 24 |
| Bennion | 28 | | | 28 |
| Boyle | 15 | 1 | | 16 |
| Chesters | 3 | | | 3 |
| Dale | 19 | | | 19 |
| Hanson | 18 | | | 18 |
| Hilditch | 27 | 1 | | 28 |
| Jones | 16 | 1 | | 17 |
| McLachlan | 23 | 1 | | 24 |
| McLenahan | 10 | | | 10 |
| Mann | 14 | | | 14 |
| Moore | 28 | 1 | | 29 |
| Rawlings | 4 | | | 4 |
| Reid | 13 | | | 13 |
| Rowley | 40 | 1 | | 41 |
| Silcock | 21 | | | 21 |
| Spence | 42 | 1 | | 43 |
| Spencer | 10 | | | 10 |
| Steward | 39 | 1 | | 40 |
| Sweeney | 1 | | | 1 |
| Taylor | 16 | 1 | | 17 |
| Thomas | 21 | | | 21 |
| Thomson | 1 | | | 1 |
| Warburton | 2 | | | 2 |
| Wilson | 28 | 1 | | 29 |

## Goalscorers

| PLAYER | LEAGUE | CUP COMPETITION FA CUP | OTHER | TOTAL |
|---|---|---|---|---|
| Rowley | 12 | | | 12 |
| Spence | 12 | | | 12 |
| Ball | 11 | | | 11 |
| Boyle | 6 | | | 6 |
| McLenahan | 6 | | | 6 |
| Hanson | 5 | | | 5 |
| Reid | 5 | | | 5 |
| Rawlings | 3 | | | 3 |
| McLachlan | 2 | | | 2 |
| Hilditch | 1 | | | 1 |
| Mann | 1 | | | 1 |
| Thomas | 1 | | | 1 |
| Warburton | 1 | | | 1 |
| Wilson | 1 | | | 1 |

## Fact File

Another less than satisfactory season with United once again completing the campaign dangerously close to the dreaded 'drop zone' and there was little comfort to be had in the FA Cup.

**MANAGER:** Herbert Bamlett

**MOST APPEARANCES:** 43 Joe Spence

**TOP SCORER:** 12 Harry Rowley, Joe Spence (all League)

**BIGGEST WIN:** 5-0 v Newcastle United, 28 December 1929, League

**HIGHEST ATTENDANCE:** 64,472 v Manchester City, 8 February 1930, League

## Final Division One Table

| | | P | W | D | L | F | A | Pts |
|---|---|---|---|---|---|---|---|---|
| 1 | Sheffield Wednesday | 42 | 26 | 8 | 8 | 105 | 57 | 60 |
| 2 | Derby County | 42 | 21 | 8 | 13 | 90 | 82 | 50 |
| 3 | Manchester City | 42 | 19 | 9 | 14 | 91 | 81 | 47 |
| 4 | Aston Villa | 42 | 21 | 5 | 16 | 92 | 83 | 47 |
| 5 | Leeds United | 42 | 20 | 6 | 16 | 79 | 63 | 46 |
| 6 | Blackburn Rovers | 42 | 19 | 7 | 16 | 99 | 93 | 45 |
| 7 | West Ham United | 42 | 19 | 5 | 18 | 86 | 79 | 43 |
| 8 | Leicester City | 42 | 17 | 9 | 16 | 86 | 90 | 43 |
| 9 | Sunderland | 42 | 18 | 7 | 17 | 76 | 80 | 43 |
| 10 | Huddersfield Town | 42 | 16 | 9 | 17 | 63 | 69 | 43 |
| 11 | Birmingham | 42 | 16 | 9 | 17 | 67 | 62 | 41 |
| 12 | Liverpool | 42 | 16 | 9 | 17 | 63 | 79 | 41 |
| 13 | Portsmouth | 42 | 15 | 10 | 17 | 66 | 62 | 40 |
| 14 | Arsenal | 42 | 14 | 11 | 17 | 78 | 66 | 39 |
| 15 | Bolton Wanderers | 42 | 15 | 9 | 18 | 74 | 74 | 39 |
| 16 | Middlesbrough | 42 | 16 | 6 | 20 | 82 | 84 | 38 |
| 17 | Manchester United | 42 | 15 | 8 | 19 | 67 | 88 | 38 |
| 18 | Grimsby Town | 42 | 15 | 7 | 20 | 73 | 89 | 37 |
| 19 | Newcastle United | 42 | 15 | 7 | 20 | 71 | 92 | 37 |
| 20 | Sheffield United | 42 | 15 | 6 | 21 | 91 | 96 | 36 |
| 21 | Burnley | 42 | 14 | 8 | 20 | 79 | 97 | 36 |
| 22 | Everton | 42 | 12 | 11 | 19 | 80 | 92 | 35 |

# Season 1930-31

## Football League Division One

| DATE | OPPONENTS | SCORE | GOALSCORERS | ATTENDANCE |
|---|---|---|---|---|
| Aug 30 | ASTON VILLA | L 3-4 | Reid, Rowley, Warburton | 18,004 |
| Sep 3 | Middlesbrough | L 1-3 | Rowley | 15,712 |
| Sep 6 | Chelsea | L 2-6 | Reid, Spence | 48,648 |
| Sep 10 | HUDDERSFIELD TOWN | L 0-6 | | 11,836 |
| Sep 13 | NEWCASTLE UNITED | L 4-7 | Reid 3, Rowley | 10,907 |
| Sep 15 | Huddersfield Town | L 0-3 | | 14,028 |
| Sep 20 | Sheffield Wednesday | L 0-3 | | 18,705 |
| Sep 27 | GRIMSBY TOWN | L 0-2 | | 14,695 |
| Oct 4 | Manchester City | L 1-4 | Spence | 41,757 |
| Oct 11 | West ham United | L 1-5 | Reid | 20,003 |
| Oct 18 | ARSENAL | L 1-2 | McLachlan | 23,406 |
| Oct 25 | Portsmouth | L 1-4 | Rowley | 19,262 |
| Nov 1 | BIRMINGHAM | W 2-0 | Gallimore, Rowley | 11,479 |
| Nov 8 | Leicester City | L 4-5 | Bullock 3, McLachlan | 17,466 |
| Nov 15 | BLACKPOOL | D 0-0 | | 14,765 |
| Nov 22 | Sheffield United | L 1-3 | Gallimore | 12,698 |
| Nov 29 | SUNDERLAND | D 1-1 | Gallimore | 10,971 |
| Dec 6 | Blackburn Rovers | L 1-4 | Rowley | 10,802 |
| Dec 13 | DERBY COUNTY | W 2-1 | Reid, Spence | 9,701 |
| Dec 20 | Leeds United | L 0-5 | | 11,282 |
| Dec 25 | Bolton Wanderers | L 1-3 | Reid | 22,662 |
| Dec 26 | BOLTON WANDERERS | D 1-1 | Reid | 12,741 |
| Dec 27 | Aston Villa | L 0-7 | | 32,505 |
| Jan 1 | LEEDS UNITED | D 0-0 | | 9,875 |
| Jan 3 | CHELSEA | W 1-0 | Warburton | 8,966 |
| Jan 17 | Newcastle United | L 3-4 | Warburton 2, Reid | 24,835 |
| Jan 28 | SHEFFIELD WEDNESDAY | W 4-1 | Hopkinson, Reid, Spence, Warburton | 6,077 |
| Jan 31 | Grimsby Town | L 1-2 | Reid | 9,305 |
| Feb 7 | MANCHESTER CITY | L 1-3 | Spence | 39,876 |
| Feb 14 | WEST HAM UNITED | W 1-0 | Gallimore | 9,745 |
| Feb 21 | Arsenal | L 1-4 | Thomson | 41,510 |
| Mar 7 | Birmingham | D 0-0 | | 17,678 |
| Mar 16 | PORTSMOUTH | L 0-1 | | 4,808 |
| Mar 21 | Blackpool | L 1-5 | Hopkinson | 13,612 |
| Mar 25 | LEICESTER CITY | D 0-0 | | 3,679 |
| Mar 28 | SHEFFIELD UNITED | L 1-2 | Hopkinson | 5,420 |
| Apr 3 | Liverpool | D 1-1 | Wilson | 27,782 |
| Apr 4 | Sunderland | W 2-1 | Hopkinson, Reid | 13,590 |
| Apr 6 | LIVERPOOL | W 4-1 | Reid 2, McLenahan, Rowley | 8,058 |
| Apr 11 | BLACKBURN ROVERS | L 0-1 | | 6,414 |
| Apr 18 | Derby County | L 1-6 | Spence | 6,610 |
| May 2 | MIDDLESBROUGH | D 4-4 | Reid 2, Bennion, Gallimore | 3,969 |

## FA Cup

| | | | | |
|---|---|---|---|---|
| Jan 10 | Stoke City | (Rd3) D 3-3 | Reid 3 | 23,415 |
| Jan 14 | STOKE CITY | (R) D 0-0* | | 22,013 |
| Jan 19 | Stoke City** | (2nd R) W 4-2 | Hopkinson 2, Spence, Gallimore | 11,788 |
| Jan 24 | Grimsby Town | (Rd4) L 0-1 | | 15,000 |

*After extra-time. **Played at Anfield, Liverpool.

## League & Cup Appearances

| PLAYER | LEAGUE | CUP COMPETITION FA CUP | TOTAL |
|---|---|---|---|
| Bennion | 36 | 4 | 40 |
| Bullock | 10 | | 10 |
| Chesters | 4 | | 4 |
| Dale | 22 | 4 | 26 |
| Gallimore | 28 | 4 | 32 |
| Hilditch | 25 | 4 | 29 |
| Hopkinson | 17 | 2 | 19 |
| Jones | 5 | | 5 |
| Lydon | 1 | | 1 |
| McLachlan | 42 | 4 | 46 |
| McLenahan | 21 | | 21 |
| Mellor | 35 | 4 | 39 |
| Parker | 9 | | 9 |
| Ramsden | 7 | 2 | 9 |
| Reid | 30 | 3 | 33 |
| Rowley | 29 | | 29 |
| Silcock | 25 | | 25 |
| Spence | 35 | 2 | 37 |
| Steward | 38 | 4 | 42 |
| Thomson | 2 | 1 | 3 |
| Williams | 3 | | 3 |
| Wilson | 20 | 2 | 22 |
| Warburton | 18 | 4 | 22 |

## Goalscorers

| PLAYER | LEAGUE | CUP COMPETITION FA CUP | TOTAL |
|---|---|---|---|
| Reid | 17 | 3 | 20 |
| Rowley | 7 | | 7 |
| Spence | 6 | 1 | 7 |
| Gallimore | 5 | 1 | 6 |
| Hopkinson | 4 | 2 | 6 |
| Warburton | 5 | | 5 |
| Bullock | 3 | | 3 |
| McLachlan | 2 | | 2 |
| Bennion | 1 | | 1 |
| McLenahan | 1 | | 1 |
| Thomson | 1 | | 1 |
| Wilson | 1 | | 1 |

## Fact File

United were relegated to Division Two following a disastrous season that saw them gather in just four points from 21 away matches.

**MANAGER:** Herbert Bamlett

**MOST APPEARANCES:** George McLachlan 46

**TOP SCORER:** Tommy Reid 20 (17 League)

**BIGGEST WIN:** 4-1 v Sheffield Wednesday, 28 January 1931, League; 4-1 v Liverpool, 3 April 1931, League

**HIGHEST ATTENDANCE:** 48,648 v Chelsea, 6 September 1930, League

## Final Division One Table

| | | P | W | D | L | F | A | Pts |
|---|---|---|---|---|---|---|---|---|
| 1 | Arsenal | 42 | 28 | 10 | 4 | 127 | 59 | 66 |
| 2 | Aston Villa | 42 | 25 | 9 | 8 | 128 | 78 | 59 |
| 3 | Sheffield Wednesday | 42 | 22 | 8 | 12 | 102 | 75 | 52 |
| 4 | Portsmouth | 42 | 18 | 13 | 11 | 84 | 67 | 49 |
| 5 | Huddersfield Town | 42 | 18 | 12 | 12 | 81 | 65 | 48 |
| 6 | Derby County | 42 | 18 | 10 | 14 | 94 | 79 | 46 |
| 7 | Middlesbrough | 42 | 19 | 8 | 15 | 98 | 90 | 46 |
| 8 | Manchester City | 42 | 18 | 10 | 14 | 75 | 70 | 46 |
| 9 | Liverpool | 42 | 15 | 12 | 15 | 86 | 85 | 42 |
| 10 | Blackburn Rovers | 42 | 17 | 8 | 17 | 83 | 84 | 42 |
| 11 | Sunderland | 42 | 16 | 9 | 17 | 89 | 85 | 41 |
| 12 | Chelsea | 42 | 15 | 10 | 17 | 64 | 67 | 40 |
| 13 | Grimsby Town | 42 | 17 | 5 | 20 | 82 | 87 | 39 |
| 14 | Bolton Wanderers | 42 | 15 | 9 | 18 | 68 | 81 | 39 |
| 15 | Sheffield United | 42 | 14 | 10 | 18 | 78 | 84 | 38 |
| 16 | Leicester City | 42 | 16 | 6 | 20 | 80 | 95 | 38 |
| 17 | Newcastle United | 42 | 15 | 6 | 21 | 78 | 87 | 36 |
| 18 | West Ham United | 42 | 14 | 8 | 20 | 79 | 94 | 36 |
| 19 | Birmingham | 42 | 13 | 10 | 19 | 55 | 70 | 36 |
| 20 | Blackpool | 42 | 11 | 10 | 21 | 71 | 125 | 32 |
| 21 | Leeds United | 42 | 12 | 7 | 23 | 68 | 81 | 31 |
| 22 | Manchester United | 42 | 7 | 8 | 27 | 53 | 115 | 22 |

## Season 1931-32

### Football League Division Two

| DATE | OPPONENTS | SCORE | GOALSCORERS | ATTENDANCE |
|---|---|---|---|---|
| Aug 29 | Bradford Park Avenue | L 1-3 | Reid | 16,239 |
| Sep 2 | SOUTHAMPTON | L 2-3 | Ferguson, Johnston | 3,507 |
| Sep 5 | SWANSEA TOWN | W 2-1 | Hopkinson, Reid | 6,763 |
| Sep 7 | Stoke City | L 0-3 | | 10,518 |
| Sep 12 | TOTTENHAM HOTSPUR | D 1-1 | Johnston | 9,557 |
| Sep 16 | STOKE CITY | D 1-1 | Spence | 5,025 |
| Sep 19 | Nottingham Forest | L 1-2 | Gallimore | 10,166 |
| Sep 26 | CHESTERFIELD | W 3-1 | Warburton 2, Johnston | 10,834 |
| Oct 3 | Burnley | L 0-2 | | 9,719 |
| Oct 10 | PRESTON NORTH END | W 3-2 | Gallimore, Johnston, Spence | 8,496 |
| Oct 17 | Barnsley | D 0-0 | | 4,052 |
| Oct 24 | NOTTS COUNTY | D 3-3 | Gallimore, Mann, Spence | 6,694 |
| Oct 31 | Plymouth Argyle | L 1-3 | Johnston | 22,555 |
| Nov 7 | LEEDS UNITED | L 2-5 | Spence 2 | 9,512 |
| Nov 14 | Oldham Athletic | W 5-1 | Johnston 2, Spence 2, Mann | 10,922 |
| Nov 21 | BURY | L 1-2 | Spence | 11,745 |
| Nov 28 | Port Vale | W 2-1 | Spence 2 | 6,955 |
| Dec 5 | MILLWALL | W 2-0 | Gallimore, Spence | 6,396 |
| Dec 12 | Bradford City | L 3-4 | Spence 2, Johnston | 13,215 |
| Dec 19 | BRISTOL CITY | L 0-1 | | 4,697 |
| Dec 25 | WOLVERHAMPTON WANDERERS | W 3-2 | Hopkinson, Reid, Spence | 33,123 |
| Dec 26 | Wolverhampton Wanderers | L 0-7 | | 37,207 |
| Jan 2 | BRADFORD PARK AVENUE | L 0-2 | | 6,056 |
| Jan 16 | Swansea Town | L 1-3 | Warburton | 5,888 |
| Sep 23 | Tottenham Hotspur | L 1-4 | Reid | 19,139 |
| Jan 30 | NOTTINGHAM FOREST | W 3-2 | Reid 3 | 11,152 |
| Feb 6 | Chesterfield | W 3-1 | Reid 2, Spence | 9,457 |
| Feb 17 | BURNLEY | W 5-1 | Johnston 2, Ridding 2, Gallimore | 11,036 |
| Feb 20 | Preston North End | D 0-0 | | 13,353 |
| Feb 27 | BARNSLEY | W 3-0 | Hopkinson 2, Gallimore | 18,223 |
| Mar 5 | Notts County | W 2-1 | Hopkinson, Reid | 10,817 |
| Mar 12 | PLYMOUTH ARGYLE | W 2-1 | Spence 2 | 24,827 |
| Mar 19 | Leeds United | W 4-1 | Reid 2, Johnston, Ridding | 13,644 |
| Mar 25 | CHARLTON ATHLETIC | L 0-2 | | 37,012 |
| Mar 26 | OLDHAM ATHLETIC | W 5-1 | Reid 3, Fitton, Spence | 17,886 |
| Mar 28 | Charlton Athletic | L 0-1 | | 16,256 |
| Apr 2 | Bury | D 0-0 | | 12,592 |
| Apr 9 | PORT VALE | W 2-0 | Reid, Spence | 10,916 |
| Apr 16 | Millwall | D 1-1 | Reid | 9,087 |
| Apr 23 | BRADFORD CITY | W 1-0 | Fitton | 17,765 |
| Apr 30 | Bristol City | L 1-2 | Black | 5,874 |
| May 7 | Southampton | D 1-1 | Black | 6,128 |

### FA Cup

| | | | | |
|---|---|---|---|---|
| Jan 9 | Plymouth Argyle | (Rd3) L 1-4 | Reid | 28,000 |

### League & Cup Appearances

| PLAYER | LEAGUE | CUP COMPETITION FA CUP | TOTAL |
|---|---|---|---|
| Bennion | 28 | 1 | 29 |
| Black | 3 | | 3 |
| Chesters | 2 | | 2 |
| Dale | 4 | | 4 |
| Dean | 2 | | 2 |
| Ferguson | 8 | | 8 |
| Fitton | 8 | | 8 |
| Gallimore | 25 | | 25 |
| Hilditch | 17 | 1 | 18 |
| Hopkinson | 19 | | 19 |
| Johnston | 28 | 1 | 29 |
| Jones | 12 | | 12 |
| Lievesley | 2 | | 2 |
| Lydon | 2 | | 2 |
| McDonald | 2 | | 2 |
| McLachlan | 28 | 1 | 29 |
| McLenahan | 11 | 1 | 12 |
| Manley | 3 | | 3 |
| Mann | 13 | | 13 |
| Mellor | 33 | 1 | 34 |
| Moody | 8 | | 8 |
| Page | 9 | | 9 |
| Parker | 8 | | 8 |
| Ridding | 14 | 1 | 15 |
| Robinson | 10 | | 10 |
| Rowley | 1 | | 1 |
| Reid | 25 | 1 | 26 |
| Silcock | 35 | 1 | 36 |
| Spence | 37 | 1 | 38 |
| Steward | 32 | 1 | 33 |
| Vincent | 16 | | 16 |
| Warburton | 7 | | 7 |
| Whittle | 1 | | 1 |
| Wilson | 9 | | 9 |

### Goalscorers

| PLAYER | LEAGUE | CUP COMPETITION FA CUP | TOTAL |
|---|---|---|---|
| Spence | 19 | | 19 |
| Reid | 17 | 1 | 18 |
| Johnston | 11 | | 11 |
| Gallimore | 6 | | 6 |
| Hopkinson | 5 | | 5 |
| Ridding | 3 | | 3 |
| Warburton | 3 | | 3 |
| Black | 2 | | 2 |
| Fitton | 2 | | 2 |
| Mann | 2 | | 2 |
| Ferguson | 1 | | 1 |

### Final Division Two Table

| | | P | W | D | L | F | A | PTS |
|---|---|---|---|---|---|---|---|---|
| 1 | WOLVERHAMPTON W | 42 | 24 | 8 | 10 | 115 | 49 | 56 |
| 2 | LEEDS UNITED | 42 | 22 | 10 | 10 | 78 | 54 | 54 |
| 3 | STOKE CITY | 42 | 19 | 14 | 9 | 69 | 48 | 52 |
| 4 | PLYMOUTH ARGYLE | 42 | 20 | 9 | 13 | 100 | 66 | 49 |
| 5 | BURY | 42 | 21 | 7 | 14 | 70 | 58 | 49 |
| 6 | BRADFORD PARK AV | 42 | 21 | 7 | 14 | 72 | 63 | 49 |
| 7 | BRADFORD CITY | 42 | 16 | 13 | 13 | 80 | 61 | 45 |
| 8 | TOTTENHAM HOTSPUR | 42 | 16 | 11 | 15 | 87 | 78 | 43 |
| 9 | MILLWALL | 42 | 17 | 9 | 16 | 61 | 61 | 43 |
| 10 | CHARLTON ATHLETIC | 42 | 17 | 9 | 16 | 61 | 66 | 43 |
| 11 | NOTTINGHAM FOREST | 42 | 16 | 10 | 16 | 77 | 72 | 42 |
| 12 | MANCHESTER UNITED | 42 | 17 | 8 | 17 | 71 | 72 | 42 |
| 13 | PRESTON NORTH END | 42 | 16 | 10 | 16 | 75 | 77 | 42 |
| 14 | SOUTHAMPTON | 42 | 17 | 7 | 18 | 66 | 77 | 41 |
| 15 | SWANSEA TOWN | 42 | 16 | 7 | 19 | 73 | 75 | 39 |
| 16 | NOTTS COUNTY | 42 | 13 | 12 | 17 | 75 | 75 | 38 |
| 17 | CHESTERFIELD | 42 | 13 | 11 | 18 | 64 | 86 | 37 |
| 18 | OLDHAM ATHLETIC | 42 | 13 | 10 | 19 | 62 | 84 | 36 |
| 19 | BURNLEY | 42 | 13 | 9 | 20 | 59 | 87 | 35 |
| 20 | PORT VALE | 42 | 13 | 7 | 22 | 58 | 89 | 33 |
| 21 | BARNSLEY | 42 | 12 | 9 | 21 | 55 | 91 | 33 |
| 22 | BRISTOL CITY | 42 | 6 | 11 | 25 | 39 | 78 | 23 |

### Fact File

United lost 7-0 against Wolverhampton Wanderers at Molineux 12 months after suffering a similar record-equalling defeat away at Aston Villa.

**SECRETARY:** Walter Crickmer

**MOST APPEARANCES:** Joe Spence 38

**TOP SCORER:** Joe Spence 19 (all League)

**BIGGEST WIN:** 5-1 v Oldham Athletic, 14 November 1931, League; 5-1 v Burnley, 17 February 1932, League; 5-1 v Oldham Athletic, 26 March 1932, League

**HIGHEST ATTENDANCE:** 37,207 v Wolverhampton Wanderers, 26 December 1931, League

# Season 1932-33

## Football League Division Two

| DATE | OPPONENTS | SCORE | GOALSCORERS | ATTENDANCE |
|---|---|---|---|---|
| Aug 27 | STOKE CITY | L 0-2 | | 24,996 |
| Aug 29 | Charlton Athletic | W 1-0 | Spence | 13,946 |
| Sep 3 | Southampton | L 2-4 | Reid, Campbell o.g. | 7,978 |
| Sep 7 | CHARLTON ATHLETIC | D 1-1 | McLenahan | 9,480 |
| Sep 10 | Tottenham Hotspur | L 1-6 | Ridding | 23,333 |
| Sep 17 | GRIMSBY TOWN | D 1-1 | Brown | 17,662 |
| Sep 24 | Oldham Athletic | D 1-1 | Spence | 14,403 |
| Oct 1 | PRESTON NORTH END | D 0-0 | | 20,800 |
| Oct 8 | Burnley | W 3-2 | Brown, Gallimore, Spence | 5,314 |
| Oct 15 | BRADFORD PARK AVENUE | W 2-1 | Reid 2 | 18,918 |
| Oct 22 | MILLWALL | W 7-1 | Reid 3, Brown 2, Gallimore, Spence | 15,860 |
| Oct 29 | Port Vale | D 3-3 | Ridding 2, Brown | 7,138 |
| Nov 5 | NOTTS COUNTY | W 2-0 | Gallimore, Ridding | 24,178 |
| Nov 12 | Bury | D 2-2 | Brown, Ridding | 21,663 |
| Nov 19 | FULHAM | W 4-3 | Gallimore 2, Brown, Ridding | 28,803 |
| Nov 26 | Chesterfield | D 1-1 | Ridding | 10,277 |
| Dec 3 | BRADFORD CITY | L 0-1 | | 28,513 |
| Dec 10 | West Ham United | L 1-3 | Ridding | 13,435 |
| Dec 17 | LINCOLN CITY | W 4-1 | Reid 3, Worthy o.g. | 18,021 |
| Dec 24 | Swansea Town | L 1-2 | Brown | 10,727 |
| Dec 26 | Plymouth Argyle | W 3-2 | Spence 2, Reid | 33,776 |
| Dec 31 | Stoke City | D 0-0 | | 14,115 |
| Jan 2 | PLYMOUTH ARGYLE | W 4-0 | Ridding 2, Chalmers, Spence | 30,257 |
| Jan 7 | SOUTHAMPTON | L 1-2 | McDonald | 21,364 |
| Jan 21 | TOTTENHAM HOTSPUR | W 2-1 | Frame, McDonald | 20,661 |
| Jan 31 | Grimsby Town | D 1-1 | Stewart | 4,020 |
| Feb 4 | OLDHAM ATHLETIC | W 2-0 | Ridding, Stewart | 15,275 |
| Feb 11 | Preston North End | D 3-3 | Dewar, Hopkinson, Stewart | 15,662 |
| Feb 22 | BURNLEY | W 2-1 | McDonald, Warburton | 18,533 |
| Mar 4 | Millwall | L 0-2 | | 22,578 |
| Mar 11 | PORT VALE | D 1-1 | Hine | 24,690 |
| Mar 18 | Notts County | L 0-1 | | 13,018 |
| Mar 25 | BURY | L 1-3 | McLenahan | 27,687 |
| Apr 1 | Fulham | L 1-3 | Dewar | 21,477 |
| Apr 5 | Bradford Park Avenue | D 1-1 | Vincent | 6,314 |
| Apr 8 | CHESTERFIELD | W 2-1 | Dewar, Frame | 16,031 |
| Apr 14 | Nottingham Forest | L 2-3 | Brown, Dewar | 12,963 |
| Apr 15 | Bradford City | W 2-1 | Brown, Hine | 11,195 |
| Apr 17 | NOTTINGHAM FOREST | W 2-1 | Hine, McDonald | 16,849 |
| Apr 22 | WEST HAM UNITED | L 1-2 | Dewar | 14,958 |
| Apr 29 | Lincoln City | L 2-3 | Dewar, Hine | 8,507 |
| May 6 | SWANSEA CITY | D 1-1 | Hine | 9,588 |

## FA Cup

| | | | | |
|---|---|---|---|---|
| Jan 14 | MIDDLESBROUGH | (Rd3) L 1-4 | Spence | 36,991 |

## League & Cup Appearances

| PLAYER | LEAGUE | CUP COMPETITION FA CUP | TOTAL |
|---|---|---|---|
| Black | 1 | | 1 |
| Brown | 25 | | 25 |
| Chalmers | 22 | 1 | 23 |
| Dewar | 15 | | 15 |
| Fitton | 4 | | 4 |
| Frame | 33 | 1 | 34 |
| Gallimore | 12 | | 12 |
| Heywood | 1 | | 1 |
| Hine | 14 | | 14 |
| Hopkinson | 6 | | 6 |
| Jones | 10 | | 10 |
| McDonald | 21 | | 21 |
| McLachlan | 17 | | 17 |
| McLenahan | 24 | 1 | 25 |
| Manley | 19 | | 19 |
| Mellor | 40 | 1 | 41 |
| Mitchell | 1 | | 1 |
| Moody | 42 | 1 | 43 |
| Page | 3 | | 3 |
| Reid | 11 | 1 | 12 |
| Ridding | 23 | 1 | 24 |
| Silcock | 27 | 1 | 28 |
| Spence | 19 | 1 | 20 |
| Stewart | 21 | 1 | 22 |
| Topping | 5 | | 5 |
| Vincent | 40 | 1 | 41 |
| Warburton | 6 | | 6 |

## Goalscorers

| PLAYER | LEAGUE | CUP COMPETITION FA CUP | TOTAL |
|---|---|---|---|
| Ridding | 11 | | 11 |
| Brown | 10 | | 10 |
| Reid | 10 | | 10 |
| Spence | 7 | 1 | 7 |
| Dewar | 6 | | 6 |
| Gallimore | 5 | | 5 |
| Hine | 5 | | 5 |
| McDonald | 4 | | 4 |
| Stewart | 3 | | 3 |
| Frame | 2 | | 2 |
| McLenahan | 2 | | 2 |
| Chalmers | 1 | | 1 |
| Hopkinson | 1 | | 1 |
| Vincent | 1 | | 1 |
| Warburton | 1 | | 1 |
| Opps' o.gs. | 2 | | 2 |

### Fact File

Joe Spence, the legendary United figure of the 1920s and 30s, severed his links with the club to join Bradford City during the 1933 close season.

**MANAGER:** Scott Duncan
**MOST APPEARANCES:** John Moody 43
**TOP SCORER:** Bill Ridding 11 (all League)
**BIGGEST WIN:** 7-1 v Millwall, 22 October 1932, League
**HIGHEST ATTENDANCE:** 36,991 v Middlesbrough, 14 January 1933, FA Cup

### Final Division Two Table

| | | P | W | D | L | F | A | Pts |
|---|---|---|---|---|---|---|---|---|
| 1 | Stoke City | 42 | 25 | 6 | 11 | 78 | 39 | 56 |
| 2 | Tottenham Hotspur | 42 | 20 | 15 | 7 | 96 | 51 | 55 |
| 3 | Fulham | 42 | 20 | 10 | 12 | 78 | 65 | 50 |
| 4 | Bury | 42 | 20 | 9 | 13 | 84 | 59 | 49 |
| 5 | Nottingham Forest | 42 | 17 | 15 | 10 | 67 | 59 | 49 |
| 6 | Manchester United | 42 | 15 | 13 | 14 | 71 | 68 | 43 |
| 7 | Millwall | 42 | 16 | 11 | 15 | 59 | 57 | 43 |
| 8 | Bradford Park A | 42 | 17 | 8 | 17 | 77 | 71 | 42 |
| 9 | Preston North End | 42 | 16 | 10 | 16 | 74 | 70 | 42 |
| 10 | Swansea Town | 42 | 19 | 4 | 19 | 50 | 54 | 42 |
| 11 | Bradford City | 42 | 14 | 13 | 15 | 65 | 61 | 41 |
| 12 | Southampton | 42 | 18 | 5 | 19 | 66 | 66 | 41 |
| 13 | Grimsby Town | 42 | 14 | 13 | 15 | 79 | 84 | 41 |
| 14 | Plymouth Argyle | 42 | 16 | 9 | 17 | 63 | 67 | 41 |
| 15 | Notts County | 42 | 15 | 10 | 17 | 67 | 78 | 40 |
| 16 | Oldham Athletic | 42 | 15 | 8 | 19 | 67 | 80 | 38 |
| 17 | Port Vale | 42 | 14 | 10 | 18 | 66 | 79 | 38 |
| 18 | Lincoln City | 42 | 12 | 13 | 17 | 72 | 87 | 37 |
| 19 | Burnley | 42 | 11 | 14 | 17 | 67 | 79 | 36 |
| 20 | West Ham United | 42 | 13 | 9 | 20 | 75 | 93 | 35 |
| 21 | Chesterfield | 42 | 12 | 10 | 20 | 61 | 84 | 34 |
| 22 | Charlton Athletic | 42 | 12 | 7 | 23 | 60 | 91 | 31 |

# Season 1933-34

## Football League Division Two

| DATE | OPPONENTS | SCORE | GOALSCORERS | ATTENDANCE |
|---|---|---|---|---|
| Aug 26 | Plymouth Argyle | L 0-4 | | 25,700 |
| Aug 30 | NOTTINGHAM FOREST | L 0-1 | | 16,934 |
| Sep 2 | LINCOLN CITY | D 1-1 | Green | 16,987 |
| Sep 7 | Nottingham Forest | D 1-1 | Stewart | 10,650 |
| Sep 9 | BOLTON WANDERERS | L 1-5 | Stewart | 21,779 |
| Sep 16 | Brentford | W 4-3 | Brown 2, Frame, Hine | 17,180 |
| Sep 23 | BURNLEY | W 5-2 | Dewar 4, Brown | 18,411 |
| Sep 30 | Oldham Athletic | L 0-2 | | 22,736 |
| Oct 7 | PRESTON NORTH END | W 1-0 | Hine | 22,303 |
| Oct 14 | Bradford Park Avenue | L 1-6 | Hine | 11,033 |
| Oct 21 | Bury | L 1-2 | Byrne | 15,008 |
| Oct 28 | HULL CITY | W 4-1 | Heywood 2, Green, Hine | 16,269 |
| Nov 4 | Fulham | W 2-0 | Stewart, Keeping o.g. | 17,049 |
| Nov 11 | SOUTHAMPTON | W 1-0 | Manley | 18,149 |
| Nov 18 | Blackpool | L 1-3 | Brown | 14,384 |
| Nov 25 | BRADFORD CITY | W 2-1 | Dewar, Barkas o.g. | 20,902 |
| Dec 2 | Port Vale | W 3-2 | Black, Brown, Dewar | 10,316 |
| Dec 9 | NOTTS COUNTY | L 1-2 | Dewar | 15,564 |
| Dec 16 | Swansea Town | L 1-2 | Hine | 6,591 |
| Dec 23 | MILLWALL | D 1-1 | Dewar | 12,043 |
| Dec 25 | GRIMSBY TOWN | L 1-3 | Vose | 29,443 |
| Dec 26 | Grimsby Town | L 3-7 | Byrne 2, Frame | 15,801 |
| Dec 30 | PLYMOUTH ARGYLE | L 0-3 | | 12,206 |
| Jan 6 | Lincoln City | L 1-5 | Brown | 6,075 |
| Jan 20 | Bolton Wanderers | L 1-3 | Ball | 11,887 |
| Jan 27 | BRENTFORD | L 1-3 | Ball | 16,891 |
| Feb 3 | Burnley | W 4-1 | Cape 2, Green, Stewart | 9,906 |
| Feb 10 | Oldham Athletic | L 2-3 | Cape, Green | 24,480 |
| Feb 21 | Preston North End | L 2-3 | Gallimore 2 | 9,173 |
| Feb 24 | BRADFORD PARK AVENUE | L 0-4 | | 13,389 |
| Mar 3 | BURY | W 2-1 | Ball, Gallimore | 11,176 |
| Mar 10 | Hull City | L 1-4 | Ball | 5,771 |
| Mar 17 | FULHAM | W 1-0 | Ball | 17,565 |
| Mar 24 | Southampton | L 0-1 | | 4,840 |
| Mar 30 | WEST HAM UNITED | L 0-1 | | 29,114 |
| Mar 31 | BLACKPOOL | W 2-0 | Cape, Hine | 20,038 |
| Apr 2 | West Ham United | L 1-2 | Cape | 20,085 |
| Apr 7 | Bradford City | D 1-1 | Cape | 9,258 |
| Apr 14 | PORT VALE | W 2-0 | Brown, McMillen | 14,777 |
| Apr 21 | Notts County | D 0-0 | | 9,645 |
| Apr 28 | SWANSEA TOWN | D 1-1 | Topping | 16,678 |
| May 5 | Millwall | W 2-0 | Cape, Manley | 24,003 |

## FA Cup

| | | | | |
|---|---|---|---|---|
| Jan 13 | PORTSMOUTH | (Rd3) D 1-1 | McLenahan | 23,283 |
| Jan 17 | Portsmouth | (R) L 1-4 | Ball | 18,748 |

## League & Cup Appearances

| PLAYER | LEAGUE | CUP COMPETITION FA CUP | TOTAL |
|---|---|---|---|
| Ball | 18 | 2 | 20 |
| Behan | 1 | | 1 |
| Black | 4 | | 4 |
| Brown | 15 | 1 | 16 |
| Byrne | 4 | | 4 |
| Cape | 17 | | 17 |
| Chalmers | 12 | | 12 |
| Dewar | 21 | | 21 |
| Frame | 18 | | 18 |
| Gallimore | 7 | | 7 |
| Green | 9 | | 9 |
| Griffiths | 10 | | 10 |
| Hall | 23 | 2 | 25 |
| Hacking | 10 | | 10 |
| Heywood | 3 | | 3 |
| Hillam | 8 | | 8 |
| Hine | 33 | 2 | 35 |
| Hopkinson | 9 | | 9 |
| Jones | 39 | 2 | 41 |
| McDonald | 4 | | 4 |
| McGillivray | 8 | 1 | 9 |
| McKay | 10 | | 10 |
| McLenahan | 22 | 2 | 24 |
| McMillen | 23 | 2 | 25 |
| Manley | 30 | 2 | 32 |
| Manns | 2 | | 2 |
| Mellor | 5 | | 5 |
| Nevin | 4 | 2 | 6 |
| Newton | 2 | | 2 |
| Ridding | 5 | | 5 |
| Robertson | 10 | | 10 |
| Silcock | 16 | 1 | 17 |
| Stewart | 25 | 2 | 27 |
| Topping | 6 | | 6 |
| Vincent | 8 | | 8 |
| Vose | 17 | 2 | 19 |
| Warburton | 2 | | 2 |

## Goalscorers

| PLAYER | LEAGUE | CUP COMPETITION FA CUP | TOTAL |
|---|---|---|---|
| Dewar | 8 | | 8 |
| Brown | 7 | | 7 |
| Cape | 7 | | 7 |
| Ball | 5 | 1 | 6 |
| Hine | 6 | | 6 |
| Green | 4 | | 4 |
| Stewart | 4 | | 4 |
| Byrne | 3 | | 3 |
| Gallimore | 3 | | 3 |
| Frame | 2 | | 2 |
| Heywood | 2 | | 2 |
| Manley | 2 | | 2 |
| Black | 1 | | 1 |
| McLenahan | | 1 | 1 |
| McMillen | 1 | | 1 |
| Topping | 1 | | 1 |
| Vose | 1 | | 1 |
| Opps' o.gs. | 2 | | 2 |

## Final Division Two Table

| | | P | W | D | L | F | A | PTS |
|---|---|---|---|---|---|---|---|---|
| 1 | Grimsby Town | 42 | 27 | 5 | 10 | 103 | 59 | 59 |
| 2 | Preston North End | 42 | 23 | 6 | 13 | 71 | 52 | 52 |
| 3 | Bolton Wanderers | 42 | 21 | 9 | 12 | 79 | 55 | 51 |
| 4 | Brentford | 42 | 22 | 7 | 13 | 85 | 60 | 51 |
| 5 | Bradford Park Av | 42 | 23 | 3 | 16 | 86 | 67 | 49 |
| 6 | Bradford City | 42 | 20 | 6 | 16 | 73 | 67 | 46 |
| 7 | West Ham United | 42 | 17 | 11 | 14 | 78 | 70 | 45 |
| 8 | Port Vale | 42 | 19 | 7 | 16 | 60 | 55 | 45 |
| 9 | Oldham Athletic | 42 | 17 | 10 | 15 | 72 | 60 | 44 |
| 10 | Plymouth Argyle | 42 | 15 | 13 | 14 | 69 | 70 | 43 |
| 11 | Blackpool | 42 | 15 | 13 | 14 | 62 | 64 | 43 |
| 12 | Bury | 42 | 17 | 9 | 16 | 70 | 73 | 43 |
| 13 | Burnley | 42 | 18 | 6 | 18 | 60 | 72 | 42 |
| 14 | Southampton | 42 | 15 | 8 | 19 | 54 | 58 | 38 |
| 15 | Hull City | 42 | 13 | 12 | 17 | 52 | 68 | 38 |
| 16 | Fulham | 42 | 15 | 7 | 20 | 48 | 67 | 37 |
| 17 | Nottingham Forest | 42 | 13 | 9 | 20 | 73 | 74 | 35 |
| 18 | Notts County | 42 | 12 | 11 | 19 | 53 | 62 | 35 |
| 19 | Swansea Town | 42 | 10 | 15 | 17 | 51 | 60 | 35 |
| 20 | Manchester United | 42 | 14 | 6 | 22 | 59 | 85 | 34 |
| 21 | Millwall | 42 | 11 | 11 | 20 | 39 | 68 | 33 |
| 22 | Lincoln City | 42 | 9 | 8 | 25 | 44 | 75 | 26 |

## Fact File

United avoided relegation to Division Three by the skin of their teeth. Needing to win their last game of the season, away at Millwall, they took the points following a 2-0 win and the Lions made the drop instead.

**MANAGER:** Scott Duncan

**MOST APPEARANCES:** Tom Jones 41

**TOP SCORER:** Neil Dewar 8 (all League)

**BIGGEST WIN:** 5-2 v Burnley, 23 September 1933, League

**HIGHEST ATTENDANCE:** 29,443 v Grimsby Town, 25 December 1933, League

# Season 1934-35

## Football League Division Two

| DATE | OPPONENTS | SCORE | GOALSCORERS | ATTENDANCE |
|---|---|---|---|---|
| Aug 25 | BRADFORD CITY | W 2-0 | Manley 2 | 27,573 |
| Sep 1 | Sheffield United | L 2-3 | Ball, Manley | 18,468 |
| Sep 3 | Bolton Wanderers | L 1-3 | Finney o.g. | 16,238 |
| Sep 8 | BARNSLEY | W 4-1 | Mutch 3, Manley | 22,315 |
| Sep 12 | BOLTON WANDERERS | L 0-3 | | 24,760 |
| Sep 15 | Port Vale | L 2-3 | Jones TJ, Mutch | 9,307 |
| Sep 22 | NORWICH CITY | W 5-0 | Cape, Jones T.J., McLenahan, Mutch, Owen | 13,052 |
| Sep 29 | SWANSEA TOWN | W 3-1 | Cape 2, Mutch | 14,865 |
| Oct 6 | Burnley | W 2-1 | Cape, Manley | 16,757 |
| Oct 13 | OLDHAM ATHLETIC | W 4-0 | Manley 2, McKay, Mutch | 29,143 |
| Oct 20 | Newcastle United | W 1-0 | Bamford | 24,752 |
| Oct 27 | WEST HAM UNITED | W 3-1 | Mutch 2, McKay | 31,950 |
| Nov 3 | Blackpool | W 2-1 | Bryant, McKay | 15,663 |
| Nov 10 | BURY | W 1-0 | Mutch | 41,415 |
| Nov 17 | Hull City | L 2-3 | Bamford 2 | 6,494 |
| Nov 24 | NOTTINGHAM FOREST | W 3-2 | Mutch 2, Hine | 27,192 |
| Dec 1 | Brentford | L 1-3 | Bamford | 21,744 |
| Dec 8 | FULHAM | W 1-0 | Mutch | 25,706 |
| Dec 15 | Bradford Park Avenue | W 2-1 | Manley, Mutch | 8,405 |
| Dec 22 | PLYMOUTH ARGYLE | W 3-1 | Bamford, Bryant, Rowley | 24,896 |
| Dec 25 | NOTTS COUNTY | W 2-1 | Mutch, Rowley | 32,965 |
| Dec 26 | Notts County | L 0-1 | | 24,599 |
| Dec 29 | Bradford City | L 0-2 | | 11,908 |
| Jan 1 | SOUTHAMPTON | W 3-0 | Cape 2, Rowley | 15,174 |
| Jan 5 | SHEFFIELD UNITED | D 3-3 | Bryant, Mutch, Rowley | 28,300 |
| Jan 19 | Barnsley | W 2-0 | Bryant, Jones T.J. | 10,177 |
| Feb 2 | Norwich City | L 2-3 | Manley, Rowley | 14,260 |
| Feb 6 | PORT VALE | W 2-1 | Jones T.J., Rowley | 7,372 |
| Feb 9 | Swansea Town | L 0-1 | | 8,876 |
| Feb 23 | Oldham Athletic | L 1-3 | Mutch | 14,432 |
| Mar 2 | NEWCASTLE UNITED | L 0-1 | | 20,728 |
| Mar 9 | West Ham United | D 0-0 | | 19,718 |
| Mar 16 | BLACKPOOL | W 3-2 | Bamford, Mutch, Rowley | 25,704 |
| Mar 23 | Bury | W 1-0 | Cape | 7,229 |
| Mar 27 | BURNLEY | L 3-4 | Boyd, Cape, McMillen | 10,247 |
| Mar 30 | HULL CITY | W 3-0 | Boyd 3 | 15,358 |
| Apr 6 | Nottingham Forest | D 2-2 | Bryant 2 | 8,618 |
| Apr 13 | BRENTFORD | D 0-0 | | 32,969 |
| Apr 20 | Fulham | L 1-3 | Bamford | 11,059 |
| Apr 22 | Southampton | L 0-1 | | 12,458 |
| Apr 27 | BRADFORD PARK AVENUE | W 2-0 | Bamford, Robertson | 8,606 |
| May 4 | Plymouth Argyle | W 2-0 | Bamford, Rowley | 10,767 |

## FA Cup

| | | | | | |
|---|---|---|---|---|---|
| Jan 12 | Bristol Rovers | (Rd3) | W 3-1 | Bamford 2, Mutch | 20,400 |
| Jan 26 | Nottingham Forest | (R) | D 0-0 | | 32,862 |
| Jan 30 | NOTTINGHAM FOREST | (Rd4) | L 0-3 | | 33,851 |

## League & Cup Appearances

| PLAYER | LEAGUE | CUP COMPETITION FA CUP | TOTAL |
|---|---|---|---|
| Ball | 6 | | 6 |
| Bamford | 19 | 3 | 22 |
| Boyd | 6 | | 6 |
| Bryant | 24 | 2 | 26 |
| Cape | 21 | 1 | 22 |
| Griffiths | 40 | 3 | 43 |
| Hacking | 22 | 2 | 24 |
| Hall | 8 | 1 | 9 |
| Hine | 4 | | 4 |
| Jones T. | 27 | 2 | 29 |
| Jones T.J. | 20 | 2 | 22 |
| Langford | 12 | | 12 |
| McKay | 38 | 3 | 41 |
| McLenahan | 10 | | 10 |
| McMillen | 4 | | 4 |
| Manley | 30 | 1 | 31 |
| Mellor | 1 | | 1 |
| Mutch | 40 | 3 | 43 |
| Owen | 15 | | 15 |
| Porter | 15 | 1 | 16 |
| Robertson | 36 | 3 | 39 |
| Rowley | 24 | 3 | 27 |
| Topping | 1 | | 1 |
| Vose | 39 | 3 | 42 |

## Goalscorers

| PLAYER | LEAGUE | CUP COMPETITION FA CUP | TOTAL |
|---|---|---|---|
| Mutch | 18 | 1 | 19 |
| Bamford | 9 | 2 | 11 |
| Manley | 9 | | 9 |
| Cape | 8 | | 8 |
| Rowley | 8 | | 8 |
| Bryant | 6 | | 6 |
| Boyd | 4 | | 4 |
| Jones T.J. | 4 | | 4 |
| McKay | 3 | | 3 |
| Ball | 1 | | 1 |
| Hine | 1 | | 1 |
| McLenahan | 1 | | 1 |
| McMillen | 1 | | 1 |
| Owen | 1 | | 1 |
| Robertson | 1 | | 1 |
| Opps' o.gs. | 1 | | 1 |

## Fact File

United failed to in their bid to return to the top grade despite putting together an impressive eight-match winning run during the first half of the season.

**MANAGER:** Scott Duncan
**MOST APPEARANCES:** Jack Griffiths, George Mutch 43
**TOP SCORER:** George Mutch 19 (18 League)
**BIGGEST WIN:** 5-0 v Norwich City, 22 September 1934, League
**HIGHEST ATTENDANCE:** 41,415 v Bury, 10 November 1934, League

## Final Division Two Table

| | | P | W | D | L | F | A | PTS |
|---|---|---|---|---|---|---|---|---|
| 1 | Brentford | 42 | 26 | 9 | 7 | 93 | 48 | 61 |
| 2 | Bolton Wanderers | 42 | 26 | 4 | 12 | 96 | 48 | 56 |
| 3 | West Ham United | 42 | 26 | 4 | 12 | 80 | 63 | 56 |
| 4 | Blackpool | 42 | 21 | 11 | 10 | 79 | 57 | 53 |
| 5 | Manchester United | 42 | 23 | 4 | 15 | 76 | 55 | 50 |
| 6 | Newcastle United | 42 | 22 | 4 | 16 | 89 | 68 | 48 |
| 7 | Fulham | 42 | 17 | 12 | 13 | 76 | 56 | 46 |
| 8 | Plymouth Argyle | 42 | 19 | 8 | 15 | 75 | 64 | 46 |
| 9 | Nottingham Forest | 42 | 17 | 8 | 17 | 76 | 70 | 42 |
| 10 | Bury | 42 | 19 | 4 | 19 | 62 | 73 | 42 |
| 11 | Sheffield United | 42 | 16 | 9 | 17 | 79 | 70 | 41 |
| 12 | Burnley | 42 | 16 | 9 | 17 | 63 | 73 | 41 |
| 13 | Hull City | 42 | 16 | 8 | 18 | 63 | 74 | 40 |
| 14 | Norwich City | 42 | 14 | 11 | 17 | 71 | 61 | 39 |
| 15 | Bradford Park Av | 42 | 11 | 16 | 15 | 55 | 63 | 38 |
| 16 | Barnsley | 42 | 13 | 12 | 17 | 60 | 83 | 38 |
| 17 | Swansea Town | 42 | 14 | 8 | 20 | 56 | 67 | 36 |
| 18 | Port Vale | 42 | 11 | 12 | 19 | 55 | 74 | 34 |
| 19 | Southampton | 42 | 11 | 12 | 19 | 46 | 75 | 34 |
| 20 | Bradford City | 42 | 12 | 8 | 22 | 50 | 68 | 32 |
| 21 | Oldham Athletic | 42 | 10 | 6 | 26 | 56 | 95 | 26 |
| 22 | Notts County | 42 | 9 | 7 | 26 | 46 | 97 | 25 |

## Season 1935-36

### Football League Division Two

| DATE | OPPONENTS | SCORE | GOALSCORERS | ATTENDANCE |
|---|---|---|---|---|
| Aug 31 | Plymouth Argyle | L 1-3 | Bamford | 22,366 |
| Sep 4 | CHARLTON ATHLETIC | W 3-0 | Bamford, Cape, Chester | 21,211 |
| Sep 7 | BRADFORD CITY | W 3-1 | Bamford 2, Mutch | 30,754 |
| Sep 9 | Charlton Athletic | D 0-0 | | 13,178 |
| Sep 14 | Newcastle United | W 2-0 | Bamford, Rowley | 28,520 |
| Sep 18 | HULL CITY | W 2-0 | Bamford 2 | 15,739 |
| Sep 21 | TOTTENHAM HOTSPUR | D 0-0 | | 34,718 |
| Sep 28 | Southampton | L 1-2 | Rowley | 17,678 |
| Oct 5 | Port Vale | W 3-0 | Mutch 2, Bamford | 9,703 |
| Oct 12 | FULHAM | W 1-0 | Rowley | 22,723 |
| Oct 19 | SHEFFIELD UNITED | W 3-1 | Cape, Mutch, Rowley | 18,636 |
| Oct 26 | Bradford Park Avenue | L 0-1 | | 12,216 |
| Nov 2 | LEICESTER CITY | L 0-1 | | 39,074 |
| Nov 9 | Swansea Town | L 1-2 | Bamford | 9,731 |
| Nov 16 | WEST HAM UNITED | L 2-3 | Rowley 2 | 24,440 |
| Nov 23 | Norwich City | W 5-3 | Rowley 3, Manley 2 | 17,266 |
| Nov 30 | DONCASTER ROVERS | D 0-0 | | 23,569 |
| Dec 7 | Blackpool | L 1-4 | Mutch | 13,218 |
| Dec 14 | NOTTINGHAM FOREST | W 5-0 | Bamford 2, Manley, Mutch, Rowley | 15,284 |
| Dec 26 | BARNSLEY | D 1-1 | Mutch | 20,993 |
| Dec 28 | PLYMOUTH ARGYLE | W 3-2 | Mutch2, Manley | 20,894 |
| Jan 1 | Barnsley | W 3-0 | Gardner, Manley, Mutch | 20,957 |
| Jan 4 | Bradford City | L 0-1 | | 11,286 |
| Jan 18 | NEWCASTLE UNITED | W 3-1 | Mutch 2, Rowley | 22,968 |
| Feb 1 | SOUTHAMPTON | W 4-0 | Mutch 2, Bryant, Curry o.g. | 23,205 |
| Feb 5 | Tottenham Hotspur | D 0-0 | | 20,085 |
| Feb 8 | PORT VALE | W 7-2 | Manley 4, Rowley 2, Mutch | 22,265 |
| Feb 22 | Sheffield United | D 1-1 | Manley | 25,852 |
| Feb 29 | BLACKPOOL | W 3-2 | Bryant, Manley, Mutch | 18,423 |
| Mar 7 | West Ham United | W 2-1 | Bryant, Mutch | 29,684 |
| Mar 14 | SWANSEA TOWN | W 3-0 | Manley, Mutch, Rowley | 27,580 |
| Mar 21 | Leicester City | D 1-1 | Bryant | 18,200 |
| Mar 28 | NORWICH CITY | W 2-1 | Rowley 2 | 31,596 |
| Apr 1 | Fulham | D 2-2 | Bryant, Griffiths | 11,137 |
| Apr 4 | Doncaster Rovers | D 0-0 | | 13,474 |
| Apr 10 | Burnley | D 2-2 | Bamford 2 | 27,245 |
| Apr 11 | BRADFORD PARK AVENUE | W 4-0 | Mutch 2, Bamford, Bryant | 33,517 |
| Apr 13 | BURNLEY | W 4-0 | Bryant 2, Rowley 2 | 39,855 |
| Apr 18 | Nottingham Forest | D 1-1 | Bamford | 12,156 |
| Apr 25 | BURY | W 2-1 | Lang, Rowley | 35,027 |
| Apr 29 | Bury | W 3-2 | Manley 2, Mutch | 31,562 |
| May 2 | Hull City | D 1-1 | Bamford | 4,540 |

### FA Cup

| | | | | |
|---|---|---|---|---|
| Jan 11 | Reading | (Rd3) W 3-1 | Mutch 2, Manley | 25,844 |
| Jan 25 | Stoke City | (Rd4) D 0-0 | | 32,286 |
| Jan 29 | STOKE CITY | (R) L 0-2 | | 34,440 |

### League & Cup Appearances

| PLAYER | LEAGUE | CUP COMPETITION FA CUP | TOTAL |
|---|---|---|---|
| Bamford | 27 | 2 | 29 |
| Breedon | 3 | | 3 |
| Brown | 40 | 3 | 43 |
| Bryant | 21 | 1 | 22 |
| Cape | 17 | | 17 |
| Chester | 13 | | 13 |
| Ferrier | 7 | 1 | 8 |
| Gardner | 12 | 2 | 14 |
| Griffiths | 41 | 3 | 44 |
| Hall | 36 | 3 | 39 |
| Lang | 4 | | 4 |
| Langford | 3 | | 3 |
| McKay | 35 | 3 | 38 |
| Manley | 31 | 3 | 34 |
| Morton | 1 | | 1 |
| Mutch | 42 | 3 | 45 |
| Owen | 2 | | 2 |
| Porter | 42 | 3 | 45 |
| Redwood | 1 | | 1 |
| Robbie | 1 | | 1 |
| Robertson | 1 | | 1 |
| Rowley | 37 | 3 | 40 |
| Vose | 41 | 3 | 44 |
| Wassall | 2 | | 2 |
| Whalley | 2 | | 2 |

### Goalscorers

| PLAYER | LEAGUE | CUP COMPETITION FA CUP | TOTAL |
|---|---|---|---|
| Mutch | 21 | 2 | 23 |
| Rowley | 19 | | 19 |
| Bamford | 16 | | 16 |
| Manley | 14 | 1 | 15 |
| Bryant | 8 | | 8 |
| Cape | 2 | | 2 |
| Chester | 1 | | 1 |
| Gardner | 1 | | 1 |
| Griffiths | 1 | | 1 |
| Lang | 1 | | 1 |
| Opps' o.gs. | 1 | | 1 |

### Fact File

Division One status was regained as the club celebrated their only championship success during the inter-war years. The team lost just once in 24 as they closed in on the title.

**MANAGER:** Scott Duncan
**MOST APPEARANCES:** George Mutch, Billy Porter 45
**TOP SCORER:** George Mutch 23 (21 League)
**BIGGEST WIN:** 7-2 v Port Vale, 8 February 1936, League
**HIGHEST ATTENDANCE:** 39,855 v Burnley, 13 April 1936, League

### Final Division Two Table

| | P | W | D | L | F | A | Pts |
|---|---|---|---|---|---|---|---|
| 1 Manchester United | 42 | 22 | 12 | 8 | 85 | 43 | 56 |
| 2 Charlton Athletic | 42 | 22 | 11 | 9 | 85 | 58 | 55 |
| 3 Sheffield United | 42 | 20 | 12 | 10 | 79 | 50 | 52 |
| 4 West Ham United | 42 | 22 | 8 | 12 | 90 | 68 | 52 |
| 5 Tottenham Hotspur | 42 | 18 | 13 | 11 | 91 | 55 | 49 |
| 6 Leicester City | 42 | 19 | 10 | 13 | 79 | 57 | 48 |
| 7 Plymouth Argyle | 42 | 20 | 8 | 14 | 71 | 57 | 48 |
| 8 Newcastle United | 42 | 20 | 6 | 16 | 88 | 79 | 46 |
| 9 Fulham | 42 | 15 | 14 | 13 | 76 | 52 | 44 |
| 10 Blackpool | 42 | 18 | 7 | 17 | 93 | 72 | 43 |
| 11 Norwich City | 42 | 17 | 9 | 16 | 72 | 65 | 43 |
| 12 Bradford City | 42 | 15 | 13 | 14 | 55 | 65 | 43 |
| 13 Swansea Town | 42 | 15 | 9 | 18 | 67 | 76 | 39 |
| 14 Bury | 42 | 13 | 12 | 17 | 66 | 84 | 38 |
| 15 Burnley | 42 | 12 | 13 | 17 | 50 | 59 | 37 |
| 16 Bradford Park Av | 42 | 14 | 9 | 19 | 62 | 84 | 37 |
| 17 Southampton | 42 | 14 | 9 | 19 | 47 | 65 | 37 |
| 18 Doncaster Rovers | 42 | 14 | 9 | 19 | 51 | 71 | 37 |
| 19 Nottingham Forest | 42 | 12 | 11 | 19 | 69 | 76 | 35 |
| 20 Barnsley | 42 | 12 | 9 | 21 | 54 | 80 | 33 |
| 21 Port Vale | 42 | 12 | 8 | 22 | 56 | 106 | 32 |
| 22 Hull City | 42 | 5 | 10 | 27 | 47 | 111 | 20 |

# Season 1936-37

## Football League Division One

| DATE | OPPONENTS | SCORE | GOALSCORERS | ATTENDANCE |
|---|---|---|---|---|
| Aug 29 | WOLVERHAMPTON WANDERERS | D 1-1 | Bamford | 42,731 |
| Sep 2 | Huddersfield Town | L 1-3 | Manley | 12,616 |
| Sep 5 | Derby County | L 4-5 | Bamford 3, Wassall | 21,194 |
| Sep 9 | HUDDERSFIELD TOWN | W 3-1 | Bamford, Bryant, Mutch | 26,839 |
| Sep 12 | MANCHESTER CITY | W 3-2 | Bamford, Bryant, Manley | 68,796 |
| Sep 19 | SHEFFIELD WEDNESDAY | D 1-1 | Bamford | 40,933 |
| Sep 26 | Preston North End | L 1-3 | Bamford | 24,149 |
| Oct 3 | ARSENAL | W 2-0 | Bryant, Rowley | 55,884 |
| Oct 10 | Brentford | L 0-4 | | 28,019 |
| Oct 17 | Portsmouth | L 1-2 | Manley | 19,845 |
| Oct 24 | CHELSEA | D 0-0 | | 29,859 |
| Oct 31 | Stoke City | L 0-3 | | 22,464 |
| Nov 7 | CHARLTON ATHLETIC | D 0-0 | | 26,084 |
| Nov 14 | Grimsby Town | L 2-6 | Bryant, Mutch | 9,844 |
| Nov 21 | LIVERPOOL | L 2-5 | Manley, Thompson | 26,419 |
| Nov 28 | Leeds United | L 1-2 | Bryant | 17,610 |
| Dec 5 | BIRMINGHAM | L 1-2 | Mutch | 16,544 |
| Dec 12 | Middlesbrough | L 2-3 | Halton, Manley | 11,790 |
| Dec 19 | WEST BROMWICH ALBION | D 2-2 | McKay, Mutch | 21,051 |
| Dec 25 | BOLTON WANDERERS | W 1-0 | Bamford | 47,458 |
| Dec 26 | Wolverhampton Wanderers | L 1-3 | McKay | 41,525 |
| Dec 28 | Bolton Wanderers | W 4-0 | Bryant 2, McKay 2 | 11,801 |
| Jan 1 | SUNDERLAND | W 2-1 | Bryant, Mutch | 46,257 |
| Jan 2 | DERBY COUNTY | D 2-2 | Rowley 2 | 31,883 |
| Jan 9 | Manchester City | L 0-1 | | 64,862 |
| Jan 23 | Sheffield Wednesday | L 0-1 | | 8,658 |
| Feb 3 | PRESTON NORTH END | D 1-1 | Wrigglesworth | 13,225 |
| Feb 6 | Arsenal | D 1-1 | Rowley | 37,236 |
| Feb 13 | BRENTFORD | L 1-3 | Baird | 31,942 |
| Feb 20 | PORTSMOUTH | L 0-1 | | 19,416 |
| Feb 27 | Chelsea | L 2-4 | Bamford, Gladwin | 16,382 |
| Mar 6 | STOKE CITY | W 2-1 | Baird, McClelland | 24,660 |
| Mar 13 | Charlton Athletic | L 0-3 | | 25,943 |
| Mar 20 | GRIMSBY TOWN | D 1-1 | Cape | 26,636 |
| Mar 26 | EVERTON | W 2-1 | Baird, Mutch | 30,071 |
| Mar 27 | Liverpool | L 0-2 | | 25,319 |
| Mar 29 | Everton | W 3-2 | Bryant, Ferrier, Mutch | 28,395 |
| Apr 3 | LEEDS UNITED | D 0-0 | | 34,429 |
| Apr 10 | Birmingham | D 2-2 | Bamford 2 | 19,130 |
| Apr 17 | MIDDLESBROUGH | W 2-1 | Bamford, Bryant | 17,656 |
| Apr 21 | Sunderland | D 1-1 | Bamford | 12,876 |
| Apr 24 | West Bromwich Albion | L 0-1 | | 16,234 |

## FA Cup

| | | | | | |
|---|---|---|---|---|---|
| Jan 16 | READING | (Rd3) | W 1-0 | Bamford | 36,668 |
| Jan 30 | Arsenal | (Rd4) | L 0-5 | | 45,637 |

## League & Cup Appearances

| PLAYER | LEAGUE | CUP COMPETITION FA CUP | TOTAL |
|---|---|---|---|
| Baird | 14 | | 14 |
| Bamford | 29 | 2 | 31 |
| Breedon | 1 | | 1 |
| Breen | 26 | 2 | 28 |
| Brown | 31 | 2 | 33 |
| Bryant | 37 | 2 | 39 |
| Cape | 4 | | 4 |
| Ferrier | 6 | | 6 |
| Gardner | 4 | | 4 |
| Gladwin | 8 | | 8 |
| Griffiths | 21 | | 21 |
| Halton | 4 | | 4 |
| John | 15 | | 15 |
| Jones | 1 | | 1 |
| Lang | 8 | 1 | 9 |
| McClelland | 5 | | 5 |
| McKay | 29 | 2 | 31 |
| McLenahan | 3 | | 3 |
| Manley | 31 | | 31 |
| Mellor | 2 | | 2 |
| Mutch | 28 | 2 | 30 |
| Porter | 2 | | 2 |
| Redwood | 21 | 1 | 22 |
| Roughton | 33 | 2 | 35 |
| Rowley | 17 | | 17 |
| Thompson | 2 | | 2 |
| Vose | 26 | 1 | 27 |
| Wassall | 7 | | 7 |
| Whalley | 19 | 2 | 21 |
| Winterbottom | 21 | 2 | 23 |
| Wrigglesworth | 7 | 1 | 8 |

## Goalscorers

| PLAYER | LEAGUE | CUP COMPETITION FA CUP | TOTAL |
|---|---|---|---|
| Bamford | 14 | 1 | 15 |
| Bryant | 10 | | 10 |
| Mutch | 7 | | 7 |
| Manley | 5 | | 5 |
| McKay | 4 | | 4 |
| Rowley | 4 | | 4 |
| Baird | 3 | | 3 |
| Cape | 1 | | 1 |
| Ferrier | 1 | | 1 |
| Gladwin | 1 | | 1 |
| Halton | 1 | | 1 |
| McClelland | 1 | | 1 |
| Thompson | 1 | | 1 |
| Wassall | 1 | | 1 |
| Wrigglesworth | 1 | | 1 |

## Final Division One Table

| | | P | W | D | L | F | A | Pts |
|---|---|---|---|---|---|---|---|---|
| 1 | Manchester City | 42 | 22 | 13 | 7 | 107 | 61 | 57 |
| 2 | Charlton Athletic | 42 | 21 | 12 | 9 | 58 | 49 | 54 |
| 3 | Arsenal | 42 | 18 | 16 | 8 | 80 | 49 | 52 |
| 4 | Derby County | 42 | 21 | 7 | 14 | 96 | 90 | 49 |
| 5 | Wolverhampton W | 42 | 21 | 5 | 16 | 84 | 67 | 47 |
| 6 | Brentford | 42 | 18 | 10 | 14 | 82 | 78 | 46 |
| 7 | Middlesbrough | 42 | 19 | 8 | 15 | 74 | 71 | 46 |
| 8 | Sunderland | 42 | 19 | 6 | 17 | 89 | 87 | 44 |
| 9 | Portsmouth | 42 | 17 | 10 | 15 | 62 | 66 | 44 |
| 10 | Stoke City | 42 | 15 | 12 | 15 | 72 | 57 | 42 |
| 11 | Birmingham | 42 | 13 | 15 | 14 | 64 | 60 | 41 |
| 12 | Grimsby Town | 42 | 17 | 7 | 18 | 86 | 81 | 41 |
| 13 | Chelsea | 42 | 14 | 13 | 15 | 52 | 55 | 41 |
| 14 | Preston North End | 42 | 14 | 13 | 15 | 56 | 67 | 41 |
| 15 | Huddersfield Town | 42 | 12 | 15 | 15 | 62 | 64 | 39 |
| 16 | WBA | 42 | 16 | 6 | 20 | 77 | 98 | 38 |
| 17 | Everton | 42 | 14 | 9 | 19 | 81 | 78 | 37 |
| 18 | Liverpool | 42 | 12 | 11 | 19 | 62 | 84 | 35 |
| 19 | Leeds United | 42 | 15 | 4 | 23 | 60 | 80 | 34 |
| 20 | Bolton Wanderers | 42 | 10 | 14 | 18 | 43 | 66 | 34 |
| 21 | Manchester United | 42 | 10 | 12 | 20 | 55 | 78 | 32 |
| 22 | Sheffield Wednesday | 42 | 9 | 12 | 21 | 53 | 69 | 30 |

### Fact File

Walter Winterbottom, who in later years was to serve with distinction as England manager, made his United debut against Leeds United at Elland Road.

**MANAGER:** Scott Duncan/Walter Crickmer (Secretary)
**MOST APPEARANCES:** Billy Bryant 39
**TOP SCORER:** Tommy Bamford 15 (14 League)
**BIGGEST WIN:** 4-0 v Bolton Wanderers, 28 December 1936, League
**HIGHEST ATTENDANCE:** 68,796 v Manchester City, 12 September 1936, League

# Season 1937-38

## Football League Division Two

| DATE | OPPONENTS | SCORE | GOALSCORERS | ATTENDANCE |
|---|---|---|---|---|
| Aug 28 | NEWCASTLE UNITED | W 3-0 | Manley 2, Bryant | 29,446 |
| Aug 30 | Coventry City | L 0-1 | | 30,575 |
| Sep 4 | Luton Town | L 0-1 | | 20,610 |
| Sep 8 | COVENTRY CITY | D 2-2 | Bamford, Bryant | 17,455 |
| Sep 11 | BARNSLEY | W 4-1 | Bamford 3, Manley | 22,394 |
| Sep 13 | Bury | W 2-1 | Ferrier 2 | 9,954 |
| Sep 18 | Stockport County | L 0-1 | | 24,386 |
| Sep 25 | SOUTHAMPTON | L 1-2 | Manley | 22,729 |
| Oct 2 | SHEFFIELD UNITED | L 0-1 | | 20,105 |
| Oct 9 | Tottenham Hotspur | W 1-0 | Manley | 31,189 |
| Oct 16 | Blackburn Rovers | D 1-1 | Bamford | 19,580 |
| Oct 23 | SHEFFIELD WEDNESDAY | W 1-0 | Ferrier | 16,379 |
| Oct 30 | Fulham | L 0-1 | | 17,350 |
| Nov 6 | PLYMOUTH ARGYLE | D 0-0 | | 18,359 |
| Nov 13 | Chesterfield | W 7-1 | Bamford 4, Baird, Bryant, Manley | 17,407 |
| Nov 20 | ASTON VILLA | W 3-1 | Bamford, Manley, Pearson | 33,193 |
| Nov 27 | Norwich City | W 3-2 | Baird, Bryant, Pearson | 17,397 |
| Dec 4 | SWANSEA TOWN | W 5-1 | Rowley 4, Bryant | 17,782 |
| Dec 11 | Bradford Park Avenue | L 0-4 | | 12,004 |
| Dec 27 | NOTTINGHAM FOREST | W 4-3 | Baird 2, McKay, Wrigglesworth | 30,778 |
| Dec 28 | Nottingham Forest | W 3-2 | Bamford, Bryant, Carey | 19,283 |
| Jan 1 | Newcastle United | D 2-2 | Bamford, Rowley | 40,088 |
| Jan 15 | LUTON TOWN | W 4-2 | Bamford, Bryant, Carey, McKay | 16,845 |
| Jan 29 | STOCKPORT COUNTY | W 3-1 | Bamford, Bryant, McKay | 31,852 |
| Feb 2 | Barnsley | D 2-2 | Rowley, Smith | 7,859 |
| Feb 5 | Southampton | D 3-3 | Redwood 2, Baird | 20,354 |
| Feb 17 | Sheffield United | W 2-1 | Bryant, Smith | 17,754 |
| Feb 19 | TOTTENHAM HOTSPUR | L 0-1 | | 34,631 |
| Feb 23 | WEST HAM UNITED | W 4-0 | Baird 2, Smith, Wassall | 14,572 |
| Feb 26 | BLACKBURN ROVERS | W 2-1 | Baird, Bryant | 30,892 |
| Mar 5 | Sheffield Wednesday | W 3-1 | Baird, Brown, Rowley | 37,156 |
| Mar 12 | FULHAM | W 1-0 | Baird | 30,363 |
| Mar 19 | Plymouth Argyle | D 1-1 | Rowley | 20,311 |
| Mar 26 | CHESTERFIELD | W 4-1 | Smith 2, Bryant, Carey | 27,311 |
| Apr 2 | Aston Villa | L 0-3 | | 54,654 |
| Apr 9 | NORWICH CITY | D 0-0 | | 25,879 |
| Apr 15 | Burnley | L 0-1 | | 28,459 |
| Apr 16 | Swansea Town | D 2-2 | Rowley, Smith | 13,811 |
| Apr 18 | BURNLEY | W 4-0 | McKay 2, Baird, Bryant | 35,808 |
| Apr 23 | BRADFORD PARK AVENUE | W 3-1 | Baird, McKay, Smith | 28,919 |
| Apr 30 | West Ham United | L 0-1 | | 14,816 |
| May 7 | BURY | W 2-0 | McKay, Smith | 53,604 |

## FA Cup

| | | | | |
|---|---|---|---|---|
| Jan 8 | YEOVIL TOWN | (Rd3) W 3-0 | Baird, Bamford, Pearson | 49,004 |
| Jan 22 | Barnsley | (Rd4) D 2-2 | Baird, Carey | 35,549 |
| Jan 26 | BARNSLEY | (R) W 1-0 | Baird | 33,601 |
| Feb 12 | Brentford | (Rd5) L 0-2 | | 24,147 |

## League & Cup Appearances

| PLAYER | LEAGUE | CUP COMPETITION FA CUP | TOTAL |
|---|---|---|---|
| Baird | 35 | 4 | 39 |
| Bamford | 23 | 4 | 27 |
| Breedon | 9 | | 9 |
| Breen | 33 | 4 | 37 |
| Brown | 28 | 3 | 31 |
| Bryant | 39 | 4 | 43 |
| Carey | 16 | 3 | 19 |
| Ferrier | 5 | | 5 |
| Gladwin | 7 | | 7 |
| Griffiths | 18 | | 18 |
| Jones | 1 | | 1 |
| McKay | 37 | 3 | 40 |
| Manley | 21 | 1 | 22 |
| Murray | 4 | | 4 |
| Mutch | 2 | | 2 |
| Pearson | 11 | 1 | 12 |
| Porter | 2 | | 2 |
| Redwood | 29 | 4 | 33 |
| Roughton | 39 | 4 | 43 |
| Rowley | 25 | 4 | 29 |
| Savage | 4 | 1 | 5 |
| Smith | 17 | | 17 |
| Thompson | 1 | | 1 |
| Vose | 33 | 4 | 37 |
| Wassall | 9 | | 9 |
| Whalley | 6 | | 6 |
| Winterbottom | 4 | | 4 |
| Wrigglesworth | 4 | | 4 |

## Goalscorers

| PLAYER | LEAGUE | CUP COMPETITION FA CUP | TOTAL |
|---|---|---|---|
| Baird | 12 | 3 | 15 |
| Bamford | 14 | 1 | 15 |
| Bryant | 12 | | 12 |
| Rowley | 9 | | 9 |
| Smith | 8 | | 8 |
| McKay | 7 | | 7 |
| Manley | 7 | | 7 |
| Carey | 3 | 1 | 4 |
| Ferrier | 3 | | 3 |
| Pearson | 2 | 1 | 3 |
| Redwood | 2 | | 2 |
| Brown | 1 | | 1 |
| Wassall | 1 | | 1 |
| Wrigglesworth | 1 | | 1 |

### Fact File

Having suffered relegation the previous season United bounced back again to grab promotion as Division Two runners-up to champions Aston Villa.

**SECRETARY:** Walter Crickmer
**MOST APPEARANCES:** Billy Bryant, George Roughton 43
**TOP SCORERS:** Tommy Bamford 15 (14 League), Harry Baird 15 (12 League)
**BIGGEST WIN:** 7-1 v Chesterfield, 13 November 1937, League
**HIGHEST ATTENDANCE:** 54,654 v Aston Villa, 2 April 1938, League

### Final Division Two Table

| | | P | W | D | L | F | A | Pts |
|---|---|---|---|---|---|---|---|---|
| 1 | Aston Villa | 42 | 25 | 7 | 10 | 73 | 35 | 57 |
| 2 | Manchester United | 42 | 22 | 9 | 11 | 82 | 50 | 53 |
| 3 | Sheffield United | 42 | 22 | 9 | 11 | 73 | 56 | 53 |
| 4 | Coventry City | 42 | 20 | 12 | 10 | 66 | 45 | 52 |
| 5 | Tottenham Hotspur | 42 | 10 | 6 | 17 | 76 | 54 | 44 |
| 6 | Burnley | 42 | 17 | 10 | 15 | 54 | 54 | 44 |
| 7 | Bradford Park Av | 42 | 17 | 9 | 16 | 69 | 56 | 43 |
| 8 | Fulham | 42 | 16 | 11 | 15 | 61 | 57 | 43 |
| 9 | West Ham United | 42 | 14 | 14 | 14 | 53 | 52 | 42 |
| 10 | Bury | 42 | 18 | 5 | 19 | 63 | 60 | 41 |
| 11 | Chesterfield | 42 | 16 | 9 | 17 | 63 | 63 | 41 |
| 12 | Luton Town | 42 | 15 | 10 | 17 | 89 | 86 | 40 |
| 13 | Plymouth Argyle | 42 | 14 | 12 | 16 | 57 | 65 | 40 |
| 14 | Norwich City | 42 | 14 | 11 | 17 | 56 | 75 | 39 |
| 15 | Southampton | 42 | 15 | 9 | 18 | 55 | 77 | 39 |
| 16 | Blackburn Rovers | 42 | 14 | 10 | 18 | 71 | 80 | 38 |
| 17 | Sheffield Wednesday | 42 | 14 | 10 | 18 | 49 | 56 | 38 |
| 18 | Swansea Town | 42 | 13 | 12 | 17 | 45 | 73 | 38 |
| 19 | Newcastle United | 42 | 14 | 8 | 20 | 51 | 58 | 36 |
| 20 | Nottingham Forest | 42 | 14 | 8 | 20 | 47 | 60 | 36 |
| 21 | Barnsley | 42 | 11 | 14 | 17 | 50 | 64 | 36 |
| 22 | Stockport County | 42 | 11 | 9 | 22 | 43 | 70 | 31 |

# Season 1938-39

## Football League Division One

| DATE | OPPONENTS | SCORE | GOALSCORERS | ATTENDANCE |
|---|---|---|---|---|
| Aug 27 | Middlesbrough | L 1-3 | Smith | 25,539 |
| Aug 31 | BOLTON WANDERERS | D 2-2 | Craven, Hubbick o.g. | 37,950 |
| Sep 3 | BIRMINGHAM | W 4-1 | Smith 2, Bryant, Craven | 22,228 |
| Sep 7 | Liverpool | L 0-1 | | 25,070 |
| Sep 10 | Grimsby Town | L 0-1 | | 14,077 |
| Sep 17 | Stoke City | D 1-1 | Smith | 21,526 |
| Sep 24 | CHELSEA | W 5-1 | Carey, Manley, Redwood, Rowley, Smith | 34,557 |
| Oct 1 | Preston North End | D 1-1 | Bryant | 25,964 |
| Oct 8 | CHARLTON ATHLETIC | L 0-2 | | 35,730 |
| Oct 15 | BLACKPOOL | D 0-0 | | 39,723 |
| Oct 22 | Derby County | L 1-5 | Smith | 26,612 |
| Oct 29 | SUNDERLAND | L 0-1 | | 33,565 |
| Nov 5 | Aston Villa | W 2-0 | Rowley, Wrigglesworth | 38,357 |
| Nov 12 | WOLVERHAMPTON WANDERERS | L 1-3 | Rowley | 32,821 |
| Nov 19 | Everton | L 0-3 | | 31,809 |
| Nov 26 | HUDDERSFIELD TOWN | D 1-1 | Hanlon | 23,164 |
| Dec 3 | Portsmouth | D 0-0 | | 18,692 |
| Dec 10 | ARSENAL | W 1-0 | Bryant | 42,008 |
| Dec 17 | Brentford | W 5-2 | Hanlon 2, Bryant, Manley, Rowley | 14,919 |
| Dec 24 | MIDDLESBROUGH | D 1-1 | Wassall | 33,235 |
| Dec 26 | LEICESTER CITY | W 3-0 | Wrigglesworth 2, Carey | 26,332 |
| Dec 27 | Leicester City | D 1-1 | Hanlon | 21,434 |
| Dec 31 | Birmingham | D 3-3 | Hanlon, McKay, Pearson | 20,787 |
| Jan 14 | GRIMSBY TOWN | W 3-1 | Rowley 2, Wassall | 25,654 |
| Jan 21 | STOKE CITY | L 0-1 | | 37,384 |
| Jan 28 | Chelsea | W 1-0 | Bradbury | 31,265 |
| Feb 4 | PRESTON NORTH END | D 1-1 | Rowley | 41,061 |
| Feb 11 | Charlton Athletic | L 1-7 | Hanlon | 23,721 |
| Feb 18 | Blackpool | W 5-3 | Hanlon 3, Bryant, Carey | 15,253 |
| Feb 25 | DERBY COUNTY | D 1-1 | Carey | 37,166 |
| Mar 4 | Sunderland | L 2-5 | Manley, Rowley | 11,078 |
| Mar 11 | ASTON VILLA | D 1-1 | Wassall | 28,292 |
| Mar 18 | Wolverhampton Wanderers | L 0-3 | | 31,498 |
| Mar 29 | EVERTON | L 0-2 | | 18,348 |
| Apr 1 | Huddersfield Town | D 1-1 | Rowley | 14,007 |
| Apr 7 | LEEDS UNITED | D 0-0 | | 35,564 |
| Apr 8 | PORTSMOUTH | D 1-1 | Rowley | 25,457 |
| Apr 10 | Leeds United | L 1-3 | Carey | 13,771 |
| Apr 15 | Arsenal | L 1-2 | Hanlon | 25,741 |
| Apr 22 | BRENTFORD | W 3-0 | Bryant, Carey, Wassall | 15,353 |
| Apr 29 | Bolton Wanderers | D 0-0 | | 10,314 |
| May 6 | LIVERPOOL | W 2-0 | Hanlon 2 | 12,073 |

## FA Cup

| | | | | |
|---|---|---|---|---|
| Jan 7 | West Bromwich Albion (Rd3) | D 0-0 | | 23,900 |
| Jan 11 | WEST BROMWICH ALBION (R) | L 1-5 | Redwood | 17,641 |

## League & Cup Appearances

| PLAYER | LEAGUE | CUP COMPETITION FA CUP | TOTAL |
|---|---|---|---|
| Bradbury | 2 | | 2 |
| Breedon | 22 | | 22 |
| Breen | 6 | | 6 |
| Brown | 3 | | 3 |
| Carey | 32 | 2 | 34 |
| Craven | 11 | | 11 |
| Dougan | 4 | | 4 |
| Gladwin | 12 | 1 | 13 |
| Griffiths | 35 | 2 | 37 |
| Hanlon | 27 | 2 | 29 |
| McKay | 20 | 2 | 22 |
| Manley | 23 | | 23 |
| Pearson | 9 | | 9 |
| Redwood | 35 | 2 | 37 |
| Roughton | 14 | | 14 |
| Rowley | 38 | 1 | 39 |
| Smith | 19 | 1 | 20 |
| Tapken | 14 | 2 | 16 |
| Vose | 39 | 1 | 40 |
| Warner | 29 | 2 | 31 |
| Wassall | 27 | 2 | 29 |
| Whalley | 2 | | 2 |
| Wrigglesworth | 12 | 2 | 14 |

## Goalscorers

| PLAYER | LEAGUE | CUP COMPETITION FA CUP | TOTAL |
|---|---|---|---|
| Hanlon | 12 | | 12 |
| Rowley | 10 | | 10 |
| Bryant | 6 | | 6 |
| Carey | 6 | | 6 |
| Smith | 6 | | 6 |
| Wassall | 4 | | 4 |
| Manley | 3 | | 3 |
| Wrigglesworth | 3 | | 3 |
| Craven | 2 | | 2 |
| Redwood | 1 | 1 | 2 |
| Bradbury | 1 | | 1 |
| McKay | 1 | | 1 |
| Pearson | 1 | | 1 |
| Opps' o.gs. | 1 | | 1 |

## Fact File

Old Trafford's biggest-ever crowd, 76,962, gather to watch Wolverhampton Wanderers beat Grimsby Town 5-1 in a FA Cup semi-final. This figure, set on 25 March 1939, stood as a record at the start of the 2003-04 season.

**SECRETARY:** Walter Crickmer
**MOST APPEARANCES:** George Vose 40
**TOP SCORER:** Jimmy Hanlon 12 (all League)
**BIGGEST WIN:** 5-1 v Chelsea, 24 September 1938, League
**HIGHEST ATTENDANCE:** 42,008 v Arsenal, 10 December 1938, League

## Final Division One Table

| | | P | W | D | L | F | A | Pts |
|---|---|---|---|---|---|---|---|---|
| 1 | Everton | 42 | 27 | 5 | 10 | 88 | 52 | 59 |
| 2 | Wolverhampton W | 42 | 22 | 11 | 9 | 88 | 39 | 55 |
| 3 | Charlton Athletic | 42 | 22 | 6 | 14 | 75 | 59 | 50 |
| 4 | Middlesbrough | 42 | 20 | 9 | 13 | 93 | 74 | 49 |
| 5 | Arsenal | 42 | 19 | 9 | 14 | 55 | 41 | 47 |
| 6 | Derby County | 42 | 19 | 8 | 15 | 66 | 55 | 46 |
| 7 | Stoke City | 42 | 17 | 12 | 13 | 71 | 68 | 46 |
| 8 | Bolton Wanderers | 42 | 15 | 15 | 12 | 67 | 58 | 45 |
| 9 | Preston North End | 42 | 16 | 12 | 14 | 63 | 69 | 44 |
| 10 | Grimsby Town | 42 | 16 | 11 | 15 | 61 | 69 | 43 |
| 11 | Liverpool | 42 | 14 | 14 | 14 | 62 | 63 | 42 |
| 12 | Aston Villa | 42 | 15 | 11 | 16 | 71 | 60 | 41 |
| 13 | Leeds United | 42 | 16 | 9 | 17 | 59 | 67 | 41 |
| 14 | Manchester United | 42 | 11 | 16 | 15 | 57 | 65 | 38 |
| 15 | Blackpool | 42 | 12 | 14 | 16 | 58 | 68 | 38 |
| 16 | Sunderland | 42 | 13 | 12 | 17 | 54 | 67 | 38 |
| 17 | Portsmouth | 42 | 12 | 13 | 17 | 47 | 70 | 37 |
| 18 | Brentford | 42 | 14 | 8 | 20 | 53 | 74 | 36 |
| 19 | Huddersfield Town | 42 | 12 | 11 | 19 | 58 | 64 | 35 |
| 20 | Chelsea | 42 | 12 | 9 | 21 | 64 | 80 | 33 |
| 21 | Birmingham | 42 | 12 | 8 | 22 | 62 | 84 | 32 |
| 22 | Leicester City | 42 | 9 | 11 | 22 | 48 | 82 | 29 |

## Season 1946-47

### Football League Division One

| DATE | OPPONENTS | SCORE | GOALSCORERS | ATTENDANCE |
|---|---|---|---|---|
| Aug 31 | GRIMSBY TOWN | W 2-1 | Rowley, Mitten | 41,025 |
| Sep 4 | Chelsea | W 3-0 | Rowley, Pearson, Mitten | 27,750 |
| Sep 7 | Charlton Athletic | W 3-1 | Hanlon, Rowley, Johnson o.g. | 44,088 |
| Sep 11 | LIVERPOOL | W 5-0 | Pearson 3, Rowley, Mitten | 41,657 |
| Sep 14 | MIDDLESBROUGH | W 1-0 | Rowley | 65,112 |
| Sep 18 | CHELSEA | D 1-1 | Chilton | 30,275 |
| Sep 21 | Stoke City | L 2-3 | Delaney, Hanlon | 41,699 |
| Sep 28 | ARSENAL | W 5-2 | Hanlon 2, Rowley 2, Wrigglesworth (pen) | 62,718 |
| Oct 5 | PRESTON NORTH END | D 1-1 | Wrigglesworth | 55,395 |
| Oct 12 | Sheffield United | D 2-2 | Rowley 2 | 35,543 |
| Oct 19 | Blackpool | L 1-3 | Delaney | 26,307 |
| Oct 26 | SUNDERLAND | L 0-3 | | 48,385 |
| Nov 2 | Aston Villa | D 0-0 | | 53,668 |
| Nov 9 | DERBY COUNTY | W 4-1 | Pearson 2, Rowley, Mitten | 57,340 |
| Nov 16 | Everton | D 2-2 | Rowley, Pearson | 45,832 |
| Nov 23 | HUDDERSFIELD TOWN | W 5-2 | Morris 2, Mitten 2, Rowley | 39,216 |
| Nov 30 | Wolverhampton Wanderers | L 2-3 | Hanlon, Delaney | 46,704 |
| Dec 7 | BRENTFORD | W 4-1 | Rowley 3, Mitten | 31,962 |
| Dec 14 | Blackburn Rovers | L 1-2 | Morris | 21,455 |
| Dec 25 | Bolton Wanderers | D 2-2 | Rowley 2 | 28,505 |
| Dec 26 | BOLTON WANDERERS | W 1-0 | Pearson | 57,186 |
| Dec 28 | Grimsby Town | D 0-0 | | 17,183 |
| Jan 4 | CHARLTON ATHLETIC | W 4-1 | Burke 2, Pearson, Buckle (pen) | 43,406 |
| Jan 18 | Middlesbrough | W 4-2 | Pearson 2, Buckle, Morris | 37,435 |
| Feb 1 | Arsenal | L 2-6 | Morris, Pearson | 29,415 |
| Feb 5 | STOKE CITY | D 1-1 | Buckle (pen) | 8,456 |
| Feb 22 | BLACKPOOL | W 3-0 | Rowley 2 (1pen), Hanlon | 29,993 |
| Mar 1 | Sunderland | D 1-1 | Delaney | 25,038 |
| Mar 8 | ASTON VILLA | W 2-1 | Burke, Pearson | 36,965 |
| Mar 15 | Derby County | L 3-4 | Burke 2, Pearson | 19,579 |
| Mar 22 | EVERTON | W 3-0 | Delaney, Burke, Warner | 43,441 |
| Mar 29 | Huddersfield Town | D 2-2 | Delaney, Pearson | 18,509 |
| Apr 5 | WOLVERHAMPTON WANDERERS | W 3-1 | Rowley 2, Hanlon | 66,967 |
| Apr 7 | LEEDS UNITED | W 3-1 | Burke 2, Delaney | 41,772 |
| Apr 8 | Leeds United | W 2-0 | Burke, McGlen | 15,528 |
| Apr 12 | Brentford | D 0-0 | | 21,714 |
| Apr 19 | BLACKBURN ROVERS | W 4-0 | Pearson 2, Rowley, Higgins o.g. | 46,196 |
| Apr 26 | Portsmouth | W 1-0 | Delaney | 30,623 |
| May 3 | Liverpool | L 0-1 | | 48,800 |
| May 10 | Preston North End | D 1-1 | Pearson | 23,278 |
| May 17 | PORTSMOUTH | W 3-0 | Morris, Rowley, Mitten | 37,614 |
| May 26 | SHEFFIELD UNITED | W 6-2 | Rowley 3, Morris 2, Pearson | 34,059 |

### FA Cup

| | | | | |
|---|---|---|---|---|
| Jan 11 | Bradford Park Avenue | W 3-0 | Rowley 2, Buckle | 26,990 |
| Jan 25 | NOTTINGHAM FOREST | L 0-2 | | 58,641 |

All home games at Maine Road, Manchester.

### League & Cup Appearances

| PLAYER | LEAGUE | CUP COMPETITION FA CUP | TOTAL |
|---|---|---|---|
| Aston | 21 | 2 | 23 |
| Buckle | 5 | 2 | 7 |
| Burke | 13 | | 13 |
| Carey | 31 | 2 | 33 |
| Chilton | 41 | 2 | 43 |
| Cockburn | 32 | | 32 |
| Collinson | 7 | | 7 |
| Crompton | 29 | 1 | 30 |
| Delaney | 37 | 2 | 39 |
| Fielding | 6 | 1 | 7 |
| Hanlon | 27 | | 27 |
| McGlen | 33 | 2 | 35 |
| Mitten | 20 | | 20 |
| Morris | 24 | 2 | 26 |
| Pearson | 42 | 2 | 44 |
| Rowley | 37 | 2 | 39 |
| Walton | 15 | | 15 |
| Warner | 34 | 2 | 36 |
| Whalley | 3 | | 3 |
| Worrall | 1 | | 1 |
| Wrigglesworth | 4 | | 4 |

### Goalscorers

| PLAYER | LEAGUE | CUP COMPETITION FA CUP | TOTAL |
|---|---|---|---|
| Rowley | 26 | 2 | 28 |
| Pearson | 19 | | 19 |
| Burke | 9 | | 9 |
| Delaney | 8 | | 8 |
| Mitten | 8 | | 8 |
| Morris | 8 | | 8 |
| Hanlon | 7 | | 7 |
| Buckle | 3 | 1 | 4 |
| Wrigglesworth | 2 | | 2 |
| Chilton | 1 | | 1 |
| McGlen | 1 | | 1 |
| Warner | 1 | | 1 |
| Opps' o.gs. | 2 | | 2 |

### Fact File

United ended the season as runners-up to champions Liverpool. It was the club's highest position in the league since winning the title in 1911.

**MANAGER:** Matt Busby
**MOST APPEARANCES:** Stan Pearson 44
**TOP SCORER:** Jack Rowley 28 (26 League)
**BIGGEST WIN:** 5-0 v Liverpool, 11 September 1946, League
**HIGHEST ATTENDANCE:** 66,967 v Wolverhampton Wanderers, 5 April 1946, League

### Final Division One Table

| | | P | W | D | L | F | A | Pts |
|---|---|---|---|---|---|---|---|---|
| 1 | Liverpool | 42 | 25 | 7 | 10 | 84 | 52 | 57 |
| 2 | Manchester United | 42 | 22 | 12 | 8 | 95 | 54 | 56 |
| 3 | Wolverhampton W | 42 | 25 | 6 | 11 | 98 | 56 | 56 |
| 4 | Stoke City | 42 | 24 | 7 | 11 | 90 | 53 | 55 |
| 5 | Blackpool | 42 | 22 | 6 | 14 | 71 | 70 | 50 |
| 6 | Sheffield United | 42 | 21 | 7 | 14 | 89 | 75 | 49 |
| 7 | Preston North End | 42 | 18 | 11 | 13 | 76 | 74 | 47 |
| 8 | Aston Villa | 42 | 18 | 9 | 15 | 67 | 53 | 45 |
| 9 | Sunderland | 42 | 18 | 8 | 16 | 65 | 66 | 44 |
| 10 | Everton | 42 | 17 | 9 | 16 | 62 | 67 | 43 |
| 11 | Middlesbrough | 42 | 17 | 8 | 17 | 73 | 68 | 42 |
| 12 | Portsmouth | 42 | 16 | 9 | 17 | 66 | 60 | 41 |
| 13 | Arsenal | 42 | 16 | 9 | 17 | 72 | 70 | 41 |
| 14 | Derby County | 42 | 18 | 5 | 19 | 73 | 79 | 41 |
| 15 | Chelsea | 42 | 16 | 7 | 19 | 69 | 84 | 39 |
| 16 | Grimsby Town | 42 | 13 | 12 | 17 | 61 | 82 | 38 |
| 17 | Blackburn Rovers | 42 | 14 | 8 | 20 | 45 | 53 | 36 |
| 18 | Bolton Wanderers | 42 | 13 | 8 | 21 | 57 | 69 | 34 |
| 19 | Charlton Athletic | 42 | 11 | 12 | 19 | 57 | 71 | 34 |
| 20 | Huddersfield Town | 42 | 13 | 7 | 22 | 53 | 79 | 33 |
| 21 | Brentford | 42 | 9 | 7 | 26 | 45 | 88 | 25 |
| 22 | Leeds United | 42 | 6 | 6 | 30 | 45 | 90 | 18 |

# Season 1947-48

## Football League Division One

| DATE | OPPONENTS | SCORE | GOALSCORERS | ATTENDANCE |
|---|---|---|---|---|
| Aug 23 | Middlesbrough | D 2-2 | Rowley 2 | 39,554 |
| Aug 27 | LIVERPOOL | W 2-0 | Morris, Pearson | 52,385 |
| Aug 30 | CHARLTON ATHLETIC | W 6-2 | Rowley 4, Morris, Pearson | 52,659 |
| Sep 3 | Liverpool | D 2-2 | Mitten, Pearson | 48,081 |
| Sep 6 | Arsenal | L 1-2 | Morris | 64,905 |
| Sep 8 | Burnley | D 0-0 | | 37,517 |
| Sep 13 | SHEFFIELD UNITED | L 0-1 | | 49,808 |
| Sep 20 | Manchester City | D 0-0 | | 71,364 |
| Sep 27 | Preston North End | L 1-2 | Morris | 34,372 |
| Oct 4 | STOKE CITY | D 1-1 | Hanlon | 45,745 |
| Oct 11 | GRIMSBY TOWN | L 3-4 | Morris, Rowley, Mitten | 40,035 |
| Oct 18 | Sunderland | L 0-1 | | 37,148 |
| Oct 25 | ASTON VILLA | W 2-0 | Delaney, Rowley | 47,078 |
| Nov 1 | Wolverhampton Wanderers | W 6-2 | Morris 2, Pearson 2, Mitten, Delaney | 44,309 |
| Nov 8 | HUDDERSFIELD TOWN | D 4-4 | Rowley 4 | 59,772 |
| Nov 15 | Derby County | D 1-1 | Carey | 32,990 |
| Nov 22 | EVERTON | D 2-2 | Morris, Cockburn | 35,509 |
| Nov 29 | Chelsea | W 4-0 | Morris 3, Rowley | 43,617 |
| Dec 6 | BLACKPOOL | D 1-1 | Pearson | 63,683 |
| Dec 13 | Blackburn Rovers | D 1-1 | Morris | 22,784 |
| Dec 20 | MIDDLESBROUGH | W 2-1 | Pearson 2 | 46,666 |
| Dec 25 | PORTSMOUTH | W 3-2 | Morris 2, Rowley | 42,776 |
| Dec 27 | Portsmouth | W 3-1 | Morris 2, Delaney | 27,674 |
| Jan 1 | BURNLEY | W 5-0 | Rowley 3, Mitten 2 | 59,838 |
| Jan 3 | Charlton Athletic | W 2-1 | Morris, Pearson | 40,484 |
| Jan 17 | ARSENAL | D 1-1 | Rowley | 83,260 |
| Jan 31 | Sheffield United | L 1-2 | Rowley | 45,189 |
| Feb 14 | PRESTON NORTH END | D 1-1 | Delaney | 61,765 |
| Feb 21 | Stoke City | W 2-0 | Pearson, Buckle (pen) | 36,794 |
| Mar 6 | SUNDERLAND | W 3-1 | Rowley, Delaney, Mitten (pen) | 55,160 |
| Mar 17 | Grimsby Town | D 1-1 | Rowley | 12,284 |
| Mar 20 | WOLVERHAMPTON WANDERERS | W 3-2 | Mitten, Morris, Delaney | 50,667 |
| Mar 22 | Aston Villa | W 1-0 | Pearson | 52,366 |
| Mar 26 | BOLTON WANDERERS | L 0-2 | | 71,623 |
| Mar 27 | Huddersfield Town | W 2-0 | Pearson, Burke | 38,266 |
| Mar 29 | Bolton Wanderers | W 1-0 | Anderson | 44,225 |
| Apr 3 | DERBY COUNTY | W 1-0 | Pearson | 49,609 |
| Apr 7 | MANCHESTER CITY | D 1-1 | Rowley | 71,690 |
| Apr 10 | Everton | L 0-2 | | 44,198 |
| Apr 17 | CHELSEA | W 5-0 | Pearson 2, Rowley, Delaney, Mitten | 43,225 |
| Apr 28 | Blackpool | L 0-1 | | 32,236 |
| May 1 | BLACKBURN ROVERS | W 4-1 | Pearson 3, Delaney | 44,439 |

## FA Cup

| DATE | OPPONENTS | ROUND | SCORE | GOALSCORERS | ATTENDANCE |
|---|---|---|---|---|---|
| Jan 10 | Aston Villa | (Rd3) | W 6-4 | Morris 2, Pearson 2, Rowley, Delaney | 58,683 |
| Jan 24 | LIVERPOOL* | (Rd4) | W 3-0 | Rowley, Morris, Mitten | 74,000 |
| Feb 7 | CHARLTON ATHLETIC** | (Rd5) | W 2-0 | Warner, Mitten | 33,312 |
| Feb 28 | PRESTON NORTH END | (Rd6) | W 4-1 | Mitten, Pearson 2, Rowley | 74,213 |
| Mar 13 | Derby County† | (SF) | W 3-1 | Pearson 3 | 60,000 |
| Apr 24 | Blackpool# | (F) | W 4-2 | Rowley 2, Pearson, Anderson | 99,842 |

*Played at Goodison Park, Liverpool. **Played at Leeds Road, Huddersfield.
†Played at Hillsborough, Sheffield. #Played at Wembley Stadium, London.
All home games at Maine Road, Manchester.

## League & Cup Appearances

| PLAYER | LEAGUE | CUP COMPETITION FA CUP | TOTAL |
|---|---|---|---|
| Aston | 42 | 6 | 48 |
| Ball | 1 | | 1 |
| Brown | 3 | | 3 |
| Buckle | 3 | | 3 |
| Burke | 6 | | 6 |
| Carey | 37 | 6 | 43 |
| Cassidy | 1 | | 1 |
| Chilton | 41 | 6 | 47 |
| Cockburn | 26 | 6 | 32 |
| Crompton | 37 | 6 | 43 |
| Dale | 2 | | 2 |
| Delaney | 36 | 6 | 42 |
| Hanlon | 8 | | 8 |
| Lowrie | 2 | | 2 |
| Lynn | 3 | | 3 |
| McGlen | 13 | | 13 |
| Mitten | 38 | 6 | 44 |
| Morris | 38 | 6 | 44 |
| Pearson | 40 | 6 | 46 |
| Pegg | 2 | | 2 |
| Rowley | 39 | 5 | 44 |
| Warner | 15 | 1 | 16 |
| Walton | 6 | | 6 |
| Worrall | 5 | | 5 |

## Goalscorers

| PLAYER | LEAGUE | CUP COMPETITION FA CUP | TOTAL |
|---|---|---|---|
| Rowley | 23 | 5 | 28 |
| Pearson | 18 | 8 | 26 |
| Morris | 18 | 3 | 21 |
| Mitten | 8 | 3 | 11 |
| Delaney | 8 | 1 | 9 |
| Anderson | 1 | 1 | 2 |
| Buckle | 1 | | 1 |
| Burke | 1 | | 1 |
| Carey | 1 | | 1 |
| Cockburn | 1 | | 1 |
| Hanlon | 1 | | 1 |
| Warner | | 1 | 1 |

## Final Division One Table

| | | P | W | D | L | F | A | Pts |
|---|---|---|---|---|---|---|---|---|
| 1 | Arsenal | 42 | 23 | 13 | 6 | 81 | 32 | 59 |
| 2 | Manchester United | 42 | 19 | 14 | 9 | 81 | 48 | 52 |
| 3 | Burnley | 42 | 20 | 12 | 10 | 56 | 43 | 52 |
| 4 | Derby County | 42 | 19 | 12 | 11 | 77 | 57 | 50 |
| 5 | Wolverhampton W | 42 | 19 | 9 | 14 | 83 | 70 | 47 |
| 6 | Aston Villa | 42 | 19 | 9 | 14 | 65 | 57 | 47 |
| 7 | Preston North End | 42 | 20 | 7 | 15 | 67 | 68 | 47 |
| 8 | Portsmouth | 42 | 19 | 7 | 16 | 68 | 50 | 45 |
| 9 | Blackpool | 42 | 17 | 10 | 15 | 57 | 41 | 44 |
| 10 | Manchester City | 42 | 15 | 12 | 15 | 52 | 47 | 42 |
| 11 | Liverpool | 42 | 16 | 10 | 16 | 65 | 61 | 42 |
| 12 | Sheffield United | 42 | 16 | 10 | 16 | 65 | 70 | 42 |
| 13 | Charlton Athletic | 42 | 17 | 6 | 19 | 57 | 66 | 40 |
| 14 | Everton | 42 | 17 | 6 | 19 | 52 | 66 | 40 |
| 15 | Stoke City | 42 | 14 | 10 | 18 | 41 | 55 | 38 |
| 16 | Middlesbrough | 42 | 14 | 9 | 19 | 71 | 73 | 37 |
| 17 | Bolton Wanderers | 42 | 16 | 5 | 21 | 46 | 58 | 37 |
| 18 | Chelsea | 42 | 14 | 9 | 19 | 53 | 71 | 37 |
| 19 | Huddersfield Town | 42 | 12 | 12 | 18 | 51 | 60 | 36 |
| 20 | Sunderland | 42 | 13 | 10 | 19 | 56 | 67 | 36 |
| 21 | Blackburn Rovers | 42 | 11 | 10 | 21 | 54 | 72 | 32 |
| 22 | Grimsby Town | 42 | 8 | 6 | 28 | 45 | 111 | 22 |

### Fact File

United claimed their first major honour in 37 years as they lifted the FA Cup after beating Blackpool 4-2 in one of the finest finals ever seen at Wembley.

**MANAGER:** Matt Busby

**MOST APPEARANCES:** Allenby Chilton 47

**TOP SCORER:** Jack Rowley 28 (23 League)

**BIGGEST WIN:** 5-0 v Burnley, 1 January 1947, League; 5-0 v Chelsea, 17 April 1948, League

**HIGHEST ATTENDANCE:** 99,842 v Blackpool, 24 April 1948, FA Cup

# Season 1948-49

## Football League Division One

| DATE | OPPONENTS | SCORE | GOALSCORERS | ATTENDANCE |
|---|---|---|---|---|
| Aug 21 | DERBY COUNTY | L 1-2 | Pearson | 52,620 |
| Aug 23 | Blackpool | W 3-0 | Mitten 2, Pearson | 36,880 |
| Aug 28 | Arsenal | W 1-0 | Mitten | 64,150 |
| Sep 1 | BLACKPOOL | L 3-4 | Delaney, Morris, Mitten (pen) | 51,187 |
| Sep 4 | HUDDERSFIELD TOWN | W 4-1 | Pearson 2, Delaney, Mitten (pen) | 57,714 |
| Sep 8 | Wolverhampton Wanderers | L 2-3 | Morris, Rowley | 42,617 |
| Sep 11 | Manchester City | D 0-0 | | 64,502 |
| Sep 15 | WOLVERHAMPTON WANDERERS | W 2-0 | Buckle, Pearson | 33,871 |
| Sep 18 | Sheffield United | D 2-2 | Buckle, Pearson | 36,880 |
| Sep 25 | ASTON VILLA | W 3-1 | Rowley 2, Mitten (pen) | 53,820 |
| Oct 2 | Sunderland | L 1-2 | Rowley | 54,419 |
| Oct 9 | CHARLTON ATHLETIC | D 1-1 | Burke | 46,964 |
| Oct 16 | Stoke City | L 1-2 | Morris | 45,830 |
| Oct 23 | BURNLEY | D 1-1 | Mitten | 47,093 |
| Oct 30 | Preston North End | W 6-1 | Pearson 2, Mitten 2, Rowley, Morris | 37,372 |
| Nov 6 | EVERTON | W 2-0 | Delaney, Morris | 42,789 |
| Nov 13 | Chelsea | D 1-1 | Rowley | 62,542 |
| Nov 20 | BIRMINGHAM CITY | W 3-0 | Morris, Rowley, Pearson | 45,482 |
| Nov 27 | Middlesbrough | W 4-1 | Rowley 3, Delaney | 31,331 |
| Dec 4 | NEWCASTLE UNITED | D 1-1 | Mitten | 70,787 |
| Dec 11 | Portsmouth | D 2-2 | Mitten (pen), McGlen | 29,966 |
| Dec 18 | Derby County | W 3-1 | Burke 2, Pearson | 31,498 |
| Dec 25 | LIVERPOOL | D 0-0 | | 47,788 |
| Dec 26 | Liverpool | W 2-0 | Pearson, Burke | 53,325 |
| Jan 1 | ARSENAL | W 2-0 | Burke, Mitten | 58,688 |
| Jan 22 | MANCHESTER CITY | D 0-0 | | 66,485 |
| Feb 19 | Aston Villa | L 1-2 | Rowley | 68,354 |
| Mar 5 | Charlton Athletic | W 3-2 | Pearson 2, Downie | 55,291 |
| Mar 12 | STOKE CITY | W 3-0 | Downie, Rowley, Mitten | 55,949 |
| Mar 19 | Birmingham City | L 0-1 | | 46,819 |
| Apr 6 | Huddersfield Town | L 1-2 | Rowley | 17,256 |
| Apr 9 | CHELSEA | D 1-1 | Mitten | 27,304 |
| Apr 15 | Bolton Wanderers | W 1-0 | Carey | 44,999 |
| Apr 16 | Burnley | W 2-0 | Rowley 2 | 37,722 |
| Apr 18 | BOLTON WANDERERS | W 3-0 | Rowley 2, Mitten | 47,653 |
| Apr 21 | SUNDERLAND | L 1-2 | Mitten (pen) | 30,640 |
| Apr 23 | PRESTON NORTH END | D 2-2 | Downie 2 | 43,214 |
| Apr 27 | Everton | L 0-2 | | 39,106 |
| Apr 30 | Newcastle United | W 1-0 | Burke | 38,266 |
| May 2 | MIDDLESBROUGH | W 1-0 | Rowley | 20,158 |
| May 4 | SHEFFIELD UNITED | W 3-2 | Mitten, Pearson, Downie | 20,880 |
| May 7 | PORTSMOUTH | W 3-2 | Rowley 2, Mitten (pen) | 49,808 |

## FA Cup

| | | | | | |
|---|---|---|---|---|---|
| Jan 8 | BOURNEMOUTH & BOSCOMBE ATHLETIC | (Rd3) | W 6-0 | Burke 2, Pearson, Rowley 2, Mitten | 55,012 |
| Jan 29 | BRADFORD PARK AVENUE | (Rd4) | D 1-1 | Mitten | 82,771 |
| Feb 5 | Bradford Park Avenue | (R) | D 1-1† | Mitten | 29,092 |
| Feb 7 | BRADFORD PARK AVENUE | (2R) | W 5-0 | Burke 2, Rowley 2, Pearson | 70,434 |
| Feb 12 | YEOVIL TOWN | (Rd5) | W 8-0 | Rowley 5, Burke 2, Mitten | 81,565 |
| Feb 26 | Hull City | (Rd6) | W 1-0 | Pearson | 55,000 |
| Mar 26 | Wolverhampton Wanderers* | (SF) | D 1-1† | Mitten | 62,250 |
| Apr 2 | Wolverhampton Wanderers** | (R) | L 0-1 | | 73,000 |

All home games at Maine Road, Manchester.
*Played at Hillsborough, Sheffield. **Played at Goodison Park, Liverpool.
† After extra-time.

## League & Cup Appearances

| PLAYER | LEAGUE | CUP COMPETITION FA CUP | TOTAL |
|---|---|---|---|
| Anderson | 15 | 1 | 16 |
| Aston | 39 | 8 | 47 |
| Ball | 8 | 1 | 9 |
| Brown | 1 | | 1 |
| Buckle | 5 | 2 | 7 |
| Burke | 9 | 6 | 15 |
| Carey | 41 | 7 | 48 |
| Cassidy | 1 | | 1 |
| Chilton | 42 | 8 | 50 |
| Cockburn | 36 | 8 | 44 |
| Crompton | 41 | 8 | 49 |
| Delaney | 36 | 6 | 42 |
| Downie | 12 | | 12 |
| Hanlon | 1 | | 1 |
| Lowrie | 8 | | 8 |
| McGlen | 23 | 8 | 31 |
| Mitten | 42 | 8 | 50 |
| Morris | 21 | 1 | 22 |
| Pearson | 39 | 8 | 47 |
| Rowley | 39 | 8 | 47 |
| Warner | 3 | | 3 |

## Goalscorers

| PLAYER | LEAGUE | CUP COMPETITION FA CUP | TOTAL |
|---|---|---|---|
| Rowley | 20 | 9 | 29 |
| Mitten | 18 | 5 | 23 |
| Pearson | 14 | 3 | 17 |
| Burke | 6 | 6 | 12 |
| Morris | 6 | | 6 |
| Downie | 5 | | 5 |
| Delaney | 4 | | 4 |
| Buckle | 2 | | 2 |
| Carey | 1 | | 1 |
| McGlen | 1 | | 1 |

## Final Division One Table

| | | P | W | D | L | F | A | Pts |
|---|---|---|---|---|---|---|---|---|
| 1 | Portsmouth | 42 | 25 | 8 | 9 | 84 | 42 | 58 |
| 2 | Manchester United | 42 | 21 | 11 | 10 | 77 | 44 | 53 |
| 3 | Derby County | 42 | 22 | 9 | 11 | 74 | 55 | 53 |
| 4 | Newcastle United | 42 | 20 | 12 | 10 | 70 | 56 | 52 |
| 5 | Arsenal | 42 | 18 | 13 | 11 | 74 | 44 | 49 |
| 6 | Wolverhampton W | 42 | 17 | 12 | 13 | 79 | 66 | 46 |
| 7 | Manchester City | 42 | 15 | 15 | 12 | 47 | 51 | 45 |
| 8 | Sunderland | 42 | 13 | 17 | 12 | 49 | 58 | 43 |
| 9 | Charlton Athletic | 42 | 15 | 12 | 15 | 63 | 67 | 42 |
| 10 | Aston Villa | 42 | 16 | 10 | 16 | 60 | 76 | 42 |
| 11 | Stoke City | 42 | 16 | 9 | 17 | 66 | 68 | 41 |
| 12 | Liverpool | 42 | 13 | 14 | 15 | 53 | 43 | 40 |
| 13 | Chelsea | 42 | 12 | 14 | 16 | 69 | 68 | 38 |
| 14 | Bolton Wanderers | 42 | 14 | 19 | 18 | 59 | 68 | 38 |
| 15 | Burnley | 42 | 12 | 14 | 16 | 43 | 50 | 38 |
| 16 | Blackpool | 42 | 11 | 16 | 15 | 54 | 67 | 38 |
| 17 | Birmingham City | 42 | 11 | 15 | 16 | 36 | 38 | 37 |
| 18 | Everton | 42 | 13 | 11 | 18 | 41 | 63 | 37 |
| 19 | Middlesbrough | 42 | 11 | 12 | 19 | 46 | 57 | 34 |
| 20 | Huddersfield Town | 42 | 12 | 10 | 20 | 40 | 69 | 34 |
| 21 | Preston North End | 42 | 11 | 11 | 20 | 62 | 75 | 33 |
| 22 | Sheffield United | 42 | 11 | 11 | 20 | 57 | 78 | 33 |

### Fact File

United's last season at Manchester City's Maine Road very nearly ended in success as the team finished second in the league and reached the FA Cup semi-final.

**MANAGER:** Matt Busby
**MOST APPEARANCES:** Allenby Chilton, Charlie Mitten 50
**TOP SCORER:** Jack Rowley 29 (20 League)
**BIGGEST WIN:** 8-0 v Yeovil Town, 12 February 1949, FA Cup
**HIGHEST ATTENDANCE:** 82,771 v Bradford Park Avenue, 29 January 1949, FA Cup

# Season 1949-50

## Football League Division One

| DATE | OPPONENTS | SCORE | GOALSCORERS | ATTENDANCE |
|---|---|---|---|---|
| Aug 20 | Derby County | W 1-0 | Rowley | 35,687 |
| Aug 24 | BOLTON WANDERERS | W 3-0 | Rowley, Mitten (pen), Gillies o.g. | 41,748 |
| Aug 27 | WEST BROMWICH ALBION | D 1-1 | Pearson | 44,655 |
| Aug 31 | Bolton Wanderers | W 2-1 | Mitten, Pearson | 36,277 |
| Sep 3 | MANCHESTER CITY | W 2-1 | Pearson 2 | 47,760 |
| Sep 7 | Liverpool | D 1-1 | Mitten | 51,587 |
| Sep 10 | Chelsea | D 1-1 | Rowley | 61,357 |
| Sep 17 | STOKE CITY | D 2-2 | Rowley 2 | 43,522 |
| Sep 24 | Burnley | L 0-1 | | 41,072 |
| Oct 1 | SUNDERLAND | L 1-3 | Pearson | 49,260 |
| Oct 8 | CHARLTON ATHLETIC | W 3-2 | Mitten 2 (1 pen), Rowley | 43,809 |
| Oct 15 | Aston Villa | W 4-0 | Mitten 2 (1 pen), Rowley, Bogan | 47,483 |
| Oct 22 | WOLVERHAMPTON WANDERERS | W 3-0 | Pearson 2, Bogan | 51,427 |
| Oct 29 | Portsmouth | D 0-0 | | 41,098 |
| Nov 5 | HUDDERSFIELD TOWN | W 6-0 | Rowley 2, Pearson 2, Delaney, Mitten | 40,295 |
| Nov 12 | Everton | D 0-0 | | 46,672 |
| Nov 19 | MIDDLESBROUGH | W 2-0 | Pearson, Rowley | 42,626 |
| Nov 26 | Blackpool | D 3-3 | Pearson 2, Bogan | 27,742 |
| Dec 3 | NEWCASTLE UNITED | D 1-1 | Mitten | 30,343 |
| Dec 10 | Fulham | L 0-1 | | 35,362 |
| Dec 17 | DERBY COUNTY | L 0-1 | | 33,753 |
| Dec 24 | West Bromwich Albion | W 2-1 | Bogan, Rowley | 46,973 |
| Dec 26 | ARSENAL | W 2-0 | Pearson 2 | 53,928 |
| Dec 27 | Arsenal | D 0-0 | | 65,133 |
| Dec 31 | Manchester City | W 2-1 | Delaney, Pearson | 63,704 |
| Jan 14 | CHELSEA | W 1-0 | Mitten | 46,954 |
| Jan 21 | Stoke City | L 1-3 | Mitten | 38,877 |
| Feb 4 | BURNLEY | W 3-2 | Rowley 2, Mitten | 46,702 |
| Feb 18 | Sunderland | D 2-2 | Rowley, Chilton | 63,251 |
| Feb 25 | Charlton Athletic | W 2-1 | Rowley, Carey | 44,920 |
| Mar 8 | ASTON VILLA | W 7-0 | Mitten 4 (3 pen), Downie 2, Rowley | 22,149 |
| Mar 11 | Middlesbrough | W 3-2 | Downie 2, Rowley | 46,702 |
| Mar 15 | LIVERPOOL | D 0-0 | | 43,456 |
| Mar 18 | BLACKPOOL | L 1-2 | Delaney | 53,688 |
| Mar 25 | Huddersfield Town | L 1-3 | Downie | 34,348 |
| Apr 1 | EVERTON | D 1-1 | Delaney | 35,381 |
| Apr 7 | BIRMINGHAM CITY | L 0-2 | | 47,170 |
| Apr 8 | Wolverhampton Wanderers | D 1-1 | Rowley | 54,296 |
| Apr 10 | Birmingham City | D 0-0 | | 35,863 |
| Apr 15 | PORTSMOUTH | L 0-2 | | 44,908 |
| Apr 22 | Newcastle United | L 1-2 | Downie | 52,203 |
| Apr 29 | FULHAM | W 3-0 | Rowley 2, Cockburn | 11,968 |

## FA Cup

| | | | | | |
|---|---|---|---|---|---|
| Jan 7 | WEYMOUTH | (Rd3) | W 4-0 | Rowley 2, Pearson, Delaney | 38,284 |
| Jan 28 | Watford | (Rd4) | W 1-0 | Rowley | 32,800 |
| Feb 11 | PORTSMOUTH | (Rd5) | D 3-3 | Mitten 2 (1 pen), Pearson | 53,688 |
| Feb 15 | Portsmouth | (R) | W 3-1 | Mitten, Downie, Delaney | 49,962 |
| Mar 4 | Chelsea | (Rd6) | L 0-2 | | 70,362 |

## League & Cup Appearances

| PLAYER | LEAGUE | CUP COMPETITION FA CUP | TOTAL |
|---|---|---|---|
| Aston | 40 | 5 | 45 |
| Ball | 13 | | 13 |
| Birch | 1 | | 1 |
| Bogan | 18 | 4 | 22 |
| Buckle | 7 | | 7 |
| Carey | 38 | 5 | 43 |
| Chilton | 35 | 5 | 40 |
| Clempson | 1 | | 1 |
| Cockburn | 35 | 5 | 40 |
| Crompton | 27 | 1 | 28 |
| Delaney | 42 | 5 | 47 |
| Downie | 18 | 2 | 20 |
| Feehan | 12 | 2 | 14 |
| Lancaster | 2 | 2 | 4 |
| Lowrie | 3 | | 3 |
| Lynn | 10 | | 10 |
| McGlen | 13 | 1 | 14 |
| McNulty | 2 | | 2 |
| Mitten | 42 | 5 | 47 |
| Pearson | 41 | 4 | 45 |
| Rowley | 39 | 5 | 44 |
| Warner | 21 | 4 | 25 |
| Whitefoot | 1 | | 1 |
| Wood | 1 | | 1 |

## Goalscorers

| PLAYER | LEAGUE | CUP COMPETITION FA CUP | TOTAL |
|---|---|---|---|
| Rowley | 20 | 3 | 23 |
| Mitten | 16 | 3 | 19 |
| Pearson | 15 | 2 | 17 |
| Downie | 6 | 1 | 7 |
| Delaney | 4 | 2 | 6 |
| Bogan | 4 | | 4 |
| Carey | 1 | | 1 |
| Chilton | 1 | | 1 |
| Cockburn | 1 | | 1 |
| Opps' o.gs. | 1 | | 1 |

## Fact File

Jeff Whitefoot, aged 16 years, 105 days, made his league bow against Portsmouth at Old Trafford on 15 April 1950, thus becoming United's youngest-ever league debutant.

**MANAGER:** Matt Busby
**MOST APPEARANCES:** Jimmy Delaney, Charlie Mitten 47
**TOP SCORER:** Jack Rowley 23 (20 League)
**BIGGEST WIN:** 7-0 v Aston Villa, 8 March 1950, League
**HIGHEST ATTENDANCE:** 70,362 v Chelsea, 4 March 1950, FA Cup

## Final Division One Table

| | | P | W | D | L | F | A | Pts |
|---|---|---|---|---|---|---|---|---|
| 1 | Portsmouth | 42 | 22 | 9 | 11 | 74 | 38 | 53 |
| 2 | Wolverhampton W | 42 | 20 | 13 | 9 | 76 | 49 | 53 |
| 3 | Sunderland | 42 | 21 | 10 | 11 | 83 | 62 | 52 |
| 4 | Manchester United | 42 | 18 | 14 | 10 | 69 | 44 | 50 |
| 5 | Newcastle United | 42 | 19 | 12 | 11 | 77 | 55 | 50 |
| 6 | Arsenal | 42 | 19 | 11 | 12 | 79 | 55 | 49 |
| 7 | Blackpool | 42 | 17 | 15 | 10 | 46 | 35 | 49 |
| 8 | Liverpool | 42 | 17 | 14 | 11 | 64 | 54 | 48 |
| 9 | Middlesbrough | 42 | 20 | 7 | 15 | 59 | 48 | 47 |
| 10 | Burnley | 42 | 16 | 13 | 13 | 40 | 40 | 45 |
| 11 | Derby County | 42 | 17 | 10 | 15 | 69 | 61 | 44 |
| 12 | Aston Villa | 42 | 15 | 12 | 15 | 61 | 61 | 42 |
| 13 | Chelsea | 42 | 12 | 16 | 14 | 58 | 65 | 40 |
| 14 | WBA | 42 | 14 | 12 | 16 | 47 | 53 | 40 |
| 15 | Huddersfield Town | 42 | 14 | 9 | 19 | 52 | 73 | 37 |
| 16 | Bolton Wanderers | 42 | 10 | 14 | 18 | 45 | 59 | 34 |
| 17 | Fulham | 42 | 10 | 14 | 18 | 41 | 54 | 34 |
| 18 | Everton | 42 | 10 | 14 | 18 | 42 | 66 | 34 |
| 19 | Stoke City | 42 | 11 | 12 | 19 | 45 | 75 | 34 |
| 20 | Charlton Athletic | 42 | 13 | 6 | 32 | 53 | 65 | 32 |
| 21 | Manchester City | 42 | 8 | 13 | 21 | 36 | 68 | 29 |
| 22 | Birmingham City | 42 | 7 | 14 | 21 | 31 | 67 | 28 |

# Season 1950-51

## Football League Division One

| DATE | OPPONENTS | SCORE | GOALSCORERS | ATTENDANCE |
|---|---|---|---|---|
| Aug 19 | FULHAM | W 1-0 | Pearson | 44,042 |
| Aug 23 | Liverpool | L 1-2 | Rowley | 30,211 |
| Aug 26 | Bolton Wanderers | L 0-1 | | 40,431 |
| Aug 30 | LIVERPOOL | W 1-0 | Downie | 34,835 |
| Sep 2 | BLACKPOOL | W 1-0 | Bogan | 53,260 |
| Sep 4 | Aston Villa | W 3-1 | Rowley 2, Pearson | 42,724 |
| Sep 9 | Tottenham Hotspur | L 0-1 | | 60,621 |
| Sep 13 | ASTON VILLA | D 0-0 | | 33,021 |
| Sep 16 | CHARLTON ATHLETIC | W 3-0 | Rowley, Pearson, Delaney | 36,619 |
| Sep 23 | Middlesbrough | W 2-1 | Pearson 2 | 48,051 |
| Sep 30 | Wolverhampton Wanderers | D 0-0 | | 45,898 |
| Oct 7 | SHEFFIELD WEDNESDAY | W 3-1 | Downie, McShane, Rowley | 40,651 |
| Oct 14 | Arsenal | L 0-3 | | 66,150 |
| Oct 21 | Portsmouth | D 0-0 | | 41,842 |
| Oct 28 | Everton | W 4-1 | Rowley 2, Pearson, Aston | 51,142 |
| Nov 4 | BURNLEY | D 1-1 | McShane | 39,454 |
| Nov 11 | Chelsea | L 0-1 | | 51,882 |
| Nov 18 | STOKE CITY | D 0-0 | | 30,031 |
| Nov 25 | West Bromwich Albion | W 1-0 | Birch | 28,146 |
| Dec 2 | NEWCASTLE UNITED | L 1-2 | Birch | 34,502 |
| Dec 9 | Huddersfield Town | W 3-2 | Aston 2, Birkett | 26,713 |
| Dec 16 | Fulham | D 2-2 | Pearson 2 | 19,649 |
| Dec 23 | BOLTON WANDERERS | L 2-3 | Pearson, Aston | 35,382 |
| Dec 25 | Sunderland | L 1-2 | Aston | 41,215 |
| Dec 26 | SUNDERLAND | L 3-5 | Bogan 2, Aston | 35,176 |
| Jan 13 | TOTTENHAM HOTSPUR | W 2-1 | Birch, Rowley | 43,283 |
| Jan 20 | Charlton Athletic | W 2-1 | Birkett, Aston | 31,978 |
| Feb 3 | MIDDLESBROUGH | W 1-0 | Pearson | 44,633 |
| Feb 17 | WOLVERHAMPTON WANDERERS | W 2-1 | Rowley, Birch | 42,022 |
| Feb 26 | Sheffield Wednesday | W 4-0 | Pearson, Downie, Rowley, Aston | 25,693 |
| Mar 3 | ARSENAL | W 3-1 | Aston 2, Downie | 46,202 |
| Mar 10 | Portsmouth | D 0-0 | | 33,148 |
| Mar 17 | EVERTON | W 3-0 | Aston, Downie, Pearson | 29,317 |
| Mar 23 | DERBY COUNTY | W 2-0 | Downie, Aston | 42,009 |
| Mar 24 | Burnley | W 2-1 | McShane, Aston | 36,656 |
| Mar 26 | Derby County | W 4-2 | Pearson, Downie, Rowley, Aston | 25,860 |
| Mar 31 | CHELSEA | W 4-1 | Pearson 3, McShane | 25,779 |
| Apr 7 | Stoke City | L 0-2 | | 25,690 |
| Apr 14 | WEST BROMWICH ALBION | W 3-0 | Rowley, Pearson, Downie | 24,764 |
| Apr 21 | Newcastle United | W 2-0 | Rowley, Pearson | 45,209 |
| Apr 28 | HUDDERSFIELD TOWN | W 6-0 | McShane 2, Aston 2, Rowley (pen), Downie | 25,560 |
| May 5 | Blackpool | D 1-1 | Downie | 22,864 |

## FA Cup

| | | | | |
|---|---|---|---|---|
| Jan 6 | OLDHAM ATHLETIC | (Rd3) W 4-1 | Pearson, Aston, Birch, Whyte o.g. | 37,161 |
| Jan 27 | LEEDS UNITED | (Rd4) W 4-0 | Pearson 3, Rowley | 55,434 |
| Feb 10 | ARSENAL | (Rd5) W 1-0 | Pearson | 55,058 |
| Feb 24 | Birmingham City | (Rd6) L 0-1 | | 50,000 |

## League & Cup Appearances

| PLAYER | LEAGUE | CUP COMPETITION FA CUP | TOTAL |
|---|---|---|---|
| Allen | 40 | 4 | 44 |
| Aston | 41 | 4 | 45 |
| Birch | 8 | 4 | 12 |
| Birkett | 9 | 4 | 13 |
| Bogan | 11 | | 11 |
| Carey | 39 | 4 | 43 |
| Cassidy | 1 | | 1 |
| Chilton | 38 | 4 | 42 |
| Clempson | 2 | | 2 |
| Cockburn | 35 | 4 | 39 |
| Crompton | 2 | | 2 |
| Delaney | 13 | | 13 |
| Downie | 29 | | 29 |
| Gibson | 32 | 3 | 35 |
| Jones | 4 | | 4 |
| Lowrie | | 1 | 1 |
| McGlen | 26 | 1 | 27 |
| McIlvenney | 2 | | 2 |
| McNulty | 4 | 1 | 5 |
| McShane | 30 | 1 | 31 |
| Pearson | 39 | 4 | 43 |
| Redman | 16 | 2 | 18 |
| Rowley | 39 | 3 | 42 |
| Whitefoot | 2 | | 2 |

## Goalscorers

| PLAYER | LEAGUE | CUP COMPETITION FA CUP | TOTAL |
|---|---|---|---|
| Pearson | 18 | 5 | 23 |
| Aston | 15 | 1 | 16 |
| Rowley | 14 | 1 | 15 |
| Downie | 10 | | 10 |
| McShane | 7 | | 7 |
| Birch | 4 | 1 | 5 |
| Bogan | 3 | | 3 |
| Birkett | 2 | | 2 |
| Delaney | 1 | | 1 |
| Opps' o.gs. | | 1 | 1 |

## Final Division One Table

| | P | W | D | L | F | A | Pts |
|---|---|---|---|---|---|---|---|
| 1 Tottenham Hotspur | 42 | 25 | 10 | 7 | 82 | 44 | 60 |
| 2 Manchester United | 42 | 24 | 8 | 10 | 74 | 40 | 56 |
| 3 Blackpool | 42 | 20 | 10 | 12 | 79 | 53 | 50 |
| 4 Newcastle United | 42 | 18 | 13 | 11 | 62 | 53 | 49 |
| 5 Arsenal | 42 | 19 | 9 | 14 | 73 | 56 | 47 |
| 6 Middlesbrough | 42 | 18 | 11 | 13 | 76 | 65 | 47 |
| 7 Portsmouth | 42 | 16 | 15 | 11 | 71 | 68 | 47 |
| 8 Bolton Wanderers | 42 | 19 | 7 | 16 | 64 | 61 | 45 |
| 9 Liverpool | 42 | 16 | 11 | 15 | 53 | 59 | 43 |
| 10 Burnley | 42 | 14 | 14 | 14 | 48 | 43 | 42 |
| 11 Derby County | 42 | 16 | 8 | 18 | 81 | 75 | 40 |
| 12 Sunderland | 42 | 12 | 16 | 14 | 63 | 73 | 40 |
| 13 Stoke City | 42 | 13 | 14 | 15 | 50 | 59 | 40 |
| 14 Wolverhampton W | 42 | 15 | 8 | 19 | 74 | 61 | 38 |
| 15 Aston Villa | 42 | 12 | 13 | 17 | 66 | 68 | 37 |
| 16 WBA | 42 | 13 | 11 | 18 | 53 | 61 | 37 |
| 17 Charlton Athletic | 42 | 14 | 9 | 19 | 63 | 80 | 37 |
| 18 Fulham | 42 | 13 | 11 | 18 | 52 | 68 | 37 |
| 19 Huddersfield Town | 42 | 15 | 6 | 21 | 64 | 92 | 36 |
| 20 Chelsea | 42 | 12 | 8 | 22 | 53 | 65 | 32 |
| 21 Sheffield Wednesday | 42 | 12 | 8 | 22 | 64 | 83 | 32 |
| 22 Everton | 42 | 12 | 8 | 22 | 48 | 86 | 32 |

### Fact File

United missed out on the league title again as they finished in the runners-up spot for the fourth time in five seasons.

**MANAGER:** Matt Busby
**MOST APPEARANCES:** John Aston 45
**TOP SCORER:** Stan Pearson 23 (18 League)
**BIGGEST WIN:** 6-0 v Huddersfield Town, 28 April 1951, League
**HIGHEST ATTENDANCE:** 66,150 v Arsenal, 14 October 1950, League

# Season 1951-52

## Football League Division One

| DATE | OPPONENTS | SCORE | GOALSCORERS | ATTENDANCE |
|---|---|---|---|---|
| Aug 18 | West Bromwich Albion | D 3-3 | Rowley 3 | 27,486 |
| Aug 22 | MIDDLESBROUGH | W 4-2 | Rowley 3, Pearson | 37,339 |
| Aug 25 | Newcastle United | W 2-1 | Rowley, Downie | 51,850 |
| Aug 29 | Middlesbrough | W 4-1 | Pearson 2, Rowley 2 | 44,212 |
| Sep 11 | Bolton Wanderers | L 0-1 | | 52,239 |
| Sep 5 | CHARLTON ATHLETIC | W 3-2 | Rowley 2, Downie | 26,773 |
| Sep 8 | STOKE CITY | W 4-0 | Rowley 3, Pearson | 43,660 |
| Sep 12 | Charlton Athletic | D 2-2 | Downie 2 | 28,806 |
| Sep 15 | Manchester City | W 2-1 | Berry, McShane | 52,571 |
| Sep 22 | Tottenham Hotspur | L 0-2 | | 70,882 |
| Sep 29 | PRESTON NORTH END | L 1-2 | Aston | 53,454 |
| Oct 6 | DERBY COUNTY | W 2-1 | Pearson, Berry | 39,767 |
| Oct 13 | Aston Villa | W 5-2 | Pearson 2, Rowley 2, Bond | 47,795 |
| Oct 20 | SUNDERLAND | L 0-1 | | 40,915 |
| Oct 27 | Wolverhampton Wanderers | W 2-0 | Pearson, Rowley | 46,167 |
| Nov 3 | HUDDERSFIELD TOWN | D 1-1 | Pearson | 25,616 |
| Nov 10 | Chelsea | L 2-4 | Pearson, Rowley | 48,960 |
| Nov 17 | PORTSMOUTH | L 1-3 | Downie | 35,914 |
| Nov 24 | Liverpool | D 0-0 | | 42,378 |
| Dec 1 | BLACKPOOL | W 3-1 | Downie 2, Rowley | 34,154 |
| Dec 8 | Arsenal | W 3-1 | Rowley, Pearson, Daniels o.g. | 55,451 |
| Dec 15 | WEST BROMWICH ALBION | W 5-1 | Pearson 2, Downie 2, Berry | 27,584 |
| Dec 22 | Newcastle United | D 2-2 | Cockburn, Bond | 45,414 |
| Dec 25 | FULHAM | W 3-2 | Bond, Rowley, Berry | 33,802 |
| Dec 26 | Fulham | D 3-3 | Rowley, Pearson, Bond | 32,671 |
| Dec 29 | BOLTON WANDERERS | W 1-0 | Pearson | 53,205 |
| Jan 5 | Stoke City | D 0-0 | | 36,389 |
| Jan 19 | MANCHESTER CITY | D 1-1 | Carey | 54,245 |
| Jan 26 | TOTTENHAM HOTSPUR | W 2-0 | Pearson, Ramsay o.g. | 40,845 |
| Feb 9 | Preston North End | W 2-1 | Aston, Berry | 38,792 |
| Feb 16 | Derby County | W 3-0 | Pearson, Rowley, Aston | 27,693 |
| Mar 1 | ASTON VILLA | D 1-1 | Berry | 39,910 |
| Mar 8 | Sunderland | W 2-1 | Rowley, Cockburn | 48,078 |
| Mar 15 | WOLVERHAMPTON WANDERERS | W 2-0 | Clempson, Aston | 45,109 |
| Mar 22 | Huddersfield Town | L 2-3 | Clempson, Pearson | 30,316 |
| Apr 5 | Portsmouth | L 0-1 | | 25,522 |
| Apr 11 | Burnley | D 1-1 | Byrne | 38,907 |
| Apr 12 | LIVERPOOL | W 4-0 | Byrne 2 (1 pen), Downie, Rowley | 42,970 |
| Apr 14 | BURNLEY | W 6-1 | Byrne 2, Rowley, Downie, Pearson, Carey | 44,508 |
| Apr 19 | Blackpool | D 2-2 | Byrne, Rowley | 29,118 |
| Apr 21 | CHELSEA | W 3-0 | Pearson, Carey, McKnight o.g. | 37,436 |
| Apr 26 | ARSENAL | W 6-1 | Rowley 3 (1 pen), Pearson 2, Byrne | 53,651 |

## FA Cup

| | | | | |
|---|---|---|---|---|
| Jan 12 | HULL CITY | (Rd3) L 0-2 | | 43,517 |

## League & Cup Appearances

| PLAYER | LEAGUE | CUP COMPETITION FA CUP | TOTAL |
|---|---|---|---|
| Allen | 33 | 1 | 34 |
| Aston | 18 | | 18 |
| Berry | 36 | 1 | 37 |
| Birch | 2 | | 2 |
| Blanchflower | 1 | | 1 |
| Bond | 19 | 1 | 20 |
| Byrne | 24 | 1 | 25 |
| Carey | 38 | 1 | 39 |
| Cassidy | 1 | | 1 |
| Chilton | 42 | 1 | 43 |
| Clempson | 8 | | 8 |
| Cockburn | 38 | 1 | 39 |
| Crompton | 9 | | 9 |
| Downie | 31 | 1 | 32 |
| Gibson | 17 | | 17 |
| Jones | 3 | | 3 |
| McGlen | 2 | | 2 |
| McNulty | 24 | 1 | 25 |
| McShane | 12 | | 12 |
| Pearson | 41 | 1 | 42 |
| Redman | 18 | | 18 |
| Rowley | 40 | 1 | 41 |
| Walton | 2 | | 2 |
| Whitefoot | 3 | | 3 |

## Goalscorers

| PLAYER | LEAGUE | CUP COMPETITION FA CUP | TOTAL |
|---|---|---|---|
| Rowley | 30 | | 30 |
| Pearson | 22 | | 22 |
| Downie | 11 | | 11 |
| Byrne | 7 | | 7 |
| Berry | 6 | | 6 |
| Aston | 4 | | 4 |
| Bond | 4 | | 4 |
| Carey | 3 | | 3 |
| Clempson | 2 | | 2 |
| Cockburn | 2 | | 2 |
| McShane | 1 | | 1 |
| Opps' o.gs. | 3 | | 3 |

## Fact File

Champions at last! United beat off a strong challenge from north London pair Arsenal and Tottenham Hotspur to land their first championship since 1911.

**MANAGER:** Matt Busby

**MOST APPEARANCES:** Allenby Chilton 43

**TOP SCORER:** Jack Rowley 30 (all League)

**BIGGEST WIN:** 6-1 v Burnley, 14 April 1952, League; 6-1 v Arsenal, 26 April 1952, League

**HIGHEST ATTENDANCE:** 70,882 v Tottenham Hotspur, 22 September 1951, League

## Final Division One Table

| | P | W | D | L | F | A | Pts |
|---|---|---|---|---|---|---|---|
| 1 Manchester United | 42 | 23 | 11 | 8 | 95 | 52 | 57 |
| 2 Tottenham Hotspur | 42 | 22 | 9 | 11 | 76 | 51 | 53 |
| 3 Arsenal | 42 | 21 | 11 | 10 | 80 | 61 | 53 |
| 4 Portsmouth | 42 | 20 | 8 | 14 | 68 | 56 | 48 |
| 5 Bolton Wanderers | 42 | 19 | 10 | 13 | 65 | 61 | 48 |
| 6 Aston Villa | 42 | 19 | 9 | 14 | 79 | 70 | 47 |
| 7 Preston North End | 42 | 17 | 12 | 13 | 74 | 54 | 46 |
| 8 Newcastle United | 42 | 18 | 9 | 15 | 98 | 73 | 45 |
| 9 Blackpool | 42 | 18 | 9 | 15 | 64 | 74 | 45 |
| 10 Charlton Athletic | 42 | 17 | 10 | 15 | 68 | 63 | 44 |
| 11 Liverpool | 42 | 12 | 19 | 11 | 57 | 61 | 43 |
| 12 Sunderland | 42 | 15 | 12 | 15 | 70 | 61 | 42 |
| 13 WBA | 42 | 14 | 13 | 15 | 74 | 77 | 41 |
| 14 Burnley | 42 | 15 | 10 | 17 | 56 | 63 | 40 |
| 15 Manchester City | 42 | 13 | 13 | 16 | 58 | 61 | 39 |
| 16 Wolverhampton W | 42 | 12 | 14 | 16 | 73 | 73 | 38 |
| 17 Derby County | 42 | 15 | 7 | 20 | 63 | 80 | 37 |
| 18 Middlesbrough | 42 | 15 | 6 | 21 | 64 | 88 | 36 |
| 19 Chelsea | 42 | 14 | 8 | 20 | 52 | 72 | 36 |
| 20 Stoke City | 42 | 12 | 7 | 23 | 49 | 88 | 31 |
| 21 Huddersfield Town | 42 | 10 | 8 | 24 | 49 | 82 | 28 |
| 22 Fulham | 42 | 8 | 11 | 23 | 58 | 77 | 27 |

## Season 1952-53

### Football League Division One

| DATE | OPPONENTS | SCORE | GOALSCORERS | ATTENDANCE |
|---|---|---|---|---|
| Aug 23 | CHELSEA | W 2-0 | Downie, Berry | 43,629 |
| Aug 27 | Arsenal | L 1-2 | Rowley | 58,831 |
| Aug 30 | Manchester City | L 1-2 | Downie | 56,140 |
| Sep 3 | ARSENAL | D 0-0 | | 39,193 |
| Sep 6 | Portsmouth | L 0-2 | | 37,278 |
| Sep 10 | Derby County | W 3-2 | Pearson 3 | 20,226 |
| Sep 13 | BOLTON WANDERERS | W 1-0 | Berry | 40,531 |
| Sep 20 | Aston Villa | D 3-3 | Rowley 2 (pens), Downie | 43,490 |
| Sep 27 | SUNDERLAND | L 0-1 | | 28,967 |
| Oct 4 | Wolverhampton Wanderers | L 2-6 | Rowley 2 | 40,132 |
| Oct 11 | STOKE CITY | L 0-2 | | 28,968 |
| Oct 18 | Preston North End | W 5-0 | Aston 2, Pearson 2, Rowley | 33,502 |
| Oct 25 | BURNLEY | L 1-3 | Aston | 36,913 |
| Nov 1 | Tottenham Hotspur | W 2-1 | Berry 2 | 44,300 |
| Nov 8 | SHEFFIELD WEDNESDAY | D 1-1 | Pearson | 48,571 |
| Nov 15 | Cardiff City | W 2-1 | Aston, Pearson | 40,096 |
| Nov 22 | NEWCASTLE UNITED | D 2-2 | Aston, Pearson | 33,528 |
| Nov 29 | West Bromwich Albion | L 1-3 | Lewis | 23,499 |
| Dec 6 | MIDDLESBROUGH | W 3-2 | Pearson 2, Aston | 27,617 |
| Dec 13 | Liverpool | W 2-1 | Aston, Pearson | 34,450 |
| Dec 20 | Chelsea | W 3-2 | Doherty 2, Aston | 23,261 |
| Dec 25 | Blackpool | D 0-0 | | 27,778 |
| Dec 26 | BLACKPOOL | W 2-1 | Carey, Lewis | 48,077 |
| Jan 1 | DERBY COUNTY | W 1-0 | Lewis | 34,813 |
| Jan 3 | MANCHESTER CITY | D 1-1 | Pearson | 47,883 |
| Jan 17 | PORTSMOUTH | W 1-0 | Lewis | 32,341 |
| Jan 24 | Bolton Wanderers | L 1-2 | Lewis | 43,638 |
| Feb 7 | ASTON VILLA | W 3-1 | Rowley 2, Lewis | 34,339 |
| Feb 18 | Sunderland | D 2-2 | Pegg, Lewis | 24,263 |
| Feb 21 | WOLVERHAMPTON WANDERERS | L 0-3 | | 38,269 |
| Feb 28 | Stoke City | L 1-3 | Berry | 30,219 |
| Mar 7 | PRESTON NORTH END | W 5-2 | Taylor 2, Pegg 2, Rowley | 52,590 |
| Mar 14 | Burnley | L 1-2 | Byrne | 45,682 |
| Mar 25 | TOTTENHAM HOTSPUR | W 3-2 | Pearson 2, Pegg | 18,384 |
| Mar 28 | Sheffield Wednesday | D 0-0 | | 36,509 |
| Apr 3 | Charlton Athletic | D 2-2 | Taylor, Berry | 41,814 |
| Apr 4 | CARDIFF CITY | L 1-4 | Byrne (pen) | 37,163 |
| Apr 6 | CHARLTON ATHLETIC | W 3-2 | Taylor 2, Rowley | 30,105 |
| Apr 11 | Newcastle United | W 2-1 | Taylor 2 | 38,970 |
| Apr 18 | WEST BROMWICH ALBION | D 2-2 | Pearson, Viollet | 31,380 |
| Apr 20 | LIVERPOOL | W 3-1 | Pearson, Rowley, Berry | 20,869 |
| Apr 25 | Middlesbrough | L 0-5 | | 34,344 |

### FA Cup

| | | | | | |
|---|---|---|---|---|---|
| Jan 10 | Millwall | (Rd3) | W 1-0 | Pearson | 35,652 |
| Jan 31 | WALTHAMSTOW AVENUE | (Rd4) | D 1-1 | Lewis | 34,748 |
| Feb 5 | Walthamstow Avenue* | (R) | W 5-2 | Pearson, Lewis, Rowley 2, Byrne (pen) | 49,119 |
| Feb 14 | Everton | (Rd5) | L 1-2 | Rowley | 77,920 |

*Played at Arsenal Stadium, London.

### FA Charity Shield

| | | | | |
|---|---|---|---|---|
| Sep 24 | NEWCASTLE UNITED | W 4-2 | Rowley 2, Downie, Byrne | 11,381 |

### Fact File

Duncan Edwards, thought by many to be the greatest United player of all-time despite losing his life, aged 21, in the Munich air disaster, made his league debut against Cardiff City at Old Trafford.

**MANAGER:** Matt Busby
**MOST APPEARANCES:** Allenby Chilton 47
**TOP SCORER:** Stan Pearson 18 (16 League)
**BIGGEST WIN:** 5-0 v Preston North End , 18 October 1952, League
**HIGHEST ATTENDANCE:** 77,920 v Everton, 14 February 1953, FA Cup

### League & Cup Appearances

| PLAYER | LEAGUE | CUP COMPETITION FA CUP | OTHER | TOTAL |
|---|---|---|---|---|
| Allen | 2 | | | 2 |
| Aston | 40 | 4 | 1 | 45 |
| Berry | 40 | 4 | 1 | 45 |
| Blanchflower | 1 | | | 1 |
| Bond | 1 | | | 1 |
| Byrne | 40 | 4 | 1 | 45 |
| Carey | 32 | 4 | 1 | 37 |
| Clempson | 4 | | | 4 |
| Cockburn | 22 | 4 | | 26 |
| Crompton | 25 | | | 25 |
| Chilton | 42 | 4 | 1 | 47 |
| Doherty | 5 | | | 5 |
| Downie | 20 | 2 | 1 | 23 |
| Edwards | 1 | | | 1 |
| Foulkes | 2 | | | 2 |
| Gibson | 20 | | 1 | 21 |
| Jones | 2 | | | 2 |
| Lewis | 10 | 4 | | 14 |
| McNulty | 23 | | 1 | 24 |
| McShane | 5 | | | 5 |
| Olive | 2 | | | 2 |
| Pearson | 39 | 4 | 1 | 44 |
| Pegg | 19 | 2 | | 21 |
| Redman | 1 | | | 1 |
| Rowley | 26 | 4 | 1 | 31 |
| Scott | 2 | | | 2 |
| Taylor | 11 | | | 11 |
| Viollet | 2 | | | 2 |
| Whitefoot | 10 | | | 10 |
| Wood | 12 | 4 | 1 | 17 |

### Goalscorers

| PLAYER | LEAGUE | CUP COMPETITION FA CUP | OTHER | TOTAL |
|---|---|---|---|---|
| Pearson | 16 | 2 | | 18 |
| Rowley | 11 | 3 | 2 | 16 |
| Lewis | 7 | 2 | | 9 |
| Aston | 8 | | | 8 |
| Berry | 7 | | | 7 |
| Taylor | 7 | | | 7 |
| Pegg | 4 | | | 4 |
| Downie | 3 | | 1 | 4 |
| Byrne | 2 | 1 | 1 | 4 |
| Doherty | 2 | | | 2 |
| Carey | 1 | | | 1 |
| Viollet | 1 | | | 1 |

### Final Division One Table

| | | P | W | D | L | F | A | PTS |
|---|---|---|---|---|---|---|---|---|
| 1 | Arsenal | 42 | 21 | 12 | 9 | 97 | 64 | 54 |
| 2 | Preston North End | 42 | 21 | 12 | 9 | 85 | 60 | 54 |
| 3 | Wolverhampton W | 42 | 19 | 13 | 10 | 86 | 63 | 51 |
| 4 | WBA | 42 | 21 | 8 | 13 | 66 | 60 | 50 |
| 5 | Charlton Athletic | 42 | 19 | 11 | 12 | 77 | 63 | 49 |
| 6 | Burnley | 42 | 18 | 12 | 12 | 67 | 52 | 48 |
| 7 | Blackpool | 42 | 19 | 9 | 14 | 71 | 70 | 47 |
| 8 | Manchester United | 42 | 18 | 10 | 14 | 69 | 72 | 46 |
| 9 | Sunderland | 42 | 15 | 13 | 14 | 68 | 82 | 43 |
| 10 | Tottenham Hotspur | 42 | 15 | 11 | 16 | 78 | 69 | 41 |
| 11 | Aston Villa | 42 | 14 | 13 | 15 | 63 | 61 | 41 |
| 12 | Cardiff City | 42 | 14 | 12 | 16 | 54 | 46 | 40 |
| 13 | Middlesbrough | 42 | 14 | 11 | 17 | 70 | 77 | 39 |
| 14 | Bolton Wanderers | 42 | 15 | 9 | 18 | 61 | 69 | 39 |
| 15 | Portsmouth | 42 | 14 | 10 | 18 | 74 | 83 | 38 |
| 16 | Newcastle United | 42 | 14 | 9 | 19 | 59 | 70 | 37 |
| 17 | Liverpool | 42 | 14 | 8 | 20 | 61 | 82 | 36 |
| 18 | Sheffield Wednesday | 42 | 12 | 11 | 19 | 62 | 72 | 35 |
| 19 | Chelsea | 42 | 12 | 11 | 19 | 56 | 66 | 35 |
| 20 | Manchester City | 42 | 14 | 7 | 21 | 72 | 87 | 35 |
| 21 | Stoke City | 42 | 12 | 10 | 20 | 53 | 66 | 34 |
| 22 | Derby County | 42 | 11 | 10 | 21 | 59 | 74 | 32 |

# Season 1953-54

## Football League Division One

| DATE | OPPONENTS | SCORE | GOALSCORERS | ATTENDANCE |
|---|---|---|---|---|
| Aug 19 | CHELSEA | D 1-1 | Pearson | 28,936 |
| Aug 22 | Liverpool | D 4-4 | Lewis, Rowley, Taylor, Byrne (pen) | 48,422 |
| Aug 26 | WEST BROMWICH ALBION | L 1-3 | Taylor | 31,806 |
| Aug 29 | NEWCASTLE UNITED | D 1-1 | Chilton | 27,837 |
| Sep 2 | West Bromwich Albion | L 0-2 | | 28,892 |
| Sep 5 | Manchester City | L 0-2 | | 53,097 |
| Sep 9 | MIDDLESBROUGH | D 2-2 | Rowley 2 | 18,161 |
| Sep 12 | Bolton Wanderers | D 0-0 | | 43,544 |
| Sep 16 | Middlesbrough | W 4-1 | Taylor 2, Rowley, Byrne (pen) | 23,607 |
| Sep 19 | PRESTON NORTH END | W 1-0 | Byrne | 41,171 |
| Sep 26 | Tottenham Hotspur | D 1-1 | Rowley | 52,837 |
| Oct 3 | BURNLEY | L 1-2 | Pearson | 37,696 |
| Oct 10 | SUNDERLAND | W 1-0 | Rowley | 34,617 |
| Oct 17 | Wolverhampton Wanderers | L 1-3 | Taylor | 40,084 |
| Oct 24 | ASTON VILLA | W 1-0 | Berry | 30,266 |
| Oct 31 | Huddersfield Town | D 0-0 | | 34,175 |
| Nov 7 | ARSENAL | D 2-2 | Blanchflower, Rowley | 28,141 |
| Nov 14 | Cardiff City | W 6-1 | Viollet 2, Taylor, Blanchflower, Berry, Rowley | 26,844 |
| Nov 21 | BLACKPOOL | W 4-1 | Taylor 3, Viollet | 49,853 |
| Nov 28 | Portsmouth | D 1-1 | Taylor | 29,233 |
| Dec 5 | SHEFFIELD UNITED | D 2-2 | Blanchflower 2 | 31,693 |
| Dec 12 | Chelsea | L 1-3 | Berry | 37,153 |
| Dec 19 | LIVERPOOL | W 5-1 | Blanchflower 2, Taylor 2, Viollet | 26,074 |
| Dec 25 | SHEFFIELD WEDNESDAY | W 5-2 | Taylor 3, Blanchflower, Viollet | 27,123 |
| Dec 26 | Sheffield Wednesday | W 1-0 | Viollet | 44,196 |
| Jan 2 | Newcastle United | W 2-1 | Blanchflower, Foulkes | 55,780 |
| Jan 16 | MANCHESTER CITY | D 1-1 | Berry | 46,379 |
| Jan 23 | BOLTON WANDERERS | L 1-5 | Taylor | 46,663 |
| Feb 6 | Preston North End | W 3-1 | Blanchflower, Rowley, Taylor | 30,064 |
| Feb 13 | TOTTENHAM HOTSPUR | W 2-0 | Taylor, Rowley | 35,485 |
| Feb 20 | Burnley | L 0-2 | | 29,576 |
| Feb 27 | Sunderland | W 2-0 | Taylor, Blanchflower | 58,440 |
| Mar 6 | WOLVERHAMPTON WANDERERS | W 1-0 | Berry | 38,939 |
| Mar 13 | Aston Villa | D 2-2 | Taylor 2 | 26,023 |
| Mar 20 | HUDDERSFIELD TOWN | W 3-1 | Viollet, Blanchflower, Rowley | 40,181 |
| Mar 27 | Arsenal | L 1-3 | Taylor | 42,753 |
| Apr 3 | CARDIFF CITY | L 2-3 | Viollet, Rowley | 22,832 |
| Apr 10 | Blackpool | L 0-2 | | 25,996 |
| Apr 16 | CHARLTON ATHLETIC | W 2-0 | Aston, Viollet | 31,876 |
| Apr 17 | PORTSMOUTH | W 2-0 | Blanchflower, Viollet | 29,663 |
| Apr 19 | Charlton Athletic | L 0-1 | | 19,111 |
| Apr 24 | Sheffield United | W 3-1 | Blanchflower, Viollet, Aston | 29,189 |

## FA Cup

| | | | | |
|---|---|---|---|---|
| Jan 9 | Burnley | (Rd3) L 3-5 | Taylor, Viollet, Aird o.g. | 54,000 |

## League & Cup Appearances

| PLAYER | LEAGUE | CUP COMPETITION FA CUP | TOTAL |
|---|---|---|---|
| Aston | 12 | | 13 |
| Crompton | 15 | | 15 |
| Blanchflower | 27 | 1 | 28 |
| Berry | 37 | 1 | 38 |
| Byrne | 41 | 1 | 42 |
| Chilton | 42 | 1 | 43 |
| Cockburn | 18 | | 18 |
| Edwards | 34 | 1 | 35 |
| Foulkes | 32 | 1 | 33 |
| Gibson | 7 | | 7 |
| Lewis | 6 | | 6 |
| McFarlane | 1 | | 1 |
| McNulty | 4 | | 4 |
| McShane | 9 | | 9 |
| Pearson | 11 | | 11 |
| Pegg | 9 | | 9 |
| Redman | 1 | | 1 |
| Rowley | 36 | 1 | 37 |
| Taylor | 35 | 1 | 36 |
| Webster | 1 | | 1 |
| Whitefoot | 38 | 1 | 39 |
| Wood | 27 | 1 | 28 |
| Viollet | 29 | 1 | 30 |

## Goalscorers

| PLAYER | LEAGUE | CUP COMPETITION FA CUP | TOTAL |
|---|---|---|---|
| Taylor | 22 | 1 | 23 |
| Blanchflower | 13 | | 13 |
| Rowley | 12 | | 12 |
| Viollet | 11 | 1 | 12 |
| Berry | 5 | | 5 |
| Byrne | 3 | | 3 |
| Aston | 2 | | 2 |
| Pearson | 2 | | 2 |
| Chilton | 1 | | 1 |
| Foulkes | 1 | | 1 |
| Lewis | 1 | | 1 |
| Opps' o.gs. | | 1 | 1 |

## Final Division One Table

| | | P | W | D | L | F | A | Pts |
|---|---|---|---|---|---|---|---|---|
| 1 | Wolverhampton W | 42 | 25 | 7 | 10 | 96 | 56 | 57 |
| 2 | WBA | 42 | 22 | 9 | 11 | 86 | 63 | 53 |
| 3 | Huddersfield Town | 42 | 20 | 11 | 11 | 78 | 61 | 51 |
| 4 | Manchester United | 42 | 18 | 12 | 12 | 73 | 58 | 48 |
| 5 | Bolton Wanderers | 42 | 18 | 12 | 12 | 75 | 60 | 48 |
| 6 | Blackpool | 42 | 19 | 10 | 13 | 80 | 69 | 48 |
| 7 | Burnley | 42 | 21 | 4 | 17 | 78 | 67 | 46 |
| 8 | Chelsea | 42 | 16 | 12 | 14 | 74 | 68 | 44 |
| 9 | Charlton Athletic | 42 | 19 | 6 | 17 | 75 | 77 | 44 |
| 10 | Cardiff City | 42 | 18 | 8 | 16 | 51 | 71 | 44 |
| 11 | Preston North End | 42 | 19 | 5 | 18 | 87 | 58 | 43 |
| 12 | Arsenal | 42 | 15 | 13 | 14 | 75 | 73 | 43 |
| 13 | Aston Villa | 42 | 16 | 9 | 17 | 70 | 68 | 41 |
| 14 | Portsmouth | 42 | 14 | 11 | 17 | 81 | 89 | 39 |
| 15 | Newcastle United | 42 | 14 | 10 | 8 | 72 | 77 | 38 |
| 16 | Tottenham Hotspur | 42 | 16 | 5 | 21 | 65 | 76 | 37 |
| 17 | Manchester City | 42 | 14 | 9 | 19 | 62 | 77 | 37 |
| 18 | Sunderland | 42 | 14 | 8 | 20 | 81 | 89 | 36 |
| 19 | Sheffield Wednesday | 42 | 15 | 6 | 21 | 70 | 91 | 36 |
| 20 | Sheffield United | 42 | 11 | 11 | 20 | 69 | 90 | 33 |
| 21 | Middlesbrough | 42 | 10 | 10 | 22 | 60 | 91 | 30 |
| 22 | Liverpool | 42 | 9 | 10 | 23 | 68 | 97 | 28 |

### Fact File

A poor start to the season – no wins in the opening eight games – damaged United's chances of recapturing the league championship.

**MANAGER:** Matt Busby
**MOST APPEARANCES:** Allenby Chilton 43
**TOP SCORER:** Tommy Taylor 23 (22 League)
**BIGGEST WIN:** 6-1 v Cardiff City, 14 November 1953, League
**HIGHEST ATTENDANCE:** 58,440 v Sunderland, 27 February 1954, League

# Season 1954-55

## Football League Division One

| DATE | OPPONENTS | SCORE | GOALSCORERS | ATTENDANCE |
|---|---|---|---|---|
| Aug 21 | PORTSMOUTH | L 1-3 | Rowley | 38,203 |
| Aug 23 | Sheffield Wednesday | W 4-2 | Blanchflower 2, Viollet 2 | 38,118 |
| Aug 28 | Blackpool | W 4-2 | Webster 2, Blanchflower, Viollet | 31,855 |
| Sep 1 | SHEFFIELD WEDNESDAY | W 2-0 | Viollet 2 | 31,371 |
| Sep 4 | CHARLTON ATHLETIC | W 3-1 | Rowley 2, Taylor | 38,105 |
| Sep 8 | Tottenham Hotspur | W 2-0 | Berry, Webster | 35,162 |
| Sep 11 | Bolton Wanderers | D 1-1 | Webster | 44,661 |
| Sep 15 | TOTTENHAM HOTSPUR | W 2-1 | Viollet, Rowley | 29,212 |
| Sep 18 | HUDDERSFIELD TOWN | D 1-1 | Viollet | 45,648 |
| Sep 25 | Manchester City | L 2-3 | Taylor, Blanchflower | 54,105 |
| Oct 2 | Wolverhampton Wanderers | L 2-4 | Rowley, Viollet | 39,617 |
| Oct 9 | CARDIFF CITY | W 5-2 | Taylor 4, Viollet | 39,378 |
| Oct 16 | Chelsea | W 6-5 | Viollet 3, Taylor 2, Blanchflower | 55,966 |
| Oct 23 | NEWCASTLE UNITED | D 2-2 | Taylor, Scoular o.g. | 29,217 |
| Oct 30 | Everton | L 2-4 | Taylor, Rowley | 63,021 |
| Nov 6 | PRESTON NORTH END | W 2-1 | Viollet 2 | 30,063 |
| Nov 13 | Sheffield United | L 0-3 | | 26,257 |
| Nov 20 | ARSENAL | W 2-1 | Blanchflower, Taylor | 33,373 |
| Nov 27 | West Bromwich Albion | L 0-2 | | 33,931 |
| Dec 4 | LEICESTER CITY | W 3-1 | Viollet, Rowley | 19,369 |
| Dec 11 | Burnley | W 4-2 | Webster 3, Viollet | 24,977 |
| Dec 18 | Portsmouth | D 0-0 | | 26,019 |
| Dec 27 | ASTON VILLA | L 0-1 | | 49,136 |
| Dec 28 | Aston Villa | L 1-2 | Taylor | 48,718 |
| Jan 1 | BLACKPOOL | W 4-1 | Blanchflower 2, Viollet, Edwards | 51,918 |
| Jan 22 | BOLTON WANDERERS | D 1-1 | Taylor | 39,873 |
| Feb 5 | Huddersfield Town | W 3-1 | Berry, Pegg, Edwards | 31,408 |
| Feb 12 | MANCHESTER CITY | L 0-5 | | 47,914 |
| Feb 23 | WOLVERHAMPTON WANDERERS | L 2-4 | Edwards, Taylor | 15,679 |
| Feb 26 | Cardiff City | L 0-3 | | 16,329 |
| Mar 5 | BURNLEY | W 1-0 | Edwards | 31,729 |
| Mar 19 | EVERTON | L 1-2 | Scanlon | 32,295 |
| Mar 26 | Preston North End | W 2-0 | Scanlon, Byrne (pen) | 13,327 |
| Apr 2 | SHEFFIELD UNITED | W 5-0 | Taylor 2, Viollet, Whelan, Berry | 21,158 |
| Apr 8 | Sunderland | L 3-4 | Edwards 2, Scanlon | 43,882 |
| Apr | Leicester City | L 0-1 | | 34,362 |
| Apr 11 | SUNDERLAND | D 2-2 | Byrne (pen), Taylor | 36,013 |
| Apr 16 | WEST BROMWICH ALBION | W 3-0 | Taylor 2, Viollet | 24,765 |
| Apr 18 | Newcastle United | L 0-2 | | 35,540 |
| Apr 23 | Arsenal | W 3-2 | Blanchflower 2, Goring o.g. | 42,754 |
| Apr 26 | Charlton Athletic | D 1-1 | Viollet | 13,149 |
| Apr 30 | CHELSEA | W 2-1 | Taylor, Scanlon | 34,933 |

## FA Cup

| | | | | |
|---|---|---|---|---|
| Jan 8 | Reading | (Rd3) D 1-1 | Webster | 26,000 |
| Jan 12 | READING | (R) W 4-1 | Webster 2, Rowley, Viollet | 24,578 |
| Jan 29 | Manchester City | (Rd4) L 0-2 | | 74,723 |

## League & Cup Appearances

| PLAYER | LEAGUE | CUP COMPETITION FA CUP | TOTAL |
|---|---|---|---|
| Bent | 2 | | 2 |
| Berry | 40 | 3 | 43 |
| Blanchflower | 29 | 3 | 32 |
| Byrne | 39 | 3 | 42 |
| Chilton | 29 | 3 | 32 |
| Cockburn | 1 | | 1 |
| Crompton | 5 | | 5 |
| Edwards | 33 | 3 | 36 |
| Foulkes | 41 | 3 | 44 |
| Gibson | 32 | 3 | 35 |
| Goodwin | 5 | | 5 |
| Greaves | 1 | | 1 |
| Jones | 13 | | 13 |
| Kennedy | 1 | | 1 |
| Pegg | 6 | | 6 |
| Rowley | 22 | 3 | 25 |
| Scanlon | 14 | | 14 |
| Taylor | 30 | 1 | 31 |
| Webster | 17 | 2 | 19 |
| Whelan | 7 | | 7 |
| Whitefoot | 24 | | 24 |
| Wood | 37 | 3 | 40 |
| Viollet | 34 | 2 | 36 |

## Goalscorers

| PLAYER | LEAGUE | CUP COMPETITION FA CUP | TOTAL |
|---|---|---|---|
| Viollet | 20 | 1 | 21 |
| Taylor | 20 | | 20 |
| Webster | 8 | 3 | 11 |
| Blanchflower | 10 | | 10 |
| Rowley | 7 | 1 | 8 |
| Edwards | 6 | | 6 |
| Scanlon | 4 | | 4 |
| Berry | 3 | | 3 |
| Byrne | 2 | | 2 |
| Pegg | 1 | | 1 |
| Whelan | 1 | | 1 |
| Opps' o.gs. | 2 | | 2 |

### Fact File

United enjoy a league double over Chelsea, including success in an 11-goal thriller at Stamford Bridge, but it was the Londoners who had the last laugh when they landed the league title.

**MANAGER:** Matt Busby

**MOST APPEARANCES:** Bill Foulkes 44

**TOP SCORER:** Dennis Viollet 21 (20 League)

**BIGGEST WIN:** 5-0 v Sheffield United, 2 April 1955, League

**HIGHEST ATTENDANCE:** 74,723 v Manchester City, 29 January 1955, FA Cup

## Final Division One Table

| | | P | W | D | L | F | A | PTS |
|---|---|---|---|---|---|---|---|---|
| 1 | CHELSEA | 42 | 20 | 12 | 10 | 81 | 57 | 52 |
| 2 | WOLVERHAMPTON W | 42 | 19 | 10 | 13 | 89 | 70 | 48 |
| 3 | PORTSMOUTH | 42 | 18 | 12 | 12 | 74 | 62 | 48 |
| 4 | SUNDERLAND | 42 | 15 | 18 | 9 | 64 | 54 | 48 |
| 5 | MANCHESTER UNITED | 42 | 20 | 7 | 15 | 84 | 74 | 47 |
| 6 | ASTON VILLA | 42 | 20 | 7 | 15 | 72 | 73 | 47 |
| 7 | MANCHESTER CITY | 42 | 18 | 10 | 14 | 76 | 69 | 46 |
| 8 | NEWCASTLE UNITED | 42 | 17 | 9 | 16 | 89 | 77 | 43 |
| 9 | ARSENAL | 42 | 17 | 9 | 16 | 69 | 63 | 43 |
| 10 | BURNLEY | 42 | 17 | 9 | 16 | 51 | 48 | 43 |
| 11 | EVERTON | 42 | 16 | 10 | 16 | 62 | 68 | 42 |
| 12 | HUDDERSFIELD TOWN | 42 | 14 | 13 | 15 | 63 | 68 | 41 |
| 13 | SHEFFIELD UNITED | 42 | 17 | 7 | 18 | 70 | 86 | 41 |
| 14 | PRESTON NORTH END | 42 | 16 | 8 | 18 | 83 | 64 | 40 |
| 15 | CHARLTON ATHLETIC | 42 | 15 | 10 | 17 | 76 | 75 | 40 |
| 16 | TOTTENHAM HOTSPUR | 42 | 16 | 8 | 18 | 72 | 73 | 40 |
| 17 | WBA | 42 | 16 | 8 | 18 | 76 | 96 | 40 |
| 18 | BOLTON WANDERERS | 42 | 13 | 13 | 16 | 62 | 69 | 39 |
| 19 | BLACKPOOL | 42 | 14 | 10 | 18 | 60 | 64 | 38 |
| 20 | CARDIFF CITY | 42 | 13 | 11 | 18 | 62 | 76 | 37 |
| 21 | LEICESTER CITY | 42 | 12 | 11 | 19 | 74 | 86 | 35 |
| 22 | SHEFFIELD WEDNESDAY | 42 | 8 | 10 | 24 | 63 | 100 | 26 |

# Season 1955-56

## Football League Division One

| DATE | OPPONENTS | SCORE | GOALSCORERS | ATTENDANCE |
|---|---|---|---|---|
| Aug 20 | Birmingham City | D 2-2 | Viollet 2 | 37,994 |
| Aug 24 | TOTTENHAM HOTSPUR | D 2-2 | Berry, Webster | 25,406 |
| Aug 27 | WEST BROMWICH ALBION | W 3-1 | Lewis, Viollet, Scanlon | 31,996 |
| Aug 31 | Tottenham Hotspur | W 2-1 | Edwards 2 | 27,453 |
| Sep 3 | Manchester City | L 0-1 | | 59,162 |
| Sep 7 | EVERTON | W 2-1 | Edwards, Blanchflower | 27,843 |
| Sep 10 | Sheffield United | L 0-1 | | 28,241 |
| Sep 14 | Everton | L 2-4 | Webster, Blanchflower | 34,897 |
| Sep 17 | PRESTON NORTH END | W 3-2 | Pegg, Viollet, Taylor | 33,078 |
| Sep 24 | Burnley | D 0-0 | | 26,873 |
| Oct 1 | LUTON TOWN | W 3-1 | Taylor 2, Webster | 34,409 |
| Oct 8 | WOLVERHAMPTON WANDERERS | W 4-3 | Taylor 2, Pegg, Doherty | 48,638 |
| Oct 15 | Aston Villa | D 4-4 | Pegg 2, Blanchflower, Webster | 29,478 |
| Oct 22 | HUDDERSFIELD TOWN | W 3-0 | Berry, Taylor, Pegg | 34,150 |
| Oct 29 | Cardiff City | W 1-0 | Taylor | 27,795 |
| Nov 5 | ARSENAL | D 1-1 | Taylor | 41,586 |
| Nov 12 | Bolton Wanderers | L 1-3 | Taylor | 38,109 |
| Nov 19 | CHELSEA | W 3-0 | Taylor 2, Byrne (pen) | 22,192 |
| Nov 26 | Blackpool | D 0-0 | | 26,240 |
| Dec 3 | SUNDERLAND | W 2-1 | Doherty, Viollet | 39,901 |
| Dec 10 | Portsmouth | L 2-3 | Taylor, Pegg | 24,594 |
| Dec 17 | BIRMINGHAM CITY | W 2-1 | Viollet, Jones | 27,704 |
| Dec 24 | West Bromwich Albion | W 4-1 | Viollet 3, Taylor | 25,168 |
| Dec 26 | CHARLTON ATHLETIC | W 5-1 | Viollet 2, Taylor, Doherty, Byrne (pen) | 44,611 |
| Dec 27 | Charlton Athletic | L 0-3 | | 42,040 |
| Dec 31 | MANCHESTER CITY | W 2-1 | Taylor, Viollet | 60,956 |
| Jan 14 | SHEFFIELD UNITED | W 3-1 | Taylor, Berry, Pegg | 30,162 |
| Jan 21 | Preston North End | L 1-3 | Whelan | 28,047 |
| Feb 4 | BURNLEY | W 2-0 | Taylor, Viollet | 27,342 |
| Feb 11 | Luton Town | W 2-0 | Viollet, Whelan | 16,354 |
| Feb 18 | Wolverhampton Wanderers | W 2-0 | Taylor 2 | 40,014 |
| Feb 25 | ASTON VILLA | W 1-0 | Whelan | 36,277 |
| Mar 3 | Chelsea | W 4-2 | Viollet 2, Taylor, Pegg | 32,050 |
| Mar 10 | CARDIFF CITY | D 1-1 | Byrne (pen) | 44,693 |
| Mar 17 | Arsenal | D 1-1 | Viollet | 50,758 |
| Mar 24 | BOLTON WANDERERS | W 1-0 | Taylor | 46,114 |
| Mar 30 | NEWCASTLE UNITED | W 5-2 | Viollet 2, Taylor, Pegg, Doherty | 58,994 |
| Mar 31 | Huddersfield Town | W 2-0 | Taylor 2 | 37,780 |
| Apr 2 | Newcastle United | D 0-0 | | 37,395 |
| Apr 7 | BLACKPOOL | W 2-1 | Berry, Taylor | 62,277 |
| Apr 14 | Sunderland | D 2-2 | McGuinness, Whelan | 19,865 |
| Apr 21 | PORTSMOUTH | W 1-0 | Viollet | 38,417 |

## FA Cup

| | | | | |
|---|---|---|---|---|
| Jan 7 | Bristol Rovers | (Rd3) L 0-4 | | 35,872 |

## League & Cup Appearances

| PLAYER | LEAGUE | CUP COMPETITION FA CUP | TOTAL |
|---|---|---|---|
| Bent | 4 | | 4 |
| Berry | 34 | 1 | 35 |
| Blanchflower | 18 | | 18 |
| Byrne | 39 | 1 | 40 |
| Colman | 25 | 1 | 26 |
| Crompton | 1 | | 1 |
| Doherty | 16 | 1 | 17 |
| Edwards | 33 | | 33 |
| Foulkes | 26 | 1 | 27 |
| Goodwin | 8 | | 8 |
| Greaves | 15 | | 15 |
| Jones | 42 | 1 | 43 |
| Lewis | 4 | | 4 |
| McGuinness | 3 | | 3 |
| Pegg | 35 | 1 | 36 |
| Scanlon | 6 | | 6 |
| Scott | 1 | | 1 |
| Taylor | 33 | 1 | 34 |
| Viollet | 34 | 1 | 35 |
| Webster | 15 | | 15 |
| Whelan | 13 | | 13 |
| Whitefoot | 15 | 1 | 16 |
| Whitehurst | 1 | | 1 |
| Wood | 41 | 1 | 42 |

## Goalscorers

| PLAYER | LEAGUE | CUP COMPETITION FA CUP | TOTAL |
|---|---|---|---|
| Taylor | 25 | | 25 |
| Viollet | 20 | | 20 |
| Pegg | 9 | | 9 |
| Berry | 4 | | 4 |
| Doherty | 4 | | 4 |
| Webster | 4 | | 4 |
| Whelan | 4 | | 4 |
| Blanchflower | 3 | | 3 |
| Byrne | 3 | | 3 |
| Edwards | 3 | | 3 |
| Jones | 1 | | 1 |
| Lewis | 1 | | 1 |
| McGuinness | 1 | | 1 |
| Scanlon | 1 | | 1 |

## Final Division One Table

| | | P | W | D | L | F | A | Pts |
|---|---|---|---|---|---|---|---|---|
| 1 | Manchester United | 42 | 25 | 10 | 7 | 83 | 51 | 60 |
| 2 | Blackpool | 42 | 20 | 9 | 13 | 86 | 62 | 49 |
| 3 | Wolverhampton W | 42 | 20 | 9 | 13 | 89 | 65 | 49 |
| 4 | Manchester City | 42 | 18 | 10 | 14 | 82 | 69 | 46 |
| 5 | Arsenal | 42 | 18 | 10 | 14 | 60 | 61 | 46 |
| 6 | Birmingham City | 42 | 18 | 9 | 15 | 75 | 57 | 45 |
| 7 | Burnley | 42 | 18 | 8 | 16 | 64 | 54 | 44 |
| 8 | Bolton Wanderers | 42 | 18 | 7 | 17 | 71 | 58 | 43 |
| 9 | Sunderland | 42 | 17 | 9 | 16 | 80 | 95 | 43 |
| 10 | Luton Town | 42 | 17 | 8 | 17 | 66 | 64 | 42 |
| 11 | Newcastle United | 42 | 17 | 7 | 18 | 85 | 70 | 41 |
| 12 | Portsmouth | 42 | 16 | 9 | 17 | 78 | 85 | 41 |
| 13 | WBA | 42 | 18 | 5 | 19 | 58 | 70 | 41 |
| 14 | Charlton Athletic | 42 | 17 | 6 | 19 | 75 | 81 | 40 |
| 15 | Everton | 42 | 15 | 10 | 17 | 55 | 69 | 40 |
| 16 | Chelsea | 42 | 14 | 11 | 17 | 64 | 17 | 39 |
| 17 | Cardiff City | 42 | 15 | 9 | 18 | 55 | 69 | 39 |
| 18 | Tottenham Hotspur | 42 | 15 | 7 | 20 | 61 | 71 | 37 |
| 19 | Preston North End | 42 | 14 | 8 | 20 | 73 | 72 | 36 |
| 20 | Aston Villa | 42 | 11 | 13 | 18 | 52 | 69 | 35 |
| 21 | Huddersfield Town | 42 | 14 | 7 | 21 | 54 | 83 | 35 |
| 22 | Sheffield United | 42 | 12 | 9 | 21 | 63 | 77 | 33 |

## Fact File

Wilf McGuinness, a future United manager, made his league debut against Wolverhampton Wanderers at Old Trafford on 8 October 1955.

**MANAGER:** Matt Busby
**MOST APPEARANCES:** Mark Jones 43
**TOP SCORER:** Tommy Taylor 25 (all League)
**BIGGEST WIN:** 5-1 v Charlton Athletic, 26 December 1955, League
**HIGHEST ATTENDANCE:** 62,277 v Blackpool, 7 April 1956, League

# Season 1956-57

## Football League Division One

| DATE | OPPONENTS | SCORE | GOALSCORERS | ATTENDANCE |
|---|---|---|---|---|
| Aug 18 | BIRMINGHAM CITY | D 2-2 | Viollet 2 | 32,752 |
| Aug 20 | Preston North End | W 3-1 | Taylor 2, Whelan | 32,569 |
| Aug 25 | West Bromwich Albion | W 3-2 | Taylor, Viollet, Whelan | 26,387 |
| Aug 29 | PRESTON NORTH END | W 3-2 | Viollet 3 | 32,515 |
| Sep 1 | PORTSMOUTH | W 3-0 | Berry, Pegg, Viollet | 40,369 |
| Sep 5 | Chelsea | W 2-1 | Taylor, Whelan | 29,082 |
| Sep 8 | Newcastle United | D 1-1 | Whelan | 50,130 |
| Sep 15 | SHEFFIELD WEDNESDAY | W 4-1 | Viollet, Whelan, Berry, Taylor | 48,078 |
| Sep 22 | MANCHESTER CITY | W 2-0 | Viollet, Whelan | 53,525 |
| Sep 29 | Arsenal | W 2-1 | Whelan, Berry (pen) | 62,479 |
| Oct 6 | CHARLTON ATHLETIC | W 4-2 | Charlton 2, Whelan, Berry | 41,439 |
| Oct 13 | Sunderland | W 3-1 | Viollet, Whelan, Morrison o.g. | 49,487 |
| Oct 20 | EVERTON | L 2-5 | Whelan, Charlton | 43,451 |
| Oct 27 | Blackpool | D 2-2 | Taylor 2 | 32,632 |
| Nov 3 | WOLVERHAMPTON WANDERERS | W 3-0 | Whelan, Taylor, Pegg | 59,835 |
| Nov 10 | Bolton Wanderers | L 0-2 | | 39,922 |
| Nov 17 | LEEDS UNITED | W 3-2 | Whelan 2, Charlton | 51,131 |
| Nov 24 | Tottenham Hotspur | D 2-2 | Berry, Colman | 57,724 |
| Dec 1 | LUTON TOWN | W 3-1 | Taylor, Edwards, Pegg | 34,736 |
| Dec 8 | Aston Villa | W 3-1 | Taylor 2, Viollet | 42,530 |
| Dec 15 | Birmingham City | L 1-3 | Whelan | 36,146 |
| Dec 26 | CARDIFF CITY | W 3-1 | Whelan, Taylor, Viollet | 28,607 |
| Dec 29 | Portsmouth | W 3-1 | Viollet, Edwards, Pegg | 32,147 |
| Jan 1 | CHELSEA | W 3-0 | Taylor 2, Whelan | 42,116 |
| Jan 12 | NEWCASTLE UNITED | W 6-1 | Whelan 2, Viollet 2, Pegg 2 | 44,911 |
| Jan 19 | Sheffield Wednesday | L 1-2 | Taylor | 51,068 |
| Feb 2 | Manchester City | W 4-2 | Viollet, Whelan, Taylor, Edwards | 63,872 |
| Feb 9 | ARSENAL | W 6-2 | Whelan 2, Berry 2 (1 pen), Edwards, Taylor | 60,384 |
| Feb 18 | Charlton Athletic | W 5-1 | Charlton 3, Taylor 2 | 16,308 |
| Feb 23 | BLACKPOOL | L 0-2 | | 42,602 |
| Mar 6 | Everton | W 2-1 | Webster 2 | 34,029 |
| Mar 9 | ASTON VILLA | D 1-1 | Charlton | 55,484 |
| Mar 16 | Wolverhampton Wanderers | D 1-1 | Charlton | 53,228 |
| Mar 25 | BOLTON WANDERERS | L 0-2 | | 60,862 |
| Mar 30 | Leeds United | W 2-1 | Berry, Charlton | 47,216 |
| Apr 6 | TOTTENHAM HOTSPUR | D 0-0 | | 60,349 |
| Apr 13 | Luton Town | W 2-0 | Taylor 2 | 21,227 |
| Apr 19 | Burnley | W 3-1 | Whelan 3 | 41,321 |
| Apr 20 | SUNDERLAND | W 4-0 | Whelan 2, Taylor, Edwards | 58,725 |
| Apr 22 | BURNLEY | W 2-0 | Webster, Dawson | 41,321 |
| Apr 27 | Cardiff City | W 3-2 | Scanlon 2, McSeveney o.g. | 17,708 |
| Apr 29 | WEST BROMWICH ALBION | D 1-1 | Dawson | 20,357 |

## FA Cup

| | | | | | |
|---|---|---|---|---|---|
| Jan 5 | Hartlepools United | (Rd3) | W 4-3 | Whelan 2, Taylor, Berry | 17,264 |
| Jan 26 | Wrexham | (Rd4) | W 5-0 | Whelan 2, Taylor 2, Byrne (pen) | 34,445 |
| Feb 16 | EVERTON | (Rd5) | W 1-0 | Edwards | 61,803 |
| Mar 2 | Bournemouth & Boscombe Athletic | (Rd6) | W 2-1 | Berry 2 (1 pen) | 28,799 |
| Mar 23 | Birmingham City* | (SF) | W 2-0 | Berry, Charlton | 65,107 |
| May 4 | Aston Villa** | (F) | L 1-2 | Taylor | 100,000 |

*Played at Hillsborough, Sheffield. **Played at Wembley Stadium, London.

## European Cup

| | | | | | |
|---|---|---|---|---|---|
| Sep 12 | Anderlecht | (PRd/1L) | W 2-0 | Viollet, Taylor | 35,000 |
| Sep 26 | ANDERLECHT† | (PRd/2L) | W10-0 | Viollet 4, Taylor 3, Whelan 2, Berry | 43,635 |
| Oct 17 | BORUSSIA DORTMUND† | (Rd1/1L) | W 3-2 | Viollet 2, Burgsmueller o.g. | 75,598 |
| Nov 21 | Borussia Dortmund | (Rd1/2L) | D 0-0 | | 45,000 |
| Jan 16 | Athletic Bilbao | (Rd2/1L) | L 3-5 | Taylor, Viollet, Whelan | 45,000 |
| Feb 6 | ATHLETIC BILBAO† | (Rd2/2L) | W 3-0 | Viollet, Taylor, Berry | 65,000 |
| Apr 11 | Real Madrid | (SF/1L) | L 1-3 | Taylor | 135.000 |
| Apr 25 | REAL MADRID | (SF/2L) | D 2-2 | Taylor, Charlton | 61,676 |

†Played at Maine Road, Manchester.

## FA Charity Shield

| | | | | |
|---|---|---|---|---|
| Oct 24 | Manchester City | W 1-0 | Viollet | 30,495 |

**MANAGER:** Matt Busby

**MOST APPEARANCES:** Johnny Berry, Bill Foulkes, Liam Whelan, Ray Wood 54

**TOP SCORER:** Tommy Taylor 34 (22 League)

**BIGGEST WIN:** 10-0 v Anderlecht, 26 September 1956, European Cup

**HIGHEST ATTENDANCE:** 135,000 v Real Madrid, 11 April 1957, European Cup

## League & Cup Appearances

| PLAYER | LEAGUE | CUP COMPETITION | | OTHER | TOTAL |
|---|---|---|---|---|---|
| | | FA CUP | EC | | |
| Bent | 6 | | | | 6 |
| Berry | 40 | 5 | 8 | 1 | 54 |
| Blanchflower | 11 | 2 | 3 | | 16 |
| Byrne | 36 | 6 | 8 | 1 | 51 |
| Charlton | 14 | 2 | 1 | | 17 |
| Clayton | 2 | | | | 2 |
| Colman | 36 | 6 | 8 | 1 | 51 |
| Cope | 2 | | | | 2 |
| Dawson | 3 | | | | 3 |
| Doherty | 3 | | | | 3 |
| Edwards | 34 | 6 | 7 | 1 | 48 |
| Foulkes | 39 | 6 | 8 | 1 | 54 |
| Gaskell | | | | 0 (1) | 0 (1) |
| Goodwin | 6 | | | | 6 |
| Greaves | 3 | | | | 3 |
| Hawksworth | 1 | | | | 1 |
| Jones | 29 | 4 | 6 | 1 | 40 |
| McGuinness | 13 | 1 | 1 | | 15 |
| Pegg | 37 | 6 | 8 | 1 | 52 |
| Scanlon | 5 | | | | 5 |
| Taylor | 32 | 4 | 8 | 1 | 45 |
| Viollet | 27 | 5 | 6 | 1 | 39 |
| Webster | 5 | 1 | | | 6 |
| Whelan | 39 | 6 | 8 | 1 | 54 |
| Wood | 39 | 6 | 8 | 1 | 54 |

## Goalscorers

| PLAYER | LEAGUE | CUP COMPETITION | | OTHER | TOTAL |
|---|---|---|---|---|---|
| | | FA CUP | EC | | |
| Taylor | 22 | 4 | 8 | | 34 |
| Whelan | 26 | 4 | 3 | | 33 |
| Viollet | 16 | | 9 | 1 | 26 |
| Berry | 8 | 4 | 2 | | 14 |
| Charlton | 10 | 1 | 1 | | 12 |
| Pegg | 6 | | | | 6 |
| Edwards | 5 | 1 | | | 6 |
| Webster | 3 | | | | 3 |
| Dawson | 2 | | | | 2 |
| Scanlon | 2 | | | | 2 |
| Colman | 1 | | | | 1 |
| Byrne | | 1 | | | 1 |
| Opps' o.gs. | 2 | | 1 | | 3 |

## Fact File

Terrific season for United as they retained the league championship, lost narrowly to Aston Villa in the FA Cup final and became the first English club to compete in the European Cup.

## Final Division One Table

| | | P | W | D | L | F | A | Pts |
|---|---|---|---|---|---|---|---|---|
| 1 | Manchester United | 42 | 28 | 8 | 6 | 103 | 54 | 64 |
| 2 | Tottenham Hotspur | 42 | 22 | 12 | 8 | 104 | 56 | 56 |
| 3 | Preston North End | 42 | 23 | 10 | 9 | 84 | 56 | 56 |
| 4 | Blackpool | 42 | 22 | 9 | 11 | 93 | 65 | 53 |
| 5 | Arsenal | 42 | 21 | 8 | 13 | 85 | 69 | 50 |
| 6 | Wolverhampton W | 42 | 20 | 8 | 14 | 94 | 70 | 48 |
| 7 | Burnley | 42 | 18 | 10 | 14 | 56 | 50 | 46 |
| 8 | Leeds United | 42 | 15 | 14 | 13 | 72 | 63 | 44 |
| 9 | Bolton Wanderers | 42 | 16 | 12 | 14 | 65 | 65 | 44 |
| 10 | Aston Villa | 42 | 14 | 15 | 13 | 65 | 55 | 43 |
| 11 | WBA | 42 | 14 | 14 | 14 | 59 | 61 | 42 |
| 12 | Birmingham City | 42 | 15 | 9 | 18 | 69 | 69 | 39 |
| 13 | Chelsea | 42 | 13 | 13 | 16 | 73 | 73 | 39 |
| 14 | Sheffield Wednesday | 42 | 16 | 6 | 20 | 82 | 88 | 38 |
| 15 | Everton | 42 | 14 | 10 | 18 | 61 | 79 | 38 |
| 16 | Luton Town | 42 | 14 | 9 | 19 | 58 | 76 | 37 |
| 17 | Newcastle United | 42 | 14 | 8 | 20 | 67 | 87 | 36 |
| 18 | Manchester City | 42 | 13 | 9 | 20 | 78 | 88 | 35 |
| 19 | Portsmouth | 42 | 10 | 13 | 19 | 62 | 92 | 33 |
| 20 | Sunderland | 42 | 12 | 8 | 22 | 67 | 88 | 32 |
| 21 | Cardiff City | 42 | 10 | 9 | 23 | 53 | 88 | 29 |
| 22 | Charlton Athletic | 42 | 9 | 4 | 29 | 62 | 120 | 22 |

# Season 1957-58

## Football League Division One

| DATE | OPPONENTS | SCORE | GOALSCORERS | ATTENDANCE |
|---|---|---|---|---|
| Aug 24 | Leicester City | W 3-0 | Whelan 3 | 40,214 |
| Aug 28 | EVERTON | W 3-0 | Taylor T., Viollet, Jones o.g. | 59,103 |
| Aug 31 | MANCHESTER CITY | W 4-1 | Edwards, Berry, Viollet, Taylor | 63,347 |
| Sep 4 | Everton | D 3-3 | Viollet, Berry, Whelan | 72,077 |
| Sep 7 | LEEDS UNITED | W 5-0 | Berry 2, Taylor T 2, Viollet | 50,842 |
| Sep 9 | Blackpool | W 4-1 | Whelan 2, Viollet 2 | 34,181 |
| Sep 14 | Bolton Wanderers | L 0-4 | | 48,003 |
| Sep 18 | BLACKPOOL | L 1-2 | Edwards | 40,763 |
| Sep 21 | ARSENAL | W 4-2 | Whelan 2, Taylor T., Pegg | 47,142 |
| Sep 28 | Wolverhampton Wanderers | L 1-3 | Doherty | 48,825 |
| Oct 5 | ASTON VILLA | W 4-1 | Taylor T. 2, Pegg, Dugdale o.g. | 43,102 |
| Oct 12 | Nottingham Forest | W 2-1 | Whelan, Viollet | 47,654 |
| Oct 19 | PORTSMOUTH | L 0-3 | | 38,253 |
| Oct 26 | West Bromwich Albion | L 3-4 | Taylor T. 2, Whelan | 52,160 |
| Nov 2 | BURNLEY | W 1-0 | Taylor T. | 49,449 |
| Nov 9 | Preston North End | D 1-1 | Whelan | 39,063 |
| Nov 16 | SHEFFIELD WEDNESDAY | W 2-1 | Webster 2 | 40,366 |
| Nov 23 | Newcastle United | W 2-1 | Edwards, Taylor T. | 53,890 |
| Nov 30 | TOTTENHAM HOTSPUR | L 3-4 | Pegg 2, Whelan | 43,077 |
| Dec 7 | Birmingham City | D 3-3 | Viollet 2, Taylor T. | 35,791 |
| Dec 14 | CHELSEA | L 0-1 | | 36,853 |
| Dec 21 | LEICESTER CITY | W 4-0 | Viollet 2, Scanlon, Charlton | 41,631 |
| Dec 25 | LUTON TOWN | W 3-0 | Edwards (pen), Taylor T., Charlton | 39,444 |
| Dec 26 | Luton Town | D 2-2 | Scanlon, Taylor T. | 26,458 |
| Dec 28 | Manchester City | D 2-2 | Viollet, Charlton | 70,483 |
| Jan 11 | Leeds United | D 1-1 | Viollet | 39,401 |
| Jan 18 | BOLTON WANDERERS | W 7-2 | Charlton 3, Viollet 2, Scanlon, Edwards (pen) | 41,141 |
| Feb 1 | Arsenal | W 5-4 | Taylor T. 2, Edwards, Charlton, Viollet | 63,578 |
| Feb 22 | NOTTINGHAM FOREST | D 1-1 | Dawson | 66,124 |
| Mar 8 | WEST BROMWICH ALBION | L 0-4 | | 63,278 |
| Mar 15 | Burnley | L 0-3 | | 37,247 |
| Mar 29 | Sheffield Wednesday | L 0-1 | | 35,608 |
| Mar 31 | Aston Villa | L 2-3 | Dawson, Webster | 16,631 |
| Apr 4 | SUNDERLAND | D 2-2 | Charlton, Dawson | 47,421 |
| Apr 5 | PRESTON NORTH END | D 0-0 | | 47,816 |
| Apr 7 | Sunderland | W 2-1 | Webster 2 | 51,302 |
| Apr 12 | Tottenham Hotspur | L 0-1 | | 59,836 |
| Apr 16 | Portsmouth | D 3-3 | Webster, Taylor E., Dawson | 39,975 |
| Apr 19 | BIRMINGHAM CITY | L 0-2 | | 38,991 |
| Apr 21 | WOLVERHAMPTON WANDERERS | L 0-4 | | 33,267 |
| Apr 23 | NEWCASTLE UNITED | D 1-1 | Dawson | 28,393 |
| Apr 26 | Chelsea | L 1-2 | Taylor E. | 45,011 |

## FA Cup

| | | | | | |
|---|---|---|---|---|---|
| Jan 4 | Workington | (Rd3) W 3-1 | Viollet 3 | 21,000 |
| Jan 25 | IPSWICH TOWN | (Rd4) W 2-0 | Charlton 2 | 53,550 |
| Feb 19 | SHEFFIELD WEDNESDAY | (Rd5) W 3-0 | Brennan 2, Dawson | 59,848 |
| Mar 1 | West Bromwich Albion | (Rd6) D 2-2 | Taylor E., Dawson | 58,250 |
| Mar 5 | WEST BROMWICH ALBION | (R) W 1-0 | Webster | 60,000 |
| Mar 22 | Fulham* | (SF) D 2-2 | Charlton 2 | 69,745 |
| Mar 26 | Fulham** | (R) W 5-3 | Dawson 3, Brennan, Charlton | 38,000 |
| May 3 | Bolton Wanderers† | (F) L 0-2 | | 99,756 |

*Played at Villa Park, Birmingham. **Played at Arsenal Stadium, London.
†Played at Wembley Stadium, London.

## European Cup

| | | | | |
|---|---|---|---|---|
| Sep 25 | Shamrock Rovers | (PRd/1L) W 6-0 | Whelan 2, Taylor T. 2, Berry, Pegg | 46,000 |
| Oct 2 | SHAMROCK ROVERS | (PRd/2L) W 3-2 | Viollet 2, Pegg | 33,754 |
| Nov 20 | DUKLA PRAGUE | (Rd1/1L) W 3-0 | Webster, Taylor T., Pegg | 60,000 |
| Dec 4 | Dukla Prague | (Rd1/2L) L 0-1 | | 35,000 |
| Jan 14 | RED STAR BELGRADE | (Rd2/1L) W 2-1 | Charlton, Colman | 60,000 |
| Feb 5 | Red Star Belgrade | (Rd2/2L) D 3-3 | Charlton 2, Viollet | 52,000 |
| May 8 | AC MILAN | (SF/1L) W 2-1 | Viollet, Taylor E. (pen) | 44,882 |
| May 14 | AC Milan | (SF/2L) L 0-4 | | 80,000 |

## FA Charity Shield

| | | | | |
|---|---|---|---|---|
| Oct 22 | ASTON VILLA | W 4-0 | Taylor T. 3, Berry | 27,923 |

**MANAGER:** Matt Busby
**MOST APPEARANCES:** Bill Foulkes 59
**TOP SCORER:** Dennis Viollet 23 (16 League)
**BIGGEST WIN:** 6-0 v Shamrock Rovers, 25 September 1957, European Cup
**HIGHEST ATTENDANCE:** 99,756 v Bolton Wanderers, 3 May 1958, FA Cup

## League & Cup Appearances

| PLAYER | LEAGUE | CUP COMPETITION | | OTHER | TOTAL |
|---|---|---|---|---|---|
| | | FA CUP | EC | | |
| Berry | 20 | | 3 | 1 | 24 |
| Blanchflower | 18 | | 2 | 1 | 21 |
| Brennan | 5 | 2 | | | 7 |
| Byrne | 26 | 2 | 6 | 1 | 35 |
| Charlton | 21 | 7 | 2 | | 30 |
| Colman | 24 | 2 | 5 | | 31 |
| Cope | 13 | 6 | 2 | | 21 |
| Crowther | 11 | 5 | 2 | | 18 |
| Dawson | 12 | 6 | | | 18 |
| Doherty | 1 | | | | 1 |
| Edwards | 26 | 2 | 5 | 1 | 34 |
| Foulkes | 42 | 8 | 8 | 1 | 59 |
| Gaskell | 3 | | | | 3 |
| Goodwin | 16 | 6 | 3 | 1 | 23 |
| Greaves | 12 | 6 | 2 | | 20 |
| Gregg | 19 | 8 | 4 | | 31 |
| Harrop | 5 | 1 | | | 6 |
| Heron | 1 | | | | 1 |
| Jones M. | 10 | 2 | 4 | | 16 |
| Jones P. | 1 | | | | 1 |
| McGuinness | 7 | | 1 | | 8 |
| Morgans | 13 | 2 | 4 | | 19 |
| Pearson | 8 | 4 | 2 | | 14 |
| Pegg | 21 | | 4 | 1 | 26 |
| Scanlon | 9 | 2 | 3 | | 14 |
| Taylor E. | 11 | 6 | 2 | | 19 |
| Taylor T. | 25 | 2 | 6 | 1 | 34 |
| Webster | 20 | 6 | 5 | | 31 |
| Whelan | 20 | | 3 | 1 | 24 |
| Viollet | 22 | 3 | 6 | 1 | 32 |
| Wood | 20 | | 4 | 1 | 25 |

## Goalscorers

| PLAYER | LEAGUE | CUP COMPETITION | | OTHER | TOTAL |
|---|---|---|---|---|---|
| | | FA CUP | EC | | |
| Viollet | 16 | 3 | 4 | | 23 |
| Taylor T. | 16 | | 3 | 3 | 22 |
| Charlton | 8 | 5 | 3 | | 16 |
| Whelan | 12 | | 2 | | 14 |
| Dawson | 5 | 5 | | | 10 |
| Webster | 6 | 1 | 1 | | 8 |
| Pegg | 4 | | 3 | | 7 |
| Edwards | 6 | | | | 6 |
| Berry | 4 | | 1 | 1 | 6 |
| Taylor E. | 2 | 1 | 1 | | 4 |
| Scanlon | 3 | | | | 3 |
| Brennan | | 3 | | | 3 |
| Colman | | | 1 | | 1 |
| Doherty | 1 | | | | 1 |
| Opps' o.gs. | 2 | | | | 2 |

## Final Division One Table

| | | P | W | D | L | F | A | Pts |
|---|---|---|---|---|---|---|---|---|
| 1 | Wolverhampton W | 42 | 28 | 8 | 6 | 103 | 47 | 64 |
| 2 | Preston North End | 42 | 26 | 7 | 9 | 100 | 51 | 59 |
| 3 | Tottenham Hotspur | 42 | 21 | 9 | 12 | 93 | 77 | 51 |
| 4 | WBA | 42 | 18 | 14 | 10 | 92 | 70 | 50 |
| 5 | Manchester City | 42 | 22 | 5 | 15 | 104 | 100 | 49 |
| 6 | Burnley | 42 | 21 | 5 | 16 | 80 | 74 | 47 |
| 7 | Blackpool | 42 | 19 | 6 | 17 | 80 | 67 | 44 |
| 8 | Luton Town | 42 | 19 | 6 | 17 | 69 | 63 | 44 |
| 9 | Manchester United | 42 | 16 | 11 | 15 | 85 | 75 | 43 |
| 10 | Nottingham Forest | 42 | 16 | 10 | 16 | 69 | 63 | 42 |
| 11 | Chelsea | 42 | 15 | 12 | 15 | 83 | 79 | 42 |
| 12 | Arsenal | 42 | 16 | 7 | 19 | 73 | 85 | 39 |
| 13 | Birmingham City | 42 | 14 | 11 | 17 | 76 | 89 | 39 |
| 14 | Aston Villa | 42 | 16 | 7 | 19 | 73 | 86 | 39 |
| 15 | Bolton Wanderers | 42 | 14 | 10 | 18 | 65 | 87 | 38 |
| 16 | Everton | 42 | 13 | 11 | 18 | 65 | 75 | 37 |
| 17 | Leeds United | 42 | 14 | 9 | 19 | 51 | 63 | 37 |
| 18 | Leicester City | 42 | 14 | 5 | 23 | 91 | 112 | 33 |
| 19 | Newcastle United | 42 | 12 | 8 | 22 | 73 | 81 | 32 |
| 20 | Portsmouth | 42 | 12 | 8 | 22 | 73 | 88 | 32 |
| 21 | Sunderland | 42 | 10 | 12 | 20 | 54 | 97 | 32 |
| 22 | Sheffield Wednesday | 42 | 12 | 7 | 23 | 69 | 92 | 31 |

## Season 1958-59

### Football League Division One

| DATE | OPPONENTS | SCORE | GOALSCORERS | ATTENDANCE |
|---|---|---|---|---|
| Aug 23 | CHELSEA | W 5-2 | Charlton 3, Dawson | 52,382 |
| Aug 27 | Nottingham Forest | W 3-0 | Charlton 2, Scanlon | 44,971 |
| Aug 30 | Blackpool | L 1-2 | Viollet | 36,719 |
| Sep 3 | NOTTINGHAM FOREST | D 1-1 | Charlton | 51,880 |
| Sep 6 | BLACKBURN ROVERS | W 6-1 | Viollet 2, Webster, Charlton 2 (1 pen), Scanlon | 65,187 |
| Sep 8 | West Ham United | L 2-3 | Webster, McGuinness | 35,672 |
| Sep 13 | Newcastle United | D 1-1 | Charlton | 60,670 |
| Sep 17 | WEST HAM UNITED | W 4-1 | Scanlon 3, Webster | 53,276 |
| Sep 20 | TOTTENHAM HOTSPUR | D 2-2 | Webster 2 | 62,277 |
| Sep 27 | Manchester City | D 1-1 | Charlton (pen) | 62,912 |
| Oct 4 | Wolverhampton Wanderers | L 0-4 | | 36,840 |
| Oct 8 | PRESTON NORTH END | L 0-2 | | 46,163 |
| Oct 11 | ARSENAL | D 1-1 | Viollet | 56,148 |
| Oct 18 | Everton | L 2-3 | Cope 2 | 64,079 |
| Oct 25 | WEST BROMWICH ALBION | L 1-2 | Goodwin | 51,721 |
| Nov 1 | Leeds United | W 2-1 | Goodwin, Scanlon | 48,574 |
| Nov 8 | BURNLEY | L 1-3 | Quixall | 48,509 |
| Nov 15 | Bolton Wanderers | L 3-6 | Dawson 2, Charlton | 33,358 |
| Nov 22 | LUTON TOWN | W 2-1 | Viollet, Charlton | 42,428 |
| Nov 29 | Birmingham City | W 4-0 | Charlton 2, Bradley, Scanlon | 28,658 |
| Dec 6 | LEICESTER CITY | W 4-1 | Viollet, Bradley, Charlton, Scanlon | 38,482 |
| Dec13 | Preston North End | W 4-3 | Bradley, Viollet, Scanlon, Charlton | 26,290 |
| Dec 20 | Chelsea | W 3-2 | Charlton, Goodwin, Scott o.g. | 48,550 |
| Dec 26 | ASTON VILLA | W 2-1 | Quixall, Viollet | 63,098 |
| Dec 27 | Aston Villa | W 2-0 | Viollet, Pearson | 56,450 |
| Jan 3 | BLACKPOOL | W 3-1 | Charlton 2, Viollet | 61,961 |
| Jan 31 | NEWCASTLE UNITED | D 4-4 | Charlton (pen), Quixall, Scanlon, Viollet | 49,008 |
| Feb 7 | Tottenham Hotspur | W 3-1 | Charlton 2 (1 pen), Scanlon | 48,401 |
| Feb 16 | Manchester City | W 4-1 | Bradley 2, Goodwin, Scanlon | 59,846 |
| Feb 21 | WOLVERHAMPTON WANDERERS | W 2-1 | Viollet, Charlton | 62,794 |
| Feb 28 | Arsenal | L 2-3 | Viollet, Bradley | 67,162 |
| Mar 2 | Blackburn Rovers | W 3-1 | Bradley 2, Scanlon | 40,401 |
| Mar 7 | EVERTON | W 2-1 | Goodwin, Scanlon | 51,254 |
| Mar 14 | West Bromwich Albion | W 3-1 | Viollet, Bradley, Scanlon | 35,463 |
| Mar 21 | LEEDS UNITED | W 4-0 | Viollet 3, Charlton (pen) | 45,473 |
| Mar 27 | PORTSMOUTH | W 6-1 | Viollet 2, Bradley, Charlton 2 (1 pen), Hayward o.g. | 52,004 |
| Mar 28 | Burnley | L 2-4 | Viollet, Goodwin | 44,577 |
| Mar 30 | Portsmouth | W 3-1 | Charlton 2, Bradley | 29,359 |
| Apr 4 | BOLTON WANDERERS | W 3-0 | Charlton, Scanlon, Viollet | 61,528 |
| Apr 11 | Luton Town | D 0-0 | | 27,025 |
| Apr 18 | BIRMINGHAM CITY | W 1-0 | Quixall (pen) | 43,006 |
| Apr 25 | Leicester City | L 1-2 | Bradley | 38,466 |

### FA Cup

| | | | | |
|---|---|---|---|---|
| Jan 10 | Norwich City | (Rd3) L 0-3 | | 38,000 |

### League & Cup Appearances

| PLAYER | LEAGUE | CUP COMPETITION FA CUP | TOTAL |
|---|---|---|---|
| Bradley | 24 | 1 | 25 |
| Brennan | 1 | | 1 |
| Carolan | 23 | 1 | 24 |
| Charlton | 38 | 1 | 39 |
| Cope | 32 | 1 | 33 |
| Crowther | 2 | | 2 |
| Dawson | 11 | | 11 |
| Foulkes | 32 | 1 | 33 |
| Goodwin | 42 | 1 | 43 |
| Gregg | 41 | 1 | 42 |
| Greaves | 34 | | 34 |
| Harrop | 5 | | 5 |
| Hunter | 1 | | 1 |
| McGuinness | 39 | 1 | 40 |
| Morgans | 2 | | 2 |
| Pearson | 4 | | 4 |
| Quixall | 33 | 1 | 34 |
| Scanlon | 42 | 1 | 43 |
| Taylor | 11 | | 11 |
| Webster | 7 | | 7 |
| Wood | 1 | | 1 |
| Viollet | 37 | 1 | 38 |

### Goalscorers

| PLAYER | LEAGUE | CUP COMPETITION FA CUP | TOTAL |
|---|---|---|---|
| Charlton | 29 | | 29 |
| Viollet | 21 | | 21 |
| Scanlon | 16 | | 16 |
| Bradley | 12 | | 12 |
| Goodwin | 6 | | 6 |
| Webster | 5 | | 5 |
| Dawson | 4 | | 4 |
| Quixall | 4 | | 4 |
| Cope | 2 | | 2 |
| McGuinness | 1 | | 1 |
| Pearson | 1 | | 1 |
| Opps' o.gs. | 2 | | 2 |

### Fact File

United signed England international Albert Quixall from Sheffield Wednesday in September 1958 for a record British transfer fee of £45,000.

**MANAGER:** Matt Busby
**MOST APPEARANCES:** Freddie Goodwin, Albert Scanlon 43
**TOP SCORER:** Bobby Charlton 29 (all League)
**BIGGEST WIN:** 6-1 v Blackburn Rovers, 6 September 1958, League; 6-1 v Portsmouth, 27 March 1959, League
**HIGHEST ATTENDANCE:** 67,162 v Arsenal, 28 February 1959, League

### Final Division One Table

| | | P | W | D | L | F | A | Pts |
|---|---|---|---|---|---|---|---|---|
| 1 | Wolverhampton W | 42 | 28 | 5 | 9 | 110 | 49 | 61 |
| 2 | Manchester United | 42 | 24 | 7 | 11 | 103 | 66 | 55 |
| 3 | Arsenal | 42 | 21 | 8 | 13 | 88 | 68 | 50 |
| 4 | Bolton Wanderers | 42 | 20 | 10 | 12 | 79 | 66 | 50 |
| 5 | WBA | 42 | 18 | 13 | 11 | 88 | 68 | 49 |
| 6 | West Ham United | 42 | 21 | 6 | 15 | 85 | 70 | 48 |
| 7 | Burnley | 42 | 19 | 10 | 13 | 81 | 70 | 48 |
| 8 | Blackpool | 42 | 18 | 11 | 13 | 66 | 49 | 47 |
| 9 | Birmingham City | 42 | 20 | 6 | 16 | 84 | 68 | 46 |
| 10 | Blackburn Rovers | 42 | 17 | 10 | 15 | 76 | 70 | 44 |
| 11 | Newcastle United | 42 | 17 | 7 | 18 | 80 | 80 | 41 |
| 12 | Preston North End | 42 | 17 | 7 | 18 | 70 | 77 | 41 |
| 13 | Nottingham Forest | 42 | 17 | 6 | 19 | 71 | 74 | 40 |
| 14 | Chelsea | 42 | 18 | 4 | 20 | 77 | 98 | 40 |
| 15 | Leeds United | 42 | 15 | 9 | 18 | 57 | 74 | 39 |
| 16 | Everton | 42 | 17 | 4 | 21 | 71 | 87 | 38 |
| 17 | Luton Town | 42 | 12 | 13 | 17 | 68 | 71 | 37 |
| 18 | Tottenham Hotspur | 42 | 13 | 10 | 19 | 85 | 95 | 36 |
| 19 | Leicester City | 42 | 11 | 10 | 21 | 67 | 98 | 32 |
| 20 | Manchester City | 42 | 11 | 9 | 22 | 64 | 95 | 31 |
| 21 | Aston Villa | 42 | 11 | 8 | 23 | 58 | 87 | 30 |
| 22 | Portsmouth | 42 | 6 | 9 | 27 | 64 | 112 | 21 |

# Season 1959-60

## Football League Division One

| DATE | OPPONENTS | SCORE | GOALSCORERS | ATTENDANCE |
|---|---|---|---|---|
| Aug 22 | West Bromwich Albion | L 2-3 | Viollet 2 | 40,076 |
| Aug 26 | CHELSEA | L 0-1 | | 57,674 |
| Aug 29 | NEWCASTLE UNITED | W 3-2 | Viollet 2, Charlton | 53,257 |
| Sep 2 | Chelsea | W 6-3 | Bradley 2, Viollet 2, Quixall, Charlton | 66,579 |
| Sep 5 | Birmingham City | D 1-1 | Quixall | 38,220 |
| Sep 9 | LEEDS UNITED | W 6-0 | Bradley 2, Charlton 2, Viollet, Scanlon | 48,407 |
| Sep 12 | TOTTENHAM HOTSPUR | L 1-5 | Viollet | 55,402 |
| Sep 16 | Leeds United | D 2-2 | Charlton, Cush o.g. | 34,048 |
| Sep 19 | Manchester City | L 0-3 | | 58,300 |
| Sep 26 | Preston North End | L 0-4 | | 35,016 |
| Oct 3 | LEICESTER CITY | W 4-1 | Viollet 2, Charlton, Quixall | 41,637 |
| Oct 10 | ARSENAL | W 4-2 | Quixall, Charlton, Viollet, Dodgin o.g. | 51,626 |
| Oct 17 | Wolverhampton Wanderers | L 2-3 | Viollet, Stuart o.g. | 45,451 |
| Oct 24 | SHEFFIELD WEDNESDAY | W 3-1 | Viollet 2, Bradley | 39,259 |
| Oct 31 | Blackburn Rovers | D 1-1 | Quixall | 39,621 |
| Nov 7 | FULHAM | D 3-3 | Viollet, Scanlon, Charlton | 44,063 |
| Nov 14 | Bolton Wanderers | D 1-1 | Dawson | 37,892 |
| Nov 21 | LUTON TOWN | W 4-1 | Viollet 2, Quixall, Goodwin | 40,572 |
| Nov 28 | Everton | L 1-2 | Viollet | 46,095 |
| Dec 5 | BLACKPOOL | W 3-1 | Pearson, Viollet 2 | 45,558 |
| Dec 12 | Nottingham Forest | W 5-1 | Viollet 3, Dawson, Scanlon | 31,666 |
| Dec 19 | WEST BROMWICH ALBION | L 2-3 | Dawson, Quixall (pen) | 33,677 |
| Dec 26 | BURNLEY | L 1-2 | Quixall | 62,376 |
| Dec 28 | Burnley | W 4-1 | Viollet 2, Scanlon 2 | 47,253 |
| Jan 2 | Newcastle United | L 3-7 | Dawson, Quixall 2 (1 pen) | 57,200 |
| Jan 16 | BIRMINGHAM CITY | W 2-1 | Quixall (pen), Viollet | 47,361 |
| Jan 23 | Tottenham Hotspur | L 1-2 | Bradley | 62,602 |
| Feb 6 | MANCHESTER CITY | D 0-0 | | 59,450 |
| Feb 13 | PRESTON NORTH END | D 1-1 | Viollet | 44,014 |
| Feb 24 | Leicester City | L 1-3 | Scanlon | 33,191 |
| Feb 27 | Blackpool | W 6-0 | Charlton 3, Viollet 2, Scanlon | 23,996 |
| Mar 5 | WOLVERHAMPTON WANDERERS | L 0-2 | | 60,560 |
| Mar 19 | NOTTINGHAM FOREST | W 3-1 | Charlton 2, Dawson | 35,269 |
| Mar 26 | Fulham | W 5-0 | Viollet 2, Dawson, Giles, Pearson | 38,250 |
| Mar 30 | Sheffield Wednesday | L 2-4 | Viollet, Charlton | 26,821 |
| Apr 2 | BOLTON WANDERERS | W 2-0 | Charlton 2 | 45,298 |
| Apr 9 | Luton Town | W 3-2 | Bradley, Dawson 2 | 21,242 |
| Apr 15 | West Ham United | L 1-2 | Dawson | 34,969 |
| Apr 16 | BLACKBURN ROVERS | W 1-0 | Dawson | 45,945 |
| Apr 18 | WEST HAM UNITED | W 5-3 | Dawson 2, Charlton 2, Quixall | 34,676 |
| Apr 23 | Arsenal | L 2-5 | Pearson, Giles | 41,057 |
| Apr 30 | EVERTON | W 5-0 | Dawson 3, Quixall, Bradley | 43,823 |

## FA Cup

| | | | | |
|---|---|---|---|---|
| Jan 9 | Derby County | (Rd3) W 4-2 | Scanlon, Charlton, Goodwin, Barrowcliffe o.g. | 33,297 |
| Jan 30 | Liverpool | (Rd4) W 3-1 | Charlton 2, Bradley | 56,736 |
| Feb 20 | SHEFFIELD WEDNESDAY | (Rd5) L 0-1 | | 66,350 |

## League & Cup Appearances

| PLAYER | LEAGUE | CUP COMPETITION FA CUP | TOTAL |
|---|---|---|---|
| Bradley | 29 | 2 | 31 |
| Brennan | 29 | 3 | 32 |
| Carolan | 41 | 3 | 44 |
| Charlton | 37 | 3 | 40 |
| Cope | 40 | 3 | 43 |
| Dawson | 22 | 1 | 23 |
| Foulkes | 42 | 3 | 45 |
| Gaskell | 9 | | 9 |
| Giles | 10 | | 10 |
| Goodwin | 18 | 1 | 19 |
| Greaves | 2 | | 2 |
| Gregg | 33 | 3 | 36 |
| Heron | 1 | | 1 |
| Lawton | 3 | | 3 |
| McGuinness | 19 | | 19 |
| Pearson | 10 | | 10 |
| Quixall | 33 | 3 | 36 |
| Scanlon | 31 | 3 | 34 |
| Setters | 17 | 2 | 19 |
| Viollet | 36 | 3 | 39 |

## Goalscorers

| PLAYER | LEAGUE | CUP COMPETITION FA CUP | TOTAL |
|---|---|---|---|
| Viollet | 32 | | 32 |
| Charlton | 18 | 3 | 21 |
| Dawson | 15 | | 15 |
| Quixall | 13 | | 13 |
| Bradley | 8 | 1 | 9 |
| Scanlon | 7 | 1 | 8 |
| Pearson | 3 | | 3 |
| Giles | 2 | | 2 |
| Goodwin | 1 | 1 | 2 |
| Opps' o.gs. | 3 | 1 | 5 |

## Fact File

Dennis Viollet grabbed 32 league goals to set a new club scoring record that was to be still in place at the conclusion of the 2002-03 campaign.

**MANAGER:** Matt Busby

**MOST APPEARANCES:** Bill Foulkes 45

**TOP SCORER:** Dennis Viollet 32 (all League)

**BIGGEST WIN:** 6-0 v Leeds United, 9 September 1959, League; 6-0 v Blackpool, 27 February 1960, League

**HIGHEST ATTENDANCE:** 66,579 v Chelsea, 2 September 1959, League

## Final Division One Table

| | | P | W | D | L | F | A | Pts |
|---|---|---|---|---|---|---|---|---|
| 1 | Burnley | 42 | 24 | 7 | 11 | 85 | 61 | 55 |
| 2 | Wolverhampton W | 42 | 24 | 6 | 12 | 106 | 67 | 54 |
| 3 | Tottenham Hotspur | 42 | 21 | 11 | 10 | 86 | 50 | 53 |
| 4 | WBA | 42 | 19 | 11 | 12 | 83 | 57 | 49 |
| 5 | Sheffield Wednesday | 42 | 19 | 11 | 12 | 80 | 59 | 49 |
| 6 | Bolton Wanderers | 42 | 20 | 8 | 14 | 59 | 51 | 48 |
| 7 | Manchester United | 42 | 19 | 7 | 16 | 102 | 80 | 45 |
| 8 | Newcastle United | 42 | 18 | 8 | 16 | 82 | 78 | 44 |
| 9 | Preston North End | 42 | 16 | 12 | 14 | 79 | 76 | 44 |
| 10 | Fulham | 42 | 17 | 10 | 15 | 73 | 80 | 44 |
| 11 | Blackpool | 42 | 15 | 10 | 17 | 59 | 71 | 40 |
| 12 | Leicester City | 42 | 13 | 13 | 16 | 66 | 75 | 39 |
| 13 | Arsenal | 42 | 15 | 9 | 18 | 68 | 80 | 39 |
| 14 | West Ham United | 42 | 16 | 6 | 20 | 75 | 91 | 38 |
| 15 | Manchester City | 42 | 17 | 3 | 22 | 78 | 84 | 37 |
| 16 | Everton | 42 | 13 | 11 | 18 | 73 | 78 | 37 |
| 17 | Blackburn Rovers | 42 | 16 | 5 | 21 | 60 | 70 | 37 |
| 18 | Chelsea | 42 | 14 | 9 | 19 | 76 | 91 | 37 |
| 19 | Birmingham City | 42 | 13 | 10 | 19 | 63 | 80 | 36 |
| 20 | Nottingham Forest | 42 | 13 | 9 | 20 | 50 | 74 | 35 |
| 21 | Leeds United | 42 | 12 | 10 | 20 | 65 | 92 | 34 |
| 22 | Luton Town | 42 | 9 | 12 | 21 | 50 | 73 | 30 |

## Season 1960-61

### Football League Division One

| DATE | OPPONENTS | SCORE | GOALSCORERS | ATTENDANCE |
|---|---|---|---|---|
| Aug 20 | BLACKBURN ROVERS | L 1-3 | Charlton | 47,778 |
| Aug 24 | Everton | L 0-4 | | 51,602 |
| Aug 31 | EVERTON | W 4-0 | Charlton, Nicholson, Dawson 2 | 51,818 |
| Sep 3 | Tottenham Hotspur | L 1-4 | Viollet | 55,445 |
| Sep 5 | West Ham United | L 1-2 | Quixall | 30,506 |
| Sep 10 | LEICESTER CITY | D 1-1 | Giles | 35,493 |
| Sep 14 | WEST HAM UNITED | W 6-1 | Charlton 2, Viollet 2, Quixall (pen), Scanlon | 33,695 |
| Sep 17 | Aston Villa | L 1-2 | Viollet | 43,593 |
| Sep 24 | WOLVERHAMPTON WANDERERS | L 1-3 | Charlton | 44,458 |
| Oct 1 | Bolton Wanderers | D 1-1 | Giles | 39,197 |
| Oct 15 | Burnley | L 3-5 | Viollet 3 | 32,011 |
| Oct 22 | NEWCASTLE UNITED | W 3-2 | Dawson, Stiles, Setters | 37,516 |
| Oct 24 | NOTTINGHAM FOREST | W 2-1 | Viollet 2 | 23,628 |
| Oct 29 | Arsenal | L 1-2 | Quixall | 45,715 |
| Nov 5 | SHEFFIELD WEDNESDAY | D 0-0 | | 36,855 |
| Nov 12 | Birmingham City | L 1-3 | Charlton | 31,549 |
| Nov 19 | WEST BROMWICH ALBION | W 3-0 | Dawson, Viollet, Quixall (pen) | 32,756 |
| Nov 26 | Cardiff City | L 0-3 | | 21,122 |
| Dec 3 | PRESTON NORTH END | W 1-0 | Dawson | 24,904 |
| Dec 10 | Fulham | D 4-4 | Charlton, Dawson, Quixall 2 (1 pen) | 23,625 |
| Dec 17 | Blackburn Rovers | W 2-1 | Pearson 2 | 17,285 |
| Dec 24 | Chelsea | W 2-1 | Charlton, Dawson | 37,601 |
| Dec 26 | CHELSEA | W 6-0 | Dawson 3, Nicholson 2, Charlton | 50,164 |
| Dec 31 | MANCHESTER CITY | W 5-1 | Charlton 2, Dawson 3 | 61,213 |
| Jan 14 | TOTTENHAM HOTSPUR | W 2-0 | Stiles, Pearson | 65,295 |
| Jan 21 | Leicester City | L 0-6 | | 31,308 |
| Feb 4 | ASTON VILLA | D 1-1 | Charlton | 33,525 |
| Feb 11 | Wolverhampton Wanderers | L 1-2 | Nicholson | 38,526 |
| Feb 18 | BOLTON WANDERERS | W 3-1 | Quixall (pen), Dawson 2 | 37,558 |
| Feb 25 | Nottingham Forest | L 2-3 | Charlton, Quixall | 26,850 |
| Mar 4 | Manchester City | W 3-1 | Dawson, Charlton, Pearson | 50,479 |
| Mar 11 | Newcastle United | D 1-1 | Charlton | 28,870 |
| Mar 18 | ARSENAL | D 1-1 | Moir | 29,732 |
| Mar 25 | Sheffield Wednesday | L 1-5 | Charlton | 35,901 |
| Mar 31 | Blackpool | L 0-2 | | 30,835 |
| Apr 1 | FULHAM | W 3-1 | Charlton, Viollet, Quixall | 24,654 |
| Apr 3 | BLACKPOOL | W 2-0 | Nicholson, Hauser o.g. | 39,169 |
| Apr 8 | West Bromwich Albion | D 1-1 | Pearson | 27,750 |
| Apr 12 | BURNLEY | W 6-0 | Viollet 3, Viollet 3 | 25,019 |
| Apr 15 | BIRMINGHAM CITY | W 4-1 | Pearson 2, Quixall (pen), Viollet | 28,376 |
| Apr 22 | Preston North End | W 4-2 | Charlton 2, Setters 2 | 21,252 |
| Apr 29 | CARDIFF CITY | D 3-3 | Charlton 2, Setters | 30,320 |

### FA Cup

| | | | | |
|---|---|---|---|---|
| Jan 7 | MIDDLESBROUGH | (Rd3) W 3-0 | Dawson 2, Cantwell | 49,184 |
| Jan 28 | Sheffield Wednesday | (Rd4) D 1-1 | Cantwell (pen) | 58,000 |
| Feb 1 | SHEFFIELD WEDNESDAY | (R) L 2-7 | Dawson, Pearson | 65,243 |

### League Cup

| | | | | |
|---|---|---|---|---|
| Oct 19 | Exeter City | (Rd1) D 1-1 | Dawson | 14,494 |
| Oct 26 | EXETER CITY | (R) W 4-1 | Quixall 2 (1 pen), Giles, Pearson | 15,662 |
| Nov 2 | Bradford City | (Rd2) L 1-2 | Viollet | 4,670 |

### Fact File

Goalkeeper Ronnie Briggs conceded a combined total 14 goals in his first three appearances for United: six in a league fixture at Leicester, one in the FA Cup fourth round against Sheffield Wednesday at Hillsborough and seven in the replay at Old Trafford.

**MANAGER:** Matt Busby
**MOST APPEARANCES:** Shay Brennan 46
**TOP SCORER:** Bobby Charlton 21 (all League)
**BIGGEST WIN:** 6-0 v Chelsea, 26 December 1960, League; 6-0 v Burnley, 12 April 1961, League
**HIGHEST ATTENDANCE:** 65,295 v Tottenham Hotspur, 14 January 1961, League

### League & Cup Appearances

| PLAYER | LEAGUE | CUP COMPETITION FA CUP | LC | TOTAL |
|---|---|---|---|---|
| Bradley | 4 | | | 4 |
| Bratt | | | 1 | 1 |
| Brennan | 41 | 3 | 2 | 46 |
| Briggs | 1 | 2 | | 3 |
| Cantwell | 24 | 3 | | 27 |
| Carolan | 2 | | 1 | 3 |
| Charlton | 39 | 3 | | 42 |
| Cope | 6 | | 1 | 7 |
| Dawson | 28 | 3 | 3 | 34 |
| Dunne | 3 | | 1 | 4 |
| Foulkes | 40 | 3 | 2 | 45 |
| Gaskell | 10 | | 1 | 11 |
| Giles | 23 | | 2 | 25 |
| Gregg | 27 | 1 | 2 | 30 |
| Haydock | 4 | | | 4 |
| Heron | 1 | | | 1 |
| Lawton | 1 | | 1 | 2 |
| Moir | 8 | | | 8 |
| Morgans | 2 | | | 2 |
| Nicholson | 31 | 3 | 3 | 37 |
| Pearson | 27 | 3 | 3 | 33 |
| Pinner | 4 | | | 4 |
| Quixall | 38 | 2 | 1 | 41 |
| Scanlon | 8 | | 3 | 11 |
| Setters | 40 | 3 | 2 | 45 |
| Stiles | 26 | 3 | 2 | 31 |
| Viollet | 24 | 1 | 2 | 27 |

### Goalscorers

| PLAYER | LEAGUE | CUP COMPETITION FA CUP | LC | TOTAL |
|---|---|---|---|---|
| Charlton | 21 | | | 21 |
| Dawson | 16 | 3 | 1 | 20 |
| Viollet | 15 | | 1 | 16 |
| Quixall | 13 | | 2 | 15 |
| Pearson | 7 | 1 | 1 | 9 |
| Nicholson | 5 | | | 5 |
| Setters | 4 | | | 4 |
| Giles | 2 | | 1 | 3 |
| Cantwell | | 2 | | 2 |
| Stiles | 2 | | | 2 |
| Moir | 1 | | | 1 |
| Scanlon | 1 | | | 1 |
| Opps' o.gs. | 1 | | | 1 |

### Final Division One Table

| | | P | W | D | L | F | A | PTS |
|---|---|---|---|---|---|---|---|---|
| 1 | Tottenham Hotspur | 42 | 31 | 4 | 7 | 115 | 55 | 66 |
| 2 | Sheffield Wednesday | 42 | 23 | 12 | 7 | 78 | 47 | 58 |
| 3 | Wolverhampton W | 42 | 25 | 7 | 10 | 103 | 75 | 57 |
| 4 | Burnley | 42 | 22 | 7 | 13 | 102 | 77 | 51 |
| 5 | Everton | 42 | 22 | 6 | 14 | 87 | 69 | 50 |
| 6 | Leicester City | 42 | 18 | 9 | 15 | 87 | 70 | 45 |
| 7 | Manchester United | 42 | 18 | 9 | 15 | 88 | 76 | 45 |
| 8 | Blackburn Rovers | 42 | 15 | 13 | 14 | 77 | 76 | 43 |
| 9 | Aston Villa | 42 | 17 | 9 | 16 | 78 | 77 | 43 |
| 10 | WBA | 42 | 18 | 5 | 19 | 67 | 71 | 41 |
| 11 | Arsenal | 42 | 15 | 11 | 16 | 77 | 85 | 41 |
| 12 | Chelsea | 42 | 15 | 7 | 20 | 98 | 100 | 37 |
| 13 | Manchester City | 42 | 13 | 11 | 18 | 79 | 90 | 37 |
| 14 | Nottingham Forest | 42 | 14 | 9 | 19 | 62 | 78 | 37 |
| 15 | Cardiff City | 42 | 13 | 11 | 18 | 60 | 85 | 37 |
| 16 | West Ham United | 42 | 13 | 10 | 19 | 77 | 88 | 36 |
| 17 | Fulham | 42 | 14 | 8 | 20 | 72 | 95 | 36 |
| 18 | Bolton Wanderers | 42 | 12 | 11 | 19 | 58 | 73 | 35 |
| 19 | Birmingham City | 42 | 14 | 6 | 22 | 62 | 84 | 34 |
| 20 | Blackpool | 42 | 12 | 9 | 21 | 68 | 73 | 33 |
| 21 | Newcastle United | 42 | 11 | 10 | 21 | 86 | 109 | 32 |
| 22 | Preston North End | 42 | 10 | 10 | 22 | 43 | 71 | 30 |

# Season 1961-62

## Football League Division One

| DATE | OPPONENTS | SCORE | GOALSCORERS | ATTENDANCE |
|---|---|---|---|---|
| Aug 19 | West Ham United | D 1-1 | Stiles | 32,628 |
| Aug 23 | CHELSEA | W 3-2 | Herd, Viollet, Pearson | 45,847 |
| Aug 26 | BLACKBURN ROVERS | W 6-0 | Charlton, Herd 2, Quixall 2 (1 pen), Setters | 45,302 |
| Aug 30 | Chelsea | L 0-2 | | 42,248 |
| Sep 2 | Blackpool | W 3-2 | Viollet 2, Charlton | 28,156 |
| Sep 9 | TOTTENHAM HOTSPUR | W 1-0 | Quixall | 57,135 |
| Sep 16 | Cardiff City | W 2-1 | Quixall (pen), Dawson | 29,251 |
| Sep 18 | Aston Villa | D 1-1 | Stiles | 38,837 |
| Sep 23 | MANCHESTER CITY | W 3-2 | Stiles, Viollet, Ewing o.g. | 56,345 |
| Sep 30 | WOLVERHAMPTON WANDERERS | L 0-2 | | 39,457 |
| Oct 7 | West Bromwich Albion | D 1-1 | Dawson | 25,645 |
| Oct 14 | BIRMINGHAM CITY | L 0-2 | | 30,674 |
| Oct 21 | Arsenal | L 1-5 | Viollet | 54,245 |
| Oct 28 | BOLTON WANDERERS | L 0-3 | | 31,442 |
| Nov 4 | Sheffield Wednesday | L 1-3 | Viollet | 35,998 |
| Nov 11 | LEICESTER CITY | D 2-2 | Giles, Viollet | 21,567 |
| Nov 18 | Ipswich Town | L 1-4 | McMillan | 25,755 |
| Nov 25 | BURNLEY | L 1-4 | Herd | 41,029 |
| Dec 2 | Everton | L 1-5 | Herd | 48,099 |
| Dec 9 | FULHAM | W 3-0 | Herd 2, Lawton | 22,193 |
| Dec 16 | WEST HAM UNITED | L 1-2 | Herd | 29,472 |
| Dec 26 | NOTTINGHAM FOREST | W 6-3 | Lawton 3, Herd, Charlton, Brennan | 30,822 |
| Jan 13 | BLACKPOOL | L 0-1 | | 26,999 |
| Jan 15 | ASTON VILLA | W 2-0 | Quixall, Charlton | 20,807 |
| Jan 20 | Tottenham Hotspur | D 2-2 | Charlton, Stiles | 55,225 |
| Feb 3 | CARDIFF CITY | W 3-0 | Stiles, Giles, Lawton | 29,200 |
| Feb 10 | Manchester City | W 2-0 | Chisnall, Herd | 49,959 |
| Feb 24 | WEST BROMWICH ALBION | W 4-1 | Charlton 2, Setters, Quixall | 32,456 |
| Feb 28 | Wolverhampton Wanderers | D 2-2 | Lawton, Herd | 27,565 |
| Mar 3 | Birmingham City | D 1-1 | Herd | 25,817 |
| Mar 17 | Bolton Wanderers | L 0-1 | | 34,366 |
| Mar 20 | Nottingham Forest | L 0-1 | | 27,833 |
| Mar 24 | SHEFFIELD WEDNESDAY | D 1-1 | Charlton | 31,322 |
| Apr 4 | Leicester City | L 3-4 | McMillan 2, Quixall (pen) | 15,318 |
| Apr 7 | IPSWICH TOWN | W 5-0 | Quixall 3, Stiles, Setters | 24,976 |
| Apr 10 | Blackburn Rovers | L 0-3 | | 14,623 |
| Apr 14 | Burnley | W 3-1 | Cantwell, Brennan (pen), Herd | 36,240 |
| Apr 16 | ARSENAL | L 2-3 | McMillan, Cantwell | 24,258 |
| Apr 21 | EVERTON | D 1-1 | Herd | 31,926 |
| Apr 23 | SHEFFIELD UNITED | L 0-1 | | 30,073 |
| Apr 24 | Sheffield United | W 3-2 | McMillan 2, Stiles | 25,324 |
| Apr 28 | Fulham | L 0-2 | | 40,113 |

## FA Cup

| | | | | | |
|---|---|---|---|---|---|
| Jan 6 | BOLTON WANDERERS | (Rd3) | W 2-1 | Herd, Nicholson | 42,202 |
| Jan 31 | ARSENAL | (Rd4) | W 1-0 | Setters | 54,082 |
| Feb 17 | SHEFFIELD WEDNESDAY | (Rd5) | D 0-0 | | 59,553 |
| Feb 21 | Sheffield Wednesday | (R) | W 2-0 | Giles, Charlton | 62,969 |
| Mar 10 | Preston North End | (Rd6) | D 0-0 | | 37,521 |
| Mar 14 | PRESTON NORTH END | (R) | W 2-1 | Charlton, Herd | 63,468 |
| Mar 31 | Tottenham Hotspur* | (SF) | L 1-3 | Herd | 65,000 |

*Played at Hillsborough, Sheffield.

## League & Cup Appearances

| PLAYER | LEAGUE | CUP COMPETITION FA CUP | TOTAL |
|---|---|---|---|
| Bradley | 6 | 1 | 7 |
| Brennan | 41 | 6 | 47 |
| Briggs | 8 | | 8 |
| Cantwell | 17 | 2 | 19 |
| Charlton | 37 | 6 | 43 |
| Chisnall | 9 | 4 | 13 |
| Dawson | 4 | | 4 |
| Dunne | 28 | 7 | 35 |
| Foulkes | 40 | 7 | 47 |
| Gaskell | 21 | 7 | 28 |
| Giles | 30 | 7 | 37 |
| Gregg | 13 | | 13 |
| Haydock | 1 | | 1 |
| Herd | 27 | 5 | 32 |
| Lawton | 20 | 7 | 27 |
| McMillan | 11 | | 11 |
| Moir | 9 | | 9 |
| Nicholson | 17 | 4 | 21 |
| Pearson | 17 | | 17 |
| Quixall | 21 | 3 | 24 |
| Setters | 38 | 7 | 45 |
| Stiles | 34 | 4 | 38 |
| Viollet | 13 | | 13 |

## Goalscorers

| PLAYER | LEAGUE | CUP COMPETITION FA CUP | TOTAL |
|---|---|---|---|
| Herd | 14 | 3 | 17 |
| Charlton | 8 | 2 | 10 |
| Quixall | 10 | | 10 |
| Stiles | 7 | | 7 |
| Viollet | 7 | | 7 |
| McMillan | 6 | | 6 |
| Lawton | 6 | | 6 |
| Setters | 3 | 1 | 4 |
| Giles | 2 | 1 | 3 |
| Brennan | 2 | | 2 |
| Cantwell | 2 | | 2 |
| Dawson | 2 | | 2 |
| Chisnall | 1 | | 1 |
| Nicholson | | 1 | 1 |
| Pearson | 1 | | 1 |
| Opps' o.gs. | 1 | | 1 |

### Fact File

United defeated Ipswich Town 5-0 at Old Trafford, just a matter of weeks before the Suffolk side were crowned league champions.

**MANAGER:** Matt Busby
**MOST APPEARANCES:** Shay Brennan, Bill Foulkes 47
**TOP SCORER:** David Herd 17 (14 League)
**BIGGEST WIN:** 6-1 v Blackburn Rovers, 26 August 1961, League
**HIGHEST ATTENDANCE:** 65,000 v Tottenham Hotspur, 31 March 1962, FA Cup

## Final Division One Table

| | | P | W | D | L | F | A | Pts |
|---|---|---|---|---|---|---|---|---|
| 1 | Ipswich Town | 42 | 24 | 8 | 10 | 93 | 67 | 56 |
| 2 | Burnley | 42 | 21 | 11 | 10 | 101 | 67 | 53 |
| 3 | Tottenham Hotspur | 42 | 21 | 10 | 11 | 88 | 69 | 52 |
| 4 | Everton | 42 | 20 | 11 | 11 | 88 | 54 | 51 |
| 5 | Sheffield United | 42 | 19 | 9 | 14 | 61 | 69 | 47 |
| 6 | Sheffield Wednesday | 42 | 20 | 6 | 16 | 72 | 58 | 46 |
| 7 | Aston Villa | 42 | 18 | 8 | 18 | 65 | 56 | 44 |
| 8 | West Ham United | 42 | 17 | 10 | 15 | 76 | 82 | 44 |
| 9 | WBA | 42 | 15 | 13 | 14 | 83 | 67 | 43 |
| 10 | Arsenal | 42 | 16 | 11 | 15 | 71 | 72 | 43 |
| 11 | Bolton Wanderers | 42 | 16 | 10 | 16 | 62 | 66 | 42 |
| 12 | Manchester City | 42 | 17 | 7 | 18 | 78 | 81 | 41 |
| 13 | Blackpool | 42 | 15 | 11 | 16 | 70 | 75 | 41 |
| 14 | Leicester City | 42 | 17 | 6 | 19 | 72 | 71 | 40 |
| 15 | Manchester United | 42 | 15 | 9 | 18 | 72 | 75 | 39 |
| 16 | Blackburn Rovers | 42 | 14 | 11 | 17 | 50 | 58 | 39 |
| 17 | Birmingham City | 42 | 14 | 10 | 18 | 65 | 81 | 38 |
| 18 | Wolverhampton W | 42 | 13 | 10 | 19 | 73 | 86 | 36 |
| 19 | Nottingham Forest | 42 | 13 | 10 | 19 | 73 | 79 | 36 |
| 20 | Fulham | 42 | 13 | 7 | 22 | 66 | 74 | 33 |
| 21 | Cardiff City | 42 | 9 | 14 | 19 | 50 | 81 | 32 |
| 22 | Chelsea | 42 | 9 | 10 | 23 | 63 | 94 | 28 |

## Season 1962-63

### Football League Division One

| DATE | OPPONENTS | SCORE | GOALSCORERS | ATTENDANCE |
|---|---|---|---|---|
| Aug 18 | WEST BROMWICH ALBION | D 2-2 | Herd, Law | 51,685 |
| Aug 22 | Everton | L 1-3 | Moir | 69,501 |
| Aug 25 | Arsenal | W 3-1 | Herd 2, Chisnall | 62,308 |
| Aug 29 | EVERTON | L 0-1 | | 63,437 |
| Sep 1 | BIRMINGHAM CITY | W 2-0 | Giles, Herd | 39,847 |
| Sep 5 | Bolton Wanderers | L 0-3 | | 44,859 |
| Sep 8 | Leyton Orient | L 0-1 | | 24,901 |
| Sep 12 | BOLTON WANDERERS | W 3-0 | Cantwell, Herd 2 | 37,721 |
| Sep 15 | MANCHESTER CITY | L 2-3 | Law 2 | 49,193 |
| Sep 22 | BURNLEY | L 2-5 | Stiles, Law | 45,954 |
| Sep 29 | Sheffield Wednesday | L 0-1 | | 40,520 |
| Oct 6 | Blackpool | D 2-2 | Herd 2 | 33,242 |
| Oct 13 | BLACKBURN ROVERS | L 0-3 | | 42,252 |
| Oct 20 | Tottenham Hotspur | L 2-6 | Herd, Quixall (pen) | 51,314 |
| Oct 27 | WEST HAM UNITED | W 3-1 | Quixall 2 (1 pen), Law | 29,204 |
| Nov 3 | Ipswich Town | W 5-3 | Law 4, Herd | 18,483 |
| Nov 10 | LIVERPOOL | D 3-3 | Herd, Quixall (pen), Giles | 43,810 |
| Nov 17 | Wolverhampton Wanderers | W 3-2 | Herd, Law 2 | 27,305 |
| Nov 24 | ASTON VILLA | D 2-2 | Quixall 2 (1 pen) | 36,852 |
| Dec 1 | Sheffield United | D 1-1 | Charlton | 25,173 |
| Dec 8 | NOTTINGHAM FOREST | W 5-1 | Herd 2, Charlton, Law, Giles | 27,946 |
| Dec 15 | West Bromwich Albion | L 0-3 | | 18,113 |
| Dec 26 | Fulham | W 1-0 | Charlton | 23,928 |
| Feb 23 | BLACKPOOL | D 1-1 | Herd | 43,121 |
| Mar 2 | Blackburn Rovers | D 2-2 | Law, Charlton | 27,924 |
| Mar 9 | TOTTENHAM HOTSPUR | L 0-2 | | 53,416 |
| Mar 18 | West Ham United | L 1-3 | Herd | 28,950 |
| Mar 23 | IPSWICH TOWN | L 0-1 | | 32,792 |
| Apr 1 | FULHAM | L 0-2 | | 28,124 |
| Apr 9 | Aston Villa | W 2-1 | Stiles, Charlton | 26,867 |
| Apr 13 | Liverpool | L 0-1 | | 51,529 |
| Apr 15 | LEICESTER CITY | D 2-2 | Herd, Charlton | 50,005 |
| Apr 16 | Leicester City | L 3-4 | Law 3 | 37,002 |
| Apr 20 | SHEFFIELD UNITED | D 1-1 | Law | 31,179 |
| Apr 22 | WOLVERHAMPTON WANDERERS | W 2-1 | Herd, Law | 36,147 |
| May 1 | SHEFFIELD WEDNESDAY | L 1-3 | Setters | 31,878 |
| May 4 | Burnley | W 1-0 | Law | 30,266 |
| May 6 | ARSENAL | L 2-3 | Law 2 | 35,999 |
| Mar 10 | Birmingham City | L 1-2 | Law | 21,814 |
| May 15 | Manchester City | D 1-1 | Quixall (pen) | 52,424 |
| May 18 | LEYTON ORIENT | W 3-1 | Law, Charlton, Charlton S o.g. | 32,759 |
| May 20 | Nottingham Forest | L 2-3 | Giles, Herd | 16,130 |

### FA Cup

| | | | | | |
|---|---|---|---|---|---|
| Mar 4 | HUDDERSFIELD TOWN | (Rd3) | W 5-0 | Law 3, Quixall, Giles | 47,703 |
| Mar 11 | ASTON VILLA | (Rd4) | W 1-0 | Quixall | 52,265 |
| Mar 16 | CHELSEA | (Rd5) | W 2-1 | Law, Quixall | 48,298 |
| Mar 30 | Coventry City | (Rd6) | W 3-1 | Charlton 2, Quixall | 44,000 |
| Apr 27 | Southampton* | (SF) | W 1-0 | Law | 65,000 |
| May 25 | Leicester City** | (F) | W 3-1 | Law, Herd 2 | 99,604 |

*Played at Villa Park, Birmingham. **Played at Wembley Stadium, London.

### League & Cup Appearances

| PLAYER | LEAGUE | CUP COMPETITION FA CUP | TOTAL |
|---|---|---|---|
| Brennan | 37 | 4 | 41 |
| Cantwell | 25 | 5 | 30 |
| Charlton | 28 | 6 | 34 |
| Chisnall | 6 | | 6 |
| Crerand | 19 | 3 | 22 |
| Dunne | 25 | 3 | 28 |
| Foulkes | 41 | 6 | 47 |
| Gaskell | 18 | 2 | 20 |
| Giles | 36 | 6 | 42 |
| Gregg | 24 | 4 | 28 |
| Haydock | 1 | | 1 |
| Herd | 37 | 6 | 43 |
| Law | 38 | 6 | 44 |
| Lawton | 12 | | 12 |
| McMillan | 4 | | 4 |
| Moir | 9 | | 9 |
| Nicholson | 10 | | 10 |
| Pearson | 2 | | 2 |
| Quixall | 31 | 5 | 36 |
| Setters | 27 | 6 | 33 |
| Stiles | 31 | 4 | 35 |
| Walker | 1 | | 1 |

### Goalscorers

| PLAYER | LEAGUE | CUP COMPETITION FA CUP | TOTAL |
|---|---|---|---|
| Law | 23 | 6 | 29 |
| Herd | 19 | 2 | 21 |
| Quixall | 7 | 4 | 11 |
| Charlton | 7 | 2 | 9 |
| Giles | 4 | 1 | 5 |
| Stiles | 2 | | 2 |
| Cantwell | 1 | | 1 |
| Chisnall | 1 | | 1 |
| Moir | 1 | | 1 |
| Setters | 1 | | 1 |
| Opps' o.gs. | 1 | | 1 |

### Final Division One Table

| | | P | W | D | L | F | A | PTS |
|---|---|---|---|---|---|---|---|---|
| 1 | Everton | 42 | 25 | 11 | 6 | 84 | 42 | 61 |
| 2 | Tottenham Hotspur | 42 | 23 | 9 | 10 | 111 | 62 | 55 |
| 3 | Burnley | 42 | 22 | 10 | 10 | 78 | 57 | 54 |
| 4 | Leicester City | 42 | 20 | 12 | 10 | 79 | 53 | 52 |
| 5 | Wolverhampton W | 42 | 20 | 10 | 12 | 93 | 65 | 50 |
| 6 | Sheffield Wednesday | 42 | 19 | 10 | 13 | 77 | 63 | 48 |
| 7 | Arsenal | 42 | 18 | 10 | 14 | 86 | 77 | 46 |
| 8 | Liverpool | 42 | 17 | 10 | 15 | 71 | 59 | 44 |
| 9 | Nottingham Forest | 42 | 17 | 10 | 15 | 67 | 69 | 44 |
| 10 | Sheffield United | 42 | 16 | 12 | 14 | 58 | 60 | 44 |
| 11 | Blackburn Rovers | 42 | 15 | 12 | 15 | 79 | 71 | 42 |
| 12 | West Ham United | 42 | 14 | 12 | 16 | 73 | 69 | 40 |
| 13 | Blackpool | 42 | 13 | 14 | 15 | 58 | 64 | 40 |
| 14 | WBA | 42 | 16 | 7 | 19 | 71 | 79 | 39 |
| 15 | Aston Villa | 42 | 15 | 8 | 19 | 62 | 68 | 38 |
| 16 | Fulham | 42 | 14 | 10 | 18 | 50 | 71 | 38 |
| 17 | Ipswich Town | 42 | 12 | 11 | 19 | 59 | 78 | 35 |
| 18 | Bolton Wanderers | 42 | 15 | 5 | 22 | 55 | 75 | 35 |
| 19 | Manchester United | 42 | 12 | 10 | 20 | 67 | 81 | 34 |
| 20 | Birmingham City | 42 | 10 | 13 | 19 | 63 | 90 | 33 |
| 21 | Manchester City | 42 | 10 | 11 | 21 | 58 | 102 | 31 |
| 22 | Leyton Orient | 42 | 6 | 9 | 27 | 37 | 81 | 21 |

### Fact File

Denis Law, soon to be crowned 'King' by the Stretford End, ended his brief exile in Italy with Torino to sign for United in August 1962.

**MANAGER:** Matt Busby
**MOST APPEARANCES:** Bill Foulkes 47
**TOP SCORER:** Denis Law 29 (23 League)
**BIGGEST WIN:** 5-0 v Huddersfield Town, 4 March 1963, FA Cup
**HIGHEST ATTENDANCE:** 99,604 v Leicester City, 25 May 1963, FA Cup

## Season 1963-64

### Football League Division One

| DATE | OPPONENTS | SCORE | GOALSCORERS | ATTENDANCE |
|---|---|---|---|---|
| Aug 24 | Sheffield Wednesday | D 3-3 | Moir, Charlton 2 | 32,177 |
| Aug 28 | IPSWICH TOWN | W 2-0 | Law 2 | 39,921 |
| Aug 31 | EVERTON | W 5-1 | Chisnall 2, Law 2, Sadler | 62,965 |
| Sep 3 | Ipswich Town | W 7-2 | Law 3 (1 pen), Sadler, Setters, Moir, Chisnall | 28,113 |
| Sep 7 | Birmingham City | D 1-1 | Chisnall | 36,874 |
| Sep 11 | BLACKPOOL | W 3-0 | Law, Charlton 2 | 47,400 |
| Sep 14 | WEST BROMWICH ALBION | W 1-0 | Sadler | 50,453 |
| Sep 16 | Blackpool | L 0-1 | | 29,806 |
| Sep 21 | Arsenal | L 1-2 | Herd | 56,776 |
| Sep 28 | LEICESTER CITY | W 3-1 | Setters, Herd 2 | 41,374 |
| Oct 2 | Chelsea | D 1-1 | Setters | 45,351 |
| Oct 5 | Bolton Wanderers | W 1-0 | Herd | 35,872 |
| Oct 19 | Nottingham Forest | W 2-1 | Chisnall, Quixall | 41,426 |
| Oct 26 | WEST HAM UNITED | L 0-1 | | 45,120 |
| Oct 28 | BLACKBURN ROVERS | D 2-2 | Quixall 2 | 41,169 |
| Nov 2 | Wolverhampton Wanderers | L 0-2 | | 34,159 |
| Nov 9 | TOTTENHAM HOTSPUR | W 4-1 | Law 3, Herd | 57,413 |
| Nov 16 | Aston Villa | L 0-4 | | 36,276 |
| Nov 23 | LIVERPOOL | L 0-1 | | 54,654 |
| Nov 30 | Sheffield United | W 2-1 | Law 2 | 30,615 |
| Dec 7 | STOKE CITY | W 5-2 | Herd, Law 4 | 52,232 |
| Dec 14 | SHEFFIELD WEDNESDAY | W 3-1 | Herd 3 | 35,139 |
| Dec 21 | Everton | L 0-4 | | 48,027 |
| Dec 26 | Burnley | L 1-6 | Herd | 35,764 |
| Dec 28 | BURNLEY | W 5-1 | Herd 2, Moore 2, Best | 47,834 |
| Jan 11 | BIRMINGHAM CITY | L 1-2 | Sadler | 44,695 |
| Jan 18 | West Bromwich Albion | W 4-1 | Charlton, Best, Law 2 | 25,624 |
| Feb 1 | ARSENAL | W 3-1 | Herd, Law, Setters | 48,340 |
| Feb 8 | Leicester City | L 2-3 | Law, Herd | 35,538 |
| Feb 19 | BOLTON WANDERERS | W 5-0 | Best 2, Herd 2, Charlton | 33,926 |
| Feb 22 | Blackburn Rovers | W 3-1 | Chisnall, Law 2 | 36,726 |
| Mar 7 | West Ham United | W 2-0 | Sadler, Herd | 27,027 |
| Mar 21 | Tottenham Hotspur | W 3-2 | Law, Moore, Charlton | 56,392 |
| Mar 23 | CHELSEA | D 1-1 | Law | 42,931 |
| Mar 27 | Fulham | D 2-2 | Herd, Law | 41,769 |
| Mar 28 | WOLVERHAMPTON WANDERERS | D 2-2 | Herd, Charlton | 44,470 |
| Mar 30 | FULHAM | W 3-0 | Crerand, Foulkes, Herd | 42,279 |
| Apr 4 | Liverpool | L 0-3 | | 52,559 |
| Apr 6 | ASTON VILLA | W 1-0 | Law | 25,848 |
| Apr 13 | SHEFFIELD UNITED | W 2-1 | Law, Moir | 27,587 |
| Apr 18 | Stoke City | L 1-3 | Charlton | 45,670 |
| Apr 25 | NOTTINGHAM FOREST | W 3-1 | Law 2, Moore | 31,671 |

### FA Cup

| | | | | | |
|---|---|---|---|---|---|
| Jan 4 | Southampton | (Rd3) | W 3-2 | Moore, Herd, Crerand | 29,164 |
| Jan 25 | BRISTOL ROVERS | (Rd4) | W 4-1 | Law 3, Herd | 55,772 |
| Feb 15 | Barnsley | (Rd5) | W 4-0 | Law 2, Best, Herd | 38,076 |
| Feb 29 | SUNDERLAND | (Rd6) | D 3-3 | Charlton, Best, Hurley o.g. | 63,700 |
| Mar 4 | Sunderland | (R) | D 2-2* | Law, Charlton | 68,000 |
| Mar 9 | Sunderland** | (2R) | W 5-1 | Law 3 (1 pen), Chisnall, Herd | 54,952 |
| Mar 14 | West Ham United† | (SF) | L 1-3 | Law | 65,000 |

*After extra-time. **Played at Leeds Road, Huddersfield.
†Played at Hillsborough, Sheffield.

### European Cup-Winners' Cup

| | | | | | |
|---|---|---|---|---|---|
| Sep 25 | Willem II | (Rd1/1L) | D 1-1 | Herd | 20,000 |
| Oct 15 | WILLEM II | (Rd1/2L) | W 6-1 | Law 3, Setters, Charlton, Chisnall | 46,272 |
| Dec 3 | Tottenham Hotspur | (Rd2/1L) | L 0-2 | | 57,447 |
| Dec 10 | TOTTENHAM HOTSPUR | (Rd2/2L) | W 4-1 | Herd 2, Charlton 2 | 48,639 |
| Feb 26 | SC LISBON | (QF/1L) | W 4-1 | Law 3 (2 pens), Charlton | 60,207 |
| Mar 18 | SC Lisbon | (QF/2L) | L 0-5 | | 50,000 |

### FA Charity Shield

| | | | | |
|---|---|---|---|---|
| Aug 17 | Everton | L 0-4 | | 54,840 |

**MANAGER:** Matt Busby
**MOST APPEARANCES:** Pat Crerand, Bill Foulkes 55
**TOP SCORER:** Denis Law 46 (30 League)
**BIGGEST WIN:** 7-2 v Ipswich Town, 3 September 1963, League
**HIGHEST ATTENDANCE:** 68,000 v Sunderland (A), 4 March 1964, FA Cup

### League & Cup Appearances

| PLAYER | LEAGUE | CUP COMPETITION | | OTHER | TOTAL |
|---|---|---|---|---|---|
| | | FA CUP | ECWC | | |
| Anderson | 2 | 1 | | | 3 |
| Best | 17 | 7 | 2 | | 26 |
| Brennan | 17 | 5 | 2 | | 24 |
| Cantwell | 28 | 2 | 4 | 1 | 35 |
| Charlton | 40 | 7 | 6 | 1 | 54 |
| Chisnall | 20 | 4 | 4 | | 28 |
| Crerand | 41 | 7 | 6 | 1 | 55 |
| Dunne | 40 | 7 | 6 | 1 | 54 |
| Foulkes | 41 | 7 | 6 | 1 | 55 |
| Gaskell | 17 | 7 | 4 | 1 | 29 |
| Gregg | 25 | | 2 | | 27 |
| Giles | | | | 1 | 1 |
| Herd | 30 | 7 | 6 | 1 | 44 |
| Law | 30 | 6 | 5 | 1 | 42 |
| Moir | 18 | | | | 18 |
| Moore | 18 | 1 | | | 19 |
| Quixall | 9 | | 3 | 1 | 13 |
| Sadler | 19 | | 2 | | 21 |
| Setters | 32 | 7 | 6 | 1 | 46 |
| Stiles | 17 | 2 | 2 | | 21 |
| Tranter | 1 | | | | 1 |

### Goalscorers

| PLAYER | LEAGUE | CUP COMPETITION | | OTHER | TOTAL |
|---|---|---|---|---|---|
| | | FA CUP | ECWC | | |
| Law | 30 | 10 | 6 | | 46 |
| Herd | 20 | 4 | 3 | | 27 |
| Charlton | 9 | 2 | 4 | | 15 |
| Chisnall | 6 | 1 | 1 | | 8 |
| Best | 4 | 2 | | | 6 |
| Moore | 4 | 1 | | | 5 |
| Sadler | 5 | | | | 5 |
| Setters | 4 | | 1 | | 5 |
| Moir | 3 | | | | 3 |
| Quixall | 3 | | | | 3 |
| Crerand | 1 | 1 | | | 2 |
| Foulkes | 1 | | | | 1 |
| Opps' o.gs. | | 1 | | | 1 |

### Fact File

George Best, who was later to become arguably the game's greatest-ever player, made his league debut against West Bromwich Albion at Old Trafford, September 1963.

### Final Division One Table

| | | P | W | D | L | F | A | Pts |
|---|---|---|---|---|---|---|---|---|
| 1 | Liverpool | 42 | 26 | 5 | 11 | 92 | 45 | 57 |
| 2 | Manchester United | 42 | 23 | 7 | 12 | 90 | 62 | 53 |
| 3 | Everton | 42 | 21 | 10 | 11 | 84 | 64 | 52 |
| 4 | Tottenham Hotspur | 42 | 22 | 7 | 13 | 97 | 81 | 51 |
| 5 | Chelsea | 42 | 20 | 10 | 12 | 72 | 56 | 50 |
| 6 | Sheffield Wednesday | 42 | 19 | 11 | 12 | 84 | 67 | 49 |
| 7 | Blackburn Rovers | 42 | 18 | 10 | 14 | 89 | 65 | 46 |
| 8 | Arsenal | 42 | 17 | 11 | 14 | 90 | 82 | 45 |
| 9 | Burnley | 42 | 17 | 10 | 15 | 71 | 64 | 44 |
| 10 | WBA | 42 | 16 | 11 | 15 | 70 | 61 | 43 |
| 11 | Leicester City | 42 | 16 | 11 | 15 | 61 | 58 | 43 |
| 12 | Sheffield United | 42 | 16 | 11 | 15 | 61 | 64 | 43 |
| 13 | Nottingham Forest | 42 | 16 | 9 | 17 | 64 | 68 | 41 |
| 14 | West Ham United | 42 | 14 | 12 | 16 | 69 | 74 | 40 |
| 15 | Fulham | 42 | 13 | 13 | 16 | 58 | 65 | 39 |
| 16 | Wolverhampton W | 42 | 12 | 15 | 15 | 70 | 80 | 39 |
| 17 | Stoke City | 42 | 14 | 10 | 18 | 77 | 78 | 38 |
| 18 | Blackpool | 42 | 13 | 9 | 20 | 52 | 73 | 35 |
| 19 | Aston Villa | 42 | 11 | 12 | 19 | 62 | 71 | 34 |
| 20 | Birmingham City | 42 | 11 | 7 | 24 | 54 | 92 | 29 |
| 21 | Bolton Wanderers | 42 | 10 | 8 | 24 | 48 | 80 | 28 |
| 22 | Ipswich Town | 42 | 9 | 7 | 26 | 56 | 121 | 25 |

## Season 1964-65

### Football League Division One

| DATE | OPPONENTS | SCORE | GOALSCORERS | ATTENDANCE |
|---|---|---|---|---|
| Aug 22 | WEST BROMWICH ALBION | D 2-2 | Law, Charlton | 52,007 |
| Aug 24 | West Ham United | L 1-3 | Law | 37,070 |
| Aug 29 | Leicester City | D 2-2 | Sadler, Law | 32,373 |
| Sep 2 | WEST HAM UNITED | W 3-1 | Connelly, Law, Best | 45,123 |
| Sep 5 | Fulham | L 1-2 | Connelly | 36,291 |
| Sep 8 | Everton | D 3-3 | Law, Connelly, Herd | 63,024 |
| Sep 12 | NOTTINGHAM FOREST | W 3-0 | Herd 2, Connelly | 45,012 |
| Sep 16 | EVERTON | W 2-1 | Best, Law | 49,968 |
| Sep 19 | Stoke City | W 2-1 | Herd, Connelly | 40,031 |
| Sep 26 | TOTTENHAM HOTSPUR | W 4-1 | Crerand 2, Law 2 | 53,058 |
| Sep 30 | Chelsea | W 2-0 | Best, Law | 60,769 |
| Oct 6 | Burnley | D 0-0 | | 30,761 |
| Oct 10 | SUNDERLAND | W 1-0 | Herd | 48,577 |
| Oct 17 | Wolverhampton Wanderers | W 4-2 | Law 2, Herd, Harris o.g. | 26,763 |
| Oct 24 | ASTON VILLA | W 7-0 | Herd 2, Law 4, Connelly | 35,807 |
| Oct 31 | Liverpool | W 2-0 | Herd, Crerand | 52,402 |
| Nov 7 | SHEFFIELD WEDNESDAY | W 1-0 | Herd | 50,178 |
| Nov 14 | Blackpool | W 2-1 | Herd, Connelly | 31,129 |
| Nov 21 | BLACKBURN ROVERS | W 3-0 | Best, Connelly, Herd | 49,633 |
| Nov 28 | Arsenal | W 3-2 | Law 2, Conelly | 59,627 |
| Dec 5 | LEEDS UNITED | L 0-1 | | 53,374 |
| Dec 12 | West Bromwich Albion | D 1-1 | Law | 28,126 |
| Dec 16 | BIRMINGHAM CITY | D 1-1 | Charlton (pen) | 25,721 |
| Dec 26 | Sheffield United | W 1-0 | Best | 37,295 |
| Dec 28 | SHEFFIELD UNITED | D 1-1 | Herd | 42,219 |
| Jan 16 | Nottingham Forest | D 2-2 | Law 2 | 43,009 |
| Jan 23 | STOKE CITY | D 1-1 | Law | 50,392 |
| Feb 6 | Tottenham Hotspur | L 0-1 | | 58,639 |
| Feb 13 | BURNLEY | W 3-2 | Best, Herd, Charlton | 38,865 |
| Feb 24 | Sunderland | L 0-1 | | 51,336 |
| Feb 27 | WOLVERHAMPTON WANDERERS | W 3-0 | Connelly, Charlton 2 | 37,018 |
| Mar 13 | CHELSEA | W 4-0 | Best, Herd 2, Law | 56,261 |
| Mar 15 | FULHAM | W 4-1 | Herd 2, Connelly 2 | 45,402 |
| Mar 20 | Sheffield Wednesday | L 0-1 | | 33,549 |
| Mar 22 | BLACKPOOL | W 2-0 | Law 2 | 42,318 |
| Apr 3 | Blackburn Rovers | W 5-0 | Charlton 3, Connelly, Herd | 29,363 |
| Apr 12 | LEICESTER CITY | W 1-0 | Herd | 34,114 |
| Apr 17 | Leeds United | W 1-0 | Connelly | 52,368 |
| Apr 19 | Birmingham City | W 4-2 | Best 2, Charlton, Cantwell | 28,907 |
| Apr 24 | LIVERPOOL | W 3-0 | Law 2, Connelly | 55,772 |
| Apr 26 | ARSENAL | W 3-1 | Best, Law 2 | 51,625 |
| Apr 28 | Aston Villa | L 1-2 | Charlton | 36,081 |

### FA Cup

| DATE | OPPONENTS | ROUND | SCORE | GOALSCORERS | ATTENDANCE |
|---|---|---|---|---|---|
| Jan 9 | CHESTER | (Rd3) | W 2-1 | Best, Kinsey | 40,000 |
| Jan 30 | Stoke City | (Rd4) | D 0-0 | | 53,009 |
| Feb 3 | STOKE CITY | (R) | W 1-0 | Herd | 50,814 |
| Feb 20 | BURNLEY | (Rd5) | W 2-1 | Law, Crerand | 54,000 |
| Mar 10 | Wolverhampton Wanderers | (Rd6) | W 5-3 | Law 2, Herd, Best, Crerand | 53,581 |
| Mar 27 | Leeds United* | (SF) | D 0-0 | | 65,000 |
| Mar 31 | Leeds United** | (R) | L 0-1 | | 46,300 |

*Played at Hillsborough, Sheffield. **Played at City Ground, Nottingham.

### Inter-Cities Fairs Cup

| DATE | OPPONENTS | ROUND | SCORE | GOALSCORERS | ATTENDANCE |
|---|---|---|---|---|---|
| Sep 23 | Djurgarden | (Rd1/1L) | D 1-1 | Herd | 6,537 |
| Oct 27 | DJURGARDEN | (Rd1/2L) | W 6-1 | Law 3 (1 pen), Charlton 2, Best | 38,437 |
| Nov 11 | Borussia Dortmund | (Rd2/1L) | W 6-1 | Charlton 3, Herd, Best, Law | 25,000 |
| Dec 2 | BORUSSIA DORTMUND | (Rd2/2L) | W 4-0 | Charlton 2, Law, Connelly | 31,896 |
| Jan 20 | Everton | (Rd3/1L) | D 1-1 | Connelly | 49,075 |
| Feb 9 | EVERTON | (Rd3/2L) | W 2-1 | Connelly, Herd | 54,397 |
| May 12 | RC Strasbourg | (QF/1L) | W 5-0 | Law 2, Connelly, Herd, Charlton | 28,914 |
| May 19 | RC STRASBOURG | (QF/2L) | D 0-0 | | 34,188 |
| May 31 | FERENCVAROS | (SF/1L) | W 3-2 | Herd 2, Law (pen) | 39,902 |
| Jun 6 | Ferencvaros | (SF/2L) | L 0-1 | | 60,000 |
| Jun 16 | Ferencvaros | (SF/PO) | L 1-2 | Connelly | 75,000 |

**MANAGER:** Matt Busby

**MOST APPEARANCES:** Shay Brennan, John Connelly, Tony Dunne, Bill Foulkes 60

**TOP SCORER:** Denis Law 39 (28 League)

**BIGGEST WIN:** 7-0 v Aston Villa, 24 October 1964, League

**HIGHEST ATTENDANCE:** 75,000 v Ferencvaros, 16 June 1965, Inter-Cities Fairs Cup

### League & Cup Appearances

| PLAYER | LEAGUE | CUP COMPETITION | | TOTAL |
|---|---|---|---|---|
| | | FA CUP | ICFC | |
| Aston | 1 | | | 1 |
| Best | 41 | 7 | 11 | 59 |
| Brennan | 42 | 7 | 11 | 60 |
| Cantwell | 2 | | | 2 |
| Charlton | 41 | 7 | 11 | 59 |
| Connelly | 42 | 7 | 11 | 60 |
| Crerand | 39 | 7 | 11 | 57 |
| Dunne A. | 42 | 7 | 11 | 60 |
| Dunne P. | 37 | 7 | 11 | 55 |
| Fitzpatrick | 2 | | | 2 |
| Foulkes | 42 | 7 | 11 | 60 |
| Gaskell | 5 | | | 5 |
| Herd | 37 | 7 | 11 | 55 |
| Kinsey | | 1 | | 1 |
| Law | 36 | 6 | 10 | 52 |
| Moir | 1 | | | 1 |
| Sadler | 6 | | | 6 |
| Setters | 5 | | 1 | 6 |
| Stiles | 41 | 7 | 11 | 59 |

### Goalscorers

| PLAYER | LEAGUE | CUP COMPETITION | | TOTAL |
|---|---|---|---|---|
| | | FA CUP | ICFC | |
| Law | 28 | 3 | 8 | 39 |
| Herd | 20 | 2 | 6 | 28 |
| Connelly | 15 | | 5 | 20 |
| Charlton | 10 | | 8 | 18 |
| Best | 10 | 2 | 1 | 13 |
| Crerand | 3 | 2 | | 5 |
| Cantwell | 1 | | | 1 |
| Kinsey | | 1 | | 1 |
| Sadler | 1 | | | 1 |
| Stiles | | | 1 | 1 |
| Opps' o.gs. | 1 | | | 1 |

### Fact File

United's Inter-Cities Fairs Cup (forerunner of the UEFA Cup) campaign stretched well into the summer with the semi-final play-off against Ferencvaros being played on 16 June in Budapest, Hungary.

### Final Division One Table

| | P | W | D | L | F | A | Pts |
|---|---|---|---|---|---|---|---|
| 1 Manchester United | 42 | 26 | 9 | 7 | 89 | 39 | 61 |
| 2 Leeds United | 42 | 26 | 9 | 7 | 83 | 52 | 61 |
| 3 Chelsea | 42 | 24 | 8 | 10 | 89 | 54 | 56 |
| 4 Everton | 42 | 17 | 15 | 10 | 69 | 60 | 49 |
| 5 Nottingham Forest | 42 | 17 | 13 | 12 | 71 | 67 | 47 |
| 6 Tottenham Hotspur | 42 | 19 | 7 | 16 | 87 | 71 | 45 |
| 7 Liverpool | 42 | 17 | 10 | 15 | 67 | 73 | 44 |
| 8 Sheffield Wednesday | 42 | 16 | 11 | 15 | 57 | 55 | 43 |
| 9 West Ham United | 42 | 19 | 4 | 19 | 82 | 71 | 42 |
| 10 Blackburn Rovers | 42 | 16 | 10 | 16 | 83 | 79 | 42 |
| 11 Stoke City | 42 | 16 | 10 | 16 | 67 | 66 | 42 |
| 12 Burnley | 42 | 16 | 10 | 16 | 70 | 70 | 42 |
| 13 Arsenal | 42 | 17 | 7 | 18 | 69 | 75 | 41 |
| 14 WBA | 42 | 13 | 13 | 16 | 70 | 65 | 39 |
| 15 Sunderland | 42 | 14 | 9 | 19 | 64 | 74 | 37 |
| 16 Aston Villa | 42 | 16 | 5 | 21 | 57 | 82 | 37 |
| 17 Blackpool | 42 | 12 | 11 | 19 | 67 | 78 | 35 |
| 18 Leicester City | 42 | 11 | 13 | 18 | 69 | 85 | 35 |
| 19 Sheffield United | 42 | 12 | 11 | 19 | 50 | 64 | 35 |
| 20 Fulham | 42 | 11 | 12 | 19 | 60 | 78 | 34 |
| 21 Wolverhampton W | 42 | 13 | 4 | 25 | 59 | 89 | 30 |
| 22 Birmingham City | 42 | 8 | 11 | 23 | 64 | 96 | 27 |

# Season 1965-66

## Football League Division One

| DATE | OPPONENTS | SCORE | GOALSCORERS | ATTENDANCE |
|---|---|---|---|---|
| Aug 21 | SHEFFIELD WEDNESDAY | W 1-0 | Herd | 37,524 |
| Aug 24 | Nottingham Forest | L 2-4 | Aston, Best | 33,744 |
| Aug 28 | Northampton Town | D 1-1 | Connelly | 21,140 |
| Sep 1 | NOTTINGHAM FOREST | D 0-0 | | 38,777 |
| Sep 4 | STOKE CITY | D 1-1 | Herd | 37,603 |
| Sep 8 | Newcastle United | W 2-1 | Herd, Law | 57,380 |
| Sep 11 | Burnley | L 0-3 | | 30,235 |
| Sep 15 | NEWCASTLE UNITED | D 1-1 | Stiles | 30,401 |
| Sep 18 | CHELSEA | W 4-1 | Charlton, Law 3 | 37,917 |
| Sep 25 | Arsenal | L 2-4 | Charlton, Aston | 56,757 |
| Oct 9 | LIVERPOOL | W 2-0 | Best, Law | 58,161 |
| Oct 16 | Tottenham Hotspur | L 1-5 | Charlton | 58,051 |
| Oct 23 | FULHAM | W 4-1 | Herd 3, Charlton | 32,716 |
| Oct 30 | Blackpool | W 2-1 | Herd 2 | 24,703 |
| Nov 6 | BLACKBURN ROVERS | D 2-2 | Charlton, Law | 38,823 |
| Nov 13 | Leicester City | W 5-0 | Herd 2, Connelly, Charlton, Best | 34,551 |
| Nov 20 | SHEFFIELD UNITED | W 3-1 | Best 2, Law | 37,922 |
| Dec 4 | WEST HAM UNITED | D 0-0 | | 32,924 |
| Dec 11 | Sunderland | W 3-2 | Best 2, Herd | 37,417 |
| Dec 15 | EVERTON | W 3-0 | Best, Herd, Charlton | 32,624 |
| Dec 18 | TOTTENHAM HOTSPUR | W 5-1 | Charlton, Law 2, Herd, Beal o.g. | 39,270 |
| Dec 27 | WEST BROMWICH ALBION | D 1-1 | Law (pen) | 54,102 |
| Jan 1 | Liverpool | L 1-2 | Law | 53,790 |
| Jan 8 | SUNDERLAND | D 1-1 | Best | 39,162 |
| Jan 12 | Leeds United | D 1-1 | Herd | 49,672 |
| Jan 15 | Fulham | W 1-0 | Charlton | 33,018 |
| Feb 29 | Sheffield Wednesday | D 0-0 | | 39,281 |
| Feb 5 | NORTHAMPTON TOWN | W 6-2 | Charlton 3, Law 2, Connelly | 34,986 |
| Feb 19 | Stoke City | D 2-2 | Herd, Connelly | 36,667 |
| Feb 26 | BURNLEY | W 4-2 | Charlton, Herd 3 | 49,892 |
| Mar 12 | Chelsea | L 0-2 | | 60,269 |
| Mar 19 | ARSENAL | W 2-1 | Law, Stiles | 47,246 |
| Apr 6 | Aston Villa | D 1-1 | Cantwell | 28,211 |
| Apr 9 | LEICESTER CITY | L 1-2 | Connelly | 42,593 |
| Apr 16 | Sheffield United | L 1-3 | Sadler | 22,330 |
| Apr 25 | Everton | D 0-0 | | 50,843 |
| Apr 27 | BLACKPOOL | W 2-1 | Law, Charlton | 26,953 |
| Apr 30 | West Ham United | L 2-3 | Cantwell, Aston | 36,416 |
| May 4 | West Bromwich Albion | D 3-3 | Herd, Aston, Dunne A. | 22,609 |
| May 7 | Blackburn Rovers | W 4-1 | Herd 2, Charlton, Sadler | 14,513 |
| May 9 | ASTON VILLA | W 6-1 | Herd 2, Sadler 2, Charlton, Ryan | 23,039 |
| May 19 | LEEDS UNITED | D 1-1 | Herd | 35,008 |

## FA Cup

| | | | | | |
|---|---|---|---|---|---|
| Jan 22 | Derby County | (Rd3) | W 5-2 | Law 2 (1 pen), Best 2, Herd | 33,827 |
| Feb 12 | ROTHERHAM UNITED | (Rd4) | D 0-0 | | 54,263 |
| Feb 15 | Rotherham United | (R) | W 1-0* | Connelly | 23,500 |
| Mar 5 | Wolverhampton Wanderers | (Rd5 | W 4-2 | Law 2, Best, Herd | 53,500 |
| Mar 26 | Preston North End | (Rd6) | D 1-1 | Herd | 37,876 |
| Mar 30 | PRESTON NORTH END | (R) | W 3-1 | Law 2, Connelly | 60,433 |
| Apr 23 | Everton** | (SF) | L 0-1 | | 60,000 |

*After extra-time. **Played at Burnden Park, Bolton.

## European Cup

| | | | | | |
|---|---|---|---|---|---|
| Sep 22 | Helsinki JK | (PRd/1L) | W 3-2 | Herd, Connelly, Law | 15,572 |
| Oct 6 | HELSINKI JK | (PRd/2L) | W 6-0 | Connelly 3, Best 2, Charlton | 30,388 |
| Nov 17 | ASK Vorwaerts | (Rd1/1L) | W 2-0 | Law, Connelly | 40,000 |
| Dec 1 | ASK VORWAERTS | (Rd1/2L) | W 3-1 | Herd 3 | 30,082 |
| Feb 2 | SL BENFICA | (Rd2/1L) | W 3-2 | Herd, Law, Foulkes | 64,035 |
| Mar 9 | SL Benfica | (Rd2/2L) | W 5-1 | Best 2, Connelly, Crerand, Charlton | 75,000 |
| Apr 13 | Partizan Belgrade | (SF/1L) | L 0-2 | | 60,000 |
| Apr 20 | PARTIZAN BELGRADE | (SF/2L) | W 1-0 | Soskic o.g. | 62,500 |

## FA Charity Shield

| | | | | |
|---|---|---|---|---|
| Aug 14 | LIVERPOOL | D 2-2 | Best, Herd | 48,502 |

**MANAGER:** Matt Busby

**MOST APPEARANCES:** Pat Crerand, Tony Dunne 56

**TOP SCORER:** David Herd 33 (24 League)

**BIGGEST WIN:** 6-0 v Helsinki JK, 6 October 1965, European Cup

**HIGHEST ATTENDANCE:** 75,000 v SL Benfica, 9 March 1966, European Cup

## League & Cup Appearances

| PLAYER | LEAGUE | CUP COMPETITION | | OTHER | TOTAL |
|---|---|---|---|---|---|
| | | FA CUP | EC | | |
| Anderson | 5 (1) | 1 | 1 | | 7 (1) |
| Aston | 23 | 2 | 2 | 1 | 28 |
| Best | 31 | 5 | 6 | 1 | 43 |
| Brennan | 28 | 5 | 5 | 1 | 39 |
| Cantwell | 23 | 2 | 3 | 1 | 29 |
| Charlton | 38 | 7 | 8 | 1 | 54 |
| Connelly | 31 (1) | 6 | 8 | | 45 (1) |
| Crerand | 41 | 7 | 7 | 1 | 56 |
| Dunne A. | 40 | 7 | 8 | 1 | 56 |
| Dunne P. | 8 | | 2 | 1 | 11 |
| Fitzpatrick | 3 (1) | | 1 | | 4 (1) |
| Foulkes | 33 | 7 | 8 | | 48 |
| Gaskell | 8 | | 1 | | 9 |
| Gregg | 26 | 7 | 5 | | 38 |
| Herd | 36 (1) | 7 | 7 | 1 | 51 (1) |
| Law | 33 | 7 | 8 | 1 | 49 |
| Noble | 2 | | | | 2 |
| Ryan | 4 | | | | 4 |
| Sadler | 10 | | | | 10 |
| Stiles | 39 | 7 | 8 | 1 | 55 |

## Goalscorers

| PLAYER | LEAGUE | CUP COMPETITION | | OTHER | TOTAL |
|---|---|---|---|---|---|
| | | FA CUP | EC | | |
| Herd | 24 | 3 | 5 | 1 | 33 |
| Law | 15 | 6 | 3 | | 24 |
| Charlton | 16 | | 2 | | 18 |
| Best | 9 | 3 | 4 | 1 | 17 |
| Connelly | 5 | 2 | 6 | | 13 |
| Aston | 4 | | | | 4 |
| Sadler | 4 | | | | 4 |
| Cantwell | 2 | | | | 2 |
| Stiles | 2 | | | | 2 |
| Crerand | | | 1 | | 1 |
| Dunne A. | 1 | | | | 1 |
| Foulkes | | | 1 | | 1 |
| Ryan | 1 | | | | 1 |
| Opps' o.gs. | 1 | | 1 | | 2 |

## Fact File

Old Trafford was used as a venue for the 1966 FIFA World Cup with Bulgaria, Hungary and Portugal all appearing in Group 3 at the stadium.

## Final Division One Table

| | | P | W | D | L | F | A | PTS |
|---|---|---|---|---|---|---|---|---|
| 1 | Liverpool | 42 | 26 | 9 | 7 | 79 | 34 | 61 |
| 2 | Leeds United | 42 | 23 | 9 | 10 | 79 | 38 | 55 |
| 3 | Burnley | 42 | 24 | 7 | 11 | 79 | 47 | 55 |
| 4 | Manchester United | 42 | 18 | 15 | 9 | 84 | 59 | 51 |
| 5 | Chelsea | 42 | 22 | 7 | 13 | 65 | 53 | 51 |
| 6 | WBA | 42 | 19 | 12 | 11 | 91 | 69 | 50 |
| 7 | Leicester City | 42 | 21 | 7 | 14 | 80 | 65 | 49 |
| 8 | Tottenham Hotspur | 42 | 16 | 12 | 14 | 75 | 66 | 44 |
| 9 | Sheffield United | 42 | 16 | 11 | 15 | 56 | 59 | 43 |
| 10 | Stoke City | 42 | 15 | 12 | 15 | 65 | 64 | 42 |
| 11 | Everton | 42 | 15 | 11 | 16 | 56 | 62 | 41 |
| 12 | West Ham United | 42 | 15 | 9 | 18 | 70 | 83 | 39 |
| 13 | Blackpool | 42 | 14 | 9 | 19 | 55 | 65 | 37 |
| 14 | Arsenal | 42 | 12 | 13 | 17 | 62 | 75 | 37 |
| 15 | Newcastle United | 42 | 14 | 9 | 19 | 50 | 63 | 37 |
| 16 | Aston Villa | 42 | 15 | 6 | 21 | 69 | 80 | 36 |
| 17 | Sheffield Wednesday | 42 | 14 | 8 | 20 | 56 | 66 | 36 |
| 18 | Nottingham Forest | 42 | 14 | 8 | 20 | 56 | 72 | 36 |
| 19 | Sunderland | 42 | 14 | 8 | 20 | 51 | 72 | 36 |
| 20 | Fulham | 42 | 14 | 7 | 21 | 67 | 85 | 35 |
| 21 | Northampton Town | 42 | 10 | 13 | 19 | 55 | 92 | 33 |
| 22 | Blackburn Rovers | 42 | 8 | 4 | 30 | 57 | 88 | 20 |

## Season 1966-67

### Football League Division One

| DATE | OPPONENTS | SCORE | GOALSCORERS | ATTENDANCE |
|---|---|---|---|---|
| Aug 20 | WEST BROMWICH ALBION | W 5-3 | Best, Stiles, Law 2, Herd | 41,343 |
| Aug 23 | Everton | W 2-1 | Law 2 | 60,657 |
| Aug 27 | Leeds United | L 1-3 | Best | 45,092 |
| Aug 31 | EVERTON | W 3-0 | Foulkes, Connelly, Law | 61,114 |
| Sep 3 | NEWCASTLE UNITED | W 3-2 | Herd, Connelly, Law | 44,448 |
| Sep 7 | Stoke City | L 0-3 | | 44,337 |
| Sep 10 | Tottenham Hotspur | L 1-2 | Law | 56,295 |
| Sep 17 | MANCHESTER CITY | W 1-0 | Law | 62,085 |
| Sep 24 | BURNLEY | W 4-1 | Law, Herd, Crerand, Sadler | 52,697 |
| Oct 1 | Nottingham Forest | L 1-4 | Charlton | 41,854 |
| Oct 8 | Blackpool | W 2-1 | Law 2 (1 pen) | 33,555 |
| Oct 15 | CHELSEA | D 1-1 | Law | 56,789 |
| Oct 29 | ARSENAL | W 1-0 | Sadler | 45,387 |
| Nov 5 | Chelsea | W 3-1 | Aston 2, Best | 55,958 |
| Nov 12 | SHEFFIELD WEDNESDAY | W 2-0 | Charlton, Herd | 46,942 |
| Nov 19 | Southampton | W 2-1 | Charlton 2 | 29,458 |
| Nov 26 | SUNDERLAND | W 5-0 | Herd 4, Law | 44,687 |
| Nov 30 | Leicester City | W 2-1 | Law, Best | 39,014 |
| Dec 3 | Aston Villa | L 1-2 | Herd | 39,937 |
| Dec 10 | LIVERPOOL | D 2-2 | Best 2 (1 pen) | 61,768 |
| Dec 17 | West Bromwich Albion | W 4-3 | Herd 3, Law | 32,080 |
| Dec 26 | Sheffield United | L 1-2 | Herd | 42,752 |
| Dec 27 | SHEFFIELD UNITED | W 2-0 | Crerand, Herd | 59,392 |
| Dec 31 | LEEDS UNITED | D 0-0 | | 53,486 |
| Jan 14 | TOTTENHAM HOTSPUR | W 1-0 | Herd | 57,366 |
| Jan 21 | Manchester City | D 1-1 | Foulkes | 62,983 |
| Feb 4 | Burnley | D 1-1 | Sadler | 40,165 |
| Feb 11 | NOTTINGHAM FOREST | W 1-0 | Law | 62,727 |
| Feb 25 | BLACKPOOL | W 4-0 | Charlton 2, Law, Hughes o.g. | 47,158 |
| Mar 3 | Arsenal | D 1-1 | Aston | 63,363 |
| Mar 11 | Newcastle United | D 0-0 | | 37,430 |
| Mar 18 | LEICESTER CITY | W 5-2 | Herd, Charlton, Aston, Law, Sadler | 50,281 |
| Mar 25 | Liverpool | D 0-0 | | 53,813 |
| Mar 27 | Fulham | D 2-2 | Best, Stiles | 47,290 |
| Mar 28 | FULHAM | W 2-1 | Foulkes, Stiles | 51,673 |
| Apr 1 | WEST HAM UNITED | W 3-0 | Charlton, Best, Law | 61,308 |
| Apr 10 | Sheffield Wednesday | D 2-2 | Charlton 2 | 51,101 |
| Apr 18 | SOUTHAMPTON | W 3-0 | Charlton, Law, Sadler | 54,291 |
| Apr 22 | Sunderland | D 0-0 | | 43,570 |
| Apr 29 | ASTON VILLA | W 3-1 | Aston, Law, Best | 55,782 |
| May 6 | West Ham United | W 6-1 | Charlton, Crerand, Foulkes, Best, Law 2 (1 pen) | 38,424 |
| May 13 | Stoke City | D 0-0 | | 61,071 |

### FA Cup

| | | | | |
|---|---|---|---|---|
| Jan 28 | STOKE CITY | (Rd3) W 2-0 | Law, Herd | 63,500 |
| Feb 18 | NORWICH CITY | (Rd4) L 1-2 | Law | 63,409 |

### League Cup

| | | | | |
|---|---|---|---|---|
| Sep 14 | Blackpool | (Rd2) L 1-5 | Herd | 15,570 |

### Fact File

A fantastic unbeaten run of 20 games during the second half of the season pushes United towards their seventh League championship.

**MANAGER:** Matt Busby
**MOST APPEARANCES:** George Best 45
**TOP SCORER:** Denis Law 23 (all League)
**BIGGEST WIN:** 6-1 v West Ham United, 6 May 1967, League
**HIGHEST ATTENDANCE:** 63,500 v Stoke City, 28 January 1967, FA Cup

### League & Cup Appearances

| PLAYER | LEAGUE | CUP COMPETITION | | TOTAL |
|---|---|---|---|---|
| | | FA CUP | LC | |
| Anderson | 0 (1) | | | 0 (1) |
| Aston | 26 (4) | | 1 | 27 (4) |
| Best | 42 | 2 | 1 | 45 |
| Brennan | 16 | | 1 | 17 |
| Cantwell | 4 | | | 4 |
| Charlton | 42 | 2 | | 44 |
| Connelly | 6 | | 1 | 7 |
| Crerand | 39 | 2 | 1 | 42 |
| Dunne A | 40 | 2 | 1 | 43 |
| Dunne P | | | 1 | 1 |
| Fitzpatrick | 3 | | | 3 |
| Foulkes | 33 | 1 | 1 | 35 |
| Gaskell | 5 | | | 5 |
| Gregg | 2 | | | 2 |
| Herd | 28 | 2 | 1 | 31 |
| Law | 36 | 2 | | 38 |
| Noble | 29 | 2 | | 31 |
| Ryan | 4 (1) | 1 | | 5 (1) |
| Sadler | 35 (1) | 2 | 1 | 38 (1) |
| Stepney | 35 | 2 | | 37 |
| Stiles | 37 | 2 | 1 | 40 |

### Goalscorers

| PLAYER | LEAGUE | CUP COMPETITION | | TOTAL |
|---|---|---|---|---|
| | | FA CUP | LC | |
| Law | 23 | 2 | | 25 |
| Herd | 16 | 1 | 1 | 18 |
| Charlton | 12 | | | 12 |
| Best | 10 | | | 10 |
| Aston | 5 | | | 5 |
| Sadler | 5 | | | 5 |
| Foulkes | 4 | | | 4 |
| Crerand | 3 | | | 3 |
| Connelly | 2 | | | 2 |
| Stiles | 3 | | | 1 |
| Opps' o.gs. | 1 | | | 1 |

### Final Division One Table

| | | P | W | D | L | F | A | Pts |
|---|---|---|---|---|---|---|---|---|
| 1 | Manchester United | 42 | 24 | 12 | 6 | 84 | 45 | 60 |
| 2 | Nottingham Forest | 42 | 23 | 10 | 9 | 64 | 41 | 56 |
| 3 | Tottenham Hotspur | 42 | 24 | 8 | 10 | 71 | 48 | 56 |
| 4 | Leeds United | 42 | 22 | 11 | 9 | 62 | 42 | 55 |
| 5 | Liverpool | 42 | 19 | 13 | 10 | 64 | 47 | 51 |
| 6 | Everton | 42 | 19 | 10 | 13 | 65 | 46 | 48 |
| 7 | Arsenal | 42 | 16 | 14 | 12 | 58 | 47 | 46 |
| 8 | Leicester City | 42 | 18 | 8 | 16 | 78 | 71 | 44 |
| 9 | Chelsea | 42 | 15 | 14 | 13 | 67 | 62 | 44 |
| 10 | Sheffield United | 42 | 16 | 10 | 16 | 52 | 59 | 42 |
| 11 | Sheffield Wednesday | 42 | 14 | 13 | 15 | 56 | 47 | 41 |
| 12 | Stoke City | 42 | 17 | 7 | 18 | 63 | 58 | 41 |
| 13 | WBA | 42 | 16 | 7 | 19 | 77 | 73 | 39 |
| 14 | Burnley | 42 | 15 | 9 | 18 | 66 | 76 | 39 |
| 15 | Manchester City | 42 | 12 | 15 | 15 | 43 | 52 | 39 |
| 16 | West Ham United | 42 | 14 | 8 | 20 | 80 | 84 | 36 |
| 17 | Sunderland | 42 | 14 | 8 | 20 | 58 | 72 | 36 |
| 18 | Fulham | 42 | 11 | 12 | 19 | 71 | 83 | 34 |
| 19 | Southampton | 42 | 14 | 6 | 22 | 74 | 92 | 34 |
| 20 | Newcastle United | 42 | 12 | 9 | 21 | 39 | 81 | 33 |
| 21 | Aston Villa | 42 | 11 | 7 | 24 | 54 | 85 | 29 |
| 22 | Blackpool | 42 | 6 | 9 | 27 | 41 | 76 | 21 |

# Season 1967-68

## Football League Division One

| DATE | OPPONENTS | SCORE | GOALSCORERS | ATTENDANCE |
|---|---|---|---|---|
| Aug 19 | Everton | L 1-3 | Charlton | 61,452 |
| Aug 23 | LEEDS UNITED | W 1-0 | Charlton | 53,016 |
| Aug 26 | LEICESTER CITY | D 1-1 | Foulkes | 51,256 |
| Sep 2 | West Ham United | W 3-1 | Kidd, Sadler, Ryan | 36,562 |
| Sep 6 | Sunderland | D 1-1 | Kidd | 51,527 |
| Sep 9 | BURNLEY | D 2-2 | Burns, Crerand | 55,809 |
| Sep 16 | Sheffield Wednesday | D 1-1 | Best | 47,274 |
| Sep 23 | TOTTENHAM HOTSPUR | W 3-1 | Best 2, Law | 58,779 |
| Sep 30 | Manchester City | W 2-1 | Charlton 2 | 62,942 |
| Oct 7 | ARSENAL | W 1-0 | Aston | 60,197 |
| Oct 14 | Sheffield United | W 3-0 | Kidd, Aston, Law (pen) | 29,170 |
| Oct 25 | COVENTRY CITY | W 4-0 | Aston 2, Best, Charlton | 54,253 |
| Oct 28 | Nottingham Forest | L 1-3 | Best | 49,946 |
| Nov 4 | STOKE CITY | W 1-0 | Charlton | 51,041 |
| Nov 8 | Leeds United | L 0-1 | | 43,999 |
| Nov 11 | Liverpool | W 2-1 | Best 2 | 54,515 |
| Nov 18 | SOUTHAMPTON | W 3-2 | Aston, Kidd, Charlton | 48,732 |
| Nov 25 | Chelsea | D 1-1 | Kidd | 54,712 |
| Dec 2 | WEST BROMWICH ALBION | W 2-1 | Best 2 | 52,568 |
| Dec 9 | Newcastle United | D 2-2 | Kidd, Dunne | 48,639 |
| Dec 16 | EVERTON | W 3-0 | Sadler, Aston, Law | 60,736 |
| Dec 23 | Leicester City | D 2-2 | Charlton, Law | 40,104 |
| Dec 26 | WOLVERHAMPTON WANDERERS | W 4-0 | Best 2, Kidd, Charlton | 63,450 |
| Dec 30 | Wolverhampton Wanderers | W 3-2 | Charlton, Aston, Kidd | 53,940 |
| Jan 6 | WEST HAM UNITED | W 3-1 | Charlton, Best, Aston | 54,498 |
| Jan 20 | SHEFFIELD WEDNESDAY | W 4-2 | Best 2, Charlton, Kidd | 55,254 |
| Feb 3 | Tottenham Hotspur | W 2-1 | Best, Charlton | 57,790 |
| Feb 17 | Burnley | L 1-2 | Best | 31,965 |
| Feb 24 | Arsenal | W 2-0 | Best, Storey o.g. | 46,417 |
| Mar 2 | CHELSEA | L 1-3 | Kidd | 62,978 |
| Mar 16 | Coventry City | L 0-2 | | 47,110 |
| Mar 23 | NOTTINGHAM FOREST | W 3-0 | Herd, Brennan, Burns | 61,978 |
| Mar 27 | MANCHESTER CITY | L 1-3 | Best | 63,004 |
| Mar 30 | Stoke City | W 4-2 | Best, Gowling, Aston, Ryan | 30,141 |
| Apr 6 | LIVERPOOL | L 1-2 | Best | 63,059 |
| Apr 12 | Fulham | W 4-0 | Best 2, Kidd, Law | 40,152 |
| Apr 13 | Southampton | D 2-2 | Charlton, Best | 30,079 |
| Apr 15 | FULHAM | W 3-0 | Charlton, Best, Aston | 60,465 |
| Apr 20 | SHEFFIELD UNITED | W 1-0 | Law | 55,033 |
| Apr 27 | West Bromwich Albion | L 3-6 | Law (pen), Kidd 2 | 43,412 |
| May 4 | NEWCASTLE UNITED | W 6-0 | Kidd 2, Best 3 (2 pens), Sadler | 59,976 |
| May 11 | SUNDERLAND | L 1-2 | Best | 62,963 |

## FA Cup

| | | | | |
|---|---|---|---|---|
| Jan 27 | TOTTENHAM HOTSPUR | (Rd3) D 2-2 | Best, Charlton | 63,500 |
| Jan 31 | Tottenham Hotspur | (R) L 0-1* | | 57,200 |

*After extra-time.

## European Cup

| | | | | |
|---|---|---|---|---|
| Sep 20 | HIBERNIANS | (Rd1/1L) W 4-0 | Law 2, Sadler 2 | 43,915 |
| Sep 27 | Hibernians | (Rd1/2L) D 0-0 | | 23,217 |
| Nov 15 | Sarajevo | (Rd2/1L) D 0-0 | | 45,000 |
| Nov 29 | SARAJEVO | (Rd2/2L) W 2-1 | Aston, Best | 62,801 |
| Feb 28 | GORNIK | (QF/1L) W 2-0 | Florenski o.g., Kidd | 63,456 |
| Mar 13 | Gornik | (QF/2L) L 0-1 | | 105,000 |
| Apr 24 | Real Madrid | (SF/1L) W 1-0 | Best | 63,500 |
| May 15 | REAL MADRID | (SF/2L) D 3-3 | Zoco o.g., Sadler, Foulkes | 125,000 |
| May 29 | SL Benfica** | (F) W 4-1* | Charlton 2, Best, Kidd | 99,882 |

*After extra-time. **Played at Wembley Stadium, London.

## FA Charity Shield

| | | | | |
|---|---|---|---|---|
| Aug 12 | TOTTENHAM HOTSPUR | D 3-3 | Charlton 2, Law | 54,106 |

### Fact File

United defeated Benfica (Portugal) 4-1, after extra-time, at Wembley to become England's first winners of the European Cup.

**MANAGER:** Matt Busby

**MOST APPEARANCES:** George Best, Bobby Charlton, Pat Crerand, Alex Stepney 53

**TOP SCORER:** George Best 32 (28 League)

**BIGGEST WIN:** 6-0 v Newcastle United, 4 May 1968, League

**HIGHEST ATTENDANCE:** 125,000 v Real Madrid, 15 May 1968, European Cup

## League & Cup Appearances

| PLAYER | LEAGUE | CUP COMPETITION | | OTHER | TOTAL |
|---|---|---|---|---|---|
| | | FA CUP | EC | | |
| Aston | 34 (3) | 2 | 9 | 1 | 46 (3) |
| Best | 41 | 2 | 9 | 1 | 53 |
| Brennan | 13 | | 3 | 1 | 17 |
| Burns | 36 | 2 | 9 | | 47 |
| Charlton | 41 | 2 | 9 | 1 | 53 |
| Crerand | 41 | 2 | 9 | 1 | 53 |
| Dunne | 37 | 2 | 9 | 1 | 49 |
| Fitzpatrick | 14 (3) | 2 | 2 | | 18 (3) |
| Foulkes | 24 | | 6 | 1 | 31 |
| Gowling | 4 (1) | | | | 4 (1) |
| Herd | 6 | 1 | 1 | | 8 |
| Kidd | 38 | 2 | 9 | 1 | 50 |
| Kopel | 1 | | | | 1 |
| Law | 23 | 1 | 3 | 1 | 28 |
| Rimmer | 1 | | | | 1 |
| Ryan | 7 (1) | | 1 | | 8 (1) |
| Sadler | 40 (1) | 2 | 9 | | 51 (1) |
| Stepney | 41 | 2 | 9 | 1 | 53 |
| Stiles | 20 | | 7 | 1 | 28 |

## Goalscorers

| PLAYER | LEAGUE | CUP COMPETITION | | OTHER | TOTAL |
|---|---|---|---|---|---|
| | | FA CUP | EC | | |
| Best | 28 | 1 | 3 | | 32 |
| Charlton | 15 | 1 | 2 | 2 | 20 |
| Kidd | 15 | | 2 | | 17 |
| Aston | 10 | | 1 | | 11 |
| Law | 7 | | 2 | 1 | 10 |
| Sadler | 3 | | 3 | | 6 |
| Burns | 2 | | | | 2 |
| Ryan | 2 | | | | 2 |
| Foulkes | 1 | | 1 | | 2 |
| Brennan | 1 | | | | 1 |
| Crerand | 1 | | | | 1 |
| Dunne | 1 | | | | 1 |
| Gowling | 1 | | | | 1 |
| Herd | 1 | | | | 1 |
| Opps' o.gs. | 1 | | 2 | | 3 |

### Final Division One Table

| | | P | W | D | L | F | A | Pts |
|---|---|---|---|---|---|---|---|---|
| 1 | Manchester City | 42 | 26 | 6 | 10 | 86 | 43 | 58 |
| 2 | Manchester United | 42 | 24 | 8 | 10 | 89 | 55 | 56 |
| 3 | Liverpool | 42 | 22 | 11 | 9 | 71 | 40 | 55 |
| 4 | Leeds United | 42 | 22 | 9 | 11 | 71 | 41 | 53 |
| 5 | Everton | 42 | 23 | 6 | 13 | 67 | 40 | 52 |
| 6 | Chelsea | 42 | 18 | 12 | 12 | 62 | 68 | 48 |
| 7 | Tottenham Hotspur | 42 | 19 | 9 | 14 | 70 | 59 | 47 |
| 8 | WBA | 42 | 17 | 12 | 13 | 75 | 62 | 46 |
| 9 | Arsenal | 42 | 17 | 10 | 15 | 60 | 56 | 44 |
| 10 | Newcastle United | 42 | 13 | 15 | 14 | 54 | 67 | 41 |
| 11 | Nottingham Forest | 42 | 14 | 11 | 17 | 52 | 64 | 39 |
| 12 | West Ham United | 42 | 14 | 10 | 18 | 73 | 69 | 38 |
| 13 | Leicester City | 42 | 13 | 12 | 17 | 64 | 69 | 38 |
| 14 | Burnley | 42 | 14 | 10 | 18 | 64 | 71 | 38 |
| 15 | Sunderland | 42 | 13 | 11 | 18 | 51 | 61 | 37 |
| 16 | Southampton | 42 | 13 | 11 | 18 | 66 | 83 | 37 |
| 17 | Wolverhampton W | 42 | 14 | 8 | 20 | 66 | 75 | 36 |
| 18 | Stoke City | 42 | 14 | 7 | 21 | 50 | 73 | 35 |
| 19 | Sheffield Wednesday | 42 | 11 | 12 | 19 | 51 | 63 | 34 |
| 20 | Coventry City | 42 | 9 | 15 | 18 | 51 | 71 | 33 |
| 21 | Sheffield United | 42 | 11 | 10 | 21 | 49 | 70 | 32 |
| 22 | Fulham | 42 | 10 | 7 | 25 | 56 | 98 | 27 |

# Season 1968-69

## Football League Division One

| DATE | OPPONENTS | SCORE | GOALSCORERS | ATTENDANCE |
|---|---|---|---|---|
| Aug 10 | EVERTON | W 2-1 | Best, Charlton | 61,311 |
| Aug 14 | West Bromwich Albion | L 1-3 | Charlton | 38,299 |
| Aug 17 | Manchester City | D 0-0 | | 63,052 |
| Aug 21 | COVENTRY CITY | W 1-0 | Ryan | 51,201 |
| Aug 24 | CHELSEA | L 0-4 | | 55,114 |
| Aug 28 | TOTTENHAM HOTSPUR | W 3-1 | Fitzpatrick 2, Beal o.g. | 62,649 |
| Aug 31 | Sheffield Wednesday | L 4-5 | Best, Law 2, Charlton | 50,490 |
| Sep 7 | WEST HAM UNITED | D 1-1 | Law | 63,274 |
| Sep 14 | Burnley | L 0-1 | | 32,935 |
| Sep 21 | NEWCASTLE UNITED | W 3-1 | Best 2, Law | 47,262 |
| Oct 5 | ARSENAL | D 0-0 | | 61,843 |
| Oct 9 | Tottenham Hotspur | D 2-2 | Crerand, Law | 56,205 |
| Oct 12 | Liverpool | L 0-2 | | 53,392 |
| Oct 19 | SOUTHAMPTON | L 1-2 | Best | 46,526 |
| Oct 26 | Queens Park Rangers | W 3-2 | Best 2, Law | 31,138 |
| Nov 2 | LEEDS UNITED | D 0-0 | | 53,839 |
| Nov 9 | Sunderland | D 1-1 | Hurley o.g. | 33,151 |
| Nov 16 | IPSWICH TOWN | D 0-0 | | 45,796 |
| Nov 23 | Stoke City | D 0-0 | | 30,562 |
| Nov 30 | WOLVERHAMPTON WANDERERS | W 2-0 | Best, Law | 50,165 |
| Dec 7 | Leicester City | L 1-2 | Law (pen) | 36,303 |
| Dec 14 | LIVERPOOL | W 1-0 | Law | 55,354 |
| Dec 21 | Southampton | L 0-2 | | 26,194 |
| Dec 26 | Arsenal | L 0-3 | | 62,300 |
| Jan 11 | Leeds United | L 1-2 | Charlton | 48,145 |
| Jan 18 | SUNDERLAND | W 4-1 | Law 3, Best | 45,670 |
| Feb 1 | Ipswich Town | L 0-1 | | 30,837 |
| Feb 15 | Wolverhampton Wanderers | D 2-2 | Charlton, Best | 44,023 |
| Mar 8 | MANCHESTER CITY | L 0-1 | | 63,264 |
| Mar 10 | Everton | D 0-0 | | 57,514 |
| Mar 15 | Chelsea | L 2-3 | James, Law (pen) | 60,436 |
| Mar 19 | QUEENS PARK RANGERS | W 8-1 | Morgan 3, Best 2, Stiles, Kidd, Aston | 36,638 |
| Mar 22 | SHEFFIELD WEDNESDAY | W 1-0 | Best | 45,527 |
| Mar 24 | STOKE CITY | D 1-1 | Aston | 39,931 |
| Mar 29 | West Ham United | D 0-0 | | 41,546 |
| Mar 31 | Nottingham Forest | W 1-0 | Best (pen) | 41,892 |
| Apr 2 | WEST BROMWICH ALBION | W 2-1 | Best 2 | 38,846 |
| Apr 5 | NOTTINGHAM FOREST | W 3-1 | Morgan 2, Best | 51,952 |
| Apr 8 | Coventry City | L 1-2 | Fitzpatrick | 45,402 |
| Apr 12 | Newcastle United | L 0-2 | | 46,379 |
| Apr 19 | BURNLEY | W 2-0 | Best, Waldron o.g. | 52,626 |
| May 17 | LEICESTER CITY | W 3-2 | Best, Morgan, Law | 45,860 |

## FA Cup

| | | | | |
|---|---|---|---|---|
| Jan 4 | Exeter City | (Rd3) W 3-1 | Fitzpatrick, Kidd, Newman o.g. | 18,500 |
| Jan 25 | WATFORD | (Rd4) D 1-1 | Law | 63,498 |
| Feb 3 | Watford | (R) W 2-0 | Law 2 | 34,000 |
| Feb 8 | Birmingham City | (Rd5) D 2-2 | Law, Best | 52,500 |
| Feb 28 | BIRMINGHAM CITY | (R) W 6-2 | Law 3 (1 pen), Crerand, Kidd, Morgan | 61,932 |
| Mar 1 | EVERTON | (Rd6) L 0-1 | | 63,464 |

## European Cup

| | | | | |
|---|---|---|---|---|
| Sep 18 | Waterford | (Rd1/1L) W 3-1 | Law 3 | 48,000 |
| Oct 2 | WATERFORD | (Rd1/2L) W 7-1 | Law 4, Burns, Charlton, Stiles | 41,750 |
| Nov 13 | ANDERLECHT | (Rd2/1L) W 3-0 | Law 2, Kidd | 51,000 |
| Nov 27 | Anderlecht | (Rd2/2L) L 1-3 | Sartori | 40,000 |
| Feb 26 | RAPID | (QF/1L) W 3-0 | Best 2, Morgan | 61,923 |
| Mar 5 | Rapid | (QF/2L) D 0-0 | | 52,000 |
| Apr 23 | AC Milan | (SF/1L) L 0-2 | | 90,000 |
| May 15 | AC MILAN | (SF/2L) W 1-0 | Charlton | 63,103 |

## Inter-Continental Cup

| | | | | |
|---|---|---|---|---|
| Sep 25 | Estudiantes* | (1L) L 0-1 | | 55,000 |
| Oct 16 | ESTUDIANTES | (2L) D 1-1 | Morgan | 63,500 |

*Played at La Bombonera, Buenos Aires.

**MANAGER:** Sir Matt Busby
**MOST APPEARANCES:** Nobby Stiles 56
**TOP SCORER:** Denis Law 30 (14 League)
**BIGGEST WIN:** 8-1 v Queens Park Rangers, 19 March 1969, League
**HIGHEST ATTENDANCE:** 90,000 v AC Milan, 23 April 1969, European Cup

## League & Cup Appearances

| PLAYER | LEAGUE | CUP COMPETITION FA CUP | CUP COMPETITION EC | OTHER | TOTAL |
|---|---|---|---|---|---|
| Aston | 13 | | | | 13 |
| Best | 41 | 6 | 6 | 2 | 55 |
| Burns | 14 (2) | 1 | 3 | 1 | 19 (2) |
| Brennan | 13 | | 3 | 1 | 17 |
| Charlton | 32 | 6 | 8 | 2 | 48 |
| Crerand | 35 | 4 | 8 | 2 | 49 |
| Dunne | 33 | 6 | 6 | 2 | 47 |
| Fitzpatrick | 28 (2) | 6 | 4 | | 38 (2) |
| Foulkes | 10 (3) | | 5 | 2 | 17 (3) |
| Gowling | 2 | | | | 2 |
| James | 21 | 6 | 2 | | 29 |
| Kidd | 28 (1) | 5 | 7 | 1 | 41 (1) |
| Kopel | 7 (1) | 1 | 1 | | 9 (1) |
| Law | 30 | 6 | 7 | 2 | 45 |
| Morgan | 29 | 5 | 4 | 2 | 40 |
| Rimmer | 4 | 1 | 2 | | 7 |
| Ryan | 6 | | 1 | 0 | 7 |
| Sadler | 26 (3) | | 5 (1) | 2 | 33 (4) |
| Sartori | 11 (2) | 2 | 2 | 0 (1) | 15 (3) |
| Stepney | 38 | 5 | 6 | 2 | 51 |
| Stiles | 41 | 6 | 8 | 1 | 56 |

## Goalscorers

| PLAYER | LEAGUE | CUP COMPETITION FA CUP | CUP COMPETITION EC | OTHER | TOTAL |
|---|---|---|---|---|---|
| Law | 14 | 7 | 9 | | 30 |
| Best | 19 | 1 | 2 | | 22 |
| Morgan | 6 | 1 | 1 | 1 | 9 |
| Charlton | 5 | | 2 | | 7 |
| Fitzpatrick | 3 | 1 | | | 4 |
| Kidd | 1 | 2 | 1 | | 4 |
| Aston | 2 | | | | 2 |
| Stiles | 1 | | 1 | | 2 |
| Burns | | | 1 | | 1 |
| Crerand | 1 | 1 | | | 1 |
| James | 1 | | | | 1 |
| Ryan | 1 | | | | 1 |
| Sartori | | | 1 | | 1 |
| Opps' o.gs. | 3 | 1 | | | 4 |

### Fact File

United failed in their attempt to become the unofficial World Club Champions following two stormy games against Estudiantes de la Plata of Argentina.

## Final Division One Table

| | | P | W | D | L | F | A | Pts |
|---|---|---|---|---|---|---|---|---|
| 1 | Leeds United | 42 | 27 | 13 | 2 | 66 | 26 | 67 |
| 2 | Liverpool | 42 | 25 | 11 | 6 | 63 | 24 | 61 |
| 3 | Everton | 42 | 21 | 15 | 6 | 77 | 36 | 57 |
| 4 | Arsenal | 42 | 22 | 12 | 8 | 56 | 27 | 56 |
| 5 | Chelsea | 42 | 20 | 10 | 12 | 73 | 53 | 50 |
| 6 | Tottenham Hotspur | 42 | 14 | 17 | 11 | 61 | 51 | 45 |
| 7 | Southampton | 42 | 16 | 13 | 13 | 57 | 48 | 45 |
| 8 | West Ham United | 42 | 13 | 18 | 11 | 66 | 50 | 44 |
| 9 | Newcastle United | 42 | 15 | 14 | 13 | 61 | 55 | 44 |
| 10 | WBA | 42 | 16 | 11 | 15 | 64 | 67 | 43 |
| 11 | Manchester United | 42 | 15 | 12 | 15 | 57 | 53 | 42 |
| 12 | Ipswich Town | 42 | 15 | 11 | 16 | 59 | 60 | 41 |
| 13 | Manchester City | 42 | 15 | 10 | 17 | 64 | 55 | 40 |
| 14 | Burnley | 42 | 15 | 9 | 18 | 55 | 82 | 39 |
| 15 | Sheffield Wednesday | 42 | 10 | 16 | 16 | 41 | 54 | 36 |
| 16 | Wolverhampton W | 42 | 10 | 15 | 17 | 41 | 58 | 35 |
| 17 | Sunderland | 42 | 11 | 12 | 19 | 43 | 67 | 34 |
| 18 | Nottingham Forest | 42 | 10 | 13 | 19 | 45 | 57 | 33 |
| 19 | Stoke City | 42 | 9 | 15 | 18 | 40 | 63 | 33 |
| 20 | Coventry City | 42 | 10 | 11 | 21 | 46 | 64 | 31 |
| 21 | Leicester City | 42 | 9 | 12 | 21 | 39 | 68 | 30 |
| 22 | QPR | 42 | 4 | 10 | 28 | 39 | 95 | 18 |

# Season 1969-70

## Football League Division One

| DATE | OPPONENTS | SCORE | GOALSCORERS | ATTENDANCE |
|---|---|---|---|---|
| Aug 9 | Crystal Palace | D 2-2 | Charlton, Morgan | 48,610 |
| Aug 13 | EVERTON | L 0-2 | | 57,752 |
| Aug 16 | SOUTHAMPTON | L 1-4 | Morgan | 46,328 |
| Aug 19 | Everton | L 0-3 | | 53,185 |
| Aug 23 | Wolverhampton Wanderers | D 0-0 | | 50,783 |
| Aug 27 | NEWCASTLE UNITED | D 0-0 | | 52,774 |
| Aug 30 | SUNDERLAND | W 3-1 | Best, Kidd, Givens | 50,570 |
| Sep 6 | Leeds United | D 2-2 | Best 2 | 44,271 |
| Sep 13 | LIVERPOOL | W 1-0 | Morgan | 56,509 |
| Sep 17 | Sheffield Wednesday | W 3-1 | Kidd, Best 2 | 39,298 |
| Sep 20 | Arsenal | D 2-2 | Best, Sadler | 59,498 |
| Sep 27 | WEST HAM UNITED | W 5-2 | Burns, Best 2, Charlton, Kidd | 58,579 |
| Oct 4 | Derby County | L 0-2 | | 40,724 |
| Oct 8 | Southampton | W 3-0 | Best, Burns, Kidd | 31,044 |
| Oct 11 | IPSWICH TOWN | W 2-1 | Best, Kidd | 52,281 |
| Oct 18 | NOTTINGHAM FOREST | D 1-1 | Best | 53,702 |
| Oct 25 | West Bromwich Albion | L 1-2 | Kidd | 45,120 |
| Nov 1 | STOKE CITY | D 1-1 | Charlton | 53,406 |
| Nov 8 | Coventry City | W 2-1 | Aston, Law | 43,446 |
| Nov 15 | Manchester City | L 0-4 | | 63,013 |
| Nov 22 | TOTTENHAM HOTSPUR | W 3-1 | Burns, Charlton 2 | 50,003 |
| Nov 29 | Burnley | D 1-1 | Best | 23,770 |
| Dec 6 | CHELSEA | L 0-2 | | 49,344 |
| Dec 13 | Liverpool | W 4-1 | Ure, Morgan, Charlton, Yeats o.g. | 47,682 |
| Dec 26 | WOLVERHAMPTON WANDERERS | D 0-0 | | 50,806 |
| Dec 27 | Sunderland | D 1-1 | Kidd | 36,504 |
| Jan 10 | ARSENAL | W 2-1 | Sartori, Morgan | 41,055 |
| Jan 17 | West Ham United | D 0-0 | | 41,643 |
| Jan 26 | LEEDS UNITED | D 2-2 | Sadler, Kidd | 59,879 |
| Jan 31 | DERBY COUNTY | W 1-0 | Charlton | 59,315 |
| Feb 10 | Ipswich Town | W 1-0 | Kidd | 29,755 |
| Feb 14 | CRYSTAL PALACE | D 1-1 | Kidd | 54,711 |
| Feb 28 | Stoke City | D 2-2 | Sartori, Morgan (pen) | 38,917 |
| Mar 17 | BURNLEY | D 3-3 | Crerand, Law, Best | 38,377 |
| Mar 21 | Chelsea | L 1-2 | Morgan | 61,479 |
| Mar 28 | MANCHESTER CITY | L 1-2 | Kidd | 59,777 |
| Mar 30 | COVENTRY CITY | D 1-1 | Kidd | 38,647 |
| Mar 31 | Nottingham Forest | W 2-1 | Gowling, Charlton | 39,228 |
| Apr 4 | Newcastle United | L 1-5 | Charlton | 43,094 |
| Apr 8 | WEST BROMWICH ALBION | W 7-0 | Fitzpatrick 2, Charlton 2, Gowling 2, Best | 26,582 |
| Apr 13 | Tottenham Hotspur | L 1-2 | Fitzpatrick | 41,808 |
| Apr 15 | SHEFFIELD WEDNESDAY | D 2-2 | Best, Charlton | 36,649 |

## FA Cup

| | | | | | |
|---|---|---|---|---|---|
| Jan 3 | Ipswich Town | (Rd3) | W 1-0 | O'Neil o.g. | 29,552 |
| Jan 24 | MANCHESTER CITY | (Rd4) | W 3-0 | Morgan (pen), Kidd 2 | 63,417 |
| Feb 7 | Northampton Town | (Rd5) | W 8-2 | Best 6, Kidd 2 | 21,771 |
| Feb 21 | Middlesbrough | (Rd6) | D 1-1 | Sartori | 40,000 |
| Feb 25 | MIDDLESBROUGH | (R) | W 2-1 | Charlton, Morgan (pen) | 63,418 |
| Mar 14 | Leeds United* | (SF) | D 0-0 | | 55,000 |
| Mar 23 | Leeds United** | (R) | D 0-0 | | 62,500 |
| Mar 26 | Leeds United† | (2R) | L 0-1 | | 56,000 |
| Apr 10 | Watford†† | (3/4PO)# | W 2-0 | Kidd 2 | 15,105 |

*Played at Hillsborough, Sheffield. **Played at Villa Park, Birmingham. After extra-time. †Played at Burnden Park, Bolton. ††Played at Arsenal Stadium, London.
# A play-off for third/fourth spots in the FA Cup was played in 1969-70 to 1973-74 incl.

## League Cup

| | | | | | |
|---|---|---|---|---|---|
| Sep 3 | MIDDLESBROUGH | (Rd2) | W 1-0 | Sadler | 38,939 |
| Sep 23 | WREXHAM | (Rd3) | W 2-0 | Kidd, Best | 48,347 |
| Oct 14 | Burnley | (Rd4) | D 0-0 | | 27,959 |
| Oct 20 | BURNLEY | (R) | W 1-0 | Best (pen) | 50,275 |
| Nov 12 | Derby County | (Rd5) | D 0-0 | | 38,895 |
| Nov 19 | DERBY COUNTY | (R) | W 1-0 | Kidd | 57,393 |
| Dec 3 | Manchester City | (SF/1L) | L 1-2 | Charlton | 55,799 |
| Dec 17 | MANCHESTER CITY | (SF/2L) | D 2-2 | Edwards, Law | 63,418 |

**MANAGER:** Wilf McGuinness
**MOST APPEARANCES:** Bobby Charlton, David Sadler 57
**TOP SCORER:** George Best 23 (15 League)
**BIGGEST WIN:** 8-2, 7 February 1970, v Northampton Town, FA Cup
**HIGHEST ATTENDANCE:** 63,418 v Manchester City, 17 December 1969, League Cup; 63,418 v Middlesbrough, 25 February 1970, FA Cup

## League & Cup Appearances

| PLAYER | LEAGUE | CUP COMPETITION | | TOTAL |
|---|---|---|---|---|
| | | FA CUP | LC | |
| Aston | 21 (1) | 1 (1) | 6 | 28 (2) |
| Best | 37 | 8 | 8 | 53 |
| Brennan | 8 (1) | 1 | 1 | 10 (1) |
| Burns | 30 (2) | 3 (1) | 6 | 39 (3) |
| Charlton | 40 | 9 | 8 | 57 |
| Crerand | 25 | 9 | 2 | 36 |
| Dunne | 33 | 7 | 8 | 48 |
| Edwards | 18 (1) | 7 | 2 | 27 (1) |
| Fitzpatrick | 20 | 1 | 5 | 26 |
| Foulkes | 3 | | | 3 |
| Givens | 4 (4) | | 1 | 5 (4) |
| Gowling | 6 (1) | | 0 (1) | 6 (2) |
| James | 2 | | 1 | 3 |
| Kidd | 33 (1) | 9 | 6 | 48 (1) |
| Law | 10 (1) | 0 (2) | 3 | 13 (3) |
| Morgan | 35 | 9 | 5 | 49 |
| Rimmer | 5 | | | 5 |
| Ryan | 0 (1) | | | 0 (1) |
| Sadler | 40 | 9 | 8 | 57 |
| Sartori | 13 (4) | 7 | 1 (2) | 21 (6) |
| Stepney | 37 | 9 | 8 | 54 |
| Stiles | 8 | 3 | 2 | 13 |
| Ure | 34 | 7 | 7 | 48 |

## Goalscorers

| PLAYER | LEAGUE | CUP COMPETITION | | TOTAL |
|---|---|---|---|---|
| | | FA CUP | LC | |
| Best | 15 | 6 | 2 | 23 |
| Kidd | 12 | 6 | 2 | 20 |
| Charlton | 12 | 1 | 1 | 14 |
| Morgan | 7 | 2 | | 9 |
| Burns | 3 | | | 3 |
| Fitzpatrick | 3 | | | 3 |
| Law | 2 | | 1 | 3 |
| Sadler | 2 | | 1 | 3 |
| Sartori | 2 | 1 | | 3 |
| Aston | 1 | | | 1 |
| Crerand | 1 | | | 1 |
| Edwards | | | 1 | 1 |
| Givens | 1 | | | 1 |
| Gowling | 3 | | | 1 |
| Ure | 1 | | | 1 |
| Opps' o.gs. | 1 | 1 | | 2 |

## Fact File

Bill Foulkes, one of United's greatest-ever servants, played his final match, against Southampton at Old Trafford, 17 years after making his debut for the club.

## Final Division One Table

| | | P | W | D | L | F | A | PTS |
|---|---|---|---|---|---|---|---|---|
| 1 | Everton | 42 | 29 | 8 | 5 | 72 | 34 | 66 |
| 2 | Leeds United | 42 | 21 | 15 | 6 | 84 | 49 | 57 |
| 3 | Chelsea | 42 | 21 | 13 | 8 | 70 | 50 | 55 |
| 4 | Derby County | 42 | 22 | 9 | 11 | 64 | 37 | 53 |
| 5 | Liverpool | 42 | 20 | 11 | 11 | 65 | 42 | 51 |
| 6 | Coventry City | 42 | 19 | 11 | 12 | 58 | 48 | 49 |
| 7 | Newcastle United | 42 | 17 | 13 | 12 | 57 | 35 | 47 |
| 8 | Manchester United | 42 | 14 | 17 | 11 | 66 | 61 | 45 |
| 9 | Stoke City | 42 | 15 | 15 | 12 | 56 | 52 | 45 |
| 10 | Manchester City | 42 | 16 | 11 | 15 | 55 | 48 | 43 |
| 11 | Tottenham Hotspur | 42 | 17 | 9 | 16 | 54 | 55 | 43 |
| 12 | Arsenal | 42 | 12 | 18 | 12 | 51 | 49 | 42 |
| 13 | Wolverhampton W | 42 | 12 | 16 | 14 | 55 | 57 | 40 |
| 14 | Burnley | 42 | 12 | 15 | 15 | 56 | 61 | 39 |
| 15 | Nottingham Forest | 42 | 10 | 18 | 14 | 50 | 71 | 38 |
| 16 | WBA | 42 | 14 | 9 | 19 | 58 | 66 | 37 |
| 17 | West Ham United | 42 | 12 | 12 | 18 | 51 | 60 | 36 |
| 18 | Ipswich Town | 42 | 10 | 11 | 21 | 40 | 63 | 31 |
| 19 | Southampton | 42 | 6 | 17 | 19 | 46 | 67 | 29 |
| 20 | Crystal Palace | 42 | 6 | 15 | 21 | 34 | 68 | 27 |
| 21 | Sunderland | 42 | 6 | 14 | 22 | 30 | 68 | 26 |
| 22 | Sheffield Wednesday | 42 | 8 | 9 | 25 | 40 | 71 | 25 |

# Season 1970-71

## Football League Division One

| DATE | OPPONENTS | SCORE | GOALSCORERS | ATTENDANCE |
|---|---|---|---|---|
| Aug 15 | LEEDS UNITED | L 0-1 | | 59,365 |
| Aug 19 | CHELSEA | D 0-0 | | 50,979 |
| Aug 22 | Arsenal | L 0-4 | | 54,117 |
| Aug 25 | Burnley | W 2-0 | Law 2 | 29,385 |
| Aug 29 | WEST HAM UNITED | D 1-1 | Fitzpatrick | 50,643 |
| Sep 2 | EVERTON | W 2-0 | Best, Charlton | 51,346 |
| Sep 5 | Liverpool | D 1-1 | Kidd | 52,542 |
| Sep 12 | COVENTRY CITY | W 2-0 | Best, Charlton | 48,939 |
| Sep 19 | Ipswich Town | L 0-4 | | 27,776 |
| Sep 26 | BLACKPOOL | D 1-1 | Best | 46,647 |
| Oct 3 | Wolverhampton Wanderers | L 2-3 | Gowling, Kidd | 38,629 |
| Oct 10 | CRYSTAL PALACE | L 0-1 | | 42,979 |
| Oct 17 | Leeds United | D 2-2 | Fitzpatrick, Charlton | 50,190 |
| Oct 24 | WEST BROMWICH ALBION | W 2-1 | Kidd, Law | 43,278 |
| Oct 31 | Newcastle United | L 0-1 | | 45,140 |
| Nov 7 | STOKE CITY | D 2-2 | Sadler, Law | 47,451 |
| Nov 14 | Nottingham Forest | W 2-1 | Gowling, Sartori | 36,364 |
| Nov 21 | Southampton | L 0-1 | | 30,302 |
| Nov 28 | HUDDERSFIELD TOWN | D 1-1 | Best | 45,306 |
| Dec 5 | Tottenham Hotspur | D 2-2 | Best, Law | 55,693 |
| Dec 12 | MANCHESTER CITY | L 1-4 | Kidd | 52,636 |
| Dec 19 | ARSENAL | L 1-3 | Sartori | 33,182 |
| Dec 26 | Derby County | D 4-4 | Kidd, Best, Law 2 | 34,068 |
| Jan 9 | Chelsea | W 2-1 | Morgan (pen), Gowling | 53,482 |
| Jan 16 | BURNLEY | D 1-1 | Aston | 40,135 |
| Jan 30 | Huddersfield Town | W 2-1 | Law, Aston | 41,464 |
| Feb 6 | TOTTENHAM HOTSPUR | W 2-1 | Morgan (pen), Best | 48,965 |
| Feb 20 | SOUTHAMPTON | W 5-1 | Gowling 4, Morgan | 36,060 |
| Feb 23 | Everton | L 0-1 | | 52,544 |
| Feb 27 | NEWCASTLE UNITED | W 1-0 | Kidd | 41,902 |
| Mar 6 | West Bromwich Albion | L 3-4 | Kidd, Best, Aston | 41,112 |
| Mar 13 | NOTTINGHAM FOREST | W 2-0 | Best, Law | 40,473 |
| Mar 20 | Stoke City | W 2-1 | Best 2 | 40,005 |
| Apr 3 | West Ham United | L 1-2 | Best | 38,507 |
| Apr 10 | DERBY COUNTY | L 1-2 | Law | 45,691 |
| Apr 12 | WOLVERHAMPTON WANDERERS | W 1-0 | Gowling | 41,886 |
| Apr 13 | Coventry City | L 1-2 | Best | 33,818 |
| Apr 17 | Crystal Palace | W 5-3 | Law 3, Best 2 | 39,145 |
| Apr 19 | LIVERPOOL | L 0-2 | | 44,004 |
| Apr 24 | IPSWICH TOWN | W 3-2 | Best (pen), Charlton, Kidd | 33,566 |
| May 1 | Blackpool | D 1-1 | Law | 29,857 |
| May 5 | Manchester City | W 4-3 | Best 2, Charlton, Law | 43,626 |

## FA Cup

| | | | | |
|---|---|---|---|---|
| Jan 2 | MIDDLESBROUGH | (Rd3) D 0-0 | | 47,824 |
| Jan 5 | Middlesbrough | (R) L 1-2 | Best | 41,000 |

## League Cup

| | | | | |
|---|---|---|---|---|
| Sep 9 | Aldershot | (Rd2) W 3-1 | Best, Kidd, Law | 18,509 |
| Oct 7 | PORTSMOUTH | (Rd3) W 1-0 | Charlton | 32,068 |
| Oct 28 | CHELSEA | (Rd4) W 2-1 | Charlton, Best | 47,565 |
| Nov 18 | CRYSTAL PALACE | (Rd5) W 4-2 | Fitzpatrick, Kidd 2, Charlton | 48,961 |
| Dec 16 | ASTON VILLA | (SF/1L) D 1-1 | Kidd | 48,889 |
| Dec 23 | Aston Villa | (SF/2L) L 1-2 | Kidd | 58,667 |

### Fact File

Alan Gowling became the latest in a long line of United players to score four goals in a game when he achieved the feat in the 5-1 win over Southampton at Old Trafford, 20 February 1971.

**MANAGER:** Wilf McGuinness/Sir Matt Busby
**MOST APPEARANCES:** Bobby Charlton 50
**TOP SCORER:** George Best 21 (18 League)
**BIGGEST WIN:** 5-1 v Southampton, 20 February 1971, League
**HIGHEST ATTENDANCE:** 59,365 v Leeds United, 15 August 1970, League

## League & Cup Appearances

| PLAYER | LEAGUE | CUP COMPETITION | | TOTAL |
|---|---|---|---|---|
| | | FA CUP | LC | |
| Aston | 19 (1) | | 3 (1) | 22 (2) |
| Best | 40 | 2 | 6 | 48 |
| Burns | 16 (4) | | 2 (1) | 18 (5) |
| Charlton | 42 | 2 | 6 | 50 |
| Crerand | 24 | 2 | 1 | 27 |
| Donald | | | 1 | 1 |
| Dunne | 35 | 2 | 5 | 42 |
| Edwards | 29 (1) | 1 | 2 | 32 (1) |
| Fitzpatrick | 35 | 2 | 6 | 43 |
| Gowling | 17 (3) | 0 (1) | 1 | 18 (4) |
| James | 13 | | 3 (1) | 16 (1) |
| Kidd | 24 (1) | 2 | 6 | 32 (1) |
| Law | 28 | 2 | 4 | 32 |
| Morgan | 25 | 2 | 2 | 29 |
| O'Neil | 1 | | | 1 |
| Rimmer | 20 | 2 | 6 | 28 |
| Sadler | 32 | 2 | 5 | 39 |
| Sartori | 2 (5) | | 1 | 3 (5) |
| Stepney | 22 | | | 22 |
| Stiles | 17 | | 2 | 19 |
| Ure | 13 | 1 | 3 | 17 |
| Watson | 8 | | 2 | 10 |
| Young | 0 (1) | | | 0 (1) |

## Goalscorers

| PLAYER | LEAGUE | CUP COMPETITION | | TOTAL |
|---|---|---|---|---|
| | | FA CUP | LC | |
| Best | 18 | 1 | 2 | 21 |
| Law | 15 | | 1 | 16 |
| Kidd | 8 | | 5 | 13 |
| Charlton | 5 | | 3 | 8 |
| Gowling | 8 | | | 8 |
| Aston | 3 | | | 3 |
| Fitzpatrick | 2 | | 1 | 3 |
| Morgan | 3 | | | 3 |
| Sartori | 2 | | | 2 |
| Sadler | 1 | | | 1 |

### Final Division One Table

| | | P | W | D | L | F | A | Pts |
|---|---|---|---|---|---|---|---|---|
| 1 | Arsenal | 42 | 29 | 7 | 6 | 71 | 29 | 65 |
| 2 | Leeds United | 42 | 27 | 10 | 5 | 72 | 30 | 64 |
| 3 | Tottenham Hotspur | 42 | 19 | 14 | 9 | 54 | 33 | 52 |
| 4 | Wolverhampton W | 42 | 22 | 8 | 12 | 64 | 54 | 52 |
| 5 | Liverpool | 42 | 17 | 17 | 8 | 42 | 24 | 51 |
| 6 | Chelsea | 42 | 18 | 15 | 9 | 52 | 42 | 51 |
| 7 | Southampton | 42 | 17 | 12 | 13 | 56 | 44 | 46 |
| 8 | Manchester United | 42 | 16 | 11 | 15 | 65 | 66 | 43 |
| 9 | Derby County | 42 | 16 | 10 | 16 | 56 | 54 | 42 |
| 10 | Coventry City | 42 | 16 | 10 | 16 | 37 | 38 | 42 |
| 11 | Manchester City | 42 | 12 | 17 | 13 | 47 | 42 | 41 |
| 12 | Newcastle United | 42 | 14 | 13 | 15 | 44 | 46 | 41 |
| 13 | Stoke City | 42 | 12 | 13 | 17 | 44 | 48 | 37 |
| 14 | Everton | 42 | 12 | 13 | 17 | 54 | 60 | 37 |
| 15 | Huddersfield Town | 42 | 11 | 14 | 17 | 40 | 49 | 36 |
| 16 | Nottingham Forest | 42 | 14 | 8 | 20 | 42 | 61 | 36 |
| 17 | WBA | 42 | 10 | 15 | 17 | 58 | 75 | 35 |
| 18 | Crystal Palace | 42 | 12 | 11 | 19 | 39 | 57 | 35 |
| 19 | Ipswich Town | 42 | 12 | 10 | 20 | 42 | 48 | 34 |
| 20 | West Ham United | 42 | 10 | 14 | 18 | 47 | 60 | 34 |
| 21 | Burnley | 42 | 7 | 13 | 22 | 29 | 63 | 27 |
| 22 | Blackpool | 42 | 4 | 15 | 23 | 34 | 66 | 23 |

# Season 1971-72

## Football League Division One

| DATE | OPPONENTS | SCORE | GOALSCORERS | ATTENDANCE |
|---|---|---|---|---|
| Aug 14 | Derby County | D 2-2 | Law, Gowling | 35,386 |
| Aug 18 | Chelsea | W 3-2 | Kidd, Morgan (pen), Charlton | 54,663 |
| Aug 20 | ARSENAL* | W 3-1 | Gowling, Charlton, Kidd | 27,649 |
| Aug 23 | WEST BROMWICH ALBION** | W 3-1 | Best 2, Gowling | 23,146 |
| Aug 28 | Wolverhampton Wanderers | D 1-1 | Best | 46,479 |
| Aug 31 | Everton | L 0-1 | | 52,151 |
| Sep 4 | IPSWICH TOWN | W 1-0 | Best | 45,656 |
| Sep 11 | Crystal Palace | W 3-1 | Kidd, Law 2 | 43,720 |
| Sep 18 | WEST HAM UNITED | W 4-2 | Best 3, Charlton | 53,339 |
| Sep 25 | Liverpool | D 2-2 | Law, Charlton | 55,642 |
| Oct 2 | SHEFFIELD UNITED | W 2-0 | Best, Gowling | 51,758 |
| Oct 9 | Huddersfield Town | W 3-0 | Best, Law, Charlton | 33,458 |
| Oct 16 | DERBY COUNTY | W 1-0 | Best | 53,247 |
| Oct 23 | Newcastle United | W 1-0 | Best | 55,603 |
| Oct 30 | LEEDS UNITED | L 0-1 | | 53,884 |
| Nov 6 | Manchester City | D 3-3 | McIlroy, Kidd, Gowling | 63,326 |
| Nov 13 | TOTTENHAM HOTSPUR | W 3-1 | McIlroy, Law 2 | 54,058 |
| Nov 20 | LEICESTER CITY | W 3-2 | Kidd, Law 2 | 48,764 |
| Nov 27 | Southampton | W 5-2 | Best 3, McIlroy, Kidd | 30,323 |
| Dec 4 | NOTTINGHAM FOREST | W 3-2 | Law, Kidd 2 | 45,411 |
| Dec 11 | Stoke City | D 1-1 | Law | 33,875 |
| Dec 18 | Ipswich Town | D 0-0 | | 29,213 |
| Dec 27 | COVENTRY CITY | D 2-2 | Law, James | 52,035 |
| Jan 1 | West Ham United | L 0-3 | | 41,990 |
| Jan 8 | WOLVERHAMPTON WANDERERS | L 1-3 | McIlroy | 47,626 |
| Jan 22 | CHELSEA | L 0-1 | | 55,927 |
| Jan 29 | West Bromwich Albion | L 1-2 | Kidd | 46,992 |
| Feb 12 | NEWCASTLE UNITED | L 0-2 | | 44,983 |
| Feb 19 | Leeds United | L 1-5 | Burns | 45,399 |
| Mar 4 | Tottenham Hotspur | L 0-2 | | 54,814 |
| Mar 8 | EVERTON | D 0-0 | | 38,415 |
| Mar 11 | HUDDERSFIELD TOWN | W 2-0 | Best, Storey-Moore | 53,581 |
| Mar 25 | CRYSTAL PALACE | W 4-0 | Gowling, Charlton, Storey-Moore, Law | 41,550 |
| Apr 1 | Coventry City | W 3-2 | Best, Storey-Moore, Charlton | 37,870 |
| Apr 3 | LIVERPOOL | L 0-3 | | 54,000 |
| Apr 4 | Sheffield United | D 1-1 | Sadler | 45,045 |
| Apr 8 | Leicester City | L 0-2 | | 35,649 |
| Apr 12 | MANCHESTER CITY | L 1-3 | Buchan | 56,362 |
| Apr 15 | SOUTHAMPTON | W 3-2 | Best (pen), Storey-Moore, Kidd | 38,437 |
| Apr 22 | Nottingham Forest | D 0-0 | | 35,063 |
| Apr 25 | Arsenal | L 0-3 | | 49,125 |
| Apr 29 | STOKE CITY | W 3-0 | Charlton, Storey-Moore, Best (pen) | 34,595 |

*Played at Anfield, Liverpool. **Played at Victoria Ground, Stoke-on-Trent.

## FA Cup

| | | | | | |
|---|---|---|---|---|---|
| Jan 15 | Southampton | (Rd3) D 1-1 | Charlton | 30,190 |
| Jan 19 | SOUTHAMPTON | (R) W 4-2 | Sadler, Aston, Best 2 | 50,956 |
| Feb 5 | Preston North End | (Rd4) W 2-0 | Gowling 2 | 27,025 |
| Feb 26 | MIDDLESBROUGH | (Rd5) D 0-0 | | 53,850 |
| Feb 29 | Middlesbrough | (R) W 3-0 | Morgan (pen), Best, Charlton | 39,683 |
| Mar 18 | STOKE CITY | (Rd6) D 1-1 | Best | 54,226 |
| Mar 22 | Stoke City | (R) L 1-2* | Best | 49,192 |

*After extra-time.

## League Cup

| | | | | |
|---|---|---|---|---|
| Sep 7 | Ipswich Town | (Rd2) W 3-1 | Morgan (pen), Best 2 | 28,143 |
| Oct 6 | BURNLEY | (Rd3) D 1-1 | Charlton | 44,600 |
| Oct 18 | Burnley | (R) W 1-0 | Charlton | 27,511 |
| Oct 27 | STOKE CITY | (Rd4) D 1-1 | Gowling | 47,062 |
| Nov 8 | Stoke City | (R) D 0-0* | | 40,805 |
| Nov 15 | Stoke City | (2R) L 1-2 | Best | 42,249 |

*After extra-time.

**MANAGER:** Frank O'Farrell

**MOST APPEARANCES:** George Best, Bobby Charlton, Brian Kidd 53

**TOP SCORER:** George Best 26 (18 League)

**BIGGEST WIN:** 5-2, 27 November 1971, v Southampton, League

**HIGHEST ATTENDANCE:** 63,326 v Manchester City, 6 November 1971, League

## League & Cup Appearances

| PLAYER | LEAGUE | CUP COMPETITION FA CUP | LC | TOTAL |
|---|---|---|---|---|
| Aston | 2 (7) | 7 (1) | 2 (2) | 11 (10) |
| Best | 40 | 7 | 6 | 53 |
| Buchan | 13 | 2 | | 15 |
| Burns | 15 (2) | 5 | 3 | 23 (2) |
| Charlton | 40 | 7 | 6 | 53 |
| Connaughton | 3 | | | 3 |
| Dunne | 34 | 4 | 3 | 41 |
| Edwards | 4 | 2 | | 6 |
| Fitzpatrick | 1 | | | 1 |
| Gowling | 35 (2) | 6 (1) | 6 | 47 (2) |
| James | 37 | 5 | 6 | 48 |
| Kidd | 34 | 4 | 5 | 53 |
| Law | 32 (1) | 7 | 2 | 41 (1) |
| McIlroy | 8 (8) | 1 (2) | 2 | 11 (10) |
| Morgan | 35 | 7 | 6 | 48 |
| O'Neil | 37 | 7 | 6 | 50 |
| Sadler | 37 | 6 | 6 | 49 |
| Sartori | 0 (2) | | 1 | 1 (2) |
| Stepney | 39 | | 6 | 45 |
| Storey-Moore | 11 | | | 11 |
| Young | 5 (2) | | | 5 (2) |

## Goalscorers

| PLAYER | LEAGUE | CUP COMPETITION FA CUP | LC | TOTAL |
|---|---|---|---|---|
| Best | 18 | 5 | 3 | 26 |
| Law | 13 | | | 13 |
| Charlton | 8 | 2 | 2 | 12 |
| Kidd | 10 | | | 10 |
| Gowling | 6 | 2 | 1 | 9 |
| Storey-Moore | 5 | | | 5 |
| McIlroy | 4 | | | 4 |
| Morgan | 1 | 1 | 1 | 3 |
| Sadler | 1 | 1 | | 2 |
| Buchan | 1 | | | 1 |
| Burns | 1 | | | 1 |
| James | 1 | | | 1 |
| Aston | | 1 | | 1 |

### Fact File

United faced Stoke City a total of seven times during the season: twice in the League, twice in the FA Cup and three times in the League Cup.

### Final Division One Table

| | | P | W | D | L | F | A | PTS |
|---|---|---|---|---|---|---|---|---|
| 1 | Derby County | 42 | 24 | 10 | 8 | 69 | 33 | 58 |
| 2 | Leeds United | 42 | 24 | 9 | 9 | 73 | 31 | 57 |
| 3 | Liverpool | 42 | 24 | 9 | 9 | 64 | 30 | 57 |
| 4 | Manchester City | 42 | 23 | 11 | 8 | 77 | 45 | 57 |
| 5 | Arsenal | 42 | 22 | 8 | 12 | 58 | 40 | 52 |
| 6 | Tottenham Hotspur | 42 | 19 | 13 | 10 | 63 | 42 | 51 |
| 7 | Chelsea | 42 | 18 | 12 | 12 | 58 | 49 | 48 |
| 8 | Manchester United | 42 | 19 | 10 | 13 | 69 | 61 | 48 |
| 9 | Wolverhampton W | 42 | 18 | 11 | 13 | 65 | 57 | 47 |
| 10 | Sheffield United | 42 | 17 | 12 | 13 | 61 | 60 | 46 |
| 11 | Newcastle United | 42 | 15 | 11 | 16 | 49 | 52 | 41 |
| 12 | Leicester City | 42 | 13 | 13 | 16 | 41 | 46 | 39 |
| 13 | Ipswich Town | 42 | 11 | 16 | 15 | 39 | 53 | 38 |
| 14 | West Ham United | 42 | 12 | 12 | 18 | 47 | 51 | 36 |
| 15 | Everton | 42 | 9 | 18 | 15 | 37 | 48 | 36 |
| 16 | WBA | 42 | 12 | 11 | 19 | 42 | 54 | 35 |
| 17 | Stoke City | 42 | 10 | 15 | 17 | 39 | 56 | 35 |
| 18 | Coventry City | 42 | 9 | 15 | 18 | 44 | 67 | 33 |
| 19 | Southampton | 42 | 12 | 7 | 23 | 52 | 80 | 31 |
| 20 | Crystal Palace | 42 | 8 | 13 | 21 | 39 | 65 | 29 |
| 21 | Nottingham Forest | 42 | 8 | 9 | 25 | 47 | 81 | 25 |
| 22 | Huddersfield Town | 42 | 6 | 13 | 23 | 27 | 59 | 25 |

# Season 1972-73

## Football League Division One

| DATE | OPPONENTS | SCORE | GOALSCORERS | ATTENDANCE |
|---|---|---|---|---|
| Aug 12 | IPSWICH TOWN | L 1-2 | Law | 51,459 |
| Aug 15 | Liverpool | L 0-2 | | 54,799 |
| Aug 19 | Everton | L 0-2 | | 52,348 |
| Aug 23 | LEICESTER CITY | D 1-1 | Best (pen) | 40,067 |
| Aug 26 | ARSENAL | D 0-0 | | 48,108 |
| Aug 30 | CHELSEA | D 0-0 | | 44,482 |
| Sep 2 | West Ham United | D 2-2 | Best, Storey-Moore | 31,939 |
| Sep 9 | COVENTRY CITY | L 0-1 | | 37,073 |
| Sep 16 | Wolverhampton Wanderers | L 0-2 | | 34,049 |
| Sep 23 | DERBY COUNTY | W 3-0 | Morgan, Storey-Moore, Davies | 48,255 |
| Sep 30 | Sheffield United | L 0-1 | | 37,347 |
| Oct 7 | West Bromwich Albion | D 2-2 | Best (pen), Storey-Moore | 39,209 |
| Oct 14 | BIRMINGHAM CITY | W 1-0 | MacDougall | 52,104 |
| Oct 21 | Newcastle United | L 1-2 | Charlton | 38,170 |
| Oct 28 | TOTTENHAM HOTSPUR | L 1-4 | Charlton | 52,497 |
| Nov 4 | Leicester City | D 2-2 | Best, Davies | 32,575 |
| Nov 11 | LIVERPOOL | W 2-0 | Davies, MacDougall | 53,944 |
| Nov 18 | Manchester City | L 0-3 | | 52,050 |
| Nov 25 | SOUTHAMPTON | W 2-1 | Davies, MacDougall | 36,073 |
| Dec 2 | Norwich City | W 2-0 | Storey-Moore, MacDougall | 35,910 |
| Dec 9 | STOKE CITY | L 0-2 | | 41,347 |
| Dec 16 | Crystal Palace | L 0-5 | | 39,484 |
| Dec 23 | LEEDS UNITED | D 1-1 | MacDougall | 46,382 |
| Dec 26 | Derby County | L 1-3 | Storey-Moore | 35,098 |
| Jan 6 | Arsenal | L 1-3 | Kidd | 51,195 |
| Jan 20 | WEST HAM UNITED | D 2-2 | Charlton (pen), Macari | 50,878 |
| Jan 24 | EVERTON | D 0-0 | | 58,970 |
| Jan 27 | Coventry City | D 1-1 | Holton | 42,767 |
| Feb 10 | WOLVERHAMPTON WANDERERS | W 2-1 | Charlton 2 (1pen) | 52,089 |
| Feb 17 | Ipswich Town | L 1-4 | Macari | 31,918 |
| Mar 3 | WEST BROMWICH ALBION | W 2-1 | Kidd, Macari | 46,735 |
| Mar 10 | Birmingham City | L 1-3 | Macari | 51,278 |
| Mar 17 | NEWCASTLE UNITED | W 2-1 | Holton, Martin | 48,426 |
| Mar 24 | Tottenham Hotspur | D 1-1 | Graham | 49,751 |
| Mar 31 | Southampton | W 2-0 | Charlton, Holton | 23,161 |
| Apr 7 | NORWICH CITY | W 1-0 | Martin | 48,593 |
| Apr 11 | CRYSTAL PALACE | W 2-0 | Kidd, Morgan | 46,891 |
| Apr 14 | Stoke City | D 2-2 | Macari, Smith o.g. | 37,051 |
| Apr 18 | Leeds United | W 1-0 | Anderson | 45,450 |
| Apr 21 | MANCHESTER CITY | D 0-0 | | 61,676 |
| Apr 23 | SHEFFIELD UNITED | L 1-2 | Kidd | 57,280 |
| Apr 28 | Chelsea | L 0-1 | | 44,184 |

## FA Cup

| | | | | | |
|---|---|---|---|---|---|
| Jan 13 | Wolverhampton Wanderers | (Rd3) | L 0-1 | | 40,005 |

## League Cup

| | | | | | |
|---|---|---|---|---|---|
| Sep 6 | Oxford United | (Rd2) | D 2-2 | Charlton, Law | 16,560 |
| Sep 12 | OXFORD UNITED | (R) | W 3-1 | Best 2, Storey-Moore | 21,486 |
| Oct 3 | Bristol Rovers | (Rd3) | D 1-1 | Morgan | 33,957 |
| Oct 11 | BRISTOL ROVERS | (R) | L 1-2 | McIlroy | 29,349 |

### Fact File

Bobby Charlton's long and illustrious career in the famous red shirt came to a close after 17 years as a first-team regular.

**MANAGER:** Frank O'Farrell/Tommy Docherty

**MOST APPEARANCES:** Martin Buchan 47

**TOP SCORER:** Bobby Charlton 7 (6 League)

**BIGGEST WIN:** 3-0 v Derby County, 23 September 1972, League

**HIGHEST ATTENDANCE:** 61,676 v Manchester City, 21 April 1973, League

## League & Cup Appearances

| PLAYER | LEAGUE | CUP COMPETITION FA CUP | LC | TOTAL |
|---|---|---|---|---|
| Anderson | 2 (5) | | | 2 (5) |
| Best | 19 | | 4 | 23 |
| Buchan | 42 | 1 | 4 | 47 |
| Charlton | 34 (2) | 1 | 4 | 39 (2) |
| Davies | 15 (1) | 1 | | 16 (1) |
| Donald | 4 | | 1 | 5 |
| Dunne | 24 | 0 (1) | 3 | 27 (1) |
| Edwards | 1 | | | 1 |
| Fletcher | 0 (2) | | | 0 (2) |
| Forsyth | 8 | 1 | | 9 |
| Fitzpatrick | 5 | | 1 | 6 |
| Graham | 18 | 1 | | 19 |
| O'Neil | 16 | | 1 | 17 |
| Holton | 15 | | | 15 |
| James | 22 | | 4 | 26 |
| Kidd | 17 (5) | 1 | 2 | 20 (5) |
| Law | 9 (2) | 1 | 2 | 12 (2) |
| MacDougall | 18 | | | 18 |
| McIlroy | 4 (6) | | 0 (3) | 4 (9) |
| Macari | 16 | | | 16 |
| Martin | 14 (2) | | | 14 (2) |
| Morgan | 39 | 1 | 4 | 44 |
| Rimmer | 4 | | | 4 |
| Sadler | 19 | 1 | 2 | 22 |
| Sidebottom | 2 | | | 2 |
| Stepney | 38 | 1 | 4 | 43 |
| Storey-Moore | 26 | | 4 | 30 |
| Watson | 3 | | 1 | 4 |
| Young | 28 (2) | 1 | 3 | 32 (2) |

## Goalscorers

| PLAYER | LEAGUE | CUP COMPETITION FA CUP | LC | TOTAL |
|---|---|---|---|---|
| Charlton | 6 | | 1 | 7 |
| Storey-Moore | 5 | | 1 | 6 |
| Best | 4 | | 2 | 6 |
| MacDougall | 5 | | | 5 |
| Macari | 5 | | | 5 |
| Davies | 4 | | | 4 |
| Kidd | 4 | | | 4 |
| Morgan | 3 | | 1 | 4 |
| Holton | 3 | | | 3 |
| Martin | 2 | | | 2 |
| Law | 1 | | 1 | 2 |
| Anderson | 1 | | | 1 |
| Graham | 1 | | | 1 |
| McIlroy | | | 1 | 1 |

### Final Division One Table

| | | P | W | D | L | F | A | Pts |
|---|---|---|---|---|---|---|---|---|
| 1 | Liverpool | 42 | 25 | 10 | 7 | 72 | 42 | 60 |
| 2 | Arsenal | 42 | 23 | 11 | 8 | 57 | 43 | 57 |
| 3 | Leeds United | 42 | 21 | 11 | 10 | 71 | 45 | 53 |
| 4 | Ipswich Town | 42 | 17 | 14 | 11 | 55 | 45 | 48 |
| 5 | Wolverhampton W | 42 | 18 | 11 | 13 | 66 | 54 | 47 |
| 6 | West Ham United | 42 | 17 | 12 | 13 | 67 | 53 | 46 |
| 7 | Derby County | 42 | 19 | 8 | 15 | 56 | 54 | 46 |
| 8 | Tottenham Hotspur | 42 | 16 | 13 | 13 | 58 | 48 | 45 |
| 9 | Newcastle United | 42 | 16 | 13 | 13 | 60 | 51 | 45 |
| 10 | Birmingham City | 42 | 15 | 12 | 15 | 53 | 54 | 42 |
| 11 | Manchester City | 42 | 15 | 11 | 16 | 57 | 60 | 41 |
| 12 | Chelsea | 42 | 13 | 14 | 15 | 49 | 51 | 40 |
| 13 | Southampton | 42 | 11 | 18 | 13 | 47 | 52 | 40 |
| 14 | Sheffield United | 42 | 15 | 10 | 17 | 51 | 59 | 40 |
| 15 | Stoke City | 42 | 14 | 10 | 18 | 61 | 56 | 38 |
| 16 | Leicester City | 42 | 10 | 17 | 15 | 40 | 46 | 37 |
| 17 | Everton | 42 | 13 | 11 | 18 | 41 | 49 | 37 |
| 18 | Manchester United | 42 | 12 | 13 | 17 | 44 | 60 | 37 |
| 19 | Coventry City | 42 | 13 | 9 | 20 | 40 | 55 | 35 |
| 20 | Norwich City | 42 | 11 | 10 | 21 | 36 | 63 | 32 |
| 21 | Crystal Palace | 42 | 9 | 12 | 21 | 41 | 58 | 30 |
| 22 | WBA | 42 | 9 | 10 | 23 | 38 | 62 | 28 |

# Season 1973-74

## Football League Division One

| DATE | OPPONENTS | SCORE | GOALSCORERS | ATTENDANCE |
|---|---|---|---|---|
| Aug 25 | Arsenal | L 0-3 | | 51,501 |
| Aug 29 | STOKE CITY | W 1-0 | James | 43,614 |
| Sep 1 | QUEENS PARK RANGERS | W 2-1 | Holton, McIlroy | 44,156 |
| Sep 5 | Leicester City | L 0-1 | | 29,152 |
| Sep 8 | Ipswich Town | L 1-2 | Anderson | 22,005 |
| Sep 12 | LEICESTER CITY | L 1-2 | Stepney (pen) | 40,793 |
| Sep 15 | WEST HAM UNITED | W 3-1 | Kidd 2, Storey-Moore | 44,757 |
| Sep 22 | Leeds United | D 0-0 | | 47,058 |
| Sep 29 | LIVERPOOL | D 0-0 | | 53,882 |
| Oct 6 | Wolverhampton Wanderers | L 1-2 | McIlroy | 32,962 |
| Oct 13 | DERBY COUNTY | L 0-1 | | 43,724 |
| Oct 20 | BIRMINGHAM CITY | W 1-0 | Stepney (pen) | 48,937 |
| Oct 27 | Burnley | D 0-0 | | 31,810 |
| Nov 3 | CHELSEA | D 2-2 | Young, Greenhoff | 48,036 |
| Nov 10 | Tottenham Hotspur | L 1-2 | Best | 42,756 |
| Nov 17 | Newcastle United | L 2-3 | Graham, Macari | 42,474 |
| Nov 24 | NORWICH CITY | D 0-0 | | 36,338 |
| Dec 8 | SOUTHAMPTON | D 0-0 | | 31,648 |
| Dec 15 | COVENTRY CITY | L 2-3 | Best, Morgan | 28,589 |
| Dec 22 | Liverpool | L 0-2 | | 40,420 |
| Dec 27 | SHEFFIELD UNITED | L 1-2 | Macari | 38,653 |
| Dec 29 | IPSWICH TOWN | W 2-0 | McIlroy, Macari | 36,365 |
| Jan 1 | Queens Park Rangers | L 0-3 | | 32,339 |
| Jan 12 | West Ham United | L 1-2 | McIlroy | 34,147 |
| Jan 19 | ARSENAL | D 1-1 | James | 38,589 |
| Feb 2 | Coventry City | L 0-1 | | 25,407 |
| Feb 9 | LEEDS UNITED | L 0-2 | | 60,025 |
| Feb 16 | Derby County | D 2-2 | Greenhoff, Houston | 29,987 |
| Feb 23 | WOLVERHAMPTON WANDERERS | D 0-0 | | 39,260 |
| Mar 2 | Sheffield United | W 1-0 | Macari | 29,203 |
| Mar 13 | Manchester City | D 0-0 | | 51,331 |
| Mar 16 | Birmingham City | L 0-1 | | 37,768 |
| Mar 23 | TOTTENHAM HOTSPUR | L 0-1 | | 36,278 |
| Mar 30 | Chelsea | W 3-1 | Morgan, Daly, McIlroy | 29,602 |
| Apr 3 | BURNLEY | D 3-3 | McIlroy, Forsyth, Holton | 33,336 |
| Apr 6 | Norwich City | W 2-0 | Macari, Greenhoff | 27,899 |
| Apr 13 | NEWCASTLE UNITED | W 1-0 | McCalliog | 44,751 |
| Apr 15 | EVERTON | W 3-0 | McCalliog 2, Houston | 48,424 |
| Apr 20 | Southampton | D 1-1 | McCalliog (pen) | 30,789 |
| Apr 23 | Everton | L 0-1 | | 46,093 |
| Apr 27 | MANCHESTER CITY | L 0-1 | | 56,996 |
| Apr 29 | STOKE CITY | L 0-1 | | 27,392 |

## FA Cup

| | | | | | |
|---|---|---|---|---|---|
| Jan 5 | PLYMOUTH ARGYLE | (Rd3) | W 1-0 | Macari | 31,810 |
| Jan 26 | IPSWICH TOWN | (Rd4) | L 1-2 | Kidd | 37,177 |

## League Cup

| | | | | | |
|---|---|---|---|---|---|
| Oct 8 | MIDDLESBROUGH | (Rd2) | L 0-1 | | 23,906 |

## League & Cup Appearances

| PLAYER | LEAGUE | CUP COMPETITION FA CUP | LC | TOTAL |
|---|---|---|---|---|
| Anderson | 11 (1) | | | 11 (1) |
| Best | 12 | | | 12 |
| Bielby | 2 (2) | | | 2 (2) |
| Buchan G. | 0 (3) | | 0 (1) | 0 (4) |
| Buchan M. | 42 | 2 | 1 | 45 |
| Daly | 14 (2) | | 1 | 15 (3) |
| Fletcher | 2 (3) | | | 2 (3) |
| Forsyth | 18 (1) | 2 | | 20 (1) |
| Graham | 23 (1) | 1 | 1 | 25 (1) |
| Greenhoff | 36 | 2 | 1 | 39 |
| Griffiths | 7 | | | 7 |
| Holton | 34 | 2 | 1 | 37 |
| Houston | 20 | | | 20 |
| James | 21 | 1 | 1 | 23 |
| Kidd | 21 | 1 (1) | 1 | 23 (1) |
| McCalliog | 11 | | | 11 |
| McIlroy | 24 (5) | 1 (1) | | 25 (6) |
| Macari | 34 (1) | 2 | 1 | 37 (1) |
| Martin | 12 (4) | 2 | | 14 (4) |
| Morgan | 41 | 2 | 1 | 44 |
| Sadler | 2 (1) | | | 2 (1) |
| Sidebottom | 2 | | | 2 |
| Stepney | 42 | 2 | 1 | 45 |
| Storey-Moore | 20 | | | 2 |
| Young | 29 | 2 | 1 | 32 |

## Goalscorers

| PLAYER | LEAGUE | CUP COMPETITION FA CUP | LC | TOTAL |
|---|---|---|---|---|
| McIlroy | 6 | | | 6 |
| Macari | 5 | 1 | | 6 |
| McCalliog | 4 | | | 4 |
| Greenhoff | 3 | | | 3 |
| Kidd | 2 | 1 | | 3 |
| Best | 2 | | | 2 |
| Holton | 2 | | | 2 |
| Houston | 2 | | | 2 |
| James | 2 | | | 2 |
| Morgan | 2 | | | 2 |
| Stepney | 2 | | | 2 |
| Anderson | 1 | | | 1 |
| Daly | 1 | | | 1 |
| Forsyth | 1 | | | 1 |
| Graham | 1 | | | 1 |
| Storey-Moore | 1 | | | 1 |
| Young | 1 | | | 1 |

### Final Division One Table

| | | P | W | D | L | F | A | Pts |
|---|---|---|---|---|---|---|---|---|
| 1 | Leeds United | 42 | 24 | 14 | 4 | 66 | 31 | 62 |
| 2 | Liverpool | 42 | 22 | 13 | 7 | 52 | 31 | 57 |
| 3 | Derby County | 42 | 21 | 14 | 11 | 52 | 42 | 48 |
| 4 | Ipswich Town | 42 | 18 | 11 | 13 | 67 | 58 | 47 |
| 5 | Stoke City | 42 | 15 | 16 | 11 | 54 | 42 | 46 |
| 6 | Burnley | 42 | 16 | 14 | 12 | 56 | 53 | 46 |
| 7 | Everton | 42 | 16 | 12 | 14 | 50 | 48 | 44 |
| 8 | QPR | 42 | 13 | 17 | 12 | 56 | 52 | 43 |
| 9 | Leicester City | 42 | 13 | 16 | 13 | 51 | 41 | 42 |
| 10 | Arsenal | 42 | 14 | 14 | 14 | 49 | 51 | 42 |
| 11 | Tottenham Hotspur | 42 | 14 | 14 | 14 | 45 | 50 | 42 |
| 12 | Wolverhampton W | 42 | 13 | 15 | 14 | 49 | 49 | 41 |
| 13 | Sheffield United | 42 | 14 | 12 | 16 | 44 | 49 | 40 |
| 14 | Manchester City | 42 | 14 | 12 | 16 | 39 | 46 | 40 |
| 15 | Newcastle United | 42 | 13 | 12 | 17 | 49 | 48 | 38 |
| 16 | Coventry City | 42 | 14 | 10 | 18 | 43 | 54 | 38 |
| 17 | Chelsea | 42 | 12 | 13 | 17 | 56 | 60 | 37 |
| 18 | West Ham United | 42 | 11 | 15 | 16 | 55 | 60 | 37 |
| 19 | Birmingham City | 42 | 12 | 13 | 17 | 52 | 64 | 37 |
| 20 | Southampton | 42 | 11 | 14 | 17 | 47 | 68 | 36 |
| 21 | Manchester United | 42 | 10 | 12 | 20 | 38 | 48 | 32 |
| 22 | Norwich City | 42 | 7 | 15 | 20 | 37 | 62 | 29 |

### Fact File

United finished the season second from bottom in the league table and were relegated to Division Two for the first time since 1937.

**MANAGER:** Tommy Docherty

**MOST APPEARANCES:** Martin Buchan, Alex Stepney 45

**TOP SCORER:** Sammy McIlroy 6 (all League), Lou Macari 6 (5 League)

**BIGGEST WIN:** 3-0 v Everton, 15 April 1974, League

**HIGHEST ATTENDANCE:** 60,025 v Leeds United, 9 February 1974, League

# Season 1974-75

## Football League Division Two

| DATE | OPPONENTS | SCORE | GOALSCORERS | ATTENDANCE |
|---|---|---|---|---|
| Aug 17 | Orient | W 2-0 | Morgan, Houston | 17,772 |
| Aug 24 | MILLWALL | W 4-0 | Daly 3 (2 pen), Pearson | 44,756 |
| Aug 28 | PORTSMOUTH | W 2-1 | Daly (pen), McIlroy | 42,547 |
| Aug 31 | Cardiff City | W 1-0 | Daly (pen) | 22,344 |
| Sep 7 | NOTTINGHAM FOREST | D 2-2 | Greenhoff, McIlroy | 40,671 |
| Sep 14 | West Bromwich Albion | D 1-1 | Pearson | 28,666 |
| Sep 16 | Millwall | W 1-0 | Daly (pen) | 16,988 |
| Sep 21 | BRISTOL ROVERS | W 2-0 | Greenhoff, Prince o.g. | 42,948 |
| Sep 25 | BOLTON WANDERERS | W 3-0 | Macari, Houston, McAllister o.g. | 47,084 |
| Sep 28 | Norwich City | L 0-2 | | 24,586 |
| Oct 5 | Fulham | W 2-1 | Pearson 2 | 26,513 |
| Oct 12 | NOTTS COUNTY | W 1-0 | McIlroy | 46,565 |
| Oct 15 | Portsmouth | D 0-0 | | 25,608 |
| Oct 19 | Blackpool | W 3-0 | Forsyth, Macari, McCalliog | 25,370 |
| Oct 26 | SOUTHAMPTON | W 1-0 | Pearson | 48,724 |
| Nov 2 | OXFORD UNITED | W 4-0 | Pearson 3, Macari | 41,909 |
| Nov 9 | Bristol City | L 0-1 | | 28,104 |
| Nov 16 | ASTON VILLA | W 2-1 | Daly 2 (1 pen) | 55,615 |
| Nov 23 | Hull City | L 0-2 | | 23,287 |
| Nov 30 | SUNDERLAND | W 3-2 | Pearson, Morgan, McIlroy | 60,585 |
| Dec 7 | Sheffield Wednesday | D 4-4 | Macari 2, Houston, Pearson | 35,067 |
| Dec 14 | ORIENT | D 0-0 | | 41,200 |
| Dec 21 | York City | W 1-0 | Pearson | 15,314 |
| Dec 26 | WEST BROMWICH ALBION | W 2-1 | McIlroy, Daly (pen) | 51,104 |
| Dec 28 | Oldham Athletic | L 0-1 | | 26,356 |
| Jan 11 | SHEFFIELD WEDNESDAY | W 2-0 | McCalliog 2 (1 pen) | 45,662 |
| Jan 18 | Sunderland | D 0-0 | | 45,976 |
| Feb 1 | BRISTOL CITY | L 0-1 | | 47,118 |
| Feb 8 | Oxford United | L 0-1 | | 15,815 |
| Feb 15 | HULL CITY | W 2-0 | Houston, Pearson | 44,712 |
| Feb 22 | Aston Villa | L 0-2 | | 40,353 |
| Mar 1 | CARDIFF CITY | W 4-0 | Houston, McIlroy, Macari, Pearson | 43,601 |
| Mar 8 | Bolton Wanderers | W 1-0 | Pearson | 38,152 |
| Mar 15 | NORWICH CITY | D 1-1 | Pearson | 56,202 |
| Mar 22 | Nottingham Forest | W 1-0 | Daly | 21,893 |
| Mar 26 | Bristol Rovers | D 1-1 | Macari | 19,337 |
| Mar 29 | YORK CITY | W 2-1 | Morgan, Macari | 46,802 |
| Mar 31 | OLDHAM ATHLETIC | W 3-2 | McIlroy, Macari, Coppell | 56,618 |
| Apr 5 | Southampton | W 1-0 | Macari | 21,866 |
| Apr 12 | FULHAM | W 1-0 | Daly | 52,971 |
| Apr 19 | Notts County | D 2-2 | Houston, Greenhoff | 17,320 |
| Apr 26 | BLACKPOOL | W 4-0 | Pearson 2, Macari, Greenhoff | 58,769 |

## FA Cup

| | | | | |
|---|---|---|---|---|
| Jan 4 | WALSALL | (Rd3) D 0-0 | | 43,353 |
| Jan 7 | Walsall | (R) L 2-3 | Daly (pen), McIlroy | 18,105 |

## League Cup

| | | | | |
|---|---|---|---|---|
| Sep 11 | CHARLTON ATHLETIC | (Rd2) W 5-1 | Macari 2, McIlroy, Houston, Warman o.g. | 21,616 |
| Oct 9 | MANCHESTER CITY | (Rd3) W 1-0 | Daly (pen) | 55,159 |
| Nov 13 | BURNLEY | (Rd4) W 3-2 | Macari 2, Morgan | 46,275 |
| Dec 4 | Middlesbrough | (Rd5) D 0-0 | | 36,005 |
| Dec 18 | MIDDLESBROUGH | (R) W 3-0 | Pearson, McIlroy, Macari | 49,501 |
| Jan 15 | NORWICH CITY | (SF/1L) D 2-2 | Macari 2 | 58,010 |
| Jan 22 | Norwich City | (SF/2L) L 0-1 | | 31,621 |

### Fact File

A highly satisfactory season, United's first out of the top grade since the World War II, ended with the club making an immediate return as Second Division champions.

**MANAGER:** Tommy Docherty
**MOST APPEARANCES:** Sammy McIlroy 51
**TOP SCORER:** Stuart Pearson 18 (17 League), Lou Macari 18 (11 League)
**BIGGEST WIN:** 5-1 v Charlton Athletic, 11 September 1974, League Cup
**HIGHEST ATTENDANCE:** 60,585 v Sunderland, 30 November 1974, League

## League & Cup Appearances

| PLAYER | LEAGUE | CUP COMPETITION FA CUP | LC | TOTAL |
|---|---|---|---|---|
| Albiston | 2 | | 1 | 3 |
| Baldwin | 2 | | | 2 |
| Buchan | 41 | 2 | 7 | 50 |
| Coppell | 9 (1) | | | 9 (1) |
| Daly | 36 (1) | 2 | 7 | 45 (1) |
| Davies | 0 (8) | 0 (2) | | 0 (10) |
| Forsyth | 39 | | 6 | 45 |
| Graham | 0 (1) | | | 0 (1) |
| Greenhoff | 39 (2) | 2 | 6 | 47 (2) |
| Holton | 14 | | 3 | 17 |
| Houston | 40 | 2 | 6 | 48 |
| James | 13 | | 2 | 15 |
| McCalliog | 20 | 1 | 5 (1) | 26 (1) |
| McCreery | 0 (2) | | | 0 (2) |
| McIlroy | 41 (1) | 2 | 7 | 50 (1) |
| Martin | 7 (1) | | 1 | 8 (1) |
| Macari | 36 (2) | 2 | 6 (1) | 44 (3) |
| Morgan | 32 (2) | 1 | 6 (1) | 39 (3) |
| Nicholl | 0 (1) | | | 0 (1) |
| Pearson | 30 (1) | 2 | 4 | 36 (1) |
| Roche | 2 | | | 2 |
| Sidebottom | 12 | 2 | 2 | 16 |
| Stepney | 40 | 2 | 7 | 49 |
| Young | 7 (8) | 2 | 1 (4) | 10 (12) |

## Goalscorers

| PLAYER | LEAGUE | CUP COMPETITION FA CUP | LC | TOTAL |
|---|---|---|---|---|
| Pearson | 17 | 1 | | 18 |
| Macari | 11 | | 7 | 18 |
| Daly | 11 | 1 | 1 | 13 |
| McIlroy | 7 | 1 | 2 | 10 |
| Houston | 6 | | 1 | 7 |
| Greenhoff | 4 | | | 4 |
| Morgan | 3 | | 1 | 4 |
| McCalliog | 3 | | | 3 |
| Coppell | 1 | | | 1 |
| Forsyth | 1 | | | 1 |
| Opps' o.gs. | 2 | | 1 | 3 |

### Final Division Two Table

| | | P | W | D | L | F | A | Pts |
|---|---|---|---|---|---|---|---|---|
| 1 | Manchester United | 42 | 26 | 9 | 7 | 66 | 30 | 61 |
| 2 | Aston Villa | 42 | 25 | 8 | 9 | 79 | 32 | 58 |
| 3 | Norwich City | 42 | 20 | 13 | 9 | 58 | 37 | 53 |
| 4 | Sunderland | 42 | 19 | 13 | 10 | 65 | 35 | 51 |
| 5 | Bristol City | 42 | 21 | 8 | 13 | 47 | 33 | 50 |
| 6 | WBA | 42 | 18 | 9 | 15 | 54 | 42 | 45 |
| 7 | Blackpool | 42 | 14 | 17 | 11 | 38 | 33 | 45 |
| 8 | Hull City | 42 | 15 | 14 | 13 | 40 | 53 | 44 |
| 9 | Fulham | 42 | 13 | 16 | 13 | 44 | 39 | 42 |
| 10 | Bolton Wanderers | 42 | 15 | 12 | 15 | 45 | 41 | 42 |
| 11 | Oxford United | 42 | 15 | 12 | 15 | 41 | 51 | 42 |
| 12 | Orient | 42 | 11 | 20 | 11 | 28 | 39 | 42 |
| 13 | Southampton | 42 | 15 | 11 | 16 | 53 | 54 | 41 |
| 14 | Notts County | 42 | 12 | 16 | 14 | 49 | 59 | 40 |
| 15 | York City | 42 | 14 | 10 | 18 | 51 | 55 | 38 |
| 16 | Nottingham Forest | 42 | 12 | 14 | 16 | 43 | 55 | 38 |
| 17 | Portsmouth | 42 | 12 | 13 | 17 | 44 | 54 | 37 |
| 18 | Oldham Athletic | 42 | 10 | 15 | 17 | 40 | 48 | 35 |
| 19 | Bristol Rovers | 42 | 12 | 11 | 19 | 42 | 64 | 35 |
| 20 | Millwall | 42 | 10 | 12 | 20 | 44 | 56 | 32 |
| 21 | Cardiff City | 42 | 9 | 14 | 19 | 36 | 62 | 32 |
| 22 | Sheffield Wednesday | 42 | 5 | 11 | 26 | 29 | 64 | 21 |

# Season 1975-76

## Football League Division One

| DATE | OPPONENTS | SCORE | GOALSCORERS | ATTENDANCE |
|---|---|---|---|---|
| Aug 16 | Wolverhampton Wanderers | W 2-0 | Macari 2 | 32,348 |
| Aug 19 | Birmingham City | W 2-0 | McIlroy 2 | 33,177 |
| Aug 23 | SHEFFIELD UNITED | W 5-1 | Pearson 2, McIlroy, Daly, Badger o.g. | 55,948 |
| Aug 27 | COVENTRY CITY | D 1-1 | Pearson | 52,169 |
| Aug 30 | Stoke City | W 1-0 | Dodd o.g. | 33,092 |
| Sep 6 | TOTTENHAM HOTSPUR | W 3-2 | Daly 2 (1pen), Pratt o.g. | 51,641 |
| Sep 13 | Queens Park Rangers | L 0-1 | | 29,237 |
| Sep 20 | IPSWICH TOWN | W 1-0 | Houston | 50,513 |
| Sep 24 | Derby County | L 1-2 | Daly | 33,187 |
| Sep 27 | Manchester City | D 2-2 | McCreery, Macari | 46,931 |
| Oct 4 | LEICESTER CITY | D 0-0 | | 47,878 |
| Oct 11 | Leeds United | W 2-1 | McIlroy 2 | 40,264 |
| Oct 18 | ARSENAL | W 3-1 | Coppell 2, Pearson | 53,885 |
| Oct 25 | West Ham United | L 1-2 | Macari | 38,601 |
| Nov 1 | NORWICH CITY | W 1-0 | Pearson | 50,587 |
| Nov 8 | Liverpool | L 1-3 | Coppell | 49,137 |
| Nov 15 | ASTON VILLA | W 2-0 | Coppell, McIlroy | 51,682 |
| Nov 22 | Arsenal | L 1-3 | Pearson | 40,102 |
| Nov 29 | NEWCASTLE UNITED | W 1-0 | Daly | 52,624 |
| Dec 6 | Middlesbrough | D 0-0 | | 32,454 |
| Dec 13 | Sheffield United | W 4-1 | Pearson 2, Hill, Macari | 31,741 |
| Dec 20 | WOLVERHAMPTON WANDERERS | W 1-0 | Hill | 44,269 |
| Dec 23 | Everton | D 1-1 | Macari | 41,732 |
| Dec 27 | BURNLEY | W 2-1 | McIlroy, Macari | 59,726 |
| Jan 10 | QUEENS PARK RANGERS | W 2-1 | Hill, McIlroy | 58,312 |
| Jan 17 | Tottenham Hotspur | D 1-1 | Hill | 49,189 |
| Jan 31 | BIRMINGHAM CITY | W 3-1 | Forsyth, Macari, McIlroy | 50,726 |
| Feb 7 | Coventry City | D 1-1 | Macari | 39,922 |
| Feb 18 | LIVERPOOL | D 0-0 | | 59,709 |
| Feb 21 | Aston Villa | L 1-2 | Macari | 50,094 |
| Feb 25 | DERBY COUNTY | D 1-1 | Pearson | 59,632 |
| Feb 28 | WEST HAM UNITED | W 4-0 | Forsyth, Macari, McCreery, Pearson | 57,220 |
| Mar 13 | LEEDS UNITED | W 3-2 | Houston, Pearson, Daly | 59,429 |
| Mar 16 | Norwich City | D 1-1 | Hill | 27,782 |
| Mar 20 | Newcastle United | W 4-3 | Pearson 2, Bird o.g., Howard o.g. | 41,427 |
| Mar 27 | MIDDLESBROUGH | W 3-0 | Daly (pen), McCreery, Hill | 58,527 |
| Apr 10 | Ipswich Town | L 0-3 | | 34,889 |
| Apr 17 | EVERTON | W 2-1 | McCreery, Kenyon o.g. | 61,879 |
| Apr 19 | Burnley | W 1-0 | Macari | 27,418 |
| Apr 21 | STOKE CITY | L 0-1 | | 53,879 |
| Apr 24 | Leicester City | L 1-2 | Coyne | 31,053 |
| May 4 | MANCHESTER CITY | W 2-0 | Hill, McIlroy | 59,528 |

## FA Cup

| | | | | | |
|---|---|---|---|---|---|
| Jan 3 | OXFORD UNITED | (Rd3) | W 2-1 | Daly 2 (pens) | 41,082 |
| Jan 24 | PETERBOROUGH UNITED | (Rd4) | W 3-1 | Forsyth, McIlroy, Hill | 56,352 |
| Feb 14 | Leicester City | (Rd5) | W 2-1 | Macari, Daly | 34,000 |
| Mar 6 | WOLVERHAMPTON WANDERERS | (Rd6) | D 1-1 | Daly | 59,433 |
| Mar 9 | Wolverhampton Wanderers | (R) | W 3-2* | Pearson, Greenhoff, Macari | 44,373 |
| Apr 3 | Derby County** | (SF) | W 2-0 | Hill 2 | 55,000 |
| May 1 | Southampton† | (F) | L 0-1 | | 99,115 |

*After extra-time. **Played at Hillsborough, Sheffield. †Played at Wembley, London.

## League Cup

| | | | | |
|---|---|---|---|---|
| Sep 10 | BRENTFORD | W 2-1 | Macari, McIlroy | 25,286 |
| Oct 8 | Aston Villa | W 2-1 | Macari, Coppell | 41,447 |
| Nov 12 | Manchester City | L 0-4 | | 50,182 |

### Fact File

United's first appearance in the FA Cup final for 13 years ended in disappointment as Bobby Stokes's lone second-half goal gave Southampton the trophy.

**MANAGER:** Tommy Docherty
**MOST APPEARANCES:** Martin Buchan, Stewart Houston 52
**TOP SCORER:** Lou Macari 15 (12 League)
**BIGGEST WIN:** 5-1 v Sheffield United, 23 August 1975, League
**HIGHEST ATTENDANCE:** 99,115 v Southampton, 1 May 1976, FA Cup

## League & Cup Appearances

| PLAYER | LEAGUE | CUP COMPETITION FA CUP | LC | TOTAL |
|---|---|---|---|---|
| Albiston | 2 (1) | | | 2 (1) |
| Buchan | 42 | 7 | 3 | 52 |
| Coppell | 39 | 7 | 3 | 49 |
| Coyne | 1 (1) | | | 1 (1) |
| Daly | 41 | 7 | 3 | 51 |
| Forsyth | 28 | 7 | | 35 |
| Greenhoff | 40 | 7 | 3 | 50 |
| Grimshaw | 0 (1) | | 0 (1) | 0 (2) |
| Hill | 26 | 7 | | 33 |
| Houston | 42 | 7 | 3 | 52 |
| Jackson | 16 (1) | | 3 | 19 (1) |
| Kelly | 0 (1) | | | 0 (1) |
| McCreery | 12 (15) | 1 (2) | 0 (1) | 13 (18) |
| McIlroy | 41 | 7 | 3 | 51 |
| Macari | 36 | 6 | | 42 |
| Nicholl | 15 (5) | 0 (2) | 3 | 18 (7) |
| Pearson | 39 | 7 | 3 | 49 |
| Roche | 4 | | 2 | 6 |
| Stepney | 38 | 7 | 2 | 47 |
| Young | 0 (1) | | | 0 (1) |

## Goalscorers

| PLAYER | LEAGUE | CUP COMPETITION FA CUP | LC | TOTAL |
|---|---|---|---|---|
| Macari | 12 | 1 | 2 | 15 |
| Pearson | 13 | 1 | | 14 |
| McIlroy | 10 | 2 | 1 | 13 |
| Daly | 7 | 4 | | 11 |
| Hill | 7 | 3 | | 10 |
| Coppell | 4 | | 1 | 5 |
| McCreery | 4 | | | 4 |
| Forsyth | 2 | 1 | | 3 |
| Houston | 2 | | | 2 |
| Coyne | 1 | | | 1 |
| Greenhoff | | 1 | | 1 |
| Opps' o.gs. | 6 | | | 6 |

### Final Division One Table

| | | P | W | D | L | F | A | Pts |
|---|---|---|---|---|---|---|---|---|
| 1 | Liverpool | 42 | 23 | 14 | 4 | 66 | 31 | 60 |
| 2 | QPR | 42 | 24 | 11 | 5 | 67 | 33 | 59 |
| 3 | Manchester United | 42 | 23 | 10 | 9 | 68 | 42 | 56 |
| 4 | Leeds United | 42 | 21 | 11 | 10 | 75 | 58 | 53 |
| 5 | Derby County | 42 | 21 | 9 | 12 | 65 | 46 | 51 |
| 6 | Ipswich Town | 42 | 16 | 14 | 12 | 54 | 48 | 46 |
| 7 | Leicester City | 42 | 13 | 19 | 10 | 48 | 51 | 45 |
| 8 | Manchester City | 42 | 16 | 11 | 14 | 64 | 44 | 43 |
| 9 | Tottenham Hotspur | 42 | 14 | 15 | 13 | 63 | 63 | 43 |
| 10 | Norwich City | 42 | 16 | 10 | 16 | 58 | 58 | 42 |
| 11 | Everton | 42 | 15 | 12 | 15 | 60 | 66 | 42 |
| 12 | Stoke City | 42 | 15 | 11 | 16 | 48 | 50 | 41 |
| 13 | Middlesbrough | 42 | 15 | 10 | 17 | 46 | 45 | 40 |
| 14 | Coventry City | 42 | 13 | 14 | 15 | 47 | 57 | 40 |
| 15 | Newcastle United | 42 | 15 | 9 | 18 | 71 | 62 | 39 |
| 16 | Aston Villa | 42 | 11 | 17 | 14 | 51 | 59 | 39 |
| 17 | Arsenal | 42 | 13 | 10 | 19 | 47 | 53 | 36 |
| 18 | West Ham United | 42 | 13 | 10 | 19 | 48 | 71 | 36 |
| 19 | Birmingham City | 42 | 13 | 7 | 22 | 57 | 75 | 33 |
| 20 | Wolverhampton W | 42 | 10 | 10 | 22 | 51 | 68 | 30 |
| 21 | Burnley | 42 | 9 | 10 | 23 | 43 | 66 | 28 |
| 22 | Sheffield United | 42 | 6 | 10 | 26 | 33 | 82 | 22 |

# Season 1976-77

## Football League Division One

| DATE | OPPONENTS | SCORE | GOALSCORERS | ATTENDANCE |
|---|---|---|---|---|
| Aug 21 | BIRMINGHAM CITY | D 2-2 | Coppell, Pearson | 58,898 |
| Aug 24 | Coventry City | W 2-0 | Hill, Macari | 26,775 |
| Aug 28 | Derby County | D 0-0 | | 34,000 |
| Sep 4 | TOTTENHAM HOTSPUR | L 2-3 | Coppell, Pearson | 60,723 |
| Sep 11 | Newcastle United | D 2-2 | Greenhoff B., Pearson | 39,037 |
| Sep 18 | MIDDLESBROUGH | W 2-0 | Pearson, McAndrew o.g. | 56,712 |
| Sep 25 | Manchester City | W 3-1 | Coppell, Daly, McCreery | 48,861 |
| Oct 2 | Leeds United | W 2-0 | Coppell, Daly | 44,512 |
| Oct 16 | West Bromwich Albion | L 0-4 | | 36,651 |
| Oct 23 | NORWICH CITY | D 2-2 | Daly (pen), Hill | 54,356 |
| Oct 30 | IPSWICH TOWN | L 0-1 | | 57,416 |
| Nov 6 | Aston Villa | L 2-3 | Pearson, Hill | 46,324 |
| Nov 10 | SUNDERLAND | D 3-3 | Greenhoff B., Hill, Pearson | 42,685 |
| Nov 20 | Leicester City | D 1-1 | Daly (pen), Hill | 26,421 |
| Nov 27 | WEST HAM UNITED | L 0-2 | | 55,366 |
| Dec 18 | Arsenal | L 1-3 | McIlroy | 39,572 |
| Dec 27 | EVERTON | W 4-0 | Greenhoff J., Hill, Macari, Pearson | 56,786 |
| Jan 1 | ASTON VILLA | W 2-0 | Pearson 2 | 55,446 |
| Jan 3 | Ipswich Town | L 1-2 | Pearson | 30,105 |
| Jan 15 | COVENTRY CITY | W 2-0 | Macari 2 | 46,568 |
| Jan 19 | BRISTOL CITY | W 2-1 | Greenhoff B., Pearson | 43,051 |
| Jan 22 | Birmingham City | W 3-2 | Greenhoff J., Houston, Pearson | 35,316 |
| Feb 5 | DERBY COUNTY | W 3-1 | Houston, Macari, Powell o.g. | 54,044 |
| Feb 12 | Tottenham Hotspur | W 3-1 | Hill, Macari, McIlroy | 46,946 |
| Feb 16 | LIVERPOOL | D 0-0 | | 57,487 |
| Feb 19 | NEWCASTLE UNITED | W 3-1 | Greenhoff J. 3 | 51,828 |
| Mar 5 | MANCHESTER CITY | W 3-1 | Coppell, Hill, Pearson | 58,595 |
| Mar 12 | LEEDS UNITED | W 1-0 | Cherry o.g. | 60,612 |
| Mar 23 | WEST BROMWICH ALBION | D 2-2 | Coppell, Hill (pen) | 51,085 |
| Apr 2 | Norwich City | L 1-2 | Powell o.g. | 24,161 |
| Apr 6 | Everton | W 2-1 | Hill 2 | 38,216 |
| Apr 9 | STOKE CITY | W 3-0 | Houston, Macari, Pearson | 53,102 |
| Apr 11 | Sunderland | L 1-2 | Hill (pen) | 38,785 |
| Apr 16 | LEICESTER CITY | D 1-1 | Greenhoff J. | 49,161 |
| Apr 19 | Queens Park Rangers | L 0-4 | | 28,848 |
| Apr 26 | Middlesbrough | L 0-3 | | 21,744 |
| Apr 30 | QUEENS PARK RANGERS | W 1-0 | Macari | 50,788 |
| May 3 | Liverpool | L 0-1 | | 50,123 |
| May 7 | Bristol City | D 1-1 | Greenhoff J. (pen) | 32,166 |
| May 11 | Stoke City | D 3-3 | Hill 2, McCreery | 24,632 |
| May 14 | ARSENAL | W 3-2 | Greenhoff J., Hill, Macari | 53,232 |
| May 16 | West Ham United | L 2-4 | Hill, Pearson | 29,311 |

## FA Cup

| | | | | | |
|---|---|---|---|---|---|
| Jan 8 | WALSALL | (Rd3) | W 1-0 | Hill | 48,870 |
| Jan 29 | QUEENS PARK RANGERS | (Rd4) | W 1-0 | Macari | 57,422 |
| Feb 26 | Southampton | (Rd5) | D 2-2 | Macari, Hill | 29,137 |
| Mar 8 | SOUTHAMPTON | (R) | W 2-1 | Greenhoff J. 2 | 58,103 |
| Mar 19 | ASTON VILLA | (Rd6) | W 2-1 | Houston, Macari | 57,089 |
| Apr 23 | LEEDS UNITED* | (SF) | W 2-1 | Greenhoff J., Coppell | 55,000 |
| May 21 | Liverpool** | (F) | W 2-1 | Pearson, Greenhoff J. | 99,252 |

*Played at Hillsborough, Sheffield. **Played at Wembley, London.

## League Cup

| | | | | | |
|---|---|---|---|---|---|
| Sep 1 | TRANMERE ROVERS | (Rd2) | W 5-0 | Daly 2, Hill, Macari, Pearson | 37,586 |
| Sep 22 | SUNDERLAND | (Rd3) | D 2-2 | Pearson, Clarke o.g. | 46,170 |
| Oct 4 | Sunderland | (R) | D 2-2* | Daly (pen), Greenhoff B. | 30,831 |
| Oct 6 | SUNDERLAND | (2R) | W 1-0 | Greenhoff B. | 47,689 |
| Oct 27 | NEWCASTLE UNITED | (Rd4) | W 7-2 | Hill 3, Coppell, Houston, Nicholl, Pearson | 52,002 |
| Dec 1 | EVERTON | (Rd5) | L 0-3 | | 57,378 |

*After extra-time.

## UEFA Cup

| | | | | | |
|---|---|---|---|---|---|
| Sep 15 | Ajax | (Rd1/1L) | L 0-1 | | 30,000 |
| Sep 29 | AJAX | (Rd1/2L) | W 2-0 | Macari, McIlroy | 58,938 |
| Oct 20 | JUVENTUS | (Rd2/1L) | W 1-0 | Hill | 59,021 |
| Nov 3 | Juventus | (Rd2/2L) | L 0-3 | | 66,632 |

**MANAGER:** Tommy Docherty
**MOST APPEARANCES:** Brian Greenhoff, Sammy McIlroy, Alex Stepney 57
**TOP SCORER:** Gordon Hill 22 (15 League)
**BIGGEST WIN:** 7-2 v Newcastle United, 27 October 1976, League Cup
**HIGHEST ATTENDANCE:** 99,252 v Liverpool, 21 May 1977, FA Cup

## League & Cup Appearances

| PLAYER | LEAGUE | CUP COMPETITION | | | TOTAL |
|---|---|---|---|---|---|
| | | FA CUP | LC | UEFA | |
| Albiston | 14 (3) | 1 | 2 (2) | 2 (1) | 19 (6) |
| Buchan | 33 | 7 | 4 | 2 | 46 |
| Clark | 0 (1) | | | | 0 (1) |
| Coppell | 40 | 7 | 5 | 4 | 56 |
| Daly | 16 (1) | 0 (1) | 6 | 4 | 26 (2) |
| Foggon | 0 (3) | | | | 0 (3) |
| Forsyth | 3 (1) | | 1 | | 4 (1) |
| Greenhoff B. | 40 | 7 | 6 | 4 | 57 |
| Greenhoff J. | 27 | 7 | | | 34 |
| Hill | 38 (1) | 7 | 6 | 4 | 55 (1) |
| Houston | 36 | 6 | 5 | 4 | 51 |
| Jackson | 2 | | 1 | | 3 |
| McCreery | 9 (16) | 0 (3) | 3 (2) | (3) | 13 (24) |
| McGrath | 2 (4) | | 0 (1) | | 2 (5) |
| McIlroy | 39 (1) | 7 | 6 | 4 | 56 (1) |
| Macari | 38 | 7 | 4 | 4 | 53 |
| Nicholl | 39 | 7 | 5 | 4 | 55 |
| Paterson | 2 | | 1 | 0 (2) | 3 (2) |
| Pearson | 39 | 7 | 4 | 3 | 53 |
| Roche | 2 | | | | 2 |
| Stepney | 40 | 7 | 6 | 4 | 57 |
| Waldron | 3 | | 1 | | 4 |

## Goalscorers

| PLAYER | LEAGUE | CUP COMPETITION | | | TOTAL |
|---|---|---|---|---|---|
| | | FA CUP | LC | UEFA | |
| Hill | 15 | 2 | 4 | 1 | 22 |
| Pearson | 15 | 1 | 3 | | 19 |
| Macari | 9 | 3 | 1 | 1 | 14 |
| Greenhoff J. | 8 | 4 | | | 12 |
| Coppell | 6 | 1 | 1 | | 8 |
| Daly | 4 | | 3 | | 7 |
| Greenhoff B. | 3 | | 2 | | 5 |
| Houston | 3 | 1 | 1 | | 5 |
| McCreery | 2 | | | | 2 |
| McIlroy | 2 | | | 1 | 1 |
| Nicholl | | | 1 | | 1 |
| Opps' o.gs. | 4 | | 1 | | 5 |

### Fact File

Gordon Hill headed United's scoring charts with 22 goals in all competitions, a brilliant total for an orthodox winger.

### Final Division One Table

| | | P | W | D | L | F | A | PTS |
|---|---|---|---|---|---|---|---|---|
| 1 | Liverpool | 42 | 23 | 11 | 8 | 62 | 33 | 57 |
| 2 | Manchester City | 42 | 21 | 14 | 7 | 60 | 34 | 56 |
| 3 | Ipswich Town | 42 | 22 | 8 | 12 | 66 | 39 | 52 |
| 4 | Aston Villa | 42 | 22 | 7 | 13 | 76 | 50 | 51 |
| 5 | Newcastle United | 42 | 18 | 13 | 11 | 64 | 49 | 49 |
| 6 | Manchester United | 42 | 18 | 11 | 13 | 71 | 62 | 47 |
| 7 | WBA | 42 | 16 | 13 | 13 | 62 | 56 | 45 |
| 8 | Arsenal | 42 | 16 | 11 | 15 | 64 | 59 | 43 |
| 9 | Everton | 42 | 14 | 14 | 14 | 62 | 64 | 42 |
| 10 | Leeds United | 42 | 15 | 12 | 15 | 48 | 51 | 42 |
| 11 | Leicester City | 42 | 12 | 18 | 12 | 47 | 60 | 42 |
| 12 | Middlesbrough | 42 | 14 | 13 | 19 | 40 | 44 | 41 |
| 13 | Birmingham City | 42 | 13 | 12 | 17 | 63 | 61 | 38 |
| 14 | QPR | 42 | 13 | 12 | 17 | 47 | 52 | 38 |
| 15 | Derby County | 42 | 9 | 19 | 14 | 50 | 55 | 37 |
| 16 | Norwich City | 42 | 14 | 9 | 19 | 47 | 64 | 37 |
| 17 | West Ham United | 42 | 11 | 14 | 27 | 46 | 65 | 36 |
| 18 | Bristol City | 42 | 11 | 13 | 18 | 38 | 48 | 35 |
| 19 | Coventry City | 42 | 10 | 15 | 17 | 48 | 59 | 35 |
| 20 | Sunderland | 42 | 11 | 12 | 19 | 46 | 54 | 34 |
| 21 | Stoke City | 42 | 10 | 14 | 18 | 28 | 51 | 34 |
| 22 | Tottenham Hotspur | 42 | 12 | 9 | 21 | 48 | 72 | 33 |

# Season 1977-78

## Football League Division One

| DATE | OPPONENTS | SCORE | GOALSCORERS | ATTENDANCE |
|---|---|---|---|---|
| Aug 21 | Birmingham City | W 4-1 | Macari 3, Hill | 58,898 |
| Aug 24 | COVENTRY CITY | W 2-1 | Hill (pen), McCreery | 55,726 |
| Aug 27 | IPSWICH TOWN | D 0-0 | | 59,547 |
| Sep 3 | Derby County | W 1-0 | Macari | 21,278 |
| Sep 10 | Manchester City | L 1-3 | Nicholl | 50,856 |
| Sep 17 | CHELSEA | L 0-1 | | 54,951 |
| Sep 24 | Leeds United | D 1-1 | Hill | 33,517 |
| Oct 1 | LIVERPOOL | W 2-0 | Macari, McIlroy | 55,089 |
| Oct 8 | Middlesbrough | L 1-2 | Coppell | 27,052 |
| Oct 15 | NEWCASTLE UNITED | W 3-2 | Coppell, Greenhoff J., Macari | 55,056 |
| Oct 22 | West Bromwich Albion | L 0-4 | | 26,822 |
| Oct 29 | Aston Villa | L 1-2 | Nicholl | 40,237 |
| Nov 5 | ARSENAL | L 1-2 | Hill | 53,055 |
| Nov 12 | Nottingham Forest | L 1-2 | Pearson | 30,183 |
| Nov 19 | NORWICH CITY | W 1-0 | Pearson | 48,729 |
| Nov 26 | Queens Park Rangers | D 2-2 | Hill 2 | 25,367 |
| Dec 3 | WOLVERHAMPTON WANDERERS | W 3-1 | Greenhoff J., McIlroy, Pearson | 48,874 |
| Dec 10 | West Ham United | L 1-2 | McGrath | 20,242 |
| Dec 17 | NOTTINGHAM FOREST | L 0-4 | | 54,374 |
| Dec 26 | Everton | W 6-2 | Macari 2, Coppell, Greenhoff J., Hill, McIlroy | 48,335 |
| Dec 27 | LEICESTER CITY | W 3-1 | Coppell, Greenhoff J., Hill | 57,396 |
| Dec 31 | Coventry City | L 0-3 | | 24,706 |
| Jan 2 | BIRMINGHAM CITY | L 1-2 | Greenhoff J. | 53,501 |
| Jan 14 | Ipswich Town | W 2-1 | McIlroy, Pearson | 23,321 |
| Jan 21 | DERBY COUNTY | W 4-0 | Hill 2 (1 pen), Buchan, Pearson | 57,115 |
| Feb 8 | BRISTOL CITY | D 1-1 | Hill (pen) | 43,457 |
| Feb 11 | Chelsea | D 2-2 | Hill (pen), McIlroy | 32,849 |
| Feb 25 | Liverpool | L 1-3 | McIlroy | 49,094 |
| Mar 1 | LEEDS UNITED | L 0-1 | | 49,101 |
| Mar 4 | MIDDLESBROUGH | D 0-0 | | 46,332 |
| Mar 11 | Newcastle United | D 2-2 | Hill, Jordan | 25,825 |
| Mar 15 | MANCHESTER CITY | D 2-2 | Hill 2 (pens) | 58,398 |
| Mar 18 | WEST BROMWICH ALBION | D 1-1 | McQueen | 46,329 |
| Mar 25 | Leicester City | W 3-2 | Greenhoff J., Hill, Pearson | 20,299 |
| Mar 27 | EVERTON | L 1-2 | Hill (pen) | 55,277 |
| Mar 29 | ASTON VILLA | D 1-1 | McIlroy | 41,625 |
| Apr 1 | Arsenal | L 1-3 | Jordan | 40,829 |
| Apr 8 | QUEENS PARK RANGERS | W 3-1 | Pearson 2 (1 pen), Grimes | 42,677 |
| Apr 15 | Norwich City | W 3-1 | Coppell, Jordan, McIlroy | 20,373 |
| Apr 22 | WEST HAM UNITED | W 3-0 | Grimes (pen), McIlroy, Pearson | 54,089 |
| Apr 25 | Bristol City | W 1-0 | Pearson | 25,858 |
| Apr 29 | Wolverhampton Wanderers | L 1-2 | Greenhoff B. | 24,774 |

## FA Cup

| | | | | |
|---|---|---|---|---|
| Jan 7 | Carlisle United | D 1-1 | Macari | 21,710 |
| Jan 11 | CARLISLE UNITED | W 4-2 | Macari 2, Pearson 2 | 54,156 |
| Jan 28 | WEST BROMWICH ALBION | D 1-1 | Coppell | 57,056 |
| Feb 1 | West Bromwich Albion | L 2-3* | Hill, Pearson | 37,086 |

*After extra-time.

## League Cup

| | | | | |
|---|---|---|---|---|
| Aug 30 | Arsenal | L 2-3 | McCreery, Pearson | 36,171 |

## European Cup-Winners' Cup

| | | | | |
|---|---|---|---|---|
| Sep 14 | St Etienne | D 1-1 | Hill | 33,678 |
| Oct 5 | ST ETIENNE* | W 2-0 | Coppell, Pearson | 31,634 |
| Oct 19 | Porto | L 0-4 | | 60,000 |
| Nov 2 | PORTO | W 5-2 | Coppell 2, Nicholl, Murca 2 o.g. | 51,831 |

*Played at Home Park, Plymouth.

## FA Charity Shield

| | | | | |
|---|---|---|---|---|
| Aug 13 | Liverpool | D 0-0* | | 81,775 |

*Shield shared six months each.

**MANAGER:** Dave Sexton
**MOST APPEARANCES:** Steve Coppell 52
**TOP SCORER:** Gordon Hill 19 (17 League)
**BIGGEST WIN:** 6-2 v Everton, 26 December 1977, League
**HIGHEST ATTENDANCE:** 81,775 v Liverpool, 13 August 1977, FA Charity Shield

## League & Cup Appearances

| PLAYER | LEAGUE | CUP COMPETITION | | | OTHER | TOTAL |
|---|---|---|---|---|---|---|
| | | FA CUP | LC | ECWC | | |
| Albiston | 27 (1) | 4 | 1 | 4 | 1 | 37 (1) |
| Buchan | 28 | 4 | 1 | 4 | 1 | 38 |
| Coppell | 42 | 4 | 1 | 4 | 1 | 52 |
| Forsyth | 3 | | | 0 (1) | | 3 (1) |
| Greenhoff B. | 31 | 1 | 1 | 2 | 1 | 36 |
| Greenhoff J. | 22 (1) | 2 (1) | | 1 | 1 | 26 (2) |
| Grimes | 7 (6) | 1 | 1 | 0 (2) | | 9 (9) |
| Hill | 36 | 3 | 1 | 4 | 1 | 45 |
| Houston | 31 | 3 | | 2 (1) | | 36 (1) |
| Jordan | 14 | 2 | | | | 16 |
| McCreery | 13 (4) | 0 (1) | 1 | 3 | 0 (1) | 17 (6) |
| McGrath | 9 (9) | | 0 (1) | 3 (1) | | 12 (11) |
| McIlroy | 39 | 4 | | 4 | 1 | 48 |
| McQueen | 14 | | | | | 14 |
| Macari | 32 | 4 | 1 | 2 | 1 | 40 |
| Nicholl | 37 | 4 | 1 | 4 | 1 | 47 |
| Pearson | 30 | 4 | 1 | 3 | 1 | 39 |
| Ritchie | 4 | | | | | 4 |
| Roche | 19 | 4 | | | | 23 |
| Rogers | 1 | | | | | 1 |
| Stepney | 23 | | 1 | 4 | 1 | 23 |

## Goalscorers

| PLAYER | LEAGUE | CUP COMPETITION | | | OTHER | TOTAL |
|---|---|---|---|---|---|---|
| | | FA CUP | LC | ECWC | | |
| Hill | 17 | 1 | | 1 | | 19 |
| Pearson | 10 | 3 | 1 | 1 | | 15 |
| Macari | 8 | 3 | | | | 11 |
| McIlroy | 9 | | | | | 9 |
| Coppell | 5 | 1 | | 3 | | 9 |
| Greenhoff J. | 6 | | | | | 6 |
| Jordan | 3 | | | | | 3 |
| Nicholl | 2 | | | 1 | | 3 |
| Grimes | 2 | | | | | 2 |
| McCreery | 1 | | 1 | | | 2 |
| Buchan | 1 | | | | | 1 |
| Greenhoff B. | 1 | | | | | 1 |
| McGrath | 1 | | | | | 1 |
| McQueen | 1 | | | | | 1 |
| Opps' o.gs. | | | | 2 | | 2 |

## Fact File

Reds boss Dave Sexton made a double transfer swoop on Elland Road early in 1978 to sign striker Joe Jordan and defender Gordon McQueen.

## Final Division One Table

| | | P | W | D | L | F | A | Pts |
|---|---|---|---|---|---|---|---|---|
| 1 | Nottingham Forest | 42 | 25 | 14 | 3 | 69 | 24 | 64 |
| 2 | Liverpool | 42 | 24 | 9 | 9 | 65 | 34 | 57 |
| 3 | Everton | 42 | 22 | 11 | 9 | 76 | 45 | 55 |
| 4 | Manchester City | 42 | 20 | 12 | 10 | 74 | 51 | 52 |
| 5 | Arsenal | 42 | 21 | 10 | 11 | 60 | 37 | 52 |
| 6 | WBA | 42 | 18 | 14 | 10 | 62 | 53 | 50 |
| 7 | Coventry City | 42 | 18 | 12 | 12 | 75 | 62 | 48 |
| 8 | Aston Villa | 42 | 18 | 13 | 11 | 57 | 42 | 46 |
| 9 | Leeds United | 42 | 18 | 10 | 14 | 63 | 53 | 46 |
| 10 | Manchester United | 42 | 16 | 10 | 16 | 67 | 63 | 42 |
| 11 | Birmingham City | 42 | 16 | 9 | 17 | 55 | 60 | 41 |
| 12 | Derby County | 42 | 14 | 13 | 15 | 54 | 59 | 41 |
| 13 | Norwich City | 42 | 11 | 18 | 13 | 52 | 66 | 40 |
| 14 | Middlesbrough | 42 | 12 | 15 | 15 | 42 | 54 | 39 |
| 15 | Wolverhampton W | 42 | 12 | 12 | 18 | 51 | 64 | 36 |
| 16 | Chelsea | 42 | 11 | 14 | 17 | 46 | 69 | 36 |
| 17 | Bristol City | 42 | 11 | 13 | 18 | 49 | 53 | 35 |
| 18 | Ipswich Town | 42 | 11 | 13 | 18 | 47 | 61 | 35 |
| 19 | QPR | 42 | 9 | 15 | 18 | 47 | 64 | 33 |
| 20 | West Ham United | 42 | 12 | 8 | 22 | 52 | 69 | 32 |
| 21 | Newcastle United | 42 | 6 | 10 | 26 | 42 | 78 | 22 |
| 22 | Leicester City | 42 | 5 | 12 | 25 | 26 | 70 | 22 |

## Season 1978-79

### Football League Division One

| DATE | OPPONENTS | SCORE | GOALSCORERS | ATTENDANCE |
|---|---|---|---|---|
| Aug 19 | BIRMINGHAM CITY | W 1-0 | Jordan | 56,139 |
| Aug 23 | Leeds United | W 3-2 | McIlroy, McQueen, Macari | 36,845 |
| Aug 26 | Ipswich Town | L 0-3 | | 21,802 |
| Sep 2 | EVERTON | D 1-1 | Buchan | 53,982 |
| Sep 9 | Queens Park Rangers | D 1-1 | Greenhoff J. | 23,477 |
| Sep 16 | NOTTINGHAM FOREST | D 1-1 | Greenhoff J. | 53,039 |
| Sep 23 | Arsenal | D 1-1 | Coppell | 45,393 |
| Sep 30 | MANCHESTER CITY | W 1-0 | Jordan | 55,301 |
| Oct 7 | MIDDLESBROUGH | W 3-2 | Macari 2, Jordan | 45,402 |
| Oct 14 | Aston Villa | D 2-2 | Macari, McIlroy | 37,667 |
| Oct 21 | BRISTOL CITY | L 1-3 | Greenhoff J. | 47,211 |
| Oct 28 | Wolverhampton Wanderers | W 4-2 | Greenhoff J. 2, Greenhoff B., Jordan | 23,979 |
| Nov 4 | SOUTHAMPTON | D 1-1 | Greenhoff J. | 46,259 |
| Nov 11 | Birmingham City | L 1-5 | Jordan | 23,877 |
| Nov 18 | IPSWICH TOWN | W 2-0 | Coppell, Greenhoff J. | 42,109 |
| Nov 21 | Everton | L 0-3 | | 42,126 |
| Nov 25 | Chelsea | W 1-0 | Greenhoff J. | 28,126 |
| Dec 9 | Derby County | W 3-1 | McIlroy, Greenhoff J., Ritchie | 23,180 |
| Dec 16 | TOTTENHAM HOTSPUR | W 2-0 | McIlroy, Ritchie | 52,026 |
| Dec 22 | Bolton Wanderers | L 0-3 | | 32,390 |
| Dec 25 | LIVERPOOL | L 0-3 | | 54,910 |
| Dec 30 | WEST BROMWICH ALBION | L 3-5 | Greenhoff B., McIlroy, McQueen | 45,091 |
| Feb 3 | ARSENAL | L 0-2 | | 45,460 |
| Feb 10 | Manchester City | W 3-0 | Coppell 2, Ritchie | 46,151 |
| Feb 24 | ASTON VILLA | D 1-1 | Greenhoff J. (pen) | 44,437 |
| Feb 28 | QUEENS PARK RANGERS | W 2-0 | Coppell, Greenhoff J. | 36,085 |
| Mar 3 | Bristol City | W 2-1 | McQueen, Ritchie | 24,583 |
| Mar 20 | Coventry City | L 3-4 | Coppell 2, McIlroy | 25,382 |
| Mar 24 | LEEDS UNITED | W 4-1 | Ritchie 3, Thomas | 51,191 |
| Mar 27 | Middlesbrough | D 2-2 | Coppell, McQueen | 20,138 |
| Apr 7 | Norwich City | D 2-2 | Macari, McQueen | 19,382 |
| Apr 11 | BOLTON WANDERERS | L 1-2 | Buchan | 49,617 |
| Apr 14 | Liverpool | L 0-2 | | 46,608 |
| Apr 16 | COVENTRY CITY | D 0-0 | | 43,035 |
| Apr 18 | Nottingham Forest | D 1-1 | Jordan | 33,074 |
| Apr 21 | Tottenham Hotspur | D 1-1 | McQueen | 36,665 |
| Apr 25 | NORWICH CITY | W 1-0 | Macari | 33,678 |
| Apr 28 | DERBY COUNTY | D 0-0 | | 42,546 |
| Apr 30 | Southampton | D 1-1 | Ritchie | 21,616 |
| May 5 | West Bromwich Albion | L 0-1 | | 27,960 |
| May 7 | WOLVERHAMPTON WANDERERS | W 3-2 | Coppell 2, Ritchie | 39,402 |
| May 16 | CHELSEA | D 1-1 | | 38,109 |

### FA Cup

| | | | | | |
|---|---|---|---|---|---|
| Jan 15 | CHELSEA | (Rd3) | W 3-0 | Coppell, Grimes, Greenhoff J. | 38,743 |
| Jan 31 | Fulham | (Rd4) | D 1-1 | Greenhoff J. | 25,229 |
| Feb 12 | FULHAM | (R) | W 1-0 | Greenhoff J. | 41,020 |
| Feb 20 | Colchester United | (Rd5) | W 1-0 | Greenhoff J. | 13,171 |
| Mar 10 | Tottenham Hotspur | (Rd6) | D 1-1 | Thomas | 51,800 |
| Mar 14 | TOTTENHAM HOTSPUR | (R) | W 2-0 | McIlroy, Jordan | 55,584 |
| Mar 31 | Liverpool* | (SF) | D 2-2 | Greenhoff B., Jordan | 52,524 |
| Apr 4 | Liverpool** | (R) | W 1-0 | Greenhoff J. | 53,069 |
| May 12 | Arsenal† | (F) | L 2-3 | McIlroy, McQueen | 99,219 |

*Played at Maine Road, Manchester. **Played at Goodison Park, Liverpool. †Played at Wembley, London.

### League Cup

| | | | | | |
|---|---|---|---|---|---|
| Aug 30 | Stockport County* | (Rd2) | W 3-2 | McIlroy, Greenhoff J. (pen), Jordan | 41,761 |
| Oct 4 | WATFORD | (Rd3) | L 1-2 | Jordan | 40,534 |

*Played at Old Trafford, Manchester.

**MANAGER:** Dave Sexton
**MOST APPEARANCES:** Steve Coppell 53
**TOP SCORER:** Jimmy Greenhoff 16 (11 League)
**BIGGEST WIN:** 4-1 v Leeds United, 24 March 1979, League
**HIGHEST ATTENDANCE:** 99,219 v Arsenal, 12 May 1979, FA Cup

### League & Cup Appearances

| PLAYER | LEAGUE | CUP COMPETITION FA CUP | LC | TOTAL |
|---|---|---|---|---|
| Albiston | 32 (1) | 7 | 2 | 41 (1) |
| Bailey | 28 | 9 | | 37 |
| Buchan | 37 | 9 | 2 | 48 |
| Connell | 2 | | | 2 |
| Coppell | 42 | 9 | 2 | 53 |
| Greenhoff B. | 32 (1) | 5 | 2 | 39 (1) |
| Greenhoff J. | 33 | 9 | 2 | 44 |
| Grimes | 5 (11) | 3 | 2 | 10 (11) |
| Houston | 21 (1) | 2 | 1 | 24 (1) |
| Jordan | 30 | 4 (1) | 2 | 36 (1) |
| McCreery | 14 (1) | | 0 (1) | 14 (2) |
| McGrath | 0 (2) | | | 0 (2) |
| McIlroy | 40 | 9 | 2 | 51 |
| McQueen | 36 | 9 | 2 | 47 |
| Macari | 31 (1) | 5 | 1 | 37 (1) |
| Moran | 1 | | | 1 |
| Nicholl | 19 (2) | 6 (2) | | 25 (4) |
| Paterson | 1 (2) | | | 1 (2) |
| Pearson | 0 | 2 | | 2 |
| Ritchie | 16 (1) | 3 (1) | | 19 (2) |
| Roche | 14 | | 2 | 16 |
| Sloan | 3 (1) | | | 3 (1) |
| Thomas | 25 | 8 | | 33 |

### Goalscorers

| PLAYER | LEAGUE | CUP COMPETITION FA CUP | LC | TOTAL |
|---|---|---|---|---|
| Greenhoff J. | 11 | 5 | 1 | 16 |
| Coppell | 11 | 1 | | 12 |
| Jordan | 6 | 2 | 2 | 10 |
| Ritchie | 9 | | | 9 |
| McIlroy | 6 | 2 | 1 | 9 |
| McQueen | 6 | 1 | | 7 |
| Macari | 6 | | | 6 |
| Greenhoff B. | 2 | 1 | | 3 |
| Buchan | 2 | | | 2 |
| Thomas | 1 | 1 | | 2 |
| Grimes | | 1 | | 1 |

### Fact File

United lost out in the FA Cup in one of the most thrilling finals ever. Called the 'five-minute' final, three goals in the dying minutes tipped the game first in United's favour but ultimately to Arsenal with Alan Sunderland's last-gasp strike.

### Final Division One Table

| | | P | W | D | L | F | A | Pts |
|---|---|---|---|---|---|---|---|---|
| 1 | Liverpool | 42 | 30 | 8 | 4 | 85 | 16 | 68 |
| 2 | Nottingham Forest | 42 | 21 | 18 | 3 | 61 | 26 | 60 |
| 3 | WBA | 42 | 24 | 11 | 7 | 72 | 35 | 59 |
| 4 | Everton | 42 | 17 | 17 | 8 | 52 | 40 | 51 |
| 5 | Leeds United | 42 | 18 | 14 | 10 | 70 | 52 | 50 |
| 6 | Ipswich Town | 42 | 20 | 9 | 13 | 63 | 49 | 49 |
| 7 | Arsenal | 42 | 17 | 14 | 11 | 61 | 48 | 48 |
| 8 | Aston Villa | 42 | 15 | 16 | 11 | 59 | 49 | 46 |
| 9 | Manchester United | 42 | 15 | 15 | 12 | 60 | 63 | 45 |
| 10 | Coventry City | 42 | 14 | 16 | 12 | 58 | 68 | 44 |
| 11 | Tottenham Hotspur | 42 | 13 | 15 | 14 | 48 | 61 | 41 |
| 12 | Middlesbrough | 42 | 15 | 10 | 17 | 57 | 50 | 40 |
| 13 | Bristol City | 42 | 15 | 10 | 17 | 47 | 51 | 40 |
| 14 | Southampton | 42 | 12 | 16 | 14 | 47 | 53 | 40 |
| 15 | Manchester City | 42 | 13 | 13 | 16 | 58 | 56 | 39 |
| 16 | Norwich City | 42 | 7 | 23 | 12 | 51 | 57 | 37 |
| 17 | Bolton Wanderers | 42 | 12 | 11 | 19 | 54 | 75 | 35 |
| 18 | Wolverhampton W | 42 | 13 | 8 | 21 | 44 | 68 | 34 |
| 19 | Derby County | 42 | 10 | 11 | 21 | 44 | 71 | 31 |
| 20 | QPR | 42 | 6 | 13 | 23 | 45 | 73 | 25 |
| 21 | Birmingham City | 42 | 6 | 10 | 26 | 37 | 64 | 22 |
| 22 | Chelsea | 42 | 5 | 10 | 27 | 44 | 92 | 20 |

# Season 1979-80

## Football League Division One

| DATE | OPPONENTS | SCORE | GOALSCORERS | ATTENDANCE |
|---|---|---|---|---|
| Aug 18 | Southampton | D 1-1 | McQueen | 21,768 |
| Aug 22 | WEST BROMWICH ALBION | W 2-0 | McQueen, Coppell | 53,377 |
| Aug 25 | Arsenal | D 0-0 | | 44,380 |
| Sep 1 | MIDDLESBROUGH | W 2-1 | Macari 2 | 51,015 |
| Sep 8 | Aston Villa | W 3-0 | Coppell, Thomas (pen), Grimes | 36,183 |
| Sep 15 | DERBY COUNTY | W 1-0 | Hill o.g. | 54,308 |
| Sep 22 | Wolverhampton Wanderers | L 1-3 | Macari | 35,503 |
| Sep 29 | STOKE CITY | W 4-0 | McQueen 2, McIlroy, Wilkins | 52,596 |
| Oct 6 | BRIGHTON & HOVE ALBION | W 2-0 | Coppell, Macari | 52,641 |
| Oct 10 | West Bromwich Albion | L 0-2 | | 27,713 |
| Oct 13 | Bristol City | D 1-1 | Macari | 28,305 |
| Oct 20 | IPSWICH TOWN | W 1-0 | Grimes | 50,826 |
| Oct 27 | Everton | D 0-0 | | 37,708 |
| Nov 3 | SOUTHAMPTON | W 1-0 | Macari | 50,215 |
| Nov 10 | Manchester City | L 0-2 | | 50,067 |
| Nov 17 | CRYSTAL PALACE | D 1-1 | Jordan | 52,800 |
| Nov 24 | NORWICH CITY | W 5-0 | Jordan 2, Moran, Coppell, Macari | 46,540 |
| Dec 1 | Tottenham Hotspur | W 2-1 | Coppell, Macari | 51,389 |
| Dec 8 | LEEDS UNITED | D 1-1 | Thomas | 57,471 |
| Dec 15 | Coventry City | W 2-1 | McQueen, Macari | 25,541 |
| Dec 22 | NOTTINGHAM FOREST | W 3-0 | Jordan 2, McQueen | 54,607 |
| Dec 26 | Liverpool | L 0-2 | | 51,073 |
| Dec 29 | ARSENAL | W 3-0 | McIlroy (pen), McQueen, Jordan | 54,295 |
| Jan 12 | Middlesbrough | D 1-1 | Thomas | 30,587 |
| Feb 2 | Derby County | W 3-1 | McIlroy, Thomas, Powell o.g. | 27,783 |
| Feb 9 | WOLVERHAMPTON WANDERERS | L 0-1 | | 51,568 |
| Feb 16 | Stoke City | D 1-1 | Coppell | 28,389 |
| Feb 23 | BRISTOL CITY | W 4-0 | Jordan 2, McIlroy, Merrick o.g. | 43,329 |
| Feb 27 | BOLTON WANDERERS | W 2-0 | McQueen, Coppell | 47,546 |
| Mar 1 | Ipswich Town | L 0-6 | | 30,229 |
| Mar 12 | EVERTON | D 0-0 | | 45,515 |
| Mar 15 | Brighton & Hove Albion | D 0-0 | | 30,243 |
| Mar 22 | MANCHESTER CITY | W 1-0 | Thomas | 56,387 |
| Mar 29 | Crystal Palace | W 2-0 | Jordan, Thomas | 33,056 |
| Apr 2 | Nottingham Forest | L 0-2 | | 31,417 |
| Apr 5 | LIVERPOOL | W 2-1 | Greenhoff J., Thomas | 57,342 |
| Apr 7 | Bolton Wanderers | W 3-1 | McQueen, Coppell, Thomas | 31,902 |
| Apr 12 | TOTTENHAM HOTSPUR | W 4-1 | Ritchie 3, Wilkins | 53,151 |
| Apr 19 | Norwich City | W 2-0 | Jordan 2 | 23,274 |
| Apr 23 | ASTON VILLA | W 2-1 | Jordan 2 | 45,201 |
| Apr 26 | COVENTRY CITY | W 2-1 | McIlroy 2 (1 pen) | 52,154 |
| May 3 | Leeds United | L 0-2 | | 39,625 |

## FA Cup

| | | | | | |
|---|---|---|---|---|---|
| Jan 5 | Tottenham Hotspur | (Rd3) | D 1-1 | McIlroy (pen) | 45,207 |
| Jan 9 | TOTTENHAM HOTSPUR | (R) | L 0-1* | | 53,762 |

*After extra-time.

## League Cup

| | | | | | |
|---|---|---|---|---|---|
| Aug 29 | Tottenham Hotspur | (Rd2/1L) | L 1-2 | Thomas | 29,163 |
| Sep 5 | TOTTENHAM HOTSPUR | (Rd2/2L) | W 3-1 | Coppell, Thomas, Miller o.g. | 48,292 |
| Sep 26 | Norwich City | (Rd3) | L 1-4 | McIlroy | 18,312 |

## League & Cup Appearances

| PLAYER | LEAGUE | CUP COMPETITION FA CUP | LC | TOTAL |
|---|---|---|---|---|
| Albiston | 25 | | 3 | 28 |
| Bailey | 42 | 2 | 3 | 47 |
| Buchan | 42 | 2 | 3 | 47 |
| Coppell | 42 | 2 | 2 | 46 |
| Greenhoff J. | 4 (1) | | | 4 (1) |
| Grime | 20 (6) | | 1 | 21 (6) |
| Houston | 14 | 2 | 1 | 17 |
| Jordan | 32 | 2 | 2 | 36 |
| Jovanovic | 1 (1) | | | 1 (1) |
| McIlroy | 41 | 2 | 2 | 45 |
| McGrath | 0 (1) | | | 0 (1) |
| McQueen | 33 | 2 | 2 | 37 |
| Macari | 39 | 2 | 3 | 44 |
| Moran | 9 | | | 9 |
| Nicholl | 42 | 2 | 3 | 47 |
| Paterson | 0 (1) | | 1 | 1 (1) |
| Ritchie | 3 (5) | | 1 (2) | 4 (7) |
| Sloan | 1 (4) | | | 1 (4) |
| Thomas | 35 | 2 | 3 | 40 |
| Wilkins | 37 | 2 | | 39 |

## Goalscorers

| PLAYER | LEAGUE | CUP COMPETITION FA CUP | LC | TOTAL |
|---|---|---|---|---|
| Jordan | 13 | | | 13 |
| Thomas | 8 | | 2 | 10 |
| Coppell | 8 | | 1 | 9 |
| Macari | 9 | | | 9 |
| McQueen | 9 | | | 9 |
| McIlroy | 6 | 1 | 1 | 8 |
| Ritchie | 3 | | | 3 |
| Grimes | 2 | | | 2 |
| Wilkins | 2 | | | 2 |
| Greenhoff J. | 1 | | | 1 |
| Moran | 1 | | | 1 |
| Opps" o.gs. | 3 | | 1 | 4 |

### Fact File

Goalkeeper Gary Bailey saved three penalties against Ipswich Town at Portman Road on 1 March – one from Frans Thijssen and a twice-taken award by Kevin Beattie – but United still lost the game 6-0.

**MANAGER:** Dave Sexton

**MOST APPEARANCES:** Gary Bailey, Martin Buchan, Jimmy Nicholl 47

**TOP SCORER:** Joe Jordan 13 (all League)

**BIGGEST WIN:** 5-0 v Norwich City, 24 November 1979, League

**HIGHEST ATTENDANCE:** 57,471 v Leeds United, 8 December 1979, League

## Final Division One Table

| | | P | W | D | L | F | A | Pts |
|---|---|---|---|---|---|---|---|---|
| 1 | Liverpool | 42 | 25 | 10 | 7 | 81 | 30 | 60 |
| 2 | Manchester United | 42 | 24 | 10 | 8 | 65 | 35 | 58 |
| 3 | Ipswich Town | 42 | 22 | 9 | 11 | 68 | 39 | 53 |
| 4 | Arsenal | 42 | 18 | 16 | 8 | 52 | 36 | 52 |
| 5 | Nottingham Forest | 42 | 20 | 8 | 14 | 63 | 43 | 48 |
| 6 | Wolverhampton W | 42 | 19 | 9 | 14 | 58 | 47 | 47 |
| 7 | Aston Villa | 42 | 16 | 14 | 12 | 51 | 50 | 46 |
| 8 | Southampton | 42 | 18 | 9 | 15 | 65 | 53 | 45 |
| 9 | Middlesbrough | 42 | 16 | 12 | 14 | 50 | 44 | 44 |
| 10 | WBA | 42 | 11 | 19 | 12 | 54 | 50 | 41 |
| 11 | Leeds United | 42 | 13 | 14 | 15 | 46 | 50 | 40 |
| 12 | Norwich City | 42 | 13 | 14 | 15 | 58 | 66 | 40 |
| 13 | Crystal Palace | 42 | 12 | 16 | 14 | 41 | 50 | 40 |
| 14 | Tottenham Hotspur | 42 | 15 | 10 | 17 | 52 | 62 | 40 |
| 15 | Coventry City | 42 | 16 | 7 | 19 | 56 | 66 | 39 |
| 16 | Brighton & HA | 42 | 11 | 15 | 16 | 47 | 57 | 37 |
| 17 | Manchester City | 42 | 12 | 13 | 17 | 43 | 66 | 39 |
| 18 | Stoke City | 42 | 13 | 10 | 19 | 44 | 58 | 36 |
| 19 | Everton | 42 | 9 | 17 | 16 | 43 | 51 | 35 |
| 20 | Bristol City | 42 | 9 | 13 | 20 | 37 | 66 | 31 |
| 21 | Derby County | 42 | 11 | 8 | 23 | 47 | 67 | 30 |
| 22 | Bolton Wanderers | 42 | 5 | 15 | 22 | 38 | 73 | 25 |

# Season 1980-81

## Football League Division One

| DATE | OPPONENTS | SCORE | GOALSCORERS | ATTENDANCE |
|---|---|---|---|---|
| Aug 16 | MIDDLESBROUGH | W 3-0 | Macari, Thomas, Grimes | 54,394 |
| Aug 19 | Wolverhampton Wanderers | L 0-1 | | 31,955 |
| Aug 23 | Birmingham City | D 0-0 | | 28,661 |
| Aug 30 | SUNDERLAND | D 1-1 | Jovanovic | 51,498 |
| Sep 6 | Tottenham Hotspur | D 0-0 | | 40,995 |
| Sep 13 | LEICESTER CITY | W 5-0 | Jovanovic 2, Grimes, Coppell, Macari | 43,229 |
| Sep 20 | Leeds United | D 0-0 | | 32,539 |
| Sep 27 | MANCHESTER CITY | D 2-2 | Albiston, Coppell | 55,918 |
| Oct 4 | Nottingham Forest | W 2-1 | Coppell, Macari | 29,801 |
| Oct 8 | ASTON VILLA | D 3-3 | McIlroy 2 (1 pen), Coppell | 38,831 |
| Oct 11 | ARSENAL | D 0-0 | | 49,036 |
| Oct 18 | Ipswich Town | D 1-1 | McIlroy (pen) | 28,572 |
| Oct 22 | Stoke City | W 2-1 | Jordan, Macari | 24,534 |
| Oct 25 | EVERTON | W 2-0 | Coppell, Jordan | 54,260 |
| Nov 1 | Crystal Palace | L 0-1 | | 31,449 |
| Nov 8 | COVENTRY CITY | D 0-0 | | 42,794 |
| Oct 12 | WOLVERHAMPTON WANDERERS | D 0-0 | | 37,959 |
| Oct 15 | Middlesbrough | D 1-1 | Jordan | 20,606 |
| Nov 22 | Brighton & Hove Albion | W 4-1 | Jordan 2, McIlroy, Duxbury | 23,401 |
| Nov 29 | SOUTHAMPTON | D 1-1 | Jordan | 46,840 |
| Dec 6 | Norwich City | D 2-2 | Coppell, Bond o.g. | 18,780 |
| Dec 13 | STOKE CITY | D 2-2 | Jordan, Macari | 39,568 |
| Dec 20 | Arsenal | L 1-2 | Macari | 33,730 |
| Dec 26 | LIVERPOOL | D 0-0 | | 57,049 |
| Dec 27 | West Bromwich Albion | L 1-3 | Jovanovic | 30,326 |
| Jan 10 | BRIGHTON & HOVE ALBION | W 2-1 | McQueen, Macari | 42,208 |
| Jan 28 | Sunderland | L 0-2 | | 31,910 |
| Jan 31 | BIRMINGHAM CITY | W 2-0 | Jordan, Macari | 39,081 |
| Feb 7 | Leicester City | L 0-1 | | 26,514 |
| Feb 17 | TOTTENHAM HOTSPUR | D 0-0 | | 40,642 |
| Feb 21 | Manchester City | L 0-1 | | 50,114 |
| Feb 28 | LEEDS UNITED | L 0-1 | | 45,733 |
| Mar 7 | Southampton | L 0-1 | | 22,698 |
| Mar 14 | Aston Villa | D 3-3 | Jordan 2, McIlroy (pen) | 42,916 |
| Mar 18 | NOTTINGHAM FOREST | D 1-1 | Burns o.g. | 38,205 |
| Mar 21 | IPSWICH TOWN | W 2-1 | Nicholl, Thomas | 46,685 |
| Mar 28 | Everton | W 1-0 | Jordan | 25,856 |
| Apr 4 | CRYSTAL PALACE | W 1-0 | Duxbury | 36,954 |
| Apr 11 | Coventry City | W 2-0 | Jordan 2 | 20,201 |
| Apr 14 | Liverpool | W 1-0 | McQueen | 31,276 |
| Apr 18 | WEST BROMWICH ALBION | W 2-1 | Jordan, Macari | 44,442 |
| Apr 25 | NORWICH CITY | W 1-0 | Jordan | 40,165 |

## FA Cup

| | | | | | |
|---|---|---|---|---|---|
| Jan 3 | BRIGHTON & HOVE ALBION | (Rd3) | D 2-2 | Thomas, Duxbury | 42,199 |
| Jan 7 | Brighton & Hove Albion | (R) | W 2-0 | Nicholl, Birtles | 26,915 |
| Jan 24 | Nottingham Forest | (Rd4) | L 0-1 | | 34,110 |

## League Cup

| | | | | | |
|---|---|---|---|---|---|
| Aug 27 | COVENTRY CITY | (Rd2/1L) | L 0-1 | | 31,656 |
| Sep 2 | Coventry City | (Rd2/2L) | L 0-1 | | 18,946 |

## UEFA Cup

| | | | | | |
|---|---|---|---|---|---|
| Sep 17 | WIDZEW LODZ | (Rd1/1L) | D 1-1 | McIlroy | 38,037 |
| Oct 1 | Widzew Lodz | (Rd1/2L) | D 0-0* | | 35,000 |

*Lost on away goals rule.

## League & Cup Appearances

| PLAYER | LEAGUE | CUP COMPETITION | | | TOTAL |
|---|---|---|---|---|---|
| | | FA CUP | LC | UEFA | |
| Albiston | 42 | 3 | 2 | 2 | 49 |
| Bailey | 40 | 3 | 2 | 2 | 47 |
| Birtles | 25 | 3 | | | 28 |
| Buchan | 26 | 2 | 2 | 2 | 32 |
| Coppell | 42 | 3 | 2 | 2 | 49 |
| Duxbury | 27 (6) | 0 (2) | | 1 (1) | 27 (9) |
| Greenhoff | 8 (1) | | 2 | 1 | 11 (1) |
| Grimes | 6 (2) | | | 2 | 8 (2) |
| Jordan | 33 | 3 | | 1 | 37 |
| Jovanovic | 19 | 1 | 2 | 2 | 24 |
| McGarvey | 0 (2) | | | | 0 (2) |
| McGrath | 1 | | | | 1 |
| McIlroy | 31 (1) | 1 | 2 | 2 | 36 (1) |
| McQueen | 11 | 2 | | | 13 |
| Macari | 37 (1) | 3 | 2 | 1 | 43 (1) |
| Moran | 32 | 1 | | 0 (1) | 33 (1) |
| Nicholl | 36 | 3 | 2 | 2 | 43 |
| Ritchie | 3 (1) | | 2 | | 5 (1) |
| Roche | 2 | | | | 2 |
| Sloan | 0 (2) | | 0 (1) | | 0 (3) |
| Thomas | 30 | 3 | 2 | 2 | 37 |
| Whelan | 0 (1) | | | | 0 (1) |
| Wilkins | 11 (2) | 2 | | | 13 (2) |

## Goalscorers

| PLAYER | LEAGUE | CUP COMPETITION | | | TOTAL |
|---|---|---|---|---|---|
| | | FA CUP | LC | UEFA | |
| Jordan | 15 | | | | 15 |
| Macari | 9 | | | | 9 |
| Coppell | 6 | | | | 6 |
| McIlroy | 5 | | | 1 | 6 |
| Jovanovic | 4 | | | | 4 |
| Duxbury | 2 | 1 | | | 3 |
| Grimes | 2 | | | | 2 |
| McQueen | 2 | | | | 2 |
| Nicholl | 1 | 1 | | | 2 |
| Thomas | 2 | 1 | | | 3 |
| Albiston | 1 | | | | 1 |
| Birtles | | 1 | | | 1 |
| Opps' o.gs. | 2 | | | | 2 |

## Final Division One Table

| | | P | W | D | L | F | A | Pts |
|---|---|---|---|---|---|---|---|---|
| 1 | Aston Villa | 42 | 26 | 8 | 8 | 72 | 40 | 60 |
| 2 | Ipswich Town | 42 | 23 | 10 | 9 | 77 | 43 | 56 |
| 3 | Arsenal | 42 | 19 | 15 | 8 | 61 | 45 | 53 |
| 4 | WBA | 42 | 20 | 12 | 10 | 60 | 42 | 52 |
| 5 | Liverpool | 42 | 17 | 17 | 8 | 62 | 42 | 51 |
| 6 | Southampton | 42 | 20 | 10 | 12 | 76 | 56 | 50 |
| 7 | Nottingham Forest | 42 | 19 | 12 | 11 | 62 | 44 | 50 |
| 8 | Manchester United | 42 | 15 | 18 | 9 | 51 | 36 | 48 |
| 9 | Leeds United | 42 | 17 | 10 | 15 | 39 | 47 | 44 |
| 10 | Tottenham Hotspur | 42 | 14 | 15 | 13 | 70 | 68 | 43 |
| 11 | Stoke City | 42 | 12 | 18 | 12 | 51 | 60 | 42 |
| 12 | Manchester City | 42 | 14 | 11 | 17 | 56 | 59 | 39 |
| 13 | Birmingham City | 42 | 13 | 12 | 17 | 50 | 61 | 38 |
| 14 | Middlesbrough | 42 | 16 | 5 | 21 | 53 | 61 | 37 |
| 15 | Everton | 42 | 13 | 10 | 19 | 55 | 58 | 36 |
| 16 | Coventry City | 42 | 13 | 10 | 19 | 48 | 68 | 36 |
| 17 | Sunderland | 42 | 14 | 7 | 21 | 52 | 53 | 35 |
| 18 | Wolverhampton W | 42 | 13 | 9 | 20 | 43 | 55 | 35 |
| 19 | Brighton & HA | 42 | 14 | 7 | 21 | 54 | 67 | 35 |
| 20 | Norwich City | 42 | 13 | 7 | 22 | 49 | 73 | 33 |
| 21 | Leicester City | 42 | 13 | 6 | 23 | 40 | 67 | 32 |
| 22 | Crystal Palace | 42 | 6 | 7 | 29 | 47 | 83 | 21 |

## Fact File

United ended the season with a run of seven consecutive victories – four of them 1-0 – but that didn't prevent manager Dave Sexton from being replaced by Ron Atkinson during the close season.

**MANAGER:** Dave Sexton

**MOST APPEARANCES:** Arthur Albiston, Steve Coppell 49

**TOP SCORER:** Joe Jordan 15 (all League)

**BIGGEST WIN:** 5-0 v Leicester City, 13 September 1980, League

**HIGHEST ATTENDANCE:** 57,049 v Liverpool, 26 December 1980, League

# Season 1981-82

## Football League Division One

| DATE | OPPONENTS | SCORE | GOALSCORERS | ATTENDANCE |
|---|---|---|---|---|
| Aug 29 | Coventry City | L 1-2 | Macari | 19,329 |
| Aug 31 | NOTTINGHAM FOREST | D 0-0 | | 51,496 |
| Sep 5 | IPSWICH TOWN | L 1-2 | Stapleton | 45,555 |
| Sep 12 | Aston Villa | D 1-1 | Stapleton | 37,661 |
| Sep 19 | SWANSEA CITY | W 1-0 | Birtles | 47,309 |
| Sep 22 | Middlesbrough | W 2-0 | Birtles, Stapleton | 19,895 |
| Sep 26 | Arsenal | D 0-0 | | 39,795 |
| Sep 30 | LEEDS UNITED | W 1-0 | Stapleton | 47,019 |
| Oct 3 | WOLVERHAMPTON WANDERERS | W 5-0 | McIlroy 3, Birtles, Stapleton | 46,837 |
| Oct 10 | Manchester City | D 0-0 | | 52,037 |
| Oct 17 | BIRMINGHAM CITY | D 1-1 | Coppell | 48,800 |
| Oct 21 | MIDDLESBROUGH | W 1-0 | Moses | 38,342 |
| Oct 24 | Liverpool | W 2-1 | Moran, Albiston | 41,438 |
| Oct 31 | NOTTS COUNTY | W 2-1 | Birtles, Moses | 45,928 |
| Nov 7 | Sunderland | W 5-1 | Stapleton 2, Birtles, Robson, Moran | 27,070 |
| Nov 21 | Tottenham Hotspur | L 1-3 | Birtles | 35,534 |
| Nov 28 | BRIGHTON & HOVE ALBION | W 2-0 | Birtles, Stapleton | 41,911 |
| Dec 5 | Southampton | L 2-3 | Robson, Stapleton | 24,404 |
| Jan 6 | EVERTON | D 1-1 | Stapleton | 40,451 |
| Jan 23 | Stoke City | W 3-0 | Birtles, Stapleton (pen), Coppell | 19,793 |
| Jan 27 | WEST HAM UNITED | W 1-0 | Macari | 41,291 |
| Jan 30 | Swansea City | L 0-2 | | 24,115 |
| Feb 6 | ASTON VILLA | W 4-1 | Moran 2, Robson, Coppell | 43,184 |
| Feb 13 | Wolverhampton Wanderers | W 1-0 | Birtles | 22,481 |
| Feb 20 | ARSENAL | D 0-0 | | 43,833 |
| Feb 27 | MANCHESTER CITY | D 1-1 | Moran | 57,830 |
| Mar 6 | Birmingham City | W 1-0 | Birtles | 19,637 |
| Mar 17 | COVENTRY CITY | L 0-1 | | 34,499 |
| Mar 20 | Notts County | W 3-1 | Coppell 2, Stapleton | 17,048 |
| Mar 27 | SUNDERLAND | D 0-0 | | 40,776 |
| Apr 3 | Leeds United | D 0-0 | | 30,953 |
| Apr 7 | LIVERPOOL | L 0-1 | | 48,371 |
| Apr 10 | Everton | D 3-3 | Coppell 2, Grimes | 29,306 |
| Apr 12 | WEST BROMWICH ALBION | W 1-0 | Moran | 38,717 |
| Apr 17 | TOTTENHAM HOTSPUR | W 2-0 | Coppell (pen), McGarvey | 50,724 |
| Apr 20 | Ipswich Town | L 1-2 | Gidman | 25,763 |
| Apr 24 | Brighton & Hove Albion | W 1-0 | Wilkins | 20.750 |
| May 1 | SOUTHAMPTON | W 1-0 | McGarvey | 40,038 |
| May 5 | Nottingham Forest | W 1-0 | Stapleton | 18,449 |
| May 8 | West Ham United | D 1-1 | Moran | 26,337 |
| May 12 | West Bromwich Albion | W 3-0 | Robson, Birtles, Coppell | 19,707 |
| May 15 | STOKE CITY | W 2-0 | Robson, Whiteside | 43,072 |

## FA Cup

| | | | | |
|---|---|---|---|---|
| Jan 2 | Watford | (Rd3) L 0-1 | | 26,104 |

## League Cup

| | | | | |
|---|---|---|---|---|
| Oct 2 | Tottenham Hotspur | (Rd2/1L) L 0-1 | | 39,333 |
| Oct 28 | TOTTENHAM HOTSPUR | (Rd2/2L) L 0-1 | | 55,890 |

## League & Cup Appearances

| PLAYER | LEAGUE | CUP COMPETITION FA CUP | LC | TOTAL |
|---|---|---|---|---|
| Albiston | 42 | 1 | 2 | 45 |
| Bailey | 39 | 1 | 2 | 42 |
| Birtles | 32 (1) | 1 | 2 | 35 (1) |
| Buchan | 27 | 1 | 2 | 30 |
| Coppell | 35 (1) | | 2 | 37 (1) |
| Davies | 1 | | | 1 |
| Duxbury | 19 (5) | | 0 (1) | 19 (6) |
| Gidman | 36 (1) | 1 | 2 | 39 (1) |
| Grimes | 9 (2) | | | 9 (2) |
| McGarvey | 10 (6) | | | 10 (6) |
| McIlroy | 12 | 1 | 1 | 14 |
| McQueen | 21 | | | 21 |
| Macari | 10 (1) | 0 (1) | | 10 (2) |
| Moran | 30 | 1 | 2 | 33 |
| Moses | 20 (1) | 1 | 1 | 22 (1) |
| Nicholl | 0 (1) | | | 0 (1) |
| Robson | 32 | 1 | 2 | 35 |
| Roche | 3 | | | 3 |
| Stapleton | 41 | 1 | 2 | 44 |
| Whiteside | 1 (1) | | | 1 (1) |
| Wilkins | 42 | 1 | 2 | 45 |

## Goalscorers

| PLAYER | LEAGUE | CUP COMPETITION FA CUP | LC | TOTAL |
|---|---|---|---|---|
| Stapleton | 13 | | | 13 |
| Birtles | 11 | | | 11 |
| Coppell | 9 | | | 9 |
| Moran | 7 | | | 7 |
| Robson | 5 | | | 5 |
| McIlroy | 3 | | | 3 |
| McGarvey | 2 | | | 2 |
| Macari | 2 | | | 2 |
| Moses | 2 | | | 2 |
| Albiston | 1 | | | 1 |
| Gidman | 1 | | | 1 |
| Grimes | 1 | | | 1 |
| Whiteside | 1 | | | 1 |
| Wilkins | 1 | | | 1 |

## Final Division One Table

| | | P | W | D | L | F | A | Pts |
|---|---|---|---|---|---|---|---|---|
| 1 | Liverpool | 42 | 26 | 9 | 7 | 80 | 32 | 87 |
| 2 | Ipswich Town | 42 | 26 | 5 | 11 | 75 | 53 | 83 |
| 3 | Manchester United | 42 | 22 | 12 | 8 | 59 | 29 | 78 |
| 4 | Tottenham Hotspur | 42 | 20 | 11 | 11 | 67 | 48 | 71 |
| 5 | Arsenal | 42 | 20 | 11 | 11 | 48 | 37 | 71 |
| 6 | Swansea City | 42 | 21 | 6 | 15 | 58 | 51 | 69 |
| 7 | Southampton | 42 | 19 | 9 | 14 | 72 | 67 | 66 |
| 8 | Everton | 42 | 17 | 13 | 12 | 56 | 50 | 64 |
| 9 | West Ham United | 42 | 14 | 16 | 12 | 66 | 57 | 58 |
| 10 | Manchester City | 42 | 15 | 13 | 14 | 49 | 50 | 58 |
| 11 | Aston Villa | 42 | 15 | 12 | 15 | 55 | 53 | 57 |
| 12 | Nottingham Forest | 42 | 15 | 12 | 15 | 42 | 48 | 57 |
| 13 | Brighton & HA | 42 | 13 | 13 | 16 | 43 | 52 | 52 |
| 14 | Coventry City | 42 | 13 | 11 | 18 | 55 | 62 | 50 |
| 15 | Notts County | 42 | 13 | 8 | 21 | 61 | 69 | 47 |
| 16 | Birmingham City | 42 | 10 | 14 | 18 | 53 | 61 | 44 |
| 17 | WBA | 42 | 11 | 11 | 20 | 66 | 57 | 44 |
| 18 | Stoke City | 42 | 12 | 8 | 22 | 44 | 63 | 44 |
| 19 | Sunderland | 42 | 11 | 11 | 20 | 39 | 61 | 44 |
| 20 | Leeds United | 42 | 10 | 12 | 20 | 39 | 61 | 42 |
| 21 | Wolverhampton W | 42 | 10 | 10 | 22 | 32 | 63 | 40 |
| 22 | Middlesbrough | 42 | 8 | 15 | 19 | 34 | 52 | 38 |

## Fact File

Bryan Robson moved to Old Trafford from West Bromwich Albion in exchange for £1.5m and signed on the pitch before the home game with Wolverhampton Wanderers.

**MANAGER:** Ron Atkinson

**MOST APPEARANCES:** Arthur Albiston, Ray Wilkins 45

**TOP SCORER:** Frank Stapleton 13 (all League)

**BIGGEST WIN:** 5-0 v Wolverhampton Wanderers, 3 October 1981, League

**HIGHEST ATTENDANCE:** 57,830 v Manchester City, 27 February 1982, League

# Season 1982-83

## Football League Division One

| DATE | OPPONENTS | SCORE | GOALSCORERS | ATTENDANCE |
|---|---|---|---|---|
| Aug 28 | BIRMINGHAM CITY | W 3-0 | Moran, Stapleton, Coppell | 48,673 |
| Sep 1 | Nottingham Forest | W 3-0 | Wilkins, Robson, Whiteside | 23,956 |
| Sep 4 | West Bromwich Albion | L 1-3 | Robson | 24,928 |
| Sep 8 | EVERTON | W 2-1 | Robson, Whiteside | 43,186 |
| Sep 11 | IPSWICH TOWN | W 3-1 | Whiteside 2, Coppell | 43,140 |
| Sep 18 | Southampton | W 1-0 | Macari | 21,700 |
| Sep 25 | ARSENAL | D 0-0 | | 43,198 |
| Oct 2 | Luton Town | D 1-1 | Grimes | 17,009 |
| Oct 9 | STOKE CITY | W 1-0 | Robson | 43,132 |
| Oct 16 | Liverpool | D 0-0 | | 40,853 |
| Oct 23 | MANCHESTER CITY | D 2-2 | Stapleton 2 | 57,334 |
| Oct 30 | West Ham United | L 1-3 | Moran | 32,478 |
| Nov 6 | Brighton & Hove Albion | L 0-1 | | 18,379 |
| Nov 13 | TOTTENHAM HOTSPUR | W 1-0 | Muhren | 47,869 |
| Nov 20 | Aston Villa | L 1-2 | Stapleton | 35,487 |
| Nov 27 | NORWICH CITY | W 3-0 | Robson 2, Muhren | 34,579 |
| Dec 4 | Watford | W 1-0 | Whiteside | 25,669 |
| Dec 11 | NOTTS COUNTY | W 4-0 | Duxbury, Stapleton, Robson, Whiteside | 33,618 |
| Dec 18 | Swansea City | D 0-0 | | 15,748 |
| Dec 27 | SUNDERLAND | D 0-0 | | 48,283 |
| Dec 28 | Coventry City | L 0-3 | | 18,945 |
| Jan 1 | ASTON VILLA | W 3-1 | Stapleton 2, Coppell | 41,545 |
| Jan 3 | WEST BROMWICH ALBION | D 0-0 | | 39,123 |
| Jan 15 | Birmingham City | W 2-1 | Robson, Whiteside | 19,333 |
| Jan 22 | NOTTINGHAM FOREST | W 2-0 | Muhren, Coppell (pen) | 38,615 |
| Feb 5 | Ipswich Town | D 1-1 | Stapleton | 23,804 |
| Feb 26 | LIVERPOOL | D 1-1 | Muhren | 57,397 |
| Mar 2 | Stoke City | L 0-1 | | 21,266 |
| Mar 5 | Manchester City | W 2-1 | Stapleton 2 | 45,400 |
| Mar 19 | BRIGHTON & HOVE ALBION | D 1-1 | Albiston | 36,264 |
| Mar 22 | WEST HAM UNITED | W 2-1 | Stapleton, McGarvey | 30,227 |
| Apr 2 | COVENTRY CITY | W 3-0 | Stapleton, Macari, Gillespie o.g. | 36,814 |
| Apr 4 | Sunderland | D 0-0 | | 31,486 |
| Apr 9 | SOUTHAMPTON | D 1-1 | Robson | 37,120 |
| Apr 19 | Everton | L 0-2 | | 21,175 |
| Apr 23 | WATFORD | W 2-0 | Grimes (pen), Cunningham | 43,048 |
| Apr 30 | Norwich City | D 1-1 | Whiteside | 22,233 |
| May 2 | Arsenal | L 0-3 | | 23,602 |
| May 7 | SWANSEA CITY | W 2-1 | Robson, Stapleton | 35,724 |
| May 9 | LUTON TOWN | W 3-0 | McGrath 2, Stapleton | 34,213 |
| May 11 | Tottenham Hotspur | L 0-2 | | 32,803 |
| May 14 | Notts County | L 2-3 | McGrath, Muhren | 14,395 |

## FA Cup

| | | | | | |
|---|---|---|---|---|---|
| Jan 8 | WEST HAM UNITED | (Rd3) | W 2-0 | Stapleton, Coppell | 44,143 |
| Jan 29 | Luton Town | (Rd4) | W 2-0 | Moses, Moran | 20,516 |
| Feb 19 | Derby County | (Rd5) | W 1-0 | Whiteside | 33,022 |
| Mar 12 | EVERTON | (Rd6) | W 1-0 | Stapleton | 58,198 |
| Apr 16 | Arsenal* | (SF) | W 2-1 | Robson, Whiteside | 46,535 |
| May 21 | Brighton & Hove Albion** | (F) | D 2-2 | Stapleton, Wilkins | 99,059 |
| May 26 | Brighton & Hove Albion** | (R) | W 4-0 | Robson 2, Muhren (pen), Whiteside | 91,534 |

*Played at Villa Park, Birmingham. **Played at Wembley, London.

## League Cup

| | | | | | |
|---|---|---|---|---|---|
| Oct 6 | AFC BOURNEMOUTH | (Rd2/1L) | W 2-0 | Stapleton, Redknapp o.g. | 22,091 |
| Oct 26 | AFC Bournemouth | (Rd2/2L) | D 2-2 | Muhren, Coppell (pen) | 13,226 |
| Nov 10 | Bradford City | (Rd3) | D 0-0 | | 15,568 |
| Nov 24 | BRADFORD CITY | (R) | W 4-1 | Albiston, Moses, Moran, Coppell | 24,981 |
| Dec 1 | SOUTHAMPTON | (Rd4) | W 2-0 | McQueen, Whiteside | 28,378 |
| Jan 19 | NOTTINGHAM FOREST | (Rd5) | W 4-0 | McQueen 2, Robson, Coppell | 44,413 |
| Feb 15 | Arsenal | (SF/1L) | W 4-2 | Coppell 2, Stapleton, Whiteside | 43,136 |
| Feb 23 | ARSENAL | (SF/2L) | W 2-1 | Moran, Coppell | 56,635 |
| Mar 26 | Liverpool† | (F) | L 1-2 | Whiteside | 99,304 |

†Played at Wembley, London.

## UEFA Cup

| | | | | | |
|---|---|---|---|---|---|
| Sep 15 | VALENCIA | (Rd1/1L) | D 0-0 | | 46,588 |
| Sep 29 | Valencia | (Rd1/2L) | L 1-2 | Robson | 35,000 |

**MANAGER:** Ron Atkinson
**MOST APPEARANCES:** Mike Duxbury 60
**TOP SCORER:** Frank Stapleton 19 (14 League)
**BIGGEST WIN:** 4-0 v Notts County, 11 December 1982, League;
4-0 v Nottingham Forest, 19 January 1983, League Cup;
4-0 v Brighton & Hove Albion, 26 May 1983, FA Cup
**HIGHEST ATTENDANCE:** 99,304 v Liverpool, 26 March 1983, League Cup

## League & Cup Appearances

| PLAYER | LEAGUE | CUP COMPETITION | | | TOTAL |
|---|---|---|---|---|---|
| | | FA CUP | LC | UEFA | |
| Albiston | 38 | 7 | 9 | 2 | 56 |
| Bailey | 37 | 7 | 9 | 2 | 55 |
| Beardsley | | | 1 | | 1 |
| Buchan | 3 | | 1 | 2 | 6 |
| Coppell | 29 | 4 | 8 | 1 (1) | 42 (1) |
| Cunningham | 3 (2) | | | | 3 (2) |
| Davies | 2 (1) | 2 | | | 2 (1) |
| Duxbury | 42 | 7 | 9 | 2 | 60 |
| Gidman | 3 | | | | 3 |
| Grimes | 15 (1) | 1 | 2 | 2 | 20 (1) |
| McGarvey | 3 (4) | | | | 3 (4) |
| McGrath | 14 | 0 (1) | 1 | | 15 (1) |
| McQueen | 37 | 7 | 8 | 1 | 53 |
| Macari | 2 (7) | 0 (1) | 2 (1) | 0 (1) | 4 (10) |
| Moran | 29 | 7 | 7 | 1 | 44 |
| Moses | 29 | 5 | 8 | 1 | 43 |
| Muhren | 32 | 6 | 8 | | 46 |
| Robson | 33 | 6 | 8 | 2 | 49 |
| Stapleton | 41 | 7 | 9 | 2 | 59 |
| Wealands | 5 | | | | 5 |
| Whiteside | 39 | 7 | 7 (2) | 2 | 55 (2) |
| Wilkins | 26 | 4 | 3 (1) | 2 | 35 (1) |

## Goalscorers

| PLAYER | LEAGUE | CUP COMPETITION | | | TOTAL |
|---|---|---|---|---|---|
| | | FA CUP | LC | UEFA | |
| Stapleton | 14 | 3 | 2 | | 19 |
| Robson | 10 | 3 | 1 | 1 | 15 |
| Whiteside | 8 | 3 | 3 | | 14 |
| Coppell | 4 | 1 | 6 | | 11 |
| Muhren | 5 | 1 | 1 | | 7 |
| Moran | 2 | 1 | 2 | | 5 |
| McGrath | 3 | | | | 3 |
| McQueen | | | 3 | | 3 |
| Albiston | 1 | | 1 | | 2 |
| Grimes | 2 | | | | 2 |
| Macari | 2 | | | | 2 |
| Moses | | 1 | 1 | | 2 |
| Wilkins | 1 | 1 | | | 2 |
| Cunningham | 1 | | | | 1 |
| Duxbury | 1 | | | | 1 |
| McGarvey | 1 | | | | 1 |
| Opps' o.gs. | 1 | | 1 | | 2 |

## Fact File

United completed an unusual 'double' over Arsenal when they defeated the North London club in the semi-final of both domestic cup competitions.

## Final Division One Table

| | P | W | D | L | F | A | Pts |
|---|---|---|---|---|---|---|---|
| 1 Liverpool | 42 | 24 | 10 | 8 | 87 | 37 | 82 |
| 2 Watford | 42 | 22 | 5 | 15 | 74 | 47 | 71 |
| 3 Manchester United | 42 | 19 | 13 | 10 | 56 | 38 | 70 |
| 4 Tottenham Hotspur | 42 | 20 | 9 | 13 | 65 | 50 | 69 |
| 5 Nottingham Forest | 42 | 20 | 9 | 13 | 62 | 50 | 69 |
| 6 Aston Villa | 42 | 21 | 5 | 16 | 61 | 50 | 68 |
| 7 Everton | 42 | 18 | 10 | 14 | 66 | 48 | 64 |
| 8 West Ham United | 42 | 20 | 4 | 18 | 68 | 62 | 64 |
| 9 Ipswich Town | 42 | 15 | 13 | 14 | 64 | 50 | 58 |
| 10 Arsenal | 42 | 16 | 10 | 16 | 58 | 56 | 58 |
| 11 WBA | 42 | 15 | 12 | 15 | 51 | 49 | 57 |
| 12 Southampton | 42 | 15 | 12 | 15 | 54 | 58 | 57 |
| 13 Stoke City | 42 | 16 | 9 | 17 | 53 | 64 | 57 |
| 14 Norwich City | 42 | 14 | 12 | 16 | 52 | 58 | 54 |
| 15 Notts County | 42 | 15 | 7 | 20 | 55 | 71 | 52 |
| 16 Sunderland | 42 | 12 | 14 | 16 | 48 | 61 | 50 |
| 17 Birmingham City | 42 | 12 | 14 | 16 | 40 | 55 | 50 |
| 18 Luton Town | 42 | 12 | 13 | 17 | 65 | 84 | 49 |
| 19 Coventry City | 42 | 13 | 9 | 20 | 48 | 59 | 48 |
| 20 Manchester City | 42 | 13 | 8 | 21 | 47 | 70 | 47 |
| 21 Swansea City | 42 | 10 | 11 | 21 | 51 | 69 | 41 |
| 22 Brighton & HA | 42 | 9 | 13 | 20 | 38 | 68 | 40 |

# Season 1983-84

## Football League Division One

| DATE | OPPONENTS | SCORE | GOALSCORERS | ATTENDANCE |
|---|---|---|---|---|
| Aug 27 | QUEENS PARK RANGERS | W 3-1 | Muhren 2 (1 pen), Stapleton | 48,742 |
| Aug 29 | NOTTINGHAM FOREST | L 1-2 | Moran | 43,005 |
| Sep 3 | Stoke City | W 1-0 | Muhren | 23,704 |
| Sep 6 | Arsenal | W 3-2 | Moran, Robson, Stapleton | 42,703 |
| Sep 10 | LUTON TOWN | W 2-0 | Albiston, Muhren | 41,013 |
| Sep 17 | Southampton | L 0-3 | | 20,674 |
| Sep 24 | LIVERPOOL | W 1-0 | Stapleton | 56,121 |
| Oct 1 | Norwich City | D 3-3 | Whiteside 2, Stapleton | 19,680 |
| Oct 15 | WEST BROMWICH ALBION | W 3-0 | Albiston, Whiteside, Graham | 42,221 |
| Oct 22 | Sunderland | W 1-0 | Wilkins (pen) | 26,826 |
| Oct 29 | WOLVERHAMPTON WANDERERS | W 3-0 | Stapleton 2, Robson | 41,880 |
| Nov 5 | ASTON VILLA | L 1-2 | Robson | 45,077 |
| Nov 12 | Leicester City | D 1-1 | Robson | 24,409 |
| Nov 19 | WATFORD | W 4-1 | Stapleton 3, Robson | 43,111 |
| Nov 27 | West Ham United | D 1-1 | Wilkins | 23,355 |
| Dec 3 | EVERTON | L 0-1 | | 43,664 |
| Dec 10 | Ipswich Town | W 2-0 | Graham, Crooks | 19,779 |
| Dec 16 | TOTTENHAM HOTSPUR | W 4-2 | Graham 2, Moran 2 | 33,616 |
| Dec 26 | Coventry City | D 1-1 | Muhren (pen) | 21,453 |
| Dec 27 | NOTTS COUNTY | D 3-3 | Moran, McQueen, Crooks | 41,544 |
| Dec 31 | STOKE CITY | W 1-0 | Graham | 40,164 |
| Jan 2 | Liverpool | D 1-1 | Whiteside | 45,122 |
| Jan 13 | Queens Park Rangers | D 1-1 | Robson | 16,309 |
| Jan 21 | SOUTHAMPTON | W 3-2 | Robson, Muhren, Stapleton | 40,371 |
| Feb 4 | NORWICH CITY | D 0-0 | | 36,851 |
| Feb 7 | Birmingham City | D 2-2 | Hogg, Whiteside | 19,957 |
| Feb 12 | Luton Town | W 5-0 | Robson 2, Whiteside 2, Stapleton | 11,265 |
| Feb 18 | Wolverhampton Wanderers | D 1-1 | Whiteside | 29,676 |
| Feb 25 | SUNDERLAND | W 2-1 | Moran 2 | 40,615 |
| Mar 3 | Aston Villa | W 3-0 | Robson, Whiteside, Moses | 32,874 |
| Mar 10 | LEICESTER CITY | W 2-0 | Hughes, Moses | 39,473 |
| Mar 17 | ARSENAL | W 4-0 | Muhren 2 (1 pen), Robson, Stapleton | 48,942 |
| Mar 31 | West Bromwich Albion | L 0-2 | | 27,954 |
| Apr 7 | BIRMINGHAM CITY | W 1-0 | Robson | 39,891 |
| Apr 14 | Notts County | L 0-1 | | 13,911 |
| Apr 17 | Watford | D 0-0 | | 20,764 |
| Apr 21 | COVENTRY CITY | W 4-1 | Hughes 2, Wilkins, McGrath | 38,524 |
| Apr 28 | WEST HAM UNITED | D 0-0 | | 44,124 |
| May 5 | Everton | D 1-1 | Stapleton | 28,817 |
| May 7 | IPSWICH TOWN | L 1-2 | Hughes | 44,257 |
| May 12 | Tottenham Hotspur | D 1-1 | Whiteside | 39,790 |
| May 16 | Nottingham Forest | L 0-2 | | 23,651 |

## FA Cup

| | | | | | |
|---|---|---|---|---|---|
| Jan 7 | AFC Bournemouth | (Rd3) | L 0-2 | | 14,782 |

## League Cup

| | | | | | |
|---|---|---|---|---|---|
| Oct 3 | Port Vale | (Rd2/1L) | W 1-0 | Stapleton | 19,885 |
| Oct 26 | PORT VALE | (Rd2/2L) | W 2-0 | Wilkins (pen), Whiteside | 23,589 |
| Nov 8 | Colchester United | (Rd3) | W 2-0 | McQueen, Moses | 13,031 |
| Nov 30 | Oxford United | (Rd4) | D 1-1 | Hughes | 13,739 |
| Dec 7 | OXFORD UNITED | (R) | D 1-1* | Stapleton | 27,459 |
| Dec 19 | Oxford United | (2R) | L 1-2* | Graham | 13,912 |

*After extra-time.

## European Cup-Winners' Cup

| | | | | | |
|---|---|---|---|---|---|
| Sep 14 | DUKLA PRAGUE | (Rd1/1L) | D 1-1 | Wilkins (pen) | 39,745 |
| Sep 27 | Dukla Prague | (Rd1/2L) | D 2-2 | Robson, Stapleton | 28,850 |
| Oct 19 | Spartak Varna | (Rd2/1L) | W 2-1 | Robson, Graham | 40,000 |
| Nov 2 | SPARTAK VARNA | (Rd2/2L) | W 2-0 | Stapleton 2 | 39,079 |
| Mar 7 | Barcelona | (Rd3/1L) | L 0-2 | | 70,000 |
| Mar 21 | BARCELONA | (Rd3/2L) | W 3-0 | Robson 2, Stapleton | 58,547 |
| Apr 11 | JUVENTUS | (SF/1L) | D 1-1 | Davies | 58,171 |
| Apr 25 | Juventus | (SF/2L) | L 1-2 | Whiteside | 64,655 |

## FA Charity Shield

| | | | | |
|---|---|---|---|---|
| Aug 20 | Liverpool** | W 2-0 | Robson 2 | 91,956 |

**Played at Wembley, London.

**MANAGER:** Ron Atkinson
**MOST APPEARANCES:** Frank Stapleton 58
**TOP SCORER:** Frank Stapleton 19 (13 League)
**BIGGEST WIN:** 5-0 v Luton Town, 12 February 1984, League
**HIGHEST ATTENDANCE:** 91,956 v Liverpool, 20 August 1983, FA Charity Shield

## League & Cup Appearances

| PLAYER | LEAGUE | CUP COMPETITION | | | OTHER | TOTAL |
|---|---|---|---|---|---|---|
| | | FA CUP | LC | ECWC | | |
| Albiston | 40 | 1 | 6 | 8 | 1 | 56 |
| Bailey | 40 | 1 | 5 | 8 | 1 | 55 |
| Blackmore | 1 | | | | | 1 |
| Crooks | 6 (1) | | | | | 6 (1) |
| Davies | 3 | | | 0 (1) | | 3 (1) |
| Dempsey | | | | 0 (1) | | 0 (1) |
| Duxbury | 39 | 1 | 6 | 8 | 1 | 55 |
| Gidman | 4 | | 1 | 1 (1) | 0 (1) | 6 (2) |
| Graham | 33 (4) | 1 | 5 | 6 (1) | 1 | 46 (5) |
| Hogg | 16 | 1 | | 4 | | 21 |
| Hughes | 7 (4) | | 1 (1) | 2 (2) | | 10 (7) |
| McGrath | 9 | | 1 | 2 | | 12 |
| McQueen | 20 | | 4 | 4 | 1 | 29 |
| Macari | 0 (5) | 0 (1) | 0 (2) | 2 | | 2 (8) |
| Moran | 38 | | 5 | 8 | 1 | 52 |
| Moses | 31 (4) | 1 | 5 (1) | 5 (1) | | 42 (6) |
| Muhren | 26 | 1 | 2 | 5 | 1 | 35 |
| Robson | 33 | 1 | 6 | 6 | 1 | 47 |
| Stapleton | 42 | 1 | 6 | 8 | 1 | 58 |
| Wealands | 2 | | 1 | | | 3 |
| Whiteside | 30 (7) | 1 | 6 | 5 (1) | 1 | 43 (8) |
| Wilkins | 42 | 1 | 6 | 6 | 1 | 56 |

## Goalscorers

| PLAYER | LEAGUE | CUP COMPETITION | | | OTHER | TOTAL |
|---|---|---|---|---|---|---|
| | | FA CUP | LC | ECWC | | |
| Stapleton | 13 | | 2 | 4 | | 19 |
| Robson | 12 | | | 4 | 2 | 18 |
| Whiteside | 10 | | 1 | 1 | | 12 |
| Muhren | 8 | | | | | 8 |
| Moran | 7 | | | | | 7 |
| Graham | 5 | | 1 | 1 | | 7 |
| Hughes | 4 | | 1 | | | 5 |
| Wilkins | 3 | | 1 | 1 | | 5 |
| Moses | 2 | | 1 | | | 3 |
| Albiston | 2 | | | | | 2 |
| Crooks | 2 | | | | | 2 |
| McQueen | 1 | | 1 | | | 2 |
| Davies | | | | 1 | | 1 |
| Hogg | 1 | | | | | 1 |
| McGrath | 1 | | | | | 1 |

### Fact File

United took four points off Liverpool, but still finished six points adrift of the Anfield club who were crowned champions at the season's close.

### Final Division One Table

| | | P | W | D | L | F | A | Pts |
|---|---|---|---|---|---|---|---|---|
| 1 | Liverpool | 42 | 22 | 14 | 6 | 73 | 32 | 80 |
| 2 | Southampton | 42 | 22 | 11 | 9 | 66 | 38 | 77 |
| 3 | Nottingham Forest | 42 | 22 | 8 | 12 | 76 | 45 | 74 |
| 4 | Manchester United | 42 | 20 | 14 | 8 | 71 | 41 | 74 |
| 5 | QPR | 42 | 22 | 7 | 13 | 67 | 37 | 73 |
| 6 | Arsenal | 42 | 18 | 9 | 15 | 74 | 80 | 63 |
| 7 | Everton | 42 | 18 | 14 | 12 | 45 | 42 | 62 |
| 8 | Tottenham Hotspur | 42 | 17 | 10 | 15 | 64 | 65 | 61 |
| 9 | West Ham United | 42 | 17 | 9 | 16 | 60 | 56 | 60 |
| 10 | Aston Villa | 42 | 17 | 9 | 16 | 59 | 61 | 60 |
| 11 | Watford | 42 | 16 | 9 | 17 | 68 | 77 | 57 |
| 12 | Ipswich Town | 42 | 15 | 9 | 19 | 55 | 57 | 53 |
| 13 | Sunderland | 42 | 13 | 13 | 16 | 42 | 53 | 52 |
| 14 | WBA | 42 | 14 | 9 | 19 | 48 | 62 | 51 |
| 15 | Leicester City | 42 | 13 | 12 | 17 | 65 | 68 | 51 |
| 16 | Luton Town | 42 | 14 | 9 | 19 | 53 | 66 | 51 |
| 17 | Norwich City | 42 | 12 | 15 | 15 | 48 | 49 | 51 |
| 18 | Stoke City | 42 | 13 | 11 | 18 | 44 | 63 | 50 |
| 19 | Coventry City | 42 | 13 | 11 | 18 | 57 | 77 | 50 |
| 20 | Birmingham City | 42 | 12 | 12 | 18 | 39 | 50 | 48 |
| 21 | Notts County | 42 | 10 | 11 | 21 | 50 | 72 | 41 |
| 22 | Wolverhampton W | 42 | 6 | 11 | 25 | 27 | 80 | 29 |

# Season 1984-85

## Football League Division One

| DATE | OPPONENTS | SCORE | GOALSCORERS | ATTENDANCE |
|---|---|---|---|---|
| Aug 25 | WATFORD | D 1-1 | Strachan (pen) | 53,668 |
| Aug 28 | Southampton | D 0-0 | | 22,183 |
| Sep 1 | Ipswich Town | D 1-1 | Hughes | 20,876 |
| Sep 5 | CHELSEA | D 1-1 | Olsen | 48,398 |
| Sep 8 | NEWCASTLE UNITED | W 5-0 | Strachan 2 (1 pen), Hughes, Moses, Olsen | 54,915 |
| Sep 15 | Coventry City | W 3-0 | Whiteside 2, Robson | 18,312 |
| Sep 22 | LIVERPOOL | D 1-1 | Strachan (pen) | 56,638 |
| Sep 29 | West Bromwich Albion | W 2-1 | Strachan (pen) | 26,401 |
| Oct 6 | Aston Villa | L 0-3 | | 37,132 |
| Oct 13 | WEST HAM UNITED | W 5-1 | Moses, McQueen, Strachan, Hughes, Brazil | 47,559 |
| Oct 20 | TOTTENHAM HOTSPUR | W 1-0 | Hughes | 54,516 |
| Oct 27 | Everton | L 0-5 | | 40,769 |
| Nov 2 | ARSENAL | W 4-2 | Strachan 2, Robson, Hughes | 32,279 |
| Nov 10 | Leicester City | W 3-2 | Strachan (pen), Hughes, Brazil | 23,840 |
| Nov 17 | LUTON TOWN | W 2-0 | Whiteside 2 | 41,630 |
| Nov 24 | Sunderland | L 2-3 | Robson, Hughes | 25,405 |
| Dec 1 | NORWICH CITY | W 2-0 | Robson, Hughes | 36,635 |
| Dec 8 | Nottingham Forest | L 2-3 | Strachan 2 (1 pen) | 25,902 |
| Dec 15 | QUEENS PARK RANGERS | W 3-0 | Gidman, Duxbury, Brazil | 36,134 |
| Dec 22 | IPSWICH TOWN | W 3-0 | Strachan (pen), Gidman, Robson | 35,168 |
| Dec 26 | Stoke City | L 1-2 | Stapleton | 20,985 |
| Dec 29 | Chelsea | W 3-1 | Stapleton, Moses, Hughes | 42,197 |
| Jan 1 | SHEFFIELD WEDNESDAY | L 1-2 | Hughes | 47,625 |
| Jan 12 | COVENTRY CITY | L 0-1 | | 35,992 |
| Feb 2 | WEST BROMWICH ALBION | W 2-0 | Strachan 2 | 36,681 |
| Feb 9 | Newcastle United | D 1-1 | Moran | 31,798 |
| Feb 23 | Arsenal | W 1-0 | Whiteside | 48,612 |
| Mar 2 | EVERTON | D 1-1 | Olsen | 51,150 |
| Mar 12 | Tottenham Hotspur | W 2-1 | Whiteside, Hughes | 42,918 |
| Mar 15 | West Ham United | D 2-2 | Stapleton, Robson | 16,674 |
| Mar 23 | ASTON VILLA | W 4-0 | Hughes 3, Whiteside | 40,941 |
| Mar 31 | Liverpool | W 1-0 | Stapleton | 34,880 |
| Apr 3 | LEICESTER CITY | W 2-1 | Robson, Stapleton | 35,590 |
| Apr 6 | STOKE CITY | W 5-0 | Hughes 2, Olsen 2, Whiteside | 42,940 |
| Apr 9 | Sheffield Wednesday | L 0-1 | | 39,380 |
| Apr 21 | Luton Town | L 1-2 | Whiteside | 10,320 |
| Apr 24 | SOUTHAMPTON | D 0-0 | | 31,291 |
| Apr 27 | SUNDERLAND | D 2-2 | Moran, Robson | 38,979 |
| May 4 | Norwich City | W 1-0 | Moran | 16,006 |
| May 6 | NOTTINGHAM FOREST | W 2-0 | Gidman, Stapleton | 41,775 |
| May 11 | Queens Park Rangers | W 3-1 | Brazil 2, Stapleton | 20,483 |
| May 13 | Watford | L 1-5 | Moran | 20,500 |

## FA Cup

| | | | | |
|---|---|---|---|---|
| Jan 5 | AFC BOURNEMOUTH | W 3-0 | McQueen, Strachan, Stapleton | 32,080 |
| Jan 26 | COVENTRY CITY | W 2-1 | McGrath, Hughes | 38,039 |
| Feb 15 | BLACKBURN ROVERS | W 2-0 | Strachan, McGrath | 22,692 |
| Mar 9 | WEST HAM UNITED | W 4-2 | Whiteside 3 (1 pen), Hughes | 46,769 |
| Apr 13 | Liverpool | D 2-2* | Hughes, Stapleton | 51,690 |
| Apr 17 | Liverpool | W 2-1** | Robson, Hughes | 45,775 |
| May 18 | Everton† | W 1-0 | Whiteside | 99,445 |

*After extra-time, played at Goodison Park, Liverpool.
**After extra-time, played at Maine Road, Manchester. †Played at Wembley, London.

## League Cup

| | | | | |
|---|---|---|---|---|
| Sep 26 | BURNLEY | W 4-0 | Hughes 3, Robson | 28,383 |
| Oct 9 | Burnley | W 3-0 | Brazil 2, Olsen | 12,690 |
| Oct 30 | EVERTON | L 1-2 | Brazil | 50,918 |

## UEFA Cup

| | | | | |
|---|---|---|---|---|
| Sep 19 | RABA VASAS ETO | W 3-0 | Robson, Muhren, Hughes | 33,119 |
| Oct 3 | Raba Vasas ETO | D 2-2 | Muhren (pen), Brazil | 26,000 |
| Oct 24 | PSV Eindhoven | D 0-0 | | 27,500 |
| Nov 7 | PSV EINDHOVEN | W 1-0 | Strachan (pen) | 39,281 |
| Nov 28 | DUNDEE UNITED | D 2-2 | Robson, Strachan (pen) | 48,278 |
| Dec 12 | Dundee United | W 3-2 | Hughes, Muhren, McGinnis o.g. | 21,821 |
| Mar 6 | VIDEOTON | W 1-0 | Stapleton | 35,432 |
| Mar 20 | Videoton | L 0-1* | | 25,000 |

*After extra-time, lost 5-4 on penalties.

## League & Cup Appearances

| PLAYER | LEAGUE | CUP COMPETITION | | | TOTAL |
|---|---|---|---|---|---|
| | | FA CUP | LC | UEFA | |
| Albiston | 39 | 7 | 3 | 8 | 57 |
| Bailey | 38 | 6 | 3 | 8 | 55 |
| Blackmore | 1 | | 1 | | 2 |
| Brazil | 17 (3) | 0 (1) | 2 (1) | 2 | 21 (5) |
| Duxbury | 27 (3) | 2 (1) | 2 | 6 | 37 (4) |
| Garton | 2 | | 1 | 0 (1) | 3 (1) |
| Gidman | 27 | 6 | 1 | 6 (1) | 40 (1) |
| Graham | | | 1 | | 1 |
| Hogg | 29 | 5 | 3 | 6 | 43 |
| Hughes | 38 | 7 | 2 | 8 | 55 |
| McGrath | 23 | 7 | | 2 | 32 |
| McQueen | 12 | 1 | | 2 2 | 15 |
| Moran | 19 | 3 | 2 | 4 | 28 |
| Moses | 26 | 3 | 3 | 6 | 38 |
| Muhren | 7 (5) | 1 | 1 | 3 | 12 (5) |
| Olsen | 36 | 6 | 2 | 6 (1) | 50 (1) |
| Pears | 4 | 1 | | | 5 |
| Robson | 32 (1) | 4 | 2 | 7 | 45 (1) |
| Stapleton | 21 (3) | 5 | 1 (1) | 4 (1) | 31 (5) |
| Strachan | 41 | 7 | 2 | 6 | 56 |
| Whiteside | 23 (4) | 6 | 1 | 4 (1) | 34 (5) |

## Goalscorers

| PLAYER | LEAGUE | CUP COMPETITION | | | TOTAL |
|---|---|---|---|---|---|
| | | FA CUP | LC | UEFA | |
| Hughes | 16 | 4 | 3 | 2 | 25 |
| Strachan | 15 | 2 | | 2 | 19 |
| Robson | 9 | 1 | 1 | 2 | 13 |
| Whiteside | 9 | 4 | | | 13 |
| Stapleton | 6 | 2 | | 1 | 9 |
| Brazil | 5 | | 3 | 1 | 9 |
| Olsen | 5 | | 1 | | 6 |
| Moran | 4 | | | | 4 |
| Gidman | 3 | | | | 3 |
| Moses | 3 | | | | 3 |
| Muhren | | | | 3 | 3 |
| McGrath | | 2 | | | 2 |
| McQueen | 1 | 1 | | | 2 |
| Duxbury | 1 | | | | 1 |
| Opps' o.g.s. | | | | 1 | 1 |

**MANAGER:** Ron Atkinson
**MOST APPEARANCES:** Arthur Albiston 57
**TOP SCORER:** Mark Hughes 25 (16 League)
**BIGGEST WIN:** 5-0 v Newcastle United, 8 September 1984, League; 5-0 v Stoke City, 6 April 1985, League
**HIGHEST ATTENDANCE:** 99,445 v Everton, 18 May 1985, FA Cup

## Final Division One Table

| | | P | W | D | L | F | A | Pts |
|---|---|---|---|---|---|---|---|---|
| 1 | Everton | 42 | 28 | 6 | 8 | 88 | 38 | 90 |
| 2 | Liverpool | 42 | 22 | 11 | 9 | 68 | 35 | 77 |
| 3 | Tottenham Hotspur | 42 | 23 | 8 | 11 | 78 | 51 | 77 |
| 4 | Manchester United | 42 | 22 | 10 | 10 | 77 | 47 | 76 |
| 5 | Southampton | 42 | 19 | 11 | 12 | 56 | 47 | 68 |
| 6 | Chelsea | 42 | 18 | 12 | 12 | 63 | 48 | 66 |
| 7 | Arsenal | 42 | 19 | 9 | 14 | 49 | 38 | 66 |
| 8 | Sheffield Wednesday | 42 | 17 | 14 | 11 | 58 | 45 | 65 |
| 9 | Nottingham Forest | 42 | 19 | 7 | 16 | 59 | 48 | 64 |
| 10 | Aston Villa | 42 | 15 | 11 | 16 | 60 | 60 | 56 |
| 11 | Watford | 42 | 14 | 13 | 15 | 81 | 71 | 55 |
| 12 | WBA | 42 | 16 | 7 | 19 | 58 | 62 | 55 |
| 13 | Luton Town | 42 | 15 | 9 | 18 | 57 | 61 | 54 |
| 14 | Newcastle United | 42 | 15 | 13 | 16 | 65 | 70 | 52 |
| 15 | Leicester City | 42 | 15 | 6 | 21 | 65 | 73 | 51 |
| 16 | West Ham United | 42 | 13 | 12 | 17 | 51 | 68 | 51 |
| 17 | Ipswich Town | 42 | 13 | 11 | 18 | 48 | 39 | 50 |
| 18 | Coventry City | 42 | 15 | 5 | 22 | 47 | 64 | 50 |
| 19 | QPR | 42 | 13 | 11 | 18 | 53 | 72 | 50 |
| 20 | Norwich City | 42 | 13 | 10 | 19 | 46 | 64 | 49 |
| 21 | Sunderland | 42 | 10 | 10 | 22 | 40 | 62 | 40 |
| 22 | Stoke City | 42 | 3 | 8 | 31 | 24 | 91 | 17 |

# Season 1985-86

## Football League Division One

| DATE | OPPONENTS | SCORE | GOALSCORERS | ATTENDANCE |
|---|---|---|---|---|
| Aug 17 | ASTON VILLA | W 4-0 | Hughes 2, Olsen, Whiteside | 49,743 |
| Aug 20 | Ipswich Town | W 1-0 | Robson | 18,777 |
| Aug 24 | Arsenal | W 2-1 | McGrath, Hughes | 37,145 |
| Aug 26 | WEST HAM UNITED | W 2-0 | Strachan, Hughes | 50,773 |
| Aug 31 | Nottingham Forest | W 3-1 | Hughes, Stapleton, Barnes | 26,274 |
| Sep 4 | NEWCASTLE UNITED | W 3-0 | Stapleton 2, Hughes | 51,102 |
| Sep 7 | OXFORD UNITED | W 3-0 | Whiteside, Robson, Barnes | 51,820 |
| Sep 14 | Manchester City | W 3-0 | Duxbury, Albiston, Robson (pen) | 48,723 |
| Sep 21 | West Bromwich Albion | W 5-1 | Brazil 2, Strachan, Stapleton, Blackmore | 25,068 |
| Sep 28 | SOUTHAMPTON | W 1-0 | Hughes | 52,449 |
| Oct 5 | Luton Town | D 1-1 | Hughes | 17,454 |
| Oct 12 | QUEENS PARK RANGERS | W 2-0 | Olsen, Hughes | 48,845 |
| Oct 19 | LIVERPOOL | D 1-1 | McGrath | 54,492 |
| Oct 26 | Chelsea | W 2-1 | Olsen, Hughes | 42,485 |
| Nov 2 | COVENTRY CITY | W 2-0 | Olsen 2 | 46,748 |
| Nov 9 | Sheffield Wednesday | L 0-1 | | 48,105 |
| Nov 16 | TOTTENHAM HOTSPUR | D 0-0 | | 54,575 |
| Nov 23 | Leicester City | L 0-3 | | 22,008 |
| Nov 30 | WATFORD | D 1-1 | Brazil | 42,181 |
| Dec 7 | IPSWICH TOWN | W 1-0 | Stapleton | 37,981 |
| Dec 14 | Aston Villa | W 3-1 | Blackmore, Strachan, Hughes | 27,626 |
| Dec 21 | ARSENAL | L 0-1 | | 44,386 |
| Dec 26 | Everton | L 1-3 | Stapleton | 42,551 |
| Jan 1 | BIRMINGHAM CITY | W 1-0 | Gibson C. | 43,095 |
| Jan 11 | Oxford United | W 3-1 | Whiteside, Hughes, Gibson C. | 13,280 |
| Jan 18 | NOTTINGHAM FOREST | L 2-3 | Olsen 2 (1 pen) | 46,717 |
| Feb 2 | West Ham United | L 1-2 | Robson | 22,642 |
| Feb 9 | Liverpool | D 1-1 | Gibson C. | 35,064 |
| Feb 22 | WEST BROMWICH ALBION | W 3-0 | Olsen 3 (2 pen) | 45,193 |
| Mar 1 | Southampton | L 0-1 | | 19,012 |
| Mar 15 | Queens Park Rangers | L 0-1 | | 23,407 |
| Mar 19 | LUTON TOWN | W 2-0 | McGrath, Hughes | 33,668 |
| Mar 22 | MANCHESTER CITY | D 2-2 | Gibson C., Strachan (pen) | 51,274 |
| Mar 29 | Birmingham City | D 1-1 | Robson | 22,551 |
| Mar 31 | EVERTON | D 0-0 | | 51,189 |
| Apr 5 | Coventry City | W 3-1 | Robson, Strachan, Gibson C. | 17,160 |
| Apr 9 | CHELSEA | L 1-2 | Olsen (pen) | 45,355 |
| Apr 13 | SHEFFIELD WEDNESDAY | L 0-2 | | 32,331 |
| Apr 16 | Newcastle United | W 4-2 | Hughes 2, Whiteside, Robson (pen) | 32,183 |
| Apr 19 | Tottenham Hotspur | D 0-0 | | 32,357 |
| Apr 26 | LEICESTER CITY | W 4-0 | Hughes, Stapleton, Blackmore, Davenport (pen) | 38,840 |
| May 3 | Watford | D 1-1 | Hughes | 18,414 |

## FA Cup

| | | | | |
|---|---|---|---|---|
| Jan 9 | ROCHDALE | (Rd3) W 2-0 | Hughes, Stapleton | 40,223 |
| Jan 25 | Sunderland | (Rd4) D 0-0 | | 35,284 |
| Jan 29 | SUNDERLAND | (R) W 3-0 | Olsen 2 (1 pen), Whiteside | 43,402 |
| Mar 5 | West Ham United | (Rd5) D 1-1 | Stapleton | 26,441 |
| Mar 9 | WEST HAM UNITED | (R) L 0-2 | | 29,733 |

## League Cup

| | | | | |
|---|---|---|---|---|
| Sep 24 | Crystal Palace | (Rd2/1L) W 1-0 | Barnes | 21,507 |
| Oct 9 | CRYSTAL PALACE | (Rd2/2L) W 1-0 | Whiteside | 26,118 |
| Oct 29 | WEST HAM UNITED | (Rd3) W 1-0 | Whiteside | 32,056 |
| Nov 26 | Liverpool | (Rd4) L 1-2 | McGrath | 41,291 |

## FA Charity Shield

| | | | | |
|---|---|---|---|---|
| Aug 10 | Everton* | L 0-2 | | 81,639 |

*Played at Wembley, London.

**MANAGER:** Ron Atkinson

**MOST APPEARANCES:** Paul McGrath 49

**TOP SCORER:** Mark Hughes 18 (17 League)

**BIGGEST WIN:** 5-1 v West Bromwich Albion, 21 September 1985, League

**HIGHEST ATTENDANCE:** 81,639 v Everton, 10 August 1985, FA Charity Shield

## League & Cup Appearances

| PLAYER | LEAGUE | CUP COMPETITION | | OTHER | TOTAL |
|---|---|---|---|---|---|
| | | FA CUP | LC | | |
| Albiston | 37 | 5 | 3 | 1 | 46 |
| Bailey | 25 | 2 | 4 | 1 | 32 |
| Barnes | 12 (1) | | 3 | | 15 (1) |
| Blackmore | 12 | 2 (2) | 2 | | 16 (2) |
| Brazil | 1 (10) | | 2 (2) | | 3 (12) |
| Davenport | 11 | | | | 11 |
| Dempsey | 1 | | | | 1 |
| Duxbury | 21 (2) | 3 | 3 | 1 | 28 (2) |
| Garton | 10 | 1 | | | 11 |
| Gibson C. | 18 | 4 | | | 22 |
| Gibson T. | 2 (5) | | | | 2 (5) |
| Gidman | 24 | 2 | 1 | 1 | 28 |
| Higgins | 6 | 2 | | | 8 |
| Hogg | 17 | | 2 | 1 | 20 |
| Hughes | 40 | 3 | 2 | 1 | 46 |
| McGrath | 40 | 4 | 4 | 1 | 49 |
| Moran | 18 (1) | 3 | 4 | | 25 (1) |
| Moses | 4 | | | 0 (1) | 4 (1) |
| Olsen | 25 (3) | 3 (2) | 3 | 1 | 32 (5) |
| Robson | 21 | 3 | 2 | 1 | 27 |
| Sivebaek | 2 (1) | | | | 2 (1) |
| Stapleton | 34 (7) | 5 | 4 | 1 | 44 (7) |
| Strachan | 27 (1) | 5 | 1 | | 33 (1) |
| Turner | 17 | 3 | | | 20 |
| Whiteside | 37 | 5 | 4 | 1 | 47 |
| Wood | 0 (1) | | | | 0 (1) |

## Goalscorers

| PLAYER | LEAGUE | CUP COMPETITION | | OTHER | TOTAL |
|---|---|---|---|---|---|
| | | FA CUP | LC | | |
| Hughes | 17 | 1 | | | 18 |
| Olsen | 11 | 2 | | | 13 |
| Stapleton | 7 | 2 | | | 9 |
| Robson | 7 | | | | 7 |
| Whiteside | 4 | 1 | 2 | | 7 |
| Gibson C. | 5 | | | | 5 |
| Strachan | 5 | | | | 5 |
| McGrath | 3 | | 1 | | 4 |
| Barnes | 2 | | 1 | | 3 |
| Blackmore | 3 | | | | 3 |
| Brazil | 3 | | | | 3 |
| Albiston | 1 | | | | 1 |
| Davenport | 1 | | | | 1 |
| Duxbury | 1 | | | | 1 |

## Fact File

Hopes of a serious title challenge mount after United open the season with a sequence of ten straight wins, but they have to settle for fourth place, 12 points behind champions Liverpool.

## Final Division One Table

| | | P | W | D | L | F | A | PTS |
|---|---|---|---|---|---|---|---|---|
| 1 | LIVERPOOL | 42 | 26 | 10 | 6 | 89 | 37 | 88 |
| 2 | EVERTON | 42 | 26 | 8 | 8 | 87 | 41 | 86 |
| 3 | WEST HAM UNITED | 42 | 26 | 6 | 10 | 74 | 40 | 84 |
| 4 | MANCHESTER UNITED | 42 | 22 | 10 | 10 | 70 | 36 | 76 |
| 5 | SHEFFIELD WEDNESDAY | 42 | 21 | 10 | 11 | 63 | 54 | 73 |
| 6 | CHELSEA | 42 | 20 | 11 | 11 | 57 | 56 | 71 |
| 7 | ARSENAL | 42 | 20 | 9 | 13 | 49 | 47 | 69 |
| 8 | NOTTINGHAM FOREST | 42 | 19 | 11 | 12 | 69 | 53 | 68 |
| 9 | LUTON TOWN | 42 | 18 | 12 | 12 | 61 | 44 | 66 |
| 10 | TOTTENHAM HOTSPUR | 42 | 19 | 8 | 15 | 74 | 52 | 65 |
| 11 | NEWCASTLE UNITED | 42 | 17 | 12 | 13 | 67 | 72 | 63 |
| 12 | WATFORD | 42 | 16 | 11 | 15 | 69 | 62 | 59 |
| 13 | QPR | 42 | 15 | 7 | 20 | 53 | 65 | 52 |
| 14 | SOUTHAMPTON | 42 | 12 | 10 | 20 | 51 | 62 | 46 |
| 15 | MANCHESTER CITY | 42 | 11 | 12 | 19 | 43 | 57 | 45 |
| 16 | ASTON VILLA | 42 | 10 | 14 | 18 | 51 | 67 | 44 |
| 17 | COVENTRY CITY | 42 | 11 | 10 | 21 | 48 | 71 | 43 |
| 18 | OXFORD UNITED | 42 | 10 | 12 | 20 | 62 | 80 | 42 |
| 19 | LEICESTER CITY | 42 | 10 | 12 | 20 | 54 | 76 | 42 |
| 20 | IPSWICH TOWN | 42 | 11 | 9 | 23 | 32 | 55 | 41 |
| 21 | BIRMINGHAM CITY | 42 | 8 | 5 | 29 | 30 | 73 | 29 |
| 22 | WBA | 42 | 4 | 11 | 27 | 35 | 89 | 24 |

# Season 1986-87

## Football League Division One

| DATE | OPPONENTS | SCORE | GOALSCORERS | ATTENDANCE |
|---|---|---|---|---|
| Aug 23 | Arsenal | L 0-1 | | 41,382 |
| Aug 25 | WEST HAM UNITED | L 2-3 | Stapleton, Davenport | 43,306 |
| Aug 30 | CHARLTON ATHLETIC | L 0-1 | | 37,544 |
| Sep 6 | Leicester City | D 1-1 | Whiteside | 16,785 |
| Sep 13 | SOUTHAMPTON | W 5-1 | Olsen (pen), Davenport, Stapleton 2, Whiteside | 40,135 |
| Sep 16 | Watford | L 0-1 | | 21,650 |
| Sep 21 | Everton | L 1-3 | Robson | 25,843 |
| Sep 28 | CHELSEA | L 0-1 | | 33,340 |
| Oct 4 | Nottingham Forest | D 1-1 | Robson | 34,828 |
| Oct 11 | SHEFFIELD WEDNESDAY | W 3-1 | Davenport 2 (1 pen), Whiteside | 45,890 |
| Oct 18 | LUTON TOWN | W 1-0 | Stapleton | 39,927 |
| Oct 26 | Manchester City | D 1-1 | Stapleton | 32,440 |
| Nov 1 | COVENTRY CITY | D 1-1 | Davenport | 36,946 |
| Nov 8 | Oxford United | L 0-2 | | 13,545 |
| Nov 15 | Norwich City | D 0-0 | | 22,684 |
| Nov 22 | QUEENS PARK RANGERS | W 1-0 | Sivebaek | 42,235 |
| Nov 29 | Wimbledon | L 0-1 | | 12,112 |
| Dec 7 | TOTTENHAM HOTSPUR | D 3-3 | Whiteside, Davenport 2 (1 pen) | 35,957 |
| Dec 13 | Aston Villa | D 3-3 | Davenport 2, Whiteside | 29,205 |
| Dec 20 | LEICESTER CITY | W 2-0 | Gibson C., Stapleton | 34,150 |
| Dec 26 | Liverpool | W 1-0 | Whiteside | 40,663 |
| Dec 27 | NORWICH CITY | L 0-1 | | 44,610 |
| Jan 1 | NEWCASTLE UNITED | W 4-1 | Jackson P. o.g., Whiteside, Stapleton, Olsen | 43,334 |
| Jan 3 | Southampton | D 1-1 | Olsen | 20,409 |
| Jan 24 | ARSENAL | W 2-0 | Olsen, Gibson T. | 51,367 |
| Feb 7 | Charlton Athletic | D 0-0 | | 15,482 |
| Feb 14 | WATFORD | W 3-1 | McGrath, Davenport (pen), Strachan | 35,763 |
| Feb 21 | Chelsea | D 1-1 | Davenport (pen) | 26,516 |
| Feb 28 | EVERTON | D 0-0 | | 47,421 |
| Mar 7 | MANCHESTER CITY | W 2-0 | Reid o.g., Robson | 48,619 |
| Mar 14 | Luton Town | L 1-2 | Robson | 12,509 |
| Mar 21 | Sheffield Wednesday | L 0-1 | | 29,888 |
| Mar 28 | NOTTINGHAM FOREST | W 2-0 | McGrath, Robson | 39,182 |
| Apr 4 | OXFORD UNITED | W 3-2 | Davenport 2, Robson | 32,443 |
| Apr 14 | West Ham United | D 0-0 | | 23,486 |
| Apr 18 | Newcastle United | L 1-2 | Strachan | 32,706 |
| Apr 20 | LIVERPOOL | W 1-0 | Davenport | 54,103 |
| Apr 25 | Queens Park Rangers | D 1-1 | Strachan | 17,414 |
| May 2 | WIMBLEDON | L 0-1 | | 31,686 |
| May 4 | Tottenham Hotspur | L 0-4 | | 36,692 |
| May 6 | Coventry City | D 1-1 | Whiteside | 23,407 |
| May 9 | ASTON VILLA | W 3-1 | Blackmore, Duxbury, Robson | 35,179 |

## FA Cup

| | | | | |
|---|---|---|---|---|
| Jan 10 | MANCHESTER CITY | (Rd3) W 1-0 | Whiteside | 54,294 |
| Jan 31 | Coventry City | (Rd4) L 0-1 | | 49,082 |

## League Cup

| | | | | |
|---|---|---|---|---|
| Sep 24 | PORT VALE | (Rd2/1L) W 2-0 | Stapleton, Whiteside | 18,906 |
| Oct 7 | Port Vale | (Rd2/2L) W 5-2 | Stapleton, Barnes, Moses 2, Davenport (pen) | 10,486 |
| Oct 29 | SOUTHAMPTON | (Rd3) D 0-0 | | 23,639 |
| Nov 4 | Southampton | (R) L 1-4 | Davenport | 17,915 |

## Fact File

Alex Ferguson became United's seventh postwar manager when he took over from Ron Atkinson in November 1986.

**MANAGER:** Ron Atkinson/Alex Ferguson
**MOST APPEARANCES:** Peter Davenport 45
**TOP SCORER:** Peter Davenport 16 (14 League)
**BIGGEST WIN:** 5-1 v Southampton, 13 September 1986, League
**HIGHEST ATTENDANCE:** 54,294 v Manchester City, 10 January 1987, FA Cup

## League & Cup Appearances

| PLAYER | LEAGUE | CUP COMPETITION FA CUP | LC | TOTAL |
|---|---|---|---|---|
| Albiston | 19 (3) | | 4 | 23 (3) |
| Barnes | 7 | | 2 | 9 |
| Bailey | 5 | | | 5 |
| Blackmore | 10 (2) | 1 | | 11 (2) |
| Davenport | 34 (5) | 1 (1) | 4 | 39 (6) |
| Duxbury | 32 | 2 | 3 | 37 |
| Garton | 9 | 2 | | 11 |
| Gibson C. | 24 | 1 | 1 | 26 |
| Gibson T. | 12 (4) | 1 (1) | 0 (2) | 13 (7) |
| Gill | 1 | | | 1 |
| Hogg | 11 | | 2 | 13 |
| McGrath | 34 (1) | 0 (1) | 4 | 38 (2) |
| Moran | 32 (1) | 2 | 2 (1) | 36 (2) |
| Moses | 17 (1) | | 4 | 21 (1) |
| O'Brien | 9 (2) | | | 9 (2) |
| Olsen | 22 (6) | 2 | 1 (1) | 25 (7) |
| Robson | 29 (1) | | 3 | 32 (1) |
| Sivebaek | 27 (1) | 2 | 1 | 30 (1) |
| Strachan | 33 (1) | 2 | 2 | 37 (1) |
| Stapleton | 25 (9) | 2 | 4 | 31 (9) |
| Turner | 23 | 2 | 4 | 29 |
| Walsh | 14 | | | 14 |
| Whiteside | 31 | 2 | 3 (1) | 36 (1) |
| Wood | 2 | | 0 (1) | 2 (1) |

## Goalscorers

| PLAYER | LEAGUE | CUP COMPETITION FA CUP | LC | TOTAL |
|---|---|---|---|---|
| Davenport | 14 | | 2 | 16 |
| Whiteside | 8 | 1 | 1 | 10 |
| Stapleton | 7 | | 2 | 9 |
| Robson | 7 | | | 7 |
| Strachan | 4 | | | 4 |
| Olsen | 3 | | | 3 |
| McGrath | 2 | | | 2 |
| Moses | | | 2 | 2 |
| Barnes | | | 1 | 1 |
| Blackmore | 1 | | | 1 |
| Duxbury | 1 | | | 1 |
| Gibson C. | 1 | | | 1 |
| Gibson T. | 1 | | | 1 |
| Sivebaek | 1 | | | 1 |
| Opps' o.gs. | 2 | | | 2 |

## Final Division One Table

| | | P | W | D | L | F | A | Pts |
|---|---|---|---|---|---|---|---|---|
| 1 | Everton | 42 | 26 | 8 | 8 | 76 | 31 | 86 |
| 2 | Liverpool | 42 | 23 | 8 | 11 | 72 | 42 | 77 |
| 3 | Tottenham Hotspur | 42 | 21 | 8 | 13 | 68 | 43 | 71 |
| 4 | Arsenal | 42 | 20 | 10 | 12 | 58 | 35 | 70 |
| 5 | Norwich City | 42 | 17 | 17 | 8 | 53 | 51 | 68 |
| 6 | Wimbledon | 42 | 19 | 9 | 14 | 57 | 50 | 66 |
| 7 | Luton Town | 42 | 18 | 12 | 12 | 47 | 45 | 66 |
| 8 | Nottingham Forest | 42 | 18 | 11 | 13 | 64 | 51 | 65 |
| 9 | Watford | 42 | 18 | 9 | 15 | 67 | 54 | 63 |
| 10 | Coventry City | 42 | 17 | 12 | 13 | 50 | 45 | 63 |
| 11 | Manchester United | 42 | 14 | 14 | 14 | 52 | 45 | 56 |
| 12 | Southampton | 42 | 14 | 10 | 18 | 69 | 68 | 52 |
| 13 | Sheffield Wednesday | 42 | 13 | 13 | 16 | 58 | 59 | 52 |
| 14 | Chelsea | 42 | 13 | 13 | 16 | 53 | 64 | 52 |
| 15 | West Ham United | 42 | 14 | 10 | 18 | 52 | 67 | 52 |
| 16 | QPR | 42 | 13 | 11 | 18 | 48 | 64 | 50 |
| 17 | Newcastle United | 42 | 12 | 11 | 19 | 47 | 65 | 47 |
| 18 | Oxford United | 42 | 11 | 13 | 18 | 44 | 69 | 46 |
| 19 | Charlton Athletic | 42 | 11 | 11 | 20 | 45 | 55 | 44 |
| 20 | Leicester City | 42 | 11 | 9 | 22 | 54 | 76 | 42 |
| 21 | Manchester City | 42 | 8 | 15 | 19 | 36 | 57 | 39 |
| 22 | Aston Villa | 42 | 8 | 12 | 22 | 45 | 79 | 36 |

# Season 1987-88

## Football League Division One

| DATE | OPPONENTS | SCORE | GOALSCORERS | ATTENDANCE |
|---|---|---|---|---|
| Aug 15 | Southampton | D 2-2 | Whiteside 2 | 21,214 |
| Aug 19 | ARSENAL | D 0-0 | | 43,893 |
| Aug 22 | WATFORD | W 2-0 | McGrath, McClair | 38,769 |
| Aug 29 | Charlton Athletic | W 3-1 | McClair, Robson, McGrath | 14,046 |
| Aug 31 | CHELSEA | W 3-1 | McClair, Strachan, Whiteside | 46,616 |
| Sep 5 | Coventry City | D 0-0 | | 27,125 |
| Sep 12 | NEWCASTLE UNITED | D 2-2 | Olsen, McClair (pen) | 45,619 |
| Sep 19 | Everton | L 1-2 | Whiteside | 38,439 |
| Sep 26 | TOTTENHAM HOTSPUR | W 1-0 | McClair (pen) | 48,087 |
| Oct 3 | Luton Town | D 1-1 | McClair | 9,137 |
| Oct 10 | Sheffield Wednesday | W 4-2 | Robson, McClair 2, Blackmore | 32,779 |
| Oct 17 | NORWICH CITY | W 2-1 | Davenport, Robson | 39,821 |
| Oct 25 | West Ham United | D 1-1 | Gibson | 19,863 |
| Oct 31 | NOTTINGHAM FOREST | D 2-2 | Robson, Whiteside | 44,669 |
| Nov 15 | LIVERPOOL | D 1-1 | Whiteside | 47,106 |
| Nov 21 | Wimbledon | L 1-2 | Blackmore | 11,532 |
| Dec 5 | Queens Park Rangers | W 2-0 | Davenport, Robson | 20,632 |
| Dec 12 | OXFORD UNITED | W 3-1 | Strachan 2, Olsen | 34,709 |
| Dec 19 | Portsmouth | W 2-1 | Robson, McClair | 22,207 |
| Dec 26 | Newcastle United | L 0-1 | | 26,461 |
| Dec 28 | EVERTON | W 2-1 | McClair 2 (1 pen) | 47,024 |
| Jan 1 | CHARLTON ATHLETIC | D 0-0 | | 37,257 |
| Jan 2 | Watford | W 1-0 | McClair | 18,038 |
| Jan 16 | SOUTHAMPTON | L 0-2 | | 35,716 |
| Jan 24 | Arsenal | W 2-1 | Strachan, McClair | 29,392 |
| Feb 6 | COVENTRY CITY | W 1-0 | O'Brien | 37,144 |
| Feb 10 | Derby County | W 2-1 | Whiteside, Strachan | 20,016 |
| Feb 13 | Chelsea | W 2-1 | Bruce, O'Brien | 25,014 |
| Feb 23 | Tottenham Hotspur | D 1-1 | McClair | 25,731 |
| Mar 5 | Norwich City | L 0-1 | | 19,129 |
| Mar 12 | SHEFFIELD WEDNESDAY | W 4-1 | Blackmore, McClair 2, Davenport | 33,318 |
| Mar 19 | Nottingham Forest | D 0-0 | | 27,598 |
| Mar 26 | WEST HAM UNITED | W 3-1 | Strachan, Anderson, Robson | 37,269 |
| Apr 2 | DERBY COUNTY | W 4-1 | McClair 3, Gibson | 40,146 |
| Apr 4 | Liverpool | D 3-3 | Robson 2, Strachan | 43,497 |
| Apr 12 | LUTON TOWN | W 3-0 | McClair, Robson, Davenport | 23,830 |
| Apr 30 | QUEENS PARK RANGERS | W 2-1 | Bruce, Parker o.g. | 35,733 |
| May 2 | Oxford United | W 2-0 | Anderson, Strachan | 8,966 |
| May 7 | PORTSMOUTH | W 4-1 | McClair 2 (1 pen), Davenport, Robson | 35,105 |
| May 9 | WIMBLEDON | W 2-1 | McClair 2 (1 pen) | 28,040 |

## FA Cup

| | | | | |
|---|---|---|---|---|
| Jan 10 | Ipswich Town | (Rd3) W 2-1 | Anderson, D'Avray o.g. | 23,012 |
| Jan 30 | CHELSEA | (Rd4) W 2-0 | Whiteside, McClair | 50,716 |
| Feb 20 | Arsenal | (Rd5) L 1-2 | McClair | 54,161 |

## League Cup

| | | | | |
|---|---|---|---|---|
| Sep 23 | HULL CITY | (Rd2/1L) W 5-0 | McGrath, Davenport, Whiteside, Strachan, McClair | 25,041 |
| Oct 7 | Hull City | (Rd2/2L) W 1-0 | McClair | 13,586 |
| Oct 28 | CRYSTAL PALACE | (Rd3) W 2-1 | McClair 2 (1 pen) | 27,283 |
| Nov 18 | Bury* | (Rd4) W 2-1 | Whiteside, McClair | 33,519 |
| Jan 20 | Oxford United | (Rd5) L 0-2 | | 12,658 |

*Played at Old Trafford, Manchester.

## Fact File

Brian McClair became the first United player to score more than 20 league goals in a season since George Best in 1967-68.

**MANAGER:** Alex Ferguson

**MOST APPEARANCES:** Brian McClair 48

**TOP SCORER:** Brian McClair 31 (20 League)

**BIGGEST WIN:** 5-0 v Hull City, 23 September 1987, League Cup

**HIGHEST ATTENDANCE:** 54,161 v Arsenal, 20 February 1988, FA Cup

## League & Cup Appearances

| PLAYER | LEAGUE | CUP COMPETITION | | TOTAL |
|---|---|---|---|---|
| | | FA CUP | LC | |
| Albiston | 5 (6) | | | 5 (6) |
| Anderson | 30 (1) | 3 | 4 | 37 (1) |
| Blackmore | 15 (7) | 1 (1) | 3 (1) | 19 (9) |
| Bruce | 21 | 3 | | 24 |
| Davenport | 21 (13) | 1 (1) | 3 (1) | 25 (15) |
| Duxbury | 39 | 3 | 5 | 47 |
| Garton | 5 (1) | | 2 (1) | 7 (2) |
| Gibson | 26 (3) | 2 | 5 | 33 (3) |
| Graham | 1 | 0 | 0 (1) | 1 (1) |
| Hogg | 9 (1) | 2 | 1 (1) | 11 (2) |
| McClair | 40 | 3 | 5 | 48 |
| McGrath | 21 (1) | | 2 | 23 (1) |
| Martin | 0 (1) | | | 0 (1) |
| Moran | 20 (1) | 1 | 2 | 23 (1) |
| Moses | 16 (1) | 1 | 1 (1) | 18 (2) |
| O'Brien | 6 (11) | 0 (2) | 0 (2) | 6 (15) |
| Olsen | 30 (7) | 2 (1) | 3 (1) | 35 (9) |
| Robson | 36 | 2 | 5 | 43 |
| Strachan | 33 (3) | 3 | 5 | 41 (3) |
| Turner | 24 | 3 | 3 | 30 |
| Walsh | 16 | | 2 | 18 |
| Whiteside | 26 (1) | 3 | 5 | 34 (1) |

## Goalscorers

| PLAYER | LEAGUE | CUP COMPETITION | | TOTAL |
|---|---|---|---|---|
| | | FA CUP | LC | |
| McClair | 24 | 2 | 5 | 31 |
| Robson | 11 | | | 11 |
| Whiteside | 7 | 1 | 2 | 10 |
| Strachan | 8 | | 1 | 9 |
| Davenport | 5 | | 1 | 6 |
| Anderson | 2 | 1 | | 3 |
| Blackmore | 3 | | | 3 |
| McGrath | 2 | | 1 | 3 |
| Bruce | 2 | | | 2 |
| Gibson | 2 | | | 2 |
| O'Brien | 2 | | | 2 |
| Olsen | 2 | | | 2 |
| Opps' o.gs. | 1 | 1 | | 2 |

## Final Division One Table

| | | P | W | D | L | F | A | Pts |
|---|---|---|---|---|---|---|---|---|
| 1 | Liverpool | 40 | 26 | 12 | 2 | 87 | 24 | 90 |
| 2 | Manchester United | 40 | 23 | 12 | 5 | 71 | 38 | 81 |
| 3 | Nottingham Forest | 40 | 20 | 13 | 7 | 67 | 39 | 73 |
| 4 | Everton | 40 | 19 | 13 | 8 | 53 | 27 | 70 |
| 5 | QPR | 40 | 19 | 10 | 11 | 48 | 38 | 67 |
| 6 | Arsenal | 40 | 18 | 12 | 10 | 58 | 39 | 66 |
| 7 | Wimbledon | 40 | 14 | 15 | 11 | 58 | 47 | 57 |
| 8 | Newcastle United | 40 | 14 | 14 | 12 | 55 | 53 | 56 |
| 9 | Luton Town | 40 | 14 | 11 | 15 | 57 | 58 | 53 |
| 10 | Coventry City | 40 | 13 | 14 | 13 | 46 | 53 | 53 |
| 11 | Sheffield Wednesday | 40 | 15 | 8 | 17 | 52 | 66 | 53 |
| 12 | Southampton | 40 | 12 | 14 | 14 | 49 | 53 | 50 |
| 13 | Tottenham Hotspur | 40 | 12 | 11 | 17 | 38 | 48 | 47 |
| 14 | Norwich City | 40 | 12 | 9 | 19 | 40 | 52 | 45 |
| 15 | Derby County | 40 | 10 | 13 | 17 | 35 | 45 | 43 |
| 16 | West Ham United | 40 | 9 | 15 | 16 | 40 | 52 | 42 |
| 17 | Charlton Athletic | 40 | 9 | 15 | 16 | 38 | 52 | 42 |
| 18 | Chelsea | 40 | 9 | 15 | 16 | 50 | 68 | 42 |
| 19 | Portsmouth | 40 | 7 | 14 | 19 | 36 | 66 | 35 |
| 20 | Watford | 40 | 7 | 11 | 22 | 27 | 51 | 32 |
| 21 | Oxford United | 40 | 6 | 13 | 21 | 44 | 80 | 31 |

# Season 1988-89

## Football League Division One

| DATE | OPPONENTS | SCORE | GOALSCORERS | ATTENDANCE |
|---|---|---|---|---|
| Aug 27 | QUEENS PARK RANGERS | D 0-0 | | 46,377 |
| Sep 3 | Liverpool | L 0-1 | | 42,026 |
| Sep 10 | MIDDLESBROUGH | W 1-0 | Robson | 40,422 |
| Sep 17 | Luton Town | W 2-0 | Davenport, Robson | 11,010 |
| Sep 24 | WEST HAM UNITED | W 2-0 | Davenport, Hughes | 39,941 |
| Oct 1 | Tottenham Hotspur | D 2-2 | Hughes, McClair | 29,318 |
| Oct 22 | Wimbledon | D 1-1 | Hughes | 12,143 |
| Oct 26 | NORWICH CITY | L 1-2 | Hughes | 36,998 |
| Oct 30 | Everton | D 1-1 | Hughes | 27,005 |
| Nov 5 | ASTON VILLA | D 1-1 | Bruce | 44,804 |
| Nov 12 | Derby County | D 2-2 | Hughes, McClair | 24,080 |
| Nov 19 | SOUTHAMPTON | D 2-2 | Robson, Hughes | 37,277 |
| Nov 23 | SHEFFIELD WEDNESDAY | D 1-1 | Hughes | 30,849 |
| Nov 27 | Newcastle United | D 0-0 | | 20,350 |
| Dec 3 | CHARLTON ATHLETIC | W 3-0 | Milne, McClair, Hughes | 31,173 |
| Dec 12 | Coventry City | L 0-1 | | 19,936 |
| Dec 17 | Arsenal | L 1-2 | Hughes | 37,422 |
| Dec 26 | NOTTINGHAM FOREST | W 2-0 | Milne, Hughes | 39,582 |
| Jan 1 | LIVERPOOL | W 3-1 | McClair, Hughes, Beardsmore | 44,745 |
| Jan 2 | Middlesbrough | L 0-1 | | 24,411 |
| Jan 14 | MILLWALL | W 3-0 | Blackmore, Gill, Hughes | 40,931 |
| Jan 21 | West Ham United | W 3-1 | Strachan, Martin, McClair | 29,822 |
| Feb 5 | TOTTENHAM HOTSPUR | W 1-0 | McClair | 41,423 |
| Feb 11 | Sheffield Wednesday | W 2-0 | McClair 2 | 34,820 |
| Feb 25 | Norwich City | L 1-2 | McGrath | 23,155 |
| Mar 12 | Aston Villa | D 0-0 | | 28,332 |
| Mar 25 | LUTON TOWN | W 2-0 | Milne, Blackmore | 36,335 |
| Mar 27 | Nottingham Forest | L 0-2 | | 30,092 |
| Apr 2 | ARSENAL | D 1-1 | Adams o.g. | 37,977 |
| Apr 8 | Millwall | D 0-0 | | 17,523 |
| Apr 15 | DERBY COUNTY | L 0-2 | | 34,145 |
| Apr 22 | Charlton Athletic | L 0-1 | | 12,055 |
| Apr 29 | COVENTRY CITY | L 0-1 | | 29,799 |
| May 2 | WIMBLEDON | W 1-0 | McClair | 23,368 |
| May 6 | Southampton | L 1-2 | Beardsmore | 17,021 |
| May 8 | Queens Park Rangers | L 2-3 | Bruce, Blackmore | 10,017 |
| May 10 | EVERTON | L 1-2 | Hughes | 26,722 |
| May 13 | NEWCASTLE UNITED | W 2-0 | McClair, Robson | 30,379 |

## FA Cup

| | | | | | |
|---|---|---|---|---|---|
| Jan 7 | QUEENS PARK RANGERS | (Rd3) | D 0-0 | | 36,222 |
| Jan 11 | Queens Park Rangers | (R) | D 2-2 | Gill, Graham | 22,236 |
| Jan 23 | QUEENS PARK RANGERS | (2R) | W 3-0 | McClair 2 (1 pen), Robson | 46,257 |
| Jan 28 | OXFORD UNITED | (Rd4) | W 4-0 | Hughes, Bruce, Phillips o.g., Robson | 47,745 |
| Feb 18 | AFC Bournemouth | (Rd5) | D 1-1 | Hughes | 12,708 |
| Feb 22 | AFC BOURNEMOUTH | (R) | W 1-0 | McClair | 52,422 |
| Mar 18 | NOTTINGHAM FOREST | (Rd6) | L 0-1 | | 55,040 |

## League Cup

| | | | | | |
|---|---|---|---|---|---|
| Sep 28 | Rotherham United | (R2/1L) | W 1-0 | Davenport | 12,588 |
| Oct 12 | ROTHERHAM UNITED | (R2/2L) | W 5-0 | McClair 3, Robson, Bruce | 20,597 |
| Nov 2 | Wimbledon | (Rd3) | L 1-2 | Robson | 10,864 |

## League & Cup Appearances

| PLAYER | LEAGUE | CUP COMPETITION | | TOTAL |
|---|---|---|---|---|
| | | FA CUP | LC | |
| Anderson | 5 (1) | | 0 (1) | 5 (2) |
| Beardsmore | 17 (6) | 3 (2) | 1 (1) | 21 (9) |
| Blackmore | 26 (2) | 5 (1) | 3 | 34 (3) |
| Brazil | 0 (1) | | | 0 (1) |
| Bruce | 38 | 7 | 3 | 48 |
| Davenport | 7 (1) | | 1 (1) | 8 (2) |
| Donaghy | 30 | 7 | | 37 |
| Duxbury | 16 (2) | | 3 | 19 (2) |
| Garton | 13 (1) | | 2 | 15 (1) |
| Gibson | 1 (1) | | 1 | 2 (1) |
| Gill | 4 (5) | 2 (2) | | 6 (7) |
| Graham | 0 | 0 (1) | | 0 (1) |
| Hughes | 38 | 7 | 3 | 48 |
| Leighton | 38 | 7 | 3 | 48 |
| McClair | 38 | 7 | 3 | 48 |
| McGrath | 18 (2) | 4 (1) | 1 | 23 (3) |
| Maiorana | 2 (4) | | | 2 (4) |
| Martin | 20 (4) | 4 (1) | | 24 (5) |
| Milne | 19 (3) | 7 | | 26 (3) |
| O'Brien | 1 (2) | | 1 | 2 (2) |
| Olsen | 6 (4) | | 1 (1) | 7 (5) |
| Robins | 1 (8) | 1 | 0 (1) | 2 (9) |
| Robson | 34 | 6 | 3 | 43 |
| Sharpe | 19 (3) | 5 (1) | 2 | 26 (4) |
| Strachan | 21 | 5 | 2 (1) | 28 (1) |
| Whiteside | 6 | | | 6 |
| Wilson | 0 (4) | 0 (2) | | 0 (6) |

## Goalscorers

| PLAYER | LEAGUE | CUP COMPETITION | | TOTAL |
|---|---|---|---|---|
| | | FA CUP | LC | |
| Hughes | 14 | 2 | | 16 |
| McClair | 10 | 3 | 3 | 16 |
| Robson | 4 | 2 | 2 | 8 |
| Bruce | 2 | 1 | 1 | 4 |
| Davenport | 2 | 1 | 1 | 4 |
| Blackmore | 3 | | | 3 |
| Milne | 3 | | | 3 |
| Beardsmore | 2 | | | 2 |
| Gill | 1 | 1 | | 2 |
| Graham | | 1 | | 1 |
| Martin | 1 | | | 1 |
| McGrath | 1 | | | 1 |
| Strachan | 1 | | | 1 |
| Opps' o.gs. | 1 | 1 | | 2 |

## Final Division One Table

| | P | W | D | L | F | A | Pts |
|---|---|---|---|---|---|---|---|
| 1 Arsenal | 38 | 22 | 10 | 6 | 73 | 36 | 76 |
| 2 Liverpool | 38 | 22 | 10 | 6 | 65 | 28 | 76 |
| 3 Nottingham Forest | 38 | 17 | 13 | 8 | 64 | 43 | 64 |
| 4 Norwich City | 38 | 17 | 11 | 10 | 48 | 45 | 62 |
| 5 Derby County | 38 | 17 | 7 | 14 | 40 | 38 | 58 |
| 6 Tottenham Hotspur | 38 | 15 | 12 | 11 | 60 | 46 | 57 |
| 7 Coventry City | 38 | 14 | 13 | 11 | 47 | 42 | 55 |
| 8 Everton | 38 | 14 | 12 | 12 | 50 | 45 | 54 |
| 9 QPR | 38 | 14 | 11 | 13 | 43 | 37 | 53 |
| 10 Millwall | 38 | 14 | 11 | 13 | 47 | 52 | 53 |
| 11 Manchester United | 38 | 13 | 12 | 13 | 45 | 35 | 51 |
| 12 Wimbledon | 38 | 14 | 9 | 15 | 50 | 46 | 51 |
| 13 Southampton | 38 | 10 | 15 | 13 | 52 | 66 | 45 |
| 14 Charlton Athletic | 38 | 10 | 12 | 16 | 44 | 58 | 42 |
| 15 Sheffield Wednesday | 38 | 10 | 12 | 16 | 34 | 51 | 42 |
| 16 Luton Town | 38 | 10 | 11 | 17 | 42 | 52 | 40 |
| 17 Aston Villa | 38 | 9 | 13 | 16 | 45 | 56 | 40 |
| 18 Middlesbrough | 38 | 9 | 12 | 17 | 44 | 61 | 39 |
| 19 West Ham United | 38 | 10 | 8 | 20 | 37 | 62 | 38 |
| 20 Newcastle United | 38 | 7 | 10 | 21 | 32 | 63 | 31 |

## Fact File

Fans' hero Mark Hughes returned to Old Trafford in June 1988 after two seasons away playing for Spanish giants Barcelona and on loan at Bayern Munich in Germany.

**MANAGER:** Alex Ferguson

**MOST APPEARANCES:** Steve Bruce, Mark Hughes, Jim Leighton, Brian McClair 48

**TOP SCORERS:** Mark Hughes 16 (14 League), Brian McClair 16 (10 League)

**BIGGEST WIN:** 5-0 v Rotherham United, 12 October 1988, League Cup

**HIGHEST ATTENDANCE:** 55,040 v Nottingham Forest, 18 March 1989, FA Cup

# Season 1989-90

## Football League Division One

| DATE | OPPONENTS | SCORE | GOALSCORERS | ATTENDANCE |
|---|---|---|---|---|
| Aug 19 | ARSENAL | W 4-1 | Bruce, Hughes, Webb, McClair | 47,245 |
| Aug 22 | Crystal Palace | D 1-1 | Robson | 22,423 |
| Aug 26 | Derby County | L 0-2 | | 22,175 |
| Aug 30 | NORWICH CITY | L 0-2 | | 41,610 |
| Sep 9 | Everton | L 2-3 | McClair, Beardsmore | 37,916 |
| Sep 16 | MILLWALL | W 5-1 | Hughes 3, Robson, Sharpe | 42,746 |
| Sep 23 | Manchester City | L 1-5 | Hughes | 43,246 |
| Oct 14 | SHEFFIELD WEDNESDAY | D 0-0 | | 41,492 |
| Oct 21 | Coventry City | W 4-1 | Bruce, Hughes 2, Phelan | 19,605 |
| Oct 28 | SOUTHAMPTON | W 2-1 | McClair 2 | 37,122 |
| Nov 4 | Charlton Athletic | L 0-2 | | 16,065 |
| Nov 12 | NOTTINGHAM FOREST | W 1-0 | Pallister | 34,182 |
| Nov 18 | Luton Town | W 3-1 | Wallace, Blackmore, Hughes | 11,141 |
| Nov 25 | CHELSEA | D 0-0 | | 46,975 |
| Dec 3 | Arsenal | L 0-1 | | 34,484 |
| Dec 9 | CRYSTAL PALACE | L 1-2 | Beardsmore | 33,514 |
| Dec 16 | TOTTENHAM HOTSPUR | L 0-1 | | 36,230 |
| Dec 23 | Liverpool | D 0-0 | | 37,426 |
| Dec 26 | Aston Villa | L 0-3 | | 41,247 |
| Dec 30 | Wimbledon | D 2-2 | Hughes, Robins | 9,622 |
| Jan 1 | QUEENS PARK RANGERS | D 0-0 | | 34,824 |
| Jan 13 | DERBY COUNTY | L 1-2 | Pallister | 38,985 |
| Jan 21 | Norwich City | L 0-2 | | 17,370 |
| Feb 3 | MANCHESTER CITY | D 1-1 | Blackmore | 40,274 |
| Feb 10 | Millwall | W 2-1 | Wallace, Hughes | 15,491 |
| Feb 24 | Chelsea | L 0-1 | | 29,979 |
| Mar 3 | LUTON TOWN | W 4-1 | McClair, Hughes, Wallace, Robins | 35,327 |
| Mar 14 | EVERTON | D 0-0 | | 37,398 |
| Mar 18 | LIVERPOOL | L 1-2 | Whelan o.g. | 46,629 |
| Mar 21 | Sheffield Wednesday | L 0-1 | | 33,260 |
| Mar 24 | Southampton | W 2-0 | Gibson, Robins | 20,510 |
| Mar 31 | COVENTRY CITY | W 3-0 | Hughes 2, Robins | 39,172 |
| Apr 14 | Queens Park Rangers | W 2-1 | Robins, Webb | 18,997 |
| Apr 17 | ASTON VILLA | W 2-0 | Robins 2 | 44,080 |
| Apr 21 | Tottenham Hotspur | L 1-2 | Bruce (pen) | 33,317 |
| Apr 30 | WIMBLEDON | D 0-0 | | 29,281 |
| May 2 | Nottingham Forest | L 0-4 | | 21,186 |
| May 5 | CHARLTON ATHLETIC | W 1-0 | Pallister | 35,389 |

## FA Cup

| DATE | OPPONENTS | ROUND | SCORE | GOALSCORERS | ATTENDANCE |
|---|---|---|---|---|---|
| Jan 7 | Nottingham Forest | (Rd3) | W 1-0 | Robins | 23,072 |
| Jan 28 | Hereford United | (Rd4) | W 1-0 | Blackmore | 13,777 |
| Feb 18 | Newcastle United | (Rd5) | W 3-2 | Robins, Wallace, McClair | 31,748 |
| Mar 11 | Sheffield United | (Rd6) | W 1-0 | McClair | 34,344 |
| Apr 8 | Oldham Athletic* | (S/F) | D 3-3† | Robson, Webb, Wallace | 44,026 |
| Apr 11 | Oldham Athletic* | (R) | W 2-1† | McClair, Robins | 35,005 |
| May 12 | Crystal Palace** | (F) | D 3-3† | Robson, Hughes 2 | 80,000 |
| May 17 | Crystal Palace** | (R) | W 1-0 | Martin | 80,000 |

*Played at Maine Road, Manchester. **Played at Wembley, London. † After extra-time.

## League Cup

| DATE | OPPONENTS | ROUND | SCORE | GOALSCORERS | ATTENDANCE |
|---|---|---|---|---|---|
| Sep 20 | Portsmouth | (Rd2/1L) | W 3-2 | Ince 2, Wallace | 18,072 |
| Oct 2 | PORTSMOUTH | (Rd2/2L) | D 0-0 | | 26,698 |
| Oct 25 | TOTTENHAM HOTSPUR | (Rd3) | L 0-3 | | 45,759 |

## League & Cup Appearances

| PLAYER | LEAGUE | CUP COMPETITION | | TOTAL |
|---|---|---|---|---|
| | | FA CUP | LC | |
| Anderson | 14 (2) | 4 | 1 | 19 (2) |
| Beardsmore | 8 (13) | 1 (2) | 1 | 10 (15) |
| Blackmore | 19 (9) | 2 (1) | | 21 (10) |
| Bosnich | 1 | | | 1 |
| Brazil | 0 (1) | | | 0 (1) |
| Bruce | 34 | 7 | 2 | 43 |
| Donaghy | 13 (1) | 1 | 3 | 17 (1) |
| Duxbury | 12 (7) | 2 (2) | 1 (1) | 15 (10) |
| Gibson | 5 (1) | 1 (1) | | 6 (2) |
| Graham | 0 (1) | | | 0 (1) |
| Hughes | 36 (1) | 8 | 3 | 47 (1) |
| Ince | 25 (1) | 6 (1) | 3 | 34 (2) |
| Leighton | 35 | 7 | 3 | 45 |
| McClair | 37 | 8 | 3 | 48 |
| Maiorana | 0 (1) | | 0 (1) | 0 (2) |
| Martin | 28 (4) | 8 | 1 | 37 (4) |
| Milne | 0 (1) | | | 0 (1) |
| Pallister | 35 | 8 | 3 | 46 |
| Phelan | 38 | 7 | 3 | 48 |
| Robins | 10 (7) | 3 (3) | | 13 (10) |
| Robson | 20 | 4 | 3 | 27 |
| Sealey | 2 | 1 | | 3 |
| Sharpe | 13 (5) | | 1 (1) | 14 (6) |
| Wallace | 23 (3) | 6 (1) | 2 | 31 (4) |
| Webb | 10 (1) | 4 | | 14 (1) |

## Goalscorers

| PLAYER | LEAGUE | CUP COMPETITION | | TOTAL |
|---|---|---|---|---|
| | | FA CUP | LC | |
| Hughes | 13 | 2 | | 15 |
| Robins | 7 | 3 | | 10 |
| McClair | 5 | 3 | | 8 |
| Wallace | 3 | 2 | 1 | 6 |
| Robson | 2 | 2 | | 4 |
| Bruce | 3 | | | 3 |
| Pallister | 3 | | | 3 |
| Blackmore | 2 | 1 | | 3 |
| Webb | 2 | 1 | | 3 |
| Beardsmore | 2 | | | 2 |
| Ince | | | 2 | 2 |
| Gibson | 1 | | | 1 |
| Phelan | 1 | | | 1 |
| Sharpe | 1 | | | 1 |
| Martin | | 1 | | 1 |
| Opps' o.gs. | 1 | | | 1 |

## Final Division One Table

| | | P | W | D | L | F | A | Pts |
|---|---|---|---|---|---|---|---|---|
| 1 | Liverpool | 38 | 23 | 10 | 5 | 78 | 37 | 79 |
| 2 | Aston Villa | 38 | 21 | 7 | 10 | 57 | 38 | 70 |
| 3 | Tottenham Hotspur | 38 | 19 | 6 | 13 | 59 | 47 | 63 |
| 4 | Arsenal | 38 | 18 | 8 | 12 | 54 | 38 | 62 |
| 5 | Chelsea | 38 | 16 | 12 | 10 | 58 | 50 | 60 |
| 6 | Everton | 38 | 17 | 8 | 13 | 57 | 46 | 59 |
| 7 | Southampton | 38 | 15 | 10 | 13 | 71 | 63 | 55 |
| 8 | Wimbledon | 38 | 13 | 16 | 9 | 57 | 50 | 55 |
| 9 | Nottingham Forest | 38 | 15 | 9 | 14 | 55 | 47 | 54 |
| 10 | Norwich City | 38 | 13 | 14 | 11 | 54 | 52 | 53 |
| 11 | QPR | 38 | 13 | 11 | 14 | 45 | 44 | 50 |
| 12 | Coventry City | 38 | 14 | 7 | 17 | 39 | 59 | 49 |
| 13 | Manchester United | 38 | 13 | 9 | 16 | 46 | 47 | 48 |
| 14 | Manchester City | 38 | 12 | 12 | 14 | 43 | 52 | 48 |
| 15 | Crystal Palace | 38 | 13 | 9 | 16 | 42 | 66 | 48 |
| 16 | Derby County | 38 | 13 | 7 | 18 | 43 | 40 | 46 |
| 17 | Luton Town | 38 | 10 | 13 | 15 | 43 | 57 | 43 |
| 18 | Sheffield Wednesday | 38 | 11 | 10 | 17 | 35 | 51 | 43 |
| 19 | Charlton Athletic | 38 | 7 | 9 | 22 | 31 | 57 | 30 |
| 20 | Millwall | 38 | 5 | 11 | 22 | 39 | 65 | 26 |

### Fact File

Alex Ferguson's first trophy success with United as the FA Cup was won without the Reds playing any of their ties at Old Trafford.

**MANAGER:** Alex Ferguson

**MOST APPEARANCES:** Brian McClair, Mike Phelan, Mark Hughes 48

**TOP SCORER:** Mark Hughes 15 (13 League)

**BIGGEST WIN:** 5-1 v Millwall, 16 September 1989, League

**HIGHEST ATTENDANCE:** 80,000 v Crystal Palace, 12 May 1990, FA Cup; 80,000 v Crystal Palace, 17 May 1990, FA Cup

# Season 1990-91

## Football League Division One

| DATE | OPPONENTS | SCORE | GOALSCORERS | ATTENDANCE |
|---|---|---|---|---|
| Aug 25 | COVENTRY CITY | W 2-0 | Bruce, Webb | 46,715 |
| Aug 28 | Leeds United | D 0-0 | | 29,174 |
| Sep 1 | Sunderland | L 1-2 | McClair | 26,105 |
| Sep 4 | Luton Town | W 1-0 | Robins | 12,576 |
| Sep 8 | QUEENS PARK RANGERS | W 3-1 | McClair, Robins 2 | 43,427 |
| Sep 16 | Liverpool | L 0-4 | | 35,726 |
| Sep 22 | SOUTHAMPTON | W 3-2 | McClair, Blackmore, Hughes | 41,228 |
| Sep 29 | NOTTINGHAM FOREST | L 0-1 | | 46,766 |
| Oct 20 | ARSENAL | L 0-1 | | 47,232 |
| Oct 27 | Manchester City | D 3-3 | Hughes, McClair 2 | 36,427 |
| Nov 3 | CRYSTAL PALACE | W 2-0 | Webb, Wallace | 45,724 |
| Nov 10 | Derby County | D 0-0 | | 21,115 |
| Nov 17 | SHEFFIELD UNITED | W 2-0 | Bruce, Hughes | 45,903 |
| Nov 25 | CHELSEA | L 2-3 | Wallace, Hughes | 37,836 |
| Dec 1 | Everton | W 1-0 | Sharpe | 32,400 |
| Dec 8 | LEEDS UNITED | D 1-1 | Webb | 40,927 |
| Dec 15 | Coventry City | D 2-2 | Hughes, Wallace | 17,106 |
| Dec 22 | Wimbledon | W 3-1 | Bruce 2 (2 pen), Hughes | 9,644 |
| Dec 26 | NORWICH CITY | W 3-0 | Hughes, McClair 2 | 39,801 |
| Dec 29 | ASTON VILLA | D 1-1 | Bruce (pen) | 47,485 |
| Jan 1 | Tottenham Hotspur | W 2-1 | Bruce (pen), McClair | 29,399 |
| Jan 12 | SUNDERLAND | W 3-0 | Hughes 2, McClair | 45,934 |
| Jan 19 | Queens Park Rangers | D 1-1 | Phelan | 18,544 |
| Feb 3 | LIVERPOOL | D 1-1 | Bruce (pen) | 43,690 |
| Feb 26 | Sheffield United | L 1-2 | Blackmore (pen) | 27,570 |
| Mar 2 | EVERTON | L 0-2 | | 45,656 |
| Mar 9 | Chelsea | L 2-3 | Hughes, McClair | 22,818 |
| Mar 13 | Southampton | D 1-1 | Ince | 15,701 |
| Mar 16 | Nottingham Forest | D 1-1 | Blackmore | 23,859 |
| Mar 23 | LUTON TOWN | W 4-1 | Bruce 2, Robins, McClair | 41,752 |
| Mar 30 | Norwich City | W 3-0 | Bruce 2 (1 pen), Ince | 18,282 |
| Apr 2 | WIMBLEDON | W 2-1 | Bruce, McClair | 36,660 |
| Apr 6 | Aston Villa | D 1-1 | Sharpe | 33,307 |
| Apr 16 | DERBY COUNTY | W 3-1 | Blackmore, McClair, Robson | 32,776 |
| May 4 | MANCHESTER CITY | W 1-0 | Giggs | 45,286 |
| May 6 | Arsenal | L 1-3 | Bruce (pen) | 40,229 |
| May 11 | Crystal Palace | L 0-3 | | 25,301 |
| May 20 | TOTTENHAM HOTSPUR | D 1-1 | Ince | 46,791 |

## FA Cup

| | | | | |
|---|---|---|---|---|
| Jan 7 | QUEENS PARK RANGERS | W 2-1 | Hughes, McClair | 35,065 |
| Jan 26 | BOLTON WANDERERS | W 1-0 | Hughes | 43,293 |
| Feb 18 | Norwich City | L 1-2 | McClair | 23,058 |

## League Cup

| | | | | | |
|---|---|---|---|---|---|
| Sep 26 | Halifax Town | (Rd2/1L) | W 3-1 | Blackmore, McClair, Webb | 6,841 |
| Oct 10 | HALIFAX TOWN | (Rd2/2L) | W 2-1 | Bruce (pen), Anderson | 22,295 |
| Oct 31 | LIVERPOOL | (Rd3) | W 3-1 | Bruce (pen), Hughes, Sharpe | 42,033 |
| Nov 28 | Arsenal | (Rd4) | W 6-2 | Blackmore, Hughes, Sharpe 3, Wallace | 40,844 |
| Jan 16 | Southampton | (Rd5) | D 1-1 | Hughes | 21,011 |
| Jan 23 | SOUTHAMPTON | (R) | W 3-2 | Hughes 3 | 41,903 |
| Feb 10 | LEEDS UNITED | (SF/1L) | W 2-1 | Sharpe, McClair | 34,050 |
| Feb 24 | Leeds United | (SF/2L) | W 1-0 | Sharpe | 32,014 |
| Apr 21 | Sheffield Wednesday* | (F) | L 0-1 | | 77,612 |

*Played at Wembley, London.

## European Cup-Winners' Cup

| | | | | | |
|---|---|---|---|---|---|
| Sep 19 | PECSI MUNKAS | (Rd1/1L) | W 2-0 | Blackmore, Webb | 28,411 |
| Oct 3 | Pecsi Munkas | (Rd1/2L) | W 1-0 | McClair | 17,000 |
| Oct 23 | WREXHAM | (Rd2/1L) | W 3-0 | McClair, Bruce (pen), Pallister | 29,405 |
| Nov 7 | Wrexham | (Rd2/2L) | W 2-0 | Robins, Bruce | 13,327 |
| Mar 6 | MONTPELLIER | (QF/1L) | D 1-1 | McClair | 41,942 |
| Mar 19 | Montpellier | (QF/2L) | W 2-0 | Blackmore, Bruce (pen) | 18,000 |
| Apr 10 | Legia Warsaw | (SF/1L) | W 3-1 | McClair, Hughes, Bruce | 20,000 |
| Apr 24 | LEGIA WARSAW | (SF/2L) | D 1-1 | Sharpe | 44,269 |
| May 15 | Barcelona** | (F) | W 2-1 | Hughes 2 | 50,000 |

**Played at Feyenoord Stadium, Rotterdam.

## FA Charity Shield

| | | | | |
|---|---|---|---|---|
| Aug 18 | Liverpool† | D 1-1 | Blackmore | 66,558 |

†Played at Wembley, London.

**MANAGER:** Alex Ferguson

**MOST APPEARANCES:** Brian McClair, Gary Pallister 58

**TOP SCORER:** Brian McClair 21 (13 League), Mark Hughes 21 (10 League)

**BIGGEST WIN:** 6-2 v Arsenal, 28 November 1990, League Cup

**HIGHEST ATTENDANCE:** 77,612 v Sheffield Wednesday, 21 April 1991, League Cup

## League & Cup Appearances

| PLAYER | LEAGUE | CUP COMPETITION | | | OTHER | TOTAL |
|---|---|---|---|---|---|---|
| | | FA CUP | LC | ECWC | | |
| Anderson | 1 | | 1 | 1 | | 3 |
| Beardsmore | 5 (7) | | 1 | 1 (1) | | 7 (8) |
| Blackmore | 35 | 3 | 9 | 9 | 1 | 57 |
| Bosnich | 2 | | | | | 2 |
| Bruce | 31 | 3 | 7 | 8 | 1 | 50 |
| Donaghy | 17 (8) | | 3 (4) | 2 (3) | 1 | 23 (15) |
| Ferguson | 2 (3) | | | | | 2 (3) |
| Giggs | 1 (1) | | | | | 1 (1) |
| Hughes | 29 (2) | 3 | 9 | 7 (1) | 1 | 49 (3) |
| Ince | 31 | 2 | 6 | 7 | 1 | 47 |
| Irwin | 33 (1) | 3 | 7 (1) | 6 | 1 | 50 (2) |
| Kanchelskis | 1 | | | | | 1 |
| Leighton | | | 1 | | | 1 |
| McClair | 34 (2) | 3 | 9 | 9 | 1 | 56 (2) |
| Martin | 7 (7) | 1 | 2 (2) | 3 (2) | | 13 (11) |
| Pallister | 36 | 3 | 9 | 9 | 1 | 58 |
| Phelan | 30 (3) | 1 | 7 (1) | 8 | 1 | 47 (4) |
| Robins | 7 (12) | 0 (1) | 0 (3) | 2 (1) | 0 (1) | 9 (18) |
| Robson | 15 (2) | 3 | 5 | 4 | | 27 (2) |
| Sealey | 31 | 3 | 8 | 8 | 1 | 51 |
| Sharpe | 20 (3) | 3 | 7 | 6 (2) | | 36 (5) |
| Wallace | 13 (6) | 0 (1) | 1 (3) | 2 (1) | 1 | 17 (11) |
| Walsh | 5 | | | 1 | | 6 |
| Webb | 31 (1) | 2 | 7 | 6 | | 46 (1) |
| Whitworth | 1 | | | | | 1 |
| Wratten | 0 (2) | | | | | 0 (2) |

## Goalscorers

| PLAYER | LEAGUE | CUP COMPETITION | | | OTHER | TOTAL |
|---|---|---|---|---|---|---|
| | | FA CUP | LC | ECWC | | |
| McClair | 13 | 2 | 2 | 4 | | 21 |
| Hughes | 10 | 2 | 6 | 3 | | 21 |
| Bruce | 13 | | 2 | 4 | | 19 |
| Blackmore | 4 | | 2 | 2 | 1 | 9 |
| Sharpe | 2 | | 6 | 1 | | 9 |
| Robins | 4 | | | 1 | | 5 |
| Webb | 3 | | 1 | 1 | | 5 |
| Wallace | 3 | | 1 | | | 4 |
| Ince | 3 | | | | | 3 |
| Giggs | 1 | | | | | 1 |
| Pallister | | | | 1 | | 1 |
| Phelan | 1 | | | | | 1 |
| Robson | 1 | | | | | 1 |
| Anderson | | | 1 | | | 1 |

### Fact File

United's first continental triumph since 1968 as Barcelona were beaten 2-1 in the European Cup-Winners' Cup final in Rotterdam.

### Final Division One Table

| | | P | W | D | L | F | A | Pts |
|---|---|---|---|---|---|---|---|---|
| 1 | Arsenal | 38 | 24 | 13 | 1 | 74 | 18 | 83 |
| 2 | Liverpool | 38 | 23 | 7 | 8 | 77 | 40 | 76 |
| 3 | Crystal Palace | 38 | 20 | 9 | 9 | 50 | 41 | 69 |
| 4 | Leeds United | 38 | 19 | 7 | 12 | 65 | 47 | 64 |
| 5 | Manchester City | 38 | 17 | 11 | 10 | 64 | 53 | 62 |
| 6 | Manchester United | 38 | 16 | 12 | 10 | 58 | 45 | 59 |
| 7 | Wimbledon | 38 | 14 | 14 | 10 | 53 | 46 | 56 |
| 8 | Nottingham Forest | 38 | 14 | 12 | 12 | 65 | 50 | 54 |
| 9 | Everton | 38 | 13 | 12 | 13 | 50 | 46 | 51 |
| 10 | Tottenham Hotspur | 38 | 11 | 16 | 11 | 51 | 50 | 49 |
| 11 | Chelsea | 38 | 13 | 10 | 15 | 58 | 69 | 49 |
| 12 | QPR | 38 | 12 | 10 | 16 | 44 | 53 | 46 |
| 13 | Sheffield United | 38 | 13 | 7 | 18 | 36 | 55 | 46 |
| 14 | Southampton | 38 | 12 | 9 | 17 | 58 | 69 | 45 |
| 15 | Norwich City | 38 | 13 | 6 | 19 | 41 | 64 | 45 |
| 16 | Coventry City | 38 | 11 | 11 | 16 | 42 | 49 | 44 |
| 17 | Aston Villa | 38 | 9 | 14 | 15 | 46 | 58 | 41 |
| 18 | Luton Town | 38 | 10 | 7 | 21 | 42 | 61 | 37 |
| 19 | Sunderland | 38 | 8 | 10 | 20 | 38 | 60 | 34 |
| 20 | Derby County | 38 | 5 | 9 | 24 | 37 | 75 | 24 |

Arsenal deducted 2 points and Manchester United 1 point for disciplinary reasons.

# Season 1991-92

## Football League Division One

| DATE | OPPONENTS | SCORE | GOALSCORERS | ATTENDANCE |
|---|---|---|---|---|
| Aug 17 | NOTTS COUNTY | W 2-0 | Hughes, Robson | 46,278 |
| Aug 21 | Aston Villa | W 1-0 | Bruce (pen) | 39,995 |
| Aug 24 | Everton | D 0-0 | | 36,085 |
| Aug 28 | OLDHAM ATHLETIC | W 1-0 | McClair | 42,078 |
| Aug 31 | LEEDS UNITED | D 1-1 | Robson | 43,778 |
| Sep 3 | Wimbledon | W 2-1 | Blackmore, Pallister | 13,824 |
| Sep 7 | NORWICH CITY | W 3-0 | Irwin, McClair, Giggs | 44,946 |
| Sep 14 | Southampton | W 1-0 | Hughes | 19,264 |
| Sep 21 | LUTON TOWN | W 5-0 | Ince, Bruce (pen), McClair 2, Hughes | 46,491 |
| Sep 28 | Tottenham Hotspur | W 2-1 | Hughes, Robson | 35,087 |
| Oct 5 | LIVERPOOL | D 0-0 | | 44,997 |
| Oct 19 | ARSENAL | D 1-1 | Bruce | 46,594 |
| Oct 26 | Sheffield Wednesday | L 2-3 | McClair 2 | 38,260 |
| Nov 2 | SHEFFIELD UNITED | W 2-0 | Kanchelskis, Hoyland o.g. | 42,942 |
| Nov 16 | Manchester City | D 0-0 | | 38,180 |
| Nov 23 | WEST HAM UNITED | W 2-1 | Giggs, Robson | 47,185 |
| Nov 30 | Crystal Palace | W 3-1 | Webb, McClair, Kanchelskis | 29,017 |
| Dec 7 | COVENTRY CITY | W 4-0 | Bruce, Webb, McClair, Hughes | 42,549 |
| Dec 15 | Chelsea | W 3-1 | Irwin, McClair, Bruce (pen) | 23,120 |
| Dec 26 | Oldham Athletic | W 6-3 | Irwin 2, McClair 2, Kanchelskis, Giggs | 18,947 |
| Dec 29 | Leeds United | D 1-1 | Webb | 32,638 |
| Jan 1 | QUEENS PARK RANGERS | L 1-4 | McClair | 38,554 |
| Jan 11 | EVERTON | W 1-0 | Kanchelskis | 46,619 |
| Jan 18 | Notts County | D 1-1 | Blackmore (pen) | 21,055 |
| Jan 22 | ASTON VILLA | W 1-0 | Hughes | 45,022 |
| Feb 1 | Arsenal | D 1-1 | McClair | 41,703 |
| Feb 8 | SHEFFIELD WEDNESDAY | D 1-1 | McClair | 47,074 |
| Feb 22 | CRYSTAL PALACE | W 2-0 | Hughes | 46,347 |
| Feb 26 | CHELSEA | D 1-1 | Hughes | 44,872 |
| Feb 29 | Coventry City | D 0-0 | | 23,967 |
| Mar 14 | Sheffield United | W 2-1 | McClair, Blackmore | 30,183 |
| Mar 18 | Nottingham Forest | L 0-1 | | 28,062 |
| Mar 21 | WIMBLEDON | D 0-0 | | 45,428 |
| Mar 28 | Queens Park Rangers | D 0-0 | | 22,603 |
| Mar 31 | Norwich City | W 3-1 | Ince 2, McClair | 17,489 |
| Apr 7 | MANCHESTER CITY | D 1-1 | Giggs | 46,781 |
| Apr 16 | SOUTHAMPTON | W 1-0 | Kanchelskis | 43,972 |
| Apr 18 | Luton Town | D 1-1 | Sharpe | 13,410 |
| Apr 20 | NOTTINGHAM FOREST | L 1-2 | McClair | 47,576 |
| Apr 22 | West Ham United | L 0-1 | | 24,197 |
| Apr 26 | Liverpool | L 0-2 | | 38,669 |
| May 2 | TOTTENHAM HOTSPUR | W 3-1 | Hughes 2, McClair | 44,595 |

## FA Cup

| | | | | | |
|---|---|---|---|---|---|
| Jan 15 | Leeds United | (Rd3) | W 1-0 | Hughes | 31,819 |
| Jan 27 | Southampton | (Rd4) | D 0-0 | | 19,506 |
| Feb 5 | SOUTHAMPTON* | (R) | D 2-2* | Kanchelskis, McClair | 33,414 |

*After extra-time, lost 4-2 on penalties.

## League Cup

| | | | | | |
|---|---|---|---|---|---|
| Sep 25 | CAMBRIDGE UNITED | (Rd2/1L) | W 3-0 | Giggs, McClair, Bruce | 30,934 |
| Oct 9 | Cambridge United | (Rd2/2L) | D 1-1 | McClair | 9,248 |
| Oct 30 | PORTSMOUTH | (Rd3) | W 3-1 | Robins 2, Robson | 29,543 |
| Dec 4 | OLDHAM ATHLETIC | (Rd4) | W 2-0 | McClair, Kanchelskis | 38,550 |
| Jan 8 | Leeds United | (Rd5) | W 3-1 | Blackmore, Kanchelskis, Giggs | 28,886 |
| Mar 4 | Middlesbrough | (SF/1L) | D 0-0 | | 25,572 |
| Mar 11 | MIDDLESBROUGH | (SF/2L) | W 2-1 | Sharpe, Giggs | 45,875 |
| Apr 12 | Nottingham Forest** | (F) | W 1-0 | McClair | 76,810 |

**Played at Wembley, London.

## European Cup-Winners' Cup

| | | | | |
|---|---|---|---|---|
| Sep 18 | Athinaikos | D 0-0 | | 5,400 |
| Oct 2 | ATHINAIKOS | W 2-0 | Hughes, McClair | 35,023 |
| Oct 23 | Atletico Madrid | L 0-3 | | 40,000 |
| Nov 6 | ATLETICO MADRID | D 1-1 | Hughes | 39,654 |

## UEFA Super Cup

| | | | | |
|---|---|---|---|---|
| Nov 19 | RED STAR BELGRADE | W 1-0 | McClair | 22,110 |

**MANAGER:** Alex Ferguson

**MOST APPEARANCES:** Brian McClair 58

**TOP SCORER:** Brian McClair 25 (18 League)

**BIGGEST WIN:** 6-3 v Oldham Athletic, 26 December 1991, League

**HIGHEST ATTENDANCE:** 76,810 v Nottingham Forest, 12 April 1992, League Cup

## League & Cup Appearances

| PLAYER | LEAGUE | CUP COMPETITION | | | OTHER | TOTAL |
|---|---|---|---|---|---|---|
| | | FA CUP | LC | ECWC | | |
| Beardsmore | | | | 1 (2) | | 1 (2) |
| Blackmore | 19 (14) | 1 | 4 (1) | 1 | 1 | 26 (15) |
| Bruce | 37 | 1 | 7 | 4 | 1 | 50 |
| Donaghy | 16 (4) | 2 | 3 (1) | | | 21 (5) |
| Ferguson | 2 (2) | | | | | 2 (2) |
| Giggs | 32 (6) | 2 (1) | 6 (2) | 1 | (1) | 41 (10) |
| Hughes | 38 (1) | 2 (1) | 6 | 4 | 1 | 51 (2) |
| Ince | 31 (2) | 3 | 6 (1) | 3 | 1 | 44 (3) |
| Irwin | 37 (1) | 3 | 7 | 2 | 1 | 50 (1) |
| Kanchelskis | 28 (6) | 2 | 4 | 1 | 1 | 36 (6) |
| McClair | 41 (1) | 3 | 8 | 4 | 1 | 57 (1) |
| Martin | 0 (1) | | 1 | 1 (2) | 1 | 3 (3) |
| Pallister | 37 (3) | 3 | 8 | 3 (1) | 1 | 52 (4) |
| Parker | 24 (2) | 3 | 6 | 2 | | 35 (2) |
| Phelan | 14 (4) | | 2 (1) | 4 | | 20 (5) |
| Robins | 1 (1) | | 0 (3) | 2 (1) | | 3 (5) |
| Robson | 26 (1) | 2 | 5 (1) | 3 | | 36 (2) |
| Schmeichel | 40 | 3 | 6 | 3 | 1 | 53 |
| Sharpe | 8 (6) | 0 (1) | 1 (3) | | | 9 (10) |
| Wallace | | | | 1 (1) | | 1 (1) |
| Walsh | 2 | | 1 | 1 | | 4 |
| Webb | 29 (2) | 3 | 6 | 3 | 1 | 42 (2) |
| Wilkinson | | | 1 | | | 1 |

## Goalscorers

| PLAYER | LEAGUE | CUP COMPETITION | | | OTHER | TOTAL |
|---|---|---|---|---|---|---|
| | | FA CUP | LC | ECWC | | |
| McClair | 18 | 1 | 4 | 1 | 1 | 25 |
| Hughes | 11 | 1 | | 2 | | 14 |
| Kanchelskis | 5 | 1 | 2 | | | 8 |
| Giggs | 4 | | 3 | | | 7 |
| Bruce | 5 | | 1 | | | 6 |
| Robson | 4 | | 1 | | | 5 |
| Irwin | 4 | | | | | 4 |
| Blackmore | 3 | | 1 | | | 4 |
| Ince | 3 | | | | | 3 |
| Webb | 3 | | | | | 3 |
| Robins | | | 2 | | | 2 |
| Sharpe | 1 | | 1 | | | 2 |
| Pallister | 1 | | | | | 1 |
| Opps' o.gs. | 1 | | | | | 1 |

## Fact File

Another first for United as Brian McClair's 14th-minute winner against Nottingham Forest at Wembley gave the club their first success in the League Cup.

## Final Division One Table

| | | P | W | D | L | F | A | Pts |
|---|---|---|---|---|---|---|---|---|
| 1 | Leeds United | 42 | 22 | 16 | 4 | 74 | 37 | 82 |
| 2 | Manchester United | 42 | 21 | 15 | 6 | 63 | 33 | 78 |
| 3 | Sheffield Wednesday | 42 | 21 | 12 | 9 | 62 | 49 | 75 |
| 4 | Arsenal | 42 | 19 | 15 | 8 | 81 | 46 | 72 |
| 5 | Manchester City | 42 | 20 | 10 | 12 | 61 | 48 | 70 |
| 6 | Liverpool | 42 | 16 | 16 | 10 | 47 | 40 | 64 |
| 7 | Aston Villa | 42 | 17 | 9 | 16 | 48 | 44 | 60 |
| 8 | Nottingham Forest | 42 | 16 | 11 | 15 | 60 | 58 | 59 |
| 9 | Sheffield United | 42 | 16 | 9 | 17 | 65 | 63 | 57 |
| 10 | Crystal Palace | 42 | 14 | 15 | 13 | 53 | 61 | 57 |
| 11 | QPR | 42 | 12 | 18 | 12 | 48 | 47 | 54 |
| 12 | Everton | 42 | 13 | 14 | 15 | 52 | 51 | 53 |
| 13 | Wimbledon | 42 | 13 | 14 | 15 | 53 | 53 | 53 |
| 14 | Chelsea | 42 | 13 | 14 | 15 | 50 | 60 | 53 |
| 15 | Tottenham Hotspur | 42 | 15 | 7 | 20 | 58 | 63 | 52 |
| 16 | Southampton | 42 | 14 | 10 | 18 | 39 | 55 | 52 |
| 17 | Oldham Athletic | 42 | 14 | 9 | 19 | 63 | 67 | 51 |
| 18 | Norwich City | 42 | 11 | 12 | 19 | 47 | 63 | 45 |
| 19 | Coventry City | 42 | 11 | 11 | 20 | 35 | 44 | 44 |
| 20 | Luton Town | 42 | 10 | 12 | 20 | 38 | 71 | 42 |
| 21 | Notts County | 42 | 10 | 10 | 22 | 40 | 62 | 40 |
| 22 | West Ham United | 42 | 9 | 11 | 22 | 37 | 59 | 38 |

# Season 1992-93

## FA Premier League

| DATE | OPPONENTS | SCORE | GOALSCORERS | ATTENDANCE |
|---|---|---|---|---|
| Aug 15 | Sheffield United | L 1-2 | Hughes | 28,070 |
| Aug 19 | EVERTON | L 0-3 | | 31,901 |
| Aug 22 | IPSWICH TOWN | D 1-1 | Irwin | 31,704 |
| Aug 24 | Southampton | W 1-0 | Dublin | 15,623 |
| Aug 26 | Nottingham Forest | W 2-0 | Hughes, Giggs | 19,694 |
| Sep 2 | CRYSTAL PALACE | W 1-0 | Hughes | 29,736 |
| Sep 6 | LEEDS UNITED | W 2-0 | Kanchelskis, Bruce | 31,296 |
| Sep 12 | Everton | W 2-0 | McClair, Bruce (pen) | 30,002 |
| Sep 19 | Tottenham Hotspur | D 1-1 | Giggs | 33,296 |
| Sep 26 | QUEENS PARK RANGERS | D 0-0 | | 33,287 |
| Oct 3 | Middlesbrough | D 1-1 | Bruce (pen) | 24,172 |
| Oct 18 | LIVERPOOL | D 2-2 | Hughes 2 | 33,243 |
| Oct 24 | Blackburn Rovers | D 0-0 | | 20,305 |
| Oct 31 | WIMBLEDON | L 0-1 | | 32,622 |
| Nov 7 | Aston Villa | L 0-1 | | 39,063 |
| Nov 21 | OLDHAM ATHLETIC | W 3-0 | McClair 2, Hughes | 33,497 |
| Nov 28 | Arsenal | W 1-0 | Hughes | 29,739 |
| Dec 6 | MANCHESTER CITY | W 2-1 | Ince, Hughes | 35,408 |
| Dec 12 | NORWICH CITY | W 1-0 | Hughes | 34,500 |
| Dec 19 | Chelsea | D 1-1 | Cantona | 34,464 |
| Dec 26 | Sheffield Wednesday | D 3-3 | McClair 2, Cantona | 37,708 |
| Dec 28 | COVENTRY CITY | W 5-0 | Giggs, Hughes, Cantona (pen), Sharpe, Irwin | 36,025 |
| Jan 9 | TOTTENHAM HOTSPUR | W 4-1 | Cantona, Irwin, McClair, Parker | 35,648 |
| Jan 18 | Queens Park Rangers | W 3-1 | Ince, Giggs, Kanchelskis | 21,117 |
| Jan 27 | NOTTINGHAM FOREST | W 2-0 | Ince, Hughes | 36,085 |
| Jan 30 | Ipswich Town | L 1-2 | McClair | 22,068 |
| Feb 6 | SHEFFIELD UNITED | W 2-1 | McClair, Cantona | 36,156 |
| Feb 8 | Leeds United | D 0-0 | | 34,166 |
| Feb 20 | SOUTHAMPTON | W 2-1 | Giggs 2 | 36,257 |
| Feb 27 | MIDDLESBROUGH | W 3-0 | Giggs, Irwin, Cantona | 36,251 |
| Mar 6 | Liverpool | W 2-1 | Hughes, McClair | 44,374 |
| Mar 9 | Oldham Athletic | L 0-1 | | 17,106 |
| Mar 14 | ASTON VILLA | D 1-1 | Hughes | 36.163 |
| Mar 20 | Manchester City | D 1-1 | Cantona | 37,136 |
| Mar 24 | ARSENAL | D 0-0 | | 37,301 |
| Apr 5 | Norwich City | W 3-1 | Giggs, Kanchelskis, Cantona | 20,582 |
| Apr 10 | SHEFFIELD WEDNESDAY | W 2-1 | Bruce 2 | 40,102 |
| Apr 12 | Coventry City | W 1-0 | Irwin | 24,249 |
| Apr 17 | CHELSEA | W 3-0 | Hughes, Cantona, Clarke o.g. | 40,139 |
| Apr 21 | Crystal Palace | W 2-0 | Hughes, Ince | 30,115 |
| May 3 | BLACKBURN ROVERS | W 3-1 | Giggs, Ince, Pallister | 40,447 |
| May 9 | Wimbledon | W 2-1 | Ince, Robson | 30,115 |

## FA Cup

| | | | | | |
|---|---|---|---|---|---|
| Jan 5 | BURY | (Rd3) | W 2-0 | Phelan, Gillespie | 30,668 |
| Jan 23 | BRIGHTON & HOVE ALBION | (Rd4) | W 1-0 | Giggs | 33,610 |
| Feb 14 | Sheffield United | (Rd5) | L 1-2 | Giggs | 27,150 |

## League Cup

| | | | | | |
|---|---|---|---|---|---|
| Sep 23 | Brighton & Hove Albion | (Rd2/1L) | D 1-1 | Wallace | 16,649 |
| Oct 7 | BRIGHTON & HOVE ALBION | (Rd2/2L) | W 1-0 | Hughes | 25,405 |
| Oct 28 | Aston Villa | (Rd3) | L 0-1 | | 35,964 |

## UEFA Cup

| | | | | | |
|---|---|---|---|---|---|
| Sep 16 | TORPEDO MOSCOW | (Rd1/1L) | D 0-0 | | 19,998 |
| Sep 29 | Torpedo Moscow | (Rd1/2L) | D 0-0* | | 11,357 |

*After extra-time, lost 4-3 on penalties.

### Fact File

Eric Cantona moved to Old Trafford from Leeds United in December 1992 and provided the final element that projected United towards their first league championship in 27 years.

**MANAGER:** Alex Ferguson
**MOST APPEARANCES:** Steve Bruce, Brian McClair, Gary Pallister 50
**TOP SCORER:** Mark Hughes 16 (15 League)
**BIGGEST WIN:** 5-0 v Coventry City, 28 December 1992, League
**HIGHEST ATTENDANCE:** 44,374 v Liverpool, 6 March 1993, League

## League & Cup Appearances

| PLAYER | LEAGUE | CUP COMPETITION | | | TOTAL |
|---|---|---|---|---|---|
| | | FA CUP | LC | UEFA | |
| Beckham | | | 0 (1) | | 0 (1) |
| Blackmore | 12 (2) | 0 (1) | 1 | 1 | 14 (3) |
| Bruce | 42 | 3 | 3 | 2 | 50 |
| Butt | 0 (1) | | | | 0 (1) |
| Cantona | 21 (1) | 1 | | | 22 (1) |
| Dublin | 3 (4) | | | | 3 (4) |
| Ferguson | 15 | | 1 | | 16 |
| Giggs | 40 (1) | 2 | 2 | 1 | 45 (1) |
| Gillespie | | 0 (1) | | | 0 (1) |
| Hughes | 41 | 2 | 3 | 2 | 48 |
| Ince | 41 | 2 | 3 | 1 | 47 |
| Irwin | 40 | 3 | 3 | 2 | 48 |
| Kanchelskis | 14 (13) | 1 | 2 (1) | 1 | 18 (14) |
| McClair | 41 (1) | 3 | 3 | 2 | 49 (1) |
| Martin | | | 1 | 1 | 2 |
| Neville G. | | | | 0 (1) | 0 (1) |
| Pallister | 42 | 3 | 3 | 2 | 50 |
| Parker | 31 | 3 | 2 | 0 (1) | 36 (1) |
| Phelan | 5 (6) | 2 | | 1 | 8 (6) |
| Robson | 5 (9) | 0 (1) | 1 | 0 (1) | 6 (11) |
| Schmeichel | 42 | 3 | 2 | 1 | 48 |
| Sharpe | 27 | 3 | | | 30 |
| Wallace | 0 (2) | 1 | 1 | 2 | 4 (2) |
| Walsh | | | 1 | 1 | 2 |
| Webb | 0 (1) | | 1 | 2 | 3 (1) |

## Goalscorers

| PLAYER | LEAGUE | CUP COMPETITION | | | TOTAL |
|---|---|---|---|---|---|
| | | FA CUP | LC | UEFA | |
| Hughes | 15 | | 1 | | 16 |
| Giggs | 9 | 2 | | | 11 |
| Cantona | 9 | | | | 9 |
| McClair | 9 | | | | 9 |
| Ince | 6 | | | | 6 |
| Bruce | 5 | | | | 5 |
| Irwin | 5 | | | | 5 |
| Kanchelskis | 3 | | | | 3 |
| Dublin | 1 | | | | 1 |
| Gillespie | | 1 | | | 1 |
| Pallister | 1 | | | | 1 |
| Parker | 1 | | | | 1 |
| Phelan | | 1 | | | 1 |
| Robson | 1 | | | | 1 |
| Sharpe | 1 | | | | 1 |
| Wallace | | 1 | | | 1 |
| Opps' o.gs. | 1 | | | | 1 |

### Final Premier League Table

| | | P | W | D | L | F | A | Pts |
|---|---|---|---|---|---|---|---|---|
| 1 | Manchester United | 42 | 24 | 12 | 6 | 67 | 31 | 84 |
| 2 | Aston Villa | 42 | 21 | 11 | 10 | 57 | 40 | 74 |
| 3 | Norwich City | 42 | 21 | 9 | 12 | 61 | 65 | 72 |
| 4 | Blackburn Rovers | 42 | 20 | 11 | 11 | 68 | 46 | 71 |
| 5 | QPR | 42 | 17 | 12 | 13 | 63 | 55 | 63 |
| 6 | Liverpool | 42 | 16 | 11 | 15 | 62 | 55 | 59 |
| 7 | Sheffield Wednesday | 42 | 15 | 14 | 13 | 55 | 51 | 59 |
| 8 | Tottenham Hotspur | 42 | 16 | 11 | 15 | 60 | 66 | 59 |
| 9 | Manchester City | 42 | 15 | 12 | 15 | 56 | 51 | 57 |
| 10 | Arsenal | 42 | 15 | 11 | 16 | 40 | 38 | 56 |
| 11 | Chelsea | 42 | 14 | 14 | 14 | 51 | 54 | 56 |
| 12 | Wimbledon | 42 | 14 | 12 | 16 | 56 | 55 | 54 |
| 13 | Everton | 42 | 15 | 8 | 19 | 53 | 55 | 53 |
| 14 | Sheffield United | 42 | 14 | 10 | 18 | 54 | 53 | 52 |
| 15 | Coventry City | 42 | 13 | 13 | 16 | 52 | 57 | 52 |
| 16 | Ipswich Town | 42 | 12 | 16 | 14 | 50 | 55 | 52 |
| 17 | Leeds United | 42 | 12 | 15 | 15 | 57 | 62 | 51 |
| 18 | Southampton | 42 | 13 | 11 | 18 | 54 | 61 | 50 |
| 19 | Oldham Athletic | 42 | 13 | 10 | 19 | 63 | 74 | 49 |
| 20 | Crystal Palace | 42 | 11 | 16 | 15 | 48 | 61 | 49 |
| 21 | Middlesbrough | 42 | 11 | 11 | 20 | 54 | 75 | 44 |
| 22 | Nottingham Forest | 42 | 10 | 10 | 22 | 41 | 62 | 40 |

# Season 1993-94

## FA Premier League

| DATE | OPPONENTS | SCORE | GOALSCORERS | ATTENDANCE |
|---|---|---|---|---|
| Aug 15 | Norwich City | W 2-0 | Giggs, Robson | 19,705 |
| Aug 18 | SHEFFIELD UNITED | W 3-0 | Keane 2, Robson | 41,949 |
| Aug 21 | NEWCASTLE UNITED | D 1-1 | Giggs | 41,829 |
| Aug 23 | Aston Villa | W 2-1 | Sharpe 2 | 39,624 |
| Aug 28 | Southampton | W 3-1 | Sharpe, Cantona, Irwin | 16,189 |
| Sep 1 | WEST HAM UNITED | W 3-0 | Sharpe, Cantona (pen), Bruce | 44,613 |
| Sep 11 | Chelsea | L 0-1 | | 37,064 |
| Sep 19 | ARSENAL | W 1-0 | Cantona | 44,009 |
| Sep 25 | SWINDON TOWN | W 4-2 | Hughes 2, Kanchelskis, Cantona | 44,583 |
| Oct 2 | Sheffield Wednesday | W 3-2 | Hughes 2, Giggs | 34,548 |
| Oct 16 | TOTTENHAM HOTSPUR | W 2-1 | Keane, Sharpe | 44,655 |
| Oct 23 | Everton | W 1-0 | Sharpe | 35,430 |
| Oct 30 | QUEENS PARK RANGERS | W 2-1 | Cantona, Hughes | 44,663 |
| Nov 3 | Manchester City | W 3-2 | Cantona 2, Keane | 35,155 |
| Nov 20 | WIMBLEDON | W 3-1 | Pallister, Hughes, Kanchelskis | 44,748 |
| Nov 24 | IPSWICH TOWN | D 0-0 | | 43,300 |
| Nov 27 | Coventry City | W 1-0 | Cantona | 17,020 |
| Dec 4 | NORWICH CITY | D 2-2 | Giggs, Cantona | 44,464 |
| Dec 7 | Sheffield United | W 3-0 | Hughes, Sharpe, Cantona | 26,746 |
| Dec 11 | Newcastle United | D 1-1 | Ince | 36,388 |
| Dec 19 | ASTON VILLA | W 3-1 | Cantona 2, Ince | 44,499 |
| Dec 26 | BLACKBURN ROVERS | D 1-1 | Ince | 44,511 |
| Dec 29 | Oldham Athletic | W 5-2 | Kanchelskis, Cantona (pen), Bruce, Giggs 2 | 44,724 |
| Jan 1 | LEEDS | D 0-0 | | 44,724 |
| Jan 4 | Liverpool | D 3-3 | Bruce, Giggs, Irwin | 42,795 |
| Jan 15 | Tottenham Hotspur | W 1-0 | Hughes | 31,343 |
| Jan 22 | EVERTON | W 1-0 | Giggs | 44,750 |
| Feb 5 | Queens Park Rangers | W 3-2 | Kanchelskis, Cantona, Giggs | 21,267 |
| Feb 26 | West Ham United | D 2-2 | Hughes, Ince | 28,832 |
| Mar 5 | CHELSEA | L 0-1 | | 44,745 |
| Mar 16 | SHEFFIELD WEDNESDAY | W 5-0 | Cantona 2, Giggs, Hughes, Ince | 43,669 |
| Mar 19 | Swindon Town | D 2-2 | Keane, Ince | 18,102 |
| Mar 22 | Arsenal | D 2-2 | Sharpe 2 | 36,203 |
| Mar 30 | LIVERPOOL | W 1-0 | Ince | 44,751 |
| Apr 2 | Blackburn Rovers | L 0-2 | | 20,886 |
| Apr 4 | OLDHAM ATHLETIC | W 3-2 | Giggs, Dublin, Ince | 44,686 |
| Apr 16 | Wimbledon | L 0-1 | | 28,553 |
| Apr 23 | MANCHESTER CITY | W 2-0 | Cantona 2 | 44,333 |
| Apr 27 | Leeds United | W 2-0 | Kanchelskis, Giggs | 41,125 |
| May 1 | Ipswich Town | W 2-1 | Cantona, Giggs | 22,559 |
| May 4 | SOUTHAMPTON | W 2-0 | Kanchelskis, Hughes | 44,705 |
| May 8 | COVENTRY CITY | D 0-0 | | 44,717 |

## FA Cup

| | | | | | |
|---|---|---|---|---|---|
| Jan 9 | Sheffield United | (Rd3) | W 1-0 | Hughes | 22,019 |
| Jan 20 | Norwich City | (Rd4) | W 2-0 | Keane, Cantona | 21,060 |
| Feb 20 | Wimbledon | (Rd5) | W 3-0 | Cantona, Ince, Irwin | 27,511 |
| Mar 12 | CHARLTON ATHLETIC | (Rd6) | W 3-1 | Kanchelskis 2, Hughes | 44,347 |
| Apr 10 | Oldham Athletic** | (SF) | D 1-1* | Hughes | 56,399 |
| Apr 13 | Oldham Athletic† | (R) | W 4-1 | Irwin, Kanchelskis, Robson, Giggs | 32,311 |
| May 14 | Chelsea** | (F) | W 4-0 | Cantona 2 (2 pens), Hughes, McClair | 79,634 |

*After extra-time. **Played at Wembley, London. †Played at Maine Road, Manchester.

## League Cup

| | | | | | |
|---|---|---|---|---|---|
| Sep 22 | Stoke City | (Rd 2/1L) | L 1-2 | Dublin | 23,327 |
| Oct 6 | STOKE CITY | (Rd2/2L) | W 2-0 | Sharpe, McClair | 41,387 |
| Oct 27 | LEICESTER CITY | (Rd3) | W 5-1 | Bruce 2, McClair, Sharpe, Hughes | 41,344 |
| Nov 30 | Everton | (Rd4) | W 2-0 | Hughes, Giggs | 34,052 |
| Jan 12 | PORTSMOUTH | (Rd5) | D 2-2 | Giggs, Cantona | 43,794 |
| Jan 26 | Portsmouth | (R) | W 1-0 | McClair | 24,950 |
| Feb 13 | SHEFFIELD WEDNESDAY | (SF/1L) | W 1-0 | Giggs | 43,294 |
| Mar 2 | Sheffield Wednesday | (SF/2L) | W 4-2 | Hughes 2, McClair, Kanchelskis | 34,878 |
| Mar 27 | Aston Villa†† | (F) | L 1-3 | Hughes | 77,231 |

††Played at Wembley Stadium, London.

## European Cup

| | | | | | |
|---|---|---|---|---|---|
| Sep 15 | Kispest Honved | (Rd1/1L) | W 3-2 | Keane 2, Cantona | 9,000 |
| Sep 29 | KISPEST HONVED | (Rd1/2L) | W 2-1 | Bruce 2 | 35,781 |
| Oct 20 | GALATASARAY | (Rd2/1L) | D 3-3 | Robson, Hakan o.g., Cantona | 39,346 |
| Nov 3 | Galatasaray | (Rd2/2L) | D 0-0 | | 40,000 |

## FA Charity Shield

| | | | | |
|---|---|---|---|---|
| Aug 7 | Arsenal# | D 1-1 | Hughes | 66,519 |

#Played at Wembley, London. United won 5-4 on penalties.

## League & Cup Appearances

| PLAYER | LEAGUE | CUP COMPETITION | | | OTHER | TOTAL |
|---|---|---|---|---|---|---|
| | | FA CUP | LC | EC | | |
| Bruce | 41 | 7 | 8 (1) | 4 | 1 | 61 (1) |
| Butt | 0 (1) | 0 (1) | | | | 0 (2) |
| Cantona | 34 | 5 | 5 4 | 1 | | 49 |
| Dublin | 1 (4) | 1 (1) | 1 (1) | 0 (1) | | 3 (7) |
| Ferguson | 1 (2) | | 1 (1) | | | 2 (3) |
| Giggs | 32 (6) | 7 | 6 (2) | 4 | 1 | 50 (8) |
| Hughes | 36 | 7 | 8 | 2 | 1 | 54 |
| Ince | 39 | 7 | 5 | 4 | 1 | 56 |
| Irwin | 42 | 7 | 8 (1) | 3 | 1 | 61 (1) |
| Kanchelskis | 28 (3) | 6 | 9 | | 1 | 44 (3) |
| Keane | 34 (3) | 6 | 6 (1) | 3 | 1 | 50 (4) |
| McClair | 12 (14) | 1 (4) | 6 (1) | | | 19 (19) |
| McKee | 1 | | | | | 1 |
| Martin | 1 | | 3 | 1 (1) | | 5 (1) |
| Neville G. | 1 | | | 0 (1) | | 1 (1) |
| Pallister | 41 | 7 | 9 | 3 | 1 | 61 |
| Parker | 39 (1) | 7 | 6 | 3 | 1 | 56 (1) |
| Phelan | 1 (1) | | 2 | 1 (3) | | 4 (4) |
| Robson | 10 (5) | 1 (1) | 5 | 4 | 0 (1) | 20 (7) |
| Schmeichel | 40 | 7 | 8 | 4 | 1 | 60 |
| Sealey | | 0 (1) | 1 | | | 1 (1) |
| Sharpe | 26 (4) | 1 (2) | 2 (2) | 4 | | 33 (8) |
| Thornley | 0 (1) | | | | | 0 (1) |
| Walsh | 2 (1) | | | | | 2 (1) |

## Goalscorers

| PLAYER | LEAGUE | CUP COMPETITION | | | OTHER | TOTAL |
|---|---|---|---|---|---|---|
| | | FA CUP | LC | EC | | |
| Cantona | 18 | 4 | 1 | 2 | | 25 |
| Hughes | 12 | 4 | 5 | | 1 | 22 |
| Giggs | 13 | 1 | 3 | | | 17 |
| Sharpe | 9 | | 2 | | | 11 |
| Kanchelskis | 6 | 3 | 1 | | | 10 |
| Bruce | 3 | | 2 | 2 | | 7 |
| Ince | 8 | 1 | | | | 9 |
| Keane | 5 | 1 | | 2 | | 8 |
| McClair | 1 | 1 | 4 | | | 6 |
| Irwin | 2 | 2 | | | | 4 |
| Robson | 1 | 1 | | 1 | | 3 |
| Dublin | 1 | | 1 | | | 2 |
| Pallister | 1 | | | | | 1 |
| Opps' o.gs. | | | | 1 | | 1 |

**MANAGER:** Alex Ferguson

**MOST APPEARANCES:** Steve Bruce, Denis Irwin 62

**TOP SCORER:** Eric Cantona 25 (18 League)

**BIGGEST WIN:** 5-0 v Sheffield Wednesday, 16 March 1994, League

**HIGHEST ATTENDANCE:** 79,634 v Chelsea, 14 May 1994, FA Cup

## Final Premier League Table

| | | P | W | D | L | F | A | PTS |
|---|---|---|---|---|---|---|---|---|
| 1 | Manchester United | 42 | 27 | 11 | 4 | 80 | 38 | 92 |
| 2 | Blackburn Rovers | 42 | 25 | 9 | 8 | 63 | 36 | 84 |
| 3 | Newcastle United | 42 | 23 | 8 | 11 | 82 | 41 | 77 |
| 4 | Arsenal | 42 | 18 | 17 | 7 | 53 | 28 | 71 |
| 5 | Leeds United | 42 | 18 | 16 | 8 | 65 | 39 | 70 |
| 6 | Wimbledon | 42 | 18 | 11 | 13 | 56 | 53 | 65 |
| 7 | Sheffield Wednesday | 42 | 16 | 16 | 10 | 76 | 54 | 64 |
| 8 | Liverpool | 42 | 17 | 9 | 16 | 59 | 55 | 60 |
| 9 | QPR | 42 | 16 | 12 | 14 | 62 | 61 | 60 |
| 10 | Aston Villa | 42 | 15 | 12 | 15 | 46 | 50 | 57 |
| 11 | Coventry City | 42 | 14 | 14 | 14 | 43 | 45 | 56 |
| 12 | Norwich City | 42 | 12 | 17 | 13 | 65 | 61 | 53 |
| 13 | West Ham United | 42 | 13 | 13 | 16 | 47 | 58 | 52 |
| 14 | Chelsea | 42 | 13 | 12 | 17 | 49 | 53 | 51 |
| 15 | Tottenham Hotspur | 42 | 11 | 12 | 19 | 54 | 59 | 45 |
| 16 | Manchester City | 42 | 9 | 18 | 15 | 38 | 49 | 45 |
| 17 | Everton | 42 | 12 | 8 | 22 | 42 | 63 | 44 |
| 18 | Southampton | 42 | 12 | 7 | 23 | 49 | 66 | 43 |
| 19 | Ipswich Town | 42 | 9 | 16 | 17 | 35 | 58 | 43 |
| 20 | Sheffield United | 42 | 8 | 18 | 16 | 42 | 60 | 42 |
| 21 | Oldham Athletic | 42 | 10 | 13 | 19 | 42 | 68 | 40 |
| 22 | Swindon Town | 42 | 5 | 15 | 22 | 47 | 100 | 30 |

# Season 1994-95

## FA Premier League

| DATE | OPPONENTS | SCORE | GOALSCORERS | ATTENDANCE |
|---|---|---|---|---|
| Aug 20 | QUEENS PARK RANGERS | W 2-0 | Hughes, McClair | 43,214 |
| Aug 22 | Nottingham Forest | D 1-1 | Kanchelskis | 22,072 |
| Aug 27 | Tottenham Hotspur | W 1-0 | Bruce | 24,502 |
| Aug 31 | WIMBLEDON | W 3-0 | Cantona, McClair, Giggs | 43,440 |
| Sep 11 | Leeds United | L 1-2 | Cantona (pen) | 39,396 |
| Sep 17 | LIVERPOOL | W 2-0 | Kanchelskis, McClair | 43,740 |
| Sep 24 | Ipswich Town | L 2-3 | Cantona, Scholes | 22,559 |
| Oct 1 | EVERTON | W 2-0 | Kanchelskis, Sharpe | 43,803 |
| Oct 8 | Sheffield Wednesday | L 0-1 | | 33,441 |
| Oct 15 | WEST HAM UNITED | W 1-0 | Cantona | 43,795 |
| Oct 23 | Blackburn Rovers | W 4-2 | Kanchelskis 2, Cantona (pen), Hughes | 30,260 |
| Oct 29 | Newcastle United | W 2-0 | Pallister, Gillespie | 43,795 |
| Nov 6 | Aston Villa | W 2-1 | Ince, Kanchelskis | 32,136 |
| Nov 10 | MANCHESTER CITY | W 5-0 | Kanchelskis 3, Cantona, Hughes | 43,738 |
| Nov 19 | CRYSTAL PALACE | W 3-0 | Irwin, Cantona, Kanchelskis | 43,788 |
| Nov 26 | Arsenal | D 0-0 | | 38,301 |
| Dec 3 | NORWICH CITY | W 1-0 | Cantona | 43,789 |
| Dec 10 | Queens Park Rangers | W 3-2 | Scholes 2, Keane | 18,948 |
| Dec 17 | NOTTINGHAM FOREST | L 1-2 | Cantona | 43,744 |
| Dec 26 | Chelsea | W 3-2 | Hughes, Cantona (pen), McClair | 31,161 |
| Dec 28 | LEICESTER CITY | D 1-1 | Kanchelskis | 43,789 |
| Dec 31 | Southampton | D 2-2 | Butt, Pallister | 15,204 |
| Jan 3 | COVENTRY CITY | W 2-0 | Scholes, Cantona (pen) | 43,130 |
| Jan 15 | Newcastle United | D 1-1 | Hughes | 34,471 |
| Jan 22 | BLACKBURN ROVERS | W 1-0 | Cantona | 43,742 |
| Jan 25 | Crystal Palace | D 1-1 | May | 18,224 |
| Feb 4 | ASTON VILLA | W 1-0 | Cole | 43,795 |
| Feb 11 | Manchester City | W 3-0 | Ince, Kanchelskis, Cole | 26,368 |
| Feb 22 | Norwich City | W 2-0 | Ince, Kanchelskis | 21,824 |
| Feb 25 | Everton | L 0-1 | | 40,011 |
| Mar 4 | IPSWICH TOWN | W 9-0 | Cole 5, Hughes 2, Keane, Ince | 43,804 |
| Mar 7 | Wimbledon | W 1-0 | Bruce | 18,224 |
| Mar 15 | TOTTENHAM HOTSPUR | D 0-0 | | 43,802 |
| Mar 19 | Liverpool | L 0-2 | | 38,906 |
| Mar 22 | ARSENAL | W 3-0 | Hughes, Sharpe, Kanchelskis | 43,623 |
| Apr 2 | LEEDS UNITED | D 0-0 | | 43,712 |
| Apr 15 | Leicester City | W 4-0 | Cole 2, Ince, Sharpe | 21,281 |
| Apr 17 | CHELSEA | D 0-0 | | 43,728 |
| May 1 | Coventry City | W 3-2 | Cole 2, Scholes | 21,885 |
| May 7 | SHEFFIELD WEDNESDAY | W 1-0 | May | 43,868 |
| May 10 | SOUTHAMPTON | W 2-1 | Cole, Irwin (pen) | 43,479 |
| May 14 | West Ham United | D 1-1 | McClair | 24,783 |

## FA Cup

| | | | | | |
|---|---|---|---|---|---|
| Jan 9 | Sheffield United | (Rd3) | W 2-0 | Hughes, Cantona | 22,322 |
| Jan 28 | WREXHAM | (Rd4) | W 5-2 | Irwin 2 (1pen), Giggs, McClair, Humes o.g. | 43,222 |
| Feb 19 | LEEDS UNITED | (Rd5) | W 3-1 | Bruce, McClair, Hughes | 42,744 |
| Mar 12 | QUEENS PARK RANGERS | (Rd6) | W 2-0 | Sharpe, Irwin | 42,830 |
| Apr 9 | Crystal Palace** | (SF) | D 2-2* | Irwin, Pallister | 38,256 |
| Apr 12 | Crystal Palace** | (R) | W 2-0 | Bruce, Pallister | 17,987 |
| May 20 | Everton† | (F) | L 0-1 | | 79,592 |

*After extra-time. **Played at Villa Park, Birmingham. †Played at Wembley, London.

## League Cup

| | | | | | |
|---|---|---|---|---|---|
| Sep 21 | Port Vale | (Rd2/1L) | W 2-1 | Scholes 2 | 18,605 |
| Oct 5 | PORT VALE | (Rd2/2L) | W 2-0 | McClair, May | 31,615 |
| Oct 26 | Newcastle United | (Rd3) | L 0-2 | | 34,178 |

## European Champions League

| | | | | | |
|---|---|---|---|---|---|
| Sep 14 | IFK GOTHENBURG | (Grp A) | W 4-2 | Giggs 2, Kanchelskis, Sharpe | 33,625 |
| Sep 28 | Galatasaray | (Grp A) | D 0-0 | | 28,605 |
| Oct 19 | BARCELONA | (Grp A) | D 2-2 | Hughes, Sharpe | 40,064 |
| Nov 2 | Barcelona | (Grp A) | L 0-4 | | 114,273 |
| Nov 23 | IFK Gothenburg | (Grp A) | L 1-3 | Hughes | 36,385 |
| Dec 7 | GALATASARAY | (Grp A) | W 4-0 | Davies, Beckham, Keane, Bulent o.g. | 39,220 |

## FA Charity Shield

| | | | | |
|---|---|---|---|---|
| Aug 14 | Blackburn Rovers†† | W 2-0 | Ince, Cantona (pen) | 60,402 |

††Played at Wembley, London.

**MANAGER:** Alex Ferguson
**MOST APPEARANCES:** 58 Gary Pallister
**TOP SCORER:** 15 Andrei Kanchelskis
**BIGGEST WIN:** 9-0 v Ipswich Town, 4 March 1995, League
**HIGHEST ATTENDANCE:** 114,273 v Barcelona, 2 November 1994, Champions League

## League & Cup Appearances

| PLAYER | LEAGUE | CUP COMPETITION | | | OTHER | TOTAL |
|---|---|---|---|---|---|---|
| | | FA CUP | LC | ECL | | |
| Beckham | 2 (2) | 1 (1) | 3 | 1 | | 7 (3) |
| Bruce | 35 | 5 | 1 | 5 (1) | 1 | 47 (1) |
| Butt | 11 (11) | 3 (1) | 3 | 5 (1) | | 22 (13) |
| Cantona | 21 | 1 | | 2 | 1 | 25 |
| Casper | | | 1 | | | 1 |
| Cole | 17 (1) | | | | | 17 (1) |
| Davies | 3 (2) | | 3 | 2 | | 8 (2) |
| Giggs | 29 | 6 (1) | | 3 | 1 | 39 (1) |
| Gillespie | 3 (6) | | 3 | | | 6 (6) |
| Hughes | 33 (1) | 6 | | 5 | 1 | 45 (1) |
| Ince | 36 | 6 | | 5 | 1 | 48 |
| Irwin | 40 | 7 | 2 | 5 | | 54 |
| Kanchelskis | 25 (5) | 2 (1) | | 5 | 1 | 33 (6) |
| Keane | 23 (2) | 6 (1) | 1 | 4 | | 34 (3) |
| McClair | 35 (5) | 6 (1) | 3 | 2 | 1 | 47 (6) |
| May | 15 (4) | 1 | 2 | 4 | 1 | 23 (4) |
| Neville G. | 16 (2) | 4 | 2 (1) | 1 (1) | | 23 (4) |
| Neville P. | 1 (1) | 1 | | | | 2 (1) |
| O'Kane | | 1 | 1 (1) | | | 2 (1) |
| Pallister | 42 | 7 | 2 | 6 | 1 | 58 |
| Parker | 1 (1) | | | 2 (1) | | 3 (2) |
| Pilkington | 0 (1) | | | | | 0 (1) |
| Schmeichel | 32 | 7 | | 3 | 1 | 43 |
| Scholes | 6 (11) | 1 (2) | 3 | 0 (2) | | 10 (15) |
| Sharpe | 26 (2) | 6 (1) | 0 (2) | 3 | 1 | 36 (5) |
| Tomlinson | | | 0 (2) | | | 0 (2) |
| Walsh | 10 | | 3 | 3 | | 16 |

## Goalscorers

| PLAYER | LEAGUE | CUP COMPETITION | | | OTHER | TOTAL |
|---|---|---|---|---|---|---|
| | | FA CUP | LC | ECL | | |
| Kanchelskis | 14 | | | 1 | | 15 |
| Cantona | 12 | 1 | | | 1 | 14 |
| Cole | 12 | | | | | 12 |
| Hughes | 8 | 2 | | 2 | | 12 |
| Ince | 5 | | | 5 | 1 | 11 |
| McClair | 5 | 2 | 1 | | | 8 |
| Scholes | 5 | | 2 | | | 7 |
| Irwin | 2 | 4 | | | | 6 |
| Sharpe | 3 | 1 | | 2 | | 6 |
| Bruce | 2 | 2 | | | | 4 |
| Giggs | 1 | 1 | | 2 | | 4 |
| Pallister | 2 | 2 | | | | 4 |
| Keane | 2 | | | 1 | | 3 |
| May | 2 | | 1 | | | 3 |
| Butt | 1 | | | | | 1 |
| Gillespie | 1 | | | | | 1 |
| Beckham | | | | 1 | | 1 |
| Davies | | | | 1 | | 1 |
| Opps' o.gs. | | 1 | | 1 | | 2 |

## Final Premier League Table

| | | P | W | D | L | F | A | Pts |
|---|---|---|---|---|---|---|---|---|
| 1 | Blackburn Rovers | 42 | 27 | 8 | 7 | 80 | 39 | 89 |
| 2 | Manchester United | 42 | 26 | 10 | 6 | 77 | 28 | 88 |
| 3 | Nottingham Forest | 42 | 22 | 11 | 9 | 72 | 43 | 77 |
| 4 | Liverpool | 42 | 21 | 11 | 10 | 65 | 37 | 74 |
| 5 | Leeds United | 42 | 20 | 13 | 9 | 59 | 38 | 73 |
| 6 | Newcastle United | 42 | 20 | 12 | 10 | 67 | 47 | 72 |
| 7 | Tottenham Hotspur | 42 | 16 | 14 | 12 | 66 | 58 | 62 |
| 8 | QPR | 42 | 17 | 9 | 16 | 61 | 59 | 60 |
| 9 | Wimbledon | 42 | 15 | 11 | 16 | 48 | 65 | 56 |
| 10 | Southampton | 42 | 12 | 18 | 12 | 61 | 63 | 54 |
| 11 | Chelsea | 42 | 13 | 15 | 14 | 50 | 55 | 54 |
| 12 | Arsenal | 42 | 13 | 12 | 17 | 52 | 49 | 51 |
| 13 | Sheffield Wednesday | 42 | 13 | 12 | 17 | 49 | 57 | 51 |
| 14 | West Ham United | 42 | 13 | 11 | 18 | 44 | 48 | 50 |
| 15 | Everton | 42 | 11 | 17 | 14 | 44 | 51 | 50 |
| 16 | Coventry City | 42 | 12 | 14 | 16 | 44 | 62 | 50 |
| 17 | Manchester City | 42 | 12 | 13 | 17 | 53 | 64 | 49 |
| 18 | Aston Villa | 42 | 11 | 15 | 16 | 51 | 56 | 48 |
| 19 | Crystal Palace | 42 | 11 | 12 | 19 | 34 | 49 | 45 |
| 20 | Norwich City | 42 | 10 | 13 | 19 | 37 | 54 | 43 |
| 21 | Leicester City | 42 | 6 | 11 | 25 | 45 | 80 | 29 |
| 22 | Ipswich Town | 42 | 7 | 6 | 29 | 36 | 93 | 27 |

# Season 1995-96

## FA Premier League

| DATE | OPPONENTS | SCORE | GOALSCORERS | ATTENDANCE |
|---|---|---|---|---|
| Aug 19 | Aston Villa | L 1-3 | Beckham | 34,655 |
| Aug 23 | WEST HAM UNITED | W 2-1 | Scholes, Keane | 31,966 |
| Aug 26 | WIMBLEDON | W 3-1 | Keane 2, Cole | 32,226 |
| Aug 28 | Blackburn Rovers | W 2-1 | Sharpe, Beckham | 29,843 |
| Sep 9 | Everton | W 3-2 | Sharpe 2, Giggs | 39,496 |
| Sep 16 | BOLTON WANDERERS | W 3-1 | Scholes 2, Giggs | 32,812 |
| Sep 23 | Sheffield Wednesday | D 0-0 | | 34,101 |
| Oct 1 | LIVERPOOL | D 2-2 | Butt, Cantona (pen) | 34,934 |
| Oct 14 | MANCHESTER CITY | W 1-0 | Scholes | 35,707 |
| Oct 21 | Chelsea | W 4-1 | Scholes 2, Giggs, McClair | 31,019 |
| Oct 28 | MIDDLESBROUGH | W 2-0 | Pallister, Cole | 36,580 |
| Nov 4 | Arsenal | L 0-1 | | 38,317 |
| Nov 18 | SOUTHAMPTON | W 4-1 | Giggs 2, Scholes, Cole | 39,301 |
| Nov 22 | Coventry City | W 4-0 | McClair 2, Beckham, Irwin | 23,400 |
| Nov 27 | Nottingham Forest | D 1-1 | Cantona (pen) | 29,263 |
| Dec 2 | CHELSEA | D 1-1 | Beckham | 42,019 |
| Dec 9 | SHEFFIELD WEDNESDAY | D 2-2 | Cantona 2 | 41,849 |
| Dec 17 | Liverpool | L 0-2 | | 40,546 |
| Dec 24 | Leeds United | L 1-3 | Cole | 39,801 |
| Dec 27 | NEWCASTLE UNITED | W 2-0 | Cole, Keane | 42,024 |
| Dec 30 | QUEENS PARK RANGERS | W 2-1 | Cole, Giggs | 41,890 |
| Jan 1 | Tottenham Hotspur | L 1-4 | Cole | 32,852 |
| Jan 13 | ASTON VILLA | D 0-0 | | 42,667 |
| Jan 22 | West Ham United | W 1-0 | Cantona | 24,197 |
| Feb 3 | Wimbledon | W 4-2 | Cantona 2 (1 pen), Cole, Perry o.g. | 25,380 |
| Feb 10 | BLACKBURN ROVERS | W 1-0 | Sharpe | 42,681 |
| Feb 21 | EVERTON | W 2-0 | Keane, Giggs | 42,459 |
| Feb 25 | Bolton Wanderers | W 6-0 | Scholes 2, Beckham, Bruce, Cole, Butt | 21,381 |
| Mar 4 | Newcastle United | W 1-0 | Cantona | 36,584 |
| Mar 16 | Queens Park Rangers | D 1-1 | Cantona | 18,817 |
| Mar 20 | ARSENAL | W 1-0 | Cantona | 50,028 |
| Mar 24 | TOTTENHAM HOTSPUR | W 1-0 | Cantona | 50,157 |
| Apr 6 | MANCHESTER CITY | W 3-2 | Cantona (pen), Cole, Giggs | 29,688 |
| Apr 8 | COVENTRY CITY | W 1-0 | Cantona | 50,332 |
| Apr 13 | Southampton | L 1-3 | Giggs | 15,262 |
| Apr 17 | LEEDS UNITED | W 1-0 | Keane | 48,382 |
| Apr 28 | NOTTINGHAM FOREST | W 5-0 | Beckham 2, Scholes, Giggs, Cantona | 53,926 |
| May 5 | Middlesbrough | W 3-0 | May, Cole, Giggs | 29,921 |

## FA Cup

| | | | | | |
|---|---|---|---|---|---|
| Jan 6 | SUNDERLAND | (Rd3) | D 2-2 | Butt, Cantona | 41,563 |
| Jan 16 | Sunderland | (R) | W 2-1 | Scholes, Cole | 21,378 |
| Jan 27 | Reading | (Rd4) | W 3-0 | Giggs, Parker, Cantona | 14,780 |
| Feb 18 | MANCHESTER CITY | (Rd5) | W 2-1 | Cantona (pen), Sharpe | 42,692 |
| Mar 11 | SOUTHAMPTON | (Rd6) | W 2-0 | Cantona, Sharpe | 45,446 |
| Mar 31 | Chelsea | (SF) | W 2-1 | Cole, Beckham | 38,421 |
| May 11 | Liverpool* | (F) | W 1-0 | Cantona | 79,007 |

*Played at Wembley, London.

## League Cup

| | | | | | |
|---|---|---|---|---|---|
| Sep 20 | YORK CITY | (Rd2/1L) | L 0-3 | | 29,049 |
| Oct 3 | York City | (Rd2/2L) | W 3-1 | Scholes 2, Cooke | 9,386 |

## UEFA Cup

| | | | | | |
|---|---|---|---|---|---|
| Sep 14 | Rotor Volgograd | (Rd1/1L) | D 0-0 | | 33,000 |
| Sep 26 | ROTOR VOLGOGRAD | (Rd1/2L) | D 2-2** | Scholes, Schmeichel | 29,724 |

**Lost on away goals rule.

### Fact File

Eric Cantona scores a stunning goal in the FA Cup final to secure yet another 'Double' for United.

**MANAGER:** Alex Ferguson
**MOST APPEARANCES:** Peter Schmeichel 45
**TOP SCORER:** Eric Cantona 19 (14 League)
**BIGGEST WIN:** 6-0 v Bolton Wanderers, 25 February 1996, League
**HIGHEST ATTENDANCE:** 79,007 v Liverpool, 11 May 1996, FA Cup

## League & Cup Appearances

| PLAYER | LEAGUE | CUP COMPETITION | | | TOTAL |
|---|---|---|---|---|---|
| | | FA CUP | LC | UEFA | |
| Beckham | 26 (7) | 3 | 2 | 2 | 33 (7) |
| Cantona | 30 | 7 | 1 | | 38 |
| Cole | 32 (2) | 7 | 1 | 1 | 41 (2) |
| Cooke | 1 (3) | | 1 (1) | 0 (1) | 2 (5) |
| Davies | 1 (5) | | 1 | 0 (1) | 2 (6) |
| Bruce | 30 | 5 | 1 (1) | 2 | 38 (1) |
| Butt | 31 (1) | 7 | | 2 | 40 (1) |
| Giggs | 30 (3) | 7 | 2 | 2 | 41 (3) |
| Irwin | 31 | 6 | 1 | 1 | 39 |
| Keane | 29 | 7 | 0 (1) | 2 | 38 (1) |
| McClair | 12 (10) | | 1 | | 13 (10) |
| McGibbon | | | 1 | | 1 |
| May | 11 (5) | 2 | | | 13 (5) |
| Neville G. | 30 (1) | 5 (1) | 1 | 1 | 37 (2) |
| Neville P. | 21 (3) | 6 (1) | 1 (1) | 1 | 29 (5) |
| O'Kane | 0 (1) | | | 1 | 1 (1) |
| Pallister | 21 | 3 | 2 | 2 | 28 |
| Parker | 5 (1) | 1 (1) | 1 | 0 (1) | 7 (3) |
| Pilkington | 2 (1) | 1 | 1 | | 4 (1) |
| Prunier | 2 | | | | 2 |
| Schmeichel | 36 | 6 | 1 | 2 | 45 |
| Scholes | 16 (10) | 0 (2) | 1 | 1 (1) | 18 (13) |
| Sharpe | 21 (10) | 4 (2) | 2 | 2 | 29 (12) |
| Thornley | 0 (1) | | | | 0 (1) |

## Goalscorers

| PLAYER | LEAGUE | CUP COMPETITION | | | TOTAL |
|---|---|---|---|---|---|
| | | FA CUP | LC | UEFA | |
| Cantona | 14 | 5 | | | 19 |
| Scholes | 10 | 1 | 2 | 1 | 14 |
| Cole | 11 | 2 | | | 13 |
| Giggs | 11 | 1 | | | 12 |
| Beckham | 7 | 1 | | | 8 |
| Keane | 6 | | | | 6 |
| Sharpe | 4 | 2 | | | 6 |
| Butt | 2 | 1 | | | 3 |
| McClair | 3 | | | | 3 |
| Bruce | 1 | | | | 1 |
| Cooke | | | 1 | | 1 |
| Irwin | 1 | | | | 1 |
| May | 1 | | | | 1 |
| Pallister | 1 | | | | 1 |
| Parker | | 1 | | | 1 |
| Schmeichel | | | | 1 | 1 |
| Opps' o.gs. | 1 | | | | 1 |

### Final Premier League Table

| | | P | W | D | L | F | A | Pts |
|---|---|---|---|---|---|---|---|---|
| 1 | Manchester United | 38 | 25 | 7 | 6 | 73 | 35 | 82 |
| 2 | Newcastle United | 38 | 24 | 6 | 8 | 66 | 37 | 78 |
| 3 | Liverpool | 38 | 20 | 11 | 7 | 70 | 34 | 71 |
| 4 | Aston Villa | 38 | 18 | 9 | 11 | 52 | 35 | 63 |
| 5 | Arsenal | 38 | 17 | 12 | 9 | 49 | 32 | 63 |
| 6 | Everton | 38 | 17 | 10 | 11 | 64 | 44 | 61 |
| 7 | Blackburn Rovers | 38 | 18 | 7 | 13 | 61 | 47 | 61 |
| 8 | Tottenham Hotspur | 38 | 16 | 13 | 9 | 50 | 38 | 61 |
| 9 | Nottingham Forest | 38 | 15 | 13 | 10 | 50 | 54 | 58 |
| 10 | West Ham United | 38 | 14 | 9 | 15 | 43 | 52 | 51 |
| 11 | Chelsea | 38 | 12 | 14 | 12 | 46 | 44 | 50 |
| 12 | Middlesbrough | 38 | 11 | 10 | 17 | 35 | 50 | 43 |
| 13 | Leeds United | 38 | 12 | 7 | 19 | 40 | 57 | 43 |
| 14 | Wimbledon | 38 | 10 | 11 | 17 | 55 | 70 | 41 |
| 15 | Sheffield Wednesday | 38 | 10 | 10 | 18 | 48 | 61 | 40 |
| 16 | Coventry City | 38 | 8 | 14 | 16 | 42 | 60 | 38 |
| 17 | Southampton | 38 | 9 | 11 | 18 | 34 | 52 | 38 |
| 18 | Manchester City | 38 | 9 | 11 | 18 | 33 | 58 | 38 |
| 19 | QPR | 38 | 9 | 6 | 23 | 39 | 57 | 33 |
| 20 | Bolton Wanderers | 38 | 8 | 5 | 25 | 39 | 71 | 29 |

# Season 1996-97

## FA Premier League

| DATE | OPPONENTS | SCORE | GOALSCORERS | ATTENDANCE |
|---|---|---|---|---|
| Aug 17 | Wimbledon | W 3-0 | Cantona, Irwin, Beckham | 25,786 |
| Aug 21 | EVERTON | D 2-2 | Cruyff, Unsworth o.g. | 54,943 |
| Aug 25 | BLACKBURN ROVERS | D 2-2 | Cruyff, Solskjaer | 54,178 |
| Sep 4 | Derby County | D 1-1 | Beckham | 18,026 |
| Sep 7 | Leeds United | W 4-0 | Butt, Poborsky, Cantona, Martyn o.g. | 39,694 |
| Sep 14 | NOTTINGHAM FOREST | W 4-1 | Solskjaer, Giggs, Cantona 2 (1 pen) | 54,984 |
| Sep 21 | Aston Villa | D 0-0 | | 39,339 |
| Sep 29 | TOTTENHAM HOTSPUR | W 2-0 | Solskjaer 2 | 54,943 |
| Oct 12 | LIVERPOOL | W 1-0 | Beckham | 55,128 |
| Oct 20 | Newcastle United | L 0-5 | | 35,579 |
| Oct 26 | Southampton | L 3-6 | Beckham, May, Scholes | 15,253 |
| Nov 2 | CHELSEA | L 1-2 | May | 55,198 |
| Nov 16 | ARSENAL | W 1-0 | Winterburn o.g. | 55,210 |
| Nov 23 | Middlesbrough | D 2-2 | Keane, May | 30,063 |
| Nov 30 | LEICESTER CITY | W 3-1 | Butt 2, Solskjaer | 55,106 |
| Dec 8 | West Ham United | D 2-2 | Solskjaer, Beckham | 25,045 |
| Dec 18 | Sheffield Wednesday | D 1-1 | Scholes | 37,671 |
| Dec 21 | SUNDERLAND | W 5-0 | Solskjaer 2, Cantona 2 (1 pen), Butt | 55,081 |
| Dec 26 | Nottingham Forest | W 4-0 | Beckham, Butt, Solskjaer, Cole | 29,032 |
| Dec 28 | LEEDS UNITED | W 1-0 | Cantona (pen) | 55,256 |
| Jan 1 | ASTON VILLA | D 0-0 | | 55,133 |
| Jan 12 | Tottenham Hotspur | W 2-1 | Solskjaer, Beckham | 33,026 |
| Jan 18 | Coventry City | W 2-0 | Giggs, Solskjaer | 23,085 |
| Jan 29 | WIMBLEDON | W 2-1 | Giggs, Cole | 55,314 |
| Feb 1 | SOUTHAMPTON | W 2-1 | Pallister, Cantona | 55,269 |
| Feb 19 | Arsenal | W 2-1 | Cole, Solskjaer | 38,172 |
| Feb 22 | Chelsea | D 1-1 | Beckham | 28,336 |
| Mar 1 | COVENTRY CITY | W 3-1 | Breen o.g., Jess o.g., Poborsky | 55,230 |
| Mar 8 | Sunderland | L 1-2 | Melville o.g. | 22,225 |
| Mar 15 | SHEFFIELD WEDNESDAY | W 2-0 | Cole, Poborsky | 55,267 |
| Mar 22 | Everton | W 2-0 | Solskjaer, Cantona | 40,079 |
| Apr 5 | DERBY COUNTY | L 2-3 | Cantona, Solskjaer | 55,243 |
| Apr 12 | Blackburn Rovers | W 3-2 | Cole, Scholes, Cantona | 30,476 |
| Apr 19 | Liverpool | W 3-1 | Pallister 2, Cole | 40,892 |
| May 3 | Leicester City | D 2-2 | Solskjaer 2 | 21,068 |
| May 5 | MIDDLESBROUGH | D 3-3 | Keane, Neville G., Solskjaer | 55,489 |
| May 8 | NEWCASTLE UNITED | D 0-0 | | 55,236 |
| May 11 | WEST HAM UNITED | W 2-0 | Solskjaer, Cruyff | 55,249 |

## FA Cup

| | | | | |
|---|---|---|---|---|
| Jan 5 | TOTTENHAM HOTSPUR | (Rd3) W 2-0 | Scholes, Beckham | 52,445 |
| Jan 25 | WIMBLEDON | (Rd4) D 1-1 | Scholes | 53,342 |
| Feb 4 | Wimbledon | (R) L 0-1 | | 25,601 |

## League Cup

| | | | | |
|---|---|---|---|---|
| Oct 23 | SWINDON TOWN | (Rd3) W 2-1 | Poborsky, Scholes | 49,305 |
| Nov 27 | Leicester City | (Rd4) L 0-2 | | 20,428 |

## European Champions League

| | | | | |
|---|---|---|---|---|
| Sep 11 | Juventus | (Grp C) L 0-1 | | 54,000 |
| Sep 25 | RAPID VIENNA | (Grp C) W 2-0 | Solskjaer, Beckham | 51,831 |
| Oct 16 | Fenerbahce | (Grp C) W 2-0 | Beckham, Cantona | 26,200 |
| Oct 30 | FENERBAHCE | (Grp C) L 0-1 | | 53,297 |
| Nov 20 | JUVENTUS | (Grp C) L 0-1 | | 53,529 |
| Dec 4 | Rapid Vienna | (Grp C) W 2-0 | Giggs, Cantona | 45,000 |
| Mar 5 | PORTO | (QF/1L) W 4-0 | May, Cantona, | 53,415 |
| Mar 19 | Porto | (QF/2L) D 0-0 | | 40,000 |
| Apr 9 | Borussia Dortmund | (SF/1L) L 0-1 | | 48,500 |
| Apr 23 | BORUSSIA DORTMUND | (SF/2L) L 0-1 | | 53,606 |

## FA Charity Shield

| | | | | |
|---|---|---|---|---|
| Aug 11 | Newcastle United* | W 4-0 | Cantona, Butt, Beckham, Keane | 73,214 |

*Played at Wembley, London.

**MANAGER:** Alex Ferguson

**MOST APPEARANCES:** Eric Cantona 50

**TOP SCORER:** Ole Gunnar Solskjaer 19 (18 League)

**BIGGEST WIN:** 5-0 v Sunderland (H), 21 December 1996, League

**HIGHEST ATTENDANCE:** 73,214 v Newcastle United, 23 April 1997, FA Charity Shield

## League & Cup Appearances

| PLAYER | LEAGUE | CUP COMPETITION | | | OTHER | TOTAL |
|---|---|---|---|---|---|---|
| | | FA CUP | LC | ECL | | |
| Appleton | | | 1 (1) | | | 1 (1) |
| Beckham | 33 (3) | 2 | | 10 | 1 | 46 (3) |
| Butt | 24 (2) | | | 8 (1) | 1 | 32 (3) |
| Cantona | 36 | 3 | | 10 | 1 | 50 |
| Casper | 0 (2) | 1 | 2 | 0 (1) | | 3 (3) |
| Clegg | 3 (1) | 1 | 1 | | | 5 (1) |
| Cole | 10 (10) | 2 (1) | | 2 (3) | | 14 (14) |
| Cooke | | | 0 (1) | | | 0 (1) |
| Cruyff | 11 (5) | | 1 | 3 (1) | 0 (1) | 15 (7) |
| Davies | | | 0 (2) | | | 0 (2) |
| Giggs | 25 (1) | 3 | | 6 (1) | 1 | 35 (2) |
| Irwin | 29 (2) | 3 | | 8 | 1 | 41 (2) |
| Johnsen | 26 (5) | 2 | | 9 | | 37 (5) |
| Keane | 21 | 3 | 2 | 6 | 1 | 32 |
| McClair | 4 (15) | 1 (2) | 2 | 0 (3) | | 7 (20) |
| May | 28 (1) | 1 | 2 | 7 (1) | 1 | 39 (2) |
| Neville G. | 30 (1) | 3 | 1 | 10 | 0 (1) | 44 (2) |
| Neville P. | 15 (3) | | 1 | 2 (2) | 1 | 19 (5) |
| O'Kane | 1 | | 1 | | | 2 |
| Pallister | 27 | 1 | | 8 | 1 | 37 |
| Poborsky | 15 (7) | 2 | 2 | 3 (3) | 0 (1) | 22 (11) |
| Schmeichel | 36 | 3 | | 9 | 1 | 49 |
| Scholes | 16 (8) | 2 | 2 | 0 (4) | 1 | 21 (12) |
| Solskjaer | 25 (8) | 0 (3) | | 8 (2) | | 33 (13) |
| Thornley | 1 (1) | | 2 | | | 3 (1) |
| van der Gouw | 2 | | 2 | 1 | | 5 |

## Goalscorers

| PLAYER | LEAGUE | CUP COMPETITION | | | OTHER | TOTAL |
|---|---|---|---|---|---|---|
| | | FA CUP | LC | ECL | | |
| Solskjaer | 18 | | | 1 | | 19 |
| Cantona | 11 | | | 3 | 1 | 15 |
| Beckham | 8 | 1 | | 2 | 1 | 12 |
| Cole | 6 | | | 1 | | 7 |
| Butt | 5 | | | | 1 | 6 |
| Scholes | 3 | 2 | 1 | | | 6 |
| Giggs | 3 | | | 2 | | 5 |
| May | 3 | | | 1 | | 4 |
| Poborsky | 3 | | 1 | | | 4 |
| Cruyff | 3 | | | | | 3 |
| Pallister | 3 | | | | | 3 |
| Keane | 2 | | | | 1 | 3 |
| Irwin | 1 | | | | | 1 |
| Neville G. | 1 | | | | | 1 |
| Opps' o.gs. | 6 | | | | | 6 |

### Fact File

Another title for United but Old Trafford was rocked as Eric Cantona announced his retirement – could the Reds survive without their Gallic talisman?

### Final Premier League Table

| | | P | W | D | L | F | A | PTS |
|---|---|---|---|---|---|---|---|---|
| 1 | MANCHESTER UNITED | 38 | 21 | 12 | 5 | 76 | 44 | 75 |
| 2 | NEWCASTLE UNITED | 38 | 19 | 11 | 8 | 73 | 40 | 68 |
| 3 | ARSENAL | 38 | 19 | 11 | 8 | 62 | 32 | 68 |
| 4 | LIVERPOOL | 38 | 19 | 11 | 8 | 62 | 37 | 68 |
| 5 | ASTON VILLA | 38 | 17 | 10 | 11 | 47 | 34 | 61 |
| 6 | CHELSEA | 38 | 16 | 11 | 11 | 58 | 55 | 59 |
| 7 | SHEFFIELD WEDNESDAY | 38 | 14 | 15 | 9 | 50 | 51 | 57 |
| 8 | WIMBLEDON | 38 | 15 | 11 | 12 | 49 | 46 | 56 |
| 9 | LEICESTER CITY | 38 | 12 | 11 | 15 | 46 | 54 | 47 |
| 10 | TOTTENHAM HOTSPUR | 38 | 13 | 7 | 18 | 44 | 51 | 46 |
| 11 | LEEDS UNITED | 38 | 11 | 13 | 14 | 28 | 38 | 46 |
| 12 | DERBY COUNTY | 38 | 11 | 13 | 14 | 45 | 58 | 46 |
| 13 | BLACKBURN ROVERS | 38 | 9 | 15 | 14 | 42 | 43 | 42 |
| 14 | WEST HAM UNITED | 38 | 10 | 12 | 16 | 39 | 48 | 42 |
| 15 | EVERTON | 38 | 10 | 12 | 16 | 44 | 57 | 42 |
| 16 | SOUTHAMPTON | 38 | 10 | 11 | 17 | 50 | 56 | 41 |
| 17 | COVENTRY CITY | 38 | 9 | 14 | 15 | 38 | 54 | 41 |
| 18 | SUNDERLAND | 38 | 10 | 10 | 18 | 35 | 53 | 40 |
| 19 | MIDDLESBROUGH | 38 | 10 | 12 | 16 | 51 | 60 | 39 |
| 20 | NOTTINGHAM FOREST | 38 | 6 | 16 | 16 | 31 | 59 | 34 |

*MIDDLESBROUGH DEDUCTED THREE POINTS FOR FAILURE TO FULFIL A FIXTURE ON A GIVEN DATE.*

# Season 1997-98

## FA Premier League

| DATE | OPPONENTS | SCORE | GOALSCORERS | ATTENDANCE |
|---|---|---|---|---|
| Aug 10 | Tottenham Hotspur | W 2-0 | Butt, Vega o.g. | 26,359 |
| Aug 13 | SOUTHAMPTON | W 1-0 | Beckham | 55,008 |
| Aug 23 | Leicester City | D 0-0 | | 21,221 |
| Aug 27 | Everton | W 2-0 | Beckham, Sheringham | 40,079 |
| Aug 30 | COVENTRY CITY | W 3-0 | Cole, Keane, Poborsky | 55,074 |
| Sep 13 | WEST HAM UNITED | W 2-1 | Keane, Scholes | 55,068 |
| Sep 20 | Bolton Wanderers | D 0-0 | | 25,000 |
| Sep 24 | CHELSEA | D 2-2 | Scholes, Solskjaer | 55,163 |
| Sep 27 | Leeds United | L 0-1 | | 39,952 |
| Oct 4 | CRYSTAL PALACE | W 2-0 | Sheringham, Hreidarsson o.g. | 55,143 |
| Oct 18 | Derby County | D 2-2 | Sheringham, Cole | 30,014 |
| Oct 25 | BARNSLEY | W 7-0 | Cole 3, Giggs 2, Scholes, Poborsky | 55,142 |
| Nov 1 | SHEFFIELD WEDNESDAY | W 6-1 | Sheringham 2, Solskjaer 2, Cole, Newsome o.g. | 55,259 |
| Nov 9 | Arsenal | L 2-3 | Sheringham 2 | 38,205 |
| Nov 22 | Wimbledon | W 5-2 | Beckham 2, Butt, Scholes, Cole | |
| Nov 30 | BLACKBURN ROVERS | W 4-0 | Solskjaer 2, Henchoz o.g., Kenna o.g. | 55,175 |
| Dec 5 | Liverpool | W 3-1 | Cole 2, Beckham | 41,027 |
| Dec 15 | ASTON VILLA | W 1-0 | Giggs | 55,151 |
| Dec 21 | Newcastle United | W 1-0 | Cole | 36,767 |
| Dec 26 | EVERTON | W 2-0 | Berg, Cole | 55,167 |
| Dec 28 | Coventry City | L 2-3 | Solskjaer, Sheringham | 23,054 |
| Jan 10 | TOTTENHAM HOTSPUR | W 2-0 | Giggs 2 | 55,281 |
| Jan 19 | Southampton | L 0-1 | | 15,241 |
| Jan 31 | LEICESTER CITY | L 0-1 | | 55,156 |
| Feb 7 | BOLTON WANDERERS | D 1-1 | Cole | 55,156 |
| Feb 18 | Aston Villa | W 2-0 | Beckham, Giggs | 39,372 |
| Feb 21 | DERBY COUNTY | W 2-0 | Giggs, Irwin (pen) | 55,170 |
| Feb 28 | Chelsea | W 1-0 | Neville P. | 35,411 |
| Mar 7 | Sheffield Wednesday | L 0-2 | | 39,427 |
| Mar 11 | West Ham United | D 1-1 | Scholes | 25,892 |
| Mar 14 | ARSENAL | L 0-1 | | 55,174 |
| Mar 28 | WIMBLEDON | W 2-0 | Johnsen, Scholes | 55,306 |
| Apr 6 | Blackburn Rovers | W 3-1 | Cole, Scholes, Beckham | 30,547 |
| Apr 10 | LIVERPOOL | D 1-1 | Johnsen | 55,171 |
| Apr 18 | NEWCASTLE UNITED | D 1-1 | Beckham | 55,194 |
| Apr 27 | Crystal Palace | W 3-0 | Scholes, Butt, Cole | 26,180 |
| May 4 | LEEDS UNITED | W 3-0 | Giggs, Irwin (pen), Beckham | 55,167 |
| May 10 | Barnsley | W 2-0 | Cole, Sheringham | 18,694 |

## FA Cup

| | | | | |
|---|---|---|---|---|
| Jan 4 | Chelsea | (Rd3) W 5-3 | Beckham 2, Cole 2, Sheringham | 34,792 |
| Jan 24 | WALSALL | (Rd4) W 5-1 | Cole 2, Solskjaer 2, Johnsen | 54,669 |
| Feb 15 | BARNSLEY | (Rd5) D 1-1 | Sheringham | 54,700 |
| Feb 25 | Barnsley | (R) L 2-3 | Sheringham, Cole | 18,665 |

## League Cup

| | | | | |
|---|---|---|---|---|
| Oct 14 | Ipswich Town | (Rd3) L 0-2 | | 22,173 |

## European Champions League

| | | | | |
|---|---|---|---|---|
| Sep 17 | 1.FC Kosice | (Grp B) W 3-0 | Irwin, Berg, Cole | 9,950 |
| Oct 1 | JUVENTUS | (Grp B) W 3-2 | Sheringham, Scholes, Giggs | 53,428 |
| Oct 22 | FEYENOORD | (Grp B) W 2-1 | Scholes, Irwin (pen) | 53,188 |
| Nov 5 | Feyenoord | (Grp B) W 3-1 | Cole 3 | 42,500 |
| Nov 27 | 1.FC KOSICE | (Grp B) W 3-0 | Cole, Sheringham, Faktor o.g. | 53,535 |
| Dec 10 | Juventus | (Grp B) L 0-1 | | 47,786 |
| Mar 4 | Monaco | (QF/1L) D 0-0 | | 15,000 |
| Mar 18 | MONACO | (QF/2L) D 1-1 | Solskjaer | 53,683 |

## FA Charity Shield

| | | | | |
|---|---|---|---|---|
| Aug 3 | Chelsea* | D 1-1 | Johnsen | 73,636 |

*Played at Wembley, London. United won 4-2 on penalties.

**MANAGER:** Alex Ferguson

**MOST APPEARANCES:** David Beckham 49

**TOP SCORER:** Andy Cole 25 (15 League)

**BIGGEST WIN:** 7-0 v Barnsley, 25 October 1997, League

**HIGHEST ATTENDANCE:** 73,636 v Chelsea, 3 August 1997, FA Charity Shield

## League & Cup Appearances

| PLAYER | LEAGUE | CUP COMPETITION | | | OTHER | TOTAL |
|---|---|---|---|---|---|---|
| | | FA CUP | LC | ECL | | |
| Beckham | 34 (3) | 3 (1) | | 8 | | 45 (4) |
| Berg | 23 (4) | 2 | | 5 (2) | 0 (1) | 30 (7) |
| Brown | 1 (1) | | | | | 1 (1) |
| Butt | 31 (2) | 1 | | 7 | 1 | 40 (2) |
| Cole | 31 (2) | 3 | 1 | 6 (1) | 1 | 42 (3) |
| Clegg | 1 (2) | 2 (1) | | 0 (1) | | 3 (4) |
| Curtis | 3 (5) | | 1 | | | 4 (5) |
| Cruyff | 3 (2) | 0 (1) | 1 | 0 (4) | 0 (1) | 4 (8) |
| Giggs | 28 (1) | 2 | | 5 | 1 | 36 (1) |
| Higginbotham | 0 (1) | | | | | 0 (1) |
| Irwin | 23 (2) | 3 (1) | 0 (1) | 6 | 1 | 33 (4) |
| Johnsen | 18 (4) | 3 | 1 | 5 | 1 | 28 (4) |
| Keane | 9 | | | 1 | 1 | 11 |
| McClair | 2 (11) | 3 | 1 | 0 (3) | | 6 (14) |
| May | 7 (2) | 1 | 1 | | | 9 (2) |
| Mulryne | 1 | 0 (1) | 1 | | | 2 (1) |
| Neville G. | 34 | 2 (1) | | 8 | | 44 (1) |
| Neville P. | 24 (6) | 3 | 1 | 5 (2) | 1 | 34 (8) |
| Nevland | 0 (1) | 2 (1) | 0 (1) | | | 2 (3) |
| Pallister | 33 | 3 | | 6 | 1 | 43 |
| Pilkington | 2 | | | | | 2 |
| Poborsky | 3 (7) | | 1 | 2 (2) | | 6 (9) |
| Schmeichel | 32 | 4 | | 7 | 1 | 44 |
| Scholes | 28 (3) | 2 | 0 (1) | 6 (1) | 1 | 37 (5) |
| Sheringham | 28 (3) | 2 (1) | | 7 | 1 | 38 (4) |
| Solskjaer | 15 (7) | 1 (1) | | 3 (3) | | 19 (11) |
| Twiss | 0 | 0 (1) | | | | 0 (1) |
| Thornley | 0 (5) | 2 | 1 | | | 3 (5) |
| van der Gouw | 4 (1) | | 1 | 1 | | 6 (1) |
| Wallwork | 0 (1) | | | | | 0 (1) |

## Goalscorers

| PLAYER | LEAGUE | CUP COMPETITION | | | OTHER | TOTAL |
|---|---|---|---|---|---|---|
| | | FA CUP | LC | ECL | | |
| Cole | 15 | 5 | | 5 | | 25 |
| Sheringham | 9 | 3 | | 2 | | 14 |
| Beckham | 9 | 2 | | | | 11 |
| Scholes | 8 | | | 2 | | 10 |
| Giggs | 8 | | | 1 | | 9 |
| Solskjaer | 6 | 2 | | 1 | | 9 |
| Irwin | 2 | | | 2 | | 4 |
| Johnsen | 2 | 1 | | | 1 | 4 |
| Butt | 3 | | | | | 3 |
| Berg | 1 | | | 1 | | 2 |
| Keane | 2 | | | | | 2 |
| Poborsky | 2 | | | | | 2 |
| Neville P. | 1 | | | | | 1 |
| Opps' o.gs. | 5 | | | 1 | | 6 |

## Fact File

At the end of the season the Reds came away empty-handed – were United's fortunes on the wane? Alex Ferguson had an answer to that question...

## Final Premier League Table

| | P | W | D | L | F | A | PTS |
|---|---|---|---|---|---|---|---|
| 1 ARSENAL | 38 | 23 | 9 | 6 | 68 | 33 | 78 |
| 2 MANCHESTER UNITED | 38 | 23 | 8 | 7 | 73 | 26 | 77 |
| 3 LIVERPOOL | 38 | 18 | 11 | 9 | 68 | 42 | 65 |
| 4 CHELSEA | 38 | 20 | 3 | 15 | 71 | 43 | 63 |
| 5 LEEDS UNITED | 38 | 17 | 8 | 13 | 57 | 46 | 59 |
| 6 BLACKBURN ROVERS | 38 | 16 | 10 | 12 | 57 | 52 | 58 |
| 7 ASTON VILLA | 38 | 17 | 6 | 15 | 49 | 48 | 57 |
| 8 WEST HAM UNITED | 38 | 16 | 8 | 14 | 56 | 57 | 56 |
| 9 DERBY COUNTY | 38 | 16 | 7 | 15 | 52 | 49 | 55 |
| 10 LEICESTER CITY | 38 | 13 | 14 | 11 | 51 | 41 | 53 |
| 11 COVENTRY CITY | 38 | 12 | 16 | 10 | 46 | 44 | 52 |
| 12 SOUTHAMPTON | 38 | 14 | 6 | 18 | 50 | 55 | 48 |
| 13 NEWCASTLE UNITED | 38 | 11 | 11 | 16 | 35 | 44 | 44 |
| 14 TOTTENHAM HOTSPUR | 38 | 11 | 11 | 16 | 44 | 56 | 44 |
| 15 WIMBLEDON | 38 | 10 | 14 | 14 | 34 | 46 | 44 |
| 16 SHEFFIELD WEDNESDAY | 38 | 12 | 8 | 18 | 52 | 67 | 44 |
| 17 EVERTON | 38 | 9 | 13 | 16 | 41 | 56 | 40 |
| 18 BOLTON WANDERERS | 38 | 9 | 13 | 16 | 41 | 61 | 40 |
| 19 BARNSLEY | 38 | 10 | 5 | 23 | 37 | 82 | 35 |
| 20 CRYSTAL PALACE | 38 | 8 | 9 | 21 | 37 | 71 | 33 |

# Season 1998-99

## FA Premier League

| DATE | OPPONENTS | SCORE | GOALSCORERS | ATTENDANCE |
|---|---|---|---|---|
| Aug 15 | LEICESTER CITY | D 2-2 | Sheringham, Beckham | 55,052 |
| Aug 22 | West Ham United | D 0-0 | | 26,039 |
| Sep 9 | CHARLTON ATHLETIC | W 4-1 | Solskjaer 2, Yorke 2 | 55,147 |
| Sep 12 | COVENTRY CITY | W 2-0 | Yorke Johnsen | 55,193 |
| Sep 20 | Arsenal | L 0-3 | | 38,142 |
| Sep 24 | LIVERPOOL | W 2-0 | Irwin (pen), Scholes | 55,181 |
| Oct 3 | Southampton | W 3-0 | Yorke, Cole, Cruyff | 15,251 |
| Oct 17 | WIMBLEDON | W 5-1 | Cole 2, Giggs, Beckham, Yorke | 55,265 |
| Oct 24 | Derby County | D 1-1 | Cruyff | 30,867 |
| Oct 31 | Everton | W 4-1 | Yorke, Cole, Blomqvist, Short o.g. | 40,079 |
| Nov 8 | NEWCASTLE UNITED | D 0-0 | | 55,174 |
| Nov 14 | BLACKBURN ROVERS | W 3-2 | Scholes 2, Yorke | 55,198 |
| Nov 21 | Sheffield Wednesday | L 1-3 | Cole | 39,475 |
| Nov 29 | LEEDS UNITED | W 3-2 | Solskjaer, Keane, Butt | 55,172 |
| Dec 5 | Aston Villa | D 1-1 | Scholes | 39,241 |
| Dec 12 | Tottenham Hotspur | D 2-2 | Solskjaer 2 | 36,079 |
| Dec 16 | CHELSEA | D 1-1 | Cole | 55,159 |
| Dec 19 | MIDDLESBROUGH | L 2-3 | Butt, Scholes | 55,152 |
| Dec 26 | NOTTINGHAM FOREST | W 3-0 | Johnsen 2, Giggs | 55,216 |
| Dec 29 | Chelsea | D 0-0 | | 34,741 |
| Jan 10 | WEST HAM UNITED | W 4-1 | Cole 2, Yorke, Solskjaer | 55,180 |
| Jan 16 | Leicester City | W 6-2 | Yorke 3, Cole 2, Stam | 22,091 |
| Jan 31 | Charlton Athletic | W 1-0 | Yorke | 20,043 |
| Feb 3 | DERBY COUNTY | W 1-0 | Yorke | 55,174 |
| Feb 6 | Nottingham Forest | W 8-1 | Yorke 2, Cole 2, Solskjaer 4 | 30,025 |
| Feb 17 | ARSENAL | D 1-1 | Cole | 55,171 |
| Feb 20 | Coventry City | W 1-0 | Giggs | 22,596 |
| Feb 27 | SOUTHAMPTON | W 2-1 | Keane, Yorke | 55,316 |
| Mar 13 | Newcastle United | W 2-1 | Cole 2 | 36,776 |
| Mar 21 | EVERTON | W 3-1 | Solskjaer, Neville G., Beckham | 55,182 |
| Apr 3 | Wimbledon | D 1-1 | Beckham | 26,121 |
| Apr 17 | SHEFFIELD WEDNESDAY | W 3-0 | Solskjaer, Sheringham, Scholes | 55,270 |
| Apr 25 | Leeds United | D 1-1 | Cole | 40,255 |
| May 1 | ASTON VILLA | W 2-1 | Beckham, Watson o.g. | 55,189 |
| May 5 | Liverpool | D 2-2 | Yorke, Irwin (pen) | 44,702 |
| May 9 | Middlesbrough | W 1-0 | Yorke | 34,665 |
| May 12 | Blackburn Rovers | D 0-0 | | 30,436 |
| May 16 | TOTTENHAM HOTSPUR | W 2-1 | Beckham, Cole | 55,189 |

## FA Cup

| | | | | | |
|---|---|---|---|---|---|
| Jan 3 | MIDDLESBROUGH | (Rd3) | W 3-1 | Cole, Irwin (pen), Giggs | 52,232 |
| Jan 24 | LIVERPOOL | (Rd4) | W 2-1 | Yorke, Solskjaer | 54,591 |
| Feb 14 | FULHAM | (Rd5) | W 1-0 | Cole | 54,798 |
| Mar 7 | CHELSEA | (Rd6) | D 0-0 | | 54,587 |
| Mar 10 | Chelsea | (R) | W 2-0 | Yorke 2 | 33,075 |
| Apr 11 | Arsenal | (SF) | D 0-0* | | 39,217 |
| Apr 14 | Arsenal | (R) | W 2-1* | Beckham, Giggs | 30,223 |
| May 22 | Newcastle United | (F) | W 2-0 | Sheringham, Scholes | 79,101 |

*After extra-time.

## League Cup

| | | | | | |
|---|---|---|---|---|---|
| Oct 28 | BURY | (Rd3) | W 2-0 | Solskjaer, Nevland | 52,495 |
| Nov 11 | NOTTINGHAM FOREST | (Rd4) | W 2-1 | Solskjaer 2 | 37,237 |
| Dec 2 | Tottenham Hotspur | (Rd5) | L 1-3 | Sheringham | 35,702 |

## European Champions League

| | | | | | |
|---|---|---|---|---|---|
| Aug 12 | LKS LODZ | (2ndQ/1L) | W 2-0 | Giggs, Cole | 50,906 |
| Aug 26 | LKS Lodz | (2ndQ/2L) | D 0-0 | | 8,000 |
| Sep 18 | BARCELONA | (Grp D) | D 3-3 | Giggs, Scholes, Beckham | 53,601 |
| Sep 30 | Bayern Munich | (Grp D) | D 2-2 | Yorke, Scholes | 75,000 |
| Oct 21 | Brøndby | (Grp D) | W 6-2 | Giggs 2, Cole, Keane, Yorke, Solskjaer | 40,315 |
| Nov 4 | BRØNDBY | (Grp D) | W 5-0 | Beckham, Cole, Neville P., Yorke, Scholes | 53,250 |
| Nov 25 | Barcelona | (Grp D) | D 3-3 | Yorke 2, Cole | 54,213 |
| Dec 9 | BAYERN MUNICH | (Grp D) | D 1-1 | Keane | 54,434 |
| Mar 3 | INTERNAZIONALE | (QF/1L) | W 2-0 | Yorke 2 | 54,430 |
| Mar 17 | Internazionale | (QF/2L) | D 1-1 | Scholes | 79,528 |
| Apr 7 | JUVENTUS | (SF/1L) | D 1-1 | Giggs | 54,487 |
| Apr 21 | Juventus | (SF/2L) | W 3-2 | Keane, Yorke, Cole | 60,806 |
| May 26 | Bayern Munich** | (F) | W 2-1 | Sheringham, Solskjaer | 90,245 |

**Played at Nou Camp, Barcelona, Spain.

## FA Charity Shield

| | | | | |
|---|---|---|---|---|
| Aug 9 | Arsenal† | L 0-3 | | 67,342 |

†Played at Wembley, London.

## League & Cup Appearances

| PLAYER | LEAGUE | CUP COMPETITION | | | OTHER | TOTAL |
|---|---|---|---|---|---|---|
| | | FA CUP | LC | ECL | | |
| Beckham | 33 (1) | 7 | 0 (1) | 12 | 1 | 53 (2) |
| Berg | 10 (6) | 5 | 3 | 3 (1) | 0 (1) | 21 (8) |
| Blomqvist | 20 (5) | 3 (2) | 0 (1) | 6 (1) | | 29 (8) |
| Brown | 11 (3) | 2 | 0 (1) | 3 (1) | | 16 (5) |
| Butt | 22 (9) | 5 | 2 | 4 (4) | 1 | 34 (13) |
| Clegg | | | 3 | | | 3 |
| Cole | 26 (6) | 6 (1) | | 10 | 1 | 43 (7) |
| Cruyff | 0 (5) | | 2 | 0 (3) | 0 (1) | 2 (9) |
| Curtis | 1 (3) | | 3 | | | 4 (3) |
| Giggs | 20 (4) | 5 (1) | 1 | 9 | 1 | 36 (5) |
| Greening | 0 (3) | 0 (1) | 3 | | | 3 (4) |
| Irwin | 26 (3) | 6 | | 12 | 1 | 45 (3) |
| Johnsen | 19 (3) | 3 (2) | 1 | 6 (2) | 1 | 30 (7) |
| Keane | 33 (2) | 7 | | 12 | 1 | 53 (2) |
| May | 4 (2) | 1 | 2 | | | 7 (2) |
| Mulryne | | | 2 | | | 0 2 |
| Neville G. | 34 | 7 | | 12 | 1 | 54 |
| Neville P. | 19 (9) | 4 (3) | 2 | 4 (2) | 0 (1) | 29 (15) |
| Nevland | | | 0 (1) | | | 0 (1) |
| Notman | | | 0 (1) | | | 0 (1) |
| Schmeichel | 34 | 8 | | 13 | 1 | 56 |
| Scholes | 24 (7) | 3 (3) | 0 (1) | 10 (2) | 1 | 38 (13) |
| Sheringham | 7 (10) | 1 (3) | 1 | 2 (2) | 0 (1) | 11 (16) |
| Solskjaer | 9 (10) | 4 (4) | 3 | 1 (5) | 0 (1) | 17 (20) |
| Stam | 30 | 6 (1) | | 13 | 1 | 50 (1) |
| van der Gouw | 4 (1) | | 3 | | | 7 (1) |
| Yorke | 32 | 5 (3) | | 11 | | 48 (3) |
| Wallwork | | | 0 (1) | | | 0 (1) |
| Wilson | | | 2 | 0 (1) | | 2 (1) |

## Goalscorers

| PLAYER | LEAGUE | CUP COMPETITION | | | OTHER | TOTAL |
|---|---|---|---|---|---|---|
| | | FA CUP | LC | ECL | | |
| Yorke | 18 | 3 | | 8 | | 29 |
| Cole | 17 | 2 | | 5 | | 24 |
| Solskjaer | 12 | 1 | 3 | 2 | | 18 |
| Scholes | 6 | 1 | | 4 | | 11 |
| Giggs | 3 | 2 | | 5 | | 10 |
| Beckham | 6 | 1 | | 2 | | 9 |
| Keane | 2 | | | 3 | | 5 |
| Sheringham | 2 | 1 | 1 | 1 | | 5 |
| Johnsen | 3 | | | | | 3 |
| Irwin | 2 | 1 | | | | 3 |
| Butt | 2 | | | | | 2 |
| Cruyff | 2 | | | | | 2 |
| Blomqvist | 1 | | | | | 1 |
| Neville G. | 1 | | | | | 1 |
| Neville P. | | | | 1 | | 1 |
| Nevland | | | 1 | | | 1 |
| Stam | 1 | | | | | 1 |
| Opps' o.gs. | 2 | | | | | 2 |

### Fact File

United win the treble – so much for the critics.

### Final Premier League Table

| | | P | W | D | L | F | A | PTS |
|---|---|---|---|---|---|---|---|---|
| 1 | MANCHESTER UNITED | 38 | 22 | 13 | 3 | 80 | 37 | 79 |
| 2 | ARSENAL | 38 | 22 | 12 | 4 | 59 | 17 | 78 |
| 3 | CHELSEA | 38 | 20 | 15 | 3 | 57 | 30 | 67 |
| 4 | LEEDS UNITED | 38 | 18 | 13 | 7 | 62 | 34 | 67 |
| 5 | WEST HAM UNITED | 38 | 16 | 9 | 13 | 46 | 53 | 57 |
| 6 | ASTON VILLA | 38 | 15 | 10 | 13 | 51 | 46 | 55 |
| 7 | LIVERPOOL | 38 | 15 | 9 | 14 | 68 | 49 | 54 |
| 8 | DERBY COUNTY | 38 | 13 | 13 | 12 | 40 | 45 | 52 |
| 9 | MIDDLESBROUGH | 38 | 12 | 15 | 11 | 48 | 54 | 51 |
| 10 | LEICESTER CITY | 38 | 12 | 13 | 13 | 40 | 46 | 49 |
| 11 | TOTTENHAM HOTSPUR | 38 | 11 | 14 | 13 | 47 | 50 | 47 |
| 12 | SHEFFIELD WEDNESDAY | 38 | 13 | 7 | 18 | 41 | 42 | 46 |
| 13 | NEWCASTLE UNITED | 38 | 11 | 13 | 14 | 48 | 54 | 46 |
| 14 | EVERTON | 38 | 11 | 10 | 17 | 42 | 47 | 43 |
| 15 | COVENTRY CITY | 38 | 11 | 9 | 18 | 39 | 51 | 42 |
| 16 | WIMBLEDON | 38 | 10 | 12 | 16 | 40 | 63 | 42 |
| 17 | SOUTHAMPTON | 38 | 11 | 8 | 19 | 37 | 64 | 41 |
| 18 | CHARLTON ATHLETIC | 38 | 8 | 12 | 18 | 41 | 56 | 36 |
| 19 | BLACKBURN ROVERS | 38 | 7 | 14 | 17 | 38 | 52 | 35 |
| 20 | NOTTINGHAM FOREST | 38 | 7 | 9 | 22 | 35 | 69 | 30 |

# Season 1999-2000

## FA Premier League

| DATE | OPPONENTS | SCORE | GOALSCORERS | ATTENDANCE |
|---|---|---|---|---|
| Aug 8 | Everton | D 1-1 | Yorke | 39,141 |
| Aug 11 | SHEFFIELD WEDNESDAY | W 4-0 | Scholes, Yorke, Cole, Solskjaer | 54,941 |
| Aug 14 | LEEDS UNITED | W 2-0 | Yorke 2 | 55,187 |
| Aug 22 | Arsenal | W 2-1 | Keane 2 | 38,147 |
| Aug 25 | Coventry City | W 2-1 | Scholes, Yorke | 22,024 |
| Aug 30 | NEWCASTLE UNITED | W 5-1 | Cole 4, Giggs | 55,190 |
| Sep 11 | Liverpool | W 3-2 | Cole, Carragher 2 o.g. | 44,929 |
| Sep 18 | WIMBLEDON | D 1-1 | Cruyff | 55,189 |
| Sep 25 | SOUTHAMPTON | D 3-3 | Yorke 2, Sheringham | 55,249 |
| Oct 3 | Chelsea | L 0-5 | | 34,909 |
| Oct 16 | WATFORD | W 4-1 | Cole 2, Yorke, Irwin (pen) | 55,188 |
| Oct 23 | Tottenham Hotspur | L 1-3 | Giggs | 36,072 |
| Oct 30 | ASTON VILLA | W 3-0 | Scholes, Cole, Keane | 55,211 |
| Nov 6 | LEICESTER CITY | W 2-0 | Cole 2 | 55,191 |
| Nov 20 | Derby County | W 2-1 | Butt, Cole | 33,370 |
| Dec 4 | EVERTON | W 5-1 | Solskjaer 4, Irwin (pen) | 55,193 |
| Dec 18 | West Ham United | W 4-2 | Yorke 2, Giggs 2 | 26,037 |
| Dec 26 | BRADFORD CITY | W 4-0 | Fortune, Yorke, Cole, Keane | 55,188 |
| Dec 28 | Sunderland | D 2-2 | Keane, Butt | 42,026 |
| Jan 24 | ARSENAL | D 1-1 | Sheringham | 58,293 |
| Jan 29 | MIDDLESBROUGH | W 1-0 | Beckham | 61,267 |
| Feb 2 | Sheffield Wednesday | W 1-0 | Sheringham | 39,640 |
| Feb 5 | COVENTRY CITY | W 3-2 | Cole 2, Scholes | 61,380 |
| Feb 12 | Newcastle United | L 0-3 | | 36,470 |
| Feb 20 | Leeds United | W 1-0 | Cole | 40,160 |
| Feb 26 | Wimbledon | D 2-2 | Cruyff, Cole | 26,129 |
| Mar 4 | LIVERPOOL | D 1-1 | Solskjaer | 61,592 |
| Mar 11 | DERBY COUNTY | W 3-1 | Yorke 3 | 61,619 |
| Mar 18 | Leicester City | W 2-0 | Beckham, Yorke | 22,170 |
| Mar 25 | Bradford City | W 4-0 | Yorke 2, Scholes, Beckham | 18,276 |
| Apr 1 | WEST HAM UNITED | W 7-1 | Scholes 3 (1 pen), Irwin, Cole, Beckham, Solskjaer | 61,611 |
| Apr 10 | Middlesbrough | W 4-3 | Giggs, Cole, Scholes, Fortune | 34,775 |
| Apr 15 | SUNDERLAND | W 4-0 | Solskjaer 2, Butt, Berg | 61,612 |
| Apr 22 | Southampton | W 3-1 | Beckham, Solskjaer, Benali o.g. | 15,245 |
| Apr 24 | CHELSEA | W 3-2 | Yorke 2, Solskjaer | 61,593 |
| Apr 29 | Watford | W 3-2 | Yorke, Giggs, Cruyff | 20,250 |
| May 6 | TOTTENHAM HOTSPUR | W 3-1 | Solskjaer, Beckham, Sheringham | 61,629 |
| May 14 | Aston Villa | W 1-0 | Sheringham | 39,217 |

## League Cup

| | | | | |
|---|---|---|---|---|
| Oct 13 | Aston Villa | L 0-3 | | 33,815 |

## European Champions League

| | | | | | |
|---|---|---|---|---|---|
| Sep 14 | CROATIA ZAGREB | (Grp D) | D 0-0 | | 53,250 |
| Sep 22 | Sturm Graz | (Grp D) | W 3-0 | Keane, Yorke, Cole | 16,480 |
| Sep 29 | OLYMPIQUE MARSEILLE | (Grp D) | W2-1 | Cole, Scholes | 53,993 |
| Oct 19 | Olympique Marseille | (Grp D) | L 0-1 | | 56,879 |
| Oct 27 | Croatia Zagreb | (Grp D) | W 2-1 | Beckham, Keane | 27,500 |
| Nov 2 | STURM GRAZ | (Grp D) | W 2-1 | Solskjaer, Keane | 53,745 |
| Nov 23 | Fiorentina | (Grp B) | L 0-2 | | 36,002 |
| Dec 8 | VALENCIA | (Grp B) | W 3-0 | Keane, Scholes, Solskjaer | 54,606 |
| Mar 1 | GIRONDINS BORDEAUX | (Grp B) | W 2-0 | Giggs, Sheringham | 59,786 |
| Mar 7 | Girondins Bordeaux | (Grp B) | W 2-1 | Keane, Solskjaer | 30,130 |
| Mar 15 | FIORENTINA | (Grp B) | W 3-1 | Cole, Keane, Yorke | 59,926 |
| Mar 21 | Valencia | (Grp B) | D 0-0 | | 40,419 |
| Apr 4 | Real Madrid | (QF/1L) | D 0-0 | | 64,119 |
| Apr 19 | REAL MADRID | (QF/2L) | L 2-3 | Beckham, Scholes (pen) | 59,178 |

## FIFA Club World Championship**

| | | | | |
|---|---|---|---|---|
| Jan 6 | Rayos Del Necaxa* | D 1-1 | Yorke | 50,000 |
| Jan 8 | Vasco Da Gama* | L 1-3 | Butt | 73,000 |
| Jan 11 | South Melbourne* | W 2-0 | Fortune 2 | 25,000 |

*Played at Maracana Stadium, Rio de Janeiro, Brazil.

**United elected to forfeit their place in the FA Cup to play in this competition.

## Inter-Continental Cup

| | | | | |
|---|---|---|---|---|
| Nov 30 | Palmeiras** | W 1-0 | Keane | 53,372 |

**Played at Olympic Stadium, Tokyo, Japan.

## UEFA Super Cup

| | | | | |
|---|---|---|---|---|
| Aug 27 | Lazio† | L 0-1 | | 14,461 |

†Played at Stade Louis II Stadium, Monaco, France.

## FA Charity Shield

| | | | | |
|---|---|---|---|---|
| Aug 1 | Arsenal†† | L 1-2 | Yorke | 70,185 |

††Played at Wembley, London.

## League & Cup Appearances

| PLAYER | LEAGUE | CUP COMPETITION | | | OTHER | TOTAL |
|---|---|---|---|---|---|---|
| | | FA CUP | LC | ECL | | |
| Beckham | 30 (1) | | | 12 | 4 (1) | 46 (2) |
| Berg | 16 (6) | | | 11 (1) | 3 | 30 (7) |
| Bosnich | 23 | | 1 | 7 | 4 | 35 |
| Butt | 21 (11) | | | 4 (2) | 4 | 29 (13) |
| Chadwick | | | 1 | | | 1 |
| Clegg | 0 (2) | | 1 | 1 (1) | | 2 (3) |
| Cole | 23 (5) | | | 13 | 4 | 40 (5) |
| Cruyff | 1 (7) | | 1 | 1 (3) | 2 (2) | 5 (12) |
| Culkin | 0 (1) | | | | | 0 (1) |
| Curtis | 0 (1) | | 1 | | 0 (1) | 1 (2) |
| Fortune | 4 (2) | | | 1 (3) | 1 (1) | 6 (6) |
| Giggs | 30 | | | 11 | 3 | 44 |
| Greening | 1 (3) | | 1 | 1 (1) | 1 (1) | 4 (5) |
| Healy | | | 0 (1) | | | 0 (1) |
| Higginbotham | 2 (1) | | 1 | 0 (1) | 1 | 4 (2) |
| Irwin | 25 | | | 13 | 4 | 42 |
| Johnsen | 2 (1) | | | 0 | | 2 (1) |
| Keane | 28 (1) | | | 12 | 4 | 44 (1) |
| May | 0 (1) | | | 1 | 0 (1) | 1 (2) |
| Neville G | 22 | | | 9 | 4 | 35 |
| Neville P | 25 (4) | | | 6 (3) | 4 (1) | 35 (8) |
| O'Shea | | | 1 | | | 1 |
| Rachubka | | | | | 0 (1) | 0 (1) |
| Scholes | 27 (4) | | | 11 | 3 | 41 (4) |
| Sheringham | 15 (12) | | | 3 (6) | 1 (4) | 19 (22) |
| Silvestre | 30 (1) | | | 2 (2) | 3 | 35 (3) |
| Solskjaer | 15 (13) | | 1 | 4 (7) | 4 (2) | 24 (22) |
| Stam | 33 | | | 13 | 5 | 51 |
| Taibi | 4 | | | | | 4 |
| Twiss | | | 1 | | | 1 |
| van der Gouw | 11 (3) | | | 7 | 2 | 20 (3) |
| Wallwork | 0 (5) | | 1 | 1 | 1 | 3 (5) |
| Wellens | | | 0 (1) | | | 0 (1) |
| Wilson | 1 (2) | | | 2 (1) | 1 | 4 (3) |
| Yorke | 29 (3) | | | 9 (2) | 3 (1) | 41 (6) |

## Goalscorers

| PLAYER | LEAGUE | CUP COMPETITION | | | OTHER | TOTAL |
|---|---|---|---|---|---|---|
| | | FA CUP | LC | ECL | | |
| Yorke | 20 | | | 2 | 2 | 22 |
| Cole | 19 | | | 3 | | 22 |
| Solskjaer | 12 | | | 3 | | 15 |
| Keane | 5 | | | 6 | 1 | 12 |
| Scholes | 9 | | | 3 | | 12 |
| Beckham | 6 | | | 2 | | 8 |
| Giggs | 6 | | | 1 | | 7 |
| Sheringham | 5 | | | 1 | | 6 |
| Butt | 3 | | | | 1 | 4 |
| Fortune | 2 | | | | 2 | 4 |
| Cruyff | 3 | | | | | 3 |
| Irwin | 3 | | | | | 3 |
| Berg | 1 | | | | | 1 |
| Opps' o.gs. | 3 | | | | | 3 |

## Final Premier League Table

| | | P | W | D | L | F | A | Pts |
|---|---|---|---|---|---|---|---|---|
| 1 | Manchester United | 38 | 28 | 7 | 3 | 97 | 45 | 91 |
| 2 | Arsenal | 38 | 22 | 7 | 9 | 73 | 43 | 73 |
| 3 | Leeds United | 38 | 21 | 6 | 11 | 58 | 43 | 69 |
| 4 | Liverpool | 38 | 19 | 10 | 9 | 53 | 34 | 67 |
| 5 | Chelsea | 38 | 18 | 11 | 9 | 53 | 34 | 65 |
| 6 | Aston Villa | 38 | 15 | 13 | 10 | 46 | 35 | 58 |
| 7 | Sunderland | 38 | 16 | 10 | 12 | 57 | 56 | 58 |
| 8 | Leicester City | 38 | 16 | 7 | 15 | 55 | 55 | 55 |
| 9 | West Ham United | 38 | 15 | 10 | 13 | 52 | 53 | 55 |
| 10 | Tottenham Hotspur | 38 | 15 | 8 | 15 | 57 | 49 | 53 |
| 11 | Newcastle United | 38 | 14 | 10 | 14 | 63 | 54 | 52 |
| 12 | Middlesbrough | 38 | 14 | 10 | 14 | 46 | 52 | 52 |
| 13 | Everton | 38 | 12 | 14 | 12 | 59 | 49 | 50 |
| 14 | Coventry City | 38 | 12 | 8 | 18 | 47 | 54 | 44 |
| 15 | Southampton | 38 | 12 | 8 | 18 | 45 | 62 | 44 |
| 16 | Derby County | 38 | 9 | 11 | 18 | 44 | 57 | 38 |
| 17 | Bradford City | 38 | 9 | 9 | 20 | 38 | 68 | 36 |
| 18 | Wimbledon | 38 | 7 | 12 | 19 | 46 | 74 | 33 |
| 19 | Sheffield Wednesday | 38 | 8 | 7 | 23 | 38 | 70 | 31 |
| 20 | Watford | 38 | 6 | 6 | 26 | 35 | 77 | 24 |

# Season 2000-01

## FA Premier League

| DATE | OPPONENTS | SCORE | GOALSCORERS | ATTENDANCE |
|---|---|---|---|---|
| Aug 20 | NEWCASTLE UNITED | W 2-0 | Johnsen, Cole | 67,477 |
| Aug 22 | Ipswich Town | D 1-1 | Beckham | 22,007 |
| Aug 26 | West Ham United | D 2-2 | Beckham, Cole | 25,998 |
| Sep 5 | BRADFORD CITY | W 6-0 | Fortune 2, Sheringham 2, Cole, Beckham | 67,447 |
| Sep 9 | SUNDERLAND | W 3-0 | Scholes 2, Sheringham | 67,503 |
| Sep 16 | Everton | W 3-1 | Butt, Giggs, Solskjaer | 38,541 |
| Sep 23 | CHELSEA | D 3-3 | Scholes, Sheringham, Beckham | 67,568 |
| Oct 1 | Arsenal | L 0-1 | | 38,146 |
| Oct 14 | Leicester City | W 3-0 | Sheringham 2, Solskjaer | 22,132 |
| Oct 21 | LEEDS UNITED | W 3-0 | Yorke, Beckham, Jones o.g. | 67,523 |
| Oct 28 | SOUTHAMPTON | W 5-0 | Cole 2, Sheringham 3 | 67,581 |
| Nov 4 | Coventry City | W 2-1 | Cole, Beckham | 21,079 |
| Nov 11 | MIDDLESBROUGH | W 2-1 | Butt, Sheringham | 67,576 |
| Nov 18 | Manchester City | W 1-0 | Beckham | 34,429 |
| Nov 25 | Derby County | W 3-0 | Sheringham, Butt, Yorke | 32,910 |
| Dec 2 | TOTTENHAM HOTSPUR | W 2-0 | Scholes, Solskjaer | 67,583 |
| Dec 9 | Charlton Athletic | D 3-3 | Giggs, Solskjaer, Keane | 20,043 |
| Dec 17 | LIVERPOOL | L 0-1 | | 67,533 |
| Dec 23 | IPSWICH TOWN | W 2-0 | Solskjaer 2 | 67,597 |
| Dec 26 | Aston Villa | W 1-0 | Solskjaer | 40,889 |
| Dec 30 | Newcastle United | D 1-1 | Beckham (pen) | 52,134 |
| Jan 1 | WEST HAM UNITED | W 3-1 | Solskjaer, Yorke, Pearce o.g. | 67,603 |
| Jan 13 | Bradford City | W 3-0 | Sheringham, Giggs, Chadwick | 20,551 |
| Jan 20 | ASTON VILLA | W 2-0 | Neville G., Sheringham | 67,533 |
| Jan 31 | Sunderland | W 1-0 | Cole | 48,260 |
| Feb 3 | EVERTON | W 1-0 | Watson o.g. | 67,528 |
| Feb 10 | Chelsea | D 1-1 | Cole | 34,960 |
| Feb 25 | ARSENAL | W 6-1 | Yorke 3, Keane, Solskjaer, Sheringham | 67,535 |
| Mar 3 | Leeds United | D 1-1 | Chadwick | 40,055 |
| Mar 17 | LEICESTER CITY | W 2-0 | Yorke, Silvestre | 67,516 |
| Mar 31 | Liverpool | L 0-2 | | 44,806 |
| Apr 10 | CHARLTON ATHLETIC | W 2-1 | Cole, Solskjaer | 67,505 |
| Apr 14 | COVENTRY CITY | W 4-2 | Yorke 2, Giggs, Scholes | 67,637 |
| Apr 21 | MANCHESTER CITY | D 1-1 | Sheringham (pen) | 67,535 |
| Apr 28 | Middlesbrough | W 2-0 | Neville P., Beckham, | 34,417 |
| May 5 | DERBY COUNTY | L 0-1 | | 67,526 |
| May 13 | Southampton | L 1-2 | Giggs | 15,526 |
| May 19 | Tottenham Hotspur | L 1-3 | Scholes | 36,072 |

## FA Cup

| | | | | | |
|---|---|---|---|---|---|
| Jan 7 | Fulham | (Rd3) | W 2-1 | Solskjaer, Sheringham | 19,178 |
| Jan 28 | WEST HAM UNITED | (Rd4) | L 0-1 | | 67,029 |

## League Cup

| | | | | | |
|---|---|---|---|---|---|
| Oct 31 | Watford | (Rd3) | W 3-0 | Solskjaer 2, Yorke | 18,871 |
| Nov 28 | Sunderland | (Rd4) | L 1-2* | Yorke | 47,543 |

*After extra-time.

## European Champions League

| | | | | | |
|---|---|---|---|---|---|
| Sep 13 | ANDERLECHT | (Grp G) | W 5-1 | Cole 3, Irwin (pen), Sheringham | 62,749 |
| Sep 19 | Dynamo Kiev | (Grp G) | D 0-0 | | 65,000 |
| Sep 26 | PSV Eindhoven | (Grp G) | L 1-3 | Scholes (pen) | 29,500 |
| Oct 18 | PSV EINDHOVEN | (Grp G) | W 3-1 | Sheringham, Scholes, Yorke | 63,313 |
| Oct 24 | Anderlecht | (Grp G) | L 1-2 | Irwin (pen) | 22,503 |
| Nov 8 | DYNAMO KIEV | (Grp G) | W 1-0 | Sheringham | 66,776 |
| Nov 21 | PANATHINAIKOS | (Grp A) | W 3-1 | Scholes 2, Sheringham | 65,024 |
| Dec 6 | Sturm Graz | (Grp A) | W 2-0 | Scholes, Giggs | 16,500 |
| Feb 14 | Valencia | (Grp A) | D 0-0 | | 49,541 |
| Feb 20 | VALENCIA | (Grp A) | D 1-1 | Cole | 66,715 |
| Mar 7 | Panathinaikos | (Grp A) | D 1-1 | Scholes | 27,231 |
| Mar 13 | STURM GRAZ | (Grp A) | W 3-0 | Butt, Sheringham, Keane | 66,404 |
| Apr 3 | BAYERN MUNICH | (QF/1L) | L 0-1 | | 66,584 |
| Apr 18 | Bayern Munich | (QF/2L) | L 1-2 | Giggs | 59,178 |

## FA Charity Shield

| | | | | |
|---|---|---|---|---|
| Aug 13 | Chelsea** | L 0-2 | | 65,148 |

**Played at Wembley, London.

**MANAGER:** Sir Alex Ferguson
**MOST APPEARANCES:** Gary Neville 49
**TOP SCORER:** Teddy Sheringham 21 (15 League)
**BIGGEST WIN:** 6-0 v Bradford City, 5 September 2000, League
**HIGHEST ATTENDANCE:** 67,637 v Coventry City, 14 April 2001, League

## League & Cup Appearances

| PLAYER | LEAGUE | CUP COMPETITION FA CUP | LC | ECL | OTHER | TOTAL |
|---|---|---|---|---|---|---|
| Barthez | 30 | 1 | | 12 | 1 | 44 |
| Beckham | 29 (2) | 2 | | 11 (1) | 1 | 43 (3) |
| Berg | 0 (1) | | | | | 0 (1) |
| Brown | 25 (3) | 1 | 1 | 9 (2) | | 36 (5) |
| Butt | 24 (4) | 2 | | 8 (3) | | 34 (7) |
| Chadwick | 6 (10) | 0 (1) | 2 | 1 (2) | | 9 (13) |
| Clegg | | | 2 | | | 2 |
| Cole | 15 (4) | 1 | | 10 | 0 (1) | 26 (4) |
| Djordjic | 0 (1) | | | | | 0 (1) |
| Fortune | 6 (1) | | 2 | 0 (1) | 0 (1) | 8 (2) |
| Giggs | 24 (7) | 2 | | 9 (2) | 1 | 36 (9) |
| Goram | 2 | | | | | 2 |
| Greening | 3 (4) | | 2 | 1 (1) | | 6 (5) |
| Healy | 0 (1) | | 0 (1) | | | 0 (2) |
| Irwin | 20 (1) | 1 | | 7 | 1 | 29 (1) |
| Johnsen | 11 | | 1 | 4 | 1 | 17 |
| Keane | 28 | 2 | | 13 | 1 | 44 |
| May | 1 (1) | | | | | 1 (1) |
| Neville G. | 32 | 2 | | 14 | 1 | 49 |
| Neville P. | 24 (5) | 1 | 2 | 4 (2) | | 31 (7) |
| O'Shea | | | 2 | | | 2 |
| Rachubka | 1 | | 0 (1) | | 1 (1) | |
| Scholes | 28 (4) | | | 12 | 1 | 41 (4) |
| Sheringham | 23 (6) | 1 (1) | | 8 (3) | 1 | 33 (10) |
| Silvestre | 25 (5) | 2 | | 13 (1) | 1 | 41 (6) |
| Solskjaer | 19 (12) | 1 (1) | 2 | 3 (8) | 1 | 26 (21) |
| Stam | 15 | 1 | | 6 | 0 (1) | 22 (1) |
| Stewart | 3 | | 0 (2) | | | 3 (2) |
| van der Gouw | 5 (5) | 1 | 2 | 2 | | 10 (5) |
| Wallwork | 4 (8) | 0 (1) | 2 | 0 (1) | | 6 (10) |
| Webber | | | 0 (1) | | | 0 (1) |
| Yorke | 15 (7) | 1 (1) | 2 | 7 (4) | 0 (1) | 25 (13) |

## Goalscorers

| PLAYER | LEAGUE | CUP COMPETITION FA CUP | LC | ECL | OTHER | TOTAL |
|---|---|---|---|---|---|---|
| Sheringham | 15 | 1 | | 5 | | 21 |
| Solskjaer | 10 | 1 | 2 | | | 13 |
| Cole | 9 | | | 4 | | 13 |
| Yorke | 9 | | 2 | 1 | | 12 |
| Scholes | 6 | | | 6 | | 12 |
| Beckham | 9 | | | | | 9 |
| Giggs | 5 | | | 2 | | 7 |
| Butt | 3 | | | 1 | | 4 |
| Keane | 2 | | | 1 | | 3 |
| Chadwick | 2 | | | | | 2 |
| Fortune | 2 | | | | | 2 |
| Irwin | | | | 2 | | 2 |
| Johnsen | 1 | | | | | 1 |
| Neville G. | 1 | | | | | 1 |
| Neville P. | 1 | | | | | 1 |
| Silvestre | 1 | | | | | 1 |
| Opps' o.gs. | 3 | | | | | 3 |

## Final Premier League Table

| | P | W | D | L | F | A | Pts |
|---|---|---|---|---|---|---|---|
| 1 Manchester United | 38 | 24 | 8 | 6 | 79 | 31 | 80 |
| 2 Arsenal | 38 | 20 | 10 | 8 | 63 | 38 | 70 |
| 3 Liverpool | 38 | 20 | 9 | 9 | 71 | 39 | 69 |
| 4 Leeds United | 38 | 20 | 8 | 10 | 64 | 43 | 68 |
| 5 Ipswich Town | 38 | 20 | 6 | 12 | 57 | 42 | 66 |
| 6 Chelsea | 38 | 17 | 10 | 11 | 68 | 45 | 61 |
| 7 Sunderland | 38 | 15 | 12 | 11 | 46 | 41 | 57 |
| 8 Aston Villa | 38 | 13 | 15 | 10 | 46 | 43 | 54 |
| 9 Charlton Athletic | 38 | 14 | 10 | 14 | 50 | 57 | 52 |
| 10 Southampton | 38 | 14 | 10 | 14 | 40 | 48 | 52 |
| 11 Newcastle United | 38 | 14 | 9 | 15 | 44 | 50 | 51 |
| 12 Tottenham Hotspur | 38 | 13 | 10 | 15 | 47 | 54 | 49 |
| 13 Leicester City | 38 | 14 | 6 | 18 | 39 | 51 | 48 |
| 14 Middlesbrough | 38 | 9 | 15 | 14 | 44 | 44 | 42 |
| 15 West Ham United | 38 | 10 | 12 | 16 | 45 | 50 | 42 |
| 16 Everton | 38 | 11 | 9 | 18 | 45 | 59 | 42 |
| 17 Derby County | 38 | 10 | 12 | 16 | 37 | 59 | 42 |
| 18 Manchester City | 38 | 8 | 10 | 20 | 41 | 65 | 34 |
| 19 Coventry City | 38 | 8 | 10 | 20 | 36 | 63 | 34 |
| 20 Bradford City | 38 | 5 | 11 | 22 | 30 | 70 | 26 |

# Season 2001-02

## FA Premier League

| DATE | OPPONENTS | SCORE | GOALSCORERS | ATTENDANCE |
|---|---|---|---|---|
| Aug 19 | FULHAM | W 3-2 | van Nistelrooy 2, Beckham | 67,534 |
| Aug 22 | Blackburn Rovers | D 2-2 | Giggs, Beckham | 29,836 |
| Aug 26 | Aston Villa | D 1-1 | Alpay o.g. | 42,632 |
| Sep 8 | EVERTON | W 4-1 | Veron, Cole, Fortune, Beckham | 67,534 |
| Sep 15 | Newcastle United | L 3-4 | van Nistelrooy, Giggs, Veron | 52,056 |
| Sep 22 | IPSWICH TOWN | W 4-0 | Solskjaer 2, Johnsen, Cole | 67,551 |
| Sep 29 | Tottenham Hotspur | W 5-3 | Cole, Blanc, van Nistelrooy, Veron, Beckham | 36,038 |
| Oct 13 | Sunderland | W 3-1 | Giggs, Cole, Varga o.g. | 48,305 |
| Oct 20 | BOLTON WANDERERS | L 1-2 | Veron | 67,559 |
| Oct 27 | LEEDS UNITED | D 1-1 | Solskjaer | 67,555 |
| Nov 4 | Liverpool | L 1-3 | Beckham | 44,361 |
| Nov 17 | LEICESTER CITY | W 2-0 | van Nistelrooy, Yorke | 67,651 |
| Nov 25 | Arsenal | L 1-3 | Scholes | 38,174 |
| Dec 1 | CHELSEA | L 0-3 | | 67,544 |
| Dec 8 | WEST HAM UNITED | L 0-1 | | 67,582 |
| Dec 12 | DERBY COUNTY | W 5-0 | Solskjaer 2, Keane, van Nistelrooy, Scholes | 67,577 |
| Dec 15 | Middlesbrough | W 1-0 | van Nistelrooy | 34,358 |
| Dec 22 | SOUTHAMPTON | W 6-1 | van Nistelrooy 3, Solskjaer, Keane, Neville P. | 67,638 |
| Dec 26 | Everton | W 2-0 | Giggs, van Nistelrooy | 39,948 |
| Dec 30 | Fulham | W 3-2 | Giggs 2, van Nistelrooy | 21,159 |
| Jan 2 | NEWCASTLE UNITED | W 3-1 | Scholes 2, van Nistelrooy | 67,646 |
| Jan 13 | Southampton | W 3-1 | van Nistelrooy, Beckham, Solskjaer | 31,858 |
| Jan 19 | BLACKBURN ROVERS | W 2-1 | van Nistelrooy (pen), Keane | 67,552 |
| Jan 22 | LIVERPOOL | L 0-1 | | 67,599 |
| Jan 29 | Bolton Wanderers | W 4-0 | Solskjaer 3, van Nistelrooy | 27,350 |
| Feb 2 | SUNDERLAND | W 4-1 | van Nistelrooy 2 (1pen), Neville P., Beckham | 67,587 |
| Feb 10 | Charlton Athletic | W 2-0 | Solskjaer 2 | 26,475 |
| Feb 23 | ASTON VILLA | W 1-0 | van Nistelrooy | 67,592 |
| Mar 3 | Derby County | D 2-2 | Scholes, Veron | 33,041 |
| Mar 6 | TOTTENHAM HOTSPUR | W 4-0 | Beckham 2, van Nistelrooy 2 (1pen | 67,599 |
| Mar 16 | West Ham United | W 5-3 | Beckham 2 (1pen), Butt, Scholes, Solskjaer | 35,281 |
| Mar 23 | MIDDLESBROUGH | L 0-1 | | 67,683 |
| Mar 30 | Leeds United | W 4-3 | Solskjaer 2, Scholes, Giggs | 40,058 |
| Apr 6 | Leicester City | W 1-0 | Solskjaer | 21,447 |
| Apr 30 | Chelsea | W 3-0 | Scholes, van Nistelrooy, Solskjaer | 41,725 |
| Apr 27 | Ipswich Town | W 1-0 | van Nistelrooy | 28,433 |
| May 8 | ARSENAL | L 0-1 | | 67,580 |
| May 11 | CHARLTON ATHLETIC | D 0-0 | | 67,571 |

## FA Cup

| DATE | OPPONENTS | ROUND | SCORE | GOALSCORERS | ATTENDANCE |
|---|---|---|---|---|---|
| Jan 6 | Aston Villa | (Rd3) | W 3-2 | van Nistelrooy 2, Solskjaer | 38,444 |
| Jan 26 | Middlesbrough | (Rd4) | L 0-2 | | 17,624 |

## League Cup

| DATE | OPPONENTS | ROUND | SCORE | GOALSCORERS | ATTENDANCE |
|---|---|---|---|---|---|
| Nov 5 | Arsenal | (Rd3) | L 0-4 | | 30,693 |

## European Champions League

| DATE | OPPONENTS | ROUND | SCORE | GOALSCORERS | ATTENDANCE |
|---|---|---|---|---|---|
| Sep 18 | LILLE | (Grp G) | W 1-0 | Beckham | 64,827 |
| Sep 25 | Deportivo La Coruna | (Grp G) | L 1-2 | Scholes | 33,108 |
| Oct 10 | Olympiakos | (Grp G) | W 2-0 | Beckham, Cole | 73,537 |
| Oct 17 | DEPORTIVO LA CORUNA | (Grp G) | L 2-3 | van Nistelrooy 2 | 65,585 |
| Oct 23 | OLYMPIAKOS | (Grp G) | W 3-0 | Solskjaer, Giggs, van Nistelrooy | 66,769 |
| Oct 31 | Lille | (Grp G) | D 1-1 | Solskjaer | 37,400 |
| Nov 20 | Bayern Munich | (Grp A) | D 1-1 | van Nistelrooy | 59,000 |
| Dec 5 | BOAVISTA | (Grp A) | W 3-0 | van Nistelrooy 2, Blanc | 66,274 |
| Feb 20 | Nantes | (Grp A) | D 1-1 | van Nistelrooy (pen) | 38,285 |
| Feb 26 | NANTES | (Grp A) | W 5-1 | Solskjaer 2, Beckham, Silvestre, van Nistelrooy (pen) | 66,492 |
| Mar 13 | BAYERN MUNICH | (Grp A) | D 0-0 | | 66,818 |
| Mar 19 | Boavista | (Grp A) | W 3-0 | Blanc, Solskjaer, Beckham (pen) | 13,223 |
| Apr 2 | Deportivo La Coruna | (QF/1L) | W 2-0 | Beckham, van Nistelrooy | 32,351 |
| Apr 10 | DEPORTIVO LA CORUNA | (QF/2L) | W 3-2 | Solskjaer 2, Giggs | 65,875 |
| Apr 24 | BAYER 04 LEVERKUSEN | (SF/1L) | D 2-2 | van Nistelrooy (pen), Zivkovic o.g. | 65,534 |
| Apr 30 | Bayer 04 Leverkusen | (SF/2L) | D 1-1 | Keane | 20,605 |

## FA Charity Shield

| DATE | OPPONENTS | SCORE | GOALSCORERS | ATTENDANCE |
|---|---|---|---|---|
| Aug 12 | Liverpool† | L 1-2 | van Nistelrooy | 70,227 |

†Played at Millennium Stadium, Cardiff.

## League & Cup Appearances

| PLAYER | LEAGUE | CUP COMPETITION | | | OTHER | TOTAL |
|---|---|---|---|---|---|---|
| | | FA CUP | LC | ECL | | |
| Barthez | 32 | 1 | | 15 | 1 | 49 |
| Beckham | 23 (5) | 1 | | 13 | 1 | 38 (5) |
| Blanc | 29 | 2 | | 15 | | 46 |
| Brown | 15 (2) | | | 5 (2) | | 20 (4) |
| Butt | 20 (5) | 2 | | 8 (1) | 1 | 31 (6) |
| Carroll | 6 (1) | 1 | 1 | 1 | | 9 (1) |
| Chadwick | 5 (3) | 1 (1) | 1 | | | 7 (4) |
| Clegg | | | 0 (1) | | | 0 (1) |
| Cole | 7 (4) | | | 1 (3) | | 8 (7) |
| Davis | | | 1 | | | 1 |
| Djordjic | | | 1 | | | 1 |
| Forlan | 6 (7) | | | 1 (4) | | 7 (11) |
| Fortune | 8 (6) | | | 3 (2) | | 11 (8) |
| Giggs | 18 (7) | 0 (1) | | 13 | 1 | 32 (8) |
| Irwin | 10 (2) | | | 8 (2) | 1 | 19 (4) |
| Johnsen | 9 (1) | | | 8 (1) | | 17 (2) |
| Keane | 28 | 2 | | 11 (1) | 1 | 42 (1) |
| May | 2 | | | 1 | | 3 |
| Nardiello | | | 0 (1) | | | 0 (1) |
| Neville G. | 31 (3) | 2 | | 14 | 1 | 48 (3) |
| Neville P. | 21 (7) | 2 | 1 | 3 (4) | | 27 (11) |
| O'Shea | 4 (5) | | 1 | 0 (3) | | 5 (8) |
| Roche | | | 1 | | | 1 |
| Scholes | 30 (5) | 2 | | 13 | 1 | 46 (5) |
| Silvestre | 31 (4) | 2 | | 10 (3) | 1 | 43 (7) |
| Solskjaer | 23 (7) | 2 | | 5 (10) | | 30 (17) |
| Stam | 1 | | | | 1 | 2 |
| Stewart | 2 (1) | | 1 | 0 (1) | | 3 (2) |
| van der Gouw | 0 (1) | | 0 (1) | | | 0 (2) |
| van Nistelrooy | 29 (3) | 0 (2) | | 14 | 1 | 44 (5) |
| Veron | 24 (2) | 1 | | 13 | | 38 (2) |
| Wallwork | 0 (1) | 1 | 1 | | | 2 (1) |
| Webber | | | 1 | | | 1 |
| Yorke | 4 (6) | 0 (1) | 1 | 1 (2) | 0 (1) | 6 (10) |

## Goalscorers

| PLAYER | LEAGUE | CUP COMPETITION | | | OTHER | TOTAL |
|---|---|---|---|---|---|---|
| | | FA CUP | LC | ECL | | |
| van Nistelrooy | 23 | 2 | | 10 | 1 | 36 |
| Solskjaer | 17 | 1 | | 7 | | 25 |
| Beckham | 11 | | | 5 | | 16 |
| Scholes | 8 | | | 1 | | 9 |
| Giggs | 7 | | | 2 | | 9 |
| Veron | 5 | | | | | 5 |
| Cole | 4 | | | 1 | | 5 |
| Keane | 3 | | | 1 | | 4 |
| Blanc | 1 | | | 2 | | 3 |
| Neville P. | 2 | | | | | 2 |
| Butt | 1 | | | | | 1 |
| Fortune | 1 | | | | | 1 |
| Johnsen | 1 | | | | | 1 |
| Silvestre | | | | 1 | | 1 |
| Yorke | 1 | | | | | 1 |
| Opps' o.gs. | 2 | | | 1 | | 3 |

## Final Premier League Table

| | | P | W | D | L | F | A | PTS |
|---|---|---|---|---|---|---|---|---|
| 1 | ARSENAL | 38 | 26 | 9 | 3 | 79 | 36 | 87 |
| 2 | LIVERPOOL | 38 | 24 | 8 | 6 | 67 | 30 | 80 |
| 3 | MANCHESTER UNITED | 38 | 24 | 5 | 9 | 87 | 45 | 77 |
| 4 | NEWCASTLE UNITED | 38 | 21 | 8 | 9 | 74 | 52 | 71 |
| 5 | LEEDS UNITED | 38 | 18 | 12 | 8 | 53 | 37 | 66 |
| 6 | CHELSEA | 38 | 17 | 13 | 8 | 66 | 38 | 64 |
| 7 | WEST HAM UNITED | 38 | 15 | 8 | 15 | 48 | 57 | 53 |
| 8 | ASTON VILLA | 38 | 12 | 14 | 12 | 46 | 47 | 50 |
| 9 | TOTTENHAM HOTSPUR | 38 | 14 | 8 | 16 | 49 | 53 | 50 |
| 10 | BLACKBURN ROVERS | 38 | 12 | 10 | 16 | 55 | 51 | 46 |
| 11 | SOUTHAMPTON | 38 | 12 | 9 | 17 | 46 | 54 | 45 |
| 12 | MIDDLESBROUGH | 38 | 12 | 9 | 17 | 35 | 47 | 45 |
| 13 | FULHAM | 38 | 10 | 14 | 14 | 36 | 44 | 44 |
| 14 | CHARLTON ATHLETIC | 38 | 10 | 14 | 14 | 38 | 49 | 44 |
| 15 | EVERTON | 38 | 11 | 10 | 17 | 45 | 57 | 43 |
| 16 | BOLTON WANDERERS | 38 | 9 | 13 | 16 | 44 | 62 | 40 |
| 17 | SUNDERLAND | 38 | 10 | 10 | 18 | 29 | 51 | 40 |
| 18 | IPSWICH TOWN | 38 | 9 | 9 | 20 | 41 | 64 | 36 |
| 19 | DERBY COUNTY | 38 | 8 | 6 | 24 | 33 | 63 | 30 |
| 20 | LEICESTER CITY | 38 | 5 | 13 | 20 | 30 | 64 | 28 |

# Season 2002-03

## FA Premier League

| DATE | OPPONENTS | SCORE | GOALSCORERS | ATTENDANCE |
|---|---|---|---|---|
| Aug 17 | WEST BROMWICH ALBION | W 1-0 | Solskjaer | 67,645 |
| Aug 23 | Chelsea | D 2-2 | Beckham, Giggs | 41,541 |
| Aug 31 | Sunderland | D 1-1 | Giggs | 47,586 |
| Sep 3 | MIDDLESBROUGH | W 1-0 | van Nistelrooy | 67,508 |
| Sep 11 | BOLTON WANDERERS | L 0-1 | | 67,623 |
| Sep 14 | Leeds United | L 0-1 | | 39,622 |
| Sep 21 | TOTTENHAM HOTSPUR | W 1-0 | van Nistelrooy | 67,611 |
| Sep 28 | Charlton Athletic | W 3-1 | Scholes, Giggs, van Nistelrooy | 23,630 |
| Oct 7 | EVERTON | W 3-0 | Scholes 2, van Nistelrooy | 67,679 |
| Oct 19 | Fulham | D 1-1 | Solskjaer | 18,103 |
| Oct 26 | ASTON VILLA | D 1-1 | Forlan | 67,619 |
| Nov 2 | SOUTHAMPTON | W 2-1 | Neville P., Forlan | 67,691 |
| Nov 9 | Manchester City | L 1-3 | Solskjaer | 34,649 |
| Nov 17 | West Ham United | D 1-1 | van Nistelrooy | 35,049 |
| Nov 23 | NEWCASTLE UNITED | W 5-3 | Scholes, van Nistelrooy 3, Solskjaer | 67,625 |
| Dec 1 | Liverpool | W 2-1 | Forlan 2 | 44,250 |
| Dec 7 | ARSENAL | W 2-0 | Veron, Scholes | 67,650 |
| Dec 14 | WEST HAM UNITED | W 3-0 | Solskjaer, Veron, Schemmel o.g. | 67,555 |
| Dec 22 | Blackburn Rovers | L 0-1 | | 30,475 |
| Dec 26 | Middlesbrough | L 1-3 | Giggs | 34,673 |
| Dec 28 | BIRMINGHAM CITY | W 2-0 | Forlan, Beckham | 67,640 |
| Jan 1 | SUNDERLAND | W 2-1 | Beckham, Scholes | 67,609 |
| Jan 11 | West Bromwich Albion | W 3-1 | van Nistelrooy, Scholes, Solskjaer | 27,129 |
| Jan 18 | CHELSEA | W 2-1 | Scholes, Forlan | 67,606 |
| Feb 1 | Southampton | W 2-0 | van Nistelrooy, Giggs | 32,085 |
| Feb 4 | Birmingham City | W 1-0 | van Nistelrooy | 29,475 |
| Feb 9 | MANCHESTER CITY | D 1-1 | van Nistelrooy | 67,646 |
| Feb 22 | Bolton Wanderers | D 1-1 | Solskjaer | 27,409 |
| Mar 5 | LEEDS UNITED | W 2-1 | Silvestre, Radebe o.g. | 67,626 |
| Mar 15 | Aston Villa | W 1-0 | Beckham | 42,602 |
| Mar 22 | FULHAM | W 3-0 | van Nistelrooy 3 (1 pen) | 67,706 |
| Apr 5 | LIVERPOOL | W 4-0 | van Nistelrooy 2 (2 pens), Giggs, Solskjaer | 67,630 |
| Apr 12 | Newcastle United | W 6-2 | Scholes 3, Solskjaer, van Nistelrooy (pen), Giggs | 52,164 |
| Apr 16 | Arsenal | D 2-2 | van Nistelrooy, Giggs | 38,164 |
| Apr 19 | BLACKBURN ROVERS | W 3-1 | van Nistelrooy, Scholes 2 | 67,626 |
| Apr 27 | Tottenham Hotspur | W 2-0 | Scholes, van Nistelrooy | 36,073 |
| May 3 | CHARLTON ATHLETIC | W 4-1 | Beckham, van Nistelrooy 3 | 67,721 |
| May 11 | Everton | W 2-1 | Beckham, van Nistelrooy (pen) | 40,168 |

## FA Cup

| | | | | |
|---|---|---|---|---|
| Jan 4 | PORTSMOUTH | (Rd3) W 4-1 | van Nistelrooy 2 (2 pens), Beckham, Scholes | 67,222 |
| Jan 26 | WEST HAM UNITED | (Rd4) W 6-0 | Giggs 2, van Nistelrooy 2, Neville P., Solskjaer | 67,181 |
| Feb 15 | ARSENAL | (Rd5) L 0-2 | | 67,209 |

## League Cup

| | | | | |
|---|---|---|---|---|
| Nov 5 | LEICESTER CITY | (Rd3) W 2-0 | Beckham, Richardson | 47,848 |
| Dec 3 | Burnley | (Rd4) W 2-0 | Forlan, Solskjaer | 22,034 |
| Dec 17 | CHELSEA | (Rd5) W 1-0 | Forlan | 57,985 |
| Jan 7 | BLACKBURN ROVERS | (SF/1L) D 1-1 | Scholes | 62,740 |
| Jan 22 | Blackburn Rovers | (SF/2L) W 3-1 | Scholes 2, van Nistelrooy (pen) | 29,048 |
| Mar 2 | Liverpool* | (F) L 0-2 | | 74,500 |

*Played at Millennium Stadium, Cardiff, Wales.

## European Champions League

| | | | | |
|---|---|---|---|---|
| Aug 14 | Zalaegerszeg | (3Q/1L) L 0-1 | | 28,500 |
| Aug 27 | ZALAEGERSZEG | (3Q/2L) W 5-0 | van Nistelrooy 2, Beckham, Scholes, Solskjaer | 66,814 |
| Sep 18 | MACCABI HAIFA | (Grp F) W 5-2 | Giggs, Solskjaer, Veron, van Nistelrooy, Forlan (pen) | 63,439 |
| Sep 24 | Bayer Leverkusen | (Grp F) W 2-1 | van Nistelrooy 2 | 22,500 |
| Oct 1 | OLYMPIAKOS | (Grp F) W 4-0 | Giggs, Veron, Solskjaer, Amanatidis o.g. | 66,902 |
| Oct 23 | Olympiakos | (Grp F) W 3-2 | Blanc, Veron, Scholes | 13,220 |
| Oct 29 | Maccabi Haifa** | (Grp F) L 0-3 | | 19,653 |
| Nov 13 | BAYER LEVERKUSEN | (Grp F) W 2-0 | Veron, van Nistelrooy | 66,185 |
| Nov 26 | Basel | (Grp D) W 3-1 | van Nistelrooy 2, Solskjaer | 29,501 |
| Dec 11 | DEPORTIVO LA CORUNA | (Grp D) W 2-0 | van Nistelrooy 2 | 67,014 |
| Feb 19 | JUVENTUS | (Grp D) W 2-1 | Brown, van Nistelrooy | 66,703 |
| Feb 25 | Juventus | (Grp D) W 3-0 | Giggs 2, van Nistelrooy | 59,111 |
| Mar 12 | BASEL | (Grp D) D 1-1 | Neville G. | 66,870 |
| Mar 18 | Deportivo La Coruna | (Grp D) L 0-2 | | 25,984 |
| Apr 8 | Real Madrid | (QF/1L) L 1-3 | van Nistelrooy | 75,000 |
| Apr 23 | REAL MADRID | (QF/2L) W 4-3 | van Nistelrooy, Beckham 2, Helguera o.g. | 66,708 |

**Played at GSP Stadium, Nicosia, Cyprus.

## League & Cup Appearances

| PLAYER | LEAGUE | CUP COMPETITION | | | TOTAL |
|---|---|---|---|---|---|
| | | FA CUP | LC | ECL | |
| Barthez | 30 | 2 | 4 | 10 | 46 |
| Beckham | 27 (4) | 3 | 5 | 10 (3) | 45 (7) |
| Blanc | 15 (4) | 1 | | 9 | 25 (4) |
| Brown | 22 | 1 (1) | 5 | 6 | 34 (1) |
| Butt | 14 (4) | 0 (2) | 0 (1) | 8 | 22 (7) |
| Carroll | 8 (2) | 1 | 2 | 3 | 14 (2) |
| Chadwick | 0 (1) | | 1 | 0 (3) | 1 (4) |
| Ferdinand | 27 (1) | 3 | 4 | 11 | 45 (1) |
| Fletcher | | | | 2 | 2 |
| Forlan | 7 (18) | 0 (2) | 3 (2) | 5 (8) | 15 (30) |
| Fortune | 5 (4) | | 1 | 3 (3) | 9 (7) |
| Giggs | 32 (4) | 3 | 4 (1) | 13 (2) | 52 (7) |
| Keane | 19 (2) | 3 | 2 | 6 | 30 (2) |
| Lynch | | | | 1 | 1 |
| May | 0 (1) | | 2 | 0 (1) | 2 (2) |
| Nardiello | | | 1 | 0 (1) | 1 (1) |
| Neville G. | 19 (7) | 3 | 5 | 8 (2) | 35 (9) |
| Neville P. | 19 (6) | 2 | 4 | 10 (2) | 35 (8) |
| O'Shea | 26 (6) | 1 | 3 | 12 (4) | 42 (10) |
| Pugh | 0 (1) | | 1 | 1 (2) | 2 (3) |
| Ricardo | 0 (1) | | | 3 (1) | 3 (2) |
| Richardson | 0 (2) | 1 | 0 (1) | 2 (3) | 3 (6) |
| Roche | 0 (1) | | | 1 | 1 (1) |
| Scholes | 31 (2) | 2 (1) | 4 (2) | 9 (1) | 46 (6) |
| Silvestre | 34 | 2 | 5 | 13 | 54 |
| Solskjaer | 29 (8) | 1 (1) | 1 (3) | 9 (5) | 40 (17) |
| Stewart | 0 (1) | 0 (1) | 1 | 0 (1) | 1 (3) |
| Timm | | | | 0 (1) | 0 (1) |
| Van Nistelrooy | 33 (1) | 3 | 4 | 10 (1) | 50 (2) |
| Veron | 21 (4) | 1 | 4 (1) | 11 | 37 (5) |
| Webber | | | | 0 (1) | 0 (1) |

## Goalscorers

| PLAYER | LEAGUE | CUP COMPETITION | | | TOTAL |
|---|---|---|---|---|---|
| | | FA CUP | LC | ECL | |
| van Nistelrooy | 25 | 4 | 1 | 14 | 44 |
| Scholes | 14 | 1 | 3 | 2 | 20 |
| Solskjaer | 9 | 1 | 1 | 4 | 15 |
| Giggs | 8 | 2 | | 4 | 14 |
| Beckham | 6 | 1 | 1 | 3 | 11 |
| Forlan | 6 | | 2 | 1 | 9 |
| Veron | 2 | | | 4 | 6 |
| Neville P. | 1 | 1 | | | 2 |
| Blanc | | | | 1 | 1 |
| Brown | | | | 1 | 1 |
| Neville G. | | | | 1 | 1 |
| Richardson | | | 1 | | 1 |
| Silvestre | 1 | | | | 1 |
| Opps' o.gs. | 2 | | | 2 | 4 |

### Fact File

Ruud van Nistelrooy's 25 league goals was the highest total for 25 years – George Best's 28 in 1967-68.

### Final Premier League Table

| | P | W | D | L | F | A | Pts |
|---|---|---|---|---|---|---|---|
| 1 Manchester United | 38 | 25 | 8 | 5 | 74 | 34 | 83 |
| 2 Arsenal | 38 | 23 | 9 | 6 | 85 | 42 | 78 |
| 3 Newcastle United | 38 | 21 | 6 | 11 | 63 | 48 | 69 |
| 4 Chelsea | 38 | 19 | 10 | 9 | 68 | 38 | 67 |
| 5 Liverpool | 38 | 18 | 10 | 10 | 61 | 41 | 64 |
| 6 Blackburn Rovers | 38 | 16 | 12 | 10 | 52 | 43 | 60 |
| 7 Everton | 38 | 17 | 8 | 13 | 48 | 49 | 59 |
| 8 Southampton | 38 | 13 | 13 | 12 | 43 | 46 | 52 |
| 9 Manchester City | 38 | 15 | 6 | 17 | 47 | 54 | 51 |
| 10 Tottenham Hotspur | 38 | 14 | 8 | 16 | 51 | 62 | 50 |
| 11 Middlesbrough | 38 | 13 | 10 | 15 | 48 | 44 | 49 |
| 12 Charlton Athletic | 38 | 14 | 7 | 17 | 45 | 56 | 49 |
| 13 Birmingham City | 38 | 13 | 9 | 16 | 41 | 49 | 48 |
| 14 Fulham | 38 | 13 | 9 | 16 | 41 | 50 | 48 |
| 15 Leeds United | 38 | 14 | 5 | 19 | 58 | 57 | 47 |
| 16 Aston Villa | 38 | 12 | 9 | 17 | 42 | 47 | 45 |
| 17 Bolton Wanderers | 38 | 10 | 14 | 14 | 41 | 51 | 44 |
| 18 West Ham United | 38 | 10 | 12 | 16 | 42 | 59 | 42 |
| 19 West Bromwich Alb | 38 | 6 | 8 | 24 | 29 | 65 | 26 |
| 20 Sunderland | 38 | 4 | 7 | 27 | 21 | 65 | 19 |

# Complete Players' Career Records

Records cover Newton Heath and Manchester United players up to and including season 2002-03

| Player | Birthplace | From | Year Joined | Year Left | To | League Apps | Sub | Goals |
|---|---|---|---|---|---|---|---|---|
| Ainsworth, A | Manchester | Ashton United | 1934 | 1935 | New Brighton | 2 | | |
| Aitken, J | Scotland | 5th King's Rifle Volunteers | 1895 | 1896 | not known | 2 | | 1 |
| Albinson, G | Prestwich | local football | 1919 | 1921 | Manchester City | | | |
| Albiston, A | Edinburgh | juniors | 1974 | 1988 | West Bromwich Albion | 364 | 15 | 6 |
| Allan, J | South Shields | Bishop Auckland | 1904 | 1905 | Bishop Auckland | 35 | | 21 |
| Allen, R | Marylebone | Queens Park Rangers | 1950 | 1953 | Altrincham | 75 | | |
| Allman A | Milton, Staffs. | Swansea Town | 1914 | 1919 | Millwall Athletic | 12 | | |
| Ambler, A | Manchester | Hyde United | 1899 | 1900 | Colne | 10 | | 1 |
| Anderson, G | Manchester | Bury | 1910 | 1911 | retired | 80 | | 37 |
| Anderson, J | Salford | juniors | 1938 | 1949 | Nottingham Forest | 33 | | 1 |
| Anderson, T | Belfast | Portadown | 1972 | 1974 | Swindon Town | 13 | 6 | 2 |
| Anderson, V | Nottingham | Arsenal | 1987 | 1991 | Sheffield Wednesday | 50 | 4 | 2 |
| Anderson, W | Liverpool | juniors | 1964 | 1967 | Aston Villa | 7 | 2 | |
| Appleton, M | Salford | juniors | 1992 | 1997 | Preston North End | | | |
| Arkesden, T | Warwick | Burton United | 1903 | 1907 | Gainsborough Trinity | 70 | | 28 |
| Asquith, B | Painthorpe | Barnsley | 1939 | 1945 | Barnsley | 1 | | |
| Astley, J | Dudley | Cradley Heath | 1924 | 1928 | Notts County | 2 | | |
| Aston, J (Snr) | Manchester | juniors | 1939 | 1954 | retired | 253 | | 29 |
| Aston, J (Jnr) | Manchester | juniors | 1964 | 1972 | Luton Town | 139 | 16 | 25 |
| Bailey, G | Ipswich | Wits Univ. (South Africa) | 1978 | 1988 | retired | 294 | | |
| Bain, D | Rutherglen | Rutherglen Glencairn | 1922 | 1924 | Everton | 22 | | |
| Bain, J | Scotland | Dundee | 1899 | 1900 | not known | 2 | | 1 |
| Bain, J | Rutherglen | Strathclyde | 1922 | 1928 | Manchester Central | 4 | | |
| Bainbridge, W | Gateshead | Ashington | 1944 | 1946 | Bury | | | |
| Baird, H | Belfast | Linfield | 1937 | 1938 | Huddersfield Town | 49 | | 15 |
| Baldwin, T | Gateshead | Millwall (loan) | 1975 | 1975 | Millwall | 2 | | |
| Ball, J | Wigan | Wigan Athletic | 1948 | 1950 | Bolton Wanderers | 22 | | |
| Ball, J | Southport | Chorley | 1928 | 1930 | Sheffield Wednesday | | | |
| | | Sheffield Wednesday | 1933 | 1934 | Huddersfield Town | 47 | | 17 |
| Ball, W | Liverpool | Blackburn Rovers | 1902 | 1903 | not known | 4 | | |
| Bamford, T | Port Talbot | Wrexham | 1934 | 1938 | Swansea Town | 98 | | 53 |
| Banks, J | West Bromwich | West Bromwich Albion | 1901 | 1903 | Plymouth Argyle | 40 | | |
| Bannister J | Leyland | Manchester City | 1906 | 1909 | Preston North End | 57 | | 7 |
| Barber, J | Salford | Clayton | 1922 | 1924 | Southport | 3 | | 1 |
| Barlow, C | Manchester | Northern Nomads | 1919 | 1922 | New Cross | 29 | | |
| Barnes, P | Manchester | Leeds United | 1984 | 1984 | Leeds United | | | |
| | | Coventry City | 1985 | 1987 | Manchester City | 19 | 1 | |
| Barrett, F | Dundee | Dundee | 1896 | 1900 | New Brighton Tower | 118 | | |
| Barson, F | Sheffield | Aston Villa | 1922 | 1928 | Watford | 140 | | 4 |
| Barthez, F | Lavelanet, France | Monaco | 2000 | | still at club | 92 | | |
| Beadsworth, A | Leicester | Preston North End | 1902 | 1903 | Swindon Town | 9 | | 1 |
| Beale ,R | Maidstone | Norwich City | 1912 | 1919 | Gillingham | 105 | | |
| Beardsley, P | Newcastle-upon-Tyne | Vancouver Whitecaps | 1982 | 1983 | Vancouver Whitecaps | | | |
| Beardsmore, R | Wigan | juniors | 1986 | 1993 | AFC Bournemouth | 30 | 26 | 4 |
| Beckett, R | not known | not known | 1896 | 1897 | not known | | | |
| Beckham, D | Leytonstone | juniors | 1993 | 2003 | Real Madrid, Spain | 237 | 28 | 62 |
| Beddow, J | Burton-upon-Trent | Burton United | 1905 | 1907 | Burnley | 33 | | 12 |
| Behan, W | Dublin | Shelbourne | 1933 | 1934 | Shelbourne | 1 | | |
| Bell, A | Cape Town, S Africa | Ayr Parkhouse | 1903 | 1913 | Blackburn Rovers | 278 | | 10 |
| Bennion, R | Wrexham | Chrichton's Athletic | 1921 | 1932 | Burnley | 286 | | 2 |
| Bent, G | Salford | juniors | 1951 | 1958 | victim, Munich air disaster | 12 | | |
| Berg, H | Eidsvoll, Norway | Blackburn Rovers | 1997 | 2000 | Blackburn Rovers | 49 | 17 | 2 |
| Berry, J | Aldershot | Birmingham City | 1951 | 1958 | retired | 247 | | 37 |
| Berry, W | Sunderland | Tottenham Hotspur | 1906 | 1909 | Stockport County | 13 | | 1 |
| Best, G | Belfast | juniors | 1963 | 1974 | Dunstable Town | 361 | | 137 |
| Bielby, P | Darlington | juniors | 1973 | 1975 | Hartlepool United | 2 | 2 | |
| Birch, B | Salford | juniors | 1948 | 1952 | Wolverhampton Wanderers | 11 | | 4 |
| Birchenough, H | Crewe | Glossop | 1902 | 1903 | Crewe Alexandra | 25 | | |
| Birkett, C | Haydock | juniors | 1950 | 1956 | Southport | 9 | | 2 |
| Birtles, G | Nottingham | Nottingham Forest | 1980 | 1982 | Nottingham Forest | 57 | 1 | 11 |
| Bissett, G | Cowdenbeath | Third Lanark | 1919 | 1921 | Wolverhampton Wanderers | 40 | | 10 |
| Black, A | Glasgow | Greenock Morton | 1932 | 1934 | St Mirren | 8 | | 3 |
| Blackmore, C | Neath | juniors | 1982 | 1994 | Middlesbrough | 150 | 36 | 19 |
| Blackmore, P | not known | not known | 1899 | 1900 | not known | 1 | | |
| Blackstock, T | Kirkaldy | Cowdenbeath | 1903 | 1907 | died playing reserve match | 34 | | |
| Blanc, L | Ales, France | Internazionale | 2001 | 2003 | retired | 44 | 4 | 1 |
| Blanchflower, J | Belfast | juniors | 1950 | 1959 | retired | 105 | | 26 |
| Blomqvist, J | Tavelsjo, Sweden | Parma | 1998 | 2001 | Everton | 20 | 5 | 1 |
| Blew, H | Wrexham | Bury | 1906 | 1906 | Manchester City | 1 | | |
| Blott, S | London | Southend United | 1908 | 1909 | Plymouth Argyle | 19 | | 2 |
| Bogan, T | Glasgow | Preston North End | 1949 | 1951 | Aberdeen | 29 | | 7 |
| Bond, J | Preston | Leyland Motors | 1950 | 1952 | Carlisle United | 20 | | 4 |
| Bonthron, R | Dundee | Dundee | 1903 | 1907 | Sunderland | 119 | | 3 |
| Booth, W | Manchester | Edge Lane | 1900 | 1901 | not known | 2 | | |

**League** = Football League and Premiership. **FAC** = FA Cup. **FLC** = Football League Cup. **Others** = FIFA Club World Championship, Inter-Continental Cup (Europe/South America), UEFA Super Cup, FA Charity Shield and Football League Test Matches.
**Sub** = substitute appearances. **From** = previous club. **To** = next club. *Only details known

| FAC | | | FLC | | | Europe | | | Others | | | Totals | | |
|---|---|---|---|---|---|---|---|---|---|---|---|---|---|---|
| Apps | Sub | Goals | Apps | Sub | Goals | Apps | Sub | Goals | Apps | Sub | Goals | Apps | Sub | Goals |
| | | | | | | | | | | | | 2 | | |
| | | | | | | | | | | | | 2 | | 1 |
| 1 | | | | | | | | | | | | 1 | | |
| 36 | | | 38 | 2 | 1 | 26 | 1 | | 3 | | | 467 | 18 | 7 |
| 1 | | 1 | | | | | | | | | | 36 | | 22 |
| 5 | | | | | | | | | | | | 80 | | |
| | | | | | | | | | | | | 12 | | |
| | | | | | | | | | | | | 10 | | 1 |
| 6 | | 2 | | | | | | | | | | 86 | | 39 |
| 6 | | 1 | | | | | | | 1 | | | 40 | | 2 |
| | | | | | | | | | | | | 13 | 6 | 2 |
| 7 | | 1 | 6 | 1 | 1 | 1 | | | | | | 64 | 5 | 4 |
| 2 | | | | | | 1 | | | | 1 | | 10 | 3 | |
| | | | 1 | 1 | | | | | | | | 1 | 1 | |
| 9 | | 5 | | | | | | | | | | 79 | | 33 |
| | | | | | | | | | | | | 1 | | |
| | | | | | | | | | | | | 2 | | |
| 29 | | 1 | | | | | | | 2 | | | 284 | | 30 |
| 5 | 2 | 1 | 12 | 3 | | 8 | | 1 | 2 | | | 166 | 21 | 27 |
| 31 | | | 28 | | | 20 | | | 2 | | | 375 | | |
| 1 | | | | | | | | | | | | 23 | | |
| | | | | | | | | | | | | 2 | | 1 |
| | | | | | | | | | | | | 4 | | |
| 1 | | 1 | | | | | | | | | | 1 | | 1 |
| 4 | | 3 | | | | | | | | | | 53 | | 18 |
| | | | | | | | | | | | | 2 | | |
| 1 | | | | | | | | | | | | 23 | | |
| | | | | | | | | | | | | | | |
| 3 | | 1 | | | | | | | | | | 50 | | 18 |
| | | | | | | | | | | | | 4 | | |
| 11 | | 4 | | | | | | | | | | 109 | | 57 |
| 4 | | 1 | | | | | | | | | | 44 | | 1 |
| 4 | | 1 | | | | | | | 2 | | | 63 | | 8 |
| 1 | | 1 | | | | | | | | | | 4 | | 2 |
| 1 | | | | | | | | | | | | 30 | | |
| | | | | | | | | | | | | | | |
| | | | 5 | | 2 | | | | | | | 24 | 1 | 4 |
| 14 | | | | | | | | | 4 | | | 136 | | |
| 12 | | | | | | | | | | | | 152 | | 4 |
| 4 | | | 4 | | | 37 | | | 2 | | | 139 | | |
| 3 | | 1 | | | | | | | | | | 12 | | 2 |
| 7 | | | | | | | | | | | | 112 | | |
| | | | 1 | | | | | | | | | 1 | | |
| 4 | 4 | | 3 | 1 | | 2 | 3 | | | | | 39 | 34 | 4 |
| | 1 | | | | | | | | | | | | 1 | |
| 22 | 2 | 6 | 10 | 2 | 1 | 79 | 4 | 15 | 8 | 2 | 1 | 356 | 38 | 85 |
| 1 | | 3 | | | | | | | | | | 34 | | 15 |
| | | | | | | | | | | | | 1 | | |
| 28 | | | | | | | | | 3 | | | 309 | | 10 |
| 15 | | 1 | | | | | | | | | | 301 | | 3 |
| | | | | | | | | | | | | 12 | | |
| 7 | | | 3 | | | 19 | 4 | 1 | 3 | 1 | | 81 | 22 | 3 |
| 15 | | 4 | | | | 11 | | 3 | 3 | | 1 | 276 | | 45 |
| 1 | | | | | | | | | | | | 14 | | 1 |
| 46 | | 21 | 25 | | 9 | 34 | | 11 | 4 | | 1 | 470 | | 179 |
| | | | | | | | | | | | | 2 | 2 | |
| 4 | | 1 | | | | | | | | | | 15 | | 5 |
| 5 | | | | | | | | | | | | 30 | | |
| 4 | | | | | | | | | | | | 13 | | 2 |
| 4 | | 1 | 2 | | | | | | | | | 63 | 1 | 12 |
| 2 | | | | | | | | | | | | 42 | | 10 |
| | | | | | | | | | | | | 8 | | 3 |
| 15 | 6 | 1 | 23 | 2 | 3 | 11 | | 2 | 2 | | 1 | 201 | 44 | 26 |
| 1 | | | | | | | | | | | | 2 | | |
| 4 | | | | | | | | | | | | 38 | | |
| 3 | | | | | | 24 | | 3 | | | | 71 | 4 | 4 |
| 6 | | 1 | | | | 5 | | | 1 | | | 117 | | 27 |
| 3 | 2 | | | 1 | | 6 | 1 | | | | | 29 | 9 | 1 |
| | | | | | | | | | | | | 1 | | |
| | | | | | | | | | | | | 19 | | 2 |
| 4 | | | | | | | | | | | | 33 | | 7 |
| 1 | | | | | | | | | | | | 21 | | 4 |
| 15 | | | | | | | | | | | | 134 | | 3 |
| | | | | | | | | | | | | 2 | | |

| Player | Birthplace | From | Year Joined | Year Left | To | League Apps | Sub | Goals |
|---|---|---|---|---|---|---|---|---|
| Bosnich, M | Sydney | Croatia Sydney | 1989 | 1991 | Croatia Sydney | | | |
| | | Aston Villa | 1999 | 2000 | Chelsea | 26 | | |
| Boyd, H | Pollokshaws | Royal Arsenal | 1897 | 1899 | Falkirk | 52 | | 32 |
| Boyd, W | Cambuslang | Sheffield United | 1935 | 1935 | Workington | 6 | | 4 |
| Boyle, T | Sheffield | Sheffield United | 1929 | 1930 | Macclesfield | 16 | | 6 |
| Bradbury, L | Northwich | Northwich Victoria | 1935 | 1937 | Northwich Victoria | 2 | | 1 |
| Bradley, W | Hyde | Bishop Auckland | 1958 | 1962 | Bury | 63 | | 20 |
| Bratt, H | Salford | juniors | 1957 | 1961 | Doncaster Rovers | | | |
| Brazil, A | Glasgow | Tottenham Hotspur | 1984 | 1986 | Coventry City | 18 | 13 | 8 |
| Brazil, D | Dublin | Rivermount B.C. | 1986 | 1992 | Cardiff City | | 2 | |
| Breedon, J | Barnsley | Sheffield Wednesday | 1935 | 1945 | Burnley | 38 | | |
| Breen T | Belfast | Belfast Celtic | 1936 | 1939 | Belfast Celtic | 65 | | 0 |
| Brennan, S | Manchester | juniors | 1955 | 1970 | Waterford | 291 | 1 | 3 |
| Brett F | Kings Norton | Aston Villa | 1921 | 1922 | Aston Villa | 10 | | 0 |
| Briggs, R | Belfast | juniors | 1960 | 1964 | Swansea Town | 9 | | |
| Brooks, W | Stalybridge | Stalybridge Rovers | 1896 | 1897 | Stalybridge Rovers | 3 | | |
| Broome, A | Unsworth | Oldham Athletic | 1923 | 1924 | Oldham Athletic | 1 | | |
| Broomfield, H | Nantwich | Bolton Wanderers | 1907 | 1908 | Manchester City | 9 | | |
| Brown, J | not known | Dundee Our Boys | 1892 | 1893 | Dundee | 7 | | |
| Brown, J | Kilmarnock | Brooklyn Wanderers | 1932 | 1934 | Brentford | 40 | | 17 |
| Brown, J | Leith | Burnley | 1935 | 1939 | Bradford Park Avenue | 102 | | 1 |
| Brown, R | West Hartlepool | not known | 1946 | 1949 | Doncaster Rovers | 4 | | |
| Brown, W | not known | Chester | 1896 | 1896 | Stockport County | 7 | | 2 |
| Brown, W | Manchester | juniors | 1996 | | still at club | 73 | 9 | |
| Bruce, S | Corbridge | Norwich City | 1987 | 1996 | Birmingham City | 309 | | 36 |
| Bryant, W | Rotherham | Rotherham Town | 1896 | 1900 | Blackburn Rovers | 109 | | 27 |
| Bryant, W | Shildon | Wrexham | 1933 | 1945 | Bradford City | 151 | | 44 |
| Buchan, G | Aberdeen | Aberdeen | 1973 | 1974 | Bury | | 3 | |
| Buchan, M | Aberdeen | Aberdeen | 1972 | 1983 | Oldham Athletic | 376 | | 4 |
| Buckle, E | Southwark | Royal Navy football | 1945 | 1949 | Everton | 20 | | 6 |
| Buckley, F | Manchester | Brighton & Hove Albion | 1906 | 1907 | Aston Villa | 3 | | |
| Bullock, J | Manchester | Chesterfield | 1930 | 1931 | Dundalk | 10 | | 3 |
| Bunce, W | not known | Stockport County | 1902 | 1903 | not known | 2 | | |
| Burgess, H | Manchester | Manchester City | 1906 | 1910 | retired | 49 | | |
| Burke, R | Dormanstown | not known | 1946 | 1949 | Huddersfield Town | 28 | | 16 |
| Burke, T | Wrexham | Liverpool Cambrians | 1886 | 1890 | Wrexham Victoria | | | |
| Burns, F | Glenboig | not known | 1964 | 1972 | Southampton | 111 | 10 | 6 |
| Butt, N | Manchester | juniors | 1993 | | still at club | 198 | 51 | 20 |
| Byrne, D | Dublin | Shamrock Rovers | 1933 | 1934 | Coleraine | 4 | | 3 |
| Byrne, R | Manchester | juniors | 1949 | 1958 | victim, Munich air disaster | 245 | | 17 |
| Cairns, J | not known | Ardwick | 1894 | 1895 | not known | 1 | | |
| Cairns, J | not known | Lincoln City | 1898 | 1898 | Berry's Association | 1 | | |
| Campbell, W | not known | Blackburn Rovers | 1894 | 1894 | Notts County | 5 | | 1 |
| Cantona, E | Paris | Leeds United | 1992 | 1997 | retired | 142 | 1 | 64 |
| Cantwell, N | Cork | West Ham United | 1960 | 1967 | retired | 123 | | 6 |
| Cape, J | Carlisle | Newcastle United | 1934 | 1937 | Queens Park Rangers | 59 | | 18 |
| Capper, A | Northwich | not known | 1911 | 1913 | Witton Albion | 1 | | |
| Carey, J | Dublin | St James' Gate | 1936 | 1953 | retired | 306 | | 17 |
| Carman, J | not known | Oldham County | 1897 | 1898 | not known | 3 | | 1 |
| Carolan, J | Dublin | Home Farm | 1956 | 1960 | Brighton & Hove Albion | 66 | | |
| Carroll, R | Enniskillen | Wigan Athletic | 2001 | | Still at club | 14 | 3 | |
| Carson, A | not known | Glasgow Thistle | 1892 | 1893 | Ardwick | 13 | | 3 |
| Cartman, H | Bolton | Bolton Wanderers | 1922 | 1923 | Tranmere Rovers | 3 | | |
| Cartwright, W | Nantwich | Crewe Alexandra | 1895 | 1905 | retired | 228 | | 8 |
| Cashmore, A | Birmingham | Stourbridge | 1913 | 1914 | Oldham Athletic | 3 | | |
| Casper, C | Burnley | juniors | 1991 | 1998 | Reading | | 2 | |
| Cassidy, J | Dalziel | Blythe | 1895 | 1900 | Manchester City | 152 | | 90 |
| Cassidy, L | Manchester | not known | 1947 | 1956 | Oldham Atheltic | 4 | | |
| Chadwick, L | Cambridge | juniors | 1997 | | still at club | 11 | 14 | 2 |
| Chalmers, W | Glasgow | Heart of Midlothian | 1932 | 1934 | Dunfermiline Athletic | 34 | | 1 |
| Chapman, W | Murton | Sheffield Wednesday | 1926 | 1928 | Watford | 26 | | |
| Charlton, R | Ashington | juniors | 1953 | 1973 | Preston North End | 604 | 2 | 199 |
| Chester, R | Long Eaton | Aston Villa | 1935 | 1935 | Huddersfield Town | 13 | | 1 |
| Chesters, A | Salford | not known | 1929 | 1933 | Exeter City | 9 | | |
| Chilton, A | South Hylton | Seaham Colliery | 1938 | 1955 | Grimsby Town | 353 | | 3 |
| Chisnall, P | Stretford | juniors | 1958 | 1964 | Liverpool | 35 | | 8 |
| Chorlton, T | Heaton Mersey | Liverpool | 1912 | 1914 | Stalybridge Celtic | 4 | | |
| Christie, D | Scotland | not known | 1907 | 1910 | not known | 2 | | |
| Christie J | Manchester | Sale Holmefield | 1902 | 1904 | Manchester City | 1 | | 0 |
| Clark, J | not known | Dundee | 1899 | 1900 | not known | 9 | | |
| Clark, J | Swansea | juniors | 1975 | 1978 | Derby County | | 1 | |
| Clarkin, J | Neilston | Glasgow Thistle | 1894 | 1896 | Blackpool | 67 | | 23 |
| Clayton, G | Chadsmoor, Staffs. | juniors | 1952 | 1959 | Tranmere Rovers | 2 | | |
| Cleaver, H | not known | Desborough | 1902 | 1903 | not known | 1 | | |
| Clegg, M | Ashton-under-Lyne | juniors | 1993 | 2002 | Oldham Athletic | 4 | 5 | |
| Clements, J | not known | Notts County | 1892 | 1894 | Rotherham Town | 36 | | |
| Clempson, F | Salford | juniors | 1948 | 1953 | Stockport County | 15 | | 2 |
| Cockburn, H | Ashton-under-Lyne | Goslings | 1943 | 1954 | Bury | 243 | | 4 |
| Cole, A | Nottingham | Newcastle United | 1995 | 2001 | Blackburn Rovers | 161 | 34 | 93 |
| Collinson, C | Middlesbrough | juniors | 1946 | 1947 | not known | 7 | | |

| FAC | | | FLC | | | Europe | | | Others | | | Totals | | |
|---|---|---|---|---|---|---|---|---|---|---|---|---|---|---|
| Apps | Sub | Goals | Apps | Sub | Goals | Apps | Sub | Goals | Apps | Sub | Goals | Apps | Sub | Goals |
| | | | | | | | | | | | | | | |
| | | | 1 | | | 7 | | | 4 | | | 38 | | |
| 7 | | 1 | | | | | | | | | | 59 | | 33 |
| | | | | | | | | | | | | 6 | | 4 |
| 1 | | | | | | | | | | | | 17 | | 6 |
| | | | | | | | | | | | | 2 | | 1 |
| 3 | | 1 | | | | | | | | | | 66 | | 21 |
| | | | 1 | | | | | | | | | 1 | | |
| | 1 | | 4 | 3 | 3 | 2 | | 1 | | | | 24 | 17 | 12 |
| | | | | | | | | | | | | | 2 | |
| | | | | | | | | | | | | 38 | | |
| 6 | | 0 | | | | | | | | | | 71 | | 0 |
| 36 | | 3 | 4 | | | 24 | | | 3 | | | 358 | 1 | 6 |
| | | | | | | | | | | | | 10 | | 0 |
| 2 | | | | | | | | | | | | 11 | | |
| | | | | | | | | | | | | 3 | | |
| | | | | | | | | | | | | 1 | | |
| | | | | | | | | | | | | 9 | | |
| | | | | | | | | | | | | 7 | | |
| 1 | | | | | | | | | | | | 41 | | 17 |
| 8 | | | | | | | | | | | | 110 | | 1 |
| | | | | | | | | | | | | 4 | | |
| | | | | | | | | | | | | 7 | | 2 |
| 4 | 1 | | 6 | 1 | | 23 | 5 | 1 | | | | 107 | 16 | 1 |
| 41 | | 3 | 32 | 2 | 6 | 25 | 1 | 6 | 4 | | | 411 | 3 | 51 |
| 14 | | 6 | | | | | | | 4 | | | 127 | | 33 |
| 9 | | | | | | | | | | | | 160 | | 44 |
| | | | | 1 | | | | | | | | | 4 | |
| 39 | | | 30 | | | 10 | | | 1 | | | 456 | | 4 |
| 4 | | 1 | | | | | | | | | | 24 | | 7 |
| | | | | | | | | | | | | 3 | | |
| | | | | | | | | | | | | 10 | | 3 |
| | | | | | | | | | | | | 2 | | |
| 3 | | | | | | | | | 2 | | | 54 | | |
| 6 | | 6 | | | | | | | 1 | | 1 | 35 | | 23 |
| 1 | | | | | | | | | | | | 1 | | |
| 11 | 1 | | 10 | 1 | 1 | 10 | 1 | | 1 | | | 143 | 13 | 7 |
| 20 | 4 | 1 | 5 | 1 | | 54 | 12 | 1 | 8 | | 2 | 285 | 68 | 24 |
| | | | | | | | | | | | | 4 | | 3 |
| 18 | | 2 | | | | 14 | | | 3 | | 1 | 280 | | 20 |
| | | | | | | | | | | | | 1 | | |
| | | | | | | | | | | | | 1 | | |
| | | | | | | | | | | | | 5 | | 1 |
| 17 | | 10 | 6 | | 1 | 16 | | 5 | 3 | | 2 | 184 | 1 | 82 |
| 14 | | 2 | | | | 7 | | | 2 | | | 146 | | 8 |
| 1 | | | | | | | | | | | | 60 | | 18 |
| | | | | | | | | | | | | 1 | | |
| 38 | | 1 | | | | | | | 2 | | | 346 | | 18 |
| | | | | | | | | | | | | 3 | | 1 |
| 4 | | | 1 | | | | | | | | | 71 | | |
| 2 | | | 3 | | | 4 | | | | | | 23 | 3 | |
| | | | | | | | | | | | | 13 | | 3 |
| | | | | | | | | | | | | 3 | | |
| 27 | | | | | | | | | 2 | | | 257 | | 8 |
| | | | | | | | | | | | | 3 | | |
| 1 | | | 3 | | | | 1 | | | | | 4 | 3 | |
| 15 | | 9 | | | | | | | 7 | | 1 | 174 | | 100 |
| | | | | | | | | | | | | 4 | | |
| 1 | 2 | | 5 | | | 1 | 5 | | | | | 18 | 21 | 2 |
| 1 | | | | | | | | | | | | 35 | | 1 |
| | | | | | | | | | | | | 26 | | |
| 79 | | 19 | 24 | | 9 | 45 | | 22 | 5 | | 2 | 757 | 2 | 249 |
| | | | | | | | | | | | | 13 | | 1 |
| | | | | | | | | | | | | 9 | | |
| 37 | | | | | | | | | 2 | | | 392 | | 3 |
| 8 | | 1 | | | | 4 | | 1 | | | | 47 | | 10 |
| | | | | | | | | | | | | 4 | | |
| | | | | | | | | | | | | 2 | | |
| | | | | | | | | | | | | 1 | | 0 |
| | | | | | | | | | | | | 9 | | |
| | | | | | | | | | | | | | 1 | |
| 5 | | | | | | | | | 2 | | | 74 | | 23 |
| | | | | | | | | | | | | 2 | | |
| | | | | | | | | | | | | 1 | | |
| 3 | 1 | | 7 | 1 | | 1 | 2 | | | | | 15 | 9 | |
| 4 | | | | | | | | | 2 | | | 42 | | |
| | | | | | | | | | | | | 15 | | 2 |
| 32 | | | | | | | | | | | | 275 | | 4 |
| 19 | 2 | 9 | 2 | | | 43 | 7 | 19 | 6 | 1 | | 231 | 44 | 121 |
| | | | | | | | | | | | | 7 | | |

| Player | Birthplace | From | Year Joined | Year Left | To | League Apps | Sub | Goals |
|---|---|---|---|---|---|---|---|---|
| Collinson, J | Manchester | | 1895 | 1901 | | 62 | | 16 |
| Colman, E | Salford | juniors | 1952 | 1958 | victim, Munich air disaster | 85 | | 1 |
| Colville, J | Not known | Annbank | 1892 | 1893 | Fairfield | 9 | | 1 |
| Connachan, J | Duntocher | Airdrieonians | 1898 | 1899 | Glossop North End | 4 | | |
| Connaughton, J | Wigan | juniors | 1965 | 1972 | Sheffield United | 3 | | |
| Connell, T | Newry | Coleraine | 1978 | 1982 | Glentoran | 2 | | |
| Connelly, J | St Helens | Burnley | 1964 | 1966 | Blackburn Rovers | 79 | 1 | 22 |
| Connor, E | Liverpool | not known | 1909 | 1911 | Sheffield United | 15 | | 2 |
| Cooke, T | Marston Green | juniors | 1992 | 1999 | Manchester City | 1 | 3 | |
| Cookson, S | Bargoed | Bargoed Town | 1914 | 1919 | not known | 12 | | |
| Cope, R | Crewe | juniors | 1950 | 1961 | Luton Town | 93 | | 2 |
| Coppell, S | Liverpool | Tranmere Rovers | 1975 | 1983 | retired | 320 | 2 | 54 |
| Coupar, J | Dundee | Dundee Our Boys | 1892 | 1893 | St Johnstone | 32 | | 9 |
| Coyne, P | Hartlepool | juniors | 1975 | 1977 | Ashton United | 1 | 1 | 1 |
| Craig, T | not known | not known | 1889 | 1891 | not known | | | |
| Craven, C | Boston | Grimsby Town | 1938 | 1938 | Birmingham | 11 | | 2 |
| Crerand, P | Glasgow | Celtic | 1963 | 1972 | retired | 304 | | 10 |
| Crompton, J | Manchester | not known | 1944 | 1956 | retired | 191 | | |
| Crooks, G | Stoke-on-Trent | Tottenham Hotspur (loan) | 1983 | 1984 | Tottenham Hotspur | 6 | 1 | 2 |
| Crowther, S | Bilston | Aston Villa | 1958 | 1958 | Chelsea | 13 | | |
| Cruyff, J | Amsterdam | Barcelona | 1996 | 2000 | Alaves | 15 | 19 | 8 |
| Culkin, N | York | York City | 1995 | 2002 | Queens Park Rangers | | 1 | |
| Cunningham, J | Glasgow | Aston Villa | 1898 | 1899 | Wigan County | 15 | | 2 |
| Cunningham, L | London | Real Madrid (loan) | 1983 | 1983 | Real Madrid | 3 | 2 | 1 |
| Curry, J | Newcastle-upon-Tyne | Scotswood | 1908 | 1911 | Southampton | 13 | | |
| Curtis, J | Nuneaton | juniors | 1995 | 2000 | Blackburn Rovers | 4 | 9 | |
| Dale, H | Stoke-on-Trent | not known | 1887 | 1892 | retired | | | |
| Dale, J | Northwich | Witton Albion | 1947 | 1948 | Port Vale | 2 | | |
| Dale, W | Manchester | Sandbach Ramblers | 1925 | 1931 | Manchester City | 64 | | |
| Dalton, E | not known | Pendlebury | 1905 | 1906 | Pendlebury | 1 | | |
| Daly, G | Dublin | Bohemians | 1973 | 1977 | Derby County | 107 | 4 | 23 |
| Davenport, P | Birkenhead | Nottingham Forest | 1986 | 1988 | Middlesbrough | 73 | 19 | 22 |
| Davidson, W | not known | Annbank | 1893 | 1895 | retired | 40 | | 2 |
| Davies, A | Manchester | juniors | 1978 | 1985 | Newcastle United | 6 | 1 | |
| Davies, J | not known | not known | 1892 | 1893 | not known | 7 | | |
| Davies, J | Cefn Mawr | Druids | 1886 | 1890 | Wolverhampton Wanderers | | | |
| Davies, L | not known | | 1886 | 1887 | not known | | | |
| Davies, R | Holywell | Portsmouth (loan) | 1974 | 1975 | Portsmouth | | 8 | |
| Davies, S | Middlewich | juniors | 1990 | 1997 | Luton Town | 4 | 7 | |
| Davies, W | Caernarfon | Manchester City | 1972 | 1973 | Blackpool | 15 | 1 | 4 |
| Davis, J | Bromsgrove | juniors | 1999 | | still at club | | | |
| Dawson, A | Aberdeen | not known | 1957 | 1961 | Preston North End | 80 | | 45 |
| Dean, H | Manchester | not known | 1931 | 1931 | Mossley | 2 | | |
| Delaney, J | Cleland | Celtic | 1946 | 1950 | Aberdeen | 164 | | 25 |
| Dempsey, M | Manchester | juniors | 1980 | 1986 | Sheffield United | 1 | | |
| Denman, J | not known | not known | 1891 | 1892 | not known | | | |
| Dennis, W | Mossley | Stalybridge Celtic | 1923 | 1924 | Chesterfield | 3 | | |
| Dewar, N | Lochgilphead | Third Lanark | 1933 | 1933 | Sheffield Wednesday | 36 | | 14 |
| Djordjic, B | Belgrade, Yugoslavia | Brommapojkarna (Sweden) | 1999 | | still at club | | 1 | |
| Doherty, J | Manchester | juniors | 1950 | 1957 | Leicester City | 25 | | 7 |
| Donaghy, B | Londonderry | Derry Celtic | 1905 | 1906 | Derry Celtic | 3 | | |
| Donaghy, M | Belfast | Luton Town | 1988 | 1992 | Chelsea | 76 | 13 | |
| Donald, I | Aberdeen | juniors | 1968 | 1973 | Partick Thistle | 4 | | |
| Donaldson, R | not known | Blackburn Rovers | 1892 | 1897 | Luton Town | 131 | | 56 |
| Donnelly* | not known | not known | 1890 | 1891 | not known | | | |
| Donnelly, A | Middleton | Heywood United | 1908 | 1911 | Heywood United | 34 | | |
| Dougan, T | Holytown | Plymouth Argyle | 1939 | 1940 | Heart of Midlothian | 4 | | |
| Doughty, J | Bilston | Druids | 1886 | 1892 | not known | | | |
| Doughty, R | Cannock Chase | Druids | 1886 | 1892 | Fairfield | | | |
| Douglas, W | Dundee | Ardwick | 1894 | 1896 | Derby County | 55 | | |
| Dow, J | Dundee | Dundee | 1894 | 1897 | Fairfield | 48 | | 6 |
| Downie, A | Dunoon | Swindon Town | 1902 | 1909 | Oldham Athletic | 172 | | 12 |
| Downie, J | Lanark | Bradford Park Avenue | 1949 | 1953 | Luton Town | 110 | | 35 |
| Draycott, W | Derby | Burton Wanderers | 1896 | 1899 | Bedminster | 81 | | 6 |
| Dublin, D | Leicester | Cambridge United | 1992 | 1994 | Coventry City | 4 | 8 | 2 |
| Duckworth, R | Manchester | Newton Heath Athletic | 1903 | 1915 | retired | 225 | | 11 |
| Dunn, W | Middlesbrough | South Bank | 1897 | 1898 | not known | 10 | | |
| Dunne, A | Dublin | Shelbourne | 1960 | 1973 | Bolton Wanderers | 414 | | 2 |
| Dunne, P | Dublin | Shamrock Rovers | 1964 | 1967 | Plymouth Argyle | 45 | | |
| Duxbury, M | Accrington | juniors | 1975 | 1990 | Blackburn Rovers | 274 | 25 | 6 |
| Dyer, J | Barnsley | Ashton Town | 1905 | 1908 | West Ham United | 1 | | |
| Earp, J | not known | not known | 1884 | 1887 | not known | | | |
| Edge, A | Stoke-on-Trent | Stoke | 1891 | 1892 | Notts Jardines | | | |
| Edmonds, H | Chryston | Bolton Wanderers | 1911 | 1912 | Glenavon | 43 | | |
| Edwards, D | Dudley | juniors | 1952 | 1958 | victim, Munich air disaster | 151 | | 20 |
| Edwards, P | Oldham | juniors | 1963 | 1973 | Oldham Athletic | 52 | 2 | |
| Ellis, D | Kirkcaldy | Maidstone United | 1923 | 1924 | St Johnstone | 11 | | |
| Erentz, F | Dundee | Dundee Our Boys | 1892 | 1902 | retired | 280 | | 9 |
| Erentz, H | Dundee | Oldham County | 1897 | 1898 | Tottenham Hotspur | 6 | | |
| Evans, G | not known | not known | 1890 | 1891 | not known | | | |
| Evans, S | Darlaston | Cardiff City | 1923 | 1925 | Pontypridd | 6 | | 2 |

| FAC | | | FLC | | | Europe | | | Others | | | Totals | | |
|---|---|---|---|---|---|---|---|---|---|---|---|---|---|---|
| Apps | Sub | Goals | Apps | Sub | Goals | Apps | Sub | Goals | Apps | Sub | Goals | Apps | Sub | Goals |
| 9 | | 1 | | | | | | | | | | 71 | | 17 |
| 9 | | | | | | 13 | | 1 | 1 | | | 108 | | 2 |
| 1 | | | | | | | | | | | | 10 | | 1 |
| | | | | | | | | | | | | 4 | | |
| | | | | | | | | | | | | 3 | | |
| | | | | | | | | | | | | 2 | | |
| 13 | | 2 | 1 | | | 19 | | 11 | | | | 112 | 1 | 35 |
| | | | | | | | | | | | | 15 | | 2 |
| | | | 1 | 2 | 1 | | 1 | | | | | 2 | 6 | 1 |
| 1 | | | | | | | | | | | | 13 | | |
| 10 | | | 1 | | | 2 | | | | | | 106 | | 2 |
| 36 | | 4 | 24 | | 9 | 11 | 1 | 3 | 1 | | | 393 | 3 | 70 |
| | | | | | | | | | 2 | | 1 | 34 | | 10 |
| | | | | | | | | | | | | 1 | 1 | 1 |
| 2 | | 1 | | | | | | | | | | 2 | | 1 |
| | | | | | | | | | | | | 11 | | 2 |
| 43 | | 4 | 4 | | | 41 | | 1 | 5 | | | 397 | | 15 |
| 20 | | | | | | | | | 1 | | | 212 | | |
| | | | | | | | | | | | | 6 | 1 | 2 |
| 5 | | | | | | 2 | | | | | | 20 | | |
| | 1 | | 5 | | | 4 | 7 | | 2 | 5 | | 26 | 32 | 8 |
| | | | | | | | | | | | | | 1 | |
| 2 | | | | | | | | | | | | 17 | | 2 |
| | | | | | | | | | | | | 3 | 2 | 1 |
| 1 | | | | | | | | | | | | 14 | | |
| | | | 5 | | | | | | | 1 | | 9 | 10 | |
| 1 | | | | | | | | | | | | 1 | | |
| | | | | | | | | | | | | 2 | | |
| 4 | | | | | | | | | | | | 68 | | |
| | | | | | | | | | | | | 1 | | |
| 9 | 1 | 5 | 17 | | 4 | 4 | | | | | | 137 | 5 | 32 |
| 2 | 2 | | 8 | 2 | 4 | | | | | | | 83 | 23 | 26 |
| 3 | | | | | | | | | 1 | | | 44 | | 2 |
| 2 | | | | | | | 1 | 1 | | | | 8 | 2 | 1 |
| 1 | | | | | | | | | 2 | | | 10 | | |
| 2 | | | | | | | | | | | | 2 | | |
| 1 | | | | | | | | | | | | 1 | | |
| | 2 | | | | | | | | | | | | 10 | |
| | | | 3 | 2 | | 3 | 1 | 1 | | | | 10 | 10 | 1 |
| 1 | | | | | | | | | | | | 16 | 1 | 4 |
| | | | 1 | | | | | | | | | 1 | | |
| 10 | | 8 | 3 | | 1 | | | | | | | 93 | | 54 |
| | | | | | | | | | | | | 2 | | |
| 19 | | 3 | | | | | | | 1 | | | 184 | | 28 |
| | | | | | | | 1 | | | | | 1 | 1 | |
| 1 | | | | | | | | | | | | 1 | | |
| | | | | | | | | | | | | 3 | | |
| | | | | | | | | | | | | 36 | | 14 |
| | | | 1 | | | | | | | | | 1 | 1 | |
| 1 | | | | | | | | | | | | 26 | | 7 |
| | | | | | | | | | | | | 3 | | |
| 10 | | | 9 | 5 | | 2 | 3 | | 1 | | | 98 | 21 | |
| | | | 2 | | | | | | | | | 6 | | |
| 16 | | 10 | | | | | | | 8 | | | 155 | | 66 |
| 1 | | | | | | | | | | | | 1 | | |
| 3 | | | | | | | | | | | | 37 | | |
| | | | | | | | | | | | | 4 | | |
| 3 | | | | | | | | | | | | 3 | | |
| 5 | | 1 | | | | | | | 3 | | | 8 | | 1 |
| 1 | | | | | | | | | 1 | | | 57 | | |
| 1 | | | | | | | | | 1 | | | 50 | | 6 |
| 19 | | 2 | | | | | | | | | | 191 | | 14 |
| 5 | | 1 | | | | | | | 1 | | 1 | 116 | | 37 |
| 10 | | | | | | | | | 4 | | | 95 | | 6 |
| 1 | 1 | | 1 | 1 | | | 1 | | | | | 6 | 11 | 3 |
| 26 | | | | | | | | | 3 | | | 254 | | 11 |
| 2 | | | | | | | | | | | | 12 | | |
| 54 | 1 | | 21 | | | 40 | | | 5 | | | 534 | 1 | 2 |
| 7 | | | 1 | | | 13 | | | 1 | | | 67 | | |
| 20 | 5 | 1 | 32 | 2 | | 17 | 1 | | 2 | | | 345 | 33 | 7 |
| | | | | | | | | | | | | 1 | | |
| 1 | | | | | | | | | | | | 1 | | |
| 3 | | | | | | | | | | | | 3 | | |
| 7 | | | | | | | | | 1 | | | 51 | | |
| 12 | | 1 | | | | 12 | | | 2 | | | 177 | | 21 |
| 10 | | | 4 | | 1 | | | | | | | 66 | 2 | 1 |
| | | | | | | | | | | | | 11 | | |
| 23 | | | | | | | | | 7 | | | 310 | | 9 |
| 3 | | | | | | | | | | | | 9 | | |
| 1 | | | | | | | | | | | | 1 | | |
| | | | | | | | | | | | | 6 | | 2 |

| Player | Birthplace | From | Year Joined | Year Left | To | League Apps | Sub | Goals |
|---|---|---|---|---|---|---|---|---|
| Fall, J | Manchester | Middlesbrough Ironopolis | 1893 | 1895 | Small Heath | 23 | | |
| Farman, A | Birmingham | Bolton Wanderers | 1889 | 1895 | not known | 51 | | 18 |
| Feehan, I | Dublin | Waterford | 1948 | 1950 | Northampton Town | 12 | | |
| Felton, G | not known | not known | 1887 | 1891 | not known | | | |
| Ferdinand, R | London | Leeds United | 2002 | | still at club | 27 | 1 | |
| Ferguson, A | Flint | Rhyl Athletic | 1927 | 1928 | Reading | 4 | | |
| Ferguson, D | Glasgow | juniors | 1988 | 1994 | Wolverhampton Wanderers | 20 | 7 | |
| Ferguson, J | Newcastle-upon-Tyne | Burton Town | 1931 | 1931 | Derry City | 8 | | 1 |
| Ferrier, R | Cleethorpes | Grimsby Town | 1935 | 1938 | Oldham Athletic | 18 | | 4 |
| Fielding, W | Hyde | Bolton Wanderers | 1947 | 1948 | not known | 6 | | |
| Fisher, J | Scotland | King's Park | 1900 | 1902 | not known | 42 | | 2 |
| Fitchett, J | Manchester | Southampton | 1903 | 1903 | Plymouth Argyle | | | |
| | | Plymouth Argyle | 1904 | 1905 | Fulham | 16 | | 1 |
| Fitton, G | Melton Mowbray | West Bromwich Albion | 1932 | 1932 | Preston North End | 12 | | 2 |
| Fitzpatrick, J | Aberdeen | juniors | 1961 | 1973 | retired | 111 | 6 | 8 |
| Fitzsimmons, D | Annbank | Annbank | 1895 | 1896 | Fairfield | 28 | | |
| Fitzsimmons, T | Annbank | Annbank | 1892 | 1894 | Annbank | 27 | | 6 |
| Fletcher, D | Edinburgh | juniors | 2000 | | still at club | | | |
| Fletcher, P | Manchester | juniors | 1969 | 1973 | Hull City | 2 | 5 | |
| Foggon, A | West Pelton | Middlesbrough | 1976 | 1976 | Sunderland | | 3 | |
| Foley, G | not known | Ashford | 1900 | 1900 | not known | 7 | | 1 |
| Ford, J | Northwich | Crewe Alexandra | 1907 | 1910 | Nottingham Forest | 5 | | |
| Forlan, D | Montevideo, Uruguay | Independiente | 2002 | | still at club | 13 | 25 | 6 |
| Forster, T | Northwich | Northwich Victoria | 1916 | 1922 | Northwich Victoria | 35 | | |
| Forsyth, A | Swinton, Lanarkshire | | 1972 | 1978 | Rangers | 99 | 2 | 4 |
| Fortune, Q | Cape Town, S Africa | Atlético Madrid | 1999 | | still at club | 23 | 13 | 5 |
| Foulkes, W | St Helens | United Juniors | 1950 | 1970 | retired | 563 | 3 | 7 |
| Fox* | not known | not known | 1914 | 1914 | not known | | | |
| Frame, T | Burnbank | Cowdenbeath | 1932 | 1936 | Southport | 51 | | 4 |
| Gallimore, S | Bucklow Hill | Witton Albion | 1929 | 1934 | Altrincham | 72 | | 19 |
| Gardner, R | Birmingham | Stourbridge | 1935 | 1937 | Sheffield United | 16 | | 1 |
| Garton, W | Salford | United Juniors | 1980 | 1990 | retired | 39 | 2 | |
| Garvey, J | Manchester | Wigan County | 1900 | 1902 | Southport Central | 6 | | |
| Gaskell, D | Orrell | juniors | 1955 | 1969 | Wrexham | 96 | | |
| Gaudie, R | Guisborough | Woolwich Arsenal | 1903 | 1904 | not known | 7 | | |
| Gibson, C | Bridport | Aston Villa | 1985 | 1990 | Leicester City | 74 | 5 | 9 |
| Gibson, R | London | Birmingham | 1921 | 1922 | not known | 11 | | |
| Gibson, T | London | Coventry City | 1986 | 1987 | Wimbledon | 14 | 9 | 1 |
| Gibson, D | Manchester | juniors | 1946 | 1955 | Sheffield Wednesday | 108 | | |
| Gidman, J | Liverpool | Everton | 1981 | 1986 | Manchester City | 94 | 1 | 4 |
| Giggs, R | Cardiff | juniors | 1990 | | still at club | 341 | 41 | 79 |
| Giles, J | Dublin | juniors | 1956 | 1963 | Leeds United | 99 | | 10 |
| Gill, A | Bradford | juniors | 1984 | 1990 | retired | 5 | 5 | 1 |
| Gillespie, K | Larne | juniors | 1991 | 1995 | Newcastle United | 3 | 6 | 1 |
| Gillespie, M | Glasgow | Lincoln City | 1896 | 1900 | not known | 74 | | 17 |
| Gipps, T | London | Barrow | 1912 | 1920 | not known | 23 | | |
| Givens, D | Dublin | juniors | 1965 | 1970 | Luton Town | 4 | 4 | 1 |
| Gladwin, G | Chesterfield | Doncaster Rovers | 1937 | | retired, injured in WWII | 27 | | 1 |
| Godsmark, G | Derby | Ashford | 1900 | 1901 | killed in Boer War | 9 | | 4 |
| Goldthorpe, E | Leeds | Bradford City | 1922 | 1925 | Rotherham United | 27 | | 15 |
| Goodwin, F | Heywood | juniors | 1953 | 1960 | Leeds United | 95 | | 7 |
| Goodwin, W | Staveley | Exeter City | 1920 | 1922 | Southend United | 7 | | 1 |
| Goram, A | Bury | Motherwell | 2001 | 2001 | Motherwell | 2 | | |
| Gotheridge, J | not known | not known | 1884 | 1887 | West Manchester | | | |
| Gourlay, J | Scotland | Annbank | 1899 | 1899 | not known | 1 | | |
| Gowling, A | Stockport | juniors | 1965 | 1972 | Huddersfield Town | 64 | 7 | 18 |
| Graham, A | Glasgow | Leeds United | 1983 | 1985 | Bradford City | 33 | 4 | 5 |
| Graham, D | Cannock | juniors | 1986 | 1991 | Barnsley | 1 | | |
| Graham, G | Bargeddie | Arsenal | 1972 | 1974 | Portsmouth | 41 | 2 | 2 |
| Graham, J | Not known | Blyth | 1893 | 1894 | not known | 4 | | |
| Grassam, W | Larbert | Celtic | 1903 | 1905 | Leyton | 29 | | 13 |
| Greaves, I | Oldham | Burton United | 1953 | 1960 | Lincoln City | 67 | | |
| Green, R | Tewkesbury | Derby County | 1933 | 1934 | Stockport County | 9 | | 4 |
| Greenhoff, B | Barnsley | juniors | 1968 | 1979 | Leeds United | 218 | 3 | 13 |
| Greenhoff, J | Barnsley | Stoke City | 1976 | 1980 | Crewe Alexandra | 94 | 3 | 26 |
| Greening, J | Scarborough | York City | 1998 | 2001 | Middlesbrough | 4 | 10 | |
| Greenwood, W | Padiham | Grimsby Town | 1900 | 1901 | not known | 3 | | |
| Gregg, H | Magherafelt | Doncaster Rovers | 1957 | 1966 | Stoke City | 210 | | |
| Griffiths, C | Pontypridd | juniors | 1970 | 1976 | Chicago Sting | 7 | | |
| Griffiths, J | Fenton | Bolton Wanderers | 1934 | 1946 | Hyde United | 168 | | 1 |
| Griffiths, W | Manchester | Berry's Association | 1899 | 1905 | Atherton CH | 157 | | 27 |
| Grimes, A | Dublin | Bohemians | 1977 | 1983 | Coventry City | 62 | 28 | 10 |
| Grimshaw, A | Manchester | juniors | 1974 | 1979 | retired | | 1 | |
| Grimwood, J | South Shields | South Shields | 1919 | 1927 | Aldershot Town | 196 | | 8 |
| Grundy, J | Bolton | Wigan County | 1895 | 1895 | Halliwell Rovers | | | |
| | | Halliwell Rovers | 1900 | 1901 | not known | 11 | | 3 |
| Gyves, W | Manchester | not known | 1890 | 1891 | not known | | | |
| Hacking, J | Blackburn | Oldham Athletic | 1934 | 1935 | Accrington Stanley | 32 | | |
| Hall, J | Bolton | Accrington Stanley | 1925 | 1927 | not known | 3 | | |
| Hall, J | Failsworth | Newton Heath Loco | 1932 | 1936 | Tottenham Hotspur | 67 | | |

| FAC | | | FLC | | | Europe | | | Others | | | Totals | | |
|---|---|---|---|---|---|---|---|---|---|---|---|---|---|---|
| Apps | Sub | Goals | Apps | Sub | Goals | Apps | Sub | Goals | Apps | Sub | Goals | Apps | Sub | Goals |
| 3 | | | | | | | | | 1 | | | 27 | | |
| 7 | | 6 | | | | | | | 3 | | 4 | 61 | | 28 |
| 2 | | | | | | | | | | | | 14 | | |
| 1 | | | | | | | | | | | | 1 | | |
| 3 | | | 4 | | | 11 | | | | | | 45 | 1 | |
| | | | | | | | | | | | | 4 | | |
| | | | 2 | 1 | | | | | | | | 22 | 8 | |
| | | | | | | | | | | | | 8 | | 1 |
| 1 | | | | | | | | | | | | 19 | | 4 |
| 1 | | | | | | | | | | | | 7 | | |
| 4 | | 1 | | | | | | | | | | 46 | | 3 |
| | | | | | | | | | | | | | | |
| 2 | | | | | | | | | | | | 18 | | 1 |
| | | | | | | | | | | | | 12 | | 2 |
| 11 | | 1 | 12 | | 1 | 7 | | | | | | 141 | 6 | 10 |
| 3 | | | | | | | | | | | | 31 | | |
| 1 | | | | | | | | | 2 | | | 30 | | 6 |
| | | | | | | 2 | | | | | | 2 | | |
| | | | | | | | | | | | | 2 | 5 | |
| | | | | | | | | | | | | | 3 | |
| | | | | | | | | | | | | 7 | | 1 |
| | | | | | | | | | | | | 5 | | |
| | 2 | | 3 | 2 | 2 | 6 | 12 | 1 | | | | 22 | 41 | 9 |
| 1 | | | | | | | | | | | | 36 | | |
| 10 | | 1 | 7 | | | | 1 | | | | | 116 | 3 | 5 |
| | | | 3 | | | 7 | 9 | | 1 | 2 | 2 | 34 | 24 | 7 |
| 61 | | | 3 | | | 52 | | 2 | 6 | | | 685 | 3 | 9 |
| 1 | | | | | | | | | | | | 1 | | |
| 1 | | | | | | | | | | | | 52 | | 4 |
| 4 | | 1 | | | | | | | | | | 76 | | 20 |
| 2 | | | | | | | | | | | | 18 | | 1 |
| 3 | | | 5 | 1 | | | 1 | | | | | 47 | 4 | |
| | | | | | | | | | | | | 6 | | |
| 16 | | | 1 | | | 5 | | | 1 | 1 | | 119 | 1 | |
| 1 | | | | | | | | | | | | 8 | | |
| 8 | 1 | | 7 | | | | | | | | | 89 | 6 | 9 |
| 1 | | | | | | | | | | | | 12 | | |
| 1 | 1 | | | 2 | | | | | | | | 15 | 12 | 1 |
| 6 | | | | | | | | | 1 | | | 115 | | |
| 9 | | | 5 | | | 7 | 2 | | 1 | 1 | | 116 | 4 | 4 |
| 39 | 4 | 9 | 21 | 5 | 6 | 77 | 5 | 19 | 10 | 1 | | 488 | 56 | 113 |
| 13 | | 2 | 2 | | 1 | | | | 1 | | | 115 | | 13 |
| 2 | 2 | 1 | | | | | | | | | | 7 | 7 | 1 |
| 1 | 1 | 1 | 3 | | | | | | | | | 7 | 7 | |
| 11 | | 4 | | | | | | | 4 | | | 89 | | 21 |
| | | | | | | | | | | | | 23 | | |
| | | | 1 | | | | | | | | | 5 | 4 | 1 |
| 1 | | | | | | | | | | | | 28 | | 1 |
| | | | | | | | | | | | | 9 | | 4 |
| 3 | | 1 | | | | | | | | | | 30 | | 16 |
| 8 | | 1 | | | | 3 | | | 1 | | | 107 | | 8 |
| | | | | | | | | | | | | 7 | | 1 |
| | | | | | | | | | | | | 2 | | |
| 1 | | | | | | | | | | | | 1 | | |
| | | | | | | | | | | | | 1 | | |
| 6 | 2 | 2 | 7 | 1 | 1 | | | | | | | 77 | 10 | 21 |
| 1 | | | 6 | | 1 | 6 | 1 | 1 | 1 | | | 47 | 5 | 7 |
| | 1 | 1 | | 1 | | | | | | | | 1 | 2 | 1 |
| 2 | | | 1 | | | | | | | | | 44 | 2 | 2 |
| | | | | | | | | | | | | 4 | | |
| 8 | | 1 | | | | | | | | | | 37 | | 14 |
| 6 | | | | | | 2 | | | | | | 75 | | |
| | | | | | | | | | | | | 9 | | 4 |
| 24 | | 2 | 19 | | 2 | 6 | | | 1 | | | 268 | 3 | 17 |
| 18 | 1 | 9 | 4 | | 1 | 2 | | | 1 | | | 119 | 4 | 36 |
| | 1 | | 6 | | | 2 | 2 | | 1 | 1 | | 13 | 14 | |
| | | | | | | | | | | | | 3 | | |
| 24 | | | 2 | | | 11 | | | | | | 247 | | |
| | | | | | | | | | | | | 7 | | |
| 8 | | | | | | | | | | | | 176 | | 1 |
| 18 | | 3 | | | | | | | | | | 175 | | 30 |
| 5 | | 1 | 6 | | 4 | 2 | | | | | | 77 | 30 | 11 |
| | | | | 1 | | | | | | | | | 2 | |
| 9 | | | | | | | | | | | | 205 | | 8 |
| | | | | | | | | | | | | | | |
| | | | | | | | | | | | | 11 | | 3 |
| 1 | | | | | | | | | | | | 1 | | |
| 2 | | | | | | | | | | | | 34 | | |
| | | | | | | | | | | | | 3 | | |
| 6 | | | | | | | | | | | | 73 | | |

| Player | Birthplace | From | Year Joined | Year Left | To | League Apps | Sub | Goals |
|---|---|---|---|---|---|---|---|---|
| Hall, P | Blackburn | Oswaldtwistle Rovers | 1903 | 1905 | Brighton & Hove Albion | 8 | | 2 |
| Halse, H | London | Southend United | 1908 | 1912 | Aston Villa | 109 | | 41 |
| Halton, R | Buxton | not known | 1936 | 1937 | Notts County | 4 | | 1 |
| Hamill, M | Belfast | Belfast Celtic | 1911 | 1914 | Belfast Celtic | 57 | | 2 |
| Hanlon, J | Manchester | Amateur | 1934 | 1948 | Bury | 64 | | 20 |
| Hannaford, C | London | Clapton Orient | 1925 | 1927 | Clapton Orient | 11 | | |
| Hanson, J | Manchester | Manchester North End | 1924 | 1931 | retired | 138 | | 47 |
| Hardman, H | Manchester | Everton | 1908 | 1909 | Bradford City | 4 | | |
| Harris, F | Manchester | Urmston OB | 1920 | 1923 | not known | 46 | | 2 |
| Harris, T | Ince-in-Makerfield | Skelmersdale United | 1926 | 1928 | Wigan Borough | 4 | | 1 |
| Harrison, C | not known | not known | 1889 | 1990 | not known | | | |
| Harrison, W | Wybunbury | Wolverhampton Wanderers | 1920 | 1922 | Port Vale | 44 | | 5 |
| Harrop, R | Manchester | juniors | 1953 | 1959 | Tranmere Rovers | 10 | | |
| Hartwell, W | not known | Kettering Town | 1904 | 1905 | Northampton Town | 3 | | |
| Haslam, G | Turton | Darwen | 1921 | 1927 | Portsmouth | 25 | | |
| Haworth, R | Lower Darwen | Hull City | 1926 | 1927 | Darwen | 2 | | |
| Hawksworth, A | Sheffield | juniors | 1952 | 1958 | not known | 1 | | |
| Hay, T | Staveley | Burslem | 1888 | 1890 | Accrington | | | |
| Haydock, F | Eccles | Amateur | 1957 | 1963 | Charlton Athletic | 6 | | |
| Hayes, V | Manchester | Newton Heath Athletic | 1901 | 1907 | Brentford | | | |
| | | Brentford | 1908 | 1910 | Bradford Park Avenue | 115 | | 2 |
| Haywood, J | Wednesbury | Hindley Central | 1913 | 1919 | not known | 26 | | |
| Healy, D | Downpatrick | juniors | 1996 | 2001 | Preston North End | | 1 | |
| Heathcote, J | not known | Berry's Association | 1899 | 1902 | not known | 7 | | |
| Henderson, W | Edinburgh | Airdrieonians | 1921 | 1925 | Preston North End | 34 | | 17 |
| Hendry, J | not known | Alloa Athletic | 1892 | 1893 | not known | 2 | | 1 |
| Henrys, A | Nottingham | unattached | 1891 | 1892 | Notts Jardines | | | |
| | | Notts Jardines | 1892 | 1893 | Leicester Fosse | 3 | | |
| Herd, D | Hamilton | Arsenal | 1961 | 1968 | Stoke City | 201 | 1 | 114 |
| Heron, T | Irvine | Portadown | 1958 | 1961 | York City | 3 | | |
| Heywood, H | Little Hulton | Northwich Victoria | 1932 | 1934 | Tranmere Rovers | 4 | | 2 |
| Higginbotham, D | Manchester | juniors | 1995 | 2000 | Derby County | 2 | 2 | |
| Higgins, M | Buxton | retired | 1985 | 1987 | Bury | 6 | | |
| Higgins, W | Smethwick | Middlesbrough | 1901 | 1902 | not known | 10 | | |
| Higson, J | not known | Manchester Wednesday | 1902 | 1902 | not known | 5 | | 1 |
| Hilditch, C | Hartford | Altrincham | 1916 | 1932 | retired | 301 | | 7 |
| Hill, G | Sunbury-on-Thames | Millwall | 1975 | 1978 | Derby County | 100 | 1 | 39 |
| Hillam, C | Burnley | Burnley | 1933 | 1934 | Clapton Orient | 8 | | |
| Hine, E | Smithy Cross | Huddersfield Town | 1933 | 1934 | Barnsley | 51 | | 12 |
| Hodge, Ja | Stenhousemuir | Stenhousemuir | 1910 | 1919 | Milwall Athletic | 79 | | 2 |
| Hodge, Jo | Stenhousemuir | Stenhousemuir | 1913 | 1919 | not known | 30 | | |
| Hodges, F | Birmingham | not known | 1919 | 1921 | Wigan Borough | 20 | | 4 |
| Hofton, L | Sheffield | Glossop | 1910 | 1919 | Denaby Main | 17 | | |
| Hogg, G | Aberdeen | juniors | 1980 | 1988 | Portsmouth | 82 | 1 | 1 |
| Holden, R | Middleton | Tonge | 1904 | 1913 | not known | 106 | | |
| Holt, E | not known | Newton Heath Athletic | 1899 | 1900 | not known | 1 | | 1 |
| Holton, J | Lesmahagow | Shrewsbury Town | 1973 | 1976 | Sunderland | 63 | | 5 |
| Homer, T | Birmingham | Kidderminster Harriers | 1909 | 1912 | not known | 25 | | 14 |
| Hood, W | not known | not known | 1892 | 1894 | not known | 33 | | 6 |
| Hooper, A | Brierley Hill | Kidderminster Harriers | 1909 | 1914 | Crystal Palace | 7 | | 1 |
| Hopkin, F | Dewsbury | Darlington | 1919 | 1921 | Liverpool | 70 | | 8 |
| Hopkins, J | Manchester | Berry's Association | 1899 | 1899 | not known | 1 | | |
| Hopkinson, S | Sheffield | Ashton National | 1929 | 1935 | Tranmere Rovers | 55 | | 10 |
| Houston, S | Dunoon | Brentford | 1973 | 1980 | Sheffield United | 204 | 1 | 13 |
| Howarth, J | Darwen | Darwen | 1921 | 1923 | not known | 4 | | |
| Howells, E | not known | not known | 1886 | 1887 | not known | | | |
| Hudson, E | Bolton | Walkden Central | 1912 | 1919 | Stockport County | 11 | | |
| Hughes, M | Wrexham | juniors | 1980 | 1986 | Barcelona | | | |
| | | Barcelona | 1988 | 1995 | Chelsea | 336 | 9 | 120 |
| Hulme, A | Manchester | Oldham Athletic | 1906 | 1909 | Nelson | 4 | | |
| Hunter, G | Peshawar, India | Chelsea | 1914 | 1915 | Portsmouth | 22 | | 2 |
| Hunter, R | Colwyn Bay | Colwyn Bay | 1956 | 1960 | Wrexham | 1 | | |
| Hunter, W | Sunderland | Barnsley | 1913 | 1913 | Clapton Orient | 3 | | 2 |
| Hurst, D | Cockermouth | Manchester City | 1902 | 1903 | not known | 16 | | 4 |
| Iddon, R | Tarleton | Chorley | 1925 | 1927 | Chorley | 2 | | |
| Ince, P | Ilford | West Ham United | 1989 | 1995 | Internazionale | 203 | 3 | 25 |
| Inglis, W | Kirkcaldy | Sheffield Wednesday | 1925 | 1930 | Northampton Town | 14 | | 1 |
| Irwin, D | Cork | Oldham Athletic | 1990 | 2002 | Wolverhampton Wanderers | 356 | 12 | 22 |
| Jackson, T | Belfast | Nottingham Forest | 1975 | 1978 | Waterford | 18 | 1 | |
| Jackson, W | Flint | St Helens Recreation | 1899 | 1902 | Barrow | 61 | | 12 |
| James, S | Coseley | juniors | 1965 | 1976 | York City | 129 | | 4 |
| Jenkyns, C | Builth | Woolwich Arsenal | 1896 | 1897 | Walsall | 35 | | 5 |
| John, R | Briton Ferry | Sheffield United | 1936 | 1937 | Newport County | 15 | | |
| Johnsen, R | Sandefjord, Norway | Besiktas (Turkey) | 1996 | 2002 | Aston Villa | 85 | 14 | 7 |
| Johnson, S | not known | Tonge | 1901 | 1902 | Heywood | 1 | | |
| Johnston, W | Edinburgh | Stockport County | 1927 | 1929 | Macclesfield | | | |
| | | Macclesfield | 1931 | 1932 | Oldham Athletic | 71 | | 24 |
| Jones, D | Ynysddu | Wigan Athletic | 1937 | 1938 | Swindon Town | 1 | | |
| Jones, M | Barnsley | juniors | 1948 | 1958 | victim, Munich air disaster | 103 | | 1 |
| Jones, O | Bangor, North Wales | Chorley | 1898 | 1899 | Bangor | 2 | | |

| FAC Apps | FAC Sub | FAC Goals | FLC Apps | FLC Sub | FLC Goals | Europe Apps | Europe Sub | Europe Goals | Others Apps | Others Sub | Others Goals | Totals Apps | Totals Sub | Totals Goals |
|---|---|---|---|---|---|---|---|---|---|---|---|---|---|---|
| | | | | | | | | | | | | 8 | | 2 |
| 15 | | 9 | | | | | | | 1 | | 6 | 125 | | 56 |
| | | | | | | | | | | | | 4 | | 1 |
| 2 | | | | | | | | | 1 | | | 60 | | 2 |
| 6 | | 2 | | | | | | | | | | 70 | | 22 |
| 1 | | | | | | | | | | | | 12 | | |
| 9 | | 5 | | | | | | | | | | 147 | | 52 |
| | | | | | | | | | | | | 4 | | |
| 3 | | | | | | | | | | | | 49 | | 2 |
| | | | | | | | | | | | | 4 | | 1 |
| 1 | | | | | | | | | | | | 1 | | |
| 2 | | | | | | | | | | | | 46 | | 5 |
| 1 | | | | | | | | | | | | 11 | | |
| 1 | | | | | | | | | | | | 4 | | |
| 2 | | | | | | | | | | | | 27 | | |
| | | | | | | | | | | | | 2 | | |
| | | | | | | | | | | | | 1 | | |
| 1 | | | | | | | | | | | | 1 | | |
| | | | | | | | | | | | | 6 | | |
| | | | | | | | | | | | | | | |
| 13 | | | | | | | | | | | | 128 | | 2 |
| | | | | | | | | | | | | 26 | | |
| | | | | 2 | | | | | | | | | 3 | |
| 1 | | | | | | | | | | | | 8 | | |
| 2 | | | | | | | | | | | | 36 | | 17 |
| | | | | | | | | | | | | 2 | | 1 |
| | | | | | | | | | | | | | | |
| 3 | | | | | | | | | | | | 6 | | |
| 35 | | 15 | 1 | | 1 | 25 | | 14 | 2 | | 1 | 264 | 1 | 145 |
| | | | | | | | | | | | | 3 | | |
| | | | | | | | | | | | | 4 | | 2 |
| | | | 1 | | | | 1 | | 1 | | | 4 | 3 | |
| 2 | | | | | | | | | | | | 8 | | |
| | | | | | | | | | | | | 10 | | |
| | | | | | | | | | | | | 5 | | 1 |
| 21 | | | | | | | | | | | | 322 | | 7 |
| 17 | | 6 | 7 | | 4 | 8 | | 2 | 1 | | | 133 | 1 | 51 |
| | | | | | | | | | | | | 8 | | |
| 2 | | | | | | | | | | | | 53 | | 12 |
| 7 | | | | | | | | | | | | 86 | | 2 |
| | | | | | | | | | | | | 30 | | |
| | | | | | | | | | | | | 20 | | 4 |
| 1 | | | | | | | | | 1 | | | 19 | | |
| 8 | | | 7 | 1 | | 10 | | | 1 | | | 108 | 2 | 1 |
| 11 | | | | | | | | | | | | 117 | | |
| | | | | | | | | | | | | 1 | | 1 |
| 2 | | | 4 | | | | | | | | | 69 | | 5 |
| | | | | | | | | | | | | 25 | | 14 |
| 3 | | | | | | | | | 2 | | | 38 | | 6 |
| | | | | | | | | | | | | 7 | | 1 |
| 4 | | | | | | | | | | | | 74 | | 8 |
| | | | | | | | | | | | | 1 | | |
| 2 | | 2 | | | | | | | | | | 57 | | 12 |
| 22 | | 1 | 16 | | 2 | 6 | 1 | | | | | 248 | 2 | 16 |
| | | | | | | | | | | | | 4 | | |
| 1 | | | | | | | | | | | | 1 | | |
| | | | | | | | | | | | | 11 | | |
| | | | | | | | | | | | | | | |
| 45 | 1 | 17 | 37 | 1 | 16 | 30 | 3 | 9 | 5 | | 1 | 453 | 14 | 163 |
| | | | | | | | | | | | | 4 | | |
| 1 | | | | | | | | | | | | 23 | | 2 |
| | | | | | | | | | | | | 1 | | |
| | | | | | | | | | | | | 3 | | 2 |
| 5 | | | | | | | | | | | | 21 | | 4 |
| | | | | | | | | | | | | 2 | | |
| 26 | 1 | 1 | 23 | 1 | 2 | 20 | | | 4 | | 1 | 276 | 5 | 29 |
| | | | | | | | | | | | | 14 | | 1 |
| 42 | 1 | 7 | 28 | 3 | | 73 | 2 | 4 | 11 | | | 510 | 18 | 33 |
| | | | 4 | | | | | | | | | 22 | 1 | |
| 3 | | 2 | | | | | | | | | | 64 | | 14 |
| 12 | | | 17 | 1 | | 2 | | | | | | 160 | 1 | 4 |
| 8 | | | | | | | | | 4 | | 1 | 47 | | 6 |
| | | | | | | | | | | | | 15 | | |
| 8 | 2 | 1 | 3 | | | 32 | 3 | | 3 | | 1 | 131 | 19 | 9 |
| | | | | | | | | | | | | 1 | | |
| | | | | | | | | | | | | | | |
| 6 | | 3 | | | | | | | | | | 77 | | 27 |
| | | | | | | | | | | | | 1 | | |
| 7 | | | | | | 10 | | | 1 | | | 121 | | 1 |
| | | | | | | | | | | | | 2 | | |

| Player | Birthplace | From | Year Joined | Year Left | To | League Apps | Sub | Goals |
|---|---|---|---|---|---|---|---|---|
| Jones, P | Salford | juniors | 1954 | 1960 | Wrexham | 1 | | |
| Jones, T | Penycae | Oswestry Town | 1924 | 1937 | Scunthorpe & Lindsay Utd | 189 | | |
| Jones, T | Tonupandy | Sheffield Wednesday | 1934 | 1935 | Watford | 20 | | 4 |
| Jordan, J | Carluke | Leeds United | 1978 | 1981 | AC Milan | 109 | | 37 |
| Jovanovic, N | Cetinje, Yugoslavia | Red Star | 1980 | 1982 | Buducnost (Yugoslavia) | 20 | 1 | 4 |
| Kanchelskis, A | Kirovograd, Ukraine | Shakhytor Donetsk | 1991 | 1995 | Everton | 96 | 27 | 28 |
| Keane, R | Cork | Nottingham Forest | 1993 | | still at club | 252 | 10 | 29 |
| Kelly, J | Carlisle | juniors | 1972 | 1977 | Chicago Sting | | 1 | |
| Kennedy, F | Bury | Rossendale United | 1923 | 1925 | Everton | 17 | | 4 |
| Kennedy, P | Dublin | juniors | 1952 | 1956 | Blackburn Rovers | 1 | | |
| Kennedy, W | not known | Ayr Parkhouse | 1895 | 1896 | Stockport County | 30 | | 11 |
| Kerr, H | not known | Ayr | 1904 | 1904 | not known | 2 | | |
| Kidd, B | Manchester | not known | 1964 | 1974 | Arsenal | 195 | 8 | 52 |
| Kinloch, J | not known | not known | 1892 | 1893 | not known | 1 | | |
| Kinsey, A | Liverpool | juniors | 1961 | 1966 | Wrexham | 1 | | 1 |
| Knowles, F | Hyde | Stalybridge Celtic | 1911 | 1919 | Hartlepools United | 46 | | 1 |
| Kopel, F | Falkirk | juniors | 1964 | 1969 | Blackburn Rovers | 8 | 2 | |
| Lancaster, J | Stockport | Heaton Norris OB | 1949 | 1950 | Accrington Stanley | 2 | | |
| Lang, T | Larkhall | Huddersfield Town | 1935 | 1937 | Swansea Town | 12 | | 1 |
| Langford, L | Sheffield | Manchester City | 1934 | 1937 | not known | 15 | | |
| Lappin, H | Manchester | Oldham Athletic | 1901 | 1903 | Grimsby Town | 27 | | 4 |
| Law, D | Aberdeen | Torino | 1962 | 1973 | Manchester City | 305 | 4 | 171 |
| Lawson, R | Bolton | Cheshire College | 1900 | 1901 | Bolton Wanderers | 3 | | |
| Lawton, N | Manchester | juniors | 1956 | 1963 | Preston North End | 36 | | 6 |
| Lee, E | not known | Hurst Ramblers | 1898 | 1900 | Hyde St George's | 11 | | 5 |
| Leigh, T | not known | Burton Swifts | 1900 | 1901 | not known | 43 | | 15 |
| Leighton, J | Johnstone | Aberdeen | 1988 | 1992 | Dundee | 73 | | |
| Leonard, H | Sunderland | Derby County | 1920 | 1921 | Heanor Town | 10 | | 5 |
| Lewis, E | Manchester | Amateur | 1949 | 1955 | Preston North End | 20 | | 9 |
| Lievesley, L | Staveley | Doncaster Rovers | 1932 | 1933 | Chesterfield | 2 | | |
| Lievesley, W | Staveley | Derby County | 1922 | 1923 | Exeter City | 2 | | |
| Linkson, O | New Barnet | The Pirates | 1908 | 1913 | Shelbourne | 55 | | |
| Livingstone, G | Dumbarton | Rangers | 1909 | 1914 | retired | 43 | | 4 |
| Lochhead, A | Busby | Heart of Midlothian | 1921 | 1925 | Leicester City | 147 | | 50 |
| Longair, W | Dundee | Dundee | 1895 | 1895 | Dundee | 1 | | |
| Longton* | not known | not known | 1885 | 1887 | not known | | | |
| Lowrie, T | Glasgow | Troon Athletic | 1947 | 1951 | Aberdeen | 13 | | |
| Lynch, M | Manchester | juniors | 1998 | | still at club | | | |
| Lydon, G | Manchester | Mossley | 1928 | 1933 | Southport | 3 | | |
| Lyner, D | Belfast | Glentoran | 1922 | 1922 | Kilmarnock | 3 | | |
| Lynn, S | St Helens | Amateur | 1935 | 1951 | Bradford Park Avenue | 13 | | |
| Lyons, G | not Known | Black Lane Temperance | 1904 | 1906 | Oldham Athletic | 4 | | |
| McBain, N | Campbeltown | Ayr United | 1921 | 1923 | Everton | 42 | | 2 |
| McCalliog, J | Glasgow | Wolverhampton Wanderers | 1974 | 1975 | Southampton | 31 | | 7 |
| McCarthy, P | not known | Skelmersdale United | 1912 | 1912 | Skelmersdale United | 1 | | |
| McCartney, J | Glasgow | Cowlairs | 1894 | 1895 | Luton Town | 18 | | 1 |
| McCartney, W | Newmilns | Hibernian | 1903 | 1904 | West Ham United | 13 | | 1 |
| McClair, B | Airdrie | Celtic | 1987 | 1998 | Motherwell | 296 | 59 | 88 |
| McClelland, J | Dysart | Bradford Park Avenue | 1936 | 1937 | not known | 5 | | 1 |
| McCrae, J | Bridge of Weir | New Brighton | 1925 | 1926 | Watford | 9 | | |
| McCreery, D | Belfast | juniors | 1972 | 1979 | Queens Park Rangers | 48 | 39 | 7 |
| MacDonald, K | Llanwrst | Cardiff City | 1923 | 1924 | Bradford Park Avenue | 9 | | 2 |
| McDonald, W | Coatbridge | Airdrieonians | 1932 | 1934 | Tranmere Rovers | 27 | | 4 |
| MacDougall, E | Inverness | AFC Bournemouth | 1972 | 1973 | West Ham United | 18 | | 5 |
| McFarlane, N | Bray | juniors | 1952 | 1956 | Waterford | 1 | | |
| McFarlane, R | Airdrie | Sunderland Albion | 1891 | 1892 | Airdrieonians | 3 | | |
| McFetteridge, D | not known | Cowlairs | 1894 | 1896 | Stockport County | 1 | | |
| McGarvey, S | Glasgow | juniors | 1979 | 1984 | Portsmouth | 13 | 12 | 3 |
| McGibbon, P | Lurgan | Portadown | 1992 | 1997 | Wigan Athletic | | | |
| McGillivray, C | East Whitburn | Celtic | 1933 | 1934 | Motherwell | 8 | | |
| McGillivray, J | Broughton | Berry's Association | 1907 | 1910 | Southport Central | 3 | | |
| McGlen, W | Bedlington | Blyth Spartans | 1946 | 1952 | Lincoln City | 110 | | 2, |
| McGrath, C | Belfast | Tottenham Hotspur | 1976 | 1981 | Tulsa Roughnecks | 12 | 16 | 1 |
| McGrath, P | London | St Patrick's Athletic | 1982 | 1989 | Aston Villa | 159 | 4 | 12 |
| McGuinness, W | Manchester | juniors | 1955 | 1960 | retired | 81 | | 2 |
| McIlroy, S | Belfast | juniors | 1969 | 1982 | Stoke City | 320 | 22 | 57 |
| McIlvenny, E | Greenock | Philadelphia Nationals | 1950 | 1953 | Waterford | 2 | | |
| McKay, W | West Benhar | Bolton Wanderers | 1934 | 1946 | Stalybridge Celtic | 171 | | 15 |
| McKee, C | Glasgow | juniors | 1989 | 1994 | Kilmarnock | 1 | | |
| McLachlan, G | Glasgow | Cardiff City | 1929 | 1933 | Chester | 110 | | 4 |
| McLenahan, H | Manchester | Stockport County | 1927 | 1936 | Notts County | 112 | | 11 |
| McMillan, S | Belfast | juniors | 1957 | 1963 | Wrexham | 15 | | 6 |
| McMillen, W | Belfast | Cliftonville | 1933 | 1936 | Chesterfield | 27 | | 2 |
| McNaught, J | Dumbarton | Linfield | 1893 | 1898 | Tottenham Hotspur | 140 | | 12 |
| McNulty, T | Salford | juniors | 1945 | 1954 | Liverpool | 57 | | |
| McPherson, F | Barrow in Furness | Barrow | 1922 | 1928 | Manchester Central | 159 | | 45 |
| McQueen, G | Kilbirnie | Leeds United | 1978 | 1985 | Seiko | 184 | | 20 |
| McShane, H | Holytown | Bolton Wanderers | 1950 | 1954 | Oldham Athletic | 56 | | 8 |
| Macari, L | Edinburgh | Celtic | 1973 | 1984 | Swindon Town | 311 | 18 | 78 |
| Mackie, C | not known | Aberdeen | 1904 | 1905 | West Ham United | 5 | | 3 |

| FAC Apps | FAC Sub | FAC Goals | FLC Apps | FLC Sub | FLC Goals | Europe Apps | Europe Sub | Europe Goals | Others Apps | Others Sub | Others Goals | Totals Apps | Totals Sub | Totals Goals |
|---|---|---|---|---|---|---|---|---|---|---|---|---|---|---|
| | | | | | | | | | | | | 1 | | |
| 11 | | | | | | | | | | | | 200 | | |
| 2 | | | | | | | | | | | | 22 | | 4 |
| 11 | 1 | 2 | 4 | | 2 | 1 | | | | | | 125 | 1 | 41 |
| 1 | | | 2 | | | 2 | | | | | | 25 | 1 | 4 |
| 11 | 1 | 4 | 15 | 1 | 3 | 7 | | 1 | 3 | | | 132 | 29 | 36 |
| 36 | 1 | 1 | 11 | 2 | | 70 | 1 | 14 | 10 | | 2 | 379 | 14 | 46 |
| | | | | | | | | | | | | | 1 | |
| 1 | | | | | | | | | | | | 18 | | 4 |
| | | | | | | | | | | | | 1 | | |
| 3 | | 1 | | | | | | | | | | 33 | | 12 |
| | | | | | | | | | | | | 2 | | |
| 24 | 1 | 8 | 20 | | 7 | 16 | | 3 | 2 | | | 257 | 9 | 70 |
| | | | | | | | | | | | | 1 | | |
| | | | | | | | | | | | | 1 | | 1 |
| 1 | | | | | | | | | | | | 47 | | 1 |
| 1 | | | | | | 1 | | | | | | 10 | 2 | |
| 2 | | | | | | | | | | | | 4 | | |
| 1 | | | | | | | | | | | | 13 | | 1 |
| | | | | | | | | | | | | 15 | | |
| | | | | | | | | | | | | 27 | | 4 |
| 44 | 2 | 34 | 11 | | 3 | 33 | | 28 | 5 | | 1 | 398 | 6 | 237 |
| | | | | | | | | | | | | 3 | | |
| 7 | | | 1 | | | | | | | | | 44 | | 6 |
| | | | | | | | | | | | | 11 | | 5 |
| 3 | | | | | | | | | | | | 46 | | 15 |
| 14 | | | 7 | | | | | | | | | 94 | | |
| | | | | | | | | | | | | 10 | | 5 |
| 4 | | 2 | | | | | | | | | | 24 | | 11 |
| | | | | | | | | | | | | 2 | | |
| 1 | | | | | | | | | | | | 3 | | |
| 4 | | | | | | | | | | | | 59 | | |
| 3 | | | | | | | | | | | | 46 | | 4 |
| 6 | | | | | | | | | | | | 153 | | 50 |
| | | | | | | | | | | | | 1 | | |
| 1 | | | | | | | | | | | | 1 | | |
| 1 | | | | | | | | | | | | 14 | | |
| | | | | | | 1 | | | | | | 1 | | |
| | | | | | | | | | | | | 3 | | |
| | | | | | | | | | | | | 3 | | |
| | | | | | | | | | | | | 13 | | |
| 1 | | | | | | | | | | | | 5 | | |
| 1 | | | | | | | | | | | | 43 | | 2 |
| 1 | | | 5 | 1 | | | | | | | | 37 | 1 | 7 |
| | | | | | | | | | | | | 1 | | |
| 1 | | | | | | | | | 1 | | | 20 | | 1 |
| | | | | | | | | | | | | 13 | | 1 |
| 39 | 6 | 14 | 44 | 1 | 19 | 17 | 6 | 5 | 3 | | 1 | 399 | 72 | 127 |
| | | | | | | | | | | | | 5 | | 1 |
| 4 | | | | | | | | | | | | 13 | | |
| 1 | 6 | | 4 | 4 | 1 | 4 | 3 | | | 1 | | 57 | 53 | 8 |
| | | | | | | | | | | | | 9 | | 2 |
| | | | | | | | | | | | | 27 | | 4 |
| | | | | | | | | | | | | 18 | | 5 |
| | | | | | | | | | | | | 1 | | |
| | | | | | | | | | | | | 3 | | |
| | | | | | | | | | | | | 1 | | |
| | | | | | | | | | | | | 13 | 12 | 3 |
| | | | | 1 | | | | | | | | | 1 | |
| 1 | | | | | | | | | | | | 9 | | |
| 1 | | | | | | | | | | | | 4 | | |
| 12 | | | | | | | | | | | | 122 | | 2 |
| | | | | 2 | | 3 | 1 | | | | | 15 | 19 | 1 |
| 15 | 3 | 2 | 13 | | 2 | 4 | | | 1 | | | 192 | 7 | 16 |
| 2 | | | | | | 2 | | | | | | 85 | | 2 |
| 35 | 3 | 6 | 25 | 3 | 6 | 10 | | 2 | 1 | | | 391 | 28 | 71 |
| | | | | | | | | | | | | 2 | | |
| 13 | | | | | | | | | | | | 184 | | 15 |
| | | | | | | | | | | | | 1 | 1 | |
| 6 | | | | | | | | | | | | 116 | | 4 |
| 4 | | 1 | | | | | | | | | | 116 | | 12 |
| | | | | | | | | | | | | 15 | | 6 |
| 2 | | | | | | | | | | | | 29 | | 2 |
| 17 | | | | | | | | | 5 | | | 162 | | 12 |
| 2 | | | | | | | | | 1 | | | 60 | | |
| 16 | | 7 | | | | | | | | | | 175 | | 52 |
| 21 | | 2 | 16 | | 4 | 7 | | | 1 | | | 229 | | 26 |
| 1 | | | | | | | | | | | | 57 | | 8 |
| 31 | 3 | 8 | 22 | 5 | 10 | 9 | 1 | 1 | 1 | | | 374 | 27 | 97 |
| 2 | | 1 | | | | | | | | | | 7 | | 4 |

| Player | Birthplace | From | Year Joined | Year Left | To | League Apps | Sub | Goals |
|---|---|---|---|---|---|---|---|---|
| Maiorana, G | Cambridge | Histon | 1988 | 1994 | retired | 2 | 5 | |
| Manley, T | Northwich | Northwich Victoria | 1930 | 1952 | retired | 188 | | 40 |
| Mann, F | Newark | Huddersfield Town | 1923 | 1930 | Mossley | 180 | | 5 |
| Mann, H | Nuneaton | Grantham Town | 1931 | 1933 | Ripley Town | 13 | | 2 |
| Manns, T | Rotherham | Burnley | 1933 | 1934 | Clapton Orient | 2 | | |
| Marshall, A | Liverpool | Stockport County | 1902 | 1903 | Portsmouth | 6 | | |
| Martin, L | Hyde | juniors | 1985 | 1994 | Celtic | 56 | 17 | 1 |
| Martin, M | Dublin | Bohemians | 1973 | 1975 | West Bromwich Albion | 33 | 7 | 2 |
| Mathieson, W | not known | Clydeside | 1892 | 1894 | Rotherham Town | 10 | | 2 |
| May, D | Oldham | Blackburn Rovers | 1994 | 2003 | free transfer | 68 | 17 | 6 |
| Meehan, T | Manchester | Rochdale | 1917 | 1920 | Chelsea | 51 | | 6 |
| Mellor, J | Oldham | Witton Albion | 1929 | 1937 | Cardiff City | 116 | | |
| Menzies, A | Blantyre | Heart of Midlothian | 1906 | 1907 | Luton Town | 23 | | 4 |
| Meredith, W | Black Park | Manchester City | 1906 | 1921 | Manchester City | 303 | | 35 |
| Mew, J | Sunderland | Marley Hill United | 1912 | 1926 | Barrow | 186 | | |
| Milarvie, R | Manchester | Derby County | 1890 | 1891 | Ardwick | | | |
| Millar, G | not known | Glasgow Perthshire | 1894 | 1895 | Chatham | 6 | | 5 |
| Miller, J | Greenock | Grimsby Town | 1924 | 1924 | York City | 4 | | 1 |
| Miller, T | Motherwell | Liverpool | 1920 | 1921 | Heart of Midlothian | 25 | | 7 |
| Milne, R | Dundee | Bristol City | 1988 | 1991 | Sing Tao | 19 | 4 | 3 |
| Mitchell, A | not known | Airdrieonians | 1892 | 1894 | Burton Swifts | 54 | | |
| Mitchell, A | Coxhoe | Darlington | 1932 | 1933 | Hull City | 1 | | |
| Mitchell, J | not known | not known | 1885 | 1888 | Bolton Wanderers | | | |
| | | Bolton Wanderers | 1888 | 1891 | not known | 3 | | |
| Mitten, C | Rangoon, Burma | Strathallan Hawthorn | 1936 | 1950 | Santa Fe | 142 | | 50 |
| Moger, H | Southampton | Southampton | 1903 | 1912 | retired | 242 | | |
| Moir, I | Aberdeen | juniors | 1958 | 1965 | Blackpool | 45 | | 5 |
| Montgomery, A | Chryston | Bury | 1905 | 1906 | Bury | 3 | | |
| Montgomery, J | Craghead | Glossop | 1915 | 1921 | not known | 27 | | 1 |
| Moody, J | Sheffield | Doncaster Rovers | 1932 | 1933 | Chesterfield | 50 | | |
| Moore, C | Cheslyn Hay | Hednesford Town | 1919 | 1931 | retired | 309 | | |
| Moore, G | Cascade | Chelsea | 1963 | 1965 | Northampton Town | 18 | | 4 |
| Moran, K | Dublin | Pegasus (Dublin) | 1978 | 1988 | Sporting Gijon | 228 | 3 | 21 |
| Morgan, H | Lanarkshire | Bolton Wanderers | 1900 | 1901 | Manchester City | 20 | | 4 |
| Morgan, W | Horwich | Horwich | 1897 | 1903 | Bolton Wanderers | 143 | | 6 |
| Morgan, W | Sauchie | Burnley | 1968 | 1975 | Burnley | 236 | 2 | 25 |
| Morgans, K | Swansea | juniors | 1955 | 1961 | Swansea Town | 17 | | |
| Morris, J | Radcliffe | juniors | 1939 | 1949 | Derby County | 83 | | 32 |
| Morrison, T | Belfast | Burnley | 1902 | 1904 | Colne | 29 | | 7 |
| Morton, B | Sheffield | Stourbridge | 1935 | 1936 | Torquay United | 1 | | |
| Moses, R | Manchester | West Bromwich Albion | 1981 | 1988 | retired | 143 | 7 | 7 |
| Muhren, A | Vollendam | Ipswich Town | 1982 | 1985 | Ajax | 65 | 5 | 13 |
| Mulryne, P | Belfast | juniors | 1994 | 1999 | Norwich City | 1 | | |
| Murray, R | Edinburgh | Heart of Midlothian | 1937 | 1938 | Bath City | 4 | | |
| Mutch, G | Aberdeen | Arbroath | 1934 | 1937 | Preston North End | 112 | | 46 |
| Myerscough, J | Galgate | Lancaster Town | 1920 | 1923 | Bradford | 33 | | 8 |
| Nardiello, D | Coventry | juniors | 1999 | | still at club | | | |
| Neville, G | Bury | juniors | 1991 | | still at club | 249 | 14 | 3 |
| Neville, P | Bury | juniors | 1993 | | still at club | 169 | 44 | 5 |
| Nevland, E | Stavanger, Norway | Viking | 1997 | 1999 | Viking | | 1 | |
| Nevin, G | Lintz | Sheffield Wednesday | 1934 | 1934 | Sheffield Wednesday | 4 | | |
| Newton, P | Whitchurch | Sandbach Ramblers | 1933 | 1934 | Tranmere Rovers | 2 | | |
| Nicholl, J | Hamilton, Canada | juniors | 1971 | 1982 | Toronto Blizzard | 188 | 9 | 3 |
| Nicholson, J | Belfast | juniors | 1958 | 1964 | Huddersfield Town | 58 | | 5 |
| Nicol, G | Saltcoats | Saltcoats Victoria | 1928 | 1929 | Brighton & Hove Albion | 6 | | 2 |
| Noble, R | Manchester | juniors | 1961 | 1969 | retired | 31 | | |
| Norton, J | Leicester | Nuneaton Town | 1913 | 1919 | Leicester City | 37 | | 3 |
| Notman, A | Edinburgh | juniors | 1995 | 2000 | Norwich City | | | |
| Nuttall, T | Bolton | Heywood United | 1910 | 1913 | Everton | 16 | | 4 |
| O'Brien, W | Dublin | Shamrock Rovers | 1986 | 1988 | Newcastle United | 16 | 15 | 2 |
| O'Brien, G | not known | not known | 1902 | 1902 | not known | 1 | | |
| O'Connell, P | Dublin | Hull City | 1914 | 1919 | Dumbarton | 34 | | 2 |
| O'Kane, J | Nottingham | juniors | 1991 | 1998 | Everton | 1 | 1 | |
| Olive, L | Salford | juniors | 1952 | 1953 | retired | 2 | | |
| Olsen, J | Fakse, Denmark | Ajax | 1984 | 1988 | Bordeaux | 119 | 20 | 21 |
| O'Neil, T | St Helens | juniors | 1968 | 1973 | Southport | 54 | | |
| O'Shea, J | Waterford | junior football | 1998 | | still at club | 30 | 11 | |
| O'Shaughnessey, T | not known | not known | 1890 | 1892 | not known | | | |
| Owen, G | Chirk | Chirk | 1889 | 1890 | West Manchester | | | |
| Owen, J | Chirk | Chirk | 1887 | 1893 | not known | | | |
| Owen, W | not known | Holywell | 1898 | 1899 | not known | 1 | | |
| Owen, W | Northwich | Macclesfield | 1934 | 1936 | Reading | 17 | | 1 |
| Page, L | Liverpool | Burnley | 1932 | 1932 | Port Vale | 12 | | |
| Pallister, G | Ramsgate | Middlesbrough | 1989 | 1998 | Middlesbrough | 314 | 3 | 12 |
| Pape, A | Elsecar | Clapton Orient | 1925 | 1925 | Fulham | 18 | | 5 |
| Parker, P | West Ham | Queens Park Rangers | 1991 | 1996 | Derby County | 100 | 5 | 1 |
| Parker, S | Hurlford | Hurlford | 1994 | 1994 | Burnley | 11 | | |
| Parker, T | Eccles | amateur | 1930 | 1932 | Bristol City | 17 | | |
| Parkinson, R | Preston | Nottingham Forest | 1899 | 1900 | not known | 15 | | 7 |
| Partridge, E | Lye | Ebbw Vale | 1920 | 1929 | Halifax Town | 148 | | 16 |

| FAC Apps | Sub | Goals | FLC Apps | Sub | Goals | Europe Apps | Sub | Goals | Others Apps | Sub | Goals | Totals Apps | Sub | Goals |
|---|---|---|---|---|---|---|---|---|---|---|---|---|---|---|
| | | | | 1 | | | | | | | | 2 | 6 | |
| 7 | | 1 | | | | | | | | | | 195 | | 41 |
| 17 | | | | | | | | | | | | 197 | | 5 |
| | | | | | | | | | | | | 13 | | 2 |
| | | | | | | | | | | | | 2 | | |
| | | | | | | | | | | | | 6 | | |
| 13 | 1 | 1 | 8 | 2 | | 6 | 6 | | 1 | | | 84 | 26 | 2 |
| 2 | | | 1 | | | | | | | | | 36 | 7 | 2 |
| | | | | | | | | | | | | 10 | | 2 |
| 6 | | | 9 | | 1 | 13 | 2 | 1 | 2 | 1 | | 98 | 20 | 8 |
| 2 | | | | | | | | | | | | 53 | | 6 |
| 6 | | | | | | | | | | | | 122 | | |
| 2 | | | | | | | | | | | | 25 | | 4 |
| 29 | | | | | | | | | 3 | | 1 | 335 | | 36 |
| 13 | | | | | | | | | | | | 199 | | |
| 1 | | | | | | | | | | | | 1 | | |
| 1 | | | | | | | | | | | | 7 | | 5 |
| | | | | | | | | | | | | 4 | | 1 |
| 2 | | 1 | | | | | | | | | | 27 | | 8 |
| 7 | | | | | | | | | | | | 26 | 4 | 3 |
| 4 | | | | | | | | | 3 | | | 61 | | |
| | | | | | | | | | | | | 1 | | |
| | | | | | | | | | | | | | | |
| | | | | | | | | | | | | 3 | | |
| 19 | | 11 | | | | | | | 1 | | | 162 | | 61 |
| 22 | | | | | | | | | 2 | | | 266 | | |
| | | | | | | | | | | | | 45 | | 5 |
| | | | | | | | | | | | | 3 | | |
| | | | | | | | | | | | | 27 | | 1 |
| 1 | | | | | | | | | | | | 51 | | |
| 19 | | | | | | | | | | | | 328 | | |
| 1 | | 1 | | | | | | | | | | 19 | | 5 |
| 18 | | 1 | 24 | 1 | 2 | 13 | 1 | | 1 | | | 284 | 5 | 24 |
| 3 | | | | | | | | | | | | 23 | | 4 |
| 9 | | 1 | | | | | | | | | | 152 | | 7 |
| 27 | | 4 | 24 | 1 | 3 | 4 | | 1 | 2 | | 1 | 293 | 3 | 34 |
| 2 | | | | | | 4 | | | | | | 23 | | |
| 9 | | 3 | | | | | | | 1 | | | 93 | | 35 |
| 7 | | 1 | | | | | | | | | | 36 | | 8 |
| | | | | | | | | | | | | 1 | | |
| 11 | | 1 | 22 | 2 | 4 | 12 | 1 | | | 1 | | 188 | 11 | 12 |
| 8 | | 1 | 11 | | 1 | 8 | | 3 | 1 | | | 93 | 5 | 18 |
| | | | 3 | | | | | | | | | 4 | | |
| | | | | | | | | | | | | 4 | | |
| 8 | | 3 | | | | | | | | | | 120 | | 49 |
| 1 | | | | | | | | | | | | 34 | | 8 |
| | | | 1 | 1 | | | 1 | | | | | 1 | 2 | |
| 28 | 2 | | 9 | 1 | | 77 | 5 | 1 | 7 | 1 | | 370 | 23 | 4 |
| 19 | 4 | 1 | 12 | 1 | | 35 | 17 | 1 | 6 | 2 | | 241 | 68 | 7 |
| 2 | | | | 2 | 1 | | | | | | | 2 | 3 | 1 |
| | | | | | | | | | | | | 4 | | |
| | | | | | | | | | | | | 2 | | |
| 22 | 4 | 1 | 14 | | 1 | 10 | | 1 | 1 | | | 235 | 13 | 6 |
| 7 | | 1 | 3 | | | | | | | | | 68 | | 6 |
| 1 | | | | | | | | | | | | 7 | | 2 |
| 2 | | | | | | | | | | | | 33 | | |
| | | | | | | | | | | | | 37 | | 3 |
| | | | | 1 | | | | | | | | | 1 | |
| | | | | | | | | | | | | 16 | | 4 |
| | 2 | | 1 | 2 | | | | | | | | 17 | 19 | 2 |
| | | | | | | | | | | | | 1 | | |
| 1 | | | | | | | | | | | | 35 | | 2 |
| 1 | | | 2 | 1 | | 1 | | | | | | 5 | 2 | |
| | | | | | | | | | | | | 2 | | |
| 13 | 3 | 2 | 10 | 3 | 1 | 6 | 1 | | 1 | | | 149 | 27 | 24 |
| 7 | | | 7 | | | | | | | | | 68 | | |
| 1 | | | 7 | | | 12 | 7 | | | | | 50 | 18 | |
| 1 | | | | | | | | | | | | 1 | | |
| 1 | | | | | | | | | | | | 1 | | |
| 6 | | | | | | | | | | | | 6 | | |
| | | | | | | | | | | | | 1 | | |
| | | | | | | | | | | | | 17 | | 1 |
| | | | | | | | | | | | | 12 | | |
| 38 | | 2 | 36 | | | 39 | 1 | 1 | 6 | | | 433 | 4 | 15 |
| | | | | | | | | | | | | 18 | | 5 |
| 14 | 1 | 1 | 15 | | | 7 | 3 | | 1 | | | 137 | 9 | 2 |
| | | | | | | | | | | | | 11 | | |
| | | | | | | | | | | | | 17 | | |
| | | | | | | | | | | | | 15 | | 7 |
| 12 | | 2 | | | | | | | | | | 160 | | 18 |

| Player | Birthplace | From | Year Joined | Year Left | To | League Apps | Sub | Goals |
|---|---|---|---|---|---|---|---|---|
| Paterson, S | Mostodloch | Nairn County | 1974 | 1980 | Hong Kong | 3 | 3 | |
| Payne, E | not known | Worcester City | 1908 | 1909 | not known | 2 | | 1 |
| Pears, S | Brandon | juniors | 1976 | 1985 | Middlesbrough | 4 | | |
| Pearson, M | Ridgeway | juniors | 1955 | 1963 | Sheffield Wednesday | 68 | | 12 |
| Pearson, S | Salford | Amateur | 1935 | 1954 | Bury | 315 | | 128 |
| Pearson, S | Hull | Hull City | 1974 | 1979 | West Ham United | 138 | 1 | 55 |
| Peddie, J | Glasgow | Newcastle United | 1902 | 1903 | Plymouth Argyle } | | | |
| | | Plymouth Argyle | 1904 | 1907 | Heart of Midlothian } | 12 | | 52 |
| Peden, J | Belfast | Linfield | 1893 | 1894 | Sheffield United | 28 | | 7 |
| Pegg, D | Doncaster | juniors | 1950 | 1958 | victim, Munich air disaster | 127 | | 24 |
| Pegg, E | Leicester | Preston North End | 1902 | 1904 | Fulham | 41 | | 13 |
| Pegg, K | Salford | amateur | 1945 | 1949 | Torquay United | 2 | | |
| Pepper, F | Sheffield | Sheffield United | 1898 | 1899 | Barnsley | 7 | | |
| Perrins, G | Birmingham | Birmingham St George | 1892 | 1896 | Luton Town | 92 | | |
| Peters, J | not known | Heywood Central | 1894 | 1896 | New Brompton | 46 | | 13 |
| Phelan, M | Nelson | Norwich City | 1989 | 1994 | West Bromwich Albion | 88 | 14 | 2 |
| Picken, J | Hurlford | Plymouth Argyle | 1905 | 1911 | Burnley | 113 | | 39 |
| Pilkington, K | Hitchin | junior football | 1992 | 1998 | Port Vale | 4 | 2 | |
| Pinner, M | Boston | amateur | 1961 | 1961 | Hendon | 4 | | |
| Poborsky, K | Czech Republic | Slavia Prague | 1996 | 1997 | Benfica | 18 | 14 | 5 |
| Porter, W | Fleetwood | Oldham Athletic | 1935 | 1944 | Hyde United | 61 | | |
| Potts, A | Cannock | Willenhall Swifts | 1913 | 1920 | Wolverhampton Wanderers | 27 | | 5 |
| Powell, J | Wrexham | Bolton Wanderers | 1886 | 1891 | not known | | | |
| Prentice, J | Glasgow | amateur | 1919 | 1920 | Swansea Town | 1 | | |
| Preston, S | Manchester | not known | 1901 | 1903 | Stockport County | 33 | | 14 |
| Prince, A | not known | Stafford Rangers | 1915 | 1915 | not known | 1 | | |
| Prince, D | not known | not known | 1893 | 1894 | not known | 2 | | |
| Prunier, W | Montreuil, France | Bordeaux | 1995 | 1996 | Bordeaux | 2 | | |
| Pugh, D | Manchester | juniors | 1999 | | still at club | | 1 | |
| Pugh, J | Hereford | Abertillery | 1922 | 1923 | Wrexham | 2 | | |
| Quin, J | Barrhead | Manchester City | 1908 | 1910 | Nelson | 2 | | |
| Quixall, A | Sheffield | Sheffield Wednesday | 1958 | 1964 | Oldham Athletic | 165 | | 50 |
| Rachubka, P | San Luis Obispo, USA | juniors | 1997 | 2002 | Charlton Athletic | 1 | | |
| Radcliffe, G | not known | not known | 1898 | 1899 | not known | 1 | | |
| Radford, C | Walsall | Walsall | 1920 | 1924 | died, motor cycle accident | 91 | | 1 |
| Ramsay, R | not known | Stoke | 1890 | 1891 | West Manchester | | | |
| Ramsden, C | South Normanton | Rotherham United | 1927 | 1932 | Manchester North End | 14 | | 3 |
| Rattigan | not known | not known | 1890 | 1891 | not known | | | |
| Rawlings, W | Andover | Southampton | 1928 | 1929 | Port Vale | 35 | | 19 |
| Read, H | Manchester | Manchester City | 1902 | 1908 | retired | 35 | | |
| Redman, W | Manchester | amateur | 1944 | 1954 | Bury | 36 | | |
| Redwood, H | St Helens | Sherdley Albion | 1933 | 1940 | died of TB | 89 | | 3 |
| Reid, T | Motherwell | Liverpool | 1929 | 1933 | Oldham Athletic | 96 | | 63 |
| Rennox, C | Shotts | Clapton Orient | 1925 | 1927 | Grimsby Town | 60 | | 24 |
| Ricardo | Madrid | Real Valladolid | 2002 | | still at club | | 1 | |
| Richards, C | Burton-upon-Trent | Leicester Fosse | 1902 | 1903 | Doncaster Rovers | 8 | | 1 |
| Richards, W | West Bromwich | West Bromwich Albion | 1901 | 1902 | Stourbridge | 9 | | 1 |
| Richardson, K | Greenwich | juniors | 2001 | | still at club | | 2 | |
| Richardson, L | Tow Law | South Shields | 1926 | 1929 | Reading | 38 | | |
| Ridding, W | Heswall | Manchester City | 1931 | 1934 | Northampton Town | 42 | | 14 |
| Ridgway, J | Manchester | West Manchester | 1895 | 1901 | Rochdale Town | 14 | | |
| Rimmer, J | Southport | juniors | 1963 | 1974 | Arsenal | 34 | | |
| Ritchie, A | Manchester | juniors | 1977 | 1981 | Brighton & Hove Albion | 26 | 7 | 13 |
| Roach, J | not known | amateur | 1941 | 1946 | not known | | | |
| Robbie, D | Motherwell | Plymouth Argyle | 1935 | 1935 | Margate | 1 | | |
| Roberts, C | Darlington | Grimsby Town | 1904 | 1913 | Oldham Athletic | 271 | | 22 |
| Roberts, R | Earlstown | Altrincham | 1912 | 1919 | not known | 2 | | |
| Roberts, W | not known | not known | 1897 | 1899 | not known | 9 | | 2 |
| Robertson, S | Dundee | Middelsbrough | 1903 | 1907 | Bradford Park Avenue | 28 | | 10 |
| Robertson, A | not known | Hibernian | 1903 | 1907 | not known | 33 | | 1 |
| Robertson, T | Lanarkshire | Dundee | 1903 | 1905 | Bathgate | 3 | | |
| Robertson, W | Falkirk | Stoke | 1934 | 1936 | Reading | 47 | | 1 |
| Robins, M | Ashton-under-Lyne | juniors | 1986 | 1992 | Norwich City | 19 | 29 | 11 |
| Robinson, J | Belfast | not known | 1919 | 1922 | Tranmere Rovers | 21 | | 3 |
| Robinson, M | Felling | Cardiff City | 1931 | 1932 | Chester | 10 | | |
| Robson, B | Chester-le-Street | West Bromwich Albion | 1981 | 1994 | Middlesbrough | 326 | 20 | 74 |
| Roche, L | Bolton | juniors | 1997 | 2003 | Burnley | 1 | | |
| Roche, P | Dublin | Shelbourne | 1973 | 1982 | Brentford | 46 | | |
| Rogers, M | Nottingham | juniors | 1975 | 1979 | Queens Park Rangers | 1 | | |
| Rothwell, C | not known | not known | 1893 | 1897 | not known | 2 | | 1 |
| Rothwell, H | not known | Glossop North End | 1902 | 1904 | Manchester City | 22 | | |
| Roughton, G | Manchester | Huddersfield Town | 1936 | 1945 | Exeter City | 86 | | |
| Round, E | Stoke-on-Trent | Oldham Athletic | 1909 | 1910 | Worksop Town | 2 | | |
| Rowe, J | Kingston-upon-Thames | Bohemians | 1914 | 1914 | Bohemians | 1 | | |
| Rowley, H | Bilston | Shrewsbury Town | 1928 | 1931 | Manchester City } | | | |
| | | Oldham Athletic | 1934 | 1937 | Burton Town } | 173 | | 55 |
| Rowley, J | Wolverhampton | Bournemouth & BA | 1937 | 1955 | Plymouth Argyle | 380 | | 182 |
| Royals, E | Fenton | Chesterton White Star | 1911 | 1920 | Northwich Victoria | 7 | | |
| Ryan, J | Stirling | juniors | 1962 | 1970 | Luton Town | 21 | 3 | 4 |
| Sadler, D | Yalding | Maidstone United | 1962 | 1973 | Preston North End | 266 | 6 | 22 |

| FAC Apps | FAC Sub | FAC Goals | FLC Apps | FLC Sub | FLC Goals | Europe Apps | Europe Sub | Europe Goals | Others Apps | Others Sub | Others Goals | Totals Apps | Totals Sub | Totals Goals |
|---|---|---|---|---|---|---|---|---|---|---|---|---|---|---|
| | | | 2 | | | | 2 | | | | | 5 | 5 | |
| | | | | | | | | | | | | 2 | | 1 |
| 1 | | | | | | | | | | | | 5 | | |
| 7 | | 1 | 3 | | 1 | 2 | | | | | | 80 | | 14 |
| 30 | | 21 | | | | | | | 1 | | | 346 | | 149 |
| 22 | | 5 | 12 | | 5 | 6 | | 1 | 1 | | | 179 | 1 | 66 |
| | | | | | | | | | | | | | | |
| 9 | | 6 | | | | | | | | | | 121 | | 58 |
| 3 | | 1 | | | | | | | 1 | | | 32 | | 8 |
| 9 | | | | | | 12 | | 4 | 2 | | | 150 | | 28 |
| 10 | | 7 | | | | | | | | | | 51 | | 20 |
| | | | | | | | | | | | | 2 | | |
| 1 | | | | | | | | | | | | 8 | | |
| 6 | | | | | | | | | 4 | | | 102 | | |
| 4 | | 1 | | | | | | | 1 | | | 51 | | 14 |
| 10 | | 1 | 14 | 2 | | 14 | 3 | | 1 | | | 127 | 19 | 3 |
| 8 | | 7 | | | | | | | 1 | | | 122 | | 46 |
| 1 | | | 1 | | | | | | | | | 6 | 2 | |
| | | | | | | | | | | | | 4 | | |
| 2 | | | 3 | | 1 | 5 | 5 | | | 1 | | 28 | 20 | 6 |
| 4 | | | | | | | | | | | | 65 | | |
| 2 | | | | | | | | | | | | 29 | | 5 |
| 4 | | | | | | | | | | | | 4 | | |
| | | | | | | | | | | | | 1 | | |
| 1 | | | | | | | | | | | | 34 | | 14 |
| | | | | | | | | | | | | 1 | | |
| | | | | | | | | | | | | 2 | | |
| | | | | | | | | | | | | 2 | | |
| | | | 1 | | | 1 | 2 | | | | | 2 | 3 | |
| | | | | | | | | | | | | 2 | | |
| | | | | | | | | | | | | 2 | | |
| 14 | | 4 | 1 | | 2 | 3 | | | 1 | | | 184 | | 56 |
| | | | | 1 | | | | | | 1 | | 1 | 2 | |
| | | | | | | | | | | | | 1 | | |
| 5 | | | | | | | | | | | | 96 | | 1 |
| 1 | | | | | | | | | | | | 1 | | |
| 2 | | | | | | | | | | | | 16 | | 3 |
| 1 | | | | | | | | | | | | 1 | | |
| 1 | | | | | | | | | | | | 36 | | 19 |
| 7 | | | | | | | | | | | | 42 | | |
| 2 | | | | | | | | | | | | 38 | | |
| 7 | | 1 | | | | | | | | | | 96 | | 4 |
| 5 | | 4 | | | | | | | | | | 101 | | 67 |
| 8 | | 1 | | | | | | | | | | 68 | | 25 |
| | | | | | | 3 | 1 | | | | | 3 | 2 | |
| 3 | | 1 | | | | | | | | | | 11 | | 2 |
| | | | | | | | | | | | | 9 | | 1 |
| 1 | | | | 1 | 1 | 2 | 3 | | | | | 3 | 6 | 1 |
| 4 | | | | | | | | | | | | 42 | | |
| 2 | | | | | | | | | | | | 44 | | 14 |
| 3 | | | | | | | | | | | | 17 | | |
| 3 | | | 6 | | | 2 | 1 | | | | | 45 | 1 | |
| 3 | 1 | | 3 | 2 | | | | | | | | 32 | 10 | 13 |
| 2 | | | | | | | | | | | | 2 | | |
| | | | | | | | | | | | | 1 | | |
| 28 | | 1 | | | | | | | 3 | | | 302 | | 23 |
| | | | | | | | | | | | | 2 | | |
| 1 | | | | | | | | | | | | 10 | | 2 |
| 6 | | | | | | | | | | | | 34 | | 10 |
| 2 | | | | | | | | | | | | 35 | | 1 |
| | | | | | | | | | | | | 3 | | |
| 3 | | | | | | | | | | | | 50 | | 1 |
| 4 | 4 | 3 | | 7 | 2 | 4 | 2 | 1 | | 1 | | 27 | 43 | 17 |
| | | | | | | | | | | | | 21 | | 3 |
| | | | | | | | | | | | | 10 | | |
| 33 | 2 | 10 | 50 | 1 | 5 | 26 | 1 | 8 | 2 | 1 | 2 | 437 | 25 | 99 |
| | | 1 | | | 1 | | | | | | 2 | 1 | | |
| 4 | | | 3 | | | | | | | | | 53 | | |
| | | | | | | | | | | | | 1 | | |
| 1 | | 2 | | | | | | | | | | 3 | | 3 |
| 6 | | | | | | | | | | | | 28 | | |
| 6 | | | | | | | | | | | | 92 | | |
| | | | | | | | | | | | | 2 | | |
| | | | | | | | | | | | | 1 | | |
| | | | | | | | | | | | | | | |
| 7 | | | | | | | | | | | | 180 | | 55 |
| 42 | | 26 | | | | | | | 2 | | 3 | 424 | | 211 |
| | | | | | | | | | | | | 7 | | |
| 1 | | | | | | 2 | | | | | | 24 | 3 | 4 |
| 22 | 1 | 1 | 22 | | 1 | 16 | | 3 | 2 | | | 328 | 7 | 27 |

| Player | Birthplace | From | Year Joined | Year Left | To | League Apps | Sub | Goals |
|---|---|---|---|---|---|---|---|---|
| Sagar, C | Daisy Hill | Bury | 1905 | 1907 | Atherton | 30 | | 20 |
| Sapsford, G | Salford | amateur | 1919 | 1922 | Preston North End | 52 | | 16 |
| Sartori, C | Calderzone, Italy | juniors | 1963 | 1972 | Bologna (Italy) | 26 | 13 | 4 |
| Sarvis, W | Merthyr Tydfil | Merthyr Town | 1922 | 1925 | Bradford City | 1 | | |
| Saunders, J | Birmingham | Middlesbrough | 1901 | 1905 | Nelson | 12 | | |
| Savage, R | Louth | Liverpool | 1938 | 1938 | Wrexham | 4 | | |
| Sawyer, F | not known | not known | 1899 | 1900 | Chorley | 2 | | |
| Scanlon, A | Manchester | juniors | 1950 | 1960 | Newcastle United | 115 | | 34 |
| Schmeichel, P | Gladsaxe, Denmark | Brøndby | 1991 | 1999 | Sporting Lisbon | 292 | | |
| Schofield, A | Liverpool | Everton | 1900 | 1907 | retired | 157 | | 30 |
| Schofield, G | Southport | not known | 1920 | 1922 | Crewe Alexandra | 1 | | |
| Schofield, J | Wigan | Ashton Town | 1903 | 1905 | Stockport County | 2 | | |
| Schofield, P | Bolton | Eccles Borough | 1921 | 1922 | Eccles United | 1 | | |
| Scholes, P | Salford | juniors | 1991 | | still at club | 206 | 54 | 68 |
| Scott, J | Motherwell | Bradford | 1921 | 1922 | St Mirren | 23 | | |
| Scott, J | Belfast | amateur | 1950 | 1956 | Grimsby Town | 3 | | |
| Sealey, L | Bethnall Green | Luton Town | 1989 | 1991 | Aston Villa | | | |
| | | Aston Villa | 1993 | 1994 | Blackpool | 33 | | |
| Setters, M | Honiton | West Bromwich Albion | 1960 | 1964 | Stoke City | 159 | | 12 |
| Sharpe, L | Halesowen | Torquay United | 1988 | 1996 | Leeds United | 160 | 33 | 21 |
| Sharpe, W | not known | | 1890 | 1892 | Oldham County | 2 | | |
| Sheldon, J | Clay Cross | Nuneaton | 1909 | 1913 | Liverpool | 26 | | 1 |
| Sheringham, E | Highams Park | Tottenham Hotspur | 1997 | 2001 | Tottenham Hotspur | 73 | 31 | 31 |
| Sidebottom, A | Barnsley | juniors | 1971 | 1976 | Huddersfield Town | 16 | | |
| Silcock, J | Wigan | Amateur | 1916 | 1934 | Oldham Athletic | 423 | | 2 |
| Silvestre, M | France | Internazionale | 1999 | | still at club | 120 | 10 | 2 |
| Sivebaek, J | Vejle, Denmark | Vejle | 1986 | 1987 | St Etienne | 29 | 2 | 1 |
| Slater, J | not known | not known | 1890 | 1893 | not known | | | |
| Sloan, T | Ballymena | Ballymena United | 1978 | 1982 | Chester | 4 | 7 | |
| Smith, A | Glasgow | Petershill | 1925 | 1927 | Preston North End | 5 | | 1 |
| Smith, J | Batley | Newcastle United | 1938 | 1946 | Blackburn Rovers | 37 | | 14 |
| Smith, L | Manchester | army football | 1902 | 1903 | New Brompton | 8 | | 1 |
| Smith, R | Halliwell | Heywood Central | 1894 | 1898 | Halliwell Rovers | | | |
| | | Wigan County | 1900 | 1901 | Bolton Wanderers | 93 | | 35 |
| Smith, T | Whitburn | Leicester City | 1924 | 1927 | Northampton Town | 83 | | 12 |
| Smith, W | not known | Stockport County | 1901 | 1902 | not known | 16 | | |
| Sneddon, J | not known | not known | 1891 | 1892 | not known | | | |
| Solskjaer, O | Kristiansund, Norway | Molde | 1996 | | still at club | 135 | 65 | 84 |
| Spence, J | Throckley | Scotswood | 1919 | 1933 | Bradford City | 481 | | 158 |
| Spencer, C | Washington | Newcastle United | 1928 | 1930 | Tunbridge Wells | 46 | | |
| Spratt, W | Huddersfield | Brentford | 1915 | 1920 | Brentford | 13 | | |
| Stacey, G | Thorpe Hesley | Barnsley | 1907 | 1915 | retired | 241 | | 9 |
| Stafford, H | Crewe | Crewe Alexandra | 1896 | 1903 | Crewe Alexandra | 183 | | |
| Stam, J | Kampen, Holland | PSV Eindhoven | 1998 | 2001 | SS Lazio | 79 | | 1 |
| Stapleton, F | Dublin | Arsenal | 1981 | 1987 | Ajax | 204 | 19 | 60 |
| Stephenson, R | not known | Talbot | 1895 | 1896 | Northern Nomads | 1 | | 1 |
| Stepney, A | Mitcham | Chelsea | 1966 | 1979 | Dallas Tornado | 433 | | 2 |
| Steward, A | Manchester | Amateur | 1920 | 1932 | Manchester North End | 309 | | |
| Stewart, M | Edinburgh | juniors | 1997 | | still at club | 5 | 2 | |
| Stewart, W | Coupar Angus | Warwick County | 1899 | 1895 | Luton Town | 76 | | 5 |
| Stewart, W | Glasgow | Cowdenbeath | 1932 | 1934 | Motherwell | 46 | | 7 |
| Stiles, N | Manchester | juniors | 1957 | 1971 | Middlesbrough | 311 | | 17 |
| Stone, H | St Albans | not known | 1893 | 1895 | Ashton North End | 6 | | |
| Storey-Moore, I | Ipswich | Nottingham Forest | 1972 | 1973 | retired | 39 | | 11 |
| Strachan, G | Edinburgh | Aberdeen | 1984 | 1989 | Leeds United | 155 | 5 | 33 |
| Street, E | Manchester | Sale Holmfield | 1902 | 1904 | not known | 1 | | |
| Sutcliffe, J | Shibden | Millwall Athletic | 1903 | 1905 | Plymouth Argyle | 21 | | |
| Sweeney, E | Rock Ferry | Flint Town | 1925 | 1930 | Charlton Athletic | 27 | | 6 |
| Taibi, M | Palermo, Italy | Venezia | 1999 | 2000 | Reggina | 4 | | |
| Tapken, N | Wallsend | Newcastle United | 1938 | 1947 | Darlington | 14 | | |
| Taylor, C | Birmingham | Redditch | 1924 | 1931 | Hyde United | 28 | | 6 |
| Taylor, E | Sunderland | Blackpool | 1958 | 1958 | Sunderland | 22 | | 2 |
| Taylor, T | Barnsley | Barnsley | 1953 | 1958 | victim, Munich air disaster | 166 | | 112 |
| Taylor, W | not known | New Mills | 1921 | 1922 | not known | 1 | | |
| Thomas, H | Swansea | Porth | 1922 | 1930 | Merthyr Town | 128 | | 12 |
| Thomas, M | Mochdre | Wrexham | 1978 | 1981 | Everton | 90 | | 11 |
| Thompson, J | Newbiggin | Blackburn Rovers | 1936 | 1938 | Gateshead | 3 | | 1 |
| Thompson, W | not known | Aston Villa | 1893 | 1894 | not known | 3 | | |
| Thomson, A | West Stanley | Morecambe | 1928 | 1931 | Southend United | 3 | | 1 |
| Thomson, E | not known | Darwen | 1906 | 1909 | Nelson | 4 | | |
| Thomson, J | Dumbarton | Renton | 1913 | 1914 | Dumbarton Harp | 6 | | 1 |
| Thornley, B | Bury | juniors | 1991 | 1998 | Huddersfield Town | 1 | 8 | |
| Timm, M | Odense, Denmark | juniors | 2001 | | still at club | | | |
| Tomlinson, G | Watford | Bradford City | 1994 | 1998 | Macclesfield Town | | | |
| Toms, W | Manchester | Eccles Borough | 1919 | 1920 | Plymouth Argyle | 13 | | 3 |
| Topping, H | Manchester | not known | 1932 | 1935 | Barnsley | 12 | | 1 |
| Tranter, W | Manchester | juniors | 1961 | 1966 | Brighton & Hove Albion | 1 | | |
| Travers, J | Newtown | Barnsley | 1914 | 1920 | Swindon Town | 21 | | 4 |
| Turnbull, A | Hurlford | Hurlford Thistle | 1906 | 1917 | killed in action, WW1 | 220 | | 90 |
| Turnbull, J | East Plain | Leyton | 1907 | 1910 | Bradford | 67 | | 36 |

| FAC | | | FLC | | | Europe | | | Others | | | Totals | | |
|---|---|---|---|---|---|---|---|---|---|---|---|---|---|---|
| Apps | Sub | Goals | Apps | Sub | Goals | Apps | Sub | Goals | Apps | Sub | Goals | Apps | Sub | Goals |
| 3 | | 4 | | | | | | | | | | 33 | | 24 |
| 1 | | 1 | | | | | | | | | | 53 | | 17 |
| 9 | | 1 | 3 | 2 | | 2 | | 1 | | 1 | | 40 | 16 | 6 |
| | | | | | | | | | | | | 1 | | |
| 1 | | | | | | | | | | | | 13 | | |
| 1 | | | | | | | | | | | | 5 | | |
| | | | | | | | | | | | | 2 | | |
| 6 | | 1 | 3 | | | 3 | | | | | | 127 | | 35 |
| 41 | | | 17 | | | 41 | | 1 | 6 | | | 398 | | 1 |
| 22 | | 5 | | | | | | | | | | 179 | | 35 |
| | | | | | | | | | | | | 1 | | |
| | | | | | | | | | | | | 2 | | |
| | | | | | | | | | | | | 1 | | |
| 12 | 8 | 5 | 10 | 4 | 8 | 62 | 11 | 20 | 8 | | | 298 | 77 | 101 |
| 1 | | | | | | | | | | | | 24 | | |
| | | | | | | | | | | | | 3 | | |
| | | | | | | | | | | | | | | |
| 4 | 1 | | 9 | | | 8 | | | 1 | | | 55 | 1 | |
| 25 | | 1 | 2 | | | 7 | | 1 | 1 | | | 194 | | 14 |
| 22 | 7 | 3 | 15 | 8 | 9 | 15 | 2 | 3 | 1 | | | 213 | 50 | 36 |
| | | | | | | | | | | | | 2 | | |
| | | | | | | | | | | | | 26 | | 1 |
| 4 | 5 | 5 | 1 | | 1 | 20 | 11 | 9 | 4 | 4 | | 102 | 51 | 46 |
| 2 | | | 2 | | | | | | | | | 20 | | |
| 26 | | | | | | | | | | | | 449 | | 2 |
| 6 | | | 5 | | | 38 | 6 | 1 | 5 | | | 174 | 16 | 3 |
| 2 | | | 1 | | | | | | | | | 32 | 2 | 1 |
| 4 | | | | | | | | | | | | 4 | | |
| | | | | 1 | | | | | | | | 4 | 8 | |
| | | | | | | | | | | | | 5 | | 1 |
| 5 | | 1 | | | | | | | | | | 42 | | 15 |
| 2 | | | | | | | | | | | | 10 | | 1 |
| | | | | | | | | | | | | | | |
| 7 | | 2 | | | | | | | 1 | | | 101 | | 37 |
| 7 | | 4 | | | | | | | | | | 90 | | 16 |
| 1 | | | | | | | | | | | | 17 | | |
| 3 | | 1 | | | | | | | | | | 3 | | 1 |
| 9 | 10 | 6 | 7 | 3 | 6 | 33 | 40 | 18 | 5 | 3 | | 189 | 121 | 114 |
| 29 | | 10 | | | | | | | | | | 510 | | 168 |
| 2 | | | | | | | | | | | | 48 | | |
| | | | | | | | | | | | | 13 | | |
| 26 | | | | | | | | | 3 | | | 270 | | 9 |
| 17 | | 1 | | | | | | | | | | 200 | | 1 |
| 7 | 1 | 1 | | | | 32 | | | 7 | 1 | | 125 | 2 | 1 |
| 21 | | 7 | 26 | 1 | 6 | 14 | 1 | 5 | 2 | | | 267 | 21 | 78 |
| | | | | | | | | | | | | 1 | | 1 |
| 44 | | | 35 | | | 23 | | | 4 | | | 539 | | 2 |
| 17 | | | | | | | | | | | | 326 | | |
| | 1 | | 2 | 2 | | | 2 | | | | | 7 | 7 | |
| 9 | | | | | | | | | 2 | | | 87 | | 5 |
| 3 | | | | | | | | | | | | 49 | | 7 |
| 38 | | | 7 | | | 36 | | 2 | 3 | | | 395 | | 19 |
| | | | | | | | | | 1 | | | 7 | | |
| | | | 4 | | 1 | | | | | | | 43 | | 12 |
| 22 | | 2 | 12 | 1 | 1 | 6 | | 2 | | | | 195 | 6 | 38 |
| 2 | | | | | | | | | | | | 3 | | |
| 7 | | | | | | | | | | | | 28 | | |
| 5 | | 1 | | | | | | | | | | 32 | | 7 |
| | | | | | | | | | | | | 4 | | |
| 2 | | | | | | | | | | | | 16 | | |
| 2 | | 1 | | | | | | | | | | 30 | | 7 |
| 6 | | 1 | | | | 2 | | 1 | | | | 30 | | 4 |
| 9 | | 5 | | | | 14 | | 11 | 2 | | 3 | 191 | | 131 |
| | | | | | | | | | | | | 1 | | |
| 7 | | 1 | | | | | | | | | | 135 | | 1 |
| 13 | | 2 | 5 | | 2 | 2 | | | | | | 110 | | 15 |
| | | | | | | | | | | | | 3 | | 1 |
| | | | | | | | | | | | | 3 | | |
| 2 | | | | | | | | | | | | 5 | | 1 |
| | | | | | | | | | | | | 4 | | |
| | | | | | | | | | | | | 6 | | 1 |
| 2 | | | 3 | | | | | | | | | 6 | 8 | |
| | | | | | | | 1 | | | | | | 1 | |
| | | | | 2 | | | | | | | | | 2 | |
| 1 | | 1 | | | | | | | | | | 14 | | 4 |
| | | | | | | | | | | | | 12 | | 1 |
| | | | | | | | | | | | | 1 | | |
| | | | | | | | | | | | | 21 | | 4 |
| 25 | | 10 | | | | | | | 2 | | 1 | 247 | | 101 |
| 9 | | 6 | | | | | | | 2 | | 3 | 78 | | 45 |

| Player | Birthplace | From | Year Joined | Year Left | To | League Apps | Sub | Goals |
|---|---|---|---|---|---|---|---|---|
| Turner* | not known | not known | 1890 | 1891 | not known | | | |
| Turner, C | Sheffield | Sunderland | 1985 | 1988 | Sheffield Wednesday | 64 | | |
| Turner, J | not known | Gravesend United | 1898 | 1899 | not known | 3 | | |
| Turner, R | not known | not known | 1898 | 1899 | Brighton United | 2 | | |
| Twiss, M | Salford | juniors | 1994 | 2000 | Port Vale | | | |
| Tyler, S | Wolverhampton | Stourbridge | 1922 | 1924 | Wolverhampton Wanderers | 1 | | |
| Ure, I | Ayr | Arsenal | 1969 | 1972 | St Mirren | 47 | | 1 |
| Valentine, R | not known | Swinton RLFC | 1904 | 1907 | Swinton RLFC | 10 | | |
| Vance, J | not known | Annbank | 1895 | 1896 | Fairfield | 11 | | 1 |
| Vincent, E | Seaham Harbour | Southport | 1932 | 1935 | Queens Park Rangers | 64 | | 1 |
| van der Gouw, R | Oldenzaal, Holland | Vitesse Arnhem | 1996 | 2002 | West Ham United | 26 | 11 | |
| van Nistelrooy, R | Oss, Holland | PSV Eindhoven | 2001 | | still at club | 62 | 4 | 48 |
| Veron, J | La Plata, Argentina | SS Lazio | 2001 | | still at club | 45 | 6 | 7 |
| Viollet, D | Manchester | juniors | 1949 | 1962 | Stoke City | 259 | | 159 |
| Vose, G | St Helens | Peasley Cross Athletic | 1933 | 1940 | Runcorn | 197 | | 1 |
| Waldron, C | Bristol | Burnley | 1976 | 1978 | Tulsa Roughnecks | 3 | | |
| Walker, D | Northwich | juniors | 1960 | 1963 | York City | 1 | | |
| Walker, R | not known | not known | 1899 | 1899 | not known | 2 | | |
| Wall, G | Boldon Colliery | Barnsley | 1906 | 1919 | Oldham Athletic | 287 | | 89 |
| Wallace, D | Greenwich | Southampton | 1989 | 1993 | Birmingham City | 36 | 11 | 6 |
| Wallwork, R | Manchester | juniors | 1994 | 2002 | West Bromwich Albion | 4 | 15 | |
| Walsh, G | Wigan | juniors | 1983 | 1995 | Middlesbrough | 49 | 1 | |
| Walton, J | Horwich | amateur | 1951 | 1952 | Bury | 2 | | |
| Walton, J | Manchester | amateur | 1940 | 1948 | Preston North End | 21 | | |
| Warburton, A | Whitefield | Sedgley Park | 1929 | 1933 | Burnley | 35 | | 10 |
| Warner, J | Birmingham | Aston Villa | 1892 | 1893 | Walsall Town Swifts | 22 | | |
| Warner, J | Trelaw | Swansea Town | 1938 | 1951 | Oldham Athletic | 105 | | 1 |
| Wassall, J | Shrewsbury | Wellington Town | 1935 | 1940 | Stockport County | 46 | | 6 |
| Watson, W | Motherwell | juniors | 1965 | 1973 | Miami Toros | 11 | | |
| Wealands, J | Darlington | Birmingham City | 1983 | 1985 | Altrincham | 7 | | |
| Webb, N | Reading | Nottingham Forest | 1989 | 1992 | Nottingham Forest | 70 | 5 | 8 |
| Webber, D | Manchester | juniors | 1998 | 2003 | Watford | | | |
| Webster, C | Cardiff | Cardiff City | 1952 | 1958 | Swansea Town | 65 | | 26 |
| Wedge, F | Dudley | Manchester Talbot | 1896 | 1898 | Chorlton-cum-Hardy | 2 | | |
| Wellens, R | Manchester | juniors | 1996 | 2000 | Blackpool | | | |
| West, E | Hucknall Torkard | Nottingham Forest | 1910 | 1916 | | 166 | | 72 |
| Wetherell, J | not known | | 1896 | 1897 | | 2 | | |
| Whalley, A | Rainford | Blackpool | 1909 | 1920 | Southend United | 97 | | 6 |
| Whalley, H | Ashton-under-Lyne | Stalybridge Celtic | 1935 | 1947 | retired | 33 | | |
| Whelan, A | Dublin | Bohemians | 1980 | 1983 | Shamrock Rovers | | 1 | |
| Whelan, L | Dublin | Home Farm | 1954 | 1958 | victim, Munich air disaster | 79 | | 43 |
| Whitefoot, J | Cheadle | juniors | 1949 | 1957 | Grimsby Town | 93 | | |
| Whitehouse, J | Birmingham | Grimsby Town | 1900 | 1903 | Manchester City | 59 | | |
| Whitehurst, W | Manchester | juniors | 1950 | 1956 | Chesterfield | 1 | | |
| Whiteside, K | Scotland | Irvine Victoria | 1907 | 1910 | Hurst | 1 | | |
| Whiteside, N | Belfast | juniors | 1981 | 1989 | Everton | 193 | 13 | 47 |
| Whitney, J | not known | not known | 1895 | 1896 | not known | | | |
| | | not known | 1900 | 1901 | not known | 3 | | |
| Whittaker, W | Manchester | Molyneaux | 1896 | 1896 | Fairfield | 3 | | |
| Whittle, J | Leigh | amateur | 1931 | 1932 | Rossendale United | 1 | | |
| Whitworth, N | Wigan | Wigan Athletic | 1990 | 1993 | Blackpool | 1 | | |
| Wilcox, T | at sea | Blackpool | 1907 | 1909 | Carlisle United | 2 | | |
| Wilkins, R | Hillingdon | Chelsea | 1979 | 1984 | AC Milan | 158 | 2 | 7 |
| Wilkinson, H | Bury | amateur | 1903 | 1904 | Hull City | 8 | | |
| Wilkinson, I | Warrington | juniors | 1989 | 1993 | Stockport County | | | |
| Williams, R | Abercanaid | Sheffield Wednesday | 1927 | 1929 | Thames Association | 31 | | 2 |
| Williams, F | Kearsley | Stalybridge Celtic | 1928 | 1930 | Altrincham | 3 | | |
| Williams, F | Manchester | Manchester City | 1902 | 1903 | not known | 8 | | |
| Williams, H | Hucknall Tankard | Chesterfield | 1922 | 1923 | Brentford | 5 | | 2 |
| Williams, H | Farmworth | Burnley | 1904 | 1908 | Leeds City | 32 | | 7 |
| Williams, J | Crewe | Macclesfield | 1905 | 1907 | not known | 3 | | 1 |
| Williams, W | not known | Bristol Rovers | 1901 | 1902 | not known | 4 | | |
| Williamson, J | Manchester | Ancoats Lads' Club | 1919 | 1921 | Bury | 2 | | |
| Wilson, D | Burnley | juniors | 1985 | 1991 | Bristol Rovers | | 4 | |
| Wilson, E | not known | not known | 1889 | 1900 | not known | | | |
| Wilson, J | Leadgate | Stockport County | 1926 | 1932 | Bristol City | 130 | | 3 |
| Wilson, M | Scunthorpe | juniors | 1995 | 2001 | Middlesbrough | 1 | 2 | |
| Wilson, T | Preston | Leeds City | 1908 | 1912 | retired | 1 | | |
| Winterbottom, W | Oldham | Mossley | 1936 | 1938 | retired | 25 | | |
| Wombwell, R | Nottingham | Bristol City | 1905 | 1907 | Heart of Midlothian | 47 | | 3 |
| Wood, J | Leven | Dumbarton | 1922 | 1923 | Lochgelly United | 15 | | 1 |
| Wood, N | Oldham | juniors | 1981 | 1987 | retired | 2 | 1 | |
| Wood, R | Hebburn-on-Tyne | Darlington | 1949 | 1958 | Huddersfield Town | 178 | | |
| Woodcock, W | Ashton-under-Lyne | Stalybridge Celtic | 1912 | 1920 | Manchester City | 58 | | 20 |
| Worrall, H | Northwich | Winsford United | 1937 | 1948 | Swindon Town | 6 | | |
| Wratten, P | Middlesbrough | juniors | 1987 | 1991 | not known | | 2 | |
| Wrigglesworth, W | South Elmsall | Wolverhampton Wanderers | 1937 | 1947 | Bolton Wanderers | | | |
| Yates, W | Birmingham | Brighton & Hove Albion | 1906 | 1907 | Heart of Midlothian | 3 | | |
| Yorke, D | Canaan, Tobago | Aston Villa | 1998 | 2002 | Blackburn Rovers | 80 | 16 | 48 |
| Young, A | Scotland | Hurlford Thistle | 1906 | 1906 | not known | 2 | | |
| Young, A | Urmston | juniors | 1968 | 1976 | Charlton Athletic | 69 | 14 | 1 |

| FAC Apps | FAC Sub | FAC Goals | FLC Apps | FLC Sub | FLC Goals | Europe Apps | Europe Sub | Europe Goals | Others Apps | Others Sub | Others Goals | Totals Apps | Totals Sub | Totals Goals |
|---|---|---|---|---|---|---|---|---|---|---|---|---|---|---|
| 1 | | | | | | | | | | | | 1 | | |
| 8 | | | 7 | | | | | | | | | 79 | | |
| 1 | | | | | | | | | | | | 4 | | |
| | | | | | | | | | | | | 2 | | |
| | 1 | | 1 | | | | | | | | | 1 | 1 | |
| | | | | | | | | | | | | 1 | | |
| 8 | | | 10 | | | | | | | | | 65 | | 1 |
| | | | | | | | | | | | | 10 | | |
| | | | | | | | | | | | | 11 | | 1 |
| 1 | | | | | | | | | | | | 65 | | 1 |
| 1 | | | 8 | 1 | | 11 | | | 2 | | | 48 | 12 | |
| 3 | 2 | 6 | 4 | | 1 | 24 | 1 | 24 | 1 | | 1 | 94 | 7 | 80 |
| 2 | | | 4 | 1 | | 24 | | 4 | | | | 75 | 7 | 11 |
| 18 | | 5 | 2 | | 1 | 12 | | 13 | 2 | | 1 | 293 | | 179 |
| 14 | | | | | | | | | | | | 211 | | 1 |
| | | | 1 | | | | | | | | | 4 | | |
| | | | | | | | | | | | | 1 | | |
| | | | | | | | | | | | | 2 | | |
| 29 | | 9 | | | | | | | 3 | | 2 | 319 | | 100 |
| 7 | 2 | 2 | 4 | 3 | 3 | 5 | 2 | | 1 | | | 53 | 18 | 11 |
| 1 | 1 | | 4 | 1 | | | 1 | | 1 | | | 10 | 18 | |
| | | | 7 | | | 6 | | | | | | 62 | 1 | |
| | | | | | | | | | | | | 2 | | |
| 2 | | | | | | | | | | | | 23 | | |
| 4 | | | | | | | | | | | | 39 | | 10 |
| | | | | | | | | | | | | 22 | | |
| 13 | | 1 | | | | | | | 1 | | | 119 | | 2 |
| 2 | | | | | | | | | | | | 48 | | 6 |
| 3 | | | | | | | | | | | | 14 | | |
| | | | 1 | | | | | | | | | 8 | | |
| 9 | | 1 | 14 | | 1 | 11 | | 1 | 1 | | | 105 | 5 | 11 |
| | | | 1 | 1 | | | 1 | | | | | 1 | 2 | |
| 9 | | 4 | | | | 5 | | 1 | | | | 79 | | 31 |
| | | | | | | | | | | | | 2 | | |
| | | | | 1 | | | | | | | | | 1 | |
| 15 | | | | | | | | | | | | 181 | | 80 |
| | | | | | | | | | | | | 2 | | |
| 9 | | | | | | | | | | | | 106 | | 6 |
| 6 | | | | | | | | | | | | 39 | | |
| | | | | | | | | | | | | | 1 | |
| 6 | | 4 | | | | 11 | | 5 | 2 | | | 98 | | 52 |
| 2 | | | | | | | | | | | | 95 | | |
| 5 | | | | | | | | | | | | 64 | | |
| | | | | | | | | | | | | 1 | | |
| | | | | | | | | | | | | 1 | | |
| 24 | | 10 | 26 | 3 | 9 | 11 | 2 | 1 | 2 | | | 256 | 18 | 67 |
| | | | | | | | | | | | | | | |
| | | | | | | | | | | | | 3 | | |
| | | | | | | | | | | | | 3 | | |
| | | | | | | | | | | | | 1 | | |
| | | | | | | | | | | | | 1 | | |
| | | | | | | | | | | | | 2 | | |
| 10 | | 1 | 14 | 1 | 1 | 8 | | 1 | 1 | | | 191 | 3 | 10 |
| 1 | | | | | | | | | | | | 9 | | |
| | | | 1 | | | | | | | | | 1 | | |
| 4 | | | | | | | | | | | | 35 | | 2 |
| | | | | | | | | | | | | 3 | | |
| 2 | | 4 | | | | | | | | | | 10 | | 4 |
| | | | | | | | | | | | | 5 | | 2 |
| 4 | | 1 | | | | | | | | | | 36 | | 8 |
| | | | | | | | | | | | | 3 | | 1 |
| | | | | | | | | | | | | 4 | | |
| | | | | | | | | | | | | 2 | | |
| | 2 | | | | | | | | | | | | 6 | |
| 1 | | | | | | | | | | | | 1 | | |
| 10 | | | | | | | | | | | | 140 | | 3 |
| | | | 2 | | | 2 | 2 | | 1 | | | 6 | 4 | |
| | | | | | | | | | | | | 1 | | |
| 2 | | | | | | | | | | | | 27 | | |
| 4 | | | | | | | | | | | | 51 | | 3 |
| 1 | | | | | | | | | | | | 16 | | 1 |
| | | | | 1 | | | | | | | | 2 | 2 | |
| 15 | | | | | | 12 | | | 3 | | | 208 | | |
| 3 | | 1 | | | | | | | | | | 61 | | 21 |
| | | | | | | | | | | | | 6 | | |
| | | | | | | | | | | | | | 2 | |
| | | | | | | | | | | | | | | |
| | | | | | | | | | | | | 3 | | |
| 6 | 5 | 3 | 3 | | 2 | 28 | 8 | 11 | 3 | 3 | 2 | 120 | 32 | 66 |
| | | | | | | | | | | | | 2 | | |
| 5 | | | 5 | 4 | | | | | | | | 79 | 18 | 1 |

## Extra Statistics

### CUP FINAL TEAM LISTS

The lists below show the details of the cup finals reached in the FA Cup, Football League Cup, European Cup and European Cup-Winners' Cup

### FA Cup Finals

Saturday 24 April 1909 (Crystal Palace, London)
**MANCHESTER UNITED 1 BRISTOL CITY 0**
Moger, Stacey, Hayes, Duckworth, Roberts, Bell, Meredith, Halse, Turnbull J., Turnbull A., Wall
**Scorer:** Turnbull A.
**Attendance:** 71,401

Saturday 24 April 1948 (Wembley, London)
**MANCHESTER UNITED 4 BLACKPOOL 2**
Crompton, Carey, Aston, Anderson, Chilton, Cockburn, Delaney, Morris, Rowley, Pearson, Mitten
**Scorers:** Rowley 2, Pearson, Anderson
**Attendance:** 99,842

Saturday 4 May 1957 (Wembley, London)
**ASTON VILLA 2 MANCHESTER UNITED 1**
Wood, Foulkes, Byrne, Colman, Blanchflower, Edwards, Berry, Whelan, Taylor, Charlton, Pegg
**Scorer:** Taylor
**Attendance:** 99,225

Saturday 3 May 1958 (Wembley, London)
**BOLTON WANDERERS 2 MANCHESTER UNITED 0**
Gregg, Foulkes, Greaves, Goodwin, Cope, Crowther, Dawson, Taylor, Charlton, Viollet, Webster
**Attendance:** 99,756

Saturday 25 May 1963 (Wembley, London)
**MANCHESTER UNITED 3 LEICESTER CITY 1**
Gaskell, Dunne, Cantwell, Crerand, Foulkes, Setters, Giles, Quixall, Herd, Law, Charlton
**Scorers:** Herd 2, Law
**Attendance:** 99,604

Saturday 1 May 1976 (Wembley, London)
**SOUTHAMPTON 1 MANCHESTER UNITED 0**
Stepney, Forsyth, Houston, Daly, Greenhoff, Buchan, Coppell, McIlroy, Pearson, Macari, Hill
**Substitute:** McCreery (Hill)
**Attendance:** 99,115

Saturday 21 May 1977 (Wembley, London)
**MANCHESTER UNITED 2 LIVERPOOL 1**
Stepney, Nicholl, Albiston, McIlroy, Greenhoff B., Buchan, Coppell, Greenhoff J., Pearson, Macari, Hill
**Substitute:** McCreery (Hill)
**Scorers:** Pearson, Greenhoff J.
**Attendance:** 99,252

Saturday 12 May 1979 (Wembley, London)
**ARSENAL 3 MANCHESTER UNITED 2**
Bailey, Nicholl, Albiston, McIlroy, McQueen, Buchan, Coppell, Greenhoff J., Jordan, Macari, Thomas
**Substitute:** Greenhoff B.
**Scorers:** McQueen, McIlroy
**Attendance:** 99,219

Saturday 21 May 1983 (Wembley, London)
**MANCHESTER UNITED 2 BRIGHTON & HOVE ALBION 2***
Bailey, Duxbury, Albiston, Wilkins, Moran, McQueen, Robson, Muhren, Stapleton, Whiteside, Davies
**Substitute:** Grimes
**Scorers:** Stapleton, Wilkins
**Attendance:** 99,059

Thursday 26 May 1983 Replay (Wembley, London)
**MANCHESTER UNITED 4 BRIGHTON & HOVE ALBION 0**
Bailey, Duxbury, Albiston, Wilkins, Moran, McQueen, Robson, Muhren, Stapleton, Whiteside, Davies
**Substitute:** Grimes
**Scorers:** Robson 2, Muhren, Whiteside
**Attendance:** 91,534

Saturday 18 May 1985 (Wembley, London)
**MANCHESTER UNITED 1 EVERTON 0***
Bailey, Gidman, Albiston, Whiteside, McGrath, Moran, Robson, Strachan, Hughes, Stapleton, Olsen.
**Substitute:** Duxbury (Albiston).
**Scorer:** Whiteside
**Attendance:** 99,445

Saturday 12 May 1990 (Wembley, London)
**MANCHESTER UNITED 3 CRYSTAL PALACE 3***
Leighton, Ince, Martin, Bruce, Phelan, Pallister, Robson, Webb, McClair, Hughes, Wallace
**Substitutes:** Robins (Pallister), Blackmore (Martin)
**Scorers:** Hughes 2, Robson
**Attendance:** 80,000

Thursday 17 May 1990 Replay (Wembley, London)
**MANCHESTER UNITED 1 CRYSTAL PALACE 0**
Sealey, Ince, Martin, Bruce, Phelan, Pallister, Robson, Webb, McClair, Hughes, Wallace
**Substitutes:** Robins, Blackmore
**Scorer:** Martin
**Attendance:** 80,000

Saturday 14 May 1994 (Wembley, London)
**CHELSEA 0 MANCHESTER UNITED 4**
Schmeichel, Parker, Irwin, Bruce, Kanchelskis, Pallister, Cantona, Ince, Keane, Hughes, Giggs
**Substitutes:** Sharpe (Irwin), McClair (Kanchelskis), Walsh
**Scorers:** Cantona 2 pens, Hughes, McClair
**Attendance:** 79,634

Saturday 20 May 1995 (Wembley, London)
**EVERTON 1 MANCHESTER UNITED 0**
Schmeichel, Neville G., Irwin, Bruce, Sharpe, Pallister, Butt, Ince, McClair, Hughes, Keane
**Substitutes:** Giggs (Bruce), Scholes (Sharpe), Walsh
**Attendance:** 79,592

Saturday 11 May 1996 (Wembley, London)
**LIVERPOOL 0 MANCHESTER UNITED 1**
Schmeichel, Neville P., Irwin, May, Beckham, Pallister, Cantona, Butt, Cole, Keane, Giggs
**Substitutes:** Sharpe, Neville G. (Beckham), Scholoes (Cole)
**Scorer:** Cantona
**Attendance:** 79,007

Saturday 22 May 1999 (Wembley, London)
**MANCHESTER UNITED 2 NEWCASTLE UNITED 0**
Schmeichel, Neville G., Neville P., May, Johnsen, Keane, Beckham, Scholes, Cole, Solskjaer, Giggs
**Substitutes:** Stam (Scholes), Sheringham (Keane), Blomqvist, van der Gouw, Yorke (Cole)
**Scorers:** Sheringham, Scholes
**Attendance:** 79,101

## Football League Cup Finals

Saturday 26 March 1983 (Wembley, London)
**LIVERPOOL 2 MANCHESTER UNITED 1**
Bailey, Duxbury, Albiston, Moses, Moran, McQueen, Wilkins, Muhren, Stapleton, Whiteside, Coppell
**Substitute:** Macari (Moran)
**Scorer:** Whiteside
**Attendance:** 99,304

Sunday 21 April 1991 (Wembley, London)
**MANCHESTER UNITED 0 SHEFFIELD WEDNESDAY 1**
Sealey, Irwin, Blackmore, Bruce, Webb, Pallister, Robson, Ince, McClair, Hughes, Sharpe
**Substitutes:** Donaghy, Phelan (Webb)
**Attendance:** 77,612

Sunday 12 April 1992 (Wembley, London)
**MANCHESTER UNITED 1 NOTTINGHAM FOREST 0**
Schmeichel, Parker, Irwin, Bruce, Phelan, Pallister, Kanchelskis, Ince, McClair, Hughes, Giggs
**Substitutes:** Webb, Sharpe (Kanchelskis)
**Scorer:** McClair
**Attendance:** 76,810

Sunday 27 March 1994 (Wembley, London)
**ASTON VILLA 3 MANCHESTER UNITED 1**
Sealey, Parker, Irwin, Bruce, Kanchelskis, Pallister, Cantona, Ince, Keane, Hughes, Giggs
**Substitutes:** Sharpe, McClair (Bruce), Walsh
**Scorer:** Hughes
**Attendance:** 77,231

Sunday 2 March 2003 (Millennium Stadium, Cardiff)
**LIVERPOOL 2 MANCHESTER UNITED 0**
Barthez, Neville G., Silvestre, Veron, Brown, Ferdinand, Beckham, Scholes, Keane, van Nistelrooy, Giggs
**Substitutes:** Neville P., Butt, Carroll, Solskjaer (Brown), O'Shea
**Attendance:** 74,500

## European Cup Finals

Wednesday 29 May 1968 (Wembley, London)
**SL BENFICA (Portugal) 1 MANCHESTER UNITED 4***
Stepney, Brennan, Dunne, Crerand, Foulkes, Stiles, Best, Kidd, Charlton, Sadler, Aston
**Substitute:** Rimmer
**Scorers:** Charlton 2, Best, Kidd
**Attendance:** 99,882

Wednesday 26 May 1999 (Nou Camp, Barcelona)
**BAYERN MUNICH 1 MANCHESTER UNITED 2**
Schmeichel, Neville G., Irwin, Blomqvist, Johnsen, Stam, Beckham, Butt, Cole, Yorke, Giggs
**Substitutes:** May, Sheringham (Blomqvist), Neville P., van der Gouw, Solskjaer (Cole), Brown, Greening
**Scorers:** Sheringham, Solskjaer
**Attendance:** 90,045

## European Cup-Winners' Cup Finals

Wednesday 15 May 1991 (Feyenoord Stadium, Rotterdam)
**BARCELONA 1 MANCHESTER UNITED 2**
Sealey, Irwin, Blackmore, Bruce, Phelan, Pallister, Robson, Ince, McClair, Hughes, Sharpe
**Substitutes:** Donaghy, Walsh, Webb, Robins, Wallace.
**Scorer:** Hughes 2
**Attendance:** 50,000

*After extra-time

*Bobby Charlton scored in United's 1968 European Cup final victory over Benfica, one of many goals in a career that spanned 20 years and 759 appearances for the Red Devils.*

## OTHER TITLES IN THE SERIES

***The Essential History of...***

***Football***

| | | |
|---|---|---|
| **Arsenal** | Rab MacWilliam/Kevin Connolly | *0 7553 1267 8* |
| **Blackburn Rovers** | Mike Jackman | *0 7553 1022 5* |
| **Celtic** | Graham McColl/George Sheridan | *0 7553 1141 8* |
| **Charlton Athletic** | Paul Clayton | *0 7553 1020 9* |
| **England** | Andrew Mourant/Jack Rollin | *0 7553 1142 6* |
| **Everton** | Mark Platt | *0 7553 1274 0** |
| **Leeds United** | Andrew Mourant | *0 7553 1170 1** |
| **Leicester City** | Tony Matthews | *0 7553 1023 3* |
| **Liverpool** | Alex Murphy/Eric Doig | *0 7553 1268 6* |
| **Manchester City** | Ian Penney | *0 7553 1168 X** |
| **Middlesbrough** | Richard Jones | *0 7553 1143 4* |
| **Newcastle United** | Paul Joannou/Bill Swann/Steve Corke | *0 7553 1270 8* |
| **Rangers** | Stephen Halliday | *0 7553 1145 0* |
| **West Bromwich Albion** | Gavin McOwan | *0 7553 1146 9* |
| **West Ham United** | Kirk Blows/Tony Hogg | *0 7553 1169 8** |

***Rugby Union***

| | | |
|---|---|---|
| **England** | Ian Malin/John Griffiths | *0 7553 1271 6* |
| **Scotland** | Nick Oswald/John Griffiths | *0 7553 1272 4* |
| **Wales** | Steve Lewis/John Griffiths | *0 7553 1273 2* |

** Trade paperback editions*

Please contact your local WHSmith store for details about ordering any of these titles.